F. Halpin Sc.

John Wilson

ÆTAT 60

W. J. WIDDLETON NY

'CHRISTOPHER NORTH'

A MEMOIR OF JOHN WILSON

LATE PROFESSOR OF MORAL PHILOSOPHY IN THE UNIVERSITY OF EDINBURGH

COMPILED

FROM FAMILY PAPERS AND OTHER SOURCES

BY HIS DAUGHTER

MRS. GORDON

WITH AN INTRODUCTION BY R. SHELTON MACKENZIE, D. C. L.

EDITOR OF THE NOCTES AMBROSIANÆ, ETC

COMPLETE IN ONE VOLUME

NEW YORK
W. J. WIDDLETON
(SUCCESSOR TO J. S. REDFIELD)
1863.

M'CREA & MILLER STEREOTYPERS,
15 Vandewater Street.
PRINTED BY C. A. ALVORD.

PREFACE TO THE AMERICAN EDITION.

John Wilson was, confessedly, the greatest magazine writer of his time. From the establishment of *Blackwood's Magazine*, to the autumn of 1852, his pen was almost exclusively employed upon that periodical. Two or three volumes of prose fiction, and an "Essay on Burns," for an edition of the peasant-poet's works, were all that Wilson wrote outside of "Maga," until he closed with the final number of the "Dies Boreales."

In the Magazine, however, his hand was to be seen, and sometimes felt, almost every month during the thirty-five years of his connection with it. His genius was as abundant as his industry was tireless. The volumes which have been selected from his writings in *Blackwood*, three of "The Recreations of Christopher North," and five of the "Noctes Ambrosianæ," imperfectly represent what he supplied. He was not only the best, but also the most fruitful of contributors.

If a man's life be written by a near relative, there usually is the disadvantage, that such a biographer has a natural tendency to take a rose-tinted view of personal character and action,—to write rather an eulogium than a fair record and a just estimate. This, independent of other causes, is mainly because of not taking an outside view of the departed; of not seeing him as he was seen by the world. Yet, of the five best literary biographies in our language (Boswell's Johnson, Crabbe's Life by his son, Moore's Byron, Lockhart's Scott, and Pierre M. Irving's Memoir of Washington Irving), three have been written by near relatives.

The present biography of John Wilson, by his daughter, is worthy, from its fairness and fulness, of a place by the others. Indeed, from Johnson to Wilson and Irving, as related in this series, the whole history of British literature, during one hundred and fifty years, may be found.

A loving daughter, solicitous for her father's reputation, Mrs Gordon writes of him with admirable impartiality. He was a man of genius, with a fountain of humanity in his great heart; a man eccentric in some things, but mean, wicked, or tricky, in none. His home affections were deep-rooted, and all who knew him loved him dearly. From the wild mirth, which he delighted to throw into the immortal "Noctes," the world who did not personally know him, fancied that Wilson was as reckless, humorsome, and jovial, as he represented their heroes to be. Mrs. Gordon's plain record shows that these very remarkable dialogues were written with prolonged toil, in a rapid manner, and upon no stronger inspiration than a chicken for dinner, and tea or cold water as the beverage to follow!

This biography may be called the key to *Blackwood's Magazine*, and particularly to the "Noctes." The mere list of Wilson's contributions, from 1826 to 1852, occupies six pages in the Appendix; and in the nine years before 1826, at least two hundred other articles were written by him. Rarely has any author exhibited such abounding industry, and, even when most careless, so little that is common-place or feeble.

The glimpses of Wilson's contemporaries, afforded by Mrs. Gordon, show us Lockhart and De Quincey, Jeffrey and Scott, Hartley Coleridge and "Delta;" and, above all, that singular "wild boar of the forest," James Hogg, the Ettrick Shepherd, the redoubtable hero of the "Noctes," and William Blackwood, the astute publisher.

Mrs. Gordon truly writes (p. 426): "There is no literary man of our land more highly prized, or better appreciated in America than Professor Wilson. In that country his name is respected, and his writings are well known. It is doubtful if in England he has so large a circle of admirers."

The great popularity of my own edition of the "Noctes Ambrosianæ," attests the accuracy of the above statement. The best personal and critical estimates of Wilson were written in this country; the first vigorously dashed off immediately after the announcement of his death in "The Citizen," by John Savage; and the other, a thoughtful and analytic estimate of his character, by Henry T. Tuckerman, which is to be found in his "Characteristics of Literature," second series.

R. SHELTON MACKENZIE.

PHILADELPHIA, *April* 4, 1863.

PREFACE.

I HAVE with much misgiving taken upon myself the duty of writing a Memoir of PROFESSOR WILSON, believing that my father's life was worthy of being recorded, and that it would bear to be truthfully told. I was well aware of the great difficulties attending its performance, and they proved not less than I anticipated; and I knew that I rendered myself liable to the charge of presumption in undertaking a task declined by abler hands. But I could not give up my persuasion that an imperfect picture of such a man was better than none at all, and in that conviction I have done what I could.

The many-sided character of the man I have not attempted to unfold; nor have I presumed to give a critical estimate of his works—they must speak for themselves. Now and then, in the course of the narrative, where letters are introduced referring to literary subjects, I have made a few observations on his writings; but in no other way, with the exception of those chapters devoted to *Blackwood's Magazine* and the Moral Philosophy chair, have I departed from my original intention of giving a simple domestic memoir. If I have in any way done justice to my father's memory in this respect, I am rewarded.

I have availed myself of the letters of my father's principal correspondents, so far as they served to throw light on the main subject, or were in themselves interesting and characteristic. I trust, in doing so, that I have inserted nothing calculated to displease or give pain to any now living. If I have erred in this or other respects, my inexperience in literary work must be my excuse.

I have spoken of the difficulties that I had to encounter. It is now my pleasing duty to thank the friends who have so kindly lent me their assistance, without which I should indeed have been much at a loss.

To my brothers, Mr. John Wilson of Billholm, Mr. Blair Wilson, and my brother-in-law, Professor Aytoun, I am indebted for memoranda and many domestic letters.

Others, too numerous to mention by name, will, I hope, accept my thanks for their courteous kindness in rendering me such service as lay in their power.

To the various students of former days, who have so heartily contributed their reminiscences of the "old man eloquent" whom they loved, I offer my most grateful thanks. Those parts of the work which are chiefly made up of such contributions, will, I am sure, be regarded by many as among its most valuable and interesting contents. To Mr. Hill Burton, the Rev. William Smith, and Mr. A. T. Innes, I am under very special obligations in this respect.

To Messrs. Blackwood I am indebted for a complete list of my father's contributions to the *Magazine* from 1826, which has enabled me to make use of autobiographic details otherwise inaccessible.

To Mr. Macduff of Bonhard, and Mr. John Boyd, Publisher, I am obliged for their kindness in placing at my disposal the correspondence connected with the publication respectively of the *Isle of Palms* and of *Janus.*

Sir David Brewster and Sheriff Cay have conferred a most valuable favor upon me in permitting the use of Mr. Lockhart's portfolios.

To my friend, Mr. Alexander Nicolson, Advocate, I am especially indebted: his warm encouragement aided my labors, and his judicious advice guided me in the arrangement of my materials, which, both in MS. and in type, he also carefully revised. The trouble which he has kindly taken in connection with this work is such as could have been expected only from one of those whom Professor Wilson loved to call his "children."

In conclusion, I may express my humble hope that this volume, however it may come short of expectation, will prove acceptable to my friends and that portion of the public who love and respect the name of JOHN WILSON.

EDINBURGH, *October*, 1862.

CONTENTS.

CHAPTER I.

BOYHOOD.

Paisley—Nursery Amusements—His First Fish—Sermon—Oure John's Teegar—Mr. Peddie's School—Life in the Mearns Manse .... Pages 1–14

CHAPTER II.

GLASGOW COLLEGE.

1797-1803.

His Father's Death—Enters College—Professor Jardine—Professor Young—Diary in 1801—Portrait by Raeburn—Student Life in Glasgow—Fondness for Barley-sugar—Walking Feats—Essay Writing—Companions—Letter to Wordsworth........ 14–32.

CHAPTER III.

LOVE AND POETRY.—LIFE AT OXFORD.

1803–'08.

Dychmont—First Love—Poems to Margaret—Oxford—Studies—Expenses—Commonplace-books—Cock-fighting—Pugilism—Leaping—Reminiscences of Magdalen College by a Fellow-student—College Anecdotes........ 32–55

CHAPTER IV.

THE ORPHAN MAID.—UNIVERSITY CAREER.

1803–'08.

Letters to Margaret and to Mr. Findlay—Letter from Mr. Blair—Letters to Mr. Findlay—Letter from Mr. Blair—Examination for his Bachelor Degree—Letters to Mr. Findlay—End of the Love Story 55–77

CHAPTER V.

LIFE AT ELLERAY.

1807–'11.

Description of Elleray—The Old Cottage—The New House—First Meeting with Wordsworth; with De Quincey—The Anglers' Tent—Mathetes—Poetic Compositions—Boating—His Fleet on Windermere—Billy Balmer—Lake escapade—Hunting a Bull—Love of Animals—His Game Birds—"A Main at Elleray"—Wrestling—"A varra bad un to Lick"—Gale House—Its Inmates—A Ball; a Regatta, etc.—Letter to Mr. Harden—Letter to De Quincey—Poetry—Letters to Mr. J. Smith, Publisher........ 77-104

CHAPTER VI.

MARRIAGE.—THE ISLE OF PALMS.

1811–'15.

Letter to Mr. Findlay, on the day of his Marriage—Letters to Mr. Smith about "The Isle of Palms"—Lines on James Grahame—Edinburgh, 53 Queen Street—Letters to Mr. Smith—Plans for future work at Elleray—Loses his Fortune—Studies for the Scottish Bar—Note from Mr. Blair—Departure from Elleray—Letter to De Quincey....................................Pages 105–119

CHAPTER VII.

LIFE IN EDINBURGH.—THE BAR.—THE HIGHLANDS.—ELLERAY.

1815–'17.

Edinburgh—Mrs. Wilson, Senior—Called to the Bar—Letter to Mrs. Wilson, from the "Head of the Yarrow"—The Shepherd at Home—An Adventure at Peebles—A Pedestrian Tour in the Highlands by Mr. and Mrs. Wilson: their Adventures—The great Caird—Letter to Hogg, giving an account of the Tour—Criticism on the Poets—Letter to Mr. Smith, proposing a new volume of Poems—Publication of "The City of the Plague"—Letters to his Wife—Letter to Mr. Smith—Letter from Jeffrey on his Poems—Loch Awe—Letter to Mrs. Wilson, from Achlian—Adventure with Tinkers—His mode of Fishing—Letters to Mrs. Wilson, from Blair-Athole and Dingwall—Adventure at Tomintoul—Mrs. Grant of Laggan's remarks on Wilson—At Elleray—Patrick Robertson....................................119–152

CHAPTER VIII.

LITERATURE.—BLACKWOOD'S MAGAZINE.

1817–'20.

His Connection with Periodical Literature—*Edinburgh Monthly Magazine*—Letter to Mrs. Wilson from Kinloch Rannoch—Review of Lalla Rookh—Fishing Tour—Letters from Jeffrey regarding Contributions for the *Edinburgh Review*—Fragment from Jeffrey regarding a Vindication of Wordsworth—State of Parties in Edinburgh in 1817—Establishment of *Blackwood*—Early Editors and Contributors—The *Scots Magazine*—A change in the Management—Number VII.—The New Contributors—The Scorpion—The Leopard—Mr. Lockhart—John Wilson—Mr. Robert Sym—James Hogg—Mystifications—Leigh Hunt and Sir J. G. Dalyell—More Mystification—Dr. James Scott, 7 Miller Street, Glasgow, *alias* The Odontist—Captain Paton's Lament—The Dilettanti Club—Letters from Mrs. Wilson to her Sister Miss Penny on the Magazine—Ensign O'Doherty—A Magazine Row, etc.—The Style of Criticism adopted—Letter to Professor Laugner—The Attack upon Professor Playfair—Ill Results—Hypocrisy Unveiled—Correspondence with the Author—Letter from Mr. Morehead—Letter to Mr. Morehead—Letter from Jeffrey, vindicating the *Edinburgh Review* from the Charge of Infidelity....................................153–198

CHAPTER IX.

MORAL PHILOSOPHY CHAIR.

1820.

Removes to Ann Street—Sir Henry Raeburn—Sir John Watson Gordon—Sir William Allan—Death of Dr. Thomas Brown—Announces himself as a Candidate for the Chair of Moral Philosophy—Sir William Hamilton—Fierce opposition by the Whig party—Letters from Mrs. Wilson on the struggle—Letters to Rev. J. Fleming and Mrs. Grant of Laggan for a Certificate as to Character—Mrs. Grant's reply—Letter from Sir Walter Scott—His Election—Letter from Mrs. Wilson on her husband's success—Letter to Mr. Smith—Preparations for his Lectures—Correspondence with Dr. Blair—A Fancy Sketch of the new Professor in his Study—Correspondence with Blair—Opening Lecture of his First Course....................................198–225

CHAPTER X.

THE PROFESSOR AND HIS CLASS.

His Syllabus—The Professor in his Sporting Jacket—Adventure in Hawick—"A little Mill"—Makes two Students at home in Ann Street—The Professor and his "Children" at St. Mary's Loch—Mr. Hill Burton's Reminiscences of the winter of 1830—A Market-day at Tarland—A kind Teacher—A Dinner at Gloucester Place—His Class—Saturday—A Snow-ball Riot—Any Old Clothes?—"Sir Peter Nimmo" and the poet Wordsworth—Dr. Syntax—A "Conservative" Meeting—Politics in the Class—Rev. Mr. Smith's Recollections of 1837—As a Lecturer—His Course for 1837-1838—Illustration, the Love of Power—His Power as an Orator—"The Demosthenes of Ireland"—An Episode in the Class-room—His Care and Industry in Examining the Students' Essays—His Kindness to them privately—The Session for 1850-1851—Mr. A. Taylor Innes—"Professor Wilson's Gold Medal"—The Origin of the Moral Faculty—His Appearance in the Class-room—An Unmannerly Student .... Pages 225-256.

CHAPTER XI.

LITERARY AND DOMESTIC LIFE.

1820–'26.

Lays from Fairy Land—Devotion to the Magazine, and Friendship for Mr. Blackwood—Lights and Shadows of Scottish Life—A Summer in Elleray once more—Letter from Mr. Blackwood—Letter from Mr. Lockhart on Mr. Leigh Hunt—The Gormandizing School of Eloquence—Miss Edgeworth, etc., etc.—Tom Purdie—Willie Laidlaw, etc.—Letters from Mr. Blackwood regarding the Magazine—Another Summer at Elleray—Letter from Mr. Blackwood—Letters from Mr. Lockhart—The People he met in London—Edward Irving's Preaching described—Party Politics—Literary Gossip—Old Slop and the *New Times*—A Daily Paper at the Breakfast-table, etc.—Letter from De Quincey—Hill on Education—The "Breeches" Review—"A Confession"—Accident to Mrs. Wilson—Letter to Mr. R. Findlay—Death of Mrs. Wilson, Senior—Letter from Principal Baird—Removal to Gloucester Place—The Proposed Chair of Political Economy—Letters from Mr. Patrick Robertson, Mr. Huskisson, Mr. Canning, and Sir Robert Peel on the Subject—Literary work—Projected "Outlines"—Correspondence of Mr. Lockhart and Mr. Wilson on "Janus"—Letters from Mr. Lockhart on Sir Walter's visit to Elleray—Letter from Professor Jameson—Letter from Mr. Lockhart on Canning—W. Maginn—Letter from Mr. Blackwood—Letter to Delta on "Janus"—Illness of Mrs. Wilson—Letter from Mr. Lockhart, on becoming Editor of the *Quarterly Review*—Work during 1826—Letters to Mrs. Wilson from Kendal—Colonsay 256-298

CHAPTER XII.

LITERARY AND DOMESTIC LIFE.

1827–'29.

As a Friendly Critic—Letter to Delta—Views on Free Trade—"Mansie Waugh," etc.—Notes to Mr. Ballantyne—Innerleithen—Letter to Mr. Fleming, Rayrig, on "Christopher North," etc.—Letters to Mrs. Wilson—Hartley Coleridge—Contributions for 1828—Letters from Allan Cunningham, regarding "The Anniversary," "Edderline's Dream," etc.—Mrs. Wilson to Miss Penny—"Evening at Furness Abbey"—Letter from James Hogg, declining an invitation to Elleray—Letter to Mr. Fleming—Letter from Thomas Carlyle—Letter from Mr. Lockhart—Contest for Oxford University, 1829—Letter to De Quincey, on his Sketch of the Professor—Thomas De Quincey—Affection for him—His visit to Gloucester Place........................... 299-328

CHAPTER XIII.

LITERARY AND DOMESTIC LIFE.—CRUISE WITH THE EXPERIMENTAL SQUADRON.

1830–'32.

Home Life in Gloucester Place—Letters to Mrs. Wilson from Penny Bridge and Westmoreland—Homeric Papers—Letter from Sotheby—Letter from Miss Watson—A Conservative Meeting and Liberal Commentary—Criticism on Tennyson—Letter to Mrs. Wilson on his Cruise with the Experimental Squadron—London—Greenwich—H. M. S. the "Vernon"—Sheerness—On board the "Vernon"—A Sailor's Death at Sea—Plymouth—The "Campeadora"—The "Vernon" -Holystoning—Off the Lizard—Land's End—Cork—London and Home.........Pages 328-359

CHAPTER XIV.

LITERARY AND DOMESTIC LIFE.

1832-'37.

Letter from an Author to a Critic—Political Feeling—Paper on Ebenezer Elliot, and Letter from him—"Come and break a ton" of iron—Letter from Mr. Audubon—From Rev. James White of Bonchurch—Letters to James Hogg—"The Shepherd's Reconciliation"—An Autumn in Ettrick—Rover and the Witch—Pets—A Dog Fight—Thirlstane Castle—Letters to Mrs. Wilson from Edinburgh—Mr. Blackwood's Illness and Death—Letters from the Clyde to Mrs. Wilson—Public Dinner at Paisley—Last Letter from Mrs. Wilson to her Sister—Illness and Death of Mrs. Wilson..359-383

CHAPTER XV.

LITERARY AND DOMESTIC LIFE.

1837-'44.

Depression of Spirits—Life at Roslin—Marriage of his Daughters—His main work that of a Teacher—His little ways at Home—Pets—The Sparrow—His Dogs: Brontë—Tory—Grog—Game Birds—A new Coop—A Note to Delta on the Dispersion of his Aviary—Work for the Year—Letters to Mr. Aird on Burns—Had Burns Family Worship at Dumfries?—The Professor's Study—Writing for Blackwood—Habits of Composition—Letter to Mr. Findlay from Rothesay—Cladich—A Fairy's Funeral—Letter to his Daughter describing Billholm—Review of Macaulay's Lays—Letter to Dr. Moir..383-407

CHAPTER XVI.

LITERARY AND DOMESTIC LIFE

1844-'48.

Characteristic Letters from John Gibson Lockhart—The Kemp Absurdity—Maga—Novel Reading, etc.—Letter to his son John on Domestic matters—"The Kemp Affair"—Walking Feats—The Burns Festival—Letter to Sheriff Gordon—Letters from Sergeant Talfourd, excusing himself from attendance at the "Festival"—Letter to Aird—Letter to his daughter Jane—Fishing in the Dochart—Letter to his daughter Jane—Maga Articles resumed in 1845—British Critics—Elleray—Letter to Sheriff Gordon, asking him to *edit* an Article of his for Blackwood—Opening of Edinburgh Philosophical Institution, of which he was elected President—Melancholy Reflections—Letter to Mr. Findlay requesting his presence at the Marriage of his son John—Visit to the newly Married Pair—Resolves not to return to Elleray—Weakness in the Hand, writes consequently with difficulty—Byron's "Address to the Ocean"—Peculiarities of Dress—Still in Mourning for his Wife— A Street Scene—A Carter defeated—Humanity to Animals—Visits to London—Sitting for a Portrait—Conversational Powers—Reminiscences of Social Meetings—Jeffrey's Receptions—Lord Robertson—The Professor's Songs—Sailor's Life at Sea—Auld Lang Syne—"A Quaint Ballad"...407-432

CHAPTER XVII.

CLOSING YEARS.

1849-'54

"Dies Boreales"—Rituals of the Church—The Scottish Service—Marriage of his youngest daughter to Professor Aytoun—Playful ways—Toilet peculiarities—His Watch—Hat—Snuff-box—Gloves, etc., etc.—Horror of Gas—Love of Children—Letter to his second son Blair, mentioning

"Billy's" Death—Letter to his son Blair—The "Dear Doctor"—From College Duties on account of Ill Health—Illness—Desire to return to his Labors—Excursion to the Highlands in search of Health—Passion for Angling—Visit to his Brother at Woodburn—Determines to retire from Active Life—Letter from the Lord Advocate to Sheriff Gordon, conveying the news of the Grant of a Pension of £300 per annum—Letter from Lord John Russell to the Lord Advocate, desiring him to have the Queen's intentions mentioned to Wilson—Receives the News—Letter of Acknowledgment to Lord John Russell—Takes up his abode at Woodburn—Last Papers for Magazine—Step feeble and unsteady—Letter to his son Blair, thanking him for supplies of Books—Macaulay a Candidate for the Representation of Edinburgh—Comes to Edinburgh and Votes for Macaulay—Letter from Macaulay to Sheriff Gordon, expressing his kindly feelings towards the Professor—Last Visit of Mr. Lockhart—Letter to Robert Findlay, congratulating him on the Marriage of his Son—At Gloucester Place again—The Last Christmas—Seized with a Shock of Paralysis—Rapid Decline—The End.......Pages 432–462

APPENDIX.

I.—Public Funeral and Proposed Statue.......463
II.—Correspondence relating to *Janus*.......464
III.—List of Professor Wilson's Contributions to *Blackwood's Magazine* from 1826.......470
INDEX.......477

LIST OF ILLUSTRATIONS.

	ARTIST.	PAGE
Portrait—from a Photograph (frontispiece), .	D. O. HILL.	
"The Strictures of the Edinburgh Review, considered at a Private Meeting of the Caput,"	J. G. LOCKHART.	54
Mr. Patrick Robertson, ...	PROF. E. FORBES.	151
The "Leopard,"	J. G. LOCKHART.	165
The "Scorpion,"	DO.	169
A Scotch Minister, ...	DO.	173
A Scotch Judge, ...	DO.	177
Mr. Gibson Lockhart, ...	DO.	185
Sir William Hamilton, ...	DO.	203

MEMOIR OF JOHN WILSON.

CHAPTER I.

BOYHOOD.

The epithets "pretty" and "pleasant," more than once applied in the writings of Professor Wilson to the place of his birth, are not those which the passing traveller would now think most appropriate to the town of Paisley, where the smoke and steam of countless factories incessantly roll over the inky waters of once fair-flowing Cart. And yet it was not the mere partiality of filial affection that made it seem both pretty and pleasant to his eyes, for such it truly was in the days when he first knew it. And has it not still its pleasant walks and pretty gardens, and its grand old Abbey? Do not green Gleniffer and Stanley Shaw still flourish near enough to be enjoyed? Is it not pleasant still to look beyond fields and trees to the sacred spot called Elderslie? And though gauze and cotton be even more than ever the chief concern of Paisley, has it not still its poets and musicians and men of taste, to make it a "pleasant" habitation, in spite of smoke and steam and sluggish waters? No native of that respectable old town need be ashamed of his birthplace, and justly is it proud of him who stands foremost among all its sons.

A somewhat gloomy-looking house in a dingy court at the head of the High Street, now used as a lecture-hall for the artisans of Paisley, is preserved as classic ground, under the name of "Wilson's Hall." In that house the poet was born, on the 18th of May, 1785. At no great distance stands the family residence, to which, after the birth of John, their first son but fourth child, Mr. and

Mrs. Wilson removed. It is a stately building, with large gardens, and an imposing entrance. The windows to the back command an extensive view of a beautiful undulating country, with the nearer prospect of a woody vale and rich sloping fields, a landscape sufficiently attractive to have awakened the love of nature in a child's heart, and to have held dominion there in after days, when memory recalled the home of youth, and those delightful pictures of boyhood's life which were immortalized in the "Recreations of Christopher North." Of Mr. Wilson, senior, I know little more than that he was a wealthy man, having realized his fortune in trade as a gauze manufacturer. The integrity of his character and his mercantile successes gave him an important position in society, and he is still remembered in Paisley as having been in his own day one of the richest and most respected of its community; while his house possessed a great attraction in his admirable and beautiful wife, a lady of rare intellect, wit, humor, wisdom, and grace. Her maiden name was Margaret Sym. Her brother Robert is not unknown to fame, as the "Timothy Tickler" of the *Noctes Ambrosianæ.* Her mother, of the Dunlops of Garnkirk, was lineally descended, by the female side, from the great Marquis of Montrose. Whether this gentle blood had any thing to do with the physical characteristics of the family or not, certain it is that Mrs. Wilson, her sons and daughters, were remarkably distinguished by personal beauty, of a refined and dignified type. An aspect so stately as that of the old lady is not often to be seen. Nor was she less gifted with qualities more durable than beauty; for ere long she was called upon, by the death of her husband, to exercise the wisdom and strength of her character in rearing a large family of sons and daughters. How well she performed that duty was best seen in the reverence and love of her children, all of whom, save two sons and a daughter, lived to shed tears over her grave, and to give proof, in their own lives, of that admirable training which had taught them betimes the way that they should go.*

* It will not be out of place here to give the names of the ten children born to Mr. Wilson and his wife:—

1. Grace Wilson, married George Cashel, Esquire, Ireland; died, 1835. 2. Jane Wilson, died unmarried, 1835. 3. Margaret Wilson, married John Ferrier, Esquire, W. S., Edinburgh; died, 1831. 4. John Wilson, married Miss Jane Penny; died, 1854. 5. Andrew Wilson, married Miss Aitken, Glasgow; died, 1812. 6. Henrietta Wilson, died young. 7. William Wilson, died in infancy 8. Robert Sym Wilson, married Miss Eliza Penny. 9. Elizabeth Wilson, married Sir John M'Neill, G. C. B. 10. James Wilson, married Miss Isabella Keith, Edinburgh; died, 1856

In his childish years, John Wilson was as beautiful and animated a creature as ever played in the sunshine. That passion for sports, and especially angling, in which his strong nature found such characteristic vent in after years, was developed at an age when most little boys are still hardly safe beyond the nurse's apron-strings. He was but three years old when he rambled off one day, armed with a willow wand, duly furnished with a thread line and crooked pin, to fish in a "wee burnie," of which he had taken note, away a good mile from home. Unknown to any one, already appreciating the fascination of an undisturbed and solitary "cast," the blue-eyed and golden-haired adventurer sallied forth to the water-side, to spend a day of unforgotten delight, lashing away at the rippling stream, with what success we may perhaps find recorded in Fytte First of "Christopher in his Sporting Jacket:"—

"A tug—a tug! With face ten times flushed and pale by turns ere you could count ten, he at last has strength, in the agitation of his fear and joy, to pull away at the monster; and there he lies in his beauty among the gowans and the greensward, for he has whapped him right over his head and far away, a fish a quarter of an ounce in weight, and, at the very least, two inches long! Off he flies, on wings of wind, to his father, mother, and sisters, and brothers and cousins, and all the neighborhood, holding the fish aloft in both hands, still fearful of its escape; and, like a genuine child of corruption, his eyes brighten at the first blush of cold blood on his small fumy fingers. He carries about with him, up-stairs and down-stairs, his prey upon a plate; he will not wash his hands before dinner, for he exults in the silver scales adhering to the thumb-nail that scooped the pin out of the baggy's maw; and at night, 'cabined, cribbed, confined,' he is overheard murmuring in his sleep—a thief, a robber, and a murderer, in his yet infant dreams!"

While the future Christopher was thus early asserting himself out of doors, the "Professor" also was displaying his capacity in the nursery. There his activity and animation kept the little circle alive from morning to night. With his sisters he was a great favorite; they looked up to his superior intelligence, and wondered at all he did. Of in-door amusements, the most exciting to their youthful minds and his precocious genius was that of pulpit oratory. One sermon he used himself to speak of as being a *chef-*

d'œuvre. So much was it appreciated, that he was continually called on to repeat it. Standing upon a chair, arranged to look as like a pulpit as possible, he would address his juvenile congregation, along with the more mature audience of nurses and other servants assembled to listen to his warning voice. The text chosen was one from his own fertile brain, drawn from that field of experience in which he was already becoming an adept, and handled not without shrewd application to moral duties. These were the words: "There was a fish, and it was a deil o' a fish, and it was ill to its young anes." In this allegory of life he displayed both pathos and humor, drawing a contrast between good and evil parents that excited sympathy and laughter, while the sermon was delivered with a vehemence of natural eloquence that, in a boy of five years old, may well have entitled him to be looked upon as a genius.

One other anecdote may here be given, which he used to tell with much humor. As a child, he was very fond of drawing, an accomplishment he regretted in after life having laid aside, before he had acquired sufficient skill to enable him to sketch from nature. One day he had copied a tiger, and, no doubt, having given to the animal considerable characteristic vigor, his mother—with natural mother's pride—treasured the specimen highly. He was not aware of the sensation this juvenile success in art had created, till one morning a visitor was announced when he was present, and was scarcely seated, ere, to his surprise, she was accosted by Mrs. Wilson with the words, pronounced in broad Scotch, as was the manner in those days with many well-educated people, "Have ye seen oure John's teegar?" when forthwith the "teegar" was exhibited to the admiring eyes of her guest. It was not long before "oure John's teegar" was well known in Paisley.*

The time had now come when the training of the nursery was to be followed by regular education at school, and John was committed to the tuition of Mr. James Peddie, English teacher, Paisley. To a child who loved to learn, the drudgery of a first apprenticeship at school would never be irksome. A year or two with Mr.

* In Flight First of "The Moors," I find an allusion to this work of art. "Strange that, with all our love of nature and of art, we never were a painter. True that in boyhood we were no contemptible hand at a lion or a tiger—and sketches by us of such cats springing or preparing to spring in keelivine, dashed off some fifty or sixty years ago, might well make Edwin Landseer stare."

Peddie prepared him to enter upon more arduous studies. He left the teacher of his childhood with regret.

The kindness and partiality with which he loved to speak of his friends in Paisley, may be seen in the words he made use of in reference to this old friend, as he was taking leave of duties he had followed for upwards of half a century. They are honorable alike to master and pupil:—

"It was his method rather to persuade than enforce, and they all saw, even amidst the thoughtlessness of boyhood, that their teacher was a good man; and therefore it was their delight and pride to please him. Sometimes a cloud would overshadow his brow, but it was succeeded by a smile of pleasure as gracious and benign as the summer sky. In his seminary, children of all ranks sat on the same form. In that school there was no distinction, except what was created by superior merit and industry, by the love of truth, and by ability. The son of the poor man was there on the same form with the sons of the rich, and nothing could ever drive him from his rightful *status* but misconduct or disobedience. No person would deny that the office of a teacher of youth was one of the most important in this world's affairs. A surly or ignorant master might scathe those blossoms, which a man of sense and reflection, by his fostering care, would rear up till they became bright consummate flowers of knowledge and virtue."

The Manse of the neighboring parish of Mearns was the next place fixed upon by Mr. Wilson to continue the education of his son; and there he found a *dolce pedagogo* fitted in every way to carry on the instruction in knowledge and virtue so well begun under the good Mr. Peddie. The Rev. George M'Latchie won no less a share of his pupil's veneration—"the minister in whose house he passed many of his sweetest youthful days, and who regarded him with a paternal, as he always looked up to *him* with a filial regard." That warm heart was ever ready with its tribute of affection to the memory of good men; and amid the tender recollections of the past, hallowed by sentiments of gratitude, no place is more touchingly alluded to than "the dear parish of Mearns." Whoever wishes to find a perfect description of its physical features, as well as most exquisite pictures of the youthful pleasures on which memory cast back a glory, must turn to the pages of the *Recreations*, particularly to the papers entitled "Our Parish," "Christopher in his Sporting Jacket," and "May Day." From the latter I cannot resist the quotation of the opening paragraph, perhaps the most beautiful of his many apostrophes to that beloved region:—

"Art thou beautiful, as of old, O wild, moorland, sylvan, and pastoral Parish! the Paradise in which our spirit dwelt beneath the glorious dawning of life—can it be, beloved world of boyhood, that thou art indeed beautiful as of old? Though round and round thy boundaries in half an hour could fly the flapping dove—though the martins, wheeling to and fro that ivied and wall-flowered ruin of a castle, central in its own domain, seem in their more distant flight to glance their crescent wings over a vale rejoicing apart in another kirk-spire, yet how rich in streams, and rivulets, and rills, each with its own peculiar murmur, art thou, with thy bold bleak exposure, sloping upwards in ever lustrous undulations to the portals of the East! How endless the interchange of woods and meadows, glens, dells, and broomy nooks, without number, among thy banks and braes! And then of human dwellings!—how rises the smoke, ever and anon, into the sky, all neighboring on each other, so that the cock-crow is heard from homestead to homestead; while, as you wander onwards, each roof still rises unexpectedly, and as solitary as if it had been far remote. Fairest of Scotland's thousand parishes—neither Highland nor Lowland—but undulating—let us again use the descriptive word—like the sea in sunset after a day of storms—yes, Heaven's blessing be upon thee! Thou art indeed beautiful as of old!"

Of the precocity of this boy there is evidence enough; but, unlike most precocious children, he was foremost in the play-ground as well as at the task. With him both work and play were equally enjoyed, and he threw his whole energy into the one or other in its turn. In school he was every inch the scholar; but when the books were laid aside, and the fresh air played on his bright cheeks, he was king of all sports, the foremost and the maddest in every jocund enterprise. A pleasant idea of the relation in which the kind minister of the Mearns stood to his pupils, is given in a note from Sir John Maxwell of Pollok, who was a schoolfellow of my father:

"He was above me in the ranks of the school, in stature, and mental acquirements. I may mention, as an illustration of the energy, activity, and vivacity of his character, that one morning, I having been permitted to go and fish in the burn near the kirk, and having caught a fine trout, was so pleased, that I repaired to the minister's study to exhibit my prize to Dr. M'Latchie, who was then reading Greek with him. He, seeing my trout, started up; and, addressing his reverend teacher, said, 'I *must* go now to fish.' Leave was granted, and I willingly resigned to him my rod and line; and before dinner he re-appeared with a large dish of fish, on which he and his companions feasted, not without that admiration of his achievement which youth delights to express and always feels."

This simple relation, to those who knew the man in after life, and have heard him speak of the happy hours which gave, in his eyes, so great a charm to "Our Parish," suggests one of those bright days he loved to wander to in memory, long after the sunny visions of youth had glided into the silent past. "Such days," says he, "seem now to us—as memory and imagination half restore and half create the past into such weather as may have shone over the bridal morn of our first parents in Paradise—to have been frequent—nay, to have lasted all the summer long—when our boyhood was bright from the hands of God. Each of those days was in itself a life!"*

It is impossible to overrate the influence of such a training as young Wilson had, during these happy years, in forming that singular character, in virtue of which he stands out as unique and inimitable among British men of genius, as Jean Paul, *Der Einzige*, among his countrymen. In no other writings do we find so inexhaustible and vivid a reminiscence of the feelings of boyhood. There was in that heart of his a perpetual well-spring of youthful emotion. In contact with him, we are made to feel as if this man were in himself the type, never to grow old, of all the glorious bright-eyed youths that we have known in the world; capable of entering, with perfect luxury of abandonment, into their wildest frolics, but also of transfiguring their pastimes into mirrors of things more sublime—of rising, without strain or artifice, from the level of common and material objects into the serene heights of poetic, philosophic, and religious contemplation. Not in vain was this brilliant youth, with his capacity for every form of activity, bodily and mental, his passionate love of nature, and his deep rev-

* "Soliloquy on the Seasons," Wilson's *Works*.

erence for all things high and pure, placed in the springtime of his days amid the manifold wholesome influences of a Scottish manse and school in the "wild, moorland, sylvan, pastoral parish" of Mearns. For truly has he himself remarked of the importance of this period of life, "Some men, it is sarcastically said, are boys all life long, and carry with them their puerility to the grave. 'Twould be well for the world were there in it more such men. By way of proving their manhood, we have heard grown-up people abuse their own boyhood, forgetting what our great philosophical poet—after Milton and Dryden—has told them, that

'The boy is father of the man,'

and thus libelling the author of their existence. . . . Not only are the foundations dug and laid in boyhood, of all the knowledge and the feelings of our prime, but the ground-flat too built, and often the entire second story of the superstructure, from the windows of which, the soul, looking out, beholds nature in her state, and leaps down, unafraid of a fall on the green or white bosom of earth, to join with hymns the front of the procession. The soul afterwards perfects her palace—building up tier after tier of all imaginable orders of architecture—till the shadowy roof, gleaming with golden cupolas, like the cloud-region of the setting sun, set the heavens ablaze."*

It were a vain task to attempt, in any words but his own, to recall some of those boyish experiences, which made that life in the Mearns so rich a seed-field of bright memories and imaginations. I must, therefore, draw upon the pages of the *Recreations* for a few pictures of "Young Kit," as he appeared to himself looked at through the vista of half a life. After describing how his youthful passion for the observation of nature impelled him, when a mere child, to wander away among the moors and woods, he goes on:—

"Once it was feared that poor wee Kit was lost; for having set off all by himself, at sunrise, to draw a night-line from the distant Black Loch, and look at a trap set for a glede, a mist overtook him on the moor on his homeward way, with an eel as long as himself hanging over his shoulder, and held him prisoner for many hours within its shifting walls, frail indeed, and opposing no resistance to the hand, yet impenetrable to the feet of fear as the stone dungeon's

* Wilson's *Works*.

thraldom. If the mist had remained, that would have been nothing; only a still cold wet seat on a stone; but as 'a trot becomes a gallop soon, in spite of curb and rein,' so a Scotch mist becomes a shower —and a shower a flood—and a flood a storm—and a storm a tempest—and a tempest thunder and lightning—and thunder and lightning heavenquake and earthquake—till the heart of poor wee Kit quaked, and almost died within him in the desert. In this age of Confessions, need we be ashamed to own, in the face of the whole world, that we sat us down and cried! The small brown moorland bird, as dry as a toast, hopped out of his heather-hole, and cheerfully cheeped comfort. With crest just a thought lowered by the rain the green-backed, white-breasted peaseweep, walked close by us in the mist; and, sight of wonder, that made even in that quandary by the quagmire our heart beat with joy—lo! never seen before, and seldom since, three wee peaseweeps, not three days old, little bigger than shrew-mice, all covered with blackish down, interspersed with long white hair, running after their mother! But the large hazel eye of the she peaseweep, restless even in the most utter solitude, soon spied us glowering at her, and her young ones, through our tears; and not for a moment doubting (Heaven forgive her for the shrewd but cruel suspicion!) that we were Lord Eglinton's gamekeeper, with a sudden shrill cry that thrilled to the marrow in our cold backbone, flapped and fluttered herself away into the mist, while the little black bits of down disappeared, like devils, into the moss. The croaking of the frogs grew terrible. And worse and worse, close at hand, seeking his lost cows through the mist, the bellow of the notorious red bull! We began saying our prayers; and just then the sun forced himself out into the open day, and, like the sudden opening of the shutters of a room, the whole world was filled with light. The frogs seemed to sink among the powheads; as for the red bull who had tossed the tinker, he was cantering away, with his tail towards us, to a lot of cows on the hill; and hark—a long, a loud, an oft-repeated halloo! Rab Roger, honest fellow, and Leezy Muir, honest lass, from the manse, in search of our dead body! Rab pulls our ears lightly, and Leezy kisses us from the one to the other, wrings the rain out of our long yellow hair (a pretty contrast to the small gray sprig now on the crown of our pericranium, and the thin tail acock behind); and by-and-by stepping into Hazel-Deanhead for a drap and a 'chitterin' piece,' by the

1*

time we reach the manse we are as dry as a whistle—take our scold and our pawmies from the minister—and, by way of punishment and penance, after a little hot whiskey-toddy, with brown sugar and a bit of bun, are bundled off to bed in the daytime!"

Could any thing be more deliciously vivid than that picture of little Kit and the maternal peaseweep "glowering" at each other in the midst of the Scotch mist?

Let us see him now a few years older, and some inches taller, armed with that remarkable piece of artillery, "Muckle-mou'd Meg," of which he has himself given this most inimitable description, or one only equalled by Hood's glorious schoolboy epistles:—

"There had been from time immemorial, it was understood, in the Manse, a duck-gun of very great length, and a musket that, according to an old tradition, had been out both in the Fifteen and Forty-five. There were ten boys of us, and we succeeded by rotation to gun or musket, each boy retaining possession for a single day only; but then the shooting season continued all the year. They must have been of admirable materials and workmanship; for neither of them so much as once burst during the Seven Years' War. The musket, who, we have often since thought, must surely rather have been a blunderbuss in disguise, was a perfect devil for kicking when she received her discharge; so much so, indeed, that it was reckoned creditable for the smaller boys not to be knocked down by the recoil. She had a very wide mouth—and was thought by us 'an awfu' scatterer;' a qualification which we considered of the very highest merit. She carried any thing we chose to put into her—there still being of all her performances a loud and favorable report—balls, buttons, chuckystanes, slugs, or hail. She had but two faults: she had got addicted, probably in early life, to one habit of burning priming, and to another of hanging fire; habits of which it was impossible, for us at least, to break her by the most assiduous hammering of many a new series of flints; but such was the high place she justly occupied in the affection and admiration of us all, that faults like these did not in the least detract from her general character. Our delight, when she did absolutely and positively and *bonâ fide* 'go off,' was in proportion to the comparative rarity of that occurrence; and as to hanging fire—why, we used to let her take her own time, contriving to keep her at the level as long as our strength sufficed, eyes shut perhaps, teeth clenched, face girning, and head slightly averted over the right shoulder, till Muckle-mou'd Meg, who, like most other Scottish females, took things leisurely, went off at last with an explosion like the blowing up of a rock."

If we would see him, at a further stage of boyhood, engaged in still more exciting and boisterous sport, we would need to go back into the *mêlée* of the "Snowball Bicker of Pedmount,"* a quiet Homeric episode, to which it is impossible to do justice by an extract. Those who care, in short, to obtain as complete a picture of that boyish life as it is possible now to have, will find it for themselves in the pages of the *Recreations*, few of which are without some tender and graphic reminiscences of his early days. They are not, of course, to be always taken as literal descriptions of things that happened exactly as there painted; for, as he himself acutely observes, giving the *rationale* of such reminiscence:—"You must know that, unless it be accompanied with imagination, memory is cold and lifeless. . . . All minds, even the dullest, remember the days of their youth; but all cannot bring back the indescribable brightness of that blessed season. They who would know what they once were, must not merely recollect, but they must imagine the hills and valleys, if any such there were, in which their childhood played. . . . To imagine what he then heard and saw, he must imagine his own nature. He must collect from many vanished hours the power of his untamed heart, and he must, perhaps, transfuse also something of his own maturer mind into these dreams of his former being, thus linking the past with the present by a continuous chain, which, though often invisible, is never broken." That my father, in these pictures of his youth, did transfuse something of his maturer mind into the vision is manifest enough, and therein lies their peculiar charm and beauty. But of the general fidelity of the impression they convey there can be no doubt. As regards in particular that surpassing excellence in all physical sports which might sometimes appear to be the exaggeration of poetic fancy, there is sufficient testimony from contemporaries. Thus a schoolfellow of his writes: "There were other boys five or six years his senior; but in all games, in running, in jumping, in hockey, he was the first and fastest; and he could run faster, and walk longer than

* Wilsons' *Works*.

any of us." Another says: "He excited our admiration by his excellence in fishing;" while, in regard to "mental superiority," he adds, "he was a capital scholar, and further in advance of the generality of the boys at Mearns than he outshone his competitors in after life."

That, with all this many-sided ability, and the undoubted consciousness of superior power, he was a prime favorite among his fellows, is not difficult to believe, when we find how affectionate and magnanimous was his nature; a nature in which the development of soul and body, of intellect and feeling, attained a harmony so rare. The combination of these gifts in such goodly proportion enabled him to enter, with a sympathy destitute of all affectation, into the feelings and pursuits of persons of the most diverse character; and throughout all the exuberance of his literary activity, much as there is in its earlier stages of impetuosity, and sometimes even *sansculottism*, there is nowhere, from beginning to end, one trace of malignity or envy. Even such was he in those happy boyish days, when he "bathed his feet in beauty" by the banks of the Yearn, and nourished "a youth sublime" in the pure and healthful atmosphere of the dear old Manse.

I pass with reluctance from this happy period, to which my father's heart ever turned with a freshness of delight which years and sorrows seemed only to increase. The chapter may fitly close with his own account of the feelings with which he bade farewell to that beloved parish, never mentioned without benediction and eulogium.

"Then this was to be our last year in the parish—now dear to us as our birthplace; nay, itself our very birthplace—for in it from the darkness of infancy had our soul been born. Once gone and away from the region of cloud and mountain, we felt that most probably never more should we return. For others, who thought they knew us better than we did ourselves, had chalked out a future life for young Christopher North—a life that was sure to lead to honor, and riches, and a splendid name. Therefore we determined, with a strong, resolute, insatiate spirit of passion, to make the most—the best—of the few months that remained to us of that, our wild, free, and romantic existence, as yet untrammelled by those inexorable laws, which, once launched into the world, all alike—young and old—must obey. Our books were flung aside—nor did our old master and minister frown, for he grudged not to the boy he loved the remnant of the dream about to be rolled away like the dawn's rosy clouds. We demanded with our eye—not with our voice—one long holiday throughout that our last autumn, on to the pale farewell blossoms of the Christmas rose. With our rod we went earlier to the loch or river; but we had not known thoroughly our own soul—for now we angled less passionately, less perseveringly, than was our wont of yore, sitting in a pensive, a melancholy, a miserable dream, by the dashing waterfall or the murmuring wave. With our gun we plunged earlier in the morning into the forest, and we returned later at eve; but less earnest, less eager, were we to hear the cushat's moan from his yew-tree—to see the hawk's shadow on the glade, as he hung aloft on the sky. A thousand dead thoughts came to life again in the gloom of the woods, and we sometimes did wring our hands in an agony of grief, to know that our eyes should not behold the birch-tree brightening there with another spring.

"Then every visit we paid to cottage or to shieling was felt to be a farewell; there was something mournful in the smiles on the sweet faces of the ruddy rustics, with their silken snoods, to whom we used to whisper harmless love-meanings, in which there was no guile. We regarded the solemn toil-and-care-worn countenances of the old with a profounder emotion than had ever touched our hearts in the hour of our more thoughtless joy; and the whole life of those dwellers among the woods, and the moors, and the mountains, seemed to us far more affecting now that we saw deeper into it, in the light of a melancholy sprung from the conviction that the time was close at hand when we should mingle with it no more. The thoughts that possessed our most secret bosom failed not by the least observant to be discovered in our open eyes. They who had liked us before, now loved us; our faults, our follies, the insolences of our reckless boyhood, were all forgotten; whatever had been our sins, pride towards the poor was never among the number; we had shunned not stooping our head beneath the humblest lintel; our mite had been given to the widow who had lost her own; quarrelsome with the young we might sometimes have been, for boyhood is soon heated, and boils before a defying eye; but in one thing at least we were Spartans—we reverèd the head of old age.

"And many at last were the kind—some the sad—farewells, ere long whispered by us at gloaming among the glens. Let them rest for ever silent amidst that music in the memory which is felt, not heard—its blessing mute though breathing, like an inarticulate prayer!"

CHAPTER II.

GLASGOW COLLEGE.

1797–1803.

"Long, long, long ago, the time when we danced hand in hand with our golden-haired sister! Long, long, long ago, the day on which she died; the hour, so far more dismal than any hour that can now darken us on this earth, when her coffin descended slowly, slowly into the horrid clay, and we were borne, deathlike and wishing to die, out of the churchyard, that from that moment we thought we could never enter more." That touching reminiscence of his golden-haired sister, which came back among the visions of a merry Christmas long after,* points to what was probably John Wilson's first deep experience of sorrow; and it is no imaginary picture of the scene it recalled. For even in those early years, and still more as life advanced, he was intensely susceptible to emotions of grief, as well as of gladness. A heavier trial awaited him at the threshold of the new life on which he was to enter after leaving the manse of Mearns in his twelfth year. He had seen the yellow leaves fall, on to the close of that last memorable autumn which finished his happy school-time, and now he was summoned home to see his father die. As he stood at the head of the grave, chief mourner, and heard the dull earth rattling over the coffin, his emotions so overcame him that he fell to the ground in a swoon, and had to be carried away. Such an effect, on a frame more than commonly robust, indicated a depth of feeling and passion not often seen in our clime among boys, or, in its outer manifestations

* "Christmas Dreams," Wilson's *Works*.

at least, among men. The aspect and the character of Wilson have sometimes suggested to the imagination those blue-eyed and long-haired Norsemen, who made their songs amid the smiting of swords, who were as swift of foot and strong of arm as they were skilled in lore and ready in counsel, fierce to their enemies, tender and true to their friends. And this little incident reminds one more of what we read in Sagas of that passionate vehemence of theirs, than any thing we are accustomed to now-a-days.

After the death of his father, he appears to have gone immediately to Glasgow University, where he entered as a student in the Latin class for the session of 1797–'98, attending other classes in due course down to 1803. During those years he resided in the family of Professor Jardine, the same prudence which had dictated the choice of his earlier instructors being here again conspicuous, and the results not less satisfactory. His life in Glasgow was a happy one; and, under the combined influences of admirable professorial instruction and a free enjoyment of good society and innocent pleasures, his character developed by natural and insensible transition from boyhood to youth, from the period of school lessons and "Muckle-mou'd Meg" to that of essay-writing and speech-making, of first love and "lines to Margaret."

Of the various professors under whom he studied, there were two who won his special love and lifelong veneration: these were Jardine and Young.* When the relationship between pupil and teacher has been cemented by feelings of respect and affection, the influence obtained over the young mind is one that does not die with the breaking of the ties that formally bound them. Of this Wilson's own experience as a professor afforded him many a delightful illustration. To Jardine, in the first place, as not only his teacher, but his private monitor and friend, he owed, he has himself said, a deep debt of gratitude. He is represented as having been "a person who, by the singular felicity of his *tact* in watching youthful minds, had done more good to a whole host of individuals, and gifted individuals too, than their utmost gratitude could ever adequately repay. They spoke of him as of a kind of intellectual father, to whom they were proud of acknowledging the eternal obligations of their intellectual being. He has created for himself a mighty family among whom his memory will long survive; by whom, all that he

* The former was Professor of Logic, the latter of Greek.

said and did—his words of kind praise and kind censure—his gravity and his graciousness—will no doubt be dwelt upon with warm and tender words and looks, long after his earthly labors shall have been brought to a close.'"*

Wilson's intercourse with Professor Young was of a nature equally friendly, and his reminiscences of that "old man eloquent" are not less pleasing:—

"We have sat," he says, "at the knees of Professor Young, looking up to his kindling or shaded countenance, while that old man eloquent gave life to every line, till Hector and Andromache seemed to our imagination standing side by side beneath a radiant rainbow glorious on a showery heaven; such, during his inspiration, was the creative power of the majesty and the beauty of their smiles and tears.

"That was long, long ago, in the Greek class of the College of Glasgow; and though that bright scholar's Greek was Scotch Greek, and all its vowels and diphthongs, and some of its consonants too, especially that glorious guttural that sounds in *lochs*, all unlike the English Greek that soon afterwards, beneath the shadow of Magdalen Tower, the fairest of all Oxford's stately structures, was poured mellifluous on our delighted ear from the lips of President Routh, the 'erudite and the wise,' still hath the music of that 'repeated strain' a charm to our souls, reminding us of life's morning march when our spirits were young, and when we could see, even as with our bodily eyes, things far away in space or time, and Troy hung visibly before us even as the sun-setting clouds. Therefore, till death, shall we love the Sixth Book of the Iliad; and, if we understand it not, then indeed has our whole life been vainer than the shadow of a dream."†

A somewhat similar account of this interesting man, from another source, is worthy of insertion here:—

"I own I was quite thunderstruck to find him passing from a transport of sheer verbal ecstasy about the particle *ἄρα*, into an ecstasy quite as vehement, and a thousand times more noble, about the deep pathetic beauty of one of Homer's conceptions in the expression of which that particle happens to occur. Such was the burst of his enthusiasm, and the enriched mellow swell of his ex-

* *Blackwood*, July, 1818.

† "Homer and his Translators," Wilson's *Works*.

panding voice, when he began to touch upon this more majestic key, that I dropped for a moment all my notions of the sharp philologer, and gazed on him with a higher delight, as a genuine lover of the soul and spirit which has been clothed in the words of antiquity.

"At the close of one of his fine excursions into this brighter field, the feelings of the man seemed to be rapt up to a pitch I never before beheld exemplified in any orator of the Chair. The tears gushed from his eyes amidst their fervid sparklings, and I was more than delighted when I looked round and found that the fire of the Professor had kindled answering flames in the eyes of not a few of his disciples."*

It may be seen from these sketches what manner of men had the moulding of that young taste in its perception of the good and beautiful. Nor could his mind fail to have been ennobled by such training. It was the means of encouraging him to cultivate the literary taste, which, in addition to the more severe routine of his studies, aided to make his memory a storehouse of knowledge, rendering him even as a boy one of the most desirable companions with his seniors.

Of the characteristic mixture of work and play which enabled him to be both an active and distinguished student, and a vivacious racer and dancer, there is fortunately some slight record extant under his own youthful hand, in the pages of a little brown memorandum-book, in which he carefully noted the chief transactions of each day from the 1st of January to the 26th of October, 1801. A very interesting and curious relic it is, if only for the light it throws on that beautiful portrait by Raeburn, now in the National Gallery, Edinburgh, which has probably disappointed so many people as a representation of young Christopher North. That slender youth, so tidily dressed in his top-boots and well-fitting coat, with face so placid, and blue eye so mild, looking as if he never could do or say anything *outré* or startling,—can that be a good picture of him we have seen and heard of as the long-maned and mighty, whose eyes were "as the lightnings of fiery flame," and his voice like an organ bass; who laid about him, when the fit was on, like a Titan, breaking small men's bones; who was loose and careless in his apparel, even as in all things he seemed too strong and primitive to heed

* *Peter's Letters.*

much the niceties of custom? So people ask and think who knew not Professor Wilson, save out of doors or in print, and who imagine that he could never have been otherwise than as they saw him in manhood or age. But true it is, that that gentle-looking cavalier represents the John Wilson in whom the deep fires of passion and the hidden riches of imagination lay still comparatively quiescent and undeveloped. For that youth, though he is a bold horseman and a matchless leaper, as well as a capital scholar and a versifier to boot, has not yet had his nature stirred by that which will presently make him talk of life as either bliss ineffable, or wretchedness insufferable. The man whom we know in after life jotting down his lectures on old backs of letters, illegible sometimes to himself, at this time keeps a neat and punctual diary, with its ink rulings for month, and week, and day, and *£ s d*, all done by his own hand; the one page containing, under the heading "Appointments, Bills, Memorandums," notes of each day's events, with the state of the weather at the week's end; the other, its careful double entry of "Received" and "Paid," duly carried over from page to page; and the expenditure in no single instance exceeding the income. It is altogether an illustration of character that might surprise the uninitiated even more than Raeburn's portrait.

As has been said, labor and pleasure seem not unequally to have divided his time. Invitations to dinner, balls, parties, etc., are frequently chronicled. A boy of sixteen might be supposed to be somewhat prematurely introduced to those social amenities. But in his case the thing does not seem to have been unnatural, or other than beneficial. No doubt his personal attractions, and a stature above his years, combined with the knowledge of his good prospects in life, made him an object of more attention than would otherwise have been the case. In the heart of this gayety, too, there are indications of marked attention to the ordinary but too often neglected minor duties of society. He makes frequent visits of politeness; he writes regularly to his mother and sisters; his respect to his grandmother and other relatives is undeviating, for upon the old lady he waits daily. Order and punctuality, in fact, seem to regulate his minutest affairs,—the more worthy of remark, as in later years these praiseworthy habits were almost entirely laid aside. It will perhaps not be altogether without interest to insert one or two of the entries from this pocket-book, even though monotonous, and to a certain extent unimportant, alluding to names of persons, the mention of which, save to a very few, will scarcely awaken any familiar associations.

The season is begun at home in Edinburgh, where his mother, with the rest of the family, had now taken up her residence. A happy band of brothers and sisters, and other relatives, there met together to welcome in the new-year. So, for a while, the dingy walls of Glasgow College, and its eight o'clock morning lectures, were shut out from thought, and the bright-hearted boy rejoiced with his friends. Before quoting from the memorandum-book its brief record of those days, which gleams out from the past like light seen from an aperture for the first time, let us hear him in maturer years recalling the memory of such scenes:—

"Merry Christmases they were indeed; one lady always presiding, with a figure that once had been the stateliest among the stately, but then somewhat bent, without being bowed down, beneath an easy weight of most venerable years. Sweet was her tremulous voice to all her grandchildren's ears. Nor did those solemn eyes, bedimmed into a pathetic beauty, in any degree restrain the glee that sparkled in orbs that had as yet shed not many tears, but tears of joy or pity.

"Whether we were indeed all so witty as we thought ourselves—uncles, aunts, brothers, sisters, nephews, nieces, cousins, and 'the rest,' it might be presumptuous in us, who were considered by ourselves and a few others not the least amusing of the whole set, at this distance of time to decide—especially in the affirmative; but how the roof did ring with sally, pun, retort, and repartee! Ay, with pun—a species of impertinence for which we have therefore a kindness even to this day. Had incomparable Thomas Hood had the good fortune to have been born a cousin of ours, how with that fine fancy of his would he have shone at those Christmas festivals, eclipsing us all! Our family, through all its different branches, has ever been famous for bad voices, but good ears; and we think we hear ourselves—all those uncles and aunts, nephews and nieces, and cousins—singing now! Easy is it to 'warble melody' as to breathe air. But we hope harmony is the most difficult of all things to people in general, for to us it was impossible; and what attempts ours used to be at seconds! Yet the most woful failures were rapturously encored; and ere the night was done we spoke with most extraordinary voices indeed, every one hoarser than another, till at last, walking home with a fair cousin, there was nothing left for it but a tender glance of the eye—a tender pressure of the hand —for cousins are not altogether sisters, and although partaking of that dearest character, possess, it may be, some peculiar and appropriate charms of their own; as didst thou, Emily the 'Wild-cap!'"

"*1st of January*, 1801.—Union with Ireland celebrated; Castle guns fired; no illumination. Called on Mr. Sym (Timothy Tickler of later date).

"*2d of January*.—Ball at our house; danced with the Misses M'Donald, Corbett, Fairfax, Chartres, Balfour, Brown, Lundie, Millar, Young."

Not too long is he to be absent from work. On the 4th of January the gayeties of home are left, and he takes a seat in the "Telegraph."

"Left Edinburgh at seven in the morning; arrived in Glasgow *safe*, and dined with my grandmother."

Items of travelling expenses make a curious comparison between the past and present cost for a similar journey:—

"For a seat in the 'Telegraph,' £1 1s.

"For the driver and guard of 'Telegraph,' 4s.

"For breakfast and waiter, 1s. 6d."

With his grandmother he was a great favorite. This lady, Mrs. Sym, lived to a good old age, as did also her husband; he being above ninety when he died. The old gentleman had considerable character, and not a little caustic humor; a quality that may be said to have pervaded the Sym family. A story is told of his having sent a note to his wine-merchant on receipt of a jar of rum, which he fancied had had more than the ordinary dilution, begging him to be so obliging, on his next order, as to send the water in one jar and the rum in another. His wife was a gentle, kind woman, and very attractive to young people, to whom she was ever ready to show attention and hospitality. She was very handsome in her youth, "stateliest among the stately," as Wilson has called her. In one of her daughter's letters, written five-and-thirty years later, there is a reminiscence of these early days:—

"Occasionally you and some other boys getting a Saturday's dinner, a good *four-hours*, and being dismissed with—'Now, you will go all away; you have gotten all your dues; and, besides, *I'm weary* *of you.*' Then, as you advanced in your academic career, came Jamie Smith, *Wee* Willy Cumin', Alick Blair, sounding out, '*Ohon a ree! ohon a ree!*' Your grandmother ready dressed at her wheel in the parlor, your aunts at their work, Blair announced in the dining-room, and *me* the only one who would join him. On entering, I find him groping in the press and *howking* out a book, part of which was read with his peculiar *burr.*"*

Many a charmed spot is mentioned in this diary. The name of Hallside, Professor Jardine's residence, is specially associated with reminiscences of pleasant society and light-hearted diversions, which show how well philosophy and geniality agreed together under that hospitable roof. The following is a specimen:—

"23*d March.*—Ran for a wager three times round the garden; accomplished it in nine minutes and a quarter. Won 5s."

Hallside is a modern house, somewhat in the style of a Scottish manse. The grounds were about seventy acres in extent, gradually sloping to the east, and bounded in part by the river Calder. On the opposite banks stood the pretty cottage *ornée* of Mrs. Jardine's brother, Mr. Lyndsay, whose wife was the niece of the celebrated Dr. Reid, the metaphysician. Their only child was a beautiful girl, whom Professor Wilson took in after years as model for the heroine of his *Trials of Margaret Lyndsay.* The charms of this agreeable neighborhood were heightened by the beauty of the situation. Calder Bank, Mr. Lyndsay's residence, commanded a fine view of Bothwell woods and castle, the gray towers of which contrasted well with the dark spreading trees that faced the ruins of Blantyre Priory, beautifying the banks of the Clyde.

Often did John Wilson and his companions from college visit those enticing scenes, and pleasant it is to find, after a lapse of sixty-one years, a memory fresh and distinct of these happy days. The "Margaret Lyndsay" of that time, now Mrs. Palmes, says:—"My knowledge of your talented father was almost confined to the period of childhood; but I well remember my own delight when the fair-haired, animated boy was my companion by the Calder, in races on

* The writer of this letter, Miss Catharine Sym, long known in Glasgow as one of its most original characters, was the only unmarried daughter of Mr. and Mrs. Sym. She was perhaps one of the wittiest women of her time, in that dry way so peculiar to Scottish nature. Before she died, not many years ago, at eighty years of age, she returned to her nephew a correspondence, and many juvenile manuscripts that had passed between them in the days of his boyhood. Not long before his death he destroyed those papers, which, had they been extant, might have supplied some interesting materials for this part of the Memoir.

Dychmont Hill, on foot or with our ponies. Whatever he did was done with all his soul, whether in boy's play or in those studies appointed him by my uncle, Professor Jardine. His beaming countenance and eager manner showed his deep interest in all he did.

"I recollect suffering from his purchase of a violin. My room was under his, and during the night and early morning hours he devoted himself to bringing out the most discordant sounds; for as he would not have a master, the difficulties to be overcome only proved an additional charm. The final result of his musical taste I do not remember. Poetry probably succeeded, for even at that early age he wrote *little* poems (long before the 'Isle of Palms'), some of which I hope were preserved."

From his journal it is to be seen he purchased other instruments besides a violin:—

"*February* 9*th*.—Got a flute and music-book to learn.

"10*th*.—Began to learn the flute by myself.

"*March* 11*th*.—Patterson came to-day. Liked Patterson pretty well; agreed with him for sixteen lessons. Terms, a guinea. Bought and paid a German flute.

"12*th*.—Played a duet with Perkins."

There is no further mention in Diary or elsewhere of this musical taste being carried out, although his playing on the flute at Elleray, long years after, is a circumstance which inclines one to believe that he continued some practice on this instrument after leaving College. He was, however, a devoted lover of music, both vocal and instrumental, though always preferring the former. His singing was charming, uncultivated as it was by study; no one could listen to it without admiration or a touched heart. His voice was exquisitely sweet,* which, combined with the pathos he infused into every note, and expressed in each word, made the pleasure of hearing him a thing to be remembered forever. His manner of singing "Auld Lang Syne" may be described as a tribute of love to the memory of the poet, whose words appeared to inspire him with something be-

* "*North*.—Do you like my voice, James? I hope you do."

"*Shepherd*.—I wad ha'e kent it, Mr. North, on the Tower o' Babel, on the day o' the great hubbub. I think Socrates maun ha'e had just sic a voice. Ye canna weel ca't saft, for even in its laigh notes there is a sort o' birr; a sort o' dirl that betokens power. Ye canna ca't hairsh, for angry as ye may be at times, its' aye in tune, frae the fineness o' your ear for music. Ye canna ca't sherp, for it's aye sae nat'ral; and flett it could never be, gin you were even gi'en ower by the doctors. It's maist the only voice I ever heard that you can say is at aince persuasive and commanding—you micht fear 't, but you maun love 't."—*Noctes*.

yond vocal melody; his sweet, solemn voice filled the air with sounds that, while they melted away, seemed still to linger on the ear, delighting the sense. Many are there who can remember the effect produced by his rendering of this beautiful song.

There is something very *naïve* in the way some of his memoranda are mixed up, in humorous contrast, the important and trivial side by side. Thus we have in one line—"Gave Archy my buckskins to clean;" and in the next, "Prize for the best specimens of the Socratic mode of reasoning given out in the Logic," followed by "Ordered a pair of corduroy breeches, tailor, Mr. Aitken;" "Began the syllogism to-day in the Logic class," and so on.

"*February* 13*th.*—Called on my grandmother; went to the sale of books; had a boxing-match of three rounds with Lloyd—beat him."

"14*th.*—General examination to-day in the Logic class;" "not examined; went to the Mearns;" "went to the sale; went to the society; the hack I had an excellent trotter; beat Fehrzyen with ease; found a sack on the road."

The result of the sale seems to have been most satisfactory. Two entries of purchases made are such as would give delight to a boy who paid due attention to his expenditure of pocket-money: "Bought Foote's Works at the sale, 2 vols., 1s. 8d.;" "also bought the *Rambler*, which Mr. Jardine was owing me."

The next item betrays a true boyish weakness, in the form of a consuming love for sweetmeats, especially of one particular sort,—thus, "For barley-sugar, 4d.;" and at another time, "For barley-sugar, at my old man's, most excellent, 6d." This taste is frequently indulged; the sum seems to increase too, by degrees, and many a shilling was spent at *Baxter's* upon this favorite luxury, for which he retained his liking even in old age.

During this winter his studies had been prosecuted with considerable assiduity, as may be gathered from his notes.

"*January* 17*th.*—Agreed to-day with Mr. Jardine to give up the Greek class, as I am too *throng.*

"20*th.*—General examination to-day; went to the Speculative Society; spoke as a stranger.

"21*st.*—Finished my exercise upon Logic.

"23*d.*—Called upon my grandmother; gave up the Greek private, finding I had too much to do this winter.

"*February* 5*th.*—Finished my Socratic mode of dialogue to-day.

"*April* 26*th.*—Got the first prize in the Logic class.

"*May* 1*st.*—Prizes distributed; got three of them."

After this date there is no more allusion made to study at College, but enough has been quoted to show how he was disposed towards it. The rest of the summer is spent in various ways amusing to boyhood, while it is evident that the more agreeable pleasure of ladies' society was not wanting to interest him. The lasting effect of love on a boy's mind is, with most, a matter of doubt; but where there is depth of character, and sincerity as well as strength of feeling, the results are not always to be judged by common experience. How it fared with him in this respect, will be touched upon in another chapter.

One or two more extracts from the Diary before this year has closed must be given. The first is characteristic of his constant energy and movement. Even a simple walk with a friend finds him wearied with any thing like delay: "Walked to Paisley with Andrew Napier; tried him a race; ran three miles on the Paisley road for a wager against a *chaise*, along with Andrew Napier; beat them *both*." Another exploit of a similar nature, at a somewhat later date, is related by a friend who was present on the occasion:*—

"He gained a bet by walking *toe and heel* three miles out and back (six miles in all) on the road to Renfrew, from the *shedding* of the roads to Renfrew and Paisley, in two minutes *within* the hour. I accompanied him on foot (but not under the restriction of toe and heel), and Willy Dunlop on horseback, to see that it was fairly won. Nobody could match your father in the college garden at 'hop, step, and jump.' Macleod (now the Rev. Dr. Norman Macleod, sen.), an active Highlander from Morven, who had also the advantage of being his senior, approached most nearly to him."

It appears that even in holiday-time he set himself to work.

"*June* 4*th.*—Finished my *poem* on Slavery.

"7*th.*—Began an essay on the Faculty of Imagination.

"*August* 17*th.*—Finished the first volume of Laing's *History of Scotland.*

"*August* 30*th.*—Made considerable progress in my essay upon Imagination; finished the second division of my exercise.

* Mr. Robert Findlay.

"31*st.*—Stayed at home all day; wrote an account of the Massacre of Glencoe."

"*September* 19*th.*—Stayed at home all day, and wrote an essay upon the Stoical Philosophy."

The notion of John Wilson having been at any time of his life an idle man, must have seemed absurd to those who knew him, though perhaps, for people who think that a hard worker must necessarily be dull and tiresome, natural enough. Even in his boyhood my father was no idler; and there remains still more convincing proof of his assiduity and love of study to be shown in his career when at Oxford. There is yet some short time to be accounted for, spent in Glasgow; and of his friendships formed at College, something may be said in this place. Boys generally combine themselves when at public schools, and other seminaries of education, into select coteries, and are as frequently judged by the qualities of their companions as by their own. The very high character of the Glasgow professors at that time almost insured a certain number of first-class youths, especially as several of them received into their own houses young men whose education was privately, as well as in their classes, under their superintendence.

Mr. Alexander Blair, to whom my father dedicated an edition of his poems, was an Englishman, and with him he began, at Glasgow, an intercourse that ripened into a lifelong friendship. This gentleman has been deterred from acquiring a prominent position in the world as a philosopher and scholar, solely by the modesty and diffidence of his character. He was my father's companion both at Glasgow and at Oxford, and in after life the Professor derived most valuable aid in his philosophical investigations from this friend, whose correspondence with him for many years was uninterrupted. It is much to be regretted that letters of so interesting and elevated a character should, with one or two exceptions, have perished. Another of those early companions was Robert Findlay of Easter Hill, grandson of an accomplished and learned doctor of divinity well known and beloved in Glasgow. He too continued a friend until death; and from him there have come to me many treasured memorials of an affection on both sides like that of brothers. Besides these two, the most intimate associates of John Wilson in those days were Mr. William Horton Lloyd, an Englishman of large fortune (whose beautiful sister married Mr. Leonard Horner), Mr.

William Dunlop, and Archibald Hamilton, a distant relative of my father, who afterwards entered the navy, and prematurely closed his promising career in the engagement off Basque Roads.

With these young men poetry was a frequent subject of discussion, and there was one poet, viz., William Wordsworth, on whose merits, then but little recognized, they found themselves unanimous. Some time before he closed his career at Glasgow University, Wilson's attention was attracted by the *Lyrical Ballads*, which had been recently published. There were at that time few eyes that had discerned in them the signs of future greatness. Among the earliest and most enthusiastic, but also most discriminating of their admirers, was young Wilson, who conveyed his sentiments to the poet in a letter of considerable length, written in a spirit of profound humility, at the same time with perfect independence of expression. It is as follows:—

"My dear Sir:—You may perhaps be surprised to see yourself addressed in this manner by one who never had the happiness of being in company with you, and whose knowledge of your character is drawn solely from the perusal of your poems. But, sir, though I am not personally acquainted with you, I may almost venture to affirm, that the qualities of your soul are not unknown to me. In your poems I discovered such marks of delicate feeling, such benevolence of disposition, and such knowledge of human nature, as made an impression on my mind that nothing will ever efface; and while I felt my soul refined by the sentiments contained in them, and filled with those delightful emotions which it would be almost impossible to describe, I entertained for you an attachment made up of love and admiration: reflection upon that delight which I enjoyed from reading your poems, will ever make me regard you with gratitude, and the consciousness of feeling those emotions you delineate makes me proud to regard your character with esteem and admiration. In whatever view you regard my behavior in writing this letter, whether you consider it as the effect of ignorance and conceit, or correct taste and refined feeling, I will, in my own mind, be satisfied with your opinion. To receive a letter from you would afford me more happiness than any occurrence in this world, save the happiness of my friends, and greatly enhance the pleasure I receive from reading your *Lyrical Ballads*. Your silence would certainly distress me; but still I would have the happiness to think that the neglect even of the virtuous cannot extinguish the sparks of sensibility, or diminish the luxury arising from refined emotions. That luxury, sir, I have enjoyed; that luxury your poems have afforded me, and for this reason I now address you. Accept my thanks for the raptures you have occasioned me, and however much you may be inclined to despise me, know at least that these thanks are sincere and fervent. To you, sir, mankind are indebted for a species of poetry which will continue to afford pleasure while respect is paid to virtuous feelings, and while sensibility continues to pour forth tears of rapture. The flimsy ornaments of language, used to conceal meanness of thought and want of feeling, may captivate for a short time the ignorant and the unwary, but true taste will discover the imposture and expose the authors of it to merited contempt. The real feelings of human nature, expressed in simple and forcible language, will, on the contrary, please those only who are capable of entertaining them, and in proportion to the attention which we pay to the faithful delineation of such feelings, will be the enjoyment derived from them. That poetry, therefore, which is the language of nature, is certain of immortality, provided circumstances do not occur to pervert the feelings of humanity, and occasion a complete revolution in the government of the mind.

"That your poetry is the language of nature, in my opinion, admits of no doubt. Both the thoughts and expressions may be tried by that standard. You have seized upon those feelings that most deeply interest the heart, and that also come within the sphere of common observation. You do not write merely for the pleasure of philosophers and men of improved taste, but for all who think—for all who feel. If we have ever known the happiness arising from parental or fraternal love; if we have ever known that delightful sympathy of souls connecting persons of different sex; if we have ever dropped a tear at the death of friends, or grieved for the misfortunes of others; if, in short, we have ever felt the more amiable emotions of human nature—it is impossible to read *your* poems without being greatly interested and frequently in raptures; your sentiments, feelings, and thoughts are therefore exactly such as ought to constitute the subject of poetry, and cannot fail of exciting interest in every heart. But, sir, your merit does not solely consist in delineating the real features of the human mind under those different aspects it assumes, when under the influence of various passions and feelings; you have, in a manner truly admirable, explained a circumstance, very important in its effects upon the soul when agitated, that has indeed been frequently alluded to, but never generally adopted by any author in tracing the progress of emotions—I mean that wonderful effect which the appearances of external nature have upon the mind when in a state of strong feeling. We must all have been sensible, that when under the influence of *grief*, Nature, when arrayed in her gayest attire, appears to us dull and gloomy, and that when our hearts bound with joy, her most deformed prospects seldom fail of pleasing. This disposition of the mind to assimilate the appearances of external nature to its own situation, is a fine subject for poetical allusion, and in several poems you have employed it with a most electrifying effect. But you have not stopped *here*, you have shown the effect which the qualities of external nature have in forming the human mind, and have presented us with several characters whose particular bias arose from that situation in which they were planted with respect to the scenery of nature. This idea is inexpressibly beautiful, and though, I confess, that to me it appeared to border upon fiction when I first considered it, yet at this moment I am convinced of its foundation in nature, and its great importance in accounting for various phenomena in the human mind. It serves to explain those diversities in the structure of the mind which have baffled all the ingenuity of philosophers to account for. It serves to overturn the theories of men who have attempted to write on human nature without a knowledge of the causes that affect it, and who have discovered greater eagerness to show their own subtlety than arrive at the acquisition of truth. May not the face of external nature through different quarters of the globe account for the dispositions of different nations? May not mountains, forests, plains, groves, and lakes, as much as the temperature of the atmosphere, or the form of government, produce important effects upon the human soul; and may not the difference subsisting between the former of these in different countries, produce as much diversity among the inhabitants as any varieties among the latter? The effect you have shown to take place in particular cases, so much to my satisfaction, most certainly may be extended so far as to authorize general inferences. This idea has no doubt struck you; and I trust that if it be founded on nature, your mind, so long accustomed to philosophical investigation, will perceive how far it may be carried, and what consequences are likely to result from it.

"Your poems, sir, are of very great advantage to the world, from containing in them a system of philosophy that regards one of the most curious subjects of investigation, and at the same time one of the most important. But your poems may not be considered merely in a philosophical light, or even as containing refined and natural feelings; they present us with a body of morality of the purest kind. They represent the enjoyment resulting from the cultivation of the social affections of our nature; they inculcate a conscientious regard to the rights of our fellow-men; they show that every creature on the face of the earth is entitled in some measure to our kindness. They prove that in every mind, *however* depraved, there exist some qualities deserving our esteem. They point out the proper way to happiness. They show that such a thing as perfect misery does not exist. They flash on our souls conviction of immortality. Considered therefore in this view, *Lyrical Ballads* is, to use your own words, the book which I value next to my Bible; and though I may, perhaps, never have the happiness of seeing you, yet I will always consider you as a friend, who has by his instructions done me a service which it never can be in my power to repay. Your instructions have afforded me inexpressible pleasure; it will be my own fault if I do not reap from them much advantage.

"I have said, sir, that in all your poems you have adhered strictly to natural feelings, and described what comes within the range of every person's observation. It is from following out this plan that, in my estimation, you have surpassed every poet both of ancient and modern times. But to me it appears that in the execution of this design you have inadvertently fallen into an error, the effects of which are, however, exceedingly trivial. No feeling, no state of mind ought, in my opinion, to become the subject of poetry, that does not please. Pleasure may, indeed, be produced in many ways, and by means that, at first sight, appear calculated to accomplish a very different end. Tragedy of the deepest kind produces pleasure of a high nature. To point out the causes of this would be foreign to the purpose. But we may lay this down as a general rule, that no description can please, where the sympathies of our soul are not excited, and no narration interest, where we do not enter into the feelings of some of the parties concerned. On this principle, many feelings which are undoubtedly natural, are improper subjects of poetry, and many situations, no less natural, incapable of being described so as to produce the grand effect of poetical composition. This, sir, I would apprehend, is reasonable, and founded on the constitution of the human mind. There are a thousand occurrences happening every day, which do not in the least interest an unconcerned spectator, though they no doubt occasion various emotions in the breast of those to whom they immediately relate. To describe these in poetry would be improper. Now, sir, I think that in several cases you have fallen into this error. You have described feelings with which I cannot sympathize, and situations in which I take no interest. I know that I can relish your beauties, and that makes me think that I can also perceive your faults. But in this matter I have not trusted wholly to my own judgment, but heard the sentiments of men whose feelings I admired, and whose understanding I respected. In a few cases, then, I think that even you have failed to excite interest. In the poem entitled 'The Idiot Boy,' your intention, as you inform us in your preface, was to trace the maternal passion through its more subtle windings. This design is no doubt accompanied with much difficulty, but, if properly executed, cannot fail of interesting the heart. But, sir, in my opinion, the manner in which you have executed this plan has frustrated the end you intended to produce by it; the affection of Betty Foy has nothing in it to excite interest. It exhibits merely the effects of that instinctive feeling inherent in the constitution of every animal. The excessive fondness of the mother disgusts us, and prevents us from sympathizing with her. We are unable to enter into her feelings; we cannot conceive ourselves actuated by the same feelings, and consequently take little or no interest in her situation. The object of her affection is indeed her son, and in that relation much consists, but then he is represented as totally destitute of any attachment towards her; the state of his mind is represented as perfectly deplorable, and, in short, to me it appears almost unnatural that a person in a state of complete idiotism should excite the warmest feelings of attachment in the breast even of his mother. This much I know, that among all the people ever I knew to have read this poem, I never met one who did not rise rather displeased from the perusal of it, and the only cause I could assign for it was the one now mentioned. This inability to receive pleasure from descriptions such as that of 'The Idiot Boy,' is, I am convinced, founded upon established feelings of human nature, and the principle of it constitutes, as I dare say you recollect, the leading feature of Smith's Theory of Moral Sentiments. I therefore think that, in the choice of this subject, you have committed an error. You never deviate from nature; in you that would be impossible; but in this case you have delineated feelings which, though natural, do not please, but which create a certain degree of disgust and contempt. With regard to the manner in which you have executed your plan, I think too great praise cannot be bestowed upon your talents. You have most admirably delineated the idiotism of the boy's mind, and the situations in which you place him are perfectly calculated to display it. The various thoughts that pass through the mother's mind are highly descriptive of her foolish fondness, her extravagant fears, and her ardent hopes. The manner in which you show how bodily sufferings are frequently removed by mental anxieties or pleasures, in the description of the cure of Betty Foy's female friend, is excessively well managed, and serves to establish a very curious and important truth. In short, every thing you proposed to execute has been executed in a masterly manner. The fault, if there be one, lies in the plan, not in the execution. This poem we heard recommended as one in your best manner, and accordingly it is frequently read in this belief. The judgment formed of it is, consequently, erroneous. Many people are displeased with the performance; but they are not careful to distinguish faults in the plan from faults in the execution, and the consequence is, that they form an improper opinion of your genius. In reading any composition, most certainly the pleasure we receive arises almost wholly from the sentiment, thoughts, and descriptions contained in it. A secondary pleasure arises from admiration of those talents requisite to the production of it. In reading 'The Idiot Boy,' all persons who allow themselves to think, must admire your talents, but they regret that they have been so employed, and while they esteem the author, they cannot help being displeased with his performance. I have seen a most excellent painting of an idiot, but it created in me inexpressible disgust. I admired the talents of the artist, but I had no other source of pleasure. The poem of 'The Idiot Boy' produced upon me an effect in every respect similar. I find that my remarks upon several of your other poems must be reserved for another letter. If you think this one deserves an answer, a letter from Wordsworth would be to me a treasure. If your silence tells me that my letter was beneath your notice, you will never again be troubled by one whom you consider as an ignorant admirer. But, if your mind be as amiable as it is reflected in your poems, you will make allowance for defects that age may supply, and make a fellow-creature happy, by dedicating a few moments to the instruction of an admirer and sincere friend,

"JOHN WILSON.

"PROFESSOR JARDINE'S COLLEGE, GLASGOW,
24*th May*, 1802.

"WILLIAM WORDSWORTH, Esq.,
Ambleside, Westmoreland, England." *

CHAPTER III.

LOVE AND POETRY.—LIFE AT OXFORD.

1803–'08.

"THEN, after all the joys and sorrows of these few years, which we now call transitory, but which our BOYHOOD felt as if they would be endless—as if they would endure forever—arose upon us the glorious dawning of another new life,—YOUTH, with its insupportable sunshine and its agitating storms. Transitory, too, we now know, and well deserving the same name of dream. But while it lasted, long, various, and agonizing, as, unable to sustain the eyes that first revealed to us the light of love, we hurried away from the parting hour, and looking up to moon and stars, invocated in sacred oaths, hugged the very heavens to our heart."

These sentences contain one among many references in my father's writings to an episode in his early life, of which, had we only these incidental and sometimes imaginative allusions to guide us, no more

* The answer to this letter will be found at page 192, vol. i., of *Memoirs of W. Wordsworth*, by C. Wordsworth, D. D., 1851. For the foregoing letter I am indebted to Mr. W. Wordsworth, son of the poet, who kindly sent it to me, and also pointed out the reply, which is introduced in the *Memoirs*, without a hint as to whom it was addressed.

could be said by the veracious biographer, than that, at the age when nature so ordains, this ardent and precocious youth was passionately in love. So brief and general a statement, however, would but very poorly express the realities of the case, or indicate the depth of the influence which that first overwhelming passion exerted on the whole nature of John Wilson. As he has himself said, "What is mere boy-love but a moonlight dream? Who would weep—who would not laugh over the catastrophe of such a bloodless tragedy? . . . But love affairs, when the lovers are full-grown men and women, though perhaps twenty years have not passed over either of their heads, are at least tragi-comedies, and, sometimes, tragedies; closing, if not in blood, although that too when the Fates are angry, yet in clouds that darken all future life, and that, now and then, lose their sullen blackness only when dissolving, through the transient sunshine, in a shower of tears." Such a love affair was this, now for the first time to be made known beyond a circle consisting of some three or four persons that are alive.

In that note-book, already made use of, the names of two ladies frequently are noted. It may be seen that his visits to them were not paid after the fashion of formal courtesy, and that Miss W. and Miss M. had made Dychmont to him a charmed place. Towards autumn, when walks along the banks of the Clyde begin to be delightful, these notices are of almost daily occurrence. One day he calls at Dychmont; then he drinks tea with Miss W. and Miss M.: he rides to Cumbernauld with Miss W.: "Very pleasant and agreeable ride;" again, "drank tea at Dychmont;" then for the next three days at home, and begins his essay "On the Faculty of Imagination;" next evening it is again, "Drank tea at Dychmont;" and so on through the month,—nothing but Dychmont, walking, riding, breakfasting, dining, supping "at Dychmont," or "with Dychmont ladies" somewhere.

This attractive place was but a simple farm-house, unadorned and almost homely, but the country around it was delightful. The hill, from which it takes its name, is part of the dukedom of Hamilton, and from its summit the valley of the Clyde, from Tinto to the mountains of the west, presents a view of great beauty. No portion of the Clyde is without beauty; for the most part, more noble than the Rhine, with a sweep of water quite as majestic, it flows through a variety of country ever embellished by its presence. Along the banks of the Clyde and Calder were all the favorite walks of John Wilson, for there were "Ha lside," "Calder Bank," "Millheugh," "Calderwood," and "Torrance," which, in later years, carried from Dychmont its attraction, and became the scene of joy and sorrow, deep as ever moved a young poet's heart.

The occupants of Dychmont were two ladies, Miss W. and Margaret, as I may simply name her; the one the guardian of the other, an "orphan-maid" of "high talent and mental graces," with fascination of manners sufficient to rivet the regard of a youth keenly alive to such charms. At the time of Wilson's residence in Glasgow these ladies were the most intimate friends he had beyond the circle of his youthful companions. During winter they lived in the College buildings, and were frequent visitors at Professor Jardine's, so that every opportunity existed for the cultivation of a friendship that gradually ripened into love, "life-deep" and passionate on the one side; on the other sincere and tender, but tranquil and self-contained, as if presaging, with woman's instinct, the envious barriers that were to keep their two lives from flowing into one.

At the date when their acquaintance began, John Wilson had that composed and perfected manner which is acquired intuitively by the gentler sex, and gives them an advantage in society rarely possessed by boys at the same age. Thus Margaret, though no longer a school-girl, was delighted to find a companion so congenial as to excite at once her interest and friendship; while young Wilson saw in the "orphan-maid" a creature to admire and love, with all that fervor which belonged to his poetical temperament. Their occupations encouraged the growth of graceful accomplishments; nor were their rides and walks merely pastimes of pleasure; sterner matter arose from those early hours, and we have words of the past that make every line of this love-passage a tale of sorrow, sad enough for tears. A few years of this bright spring-tide of youth pass away, and one heart feels the gentle quiet of its womanly interest gliding insensibly and surely into something more deep and agitating, as does the dewy calm of daybreak into the fervent splendor of noon. The love of a poet is seldom so submissive as that which long ago wrote its touching confession in these words:—

"Brama assai, poco spera, e nulla chiede."

Trace this story further, and we see two years later that deeper feelings were brought into play; and though the high-minded Margaret gave no assurance to her lover entitling him to regard her heart as bound to him, it is at least apparent that when, at the end of that time, he left Scotland for Oxford, their communings had been such that the heart of the young poet looked back to them as recalling memories of "unmingled bliss." There is in the essay on "Streams" an imaginative episode, manifestly *founded* on reality; but as manifestly designed to be a skilful mystification of his real and unforgotten experience. As he *naïvely* hints at the end, "there is some truth in it;" truth to this extent, undoubtedly, that in "that gloomy but ever-glorious glen," of which he speaks, young John Wilson and Margaret did meet many a time, and hold sweet converse together; that to her sympathizing ear he poured forth the aspirations of as pure and ardent a love as ever dwelt in the breast of youth; and that the recollection of those happy hours, and of her many modest charms, working in a nature of fiery susceptibility and earnestness, drove him afterwards, when clouds came over the heaven of his dreams, to the very brink of despair. The coloring of imagination has transformed the picture in "Streams" into a vision of things that never were; but there is no fiction in the description of that passion as having "stormed the citadel of his heart, and put the whole garrison to the sword," or, elsewhere, as "a life-deep love, call it passion, pity, friendship, brotherly affection, all united together by smiles, sighs, and tears."

Of his life, from the date last mentioned to the time of his leaving Glasgow for Oxford, I have unfortunately no memorial in the shape of letters, his correspondence with his aunt already referred to, who was his confidante and constant correspondent throughout, having been irretrievably lost. There has come to my hands, however, a memorial of his love for Margaret, consisting of an octavo volume of "Poems" in MS., written in that fair and beautiful hand which he wrote up to the time when (it is no fancy to say so) the "fever of the soul" begins to show itself in the impetuous tracings of his pen. It is without date, but must have been written before he left Glasgow. On the title-page, facing which are two dedicatory verses, is the inscription, "Poems on various subjects, by John Wilson," with a poetical quotation below. On the next leaf is this inscription:—

TO
MARGARET,
THE FOLLOWING LITTLE POEMS,
WHICH OWE ANY BEAUTY THEY POSSESS
TO THE DELICACY OF HER FEELINGS,
AND THE EMOTIONS SHE HAS INSPIRED,
ARE, AS A SMALL MARK
OF HIS ESTEEM AND REGARD,
INSCRIBED
BY HER WARMEST FRIEND AND SINCEREST ADMIRER,
JOHN WILSON.*

After this comes an elaborate preface of thirty-eight MS. pages, which, considering that it was the composition of a youth under eighteen, is very remarkable for the ease and grace of the style, the knowledge of poetical literature, the acute critical faculty, and the judicious and elevated sentiments which it displays. This Preface, and the poetical compositions to which it is prefixed, indicate sufficiently that the person to whom they were addressed must have possessed no ordinary mental qualities, and that the relation between her and the writer was founded on a true congeniality of feeling.

The poems are thirty-eight in number, including an "Answer" by Margaret to "Lines" of his. The titles, copied from the table of contents, are given below.† There are few of these compositions

* Then follow on the next page these lines:—

TO MARGARET.

If this small offering of a grateful heart
The thrill of pleasure to thy soul impart,
Or teach it e'er that magic charm to feel,
Which thy tongue knows so sweetly to reveal,
Blessed be the breathing language of the line
That speaks of grace and virtues such as thine;
Blessed be those hours, when, warmed by love and thee,
I poured the verse in trembling ecstasy!
Oh that the music which these lines contain
Flowed like the murmurs of thy holy strain,
When thy soft voice, clear-swelling, loves to pour
The tones of feeling in her pensive hour, etc.

† *Contents.*—Poem on the Immortality of the Soul. Henry and Helen; a Tale. Caledonia, or Highland Scenery. Verses to a Lady weeping at a Tragedy. The Disturbed Spirit; a Fragment. The Song of the Shipwrecked Slave. The Prayer of the Orphan. The Fate of Beauty. Feeling at parting from a beloved object. Lines on hearing a Lady play upon the Harp. Anna; a Song. Love. Florentine. Parental Affection. Elegy on the Death of Dr. Lockhart. Lines suggested by the fate of Governor Wall. Lines addressed to the Glasgow Volunteers. Osmond; an imitation of M. G. Lewis. The Pains of Memory. The Sun shines bright, etc. I know some people in this world, etc. A Wish. The Child of Misfortune. Mary. To a Lady who said she was not

in which there is not some fond allusion to the lady of his love, and the blissful hours spent by her side. The verses are often commonplace enough; but the sentiments are never other than refined. The adoration is unmistakably genuine, and, though fervent, respectful; tinged with a sense of gratitude that touches the sympathies even now. Occasionally the strain rises above mere versification into something of real poetry. I refer to this collection not because of its literary merits, but solely on account of its relation to his "Margaret," of whom, and the story of their love, more authentic accounts will be given from his correspondence.

From these gentle occupations, however, Wilson was called away to new scenes and pursuits, fitted to bring forth the whole energies of his many-sided character, but not of power enough to deaden in his heart the recollection of that beloved glen, of Bothwell Banks and Cruikstone's hoary walls, of Dychmont Hill and "her the Orphan Maid, so human yet so visionary," that made their very names dear to him forever.

"Many-towered Oxford" now summoned the young scholar away from the pleasant companionship of his Glasgow friends; and, in the month of June, 1803, he entered as a gentleman-commoner of Magdalen College. Full of life and enthusiasm, tall, strong, and graceful, quick-witted, well-read, and eloquent, of open heart and open hand, apt for all things honorable and manly, a more splendid youth of nineteen had seldom entered the "bell-chiming and cloistered haunts of Rhedicyna." The effect produced on his mind by the ancient grandeurs of Oxford, naturally stimulated his poetical temperament and heightened the interest of every study. For there hovered constantly around him suggestions of the high and solemn; he felt that he was in an abode fit for great men and sages, and his soul was elevated by the contemplation of his scholastic home. Beautifully does he recall in after days the memory of that inspiring time, when, in the fulness of hope and vigor, the fields of the future opened out before him, stretching upwards to the heights of fame, a-glitter in the dew of life's morning:—

"For having bidden farewell to our sweet native Scotland, and

a good judge of Poetry. Lines written at Bothwell Castle. Lines written at Cruikstone Castle. Lines written in Kenmore Hermitage. Lines written at Evening. Prince Charles's Address to his Army before the Battle of Culloden. Who to the pomp of burnish'd gold, etc. Petition of the Mearns Muir. Lines written in a glen by moonlight. Answer to the above Lines. The Feelings of Love. The Farewell.

kissed, ere we parted, the grass and the flowers with a show of filial tears—having bidden farewell to all her glens, now a-glimmer in the blended light of imagination and memory, with their cairns and kirks, their low-chimneyed huts and their high-turreted halls, their free-flowing rivers and lochs dashing like seas—we were all at once buried not in the Cimmerian gloom, but the cerulean glitter, of Oxford's ancient academic groves. The genius of the place fell upon us. Yes! we hear now, in the renewed delight of the awe of our youthful spirit, the pealing organ in that chapel called the Beautiful; we see the saints on the stained windows; at the altar the picture of one up Calvary meekly bearing the cross! It seemed, then, that our hearts had no need even of the kindness of kindred—of the country where we were born, and that had received the continued blessings of our enlarging love! Yet away went, even then, sometimes our thoughts to Scotland, like carrier-pigeons wafting love-messages beneath their unwearied wings! They went and they returned, and still their going and coming was blessed. But ambition touched us, as with the wand of a magician from a vanished world and a vanished time. The Greek tongue—multitudinous as the sea—kept like the sea sounding in our ears, through the stillness of that world of towers and temples. Lo! Zeno, with his arguments hard and high, beneath the porch! Plato divinely discoursing in grove and garden! The Stagyrite searching for truth in the profounder gloom! The sweet voice of the smiling Socrates, cheering the cloister's shade and the court's sunshine! And when the thunders of Demosthenes ceased, we heard the harping of the old blind glorious Mendicant, whom, for the loss of eyes, Apollo rewarded with the gift of immortal song! And that was our companionship of the dead!"*

Yet these new feelings, and all that fascination which belongs to novelty in "men and manners," could not efface the image of his old familiar Scottish home; and he writes:—

"It is not likely that I will ever like any place of study, that I may chance to live in again, so well as Glasgow College. Attachments formed in our youth, both to places and persons, are by far the strongest that we ever entertain.

"I consider Glasgow College as my mother, and I have almost a son's affection for her. It was there I gathered any ideas I may

* Old North and Young North," Wilson's *Works*.

possess; it was there I entered upon the first pursuits of study that I could fully understand or enjoy; it was there I formed the first binding and eternal friendships; in short, it was there I passed the happiest days of my life.

"I may even there have met with things to disturb me, but that was seldom; and I would, without hesitation, enter into an agreement with Providence, that my future life should be as happy as those days. I dare say I left Glasgow at the time I should have left it; my dearest companions had either gone before me, or were preparing to follow me; and had I stayed another year, perhaps my last best friends, Miss W. and Miss M., would not have been in College buildings; in that case I might as well have been at Japan."

In this honest and unaffected language may be traced that power of local attachment, that clothed every home he found with a sacred interest, interweaving into all the dreams of his memory associations that recalled either some day of unalloyed joy, or some moments of sorrow, hallowed in memory with the "tender grace of a day that is dead."

Of his studies and manner of life at Oxford I have no very minute or extensive memorials. That he was a hard student is sufficiently proved, both by the relics of his industry and by the manner in which he passed his final examination. That he also tasted of the pleasures and diversions open to a lively young Oxonian, possessed of abundant resources,* is only to say that he *was* a young man, and lived at Oxford for three years and a half. But the general impression that he led what is called a "fast life," and was not a reading man, is by no means correct. His wonderful physical powers gave him indeed great advantages, enabling him to overtake a larger amount of work in a short time than weaker frames could attempt, and to recover with rapidity the loss of hours spent in depressing gloom or hilarious enjoyment. But with all his unaffected relish for the delights of sense, his was a soul that could never linger long among them, without making them "stepping-stones to

* His father had left him an unencumbered fortune of £50,000. I find the following calculation in one of his memorandum-books, apparently made soon after his coming to Oxford:—"Expenses necessary for an Oxford life for five months amount to about £170; that doubled, to £340; and for the other two months, £50, makes £400 the very least possible." I am afraid the "necessary" expenses turned out to be very far short of the actual. The book contains an account of expenditure somewhere up to the month of October 1803, amounting to about £150, which may be considered moderate. But not long after there occurs this significant note:—"I find that I cannot balance my accounts, therefore will henceforth keep only general ones."

higher things." Many, doubtless, were his wild pranks and jovial adventures, and for a brief space, as we shall find, he gave himself up, in the agony of blighted hopes, to "unbridled dissipation," if so he might drown the memory of an insupportable grief. All such excess, however, was alien to his nature, which from childhood to old age, preserved that freshness and purity of feeling imparted by Heaven to all true poets, and in few instances utterly lost.

His life at Magdalen College, and his arrangements in regard to his studies, were marked by the same attention to order as had directed his daily course when in Glasgow. It was not till some time after he had left Scotland, that the agitation of harassing thoughts caused a change in the steadiness of his habits, leading him into strange eccentricities in search of peace. But the restlessness and occasional deep depression of his spirit were never of long continuance, otherwise the result might have been destructive. Fortunately, the strength and buoyancy of his nature were too great to be overcome, and he passed naturally from one condition of feeling to another, according as his spirit was soothed or agitated by outward circumstances. Thus, in the midst of all his sorrows, he is found throwing himself not unfrequently into the full tide of the life that surrounds him, as if he had no other thought; while again he springs off upon some distant walk that takes him miles away, to seek solace in the solitude of the valleys, or drown care among the crowds of a city. Nothing, however, damped his ardor in acquiring knowledge, or in expressing admiration for those who inspired it by their writings. The heroes he worshipped were numerous; and those he loved best have had their beauties recorded in essays of much discriminating power and taste.

One of his first steps for methodizing the results of his study, and improving his mind, was the commencement of a commonplace-book, a valuable exercise which he had already begun on a small scale in Glasgow, probably by the advice of Professor Jardine. Of these commonplace-books several volumes more or less complete are still extant, giving evidence of an industry and a systematic habit of study very inconsistent with the notion that the writer was an idle or desultory student.*

* "Volume I." is prefaced in the following philosophical style, a few days after his arrival in Oxford: the elaborate plan of study indicated was not, of course, rigidly adhered to:—

"In the following pages I propose to make such remarks upon the various subjects of polite literature as have been suggested to my mind during the course of my studies, by the perusal of

It will be observed, from the extracts I have subjoined, that he writes of the manner in which his work is to be arranged with considerable confidence; a tone observable in all he says, not the result of mere youthful self-complacency, but of that consciousness of power which accompanies genius, quickened by the freshness of new studies, and an increasing capacity to discern and appreciate the beauties and difficulties of the subjects laid before him. The various compositions resulting from the above plan, which have been preserved, give the same impression of easy power and well-balanced judgment, combined with a sensitiveness keenly alive to delicacy of thought, and a ready sympathy with those feelings which are excited by natural causes. Unlike most juvenile essays, they display no affected or maudlin sentiment; there is no exaggeration or "fine writing;" the characteristic qualities, in fact, are clearness and sagacity, the true foundations of good criticism; forming, in conjunction with wide knowledge and sympathies, the *beau-idéal*, afterwards in him exemplified, of what a critic should be, whose judgments will live as *parts* of literature, and not merely talk *about* it. As an example of the qualities now indicated, I may mention

writers upon the different branches of human knowledge; reflections upon law, history, philosophy, theology, and poetry, will be classed under separate heads; and if my information upon the useful and interesting subject of political economy can be reduced to any short discussions upon disputed or fundamental principles, or to a collection of maxims, such as form the groundwork of wider inquiries, observations upon the different theories of economists will form part of my projected plan. In following out this general view, it will frequently happen that I shall have occasion to enter fully into the discussion of questions that have been merely suggested to me by the allusion of authors; and, accordingly, essays of some length will constitute a considerable part of my plan.

"With regard to the department of poetry, original verses of my own composition will be frequently introduced, sometimes with the view to illustrate a principle, and often with no other end than self-gratification.

"If, in the course of my epistolary correspondence, any interesting subjects of literature should be discussed, thoughts thus communicated to me will be inserted in the words of the writer, under the head to which they may belong, and accompanied by my own remarks upon them.

"Should any reflections upon men and manners occur to my mind, even with regard to the general characters of mankind, or the particular dispositions of acquaintances and friends, they shall be written down as they occur, without any embellishment.

"In short, this commonplace-book, or whatever else it may be called, will contain, as far as it goes, a faithful representation of the state of my mind, both in its moments of study and retirement. I will endeavor to concentrate the different radii of information upon literary topics, impressions with regard to human life, and feelings of my own heart, in cases when that can be done with good effect. In referring to these pictures of my mind at different periods, I shall be able to estimate the progress I have made in intellectual acquirements, and the various changes that have taken place in my modes of thinking and feeling.

"I shall learn to know myself. In future times it will be pleasing to behold what I once was and what I once thought; and if I contemplate the acquirements of my youth with any thing like contempt, it will, I trust, proceed from a conviction of real superiority and virtue.

"MAGDALEN COLLEGE, *June* 8, 1803."

an essay out of the first of these two commonplace-books, "On the Poetry of Drummond," showing a most discriminating appreciation of a poet whose genius, as he justly says, has never received due acknowledgment. This essay is followed by a very elaborate and ingenious dissertation on the question, "Why have the Egyptians never been remarkable for poetry?" a curious question, which, so far as I am aware, has never formed the subject of special observation. A considerable portion of the volume is occupied with a translation of Sir William Jones's Observations on Eastern Poetry, and of the specimens, which are very happily rendered. Under date June 27th is the sketch of a proposed poem on the flight of the Israelites out of Egypt, which does not appear, however, to have been entered on. A volume seems to have been set aside for each of the chief branches of study, which from time to time engaged his attention. Some of these are probably lost; and those which remain want a good many leaves in some places. One bears the heading LAW, and contains a survey of the municipal law of England, apparently founded on Blackstone. Another is headed THEOLOGY, and contains a careful review and summary of the evidences of Christianity, based on the study of Paley. Another was intended for HISTORY, but contains, besides some general observations on the study of History, only an essay "concerning Ireland." Another, devoted to his miscellaneous subjects, contains a considerable number of essays and reflections, some pretty elaborate, and displaying a remarkable grasp and comprehensiveness of mind as well as vivacity and grace of style. The following are some of the subjects treated of: The Fear of Death; Female Beauty; Dissipation; Chastity; Religious Worship; The Old Ballad Mania; The Edinburgh Review; The Study of History; The Neglect of Genius in Britain; The Present State of Europe; Longinus as a Critic; The Tendency of Little's Poems; Duelling; Modern Poetry; The Martial Character of the Danes; The Decline of the Moorish Power in Spain; The Influence of Climate. These interesting volumes indicate altogether a very extensive range of study, and thorough mastery of particular topics. It must be remembered, too, that these were but the occasional exercises which filled up the intervals of a complete and successful course of classical study. The various poetical effusions and sketches for proposed poems, with which some of the volumes are to a great extent filled, belong manifestly to a later period. The most important among these are the original draught of several cantos of the "Isle of Palms," which will call for due notice in a subsequent chapter.

The choice of friends is one of those things which most bring out a man's character and power of discrimination. On this topic I find the following sentences addressed to Margaret:—

"—— is a being in whom I have been most grievously disappointed. When I was first introduced to him, I was prejudiced in his favor, for three reasons:—*First*, He was grave, and did not take great part in the conversation, which turned chiefly upon dogs and horses! *secondly*, He was, as I thought, something like Alexander Blair; and, *thirdly*, I was informed he studied a great deal. I accordingly thought that I had fallen upon a good companion. For some time I believed that I had formed a right judgment, thought him a sensible fellow, and, from obscure hints that he dropped, took it into my head that he was a poet. Having, however, one day got into an argument with him concerning the meaning of a line in Homer, I observed an ignorance in him which I was sorry for, and a degree of stupid obstinacy that I despised. This passed; and speaking one day of the Prince, commonly called the 'Pretender,' he thought proper to remark that his title to the throne was no greater than mine.

"With this I did not altogether agree, and having stated my reasons for dissenting from him, discovered that he was entirely ignorant of the history of his own country. Ignorance so gross as this is at all times pitiable, but more so when disguised under pretended knowledge. I accordingly gradually withdrew from his acquaintance, always preserving strict civility and politeness. At last, having judged it proper to be witty towards me, I wrote an epigram upon him, which it seems he did not like; so he now keeps a very respectful distance. He is a compound of good-nature, obstinacy, ignorance, honor, and conceit, but the bad ingredients are strongest."

The next portrait is of a more pleasing nature:—

"—— is a youth of such reserved manners, that although I was first introduced to him, I scarcely spoke twenty words to him to which I received any other answer than Yes, or No, for the first twenty days. Now, I know him rather better, and begin to like him.

"He sometimes condescends to laugh at a joke, but never to make one. He is a very close student, and I believe the first scholar in the College among the gentlemen-commoners. His father is the best Greek scholar in England, and I have given this youth the surname of Sophocles, a famous Greek tragedian. He has a taste for the Fine Arts, and paints, and plays upon the piano; but he is the worst hand at both I ever saw or heard. He is good-natured, and a gentleman."

Another still more genial companion is spoken of in the same letter:—

"—— is a young man of large fortune, and still larger prospects, so he does not think it worth his while to study much; but he is naturally very clever; is an elegant classical scholar, writes good verses, and has very amiable dispositions. He lives in the same stair with me, so we are often together, and I am very fond of him. His cousin is also a clever fellow, has lived long in dashing life in London, and is intimate with Kinnaird, Lamb, Lewis, Moore, and other wits in London; 'a merrier man, within the limits of becoming mirth, I never spent an hour's talk withal.' He delights in quizzical verses, and we are writing together a poem called *Magdalen College*, which, should we ever complete, I will send to you."

The journal breaks off here, and we find no more such familiar sketches of "men and manners," but more serious matter, for whatever bears upon work is treated with earnest respect. His obviously methodical study obtained for him that clearness of perception and correctness of knowledge, without which no mind perfectly performs its work. Accuracy may in fact be called the foundation and the stronghold of all properly directed mental energy. There is no fault more common than want of accuracy, and none that might be so easily cured. Great intellect never has it, though cleverness may; and there was no fault of which my father was more intolerant. He often used to say to his children, in a spirit of fun, "You know I am never wrong? Whatever I state is correct; whatever I say is right." It was truly the case with regard to his information.

The early efforts of genius are always interesting, and in his case they are enhanced in value, when it is considered with what they were combined. Very rarely does it happen that the same individual possesses an equal proportion of mental and bodily activity, of intellect and imagination; and the seductions that lie in the way of a youth so gifted, whose path of life is smoothed by fortune, must be taken into account in estimating the use made of his powers. No doubt conscious strength is in itself a spur to high achievements, and the enviable possession of great gifts of mind and body gives, as it were, two lives, fitting a man for a Titan's work. It was this combination of gifts that made Wilson singular among the men of his time; and the preservation of their harmony was proof that, amid the various influences tending to overthrow the balance, a healthy moral nature reigned supreme. The hard-working intellect was not led astray by the fertile imagination; the indefatigable bodily energy and exuberant sportiveness were still subservient to reason; and all worked healthily together, despite the recurring gloom of cheerless days, and the restless wanderings that hardly brought repose.

Judged by his poems alone, Wilson was to be classed with the most refined and sensitive of idealists; tested by some of his prose writings and his professional reputation, he was one of the most acute and eloquent of moralists. That such a man should have delighted in angling and in boating, in walking, running, and leaping, is not extraordinary; but that he should also have practically encouraged and greatly enjoyed the ruder pastimes of wrestling, boxing, and cock-fighting, may appear to some people anomalous. For the notion is not yet wholly extinct, that a poet should be a delicate and dreamy being, all heart and nerves, and certainly destitute of muscles; while the philosopher is held bound to be solemn and dyspeptic, dwelling in a region of clouds remote from all the business and pleasures of men. It is unnecessary, I presume, to show the absurdity of such views. But neither is it necessary to say a word in favor of the cock-pit or the prize-ring. Suffice it, that at the time when my father studied at Oxford, there were few young gentlemen, with any pretensions to manliness, by whom these now proscribed amusements were not zealously patronized. The fashions change with the generations, and the fox-hunter may ere long be considered a barbarian, and the deer-stalker a kind of assassin. Certain it is, that literary men do not now patronize cock-fighting, and the world would probably be scandalized to hear of Mr. Dickens inviting a party of friends to "a main."* Yet about this time there

* Although it has been said that the sage and refined Henry Mackenzie did not consider it inconsistent with his character to patronize this amusement, I must omit his name from the number. He was very fond of field-sports, but I am assured, on the best authority, that there is not a word of truth in the tradition, nor in the following capital story, quoted from Burgon's *Life of Tytler*:—"Drinking tea there (at Woodhouselee) one evening, we waited some time for Mr. Mackenzie's appearance; he came in at last, heated and excited: 'What a glorious evening I have had!' We thought he spoke of the weather, which was beautiful; but he went on to detail the intense en-

was a regular cock-pit in Edinburgh, patronized by "many gentlemen still alive," says the editor of Kay's *Biographical Sketches* in 1842, who would not, perhaps, relish being reminded of "their early passion for the birds."* John Wilson was a keen patron of this exciting, though, to our eyes, cruel amusement; so much so, that at Elleray he kept, as we shall presently find, a most extensive establishment of cocks, whose training and destinies evidently occupied no small share of his attention. While unable to appreciate fully the merits of this ancient but now almost extinct amusement, I would observe that, in his case, the mere pleasure in the exhibition of animal courage was connected with a more deep and comprehensive delight in the animals themselves. For, from those earliest days, when he made the acquaintance of peaseweeps in the midst of lightning and rain, he had been a keen observer of the habits of all kinds of birds; and he never ceased to take a special interest in them and their ways. I would also remark, that even in those years of student life, when he mixed with all sorts of company, and took his pleasure from the most diversified sources, the study of human nature was truly a great part of his enjoyment. He went among the various grades of men and character much as a geologist goes peering among the strata of the earth; and as a naturalist is not blamed who has his pet beasts and insects, to us repulsive, so perhaps may such a student of men and their manners be rightly fulfilling his vocation, even when he descends to occasional companionship with the stranger types of humanity.

Of his pugilistic skill, it is said by Mr. De Quincey, that "there was no man who had any talents, real or fancied, for thumping or being thumped, but he had experienced some *preeing* of his merits from Mr. Wilson. All other pretensions in the gymnastic arts he took a pride in humbling or in honoring; but chiefly his examinations fell upon pugilism; and not a man, who could either 'give' or 'take,' but boasted to have punished, or to have been punished by *Wilson of Mallen's*."†

One anecdote may suffice in illustration of this subject, having, I

joyment he had had in a cock-fight. Mrs. Mackenzie listened some time in silence; then looking up in his face, she exclaimed in her gentle voice, 'Oh, Harry, Harry, your feeling is all on paper!'"

* A few years earlier a "main" was fought in the kitchen of the Assembly Rooms, then unfinished, between the counties of Lanark and Haddington, of which Kay gives a vivid picture,—photographing the better known cockers who were present on the occasion.

† *Edinburgh Literary Gazette*, vol. i., No. 6.

believe, the merit of being true. Meeting one day with a rough and unruly wayfarer, who showed inclination to pick a quarrel, concerning right of passage across a certain bridge, the fellow obstructed the way, and making himself decidedly obnoxious, Wilson lost all patience, and offered to fight him. The man made no objection to the proposal, but replied that he had better not fight with *him*, as he was so and so, mentioning the name of a (then not unknown) pugilist. This statement had, as may be supposed, no effect in damping the belligerent intentions of the Oxonian; he knew his own strength, and his skill too. In one moment off went his coat, and he set to upon his antagonist in splendid style. The astonished and *punished* rival, on recovering from his blows and surprise, accosted him thus: "You can only be one of the two; you are either Jack Wilson or the Devil." This encounter, no doubt, led, for a short time, to fraternity and equality over a pot of porter.

His attainments as a leaper were more remarkable. For this exercise he had, in the words of the writer already quoted, "two remarkable advantages. A short trunk and remarkably long legs gave him one-half his advantage in the noble science of leaping; the other half was pointed out to me by an accurate critic in these matters, as lying in the particular conformation of his foot, the instep of which is arched, and the back of the heel strengthened in so remarkable a way, that it would be worth paying a penny for a sight of them." After referring to the boastful vanity of the celebrated Cardinal du Perron on this point, he adds:—"The Cardinal, by his own account, appears to have been the flower of Popish leapers; and, with all deference to his Eminence, upon a better assurance than that, Professor Wilson may be rated, at the time I speak of, as the flower of all Protestant leapers. Not having the Cardinal's foible of connecting any vanity with this little accomplishment, knowing exactly what could, and what could *not* be effected in this department of gymnastics, and speaking with the utmost simplicity and candor of his failures and his successes alike, he might always be relied upon, and his statements were constantly in harmony with any collateral testimony that chance happened to turn up."

His most remarkable feat of this kind, the fame of which still lingers round the spot where it took place, is thus referred to by himself:—"A hundred sovereigns to five against any man in England doing twenty-three feet on a dead level, with a run and a leap on a slightly inclined plane, perhaps an inch to a yard. We have seen twenty-three feet done in great style, and measured to a nicety, but the man who did it (aged twenty-one, height, five feet eleven inches, weight, eleven stone) was admitted to be (Ireland excepted) the best far leaper of his day in England."*

This achievement, worthy of one of Dr. Dasent's favorite heroes, took place in the presence of many spectators, at a bend of the Cherwell, a tributary of the Isis, where it glides beautifully through the enamelled meads of Christ Church, the leap being taken across the stream.

To one so full of life, and of the enjoyment of it in its various phases, Oxford was prolific ground for the exercise of his vivacious spirit; and it will naturally be expected that, in connection with this period, there are many curious stories to unfold. But the flight of years soon obliterates the traces of past adventures; very few of the contemporaries of those pleasant days survive; and I am sorry, therefore, to say, that I have been able to gather but few authentic details regarding this portion of my father's life. Every one knows how a story, when it has passed from its original source, is, in an incredibly short space of time, so metamorphosed, as not again to be recognizable; complexion, manner, matter, all changed—just as if loving and making a lie were a matter of duty. Sensible persons, too, are sometimes found credulous of strange tales; while the world in general is ever ready to pick up the veriest rubbish, and complacently exclaim, "How characteristic; so like the man." Few men have had more fables thus circulated regarding them than my father. Perhaps the most foolish story that was ever told of him, is one that William and Mary Howitt allude to with wise incredulity, in their pleasant yet somewhat incorrect memorial of him, and which now, to the disappointment of not a few, must be denied *in toto*. It was said that, when wandering in Wales, he joined a gang of gipsies, and married a girl belonging to that nomade tribe, and lived with her for some time among the mountains. That he had acted along with strolling players, and that there was one company to which he was kind and generous, is quite true; but that he lived with them, or any other adventurers, is mere romance, "the baseless fabric of a vision."

A journal of his wanderings through Wales and the south of

* "Essay on Gymnastics."

England, the Lake District, the Highlands, and Ireland, would have been more amusing than most books of travel, for we have his own word for it that they were sometimes "full of adventure and scrape." But of these journeys he kept no record, and all that can now be gleaned is an incidental allusion here and there in his works.*

The circle of his acquaintance at Oxford was most extensive, from the learned President of his College, Dr. Routh, with whom, as De Quincey says, "he enjoyed an unlimited favor," down through "an infinite gamut of friends and associates, running through every key, the diapason closing full in groom, cobbler, and stable-boy." But though a universal favorite, his circle of intimate friends was more select. Among these were Mr. Home Drummond (of Blair-Drummond), Mr. Charles Parr Burney, Reginald Heber; Mr. Sibthorpe, brother of the late Colonel Sibthorpe; Mr. N. Ellison, Mr. Charles Edward Grey. None of these gentlemen was of his own college.

An anecdote may here be given, illustrating a somewhat unusual mode of shutting up a proctor. One evening one of these important functionaries was aroused to the exercise of his authority by a considerable noise in the High Street. Coming forth to challenge the authors of the unlawful uproar, he found that "Wilson of Magdalen's" was the prime author of the disturbance. Remonstrance and warning were alike thrown away on the indomitable youth; he had put on his "boldest suit of mirth, for he had friends that purposed merriment." Nothing could be made of him. In vain the proctor advanced; he was received with speeches, and a perfect flood of words. The idea of repose was flouted by this incorrigible youth. Still the proctor protested, until he was fairly driven away by Wilson repeating to him, with imperturbable gravity, nearly the whole of Pope's "Essay on Man."

I am glad to be able to make up, in some respects, for the meagreness of these outlines, by some very interesting reminiscences kindly furnished by one who truly says, that he is "perhaps the only per

* "'*The Tipperary shillelaghs came tumbling about his nob as thick as grass.*' This is a sweet pastoral image, which we ourselves once heard employed by a very delicate and modest young woman in a cottage near Limerick, when speaking of the cudgels in an affray. A broken head is in Ireland always spoken of in terms of endearment; much of the same tender feeling is naturally transferred to the shillelagh that inflicted it. 'God bless your honor!' said the same gentle creature to us while casting an affectionate look of admiration on our walking-stick. '*You would give a swate blow with it.*'"—*Blackwood*, vol. v., p. 667.

son now living who could give so many details at the end of half a century."

"I became acquainted with the late Professor Wilson at Magdalen College, Oxford, about the year 1807 or 1808. He had already graduated, taken even (as I best recollect) his Master's degree, when I entered that College as a gentleman-commoner. His personal appearance was very remarkable; he was a powerfully built man, of great muscular strength, about five feet ten inches high, a very broad chest, wearing a great profusion of hair and *enormous* whiskers, which in those days were very unusually seen, particularly in the University. He was considered the strongest, most athletic, and most active man of those days at Oxford; and certainly created more interest among the gownsmen than any of his contemporaries, having already greatly distinguished himself in the schools, and as a poet.

"The difference of our standing in the College, as well as of our ages and pursuits, did not allow of our forming any *close* intimacy, and we seldom met but in our common room, to which the gentlemen-commoners retired from the dining-hall for wine and dessert, to spend the evening, and to sup, etc.

"I am not able to say who were Wilson's intimates in the University; he certainly had none in the College. I rather think he was much with Mr. Gaisford, the celebrated Grecian. I think of *our* men, Mr. Edward Synge, of the county of Clare, saw the most of him. The fact is we were all *pigmies*, both physically and mentally, to him, and therefore unsuited to general companionship. It was therefore in the conviviality of our common room, to which Wilson so much contributed, and which he so thoroughly himself enjoyed, that we had the opportunity of appreciating this (even then) extraordinarily gifted man, who combined the simplicity of a child with the learning of a sage. He was sometimes, but rarely, silent, abstracted for a time, which I attributed to his mind being then occupied with composition. He never seemed unhappy.

"It was the habit and fashion of those days to drink what would now be considered freely; the observance was not neglected at *Maudlin*, though never carried to excess. Wilson's great conversational powers were drawn out during these social hours. He delighted in discussions, and would often advance paradoxes, even in order to raise a debate. It was evident that (like Dr. Johnson) he had not determined which side of the argument he would take upon the question he had raised. Once he had decided *that* point, he opened with a flow of eloquence, learning, and wit, which became gradually an absolute torrent, upon which he generally tided into the small hours. No interruption, no difference of opinion, however warmly expressed, could ruffle for a moment his imperturbable good temper. He was certainly one of the most charming social companions it has ever been my lot to meet, although I have known some of the most agreeable and witty that Ireland has produced. There was a versatility of talent and eloquence (*not of opinions*) in Wilson, such as I have never seen equalled. I have heard him with equal cleverness argue in favor and disparagement of constitutional, absolute, and democratic forms of government; one evening you would suppose him to be (*as he really was*) a most determined, unbending Tory; the next he assumed to be a thorough Whig of the old school; on a third, you would conclude him to be a violent and dangerous democrat! You could never suppose that the same man could uphold and decry, with equal talent, propositions so opposite: and yet he did, and was equally persuasive and conclusive upon each. In the same manner with religious discussions: to-day there could be no more energetic and able 'defender of the faith;' to-morrow he would advance Voltaireism, Hobbism, and Gibbonism enough to induce those who did not know him to conclude that he was a thorough unbeliever. He was, on the contrary, of a highly pious and religious mind. I may sum up his characteristics, as they appeared to me, in a few words: simplicity, kindness, learning, with *chivalry;* for certainly his views and sentiments were highly chivalrous, and had he lived in those days, he would have been found among the foremost of 'les preux chevaliers.'

"The established rule of our common room was, that no one should appear there without being in full evening dress; non-compliance involved a fine of one guinea, which Wilson had more than once incurred and paid. Having one day come in in his morning garb, and paid down the fine, he asked, 'What then do you consider dress?' 'Silk stockings,' etc., etc., was the answer. The next day came Wilson, looking very well satisfied with himself, and with us all. 'Now,' he cried, 'all is right, I hope to have no more fines to pay; you see I have complied with the rules,' pointing to his silk stockings, which he had very carefully *drawn over* the coarse woollen walking stockings which he wore usually; his strong shoes he still retained!

"He told us one evening that he imagined he had a taste for, and might become proficient in music, and that he would commence to practise the French horn! which he did accordingly, commencing after we had broken up for the night, which was generally long after twelve. Some days after, old Dr. Jenner, one of the Fellows, accosted me with piteous tones and countenance: 'Oh, Southwell! do, for pity's sake, use your influence with Wilson to choose some other time for his music-lessons; I never get a wink of sleep after he commences!' I accordingly spoke to him; he seemed quite surprised that his dulcet notes could have disturbed his neighbors; but he was too good-natured to persevere, and, as far as I know, his musical talents were no further cultivated. Being a Master of Arts, he was no longer subject to college discipline, and might have, if he wished, accompanied his horn with a big drum! One of his great amusements was to go to the 'Angel Inn,' about midnight, when many of the up and down London coaches met; there he used to preside at the passengers' supper-table, carving for them, inquiring all about their respective journeys, why and wherefore they were made, who they were, etc.; and in return, astonishing them with his wit and pleasantry, and sending them off wondering *who and what* HE *could be!* He frequently went from the 'Angel' to the 'Fox and Goose,' an early 'purl and gill' house, where he found the coachman and guards, etc., preparing for the coaches which had left London late at night; and there he found an audience, and sometimes remained till the college-gates were opened, rather (I believe) than rouse the old porter, Peter, from his bed to open for him expressly. It must not be supposed, that in these strange meetings he indulged in *intemperance;* no such thing; he went to such places, I am convinced, to study character, in which they abounded. I never saw him show the slightest appearance even of drink, notwithstanding our wine-drinking, suppers, punch, and smoking in the common room, to very late hours. I never shall forget his figure, sitting with a long earthen pipe, a great *tie* wig on; those wigs had descended, I fancy, from the days of Addison (who had been a member of our College), and were worn by us all (in order, I presume, to preserve our hair and dress from

"The strictures of the *Edinburgh Review* considered at a private meeting of the Caput, A. D. 1810."

tobacco smoke) when smoking commenced, after supper; and a strange appearance we made in them!

"His pedestrian feats were marvellous. On one occasion, having been absent a day or two, we asked him, on his return to the common room, where he had been? He said, in London. When did you return? This morning. How did you come? On foot. As we all expressed surprise, he said: 'Why, the fact is, I dined yesterday with a friend in Grosvenor (I think it was) Square, and as I quitted the house, a fellow who was passing was impertinent and insulted me, upon which I knocked him down; and as I did not choose to have myself called in question for a street row, I at once started, as I was, in my dinner dress, and never stopped until I got to the College gate this morning, as it was being opened.' Now this was a walk of fifty-eight miles at least, which he must have got over in eight or nine hours at most, supposing him to have left the dinner-party at nine in the evening.*

"He had often spoken to me when at Oxford of a protracted foot-tour which he had made in Ireland some years previous, and about which there appeared to me a sort of mystery, which he did not explain.

"R. H. S."†

CHAPTER IV.

THE ORPHAN MAID.—UNIVERSITY CAREER.

1803–'08.

The course of true love, whether calm or troubled, whether issuing in sunshine or in storm, is "an old, old story;" but it is one that sums up the chiefest joys and sorrows of men and women, and

* Mr. Southwell's statement may seem an exaggeration; but a reference to Mr. Findlay's account, at p. 24, will show that my father had easily performed six miles an hour in what I take for granted to be a more difficult mode of progression than the ordinary, viz., "toe and heel."

†As a tail-piece to Mr. Southwell's letter, I take the liberty of inserting here one of Mr. Lockhart's Hogarthian sketches, containing, I have no doubt, correct if not very flattering portraits of some of the Oxford dignitaries of that day. The "strictures of the *Edinburgh Review*," which appear to have excited so much dissatisfaction, were contained in two articles in the *Review* of July, 1809, and of April, 1810, in which some of the weak points of the contemporary system of education at Oxford were handled with a roughness characteristic of the criticism of that period.

can only be regarded with indifference by those who are dead to the influence of all deep and worthy emotions. The best and brightest spirits have shown how their lives were ennobled by the passion of love, the faith and purity of which in one heart were the spring of the finest song that ever immortalized genius, and the highest compliment that ever was paid to woman. Should it sometimes happen, when the heart is overburdened with its weight of sorrow, that comfort and forgetfulness are sought in the tumultuous excitements of life, it does not always follow that nature becomes lowered, any more than that love is quenched; for nothing in reality can soothe an unfeigned grief but resolution to bear it. Those who can endure a sorrow, whatever its cause, elevate thereby their moral being, experiencing soon that all comfort from outward sources is but vanity. A strong and uncorrupted soul rises ere long above the aid of idle pleasures, and gratefully turns to the wisdom that teaches submission, believing,

"Tal pose in pace uno ed altro disio."

So was it with John Wilson, to the story of whose early love we now again turn. The reader may have ere this imagined that it was to be heard of no more; that Oxford and its varied excitements had deadened the recollection of Dychmont and Bothwell Banks. So little was it thus, that from all the evidence which letters supply, there seems to have been no portion of his time, during the seven years preceding his permanent settlement at Elleray, in which his love for Margaret did not influence the tenor of his existence, inspiring him at one time with ardent hope, oftener sinking him into the deepest anguish, from which he at times sought escape in assumed indifference or reckless dissipation. It shows how little the outward life of such a man can reveal of his whole nature and actual history, that but for these letters we could not have had even a glimpse of what was in reality the dominant thought of his life at Oxford, nor ever known of the trial which brought out so strongly the nobleness of his nature and the depth of his filial love. Had it not been that so many years of his life were spent in the indulgence of a fond hope and engrossing passion, ending in a sacrifice to duty such as few men of spirit so impetuous have ever made, this tale had not been told. It may well move the admiration of all who reverence the power of self-control in tutoring the heart, while its brightest dreams are still objects of faith. It will be seen from these letters how hard it must have been for him to bend before obstructions, of whose reality and strength he was long in utter ignorance.

Of all his letters to Margaret, the only one that survives of what must have been an extensive correspondence, is one written soon after his arrival at Oxford. Of hers to him there is, I regret to say, none to be found. The pensive simplicity that pervades it is in entire harmony with the strain of the "Poems," and, like the portrait by Raeburn, will perhaps surprise those who may have expected to find young Christopher North addressing the lady of his love in the impassioned and eloquent style of a troubadour. The thing was much too genuine for that:—

"MAGDALEN COLLEGE, OXFORD, *June* 12, 1803.

"Next to seeing yourself, my dear Margaret, and the greatest pleasure I know upon this earth, is that of seeing your writing; and I cannot describe what I felt when I read your letter, even although it contained some little censure for not having written you ere this. When I knew by the direction who it was from, my heart leaped within my breast, and I read it over and over again without intermission, so rejoiced was I to hear from one so dear to me as you are. Indeed I must confess that I was always afraid you would not write me, although this was more an unaccountable presentiment than an apprehension for which, after your promise, I could assign any reason. But where the strongest wishes are, there also are the strongest fears. I see now, however, that you really will write me, and that, I trust, often. What a wretch, therefore, would I be, were I to deprive myself of such a blessing by my own foolishness! When I read your letters, I will be with you in spirit, notwithstanding the distance between this place and Dychmont. My silence was far from proceeding out of forgetfulness of my promise to write you. Before I could have forgot that, I must have forgot you, which never will be to my dying moment; and should it ever happen, may my God forget me. The truth is, I had several reasons for not writing you sooner. I wished first to have seen your picture, which has not yet arrived, and indeed has scarcely had sufficient time yet. But I should have written you notwithstanding that, had I been able, but believe me when I tell you, that hitherto I was not.

"Whenever I thought of writing to you, I thought of the distance I was from you, of the sadness I suffered when I bade you farewell, and the loss of almost all the happiness I enjoy in this world by no longer seeing you. All this quite overpowered me, and I could no more have written to you than I could tell you that forenoon I last saw you not to forget me when I was away. Your letter has revived me; and if you have any regard for me, which I believe you have, oh, write often, often! You know I am unhappy; comfort me, comfort me! A few lines will delight me, and you are too kind to refuse me such a gratification. It will also serve to keep you in remembrance of me, when perhaps you might otherwise forget me, which, should it ever happen, would complete my sum of wretchedness. If hearing from me will afford you any pleasure, I will write as often as you choose—a small mark of affection surely to one, to serve whom I would endure any thing on the face of the earth. It will also afford myself greater pleasure than you. When I left you, my dear Margarèt, you know that I was afraid that Oxford would be to me a dull, unhappy place. You seemed to think not yourself, and believed that the change of situation and novelty of company would make me forget any thing that distressed me, and even make me think less on those friends I had left.

"Perhaps though you said this, you did not exactly think it, and wished only to comfort me, which you have so often and so sweetly done. All my suspicions have been verified, and how indeed could it be otherwise? Oxford is a gay place most certainly, and, I dare say, to people whose minds are at ease, a pleasant one; but to me it appears very different. It is true, that when I was in Glasgow I endeavored to dissipate my melancholy by company, for which I could often feel nothing but contempt, and by pursuits which I heartily despised. I imagined such a course of life might have moderated the violence of what my mind suffered, and I had certainly acquired such a portion of self-command as frequently to appear the happiest and most indifferent person in company. But this conduct did not do. When alone I was worse than ever, and, added to my other distress, had the idea of being guilty of deception, and following conduct unworthy of myself. Accordingly here I follow another plan. I do not dissipate; I live retired. I have no need to follow a course of deception, which, if long persevered in, I could imagine capable in some measure of deadening the sense of right and wrong, and which is at all events grating to the soul. I now try to read, and have, since I came here, read a great deal; but all won't do; my mind is ill at ease. Once, when I was unhappy, I had only to step across the street, hear your voice, see your face, and take hold of your hand, and for a time I forgot all my sorrow. This now I cannot do. At night I sit in a lonely room, nobody within many miles of me I love, left to my own meditations and the power of darkness, which I have long detested.

"I think of sad things, and weep the more, because I have no hope of relief. In such moments what a treasure will your picture be to me! How it will delight me; make me forget every thing on earth but you, and you looking like what you were when you agreed at last to give it to me. Would to God it were here! When, Margaret, you see how happy it will make me, how could you refuse it? And yet to give it me was goodness I had no title to expect, and for which I will often thank you in moments of stillness and solitude. Oh, what a treasure is a friend like you! How little is real friendship understood! Who could ever conceive the happiness I have felt when with you, or so much as dream the misery I endured when I left you for a long, long time! As long as there is a moon or stars in the firmament will I remember you; and when I look on either, the recollection of Dychmont Hill, the house, the trees, the wooden seat, which I am grieved is away, will enter my mind, and make me live over again the happiest period of my existence. Last night I was in heaven. I dreamed that I was sitting in the drawing-room at College Buildings with you alone, as I have often done. The room was dark, the window-shutters close; the fire was little and just twinkling. I had my feet upon the fender; you were sitting in the arm-chair; I was beside you; your hand was in mine; we were speaking of my going to Oxford; you were promising to write me; I was sad, but happy; somebody opened the door, and I awoke alone and miserable.

"I have given you my promise not to think of a plan you dissuaded me from carrying into execution. Be assured that I never will change my mind. I consider you as my better angel, for using your simple eloquence to make me abandon the project. It would have been cruel to my dearest friends, and perhaps useless to myself.

"Let none, not even Miss W., see this. Heaven protect you, my dear Margaret, and love you as well as your affectionate friend,

"JOHN WILSON."

The plan here referred to was a romantic project which he had entertained of going with the expedition of 1804, being Park's second journey to the interior of Africa. Apparently, the hostile influences which ultimately prevailed in dividing him and Margaret had begun, before he left Glasgow, to disturb the current of his felicity. However extravagant the idea of a journey to Timbuctoo may appear as a medicine for disappointed love, he unquestionably meant it; and with all the hardships and dangers connected with such an enterprise, it was one highly calculated to excite his imagination and love of adventure. A very old friend thus writes regarding it:—"He had certainly a wild project of going there, and used to talk of it in his usual enthusiastic way. But I did not imagine it had taken any hold of him till one day he astonished me by appearing in a complete sailor's dress, and told me he was going to join the expedition to Africa. I used all my influence to dissuade him from such a foolish proceeding. You may suppose what dismay he would have occasioned in his own family, who almost worshipped him." To them he never communicated his intentions in the matter, which only became known long after the project had been abandoned.

The next letter from which I shall quote is addressed to his dear friend, Findlay. The post-mark bears the date of "August 16, 1803." What had occurred between that and the month of June to give rise to expressions of despondency so unmeasured, can only be conjectured to have been a further development of the cause of distress alluded to in the letter to Margaret.

. . . "Since I saw you, my mental anguish has been as great as ever. I feel that I am doomed to be eternally wretched, and that I am cut out from all the most amiable and celestial feelings of human nature. . . . At particular times I am perfectly distracted, and hope that at last the torment my mind suffers may waste a frame that is by nature too strong easily to be destroyed. I dare say few would leave life with fewer lingering looks cast behind. My abilities, understanding, and affections are all going to destruction. I can do nothing; I can't, by Heavens! even assume that appearance of indifference and gayety I once did, without a struggle that I cannot support. I started in the career of early life as fair as that of any of my companions, and had, I confess, many hopes of being something in the world. But all these are blasted; I cannot understand any thing that I read, and nothing in the world gives, or ever will give me pleasure. I see others enjoying the world, and likely to become respectable and useful members of society; for myself, I expect to be looked at as a being who wants a mind, and to feel inwardly all the torments of hell. By Heavens! I will, perhaps, some day blow my brains out, and there is an end of the matter. If you will take the trouble, when you have nothing else to do, of writing now and then to me, I know it will be one of those few things that keep my heart from dying in my breast, and depend upon it, that every word coming from one whom I regard so dearly as you, will be interesting to me. What the happiness is which you so pleasantly allude to, I cannot understand, unless it be that J. S., yourself, Blair, and I are soon to meet. I will be glad to see you, but the word happy will never again be joined to the name of "JOHN WILSON."

The next letter, marked "September, 1803," shows an improvement in spirits:—

"Your former letters, my dear Bob, so far from offending, or giving me an idea that you are addicted to frivolous levity, relieved in a great measure the burden of my heart. Although few, perhaps, ever suffered more from mental anguish in a short time than I have done, this suffering has not had the effect of making me look gloomy disapprobation upon the happiness of others. I feel, if all went well with me, I would be one of the happiest of beings that ever saw the light of heaven, and that nothing would be too insignificant to delight me. This conviction has never quitted my heart even in its darkest moments, and has been the means of making me look with complacency upon every kind of innocent and reasonable enjoyment.

"The little girl who brings the newspaper into the room, and trips smilingly along the floor, gives me something like happiness; for, wherever I see joy and peace, I take a sad delight in looking at it. When your letters showed me how pleased you were with your new situation, and that nothing disturbed you there, it gave me much pleasure, therefore I hope you will not leave off that light and happy strain which pervaded them.

"I know that you and I are sworn friends, and that you are interested in every thing that concerns me. Nothing, therefore, in your behavior towards me, will ever appear unfeeling; and what you are afraid I might have mistaken for indifference, I know to be the hallowed voice of friendship. Were you here, I would have an opportunity of pouring out my whole soul to you, and in that I would find much relief.

"But a letter is such a short thing, and to me, sorrow is when written so unintelligible, that in cases of absence I am convinced it is best to say little upon such mournful topics.

"If writing to you, and hearing from you, can divert my attention from my own mind, much is accomplished; and I assure you that your letters, with the minute superscription, effected this end. Before I go further, your resolution to be sorrowful because I might be happier is very injudicious, upon this principle, that while it hurts yourself, so likewise does it him whom you mean to benefit."

To divert his thoughts, he went off in these autumnal days on one of those long solitary rambles which often landed him unpremeditatedly at night in an unknown region, some fifty miles from his starting-point. A glimpse of one of these excursions is afforded in the next letter, the greater portion of which, however, is occupied with an outpouring of his woes. These seem to have received fresh stimulus from an ungrounded alarm that a rival had come between him and the dear object of his anxieties.

"I have been expecting to hear from you for some time past; that is to say, I would not have been greatly astonished though I had heard from you, neither am I in the least surprised that you have not written. As I feel, however, what Wordsworth and other gentlemen of his stamp would think proper to call 'impulse to write 'mid deepest solitude,' I have disregarded entirely the great advance upon the price of writing materials, and will add to the revenue of the Post-Office by the postage of one letter, which you will never grudge to pay, when you have discovered the hidden soul which pervades these effusions. I have lately returned from a walk over a pretty wide extent of country, during which, if at particular times blistered soles and stiff joints did not vastly increase the pleasures of reflection, other moments amply recompensed me, and gave me enjoyment, though not unalloyed, of as perfect a kind as the general nature of frail humanity, assisted by the workings of particular melancholy, could possibly admit. Without being able to assign any reason for my conduct, though I entered into many philosophical inquiries concerning all the possible combinations of motives, I arrived at Coventry, distant from Oxford fifty miles. The days of riding naked upon horseback being gone, I beheld no elegant nude bestriding a prancing courser, therefore I met with no gratification in the assumed character of peeping Tom. From this foolish place I went to Nottingham, distant fifty-one miles, and stayed there three days."

Here he abruptly dismisses his pedestrian adventures, and enters on the subject more near his heart.

. . . "What will time do to such love as mine? It is not passion founded on whim and fancy; it is not a feeling of her excellent disposition resembling friendship; it is not a regard that intimacy preserved, but whose force absence may diminish. Such feelings constitute the common love of common souls. But with me the case is different. No holy throb ever agitates my heart; no idea of future happiness ever elevates my spirit; no rush of tenderness ever warms every fibre of my frame, that Margaret is not the cause and object of such emotions. If such a being were to confess she loved me; if she were to sink upon my breast with love and fondness, I would be the happiest being that ever lived among men. I feel I have a mind that could then exert itself, and a heart that would love all the human race. But if this union is denied me; if she I love reposes on the bosom of another,—then is the chain broke which bound me to the world; I have nothing to live for; all is dark, solitary, cold, wild, and fearful. When Margaret is married, on that night that gives her to another, if I am in any part of this island, you must pass that night with me. Blair will do the same. I don't expect, indeed I won't suffer either of you to soothe the agony of my soul, for that surely were a vain attempt. But you will sit with me. I know I could never pass that night alone. I would crush to death this cursed heart which has so long tormented me, and bless with my latest breath my own Margaret; for she is mine in the secret dwellings of the soul, and not a power in the universe shall tear her from that hospitable home. When I consider the ways of Providence I am astonished. Whoever marries her, let his virtues be what they may, I know he never could make her as happy as I could. He would not love her with so vast and yet so tender a love."

With a true poet's mind, he fears the change an unworthy helpmate would bring to her refined and enlightened spirit:—

"If my rival in her affections were a being superior to myself, I would not repine; at least, not so much as I now do, when I am afraid he is unworthy of her and inferior to me. Does Margaret prefer this man to me? That she does I am afraid is too true. Will he make her as happy as I could? Can he like her as well as I do? Both suppositions are impossible. The wife of a soldier seldom sees intellectual scenes; and, in progress of time, that angel Margaret, for whom I would sacrifice every thing on earth, may become—oh, I shudder to think of it!—a person of common feelings,* and laugh at all I have said to her, at my misery, my love, and my delusions. Such are often the transmigrations of spirit; or, rather, the transformations which Providence permits to humble the hopes and destroy the happiness of those it made capable of prodigious enjoyment. May I never live to see that day!"

After relieving his breast by this outburst, he returns to his walking:—

"I had almost forgot our walking match. I went from Nottingham to Birmingham. There I met Blair. . . . He intends visiting me, perhaps at Christmas; but I will tell you, however, when I expect him, and you must try to spare a few days from that eternal copying of letters, and see what an appearance an old friend cuts in purgatory.

"I have sent—at least, am going to send—you a small parcel, containing the sermon I wrote, and a letter to Margaret. You may open the parcel, and read the sermon, if you choose. Pack them up in your best manner, and direct them to Miss M., College Buildings, Glasgow. I suppose you have safe communication with Glasgow, for I would not for the world the parcel was lost, as the letter is not for every eye, and contains secret feelings.

* This reminds one of *Locksley Hall*:—

"Is it well to wish thee happy?—having known me, to decline
On a range of lower feelings, and a narrower heart than mine!
Yet it shall be: thou shalt lower to his level day by day,
What is fine within thee growing coarse to sympathize with clay."

"Isabella S., I understand, is married. I wish her all possible joy. For God's sake, take care who thou fallest in love with! I wish I had done so, faith!

"The sooner you send Margaret the parcel the better, for I should have written her before now, and she will be wondering at my silence. And let it be safe. Write me when convenient, and don't be interrupted by your mercenary concerns and employments. I would have given you another sheet, from which you are saved by the entrance of the drill-sergeant, who has come to teach me how to fight the French, if they come. I am their man. 'God save the king!' "Yours,

"J. Wilson.

"Oxford, 12*th October*, 1803."

The next letter in the series is from Blair to Findlay, showing how deeply these two friends entered into the feelings of one whose trust in them was as that of a brother. It is dated

"Hill Top, *January* 19, 1804.

"The vacation is over next Tuesday week. I left him on Monday morning last; but one of the gentlemen-commoners came to Oxford for two or three days, and breakfasted, dined, and supped with us on Sunday, so that I had no opportunity of speaking to him on many things of which I wished to have talked to him. From this, it happened that I said nothing to him of what we talked over that Wednesday night. If I had not thought we should have had all Sunday night to ourselves, I would certainly have spoken of it before; but it is a subject on which I dare not speak to him, except at those moments when he seems happier than usual from my presence. If he is gloomy and dejected, as he is sometimes with me, I know that his mind will be shut to all reasonings favorable to his happiness; and that to touch on that subject would be merely to give him occasion to overwhelm me with one of those long bursts of passion and misery to which I can make no answer. He was out of spirits the first two days I was there; and I thought it most probable that in the last evening he would, from the idea of my going so soon, feel a greater degree of kindness and affection for me, which would keep his mind in a state of gentle feeling, and dispose it more easily to think happily of himself. If we had been alone that night, I should have talked it all over with him. I am doubtful whether I ought to write to him about it."

This affectionate friend did write to him on the subject, and a few days later he again addresses Findlay:—

"HILL TOP, *Sunset, Tuesday,* 1804.

"I am writing to Wilson, and shall send the letter to-morrow, so that he will get it on Thursday morning. I tell him why I am convinced that he is loved; and what I fear she may be induced to do, both from her delicacy and just pride, which must shrink from the idea of the disapprobation of relations, and from her scrupulous sense of right, which makes her refuse to separate him from those relations. I will say, that she is now guided in every thing she does by the resolution she has formed since he left her, of sacrificing her happiness to her sense of right (she may perhaps think) to his happiness; and I will, on that account, caution him against writing to her on that subject, because she might have strength of mind to write a refusal, that would blast all his hopes, and make him never dare to speak of it to her again. My wish is that he should see her next summer, and force from her a confession of her feelings.

"See what he thinks about P—. He has talked to me as if he feared she was attached to him. P— left his country when she knew nothing more of Wilson than that he was a fine boy, and I think it very probable at that time she might feel a grateful attachment to him for his love to her, and what she might think his generosity. Does Wilson know so little of her and of himself as to dream for a moment that, after knowing him as she has done for these last three years, her heart can still hold by one wish to such a man as P—? If she has formed any engagement to such a man as P—, God help us! I cannot think it possible. If it had been, she must have acted differently. Her love might overpower in her for a time her sense of what she thinks she owes to the order of society; while her only restraint was the idea that she ought not to separate Wilson from all his family connections. I can conceive her doing all that she has done with the purest and most virtuous mind, for she acted under a great degree of delusion; I am convinced she did not suspect the consequences to her own heart or to Wilson's. But if she could in the slightest degree look on herself as the property of another, every thing becomes utterly incomprehensible; a positive engagement leaves no room for delusion, and in that situation a woman of delicate feelings has but one way of acting. I have not time for more. "Yours ever,

"ALEX. BLAIR."

The next letter in my possession is dated March 7, 1804,* and may be inserted below for the sake of chronological order, as showing the kind of studies which were meantime engaging his attention.

From this date down to September of the same year there is no record of his doings. Blair writing to Findlay, September 30th, says:—"I imagine Wilson should be in London about this time to meet his mother. I have not seen him this summer." It may be inferred that he was occupied during the spring with his studies, and struggling as best he could to overcome the dejection of spirits, which, judging from the next letter, did not for a time pass away. During the summer, he went off on a long excursion through Wales, to which he subsequently alludes in no very agreeable terms. It could not fail, however, to arouse his poetic sensibilities, and in one of the commonplace-books I find a sketch of an intended poem on this subject, entitled "Hints for the Pedestrian."

The next glimpse of him from correspondence is in a letter from Blair to Findlay, of date November 24, 1804:—

"Wilson has been walking about in Wales all this summer, and is now at Oxford again. I have not once seen him. He says he is going to Scotland in about five weeks. I believe he had better not.

* It is little more than a mere catalogue of books, but the playful tone in which the commission is rendered, gives interest and not a little character to the document.

"BOB, you scoundrel, DID you get my last letter? If you can get any bookseller to trust me under my own name, or me under your name, for the following books, until this time twelvemonths, buy them, and send them down as soon as possible. I think that, with proper management, you may manage to get it done.

"1. Ferguson's Roman Republic, in octavo; don't buy it unless in octavo. 2. Mitford's Greece, in octavo; don't buy it unless in octavo. 3. Stewart's edition of Reid's Philosophy. This book is only in octavo, therefore don't buy it unless in octavo. 4. Malthus's Essay on Population—an excellent book—read part of it; most acute thing of the present day. 5. Godwin's Political Justice; don't buy it unless in octavo. 6. Gillies' Greece in octavo; don't buy it unless in octavo. 7. Pinkerton's Ancient Scottish Poems; recollect this is not his Ancient Comic Ballads. 8. All Ritson's publications, except English Romances, and Essay on Abstinence from Animal Food. 9. Hartley on Man; last edition in three vols. octavo, with notes by some foreigner or another. 10. Rousseau's Works, if cheap and complete; thirty-four volumes, or perhaps less; but complete, certainly complete. 11. Regnier's History, if tolerably cheap. 12. Turner's History of the Anglo-Saxons, three vols. 13. Any good edition of Gilbert Stuart's Works; also, Mallet's Northern Antiquities, translated. 15. Bisset's History of this Country. 16. All Pinkerton's works indeed you may buy, except his Geography. If possible, let them all be *in boards*.

"J. WILSON.

"MAGDALEN COLLEGE, *March*, 1804,
"*Tuesday Evening*."

John Finlay * is to come back with him. I expect to be in London about the middle or end of January, and I suppose Finlay will come while I am there, and we may settle him comfortably. Wilson says, in speaking of some prize he means to undertake, that he feels the vigor of his mind returning. God grant it! If he will promise to return happy, which I think he may do, from Scotland, his going will be a blessed event; but if he is to come away again in the same miserable uncertainty, it will destroy the little calm he has gained, and repeat the same sufferings with less strength to bear them. I shall see him before he goes."

Soon after this he was seized with a fit of illness, which caused much concern to his affectionate correspondents, Blair and Findlay. He quickly recovered, however; and his brother Andrew, then serving at Chatham, on board H. M. S. "Magicienne," writes to Robert on the 7th of December, "that he had found him in very good health, but in very bad spirits." His own account of the matter in a letter to Findlay, of December 10, 1804, is sufficiently plain, and needs no comment:—

"Though well when Andrew came here, as bad luck would have it, I was taken ill before he left me, but not dangerously, and I am rather better. I believe my complaint is nervous, and mortally affects my spirits. I have a constant beating at my heart, and a wavering of thought resembling a sort of derangement; but I have been bled and feel better.

"This wretched complaint has been brought on by my late attempt to bury in unbridled dissipation the recollection of blasted hopes. But God's will be done."

Between this date and the next letter, there is a gap of ten months. Of what passed in the interval, there is no memorial beyond the allusions in his letter, from which we gather that he travelled during the summer in the north of England and in Ireland; that a considerable portion of the holidays was spent among the Lakes; and that there and then he seized the opportunity offered of becoming the proprietor of Elleray, one of the loveliest spots in which a poet ever fixed his home. This letter is dated London, October 3, 1805, and is written in a cheerful strain, yet betraying

* John Finlay, a young poet of great promise, author of *Wallace, or the Vale of Ellerslie; Historical and Romantic Ballads*, etc. etc., was born in 1782, and died at Moffat in 1810. Wilson wrote an account of his life and writings in *Blackwood* for November, 1817.

the overhanging of the clouds, which were deepening over his love-prospects, though for a brief space breaking into delusive sunshine: *—

"LONDON, *October* 3, 1805.

"MY DEAR BOB:—I received your letter in a wonderfully short time after it was written, considering the extensive tour of his Majesty's dominion it had judged it expedient to take before condescending to pay me a visit. It spent the greatest part of the summer in visiting Oxford, London, Scarborough, Harrowgate, Edinburgh, and the various post-towns of Westmoreland, Cumberland, and Lancashire. When it finally reached me, its visage was wofully begrimed with dirt, and its sides squeezed into a shape far from epistolary. It truly cut a most ridiculous appearance, and, indeed, was ashamed of itself, for it made its escape from my possession the day after I first cast salt upon its tail; and as I have never seen it since, I am led to suppose that it may have once more set out on its travels, in which case you probably will meet with it soon in Glasgow.

"I was not a little provoked to find, that during my solitary rambles in Ireland, you were improving yourself in polite accomplishments among the mountains of Wales. The rapidity with which you travelled seems to have been astonishing and praiseworthy.

"I do not feel myself in a mood just now to give you any account of my Irish expedition, which afforded me all the possible varieties of pain, and a good many modifications of pleasure. It was prolific in adventure and scrape, and made me acquainted with strange bed-fellows. Had you been with me, I am sure we would have enjoyed it more than you can well imagine. I have spent this summer at Scarborough, Harrowgate, and the Lakes. The weather has been sufficiently bad to provoke an old sow to commit suicide—a fact which actually took place near Ambleside. The creature cut its throat with a hand-saw.

" . . . . I have bought some ground on Windermere Lake, but whether in future years I may live there, I know not. I think that a settled life will never do for me; and I often lament that I did

* As he in after life said, "Sometimes, my dear Shepherd, my life from eighteen to twenty-four is an utter blank, like a moonless midnight; at other times, oh! what a refulgent day!"—*Noctes*, xxxv.

not enter the army or navy, a thing which is now entirely impossible. While I keep moving, life goes on well enough, but whenever I pause, the fever of the soul begins.

"John Wilson."

There is no letter again for a period of six months; and we are left to imagine that the interval was filled up with alternations of gloom and gayety, of hard study and hard living. He was giving himself, like the royal preacher, not only "to know wisdom," but to know also "madness and folly." The mention of Margaret is briefer than hitherto, even slightly suggestive of constraint, and one begins to see some shadowing of the truth in that sentence of the Essay on "Streams:"—"For two years of absence and of distance brought a strange, dim, misty haze over the fires—supposed unquenchable—of our hearts; then came suspicion, distrust, wrathful jealousy, and stone-eyed despair!" It had not come to that yet, for, before the curtain closes on this love-drama, there is one glimpse of ecstatic happiness, followed only by deeper gloom and unbroken silence.

The next letter is addressed to Findlay, and dated

"Oxford, *April* 13, 1806.

"My dearest Robert:—If I have not answered your letter so soon as perhaps I should have done, it was neither from being indifferent to the very agreeable contents of it, nor careless of that happiness which I see awaits you in life, and which no soul on earth better deserves than you. Most genuine satisfaction it did give me to hear of the kindness which your father's memory has procured you.

"In your case it may justly be said that a good man's righteousness is an inheritance to his children. That happiness, prosperity, and peace may ever attend you, is a wish I need not express to one who knows me so well as you do. As to myself, I have not a very great deal to say. I am going on pretty much in the old way, sometimes unhappy enough, God knows! and at other times tolerably comfortable.

"I believe that I live rather too hard, and I have formed a very determined resolution to change my ways; but it is one thing to make a resolution, and another to keep it. I have certainly led a dissipated life for some time, but,

"'Wine, they say, drives off despair,
And bids even hope remain,
And that is sure a reason fair
To fill my glass again.'

"I expected to have heard something from D., informing me of your intention relative to our summer tour to the Lakes. I wrote him how I was situated at present; but I would like to hear how your intentions are, as I might perhaps accommodate myself in a great measure to them. I am uncertain whether I shall be in Scotland again for some years. If you could meet me at the Lakes in July early, even without our other friends, I think we might pass the time most happily. But I expect to hear from you very soon at great length. By the by, I know not what excuse to make for not having visited Torrance. If ever you see Margaret, I wish you would tell how happy you know I would have been to see her, but that it could have been only for an hour or two, and that I therefore put off the happiness till I could stay a day or two with her in a few months. Perhaps she may attribute to coldness what arose from the deepness of love. It will give me sincere happiness to hear often and soon from you. Every thing interesting to you will interest me, so omit nothing of that kind.

"Remember me kindly to Finlay and Smith, and to all you love, mother and sisters. Blair is with me, and wishes you well.

"Yours ever,

"JOHN WILSON."

It would appear from the following letter, written from his mother's house in Edinburgh, that the tour to the Lakes was changed for one in the Highlands of Scotland, which, during the space of six weeks' time, was agreeably spent by the aforesaid friends:

"53 QUEEN STREET, EDINBURGH,
July 29, 1806.

"MY DEAR BOB:—I have long been conjecturing the reason of your unconjecturable silence. What in the name of wonder are you about? I had a letter from Dunlop, telling me you proposed accompanying us to the Highlands. I hope you will do so. Both Dunlop and myself are good fellows, but we should get d—ly tiresome without a third. I think the best way will be to meet at

Stirling. I shall be there on Saturday, the 9th, by five o'clock, and whoever arrives first can order dinner for the others. You can let me know of the inn we had best go to. It would be a foolish waste of time for you and Dunlop to come to Edinburgh, except in the case of going to St. Andrews, which I strongly give my vote against. "I am thine ever,

"JOHN WILSON."

There are no more letters dated from Oxford or elsewhere for some months. The next to which we come is, however, of deep interest. It is from Blair to Findlay, of date March 19, 1807, giving an account of Wilson's examination for his Bachelor Degree:—

"MY DEAR ROBERT:—About a fortnight ago, Wilson wrote to me to desire I would go to him immediately, and he would tell me what had happened with regard to *her*. I went, of course, and found him very much distressed, with a degree of anxiety that I could not have conceived, about his examination, which was to come on in a few days. If his mind had had its former strength, this, he said, would not have affected him, but after what had happened to him, he had no strength left. The terror of this examination preyed so on his mind, that for ten days before I saw him he had scarcely slept any night more than an hour or two. I wish to know from you what it is that has happened in Scotland, that has shaken his mind to this degree, for he has not spoken a word on the subject to me; and I could not begin to speak of it, after having seen, as I have seen, the state into which it threw him, to give way to his feelings. I could not begin a conversation that was to terminate in such bursts of anguish as I have witnessed.

"Write to me as soon as you can to tell me this, though you should have time to write nothing more. When he walked from this college to the schools, he went along in full conviction that he was to be plucked. His examination was, as might naturally be expected, the most illustrious within the memory of man. Sotheby was there, and declared it was worth coming from London to hear him translate a Greek chorus. I was exceedingly pleased with Shepherd, his examiner, who seemed highly delighted at having got hold of him, and took much pains to show him off. Indeed he is given to show people off; and those who know little are said not to relish the operation, so that his name is a name of terror, but nothing could be luckier for John than his strict, close style of examination.

"The mere riddance of that burden, which had sat so long on his thoughts, was enough to make him dance; but he was also elated with success and applause, and was in very high spirits after it. I left him last night."

The examination was truly, to use his private tutor's expression, a "glorious" one. "*It marked the scholar*," is the measured but emphatic phrase of the formidable Mr. Shepherd, in referring to it. "I can never forget," said another of the examiners, the Rev. Richard Dixon, Fellow and Tutor of Queen's, "the very splendid examination which you passed in this University; an examination which afforded the strongest proofs of very great application, and genius, and scholarship, and which produced such an impression on the minds of the Examiners, as to call forth (a distinction very rarely conferred) the public expression of our approbation and thanks."*

* From subsequent testimonies regarding his Oxford studies and reputation, a few may in this place be inserted. The Rev. Benjamin Cheese, who was his private tutor during the last two years of his University course, thus referred to that period:—"Among all my pupils I never met with one who read with greater zest the sublime pages of the Greek tragedians, or penetrated with the same rapid acuteness into the abstruse difficulties of Aristotle. The analyses which you then made for me of the Ethics, Rhetoric, and Poetics of that great philosopher, I still preserve as a memorial of you. I never refer to them without regretting that your Oxford examination for a degree took place previously to the introduction of the new system, under which men are now arranged in distinct classes, according to their real merits, as I am well assured that the public appearance which you *then* made (for I was myself present on the glorious occasion) would *now* fully entitle you to the very highest honors which our University can bestow."

"He was always considered by me," writes the Rev. William Russell, Fellow of Magdalen College, "and by other members of the College in which we were educated, to be a man of strong powers of mind, great industry and zeal for learning, and no ordinary degree of taste. His college exercises and compositions invariably displayed much genius and skill in argument; and the small poem on Sculpture, Architecture, and Painting, which gained the University Prize, given by the late Sir Roger Newdigate, on the first year of its establishment, was esteemed on all hands to be a superior specimen of talent. And I can truly say, that the reputation he acquired during his residence in Oxford, not only in our own Society, but in the University at large, remains fresh amongst us, though many years have elapsed since he left us, and many others of high talent have arisen during that period to attract our admiration."

The venerable President of his College, Dr. Routh, bore similar testimony:—"I can safely say, that amongst the non-foundationers of Magdalen College, who are generally about twelve in number, I do not recollect any one, during my long residence in it, who has had an equal share of reputation with yourself for great natural abilities, united with extensive literary acquirements. I remember the satisfaction I generally felt at the appearance you made at the examinations in classical authors, held thrice in the year within the College, and have often perused with delight that elegant composition which obtained a University prize, and whose only fault seemed to be that it was too short."

The Rev. Charles Thorp, formerly a Fellow of University College, Oxford, says, "Your char-

Little did these Examiners and admiring friends imagine with what feelings John Wilson had walked into the schools that morning, "in the full conviction that he was to be plucked." Little did they know, as they propounded difficulties in Greek choruses and the *Ethics*, of the more oppressing thought that had made the last ten nights so dreadful,—"what had happened with regard to *her!*" Compared with that, what to him was Hecuba, or Antigone either? On this subject, let it be noted, he did not open his lips to the beloved friend whom he had expressly summoned, that he might tell him "what had happened." And that sympathizing friend, who had hastened to hear and to console, religiously held his peace, and "could not begin to speak of it, after having seen the state into which it threw him;" and had to go elsewhere for information. It is altogether a singular exhibition of character on both sides, reminding one of those old Easterns who sat seven days speechless before their friend, "for they saw that his grief was very great."

What it was that had "happened with regard to *her*," to bring him to this state of wretchedness, may be gathered from his own letter, apparently written about the same time, to Findlay:—

"*October* 19, 1807.

"MY DEAREST ROBERT:—I have often wished to write to you, but to such an intimate friend as you I know not how to speak. There is not one ray of hope that I shall ever be able to make my mother listen for a moment to the subject nearest my heart. I know her violent feelings too well; I even know this, that if I were to acquaint her with my love for Margaret, we never could again be on the footing of mother and son.

acter and talents were known to me when I was a tutor at Oxford, and yourself a student there, before I had the pleasure of a personal acquaintance with you; an acquaintance I sought and prized, and have always wished to improve." "Those who, like myself," says Archdeacon Burney, "loved and admired you at Oxford, would, I am sure, feel pleasure in bearing a just testimony to your acuteness of discrimination, your keen spirit of inquiry, your extended reading, your copiousness in illustration, which even then rendered you eminent above your fellows." "The course of studies at Oxford," says Sir Charles E. Grey (formerly of Oriel College, Oxford, afterwards Chief-Justice of Bengal), "had shortly before been placed upon a new and excellent footing; and I shall always consider it a fortunate incident in my life that I fell on that period when all members of the University were full of zeal for the new improvements, and were engaging in the course that was opened for them with an ardor which it was not to be hoped could be sustained for many years. With what eagerness and assiduity were the writings of the moral philosophers, orators, historians, and tragedians of Greece and Rome read, and almost learned by heart. The distinguished examination which you passed, the prize which you obtained, and the general reputation which you acquired, are proofs that you were amongst the most successful students of the day."

"All this may be to you inexplicable; that I cannot help; that it is the fact, I know to my sorrow. Blair is with me, and unless he had been so, I must have died. Before my examination, my state of mind got dreadful. He sat up several nights with me, and at last I was examined and got my degree 'cum laude,' a matter certainly of indifference to me. I do not wish you to come to London if you could, for I shall not be there. The only reason I have for writing is to show you how perfectly I am your friend, and ever will be so, for by your last I saw my silence had surprised you. If I feel more at home to-morrow, I will write you again, but unless I saw yourself I could not tell you my feelings and future plans of existence, which must be joyless and unendeared. Thine eternally,

"J. Wilson."

"Oxford, 1807.

"My dear Bob:—I received your letter this morning, and it has confirmed me in what I feared, that I have written some infernal thing or another to Margaret: the truth is, that about the time I wrote her I was in a curious way, as indeed I am now, from having taken laudanum, not exactly with a view to annihilation, but spirits. That blessed beverage played the devil with my intellects, and absolutely destroyed my capacity of distinguishing right from wrong, or what was serious from ludicrous. At times I was in the same state as if I were as drunk as Chloe; and at others, sober, sad, and sunk in despair and misery. If this be any excuse to you for what I may have said, of which I do not recollect one word, you can employ it as such; if not, you are a severer judge than I have ever yet found you. As to saying any thing savage to Margaret, I scarcely think that possible, for why should even a madman do that? I have since written her, and hope whatever offences I have committed, I have her forgiveness. If you regard my soul, go again to her and try to explain my conduct as best you can, for I am unable to justify myself, my thoughts are so dreadful when I wish to write to her. This love of mine has been a fine thing; first kept me many years in misery, and now perhaps alienated from me the friendship and good opinion of those I love and regard; however, I need not expatiate much on that. As to the other parts of your letter, I can say nothing to them. Do you really imagine that I would easily give up the prospect of eternal felicity? I have corresponded with

——— often upon the subject, and know too well how it is. I shall not injure them so far as to let you know all they have said on the subject; the enclosed letter may give you some faint idea of it, as it is the mildest and most fitted to inspire hope of them all.

"J. W."

We are now approaching the close of this tender episode. That summer the lovers met, and the obstructing clouds for a brief space clear away in the light of mutual confidence and utter joy. But the obstacles remain, nevertheless; and as soon as he is left alone, he becomes a prey to the most distracting fears and perplexities. Thus he writes to his dear Robert from "Bowness," some time, as I conjecture, in the autumn of 1807:—

"MY DEAREST ROBERT:—I have often said that I would write you a long letter, and as often have I tried it; but such a crowd of feelings of all different kinds comes across my heart, that I sit for hours with a paper before me, and never write a single word. Indeed, even if we were together, I know not if I could say much to you, for with me all is strange and inextricable perplexity. I love, and am beloved to distraction, and often the gleams of hope illumine the path of futurity with a glory hardly to be looked at; while, again, extravagance of love seems only extravagance of folly, and excess of fondness excess of despair. I am betimes the most miserable and the happiest of created beings. So far I am better than during former years, when I had no hope, no wish to live. Now, indeed, my sadness almost wholly regards Margaret. For myself, I have been inured to wretchedness, and though, in some respects, or as far as it made me a man of worse conduct than of principles, I have yielded to the common effect of misery, in future I could look forward to dreary solitude of spirit with some tolerable degree of composure. But for her, whose peace is far dearer to me than my own, I have many dreadful anticipations. Should our union be rendered impracticable, and Miss W. to die, an event which, I trust in God, is far, far distant, God only knows what would become of her."

In anticipation of these obstacles being removed, he turns his thoughts to home, and addresses a beautiful short poem ("My Cottage") to Margaret. His spirit then did

"Travel like a summer sun,
Itself all glory, and its path all joy;"*

but this bright change was of brief duration. The curious would doubtless desire to know something more of why this "love never found its earthly close," while others will rest satisfied with such conclusions as may be drawn from the following expressions, met with in letters addressed to his dear friend, Robert Findlay: "I feel myself in a great measure an alien in my own family, and all this is the consequence of that my most unfortunate attachment." And once more, in allusion to this subject, he says: "I know enough now to know that my mother would die if this happened."

The following fragment will terminate this story:—

"I have made up my mind not to visit Torrance at present, in which case I must not come to Glasgow. This resolution, I hope, is right. It has been made after many an hour of (painful) reflection. This I know, that were I to go, I could not bear to look on my mother's face, a feeling which must not be mine. Enclosed is a letter to Margaret. If you could take it yourself, and see how it is received, it would please me much; yet there may be people there, in which case that would be useless.

"Thine till death in joy or sorrow.

"BOWNESS, *December* 22."

We know not how they parted, but this we may imagine, that "they caught up the whole of love, and uttered it," and bade adieu forever.

CHAPTER V.

LIFE AT ELLERAY.

1807–1811.

IN 1807, John Wilson concluded his University career, the brilliancy of which, for many years, gave his name a prestige worthy of long remembrance within the academic walls of Oxford. He loved the beautiful fields of England, and, with all the world before him where to choose a place of rest, he turned his steps from his

* *Miscellaneous Poems.*

Alma Mater, to that lovely land where cluster the fair lakes of Cumberland and Westmoreland. Having selected a home on the banks of Windermere, we find him there in the prime of youth, with that keen nature of his alternating between light and shade, and every possible humor attendant on the impulses of an ardent heart, yet uneasy with a burden which there was none other to share. Possibly the restless life he led began in a hope of self-forgetfulness; yet there was at the same time, in the conscious possession of so much bodily strength, and that unceasing activity of spirit, an irrepressible desire to exercise every faculty. To many his life in Westmoreland may appear to have been one of idleness, but not to those who, with a kindly discernment of human nature, see the advantages which varied experience gives to a strong mind.

We now follow him to Elleray. For a description of this beautiful spot I gladly avail myself of the striking description of Mr. De Quincey:*—

"With the usual latitude of language in such cases, I say *on* Windermere; but in fact this charming estate lies far above the lake; and one of the most interesting of its domestic features is the foreground of the rich landscape which connects, by the most gentle scale of declivities, this almost aërial altitude [as, for *habitable* ground, it really is] with the sylvan margin of the deep water which rolls a mile and a half below. When I say a mile and a half, you will understand me to compute the descent according to the undulations of the ground; because else the perpendicular elevation above the level of the lake cannot be above one-half of that extent. Seated on such an eminence, but yet surrounded by foregrounds of such quiet beauty, and settling downwards towards the lake by such tranquil steps as to take away every feeling of precipitous or dangerous elevation, Elleray possesses a double character of beauty rarely found in connection; and yet each, by singular good fortune, in this case, absolute and unrivalled in its kind. Within a bowshot of each other may be found stations of the deepest seclusion, fenced in by verdurous walls of insuperable forest heights, and presenting a limited scene of beauty—deep, solemn, noiseless, severely sequestered—and other stations of a magnifi-

* Letter addressed to the *Edinburgh Literary Gazette*, 1829, a forgotten newspaper, of which there were only two vols. published.

cence so gorgeous as few estates in this island can boast, and of those few, perhaps, none in such close connection with a dwelling-house. Stepping out from the very windows of the drawing-room, you find yourself on a terrace which gives you the feeling of a 'specular height,' such as you might expect on Ararat, or might appropriately conceive on 'Athos seen from Samothrace.' The whole course of a noble lake, about eleven miles long, lies subject to your view, with many of its islands, and its two opposite shores so different in character—the one stern, precipitous, and gloomy; the other (and luckily the hither one), by the mere bounty of nature and of accident—by the happy disposition of the ground originally, and by the fortunate equilibrium between the sylvan tracks, meandering irregularly through the whole district, and the proportion left to verdant fields and meadows, wearing the character of the richest park scenery; except indeed that this character is here and there a little modified by a quiet hedge-row, or the stealing smoke which betrays the embowered cottage of a laborer. But the sublime, peculiar, and not-to-be-forgotten feature of the scene is the great system of mountains which unite about five miles off, at the head of the lake, to lock in and enclose this noble landscape. The several ranges of mountains which stand at various distances within six or seven miles of the little town of Ambleside, all separately various in their forms, and all eminently picturesque, when seen from Elleray, appear to blend and group as parts of one connected whole; and, when their usual drapery of clouds happens to take a fortunate arrangement, and the sunlights are properly broken and thrown from the most suitable quarter of the heavens, I cannot recollect any spectacle in England or Wales, of the many hundreds I have seen, bearing a local, if not a national reputation for magnificence of prospect, which so much dilates the heart with a sense of power and aërial sublimity as this terrace-view from Elleray."

At the time when my father purchased Elleray, there was no suitable dwelling-house on the estate. A rustic cottage indeed there was, which, with the addition of a drawing-room thrown out at one end, was made capable for many a year to come of meeting the hospitable system of life adopted by its owner. It was built of common stone, but it might have been marble for aught that the eye could tell. Pretty French windows opened to the ground, and were the only uncovered portion of it; all else was a profusion of jessamine, clematis, and honeysuckle. A trellised entrance, clustering with wild roses, led to the chief part of the dwelling. Beyond the dining-room windows was the entrance to the kitchen and other parts of the house, only differing from the first door in being made of the dark blue slate of the country, and unadorned by roses. The bedroom windows to the front, peeped out from their natural festoons unshaded by other curtains, while the cottage was protected by a fine old sycamore-tree that, standing on a gentle eminence, sent its spreading branches and umbrageous foliage far over the roof, just leaving room enough for the quaint, picturesque chimneys to send their curling smoke into the air.* The little cottage lay beneath the shelter of a well-wooded hill, that gave a look of delightful retirement and comfort to its situation; a poet's home it might well be called. The lofty peaks of the Langdale Pikes ever greeted the eye, in the dark shadows of evening or glittering beneath a noonday sun; and Windermere as seen from Elleray was seen best—every point and bay, island and cove, lay there unveiled. Perhaps in the clearing away of mist in early morning the scene was most refreshing, as bit by bit a dewy green cluster of trees appears, and then a gleam of water, with some captive cloud deep set in its light, a mountain base, or far-off pasture, the well-defined colors of rich middle-distance creating impatience for a perfect picture; when all at once the obscuring vapors passed away, and the whole landscape was revealed.

Although this picturesque cottage remained the dwelling-house till 1825, my father began to build in the year 1808 a mansion of more elegant proportions, after plans of his own. We may gather some idea of what these plans were by referring to his ideal description of Buchanan Lodge. The whole tenement was to be upon the ground flat. "I abhor stairs," said he, "and there can be no peace in any mansion where heavy footsteps may be heard over head. Suppose three sides of a square. You approach the front by a fine serpentine avenue, and enter slap-bang through a wide glass-door

* Of this sycamore he often spoke. "Never in this well-wooded world," soliloquized the poet, "not even in the days of the Druids, could there have been such another tree! It would be easier to suppose two Shaksperes. Yet I have heard people say it is far from being a large tree. A small one it cannot be, with a house in its shadow—an unawakened house that looks as if it were dreaming. True, 'tis but a cottage, a Westmoreland cottage. But then it has several roofs shelving away there in the lustre of loveliest lichens; each roof with its own assortment of doves and pigeons preening their pinions in the morning pleasance. Oh, sweetest and shadiest of all sycamores, we love thee beyond all other trees!"

into a green-house, a conservatory of every thing rich and rare in the world of flowers. Folding-doors are drawn noiselessly into the walls as if by magic, and lo! drawing-room and dining-room stretching east and west in dim and distant perspective. Another side of the square contains kitchen, servants' rooms, etc.; and the third side my study and bedrooms, all still, silent, composed, standing obscure, unseen, unapproachable, holy! The fourth side of the square is not; shrubs and trees and a productive garden shut me in from behind, while a ring fence enclosing about five acres, just sufficient for my nag and cow, form a magical circle into which nothing vile or profane can intrude."

The new house at Elleray, of which this was an ideal description, was, as Mr. De Quincey remarked, a silent commentary on its master's state of mind, and an exemplification of his character. The plan, when completed, which in appearance had been extravagant, turned out in reality to have been calculated with the coolest judgment and nicest foresight of domestic needs.

In this beautiful retirement the young poet was now at liberty to enjoy all the varied delights of poetic meditation, of congenial society, and of those endless out-door recreations which constituted no small part of his life. Soon did his presence become identified with every nook and corner of that lake region. In the mountain pass, by the lonely stream, on the waters of the lake, by night and by day, in the houses of the rich and the poor, he came to be recognized as a familiar and welcome presence. Often would the early morning find him watching the rising mist, until the whole landscape lay clear before his enraptured eyes, and the fresh beauty of the hour invited him to a long day's ramble into the heart of the valley. Though much given, as of old, to solitary wanderings, he did not neglect to cultivate the society of the remarkable men whom he found in that district, when he took up his residence at Elleray,—Wordsworth at Rydal, Southey and Coleridge at Keswick, Charles Lloyd at Brathay, Bishop Watson at Calgarth, the Rev. Mr. Fleming at Rayrig, and other friends of lesser note, but not less pleasant memory, in and around Ambleside.

The first meeting with Wordsworth did not take place till the year 1807, the poet and his family having lived the greater part of that year at Colerton, returning to Grasmere in the spring of 1808. At his house there, towards the latter end of that year, Wilson met

De Quincey. Strange to say, they had, when at Oxford, remained unknown to each other; but here, attracted by the same influence, a mutual friendship was not long in being formed, which endured—independent of years of separation and many caprices of fortune—till death divided them. The graces of nature with which De Quincey was endowed fascinated my father, as they did every mind that came within the sphere of his extraordinary power in the days of his mental vigor, ere that sad destiny—for so it may be called—overtook him, which the brightness and strength of his intellect had no power to avert. The first impressions of the "Opium Eater" must be given in his own graphic words:*—"I remember the whole scene as circumstantially as if it belonged to but yesterday. In the vale of Grasmere—that peerless little vale, which you and Gray the poet and so many others have joined in admiring as the very Eden of English beauty, peace, and pastoral solitude—you may possibly recall, even from that flying glimpse you had of it, a modern house called Allanbank, standing under a low screen of woody rocks which descend from the hill of Silver How, on the western side of the lake. This house had been then recently built by a worthy merchant of Liverpool; but for some reason of no importance to you and me, not being immediately wanted for the family of the owner, had been let for a term of three years to Mr. Wordsworth. At the time I speak of, both Mr. Coleridge and myself were on a visit to Mr. Wordsworth; and one room on the ground floor, designed for a breakfasting-room, which commands a sublime view of the three mountains—Fairfield, Arthur's Chair, and Seat Sandal (the first of them within about 400 feet of the highest mountains in Great Britain)—was then occupied by Mr. Coleridge as a study. On this particular day, the sun having only just set, it naturally happened that Mr. Coleridge—whose nightly vigils were long—had not yet come down to breakfast; meantime, and until the epoch of the Coleridgian breakfast should arrive, his study was lawfully disposable to profaner uses. Here, therefore, it was, that, opening the door hastily in quest of a book, I found seated, and in earnest conversation, two gentlemen: one of them my host, Mr. Wordsworth, at that time about thirty-seven or thirty-eight years old; the other was a younger man by good sixteen or seventeen years, in a sailor's dress, manifestly in robust health, *fervidus juventa*, and wearing upon his countenance

* Disinterred from th columns of the *Edinburgh Literary Gazette.*

a powerful expression of ardor and animated intelligence, mixed with much good-nature. '*Mr. Wilson of Elleray*'—delivered as the formula of introduction, in the deep tones of Mr. Wordsworth—at once banished the momentary surprise I felt on finding an unknown stranger where I had expected nobody, and substituted a surprise of another kind: I now well understood who it was that I saw; and there was no wonder in his being at Allanbank, Elleray standing within nine miles; but (as usually happens in such cases), I felt a shock of surprise on seeing a person so little corresponding to the one I had half unconsciously prefigured. . . . Figure to yourself, then, a tall man, about six feet high, within half an inch or so, built with tolerable appearance of strength; but at the date of my description (that is, in the very spring-tide and blossom of youth), wearing, for the predominant character of his person, lightness and agility, or (in our Westmoreland phrase) *lishness*; he seemed framed with an express view to gymnastic exercises of every sort. . . . Viewed, therefore, by an eye learned in gymnastic proportions, Mr. Wilson presented a somewhat striking figure; and by some people he was pronounced with emphasis a fine-looking young man; but others, who less understood, or less valued these advantages, spoke of him as nothing extraordinary. Still greater division of voices I have heard on his pretensions to be thought handsome. In my opinion, and most certainly in his own, these pretensions were but slender. His complexion was too florid; hair of a hue quite unsuited to that complexion; eyes not good, having no apparent depth, but seeming mere surfaces; and, in fine, no one feature that could be called fine, except the lower region of his face, mouth, chin, and the parts adjacent, which were then (and perhaps are now) truly elegant and Ciceronian. Ask in one of your public libraries for that little quarto edition of the Rhetorical Works of Cicero, edited by Shutz (the same who edited Æschylus), and you will there see (as a frontispiece to the first volume), a reduced whole length of Cicero from the antique; which in the mouth and chin, and indeed generally, if I do not greatly forget, will give you a lively representation of the contour and expression of Professor Wilson's face. Taken as a whole, though not handsome (as I have already said), when viewed in a quiescent state, the head and countenance are massy, dignified, and expressive of tranquil sagacity. . . . Note, however, that of all this array of personal features, as I have here described them, I then saw nothing at all, my attention being altogether occupied with Mr. Wilson's conversation and demeanor, which were in the highest degree agreeable; the points which chiefly struck me being the humility and gravity with which he spoke of himself, his large expansion of heart, and a certain air of noble frankness which overspread every thing he said; he seemed to have an intense enjoyment of life; indeed, being young, rich, healthy, and full of intellectual activity, it could not be very wonderful that he should feel happy and pleased with himself and others; but it was somewhat unusual to find that so rare an assemblage of endowments had communicated no tinge of arrogance to his manner, or at all disturbed the general temperance of his mind."

Many were the pleasant days spent by these friends together; many the joyous excursions among the hills and valleys of the lake country. One memorable gathering is still remembered in the lone places of the mountains, and spoken of to the stranger wandering there. One lovely summer day, in the year 1809, the solitudes of Eskdale were invaded by what seemed a little army of anglers. It consisted of thirty-two persons, ten of whom were servants brought to look after the tents and baggage necessary for a week's sojourn in the mountains. This camp with its furniture was carried by twelve ponies. Among the gentlemen of the party were Wilson, Wordsworth, De Quincey, Alexander Blair, two Messrs. Astley, Humphries, and some others whose names have escaped notice. After passing through Eskdale, and that solemn tract of country which opens upon Wastwater, they there pitched their tent, and roaming far and near from that point, each took his own way till evening hours assembled them together.

The beauty of the scenes through which they rambled, the fine weather, and, above all, that geniality of taste and disposition which had brought them together, made the occasion one of unforgotten satisfaction. It formed the theme of one of Wilson's most beautiful minor poems, entitled the "Anglers' Tent," which was written soon after at Elleray, where Wordsworth was then living. One morning a great discussion took place between the poets about a verse Wilson had some difficulty in arranging. At last, after much trying and questioning, it was made out between them:—

"The placid lake that rested far below,
Softly embosoming another sky,

Still as we gazed assumed a lovelier glow,
And seemed to send us looks of amity."

The troublesome line was—

"Softly embosoming another sky."

In a letter I received from Dr. Blair, he says:—"'The Friend' was going on at that time—Coleridge living at Wordsworth's—Wordsworth making, and reading to us as he made them, the 'Sonnets to the Tyrolese,' first given in 'The Friend;' and from Elleray that winter went 'Mathetes.'* I remember that De Quincey was with us at the time. He may have given some suggestions besides, but we certainly owed to him our signature."

Of my father's poetic compositions during these years I shall speak presently. I find in one of his commonplace-books some unpublished verses, which may, however, be inserted here, if only in illustration of what at this time was a frequent practice of his, and continued to be indulged in for many years of his after life, viz., the habit of walking in solitude during the hours of night. In spite of his generally even flow of good spirits, and his lively enjoyment of social pleasures, it seemed as if in the depths of his heart he craved some influence more soothing and elevating than even the most congenial companionship could afford. In these silent hours, whether pacing among the hills, or resting in contemplation of the glories of the earth and sky, the solemnity of feeling which was thus induced found natural expression in words of religious adoration. At the head of the lake stood the mansion of Brathay, the property of Allan Harden, Esq. There, on his way for a midnight ramble, did he often gain admittance, and, for some time, hold converse with his friend, before taking his solitary way to the mountains, within the deep shadows of which he would wander for hours, engaged in what he appropriately calls

"MIDNIGHT ADORATION.

"Beneath the full-orb'd moon, that bathed in light
The mellow'd verdure of Helvellyn's steep,
My spirit teeming with creations bright,
I walked like one who wanders in his sleep!

* A letter on Education, the joint composition of Wilson and Blair, addressed to the editor of "The Friend."

"The glittering stillness of the starry sky
Shone in my heart as in the waveless sea;
And rising up in kindred majesty,
I felt my soul from earthly fetters free!

"Joy filled my being like a gentle flood;
I felt as living without pulse or breath;
Eternity seem'd o'er my heart to brood,
And, as a faded dream, I thought of death.

"Through the hush'd air awoke mysterious awe;
God cheer'd my loneliness with holy mirth;
And in this blended mood I clearly saw
The moving spirit that pervades the earth.

"While adoration blessed my inward sense
I felt how beautiful this world could be,
When clothed with gleams of high intelligence
Born of the mountain's still sublimity.

"I sunk in silent worship on my knees,
While night's unnumber'd planets roll'd afar;
Blest moment for a contrite heart to seize—
Forgiving love shone forth in every star!

"The mighty moon my pensive soul subdued
With sorrow, tranquil as her cloudless ray,
Mellowing the transport of her loftiest mood
With conscious glimmerings of immortal day.

"I felt with pain that life's perturbèd wave
Had dimm'd the blaze to sinless spirits given;
But saw with joy, reposing on the grave,
The seraph Hope that points the way to heaven.

"The waveless clouds that hung amid the light,
By Mercy's hand with braided glory wove,
Seem'd, in their boundless mansions, to my sight,
Like guardian spirits o'er the land they love.

"My heart lay pillowed on their wings of snow,
Drinking the calm that slept on every fold,
Till memory of the life she led below
Seem'd like a tragic tale to pity told.

"When visions from the distant world arose—
How fair the gleams from memory's mystic urn;
How did my soul, 'mid Nature's blest repose,
To the soft bosom of affection turn!

"Then sinless grew my hopes, my wishes pure,
Breeding a seraph loftiness of soul;
Though free from pride, I felt of heaven secure
A step, a moment from the eternal goal!

"Those fearful doubts that strike the living blood,
Those dreams that sink the heart, we know not why,
Were changed to joy by this mysterious mood,
Sprung from the presence of Eternity.

"I saw, returning to its fount sublime,
The flood of being that from Nature flowed;
And then, displaying at the death of time
The essence and the lineaments of God!

"Thus pass'd the midnight hour, till from the wave
The orient sun flamed slowly up the sky;
Such a blest spirit found illumined gaze,
And seem'd to realize my vision high."

Another extract from the same book contains a touching record of the associations connected with a summer day's ramble with Wordsworth upon the slopes of Helvellyn. It appears to be an outline in prose of what was meant to form the subject of a poem, to be entitled Red Tarn, and is as follows:—

"Address to the reader about the reports he may have heard about the beauty and sublimity of the lakes.

"He probably has resolved to go up to Helvellyn to admire the sublimity of that mountain: this is right. Now beneath that mountain there is a little tarn which you will see. I will tell you something about that tarn. Two persons were sitting silent and alone beside that tarn, looking steadfastly on the water, and lost in thought. These were two brothers who dearly loved each other, and had done so from earliest youth to manhood.* The one was a man of genius and a poet, who lived among these mountains enjoying his own thoughts. The other younger by a few years, and had gone to sea, but had lately returned to see his brother, and resolved to live with him. His brother accompanied him across the hills on his way to join his ship for the last time, and here they sat, about to part. They had talked over their future plans of happiness when they were again to meet, and of their simple sports. As their last

* Wordsworth and a brother who was afterwards drowned.

act, they agreed to lay the foundation-stone of a little fishing-hut, and this they did with tears.

"They parted there, in that dim and solemn place, and recommended each other to God's eternal care.

"The one brother was drowned at sea. After the first agony was over, the recollection of that parting flashed upon the mind of the survivor; he at last found courage to go there, and in a state of blindness and desolation sat down upon the very stone. At last he opened his eyes, the tarn smiling with light; the raven croaking as before when they parted; all the crags seem the same; the sheep are in the same figures browsing before them; he almost expects to find his brother at his side; he then thinks of shipwreck and agony of all kinds.

"Next time he sits calmly and thinks upon it all; he even now loves the spot, and can talk of it.

"I one sweet summer day went along with him and heard the melancholy tale.

"Then, whoever goes to that sublime solitude, muse with holy feelings, and with the wildness of nature join human sympathies."

But there were other pursuits besides poetry that formed a part of my father's life at Elleray too prominent and characteristic to be passed unnoticed. Of these his various commonplace-books contain not a few memoranda, strangely intermixed with matters of a graver or more sentimental kind. Among the other amusements with which he diversified life in the country, boating was one of the principal. As may be supposed, this was a favorite diversion in the lake country, and Wilson's taste for it was cultivated with a zeal that, in fact, became a passion. The result was a degree of skill and hardihood beyond that of most amateurs. He had a small fleet on Windermere, the expense of maintaining which was undoubtedly very considerable.* Of the numerous boatmen required to man these vessels there was one whose name became at Elleray familiar as a household word—the faithful Billy Balmer. Billy was the neatest and best rower on Windermere, and knew that beauteous water from head to foot, in all her humors, from sunrise to night-

* Among the miscellaneous jottings, from which I have been extracting above, I find such items as the following:—"Endeavor, and masts and sails, £160; ballast, £15–£175;" "Eliza, £30;" "Endeavor, £150;" "Palafox, £20;" "Jane, £180;" "additional Endeavor, £25;" "Clyde, Billy, Snail, £10." The names of his sailing vessels were—The Endeavor, The Eliza, The Palafox, The Roscoe, The Clyde, The Jane, The Billy, besides a fine ten-oared Oxford barge, called Nil Timeo.

fall, and even later. There was not a more skilful boatman, or a steadier steersman on the lake, and he was about the best judge of a pretty craft and good sailing to be found. He could sing a sailor's song, had an undeniable love of fun, understood humor, and felt the difference of wit. No one knew how to tell a story better, and with a due unction of excusable exaggeration combined with reality; and in every tale of Billy his master was invariably the hero. He was a little man, weather-beaten in complexion, and much marked from smallpox. His hair was of a light sandy color; his eyes blue and kindly in expression, as was also his smile; his gait, rather doglike, not quite straight ahead, but, like that honest animal, he was sure-footed, and quick in getting over the ground. That pleasant broad Westmoreland dialect of his, too, gave peculiar character to his voice; and there is a grateful remembrance of the hearty grasp of his little, hard, horny hand when it greeted welcome, or bade adieu, while the whole picture of the man, in his blue dress, sailor fashion, stands distinctly before me, either as he steered the "Endeavor" or mowed the grass on the lawn at Elleray.*

One or two anecdotes still linger about the country, showing how recklessly Wilson could expose himself at all hours to the chances of the weather. Cold, snow, wind, and rain were no obstacles; nothing could repress the impulse that drove him forth to seek nature in all her moods. During a stormy December night, when the snow was falling fast, with little or no light in the heavens, he took a fancy to tempt the waters of Windermere, and setting off with the never-failing Billy, they took boat from Miller-ground and steered for Bowness. In a short time all knowledge of the point to which they were bound was lost. The darkness became more dismal every moment; the cold was intolerable. Several hours were spent in this dreary position, poor Billy in despair, expecting every instant would find them at the bottom of the lake, when suddenly the skiff went aground. The oars were not long in being made use of to discover the nature of their disaster, what and where they had struck, when, to their great satisfaction, a landing-

* "Seldom rose we," said my father in after years, "from our delightful dormitory till, about twelve o'clock, we heard the south breeze come pushing up from the sea. Then Billy used to tap at our door, with his tarry paw, and whisper, 'Master, Peggs is ready. I have brailed up the foresail; her jigger sits as straight as the Knave of Clubs, and we have ballasted with sand-bags. We'se beat the Liverpoolean to-day, Master.' Then I rose." See also Wilson's *Works.*

place was found. They had been beating about Miller-ground all the time, scarcely a stone's-throw from their starting-place. Billy's account of the story was, "that Master was well-nigh frozen to death, and had icicles a finger-length hanging from his hair and beard." This adventure ended in the toll-keeper on the Ambleside road being knocked up from his slumbers, and their spending the rest of the night with him, seated by a blazing fire, telling stories and drinking ale, a temptation to which Billy had no difficulty in yielding.

These lake escapades were not confined to boating. Riding one day with his friend, Mr. Richard Watson, by the margin of Rydal Lake, my father's horse became restive. Finding that no ordinary process would soothe the animal, he turned his head to the lake, with the intention of walking gently among the oozy reeds that grew on its banks, when, quite forgetful or heedless that they suddenly sloped to the water, the horse and his rider were in a moment plunged beyond their depth. Having got into deep waters, there was nothing for it but to swim through them; and presently he became aware that his friend's horse, true to the lead, was following close behind. Fortunately the lake was not very broad, and their passage across was soon made, though not without some little feeling of apprehension; for his friend Watson could not swim a stroke.

This equestrian performance suggests a story of another kind of diversion in which, according to Mr. De Quincey's account, my father occasionally indulged at Elleray. It is best given in the Opium-Eater's own words:—"Represent to yourself the earliest dawn of a fine summer's morning, time about half-past two o'clock. A young man, anxious for an introduction to Mr. Wilson, and as yet pretty nearly a stranger to the country, has taken up his abode in Grasmere, and has strolled out at this early hour to that rocky and moorish common (called the White Moss) which overhangs the Vale of Rydal, dividing it from Grasmere. Looking southwards in the direction of Rydal, suddenly he becomes aware of a huge beast advancing at a long trot, with the heavy and thundering tread of a hippopotamus, along the public road. The creature is soon arrived within half a mile of his station; and by the gray light of morning is at length made out to be a bull apparently flying from some unseen enemy in his rear. As yet, however, all is mystery;

but suddenly three horsemen double a turn in the road, and come flying into sight with the speed of a hurricane, manifestly in pursuit of the fugitive bull: the bull labors to navigate his huge bulk to the moor, which he reaches, and then pauses, panting, and blowing out clouds of smoke from his nostrils, to look back from his station amongst rocks and slippery crags upon his hunters. If he had conceited that the rockiness of the ground had secured his repose, the foolish bull is soon undeceived; the horsemen, scarcely relaxing their speed, charge up the hill, and speedily gaining the rear of the bull, drive him at a gallop over the worst part of that impracticable ground down into the level ground below. At this point of time the stranger perceives, by the increasing light of the morning, that the hunters are armed with immense spears fourteen feet long. With these the bull is soon dislodged, and scouring down to the plain below, he and the hunters at his tail take to the common at the head of the lake, and all, in the madness of the chase, are soon half ingulfed in the swamps of the morass. After plunging together for ten or fifteen minutes, all suddenly regain the *terra firma*, and the bull again makes for the rocks. Up to this moment there had been the silence of ghosts; and the stranger had doubted whether the spectacle were not a pageant of aërial spectres, ghostly huntsmen, ghostly lances, and a ghostly bull. But just at this crisis, a voice (it was the voice of Mr. Wilson) shouted aloud, 'Turn the villain; turn that villain; or he will take to Cumberland.' The young stranger did the service required of him; the villain was turned and fled southwards; the hunters, lance in rest, rushed after him; all bowed their thanks as they fled past; the fleet cavalcade again took the high road; they doubled the cape which shut them out of sight; and in a moment all had disappeared, and left the quiet valley to its original silence, whilst the young stranger and two grave Westmoreland 'statesmen' (who by this time had come into sight upon some accident or other) stood wondering in silence, and saying to themselves, perhaps,

> 'The earth hath bubbles as the water hath;
> And these are of them!'

"But they were no bubbles: the bull was a substantial bull; and took no harm at all from being turned out occasionally at midnight for a chase of fifteen or eighteen miles. The bull, no doubt, used to wonder at this nightly visitation; and the owner of the bull must sometimes have pondered a little on the draggled state in which the swamps would now and then leave his beast; but no other harm came of it." *

His love of animals has already been noticed.† Next to his boats, if not claiming an equal share of attention, came his game-cocks; these afforded a favorite pastime while he was at Oxford. As other men keep their studs, and are careful of the pedigree and training of their racers, so did Wilson watch with studious solicitude over the development and reputation of his game-birds. The setting down of hens to hatch was registered as duly and gravely as an astronomer notes the transit of the planets; the number of eggs, the day of the month, and sometimes even the hour of the day being carefully specified.‡

In one of the MS. books containing the principal portion of *The Isle of Palms*, I find many of these quaint entries in most eccentric juxtaposition to notes of a very different kind.§ Along with

* Letter in *Edinburgh Literary Gazette.*

† Of this there are numberless indications in his works. Birds were his special favorites, but he was a general lover of animals, beasts, birds, and insects. Even that, to most people, unpleasant creature the spider, was interesting to him; and the *Noctes* contain sundry references to his observations on their habits. "I love spiders," he says; "look at the lineal descendant of Arachne; how beautifully she descends from the chair of Christopher North to the lower regions of our earth." See *Works*, vol. i., 120; vol. ii., 148, 178, 230, 252, 262. Regarding his qualifications as a naturalist, De Quincey writes:—"Perhaps you already know from your countryman Audubon, that the Professor is himself a naturalist, and of original merit; in fact, worth a score of such meagre bookish naturalists as are formed in museums and by second-hand acts of memory; having (like Audubon) built much of his knowledge upon personal observation. Hence he has two great advantages; one, that his knowledge is accurate in a very unusual degree; and another, that this knowledge, having grown up under the inspiration of a real interest and an unaffected love for its objects—commencing, indeed, at an age when no affectation in matters of that nature could exist—has settled upon those facts and circumstances which have a true philosophical value: habits, predominant affections, the direction of instincts, and the compensatory processes where these happen to be thwarted—on all such topics he is learned and full; whilst, on the science of measurements and proportions, applied to dorsal fins and tail-feathers, and on the exact arrangement of colors, &c.—that petty upholstery of nature, on which books are so tedious and elaborate—not uncommonly he is negligent or forgetful."

‡ The following are some specimens from his memoranda:

"Small Paisley hen set herself with no fewer than nine eggs on Monday, the 6th of July. Black Edinburgh hen was set on Tuesday, the 23d of June, with twelve eggs—middle of the day. Large Paisley hen was set on Wednesday, the 24th of June, with twelve eggs—middle of the day; one egg laid the day after she was set. Red pullet in Josie's barn was set with nine eggs on Thursday, the 2d of July. Sister to the above, was set with five eggs same day, but they had been sat upon a day or two before. Small black muffled hen set herself with about eight eggs on Monday night, or Tuesday morning, 7th July."

§ Side by side with those beautiful lines beginning—

"Oh, Fairy Child! what can I wish for thee?
Like a perennial flow'ret may'st thou be,
That spends its life in beauty and in bliss;

calculations of the number of lines to be allotted to various proposed poems, such as "St. Hubert," "The Manse," "The Ocean Queen," there are elaborate memoranda of the "broods proposed for next spring." "The spangled cock," and "Lord Derby," the black brass-winged cock, bred from Caradice with the Keswick Gray," the "Red Liverpool hen," the "Paisley hen," large and small, and many other distinguished fowls, take a prominent position in these curious lists. The name of "Lord Derby," in particular, from its frequent occurrence, implies that that high-bred animal, doubtless of the Knowsley stock, was one of the prime favorites of the establishment. The phraseology and figures in these memoranda are sometimes altogether unintelligible to the uninitiated.

Of the many fields of fame on which "Lord Derby," "Caradice," and their fellows must have distinguished themselves, there is but one brief record. It is given by one of a party present (James Newby), who recollects "a main of cocks being fought in the drawing-room at Elleray, before the flooring was laid down, and its being covered with sods for this occasion. The rival competitors were Mr. Wilson and Mr. Richard Watson. All the neighboring farmers were invited, and, after the sport, entertained at a *genteel* supper served from Mrs. Ullock's. Wilson was the victor, and won a handsome silver drinking-cup, bearing an inscription, with date, etc."

The solemnity of these proceedings illustrates the enthusiasm with which this sport was cultivated in those days by such amateurs as Wilson, who really believed that they were keeping up one of the characteristic and time-honored institutions of the country.*

Soft on thee fall the breath of time,
And still retain in heavenly clime
The bloom that charms in this"—

is ranged the following "List of Cocks for a main with W. and T.," of which a specimen may suffice:—

1. A heavy cock from Dobinson	£5	8 0
2. " " from Keene	5	8 0
3. " " "	5	8 0
4. Piled cock, Oldfield	5	2 0

"Lord Derby" comes in as No. 13, £4 10s., and the total makes up 22 birds. Of these "13 are to be chosen for the main, and perhaps two byes. J. W."

* Before passing from the subject, I may mention an amusing illustration of it, showing that, at a date considerably more recent than that of the above event, the rearing of game-cocks was zealously practised in Scotland by some worthy gentlemen of the old school. One Sunday, in St. John's Chapel, Edinburgh, an old gentleman, a friend of my father's, was sitting gravely in his

Wrestling has always been the principal athletic exercise in the north of England, particularly in Cumberland, where it is still practised perhaps more generally than in any other part of the kingdom. "It is impossible," says the Professor, "to conceive the intense and passionate interest taken by the whole northern population in this most rural and muscular amusement. For weeks before the great Carlisle annual contest nothing else is talked of on road, field, flood, foot, or horseback; we fear it is thought of even in church, which we regret and condemn; and in every little comfortable 'public' within a circle of thirty miles' diameter, the home-brewed quivers in the glasses on the oaken tables to knuckles smiting the board, in corroboration of the claims to the championship of a Grahame, a Cass, a Laugklen, Solid Yaik, a Wilson, or a Wightman. A political friend of ours, a stanch fellow, in passing through the Lakes last autumn, heard of nothing but the contest for the county, which he had understood would lie between Lord Lowther (the sitting member) and Mr. Brougham. But, to his sore perplexity, he heard the names of new candidates, to him hitherto unknown; and on meeting us at that best of inns, 'White Lion,' Bowness, he told us with a downcast and serious countenance that Lord Lowther would be ousted, for that the struggle, as far as he could learn, would ultimately be between Thomas Ford of Egremont, and William Richardson of Caldbeck, men of no landed property, and probably radicals!"*

During my father's residence at Elleray, and long after he became Professor, he steadily patronized this manly amusement, and though, as the historian of the subject, Litt,† remarks, "he never sported his figure in the ring," he was not without skill and practice in the art, being, as an old wrestler declared, "a varra bad un to lick," which one can readily believe. He gave prizes and belts for the Ambleside competitions, such as had never been offered before, and the historian above mentioned describes in glowing terms how much the success of the annual sports in the neighborhood was owing to his liberal encouragement. In some of his let-

seat, when a lady in the same pew moved up, wishing to speak to him. He kept edging cautiously away from her, till at last, as she came nearer, he hastily muttered out: "Sit yont, Miss ——, sit yont! Dinna ye ken ma pouch is fu' o' gemm eggs!"

* *Blackwood*, December, 1823.

† *Wrestliana; or, an Historical Account of Ancient and Modern Wrestling.* By William Litt. 12mo. Whitehaven.

ters in after years, we shall meet with allusions to this subject, which he considered not unworthy of a special article in *Blackwood.* Speaking of the beauty of the spectacle presented by the ring at Carlisle, he thus amusingly parodied Wordsworth's lines on a hedge-sparrow's nest, which, he says, by a slight alteration, "eggs to men, and so forth, become a sensible enough exclamation in such a case:"—

> "See, two strong men are struggling there,*
> Few visions have I seen more fair,
> Or many prospects of delight
> More pleasing than that simple sight."

These imperfect reminiscences of my father's out-door life at Elleray may be appropriately closed by an extract from a clever little work recently published.† The author, Mr. Waugh, in his wanderings in Westmoreland, encountered at Wastdale Head, in the person of the innkeeper there, one of the most characteristic specimens that could well be found of a genuine old Laker, William Ritson. "I was most interested," says the writer, "in Ritson's anecdotes of famous men who visited Wastdale. He had wandered many a day with Professor Wilson, Wordsworth, De Quincey, and others. Ritson had been a famous wrestler in his youth, and had won many a country belt in Cumberland. He once wrestled with Wilson, and threw him twice out of three falls. But he owned the Professor was 'a varra bad un to lick.' Wilson beat him at jumping. He could jump twelve yards in three jumps, with a great stone in each hand. Ritson could only manage eleven and three quarters. 'T' first time 'at Professor Wilson cam to Wastd'le Head,' said Ritson, 'he hed a tent set up in a field, an' he gat it weel stock't wi' bread an' beef, an' cheese, an' rum, an' ale, an' sic like. Then he gedder't up my granfadder, an' Thomas Tyson, an' Isaac Fletcher, an' Joseph Stable, an' aad Robert Grave, an' some mair, an' there was gay deed amang em. Then, nowt would sarra, bud he mun hev a boat, an' they mun all hev a sail. Well, when they gat into t' boat, he tell't un to be particklar careful, for he was liable to git giddy in t' head, an' if yan ov his giddy fits sud chance to cum on, he mud happen tummle into t' watter. Well that pleased 'em all

* In the original—
"See, five blue eggs are shining there."

† *Rambles in the Lake Country.* By Edwin Waugh. 12mo. London, Whittaker.

gaily weel, an' they said they'd tak varra girt care on him. Then he leaned back an' called oot that they mun pull quicker. So they did, and what does Wilson do then but topples ower eb'm ov his back i' t' watter with a splash. Then there was a girt cry—" 'Eh, Mr. Wilson's i' t' watter !" an yan click't, an' anudder click't, but nean o' them could get hod on him, an' there was sic a scrowe as nivver. At last, yan o' them gat him round t' neck as he popped up at teàl o' t' boat, an' Wilson taad him to kep a good hod, for he mud happen slip him ageàn. But what, it was nowt but yan ov his bit o' pranks, he was snurkin' an' laughin' all t' time. Wilson was a fine, gay, girt-hearted fellow, as strang as a lion, an' as lish as a trout, an' he hed sic antics as nivver man hed. Whativver ye sed tull him ye'd get yowr change back for it gaily soon. . . . Aa remember, there was a " Murry Neet" at Wastd'le Head that varra time, an' Wilson an' t' aad parson was there amang t' rest. When they'd gotten a bit on, Wilson med a sang aboot t' parson. He med it reight off o' t' stick end. He began wi' t' parson first, then he gat to t' Pope, an' then he turned it to t' devil, an' sic like, till he hed 'em fallin' off their cheers wi' fun. T' parson was quite astonished, an' rayder vex't an' all, but at last he burst oot laughin' wi' t' rest. He was like. Naabody could stand it. . . . T' seàm neet there was yan o' their wives cum to fetch her husband heàm, an' she was rayder ower strang i' t' tung wi' him afore t' heàl comp'ny. Well, he took it all i' good pairt, but as he went away he shouted oot t' aad minister, 'Od dang ye, parson, it wor ye at teed us two tegidder ! . . . It was a' life an' murth amang us, as lang as Professor Wilson was at Wastd'le Head.' "

In the same year that Wilson settled at Elleray, an agreeable addition was made to the society of the neighborhood by the arrival of a family of the name of Penny, who took up their abode at Gale House, Ambleside. The Misses Penny were the daughters of a Liverpool merchant, and removed to Windermere for the sake of its proximity to the residence of their eldest sister, who had been married for some years to Mr. James Penny Machell, of Hollow Oak and Penny Bridge. Wilson soon became acquainted with these ladies, and an intimacy gradually sprung up with the fair inhabitants of Gale House, which by and by led to frequent mention of his name in the correspondence of Miss Jane Penny. Writing in girlish confidence to a friend who has sent her a piece of dress, she informs her that "the jacket has been much admired; I wore it at a ball at Kendal, and there was only one like it in the room—that was worn by Lady Lonsdale; it will always remind me of one of the pleasantest evenings I ever spent. I danced with Mr. Wilson; *he* is the only one of my partners worth mentioning."

It is not very difficult to perceive why it was one of the "pleasantest evenings" ever spent.

A ball or party seldom took place at Ambleside or elsewhere in the neighborhood, at which Mr. Wilson and Miss Jane Penny were not present. De Quincey, speaking of the gayeties at Low Brathay, the residence of his friend Charles Lloyd, says that at one of the social gatherings there he "saw Wilson in circumstances of animation, and buoyant with youthful spirits. . . . He, by the way, was the best male dancer (not professional) I have ever seen. . . . Here also danced the future wife of Professor Wilson, Miss Jane P[enny], at that time the leading belle of the Lake country." They were, undoubtedly, a couple of very uncommon personal attractions. A spectator at a ball given in Liverpool in those days, relates that when Mr. Wilson entered the room with Miss Penny on his arm, the dancers stopped and cheered them, in mere admiration of their appearance.

Another extract from a letter of Miss Penny gives some further information about Mr. Wilson. There had been a regatta at Windermere:—

"It proved universally pleasant. I think I never enjoyed any thing more than I did that week. The day of the regatta we spent the morning at Mr. Bolton's, Storr's Hall, and sailed upon the lake the greater part of the day. We had the honor of being steered by a *real* midshipman, a strikingly fine young man of the name of Fairer. Mr. Wilson gave us a ball at the Inn in the evening. I had the honor of opening it with him, and of course I spent a charmingly delightful evening. We are likely to have a most delightful acquisition to our society this winter in Mrs. and Miss Wilson, mother and sister to our favorite. They are very nice people indeed. I think Mrs. Wilson one of the finest and most ladylike women I have seen for a long time. They mean to be at Elleray all winter, which will make it very pleasant to us. I hope we shall see a great deal of them. Mr. Wilson is flirting with a pretty little widow who lives in Kendal. She is generally admired by the male part of creation, but not by our sex. I think her appearance is very pretty, particularly her figure, but I think her deficient in feminine propriety and modesty. Her husband has been dead some years; she was married at fourteen, and is still quite a girl in appearance. I don't know whether Mr. Wilson's attentions to her will end in a marriage, but I hope not, for his sake. I think he is deserving a very superior woman."

There is a pretty touch of female character about this relation; the evident *penchant* for Mr. Wilson, the reserved manner of speaking of him, the slight grudge, if so it may be called, against the "little widow," the constant recurrence to his name, the interest taken in those belonging to him, all declare very plainly how much *tendresse* there lay in the wish, "he deserves a very superior woman." And most truly did he obtain one.

The flirting with the "little widow" was but the amusement of idle hours, and Wilson had now begun seriously to feel the want, as he called it himself, of "an anchor," without which, he said, he should "keep beating about the great sea of life to very little purpose." A closer intimacy with Miss Jane Penny revealed qualities more precious than those which shine most in the light of ball-rooms, and he found that "the belle of the lake district" was also such a woman as was worthy of his whole heart's love, and wanted no quality to fit her for giving happiness and dignity to his life. It took some time, however, before his mind settled down to this conclusion. The image of Margaret still rose before him tenderly in his solitary hours: he had as yet found no woman's heart in which he could confide so utterly as he had done in hers. Among other projects to divert his thoughts, he meditated an expedition into Spain along with Blair and De Quincey; and in the course of the year 1809, he and the former occupied themselves for some time assiduously in the study of Spanish, in order to qualify themselves for enjoying the journey. The intelligence of Bonaparte's fresh descent upon that country caused the breaking off alike of their plan and their studies.

The following letter, addressed about this time to his friend Mr. Harden, who was about to proceed to Edinburgh to edit the *Caledonian Mercury*,* gives some idea of the state of his mind and prospects:—

* Mr. Allan ,the proprietor, was Mr. Harden's father-in-law.

"MY DEAR HARDEN:—I received your interesting letter this morning about an hour ago, and cannot delay answering it for a single day, deeply concerned as I feel myself in every thing that regards your happiness. That you are to leave the clouds and mountains of this our delightful land, gives me, as far as my selfish emotions go, much real pain. I need not say how many happy days I have passed at Brathay, and how affectionately I regard the family living within its walls. Our friendship, which I fear not, in spite of absence or distance, will continue with unabated sincerity, was voluntary on both sides; and, during the few years we have known each other, neither of us has found cause to repent of the affection bestowed. That the determination you have formed is in all respects right, I firmly believe, and the consciousness of having in part sacrificed enjoyments so dear to you, for the sake of those you tenderly love, will no doubt forever secure your happiness.

"After all, you will appear to me in the light of a distant neighbor, and when you have leisure to come to your beloved and beauteous lakes, if the smoke of Elleray is on the air, you know where you and yours will experience an affectionate welcome.

"That you will find the paper a good concern there is no doubt; and, at the same time, I cannot see that there will be any thing very irksome in it. Living at this distance, and being no very vehement admirer of daily politics, I fear it will not be often in my power to give you effectual assistance. Any thing I can do will at all times be cheerfully communicated. And, in the first place, a copy of the paper will not be amiss. Please mark what are your lucubrations. Of Oxford politics I neither know much nor care a great deal. Oxford has long been sunk beneath the love or admiration of thoughtful men, in spite of all her magnificence and all her learning. The contest has ere now been decided, though I have not heard the result. If I find that any thing interesting can be said on the election of the Chancellor,* I shall transmit it to you in a frank, and you can either burn it or print it, as you think proper.

"On this subject, therefore, let me conclude with every warm wish for your success; and may your residence in Edinburgh afford every enjoyment you can desire.

"As for myself, all my plans of delight and instruction, at least on one great subject, are for the present abandoned. It would be

* Lord Grenville.

tedious to enter into a detail of all unlucky causes which have occasioned this. Such as they are, they could not in the present juncture be avoided; and I have at least the satisfaction to know, that my plans failed not from any want of zeal or determination on my part.

"I have not, however, by any means relinquished my scheme of going to Spain, and whether we shall meet this summer or not seems very doubtful. I agree with you that travelling will make me, for some years at least, happier than any thing else. The knowledge it bestows can be acquired by no other means, and, unless a man be married, it seems very absurd to remain, during the prime of his youth, in one little corner of the world, beautiful and glorious as that corner may be. I do not, I hope, want either ballast or cargo or sail, but I do want an anchor most confoundedly, and, without it, shall keep beating about the great sea of life to very little purpose. Since I left Edinburgh, I have had a very dear old friend staying with me, and we have studied to the wonder of the three counties. We have made some progress in Spanish, though not much, the perplexity attending our change of scheme having occasioned some little interruption. I have written many poems, some of considerable length, which I may some night or other repeat to you over a social glass, or a twinkling fire.

"A little elegy I wrote on poor little Margaret Harden* last spring, and which I promised to send to your mother, has been lost. I shall, however, endeavor to recollect it the first time I can vividly recall the melancholy event that gave rise to it. Let it be considered as the affectionate sympathy of a friend. I am, you know, the worst correspondent breathing; yet to hear from you often and minutely, as to your pleasures and occupations, will always afford me genuine satisfaction.

"While I write this, your paintings of Stavely and the Brathay smile sweetly upon me, though all without doors is wild and stormy, it being the most complete hurricane I ever saw at Elleray. The windows of the parlor have, during the night, been almost entirely destroyed, and the floor is literally swimming. I cannot conclude without again observing what pleasure I shall have in hearing from you, especially while you are just entering on such a new scheme of life."

* A daughter of his friend.

About the same time he took an excursion into Scotland. Before starting, he addressed De Quincey as follows:—

"MY DEAR DE QUINCEY:—I am obliged to leave this to-morrow for Glasgow. I therefore trouble you with this note in case you should think of coming over during my absence. I expect to return to Elleray in a few days, yet there is an uncertainty attending every motion of mine, and possibly of yours also. If you are ready for a start, I will go with you to-morrow on foot through Kentmere and Hawesdale to Penrith, and on Monday you can easily return by Ulleswater to Grasmere. The fine weather may induce you.* If you feel a wish to look at Glasgow and Edinburgh, would you take a trip with me on the top of the coach? I will pledge myself to return with you within eight days. If so, or if you agree to the first plan only, my pony or horse is with my servant who carries this, and you can come here upon it. I hope you will do so. There is no occasion for wardrobe. I take nothing with me, and we can get a change of linen. The expense will be small to us.

"Yours ever affectionately,

"JOHN WILSON.

"ELLERAY, *Saturday*, 1809."

Of this pedestrian excursion we have a glimpse in the biographical notice of his friend John Finlay, with whom they spent a few hours at Moffat.†

I now come to speak of his poetry, and I am fortunately enabled, from the preservation of his letters to his friend Mr. John Smith, the Glasgow publisher, to give some account of his first publication, for which the materials should otherwise have been wanting. The first trace I find in MS. of poems afterwards published is in the year 1807. A small note-book contains a considerable number of sonnets, composed in the autumn of that year, a selection from which appeared among the miscellaneous pieces appended to *The Isle of Palms*. His commonplace-books contain the whole of the latter

* The proposal to walk over so much ground proclaims De Quincey to have been no weak pedestrian. Although he was a man considerably under height and slender of form, he was capable of undergoing great fatigue, and took constant exercise. The very fact of his being a walking companion of Wilson's speaks well for his strength, which was not unfrequently taxed when such a tryst was kept. Perhaps, in later years, of the two men he preserved his activity more entire.

† *Blackwood*, vol. ii., p. 188.

poem, parts of it apparently written down for the first time, and other parts being final copies of the work as sent for revision to his friend Blair. The alterations in the first draught are more of entire passages than of phrases. It is evident that he never composed without first forming a clear conception of what he intended to embody in each particular poem. The prose outlines of some pieces in these books are sometimes so full as to require only their translation into verse to entitle them to the name of poems. Of this the sketch entitled "Red Tarn," already given, may be taken as a specimen. The contents of these books show, in fact, that poetry was not a mere amusement with him, but a serious study, and that he had in those days very extensive plans of composition, on which he entered with an earnest desire to use well the gifts with which he had been endowed.*

His first communication on the subject to Mr. Smith is from Edinburgh, and is as follows:—

"EDINBURGH, 53 QUEEN STREET,
Wednesday Evening, December 13, 1810.

"DEAR SIR:—I have, during the last three years, written a number of poems on various subjects, from which I intend to form a selection for the press. The principal poem, entitled *The Isle of Palms*, which will give its name to the volume, is descriptive of sea and island scenery, and contains a love-story. It is nearly 2,000 lines. The second is entitled "The Anglers' Tent." It contains nearly forty stanzas of seventeen lines each, in the same measure as Collins' Ode on the Superstitions of the Highlands. The third is a blank-verse poem upon Oxford. The rest it is needless to particularize. I can furnish as many poems as will make a volume of 350 or 400 pages. As you have an opportunity of knowing the probable merit of any works of mine from Finlay, Blair, and others, I offer my poems in the first place to you. In a publication of such

* Dr. Blair, in a letter, has expressed to me the following opinion:—"I have been always at a loss to know why your father did not follow further his youthful impulsion towards verse. I thought him endowed beyond all the youthful poets of his day, and in some powers beyond any of his contemporaries. I believe he had more of absolute deep and glowing enthusiasm than any of them. He might require a severe intellectual discipline and learned study to balance that natural fire and energy for the composition of a great work. But he had both will and ability for severe thought, and he had the capacity for searching and comprehensive inquiry, and such a wonderful power of storing materials and of managing them to his use, that I never could, nor can I now, understand why, loving poetry as he did, he left it. He had a flood of eloquence which not one of the other poets who have lived in his day had or has." This is the opinion of the man most familiar with my father's mind.

magnitude, I feel my own character deeply concerned, and will therefore insert nothing that does not please myself. The volume might in size resemble the octavo edition of the *Lady of the Lake*, and sell for the same price.

"If you are willing to purchase from me the copyright of 400 pages, such as I have described, I am ready to listen to your terms. I may, without presumption, say that at Oxford my name would sell many copies, nor am I unknown either in Cambridge or London. But you will judge for yourself. I am not a man who would thoughtlessly risk his reputation by a trivial or careless publication.

"I would prefer disposing entirely of the copyright to any other plan, as I wish to be free from all trouble or anxiety about it. In the case of a first publication I know that booksellers ought to be cautious. But I am now past the days of boyhood, and I feel that I shall come before the world, if not in the fulness of my strength, at least with few youthful weaknesses.

"As I am uncertain of being soon in Glasgow, I shall expect an answer to this as quickly as convenient to yourself. Should we agree about this volume, I have other works in contemplation that I know will attract public notice. I am, sir, your obedient servant,

"JOHN WILSON."

A few days subsequently he replied to Mr. Smith's proposals; part of which was that the work should be printed by Ballantyne:—

"MY DEAR SIR:—Your proposals seem perfectly reasonable and honorable, and I have no objection to agree to them. I have to mention, however, that it will be impossible for me to have my poems ready for publication as soon as you wish. I was indeed ignorant of the season of publication, and also imagined that the printing would take much more time than I understand it will do.

"For a few months to come my time will not, I fear, be at my own disposal; for besides several important engagements, I have been very unwell lately, and may perhaps be obliged to take a short voyage somewhere. Considering all these circumstances, it would seem that the publication of my poems must be deferred for a considerable time. Perhaps, on the whole, this may be of advantage.

"I cannot believe that a volume of that size could be printed in less than four months from the commencement of printing it. You will consider, therefore, of this hasty note, and arrange matters with Ballantyne, etc., etc. I am, yours truly,

"JOHN WILSON."

In April, 1811, he writes from Elleray. He is on the eve of being married, and wants all the ready money he can get. He proposes, therefore, to dispense with some of those standard works "which no gentleman's library should be without,"—Annual Registers, Parliamentary Histories, Statistical Accounts, best editions of various Classics in Russia, etc., etc.

"ELLERAY, *Tuesday morning* (*April*, 1811).

"MY DEAR SIR:—Since my arrival here I have been tolerably busy, and have written several small poems that please me, and it is to be hoped will produce the same effect on several thousand of the judicious part of the reading world.

"My second longest poem I have also given the last polish to, and it now looks very imposingly. In a week or two, when the spring has a little advanced, I shall emigrate to the 'Isle of Palms,' and build myself a cottage there, both elegant and commodious, and subject to no taxation. I have this day written to Blair about Finlay, and expect to hear all particulars from him. If any thing further has occurred about his affairs in Glasgow, I should like to hear from you.

"The principal object of my present letter is to speak to you about some books I wish to part with, being either tired of them or having duplicates.

"The following is a list of some of the best. If they suit you, you will take them, or any part of them, *at your own price*, most of them being books that you could sell easily. . . .

"Out of these, I think, you might find some that might suit you well. I go to Liverpool to-morrow, to James Penny, Esq., Seel street, where I should like to hear from you on receipt of this. You might make something upon them, and I be enabled to take a little longer marriage jaunt, in these hard times money being scarce.

"On my return, I shall send you some portion of my manuscript, of which, if you make any use beyond yourself, I don't fear it will be judicious. Remember that few are entitled to pass judgment on poetry. I am, dear sir, yours very truly, JOHN WILSON.

"*P. S.*—Should you ever publish any edition of any poet, and wish for preface, etc., you know where to apply."

CHAPTER VI.

MARRIAGE.—"THE ISLE OF PALMS."

1811–1815.

On the 11th of May, 1811, the following letter was written by Wilson to his friend Mr. Findlay:—

"Ambleside, *May* 11, 1811.

"Dearest Robert:—I was this morning married to Jane Penny, and doubt not of receiving your blessing, which, from your brotherly heart, will delight me, and doubtless not be unheard by the Almighty. She is in gentleness, innocence, sense, and feeling, surpassed by no woman, and has remained pure, as from her Maker's hands. Surely if I know myself I am not deficient in kindness and gentleness of nature, and will to my dying hour love, honor, and worship her. It is a mild and peaceful day, and my spirit feels calm and blest. You know what it is to possess a beloved woman's affections, and such possession now makes me return grateful thanks to my God, and remember former afflictions with resignation and gratitude. On this tranquil day of nature and delight, to think of my earliest, best, oh! best-beloved friend, I may say, adds a solemn feeling to my dreams, and your most affectionate heart will, I am sure, be made glad to hear such words from my lips. In my heart you will ever live among images of overpowering tenderness, and to hear from you when convenient will ever gladden him who never felt, thought, or uttered word to you but those of affection and gratitude. God bless you, my dearest Robert, your wife, and all that you love! "I am your kindest brother,

"John Wilson."

I don't know if any man ever conveyed the intimation of his marriage in terms more unaffectedly beautiful than these. In their quiet depth of natural affection that inner spirit is truly revealed, which, amid all varieties of energy and enjoyment, ever found its most congenial life among the tender sanctities of home, and connected its highest delights with a genuine sense of religion. Thenceforth his life had a deeper purpose, and his home was a place of pure sunshine, whatever clouds darkened the sky without. Of her who made it so, it may be said, she was

> "A blooming lady—a conspicuous flower;
> Admired for beauty, for her sweetness praised;
> Whom he had sensibility to love,
> Ambition to attempt, and skill to win;"

one in whose gentleness and goodness he found long years of happiness.

His energies were not called forth by the mere humor of the hour to prove what they were, but by the solemn realization of the high purpose for which they were given.

He did not make the usual wedding tour, but took his bride directly to his cottage home. The fascination of his new life did not, however, engross him to the exclusion of work, much temptation as there was to a blissful idleness in his lot. The various expensive tastes he indulged, as well as his generous habits, could not have been so constantly exercised, had he not been in the enjoyment of a large fortune. No doubt he lived both at Oxford and Elleray with the free munificence of one who understood the charms of hospitality, and the satisfaction of bestowing pleasure upon others, but at neither period was he wasteful or careless of money. At the time of his marriage, therefore, he was in easy circumstances, and his wife's fortune, added to his own, made him a rich man. There was no care for the future; worldly matters were in a smiling condition; every thing around the young couple was *couleur de rose.* Days passed away quickly; nothing disturbed the life of love and peace spent in that beautiful cottage home. Time brought with it only increase of happiness. Children were born; and to live at Elleray forever was the design of the poet, who loved to look upon

> "The glorious sun
> That made Winander one wide wave of gold,
> When first in transport from the mountain-top
> He hailed the heavenly vision."

These halcyon days were ere long interrupted by misfortune. But though that stern schooling was necessary to the full development of Wilson's character and powers, he had already, as we have seen, determined to give the world some fruit of his meditative hours during these apparently idle years at Elleray.

Three months after his marriage he again addressed Mr. Smith on the subject of his poems:—

"ELLERAY, *August* 11, 1811.

"It is now so long since you have heard from me, that I dare say you begin to entertain rational doubts of my existence. I am, however, alive and well; better both in mind and body than when I last saw you, and unless the damnation of my poems affect my health and spirits, likely for a considerable time to be off the sick-list.

"So many things have occurred, if not to occupy, at least to interrupt my time since my marriage, which took place on the 11th of May, that I thought it best not to write you till I found myself in some measure settled, and in a hopeful way of doing some good. I have written a considerable number of poems of a smaller size since my marriage, so that were the first poems of the collection finished, I think I have MS. enough for a volume of 400 pages, which I am desirous it should be. I know not how it is, but I have felt a strange disinclination to work at the longest poem; but on receiving your answer, all minor occupations shall be laid aside, and the work be proceeded with in good earnest. Indeed, such is my waywardness of fancy, that I feel constantly impelled to write each day on a different subject, which I should be prevented from doing were a day fixed for the commencement of the printing. Suppose we say that on the 1st of October every thing shall be ready for going to press; and if so, you may depend upon it that the press shall never be allowed to remain idle one day for want of matter. It would be most satisfactory for me to retain the MS. of my poems in my own hands, except such quantity as need be in the printer's hands. Thus, I will send the longest poem by cantos, there being four, and so on. I cannot in a letter sufficiently explain my reasons for wishing this; but unless you agree to it, it will be very painful to me, and I am confident it will be for the interest of the work. With respect to preface, I am doubtful if I shall have one; if so, it will consist of a very few pages, two or three at the most. I suppose the preface will be numbered separately from the poems, and therefore may be printed after them, should I like it, and in like manner the title-page, etc.

"With respect to the size of the volume, I am still partial to that of *Marmion;* or, if you choose, a little smaller, only as many or more lines in each page. A thinly printed book of that size looks very badly. There will be verses of many different measures, though none exceeding twelve syllables. I think that a rather smaller type would look better, since the poems are miscellaneous. But all these particulars I leave to yourself. I shall expect to hear from you as soon as you can decidedly fix matters with me, and I hope that you will find me a tractable and reasonable author. The sooner every thing is fixed the better, as otherwise I shall never set to with invincible fury. If the printing can commence by the beginning of October, the first book of the *Isle of Palms* will be sent to you by the tenth of September. You should also advertise the work in the literary notices of the Reviews, and immediately; but all this I will leave to yourself."

"ELLERAY, KENDAL, *September* 17, 1811.

"DEAR SMITH:—I send you at last the first canto of the *Isle of Palms*, ready for the press.

"I had expected Mr. Blair here to revise the poem, but he did not come, so I had to send it to him, and he returned it only yesterday, without any alteration (though with many compliments), and I had to fill up the blanks myself. The manuscript is in Mr. Blair's handwriting, and is, I trust, legible. As to punctuation, I suppose the printer uses his discretion.

"I am going on correcting and writing, and certainly never will keep the press waiting for me. The proofs will, of course, be sent to me; but I conceive that double proofs are altogether unnecessary.

"Let it go to press immediately, and write me when you think it right to inform me of your proceedings.

"This first canto will, I believe, occupy 32 pages at all events, as there are nearly 600 lines.

"You will give strict injunctions to Ballantyne to let no one see the proof-sheets. For the *Isle of Palms* is a wild tale, and must not be judged of piecemeal. But there are many reasons for this.

"J. WILSON."

"ELLERAY, *Sept.* 27 *and* 28, 1811.

"I am glad that you are pleased with the manuscript on the whole. The introductory stanzas are perhaps not, at first reading, and in manuscript, very perspicuous; but they were written upon principle, and will, I doubt not, give pleasure when the canto is thought of together, and distinctly embraced in one whole. Blair and Wordsworth were both delighted with them, and, as I shall have a very short preface, I am not afraid of their seeming obscure. At the same time, I shall be obliged to you for any remarks of the kind, as, though I have written nothing without due thought, all hints should be, and will be attended to, and gratefully received.

"I am in daily expectation of receiving the second canto from Blair, written over in the same manner, and think you may be expecting it on Thursday. Indeed, fear not of having regular and sufficient supplies.

"The whole *Isle of Palms* is of a wild character, though, I trust, sufficiently interspersed and vivified with human feelings to interest generally and deeply. Its wildness and romantic character, being qualities that suffer greatly by piecemeal quotation, render me desirous of its being seen entire or not at all; but still this is not a matter of much importance, as I fear nothing when the poem comes before the public. I know the public taste, and neither will violate nor cringe to it, and, with its own merits, and the respectable way in which it will be given to the world, I am fearless of its success. I find that the *Isle of Palms* will be nearer 3,000 than 2,000 lines. Of the other poems, I know there are many that will be more popular, and therefore I expect that, as the printing proceeds, you will see reason to confide in those hopes of my success, which you have already been good enough to entertain.

"On the whole, I think Ballantyne ought to print the work, if you can make good terms with him. Blue stockings are dirty things, but not very deleterious.

"Next letter, I expect to hear from you positively when you begin printing, that I may never be from home, and keep the devils from getting cool. In ten days I shall have sent you the first three cantos, containing above 2,000 lines, and then I am not afraid of my heels being pressed upon, as correction will be my only task.

"All the booksellers in Oxford know me well. Indeed, I once talked to Parker about publishing some poems there, but, though he was most willing to undertake it, I afterwards changed my mind, for the University is but a dullish spot, though undoubtedly many copies will be sold there.

"The whole copy shall be sent in Blair's writing, or in a hand still better; and if there are any directions necessary about correcting the press, of which you think it probable I may be ignorant, you will instruct me. I am still in hopes of Blair coming here soon.

"Poor Grahame, I hear, is gone; let me hear some particulars; he was a truly estimable being."

The reference here is to the Rev. James Grahame, author of "The Sabbath," and other poems. My father greatly esteemed him and his poetry, and at this time composed an Elegy to his memory,* which was published anonymously while the *Isle of Palms* was going through the press.

Another letter is sent by and by along with the third canto of the *Isle of Palms*, which had been kept some time by Mr. Blair. He says:—"I expect you will like it fully more than any of the preceding; and Blair thinks it equal to any poetry of modern times. The fourth canto I will send to him this day; so Ballantyne will have it in time, although I fear he has been stopped for want of this one, which will never again be owing to me.

"I have had a long letter from John Ballantyne, most anxiously requesting a share in the work, or any concern in it that I would grant, so that his name should appear in the imprint. He wishes to have 500 copies to [sell], but on what terms I do not very clearly understand.

"I think that if he could be allowed some kind of share or connection with it, it might be well, as he has, I suppose, good connections. I wish to hear from you immediately upon this subject, and I cannot answer his letter till I know your wishes and views on it. It augurs well, his anxiety. Should you wish to see his letter? He says that Longman is now preparing his winter catalogue; and that insertion of the title there would *double* the *first demand*. This seems fudge, although same time it should be sent for insertion in that catalogue, of which you probably know more than I do. I have advertised the work in the Kendal paper, and shall in one or two of the Liverpool.

"Let me hear from you if the paper has been sent to Ballantyne, and if you think the work may be out by Christmas. Stir Ballan-

* "Lines sacred to the Memory of the Rev. James Grahame, author of 'The Sabbath,' &c. 'A man he was to all the country dear.' 4to. Glasgow: Smith & Son."

tyne up with a long pole, and henceforth depend upon my being punctual."

From these and other letters, it will be seen that the poet was by no means a careless man of business; and that if he was pretty confident of success, he did not neglect any means to secure it.

In his next letter he complains bitterly of the delay in the printing, not having heard from Ballantyne for a month, and then proceeds to give some practical suggestions regarding the lines on Grahame:—

"The copies of the 'Lines, etc.,' came safely to hand. They are exceedingly well printed and accurate in all respects. One copy I gave to Lloyd; the other to my wife's sister, both of whom were greatly pleased. I find that it will be in my power to distribute a few copies without suspicion; and there is a bookseller in Kendal who would, I think, dispose of half a dozen very easily. Send me, therefore, per coach, a dozen copies; six to my own account, and six for the trade, which I will send to the bookseller in Kendal; and if he sells them, he will account to me for them. Let me hear how they take; now that Edinburgh is filling, perhaps some copies will be going off. I would wish a copy to be sent to Mr. Alison, and one to Mr. Morehead, the Episcopal clergyman in Edinburgh, with 'from the author' on the title-page. Grahame was known about Carlisle, and I should think some of the trade there would take copies; Durham also. Are there any inquiries made after the author? Is it attributed to any one? You should tell a paragraph to be extracted from it in each of the Edinburgh papers; perhaps the same two as in the Glasgow papers. Some copies would sell in Oxford if seen there; I should also think in Liverpool. A passage ought also to appear in the *London Courier* and in the *Scots Magazine;* and also very early in other magazines. It is perhaps not worth all this trouble."

The elegy attracted considerable attention, and a second edition was soon called for. His next letter is written in December:—

"I have had many letters from Edinburgh highly commending the 'Lines,' which I understand are considerable favorites there, though I find I am strongly suspected in that quarter. With respect to giving my name, you may now use your own discretion."

At Christmas he was in Edinburgh at his mother's with his young wife and her sisters. He writes to Mr. Smith:—

"The volume gets on tolerably. Page 250 has gone to press this day. All the manuscript is in Ballantyne's hands. He thinks the volume would not be the worse of being 450 pages. In that case, would you wish the lines on Grahame to be included? Fergusson, Cranstoun, and Glassford think them better than any thing Grahame himself has written. The *Eclectic* is favorable enough, but stupid enough too! Who, in writing an elegy, would give a critical dissertation on a poem? The motto is a good one, and the punctuation excellent, except in two cases, which do not destroy the sense.

"Walter Scott talks to me in great terms of what he has seen of the 'Isle.'* The elder Ballantyne is in raptures, and prophesies great popularity. Considerable expectations are formed here among the blues of both sexes, and I am whirled into the vortex of fashion here in consequence.

"I shall say nothing to any one of the dedication. Send Mr. M'Latchie a copy of the 'Lines,' 'with the author's affectionate regard,' and one to Mr. Gill with my 'respectful compliments.'

"You ought certainly to come here before the publication, and soon, to arrange every thing. I think we shall attract some attention."

A little glimpse of the life at 53 Queen street, and the pleasant footing subsisting between the relatives gathered there, is afforded in a note of young Mrs. Wilson's about this time to her sister. She thanks "Peg" for her note, which, she says, "was sacred to myself. It is not my custom, you may tell her, to show my letters to John." She goes on to speak of Edinburgh society, dinners and evening parties, and whom she most likes. The Rev. Mr. Morehead is "a great favorite;" Mr. Jeffrey is a "horrid little man," but "held in as high estimation here as the Bible." Mrs. Wilson, senior, gives a ball, and 150 people are invited. "The girls are looking forward to it with great delight. Mrs. Wilson is very nice with them, and lets them ask anybody they like. There is not the least restraint put upon them. John's poems will be sent from here next week. The large size is a guinea, and the small one twelve shillings."

* Sir Walter, writing to Miss Joanna Baillie about this time, says:—"The author of the elegy upon poor Grahame is John Wilson, a young man of very considerable poetical powers. He is now engaged upon a poem called the 'Isle of Palms,' something in the style of Southey. He is an eccentric genius, and has fixed himself on the banks of Windermere, but occasionally resides in Edinburgh, where he now is. He seems an excellent, warm-hearted, and enthusiastic young man: something too much, perhaps, of the latter quality, places him among the list of originals."

After sundry delays from want of paper or other causes, the volume duly appeared on the 20th of February, 1812, entitled, *The Isle of Palms, and other Poems*, by John Wilson. The potent name of Longman, whose catalogue could work such wonders, came first, followed by those of Ballantyne and Co., Edinburgh, and John Smith and Son, Glasgow. It was affectionately dedicated to the author's old teachers, Professors Jardine and Young. How the work was received may be gathered from his own letters. Poets are seldom entirely satisfied with the reception of their works. The author of the *Isle of Palms* had no great reason to complain, and he did not do so. At any rate, any dissatisfaction he felt, as will be seen, took the very practical form of urging all legitimate means for promoting the sale of the work.

TO MR. SMITH.

"53 QUEEN STREET, 1*st April*, 1812.
A day consecrated to Poets.

"My long-delayed visit to Glasgow has been entirely put a stop to by the miserable weather and other causes, till I find that it will not be in my power to make it out at all for nearly two months to come. Mrs. Wilson is in that state now that I could not comfortably leave her, and therefore it will not be in my power to see you till the time I mention.

"From your last letter it would appear that the *Isle of Palms* has hitherto been tolerably successful. In Edinburgh it is much read, praised, etc., but I question if the sale of it has been very great. A less enterprising set of men than Edinburgh booksellers I never had the misfortune to meet with.

"From what you told me, I doubt not that Longman will advertise it properly. I have certainly seen it occasionally in several papers, but not so often as many other volumes of far less moment (poetical); and almost all the booksellers I have spoken to here agree in stating, that the London advertising is very dull and insufficient. I mention this as I hear it, without supposing for an instant that any thing will be wanting on your part to forward the sale of the volume. It seems evident to me that some steps should be taken to make the volume known better than it is, and first of all by inserting occasional extracts in newspapers. I shall take care to do something in the Edinburgh and London papers. But what is of more importance is the provincial sale in England. Considerable inquiry was made after them in Liverpool; and had there been copies there, many would have sold. And I think you should still establish some correspondence with the booksellers there. Two hundred of Crabbe's poems were sold in Liverpool. In Manchester, many, many books are sold; one shop of considerable magnitude is kept by a Mr. Ford. But it seems certain to my mind that you must bestir yourself through the towns of England, for the people are so stupid as not to know where to send for them, unless they come to the town where they live. This I had proof of from Liverpool in abundance.

"I have sent Southey a copy. He will, I know, review it in the *Quarterly*, if he likes it, which I think probable; otherwise he will not. Jeffrey likes it much; but will very likely abuse it for all that. I see it will be reviewed in the next *Edinburgh Quarterly Review*, but I suppose it is a despicable effort; its praise or blame will be alike indifferent.

"I find that people distrust their own judgment more than I had ever believed possible, and durst not admire any thing till they can quote authorities. I shall be happy to hear from you when at leisure. Glasgow criticism is not worth regarding; but I wish to hear from you an exact account of the number of copies sold by you in Glasgow, etc., to the public, and also of the number which you have altogether disposed of to the Edinburgh booksellers; London and Oxford, too, if you have heard any thing from those quarters. I have as yet had no correspondence with England about it; here I am not a little caressed by the great, but I would excuse their caresses, if the public would buy my volume. If the volume do ultimately succeed, and nothing has yet occurred to make me suppose that it will not, then I shall in a year or two come before it again in strength; but if not, I shall court the Muse no more.

"Have any of my poems gone to Paisley or to the Sister Isle? Give me the names of as many of the purchasers as you can. Have you ever sent Watson his copies? for they had not been seen at Calgarth so late as last week, and I suppose the Kendal bookseller sent his there. Have any been sent to Cambridge or Birmingham? two places, by the by, well joined together. The longer your letter is the better, and by making a parcel of it, you may send the letters of the Oxford booksellers, and any thing else you desire, but taking care not to write till you have time to send me a full and long letter."*

In the next number of the *Edinburgh Review* appeared a criticism of the *Isle of Palms*, what publishers would call a "favorable notice," but, it would appear, not quite to the taste of the author. He would probably have preferred a good "cutting up" to the measured and somewhat patronizing approval of the reviewer. On the 3d of May, he writes to Mr. Smith:—

"I write this in great haste, it being near two o'clock on Sunday morning, and at eight I leave Edinburgh on a fishing excursion to Kelso for a week.

"Jeffrey's review is beggarly. I don't much like the extract; it is too much of an excerpt, too quackish; but please yourself. The other review is a masterpiece of nonsense and folly."

Soon after he writes again from Elleray:—

"I am meditating many other poems, and probably shall begin to write soon. I know that I can in a year write another volume that will make the *Isle* hide its head. But unless the *Isle* travels the Continent a little more before that time, I shall not throw pearls before swine in a hurry."

"ELLERAY, *Monday morning*,
"*Nov.* 23, 1812.

"MY DEAR SMITH:—The day after I received your last, I left Elleray for Ireland, on a visit to my sister, who lives near Killarney. I stayed there a month, and on my return have received the melancholy intelligence of my dear brother's death.† Since then I have not had the power of thinking of my literary concerns. We often know not how dearly we love our near relations, till called on to

* The anxiety and disappointment of the author as to the early sale of the volume does not seem altogether unreasonable, when we find that in Edinburgh, where the chief demand was to be looked for, "the trade" received the work so cautiously, as the following "subscription list" indicates:—"*The Isle of Palms, and other Poems.* By John Wilson. Demy 8vo, retail at 12s.; under 10, 8s. 6d.; above, 8s. A few copies Royal 8vo at sub. John Ballantyne & Co., two hundred copies, demy; Manners & Miller, twenty-five; Archd. Constable & Co., twenty-five copies; Jno. Anderson, twenty-five copies; Wm. Blackwood, six copies."

The last item in the list looks specially curious now; but at that time Mr. Blackwood's business was in its infancy, and the future Christopher North was unknown to him.

About the same time Longman & Co. wrote to Mr. Smith, to report the London "subscription:"—"We received a copy of Wilson's Poems from Ballantynes, and our clerk, who subscribes our books, took it round the trade yesterday and this morning; but as the author is not known amongst the London booksellers, we are sorry to say we have been enabled to subscribe only between forty-five and fifty, though, from what you say of the merit of the work, and what we hear of it from other quarters, we have no doubt of its selling very well here when it is known."

† His brother Andrew.

mourn over their graves. I know that I tenderly loved my dear brother, but his death has affected me more than I could have imagined, and I yet feel as if I could never again be happy or cheerful enough to resume my former occupations.

"I leave every thing relating to my poems to your own judgment. If they do not sell, my poetry never will; for though I may write better, they are good enough for popularity—far better than many that circulate widely—and they deserve to sell.

"Southey would have gladly reviewed them in the *Quarterly*, but found it impossible, without speaking at length of himself and Wordsworth; so he from conscience declined it. Blair I have heard nothing of since I saw you, nor am I likely to hear. A book must ultimately owe its circulation to itself, and not to the grace of reviewers. Take such steps about a second edition as you choose. I would advise, if there be one, no more than 750 copies. I will add no new poems, nor preface, nor note.

"I would fain write you at greater length, but feel unable. Let the beginning of my letter be my excuse."

The extent of his plans of composition at this time is indicated by a "List of subjects for meditation," in one of his books, containing no less than 131 titles of proposed poems. In what spirit he entered on his work, the following note, written in his commonplace-book, may illustrate:—

"*June* 12, 1812.—Expected that a volume will be completed by June 12, 1814. May the Almighty enlighten my mind, so that I may benefit my fellow-creatures, and discharge the duties of my life.—J. W."*

The list of subjects begins on the opposite page, and the proposed character of the strain in each case is indicated by such notes as these:—

"Red Tarn—melancholy and mournful.

"The widow—beautiful and fanciful.

"A poet—characteristic and copious.

* It will not, I hope, diminish in any reader's eyes the respect due to this solemn and surely most heartfelt aspiration, that it is copied from a page, never meant for other eyes to see, beginning with so different a kind of memorandum as this—"Small black muffled hen set herself with about eight eggs on Monday night or Tuesday morning, 7th July." So far am I from being offended by this curious contrast, that I specially note the fact as a characteristic illustration of the wholeness and sincerity of the man, who, whether it were high poetic meditation or the breeding of game-cocks that occupied him, did it with all his heart and strength, each in its season.

"On the death of Gough among the hills—different view of it from W. and Scott.

"City after a plague—awful and wild, solemn.

"Town and country—vigorous and bold.

"On the Greek sculpture—in strong heroics.

"The murderer and the babe—a contrast; the moral to be—to watch well our own hearts against vice."

A calculation is then given for a volume of 500 pages out of a selection of this large list, in which 170 are allotted to "St. Hubert," and 50 each to "The Manse" and "The Ocean Queen," and to the "City after a Plague" only 5. The proposed volume did not appear till January, 1816, not from any lack of materials, but in consequence of a change of plan, the "City after a Plague" having developed into a drama, instead of St. Hubert, while of the other subjects very few were ever wrought out, and some that were have been withheld from posterity. Of subjects completed and published, the titles of some will be recognized from the above extract. It is perhaps to be regretted that so rich a promise did not come to perfection; but it was no sudden or fortuitous impulse that made the poet choose to develop his poetical powers in another form than that of verse.

So much meantime of poetry. Of the four happy years that were passed in the cottage at Elleray, from 1811 to 1815, there is little to be recorded. It would appear that in the former year he had come to the resolution of joining the Scottish Bar, and, in that view, became a member of the Speculative Society, then in a highly flourishing condition. He must of course have spent some part of the succeeding winters in Edinburgh, but the only trace of the matter I find is the following allusion in a letter from his friend Blair, dated December, 1813:—

"MY DEAR JOHN:—I desire very much to hear further from you, and to know how your great soul accommodates itself to the Law Class, and other judicial sufferings and degradations, and more about your Greek and polite literature."

I find also, that he opened, on the 4th of January, 1814, the debate in the Speculative Society—topic, "Has the War on the Continent been glorious to the Spanish nation?"—in the affirmative, when the majority of the Society voted with him. He only wrote, it appears, one Essay for that Society on "some political institutions of military origin," of which there are some traces in one of his MS. books.

This happy life at Elleray was soon to come to a close. In the fourth year from the date of his marriage, there came a calamity so heavy and unlooked for that the highest fortitude was required to meet it, as it was met, bravely and cheerfully.

The circumstances which occurred to make it absolutely necessary to leave Elleray were of a most painful nature, inasmuch as they not only deprived Wilson of his entire fortune, but in that blow revealed the dishonesty of one closely allied to him by relationship, and in whom years of unshaken trust had been reposed. An uncle had acted the part of "unjust steward," and, by his treachery, overwhelmed his nephew in irretrievable loss. A sudden fall from affluence to poverty is not a trial easily borne, especially when it comes through the fault of others; but Wilson's nature was too strong and noble to bow beneath the blow. On the contrary, with a virtue rarely exemplified, he silently submitted to the calamity, and generously assisted in contributing to the support of his relative, who, in the ruin of others, had also ruined himself. Here was a practical illustration of moral philosophy, more eloquent, I think, than even the Professor's own lectures, when he came to teach what he had practised. In such a noble spirit, and with a conscience void of offence, he prepared to quit the beautiful home where he had hoped to pass his days, and set his face firmly to meet the new conditions of life which his lot imposed. The following letter to De Quincey describes his journey from Elleray with his wife and infant family:—

"PENRITH, CROWN INN,
"*Friday Evening, half-past Six*, 1815.

"MY DEAR FRIEND:—I found that it was impossible to see you again at your cottage before taking leave of Elleray. The tempestuous weather prevented me from going to Kendal on the day I had fixed, so I was forced to go on Thursday, a cold, rainy, and stormy day. Had I returned in the afternoon, I certainly would have cantered over to Grasmere for a parting grasp of cordiality and kindness; but I did not return to Elleray till near eleven o'clock. We rose this morning at six, and got under weigh at eight. We arrived here about five, and the children being fatigued, we propose to lie to during the night. The post-boy being about to return to Ambleside, I gave Keir this note, which has no other object than to kindly wish you all peace, and such happiness as you deserve till we meet again. If I cannot pay you a visit at Christmas, we shall surely meet early in summer. I will write you from Edinburgh soon.

"Blair left Elleray on an opposite tack this morning; weather hazy with heavy squalls from the northwest. Mrs. Wilson begs to be kindly remembered to you, and so would doubtless the progeny were they of maturer age and awake. Yours with true affection,

"JOHN WILSON.

"My books had not been sent to Elleray from the 'stamp-master's' * when I took my departure. If they still linger with fond, reluctant, amorous affection near Green's rotundities, perhaps you might wish to see those about Spain. If so, order them all to your cottage. The dinner in honor of Blucher and the Crown Prince at Ambleside, was, I understood, attended only by the Parson, the Apothecary, the Limner;—the King, Lord North, and Mr. Fury, signifying nothing.

"Vale! iterumque, vale!"

CHAPTER VII.

LIFE IN EDINBURGH.—THE BAR.—THE HIGHLANDS.—ELLERAY.

1815–1817.

JOHN WILSON's new home was now in Edinburgh. His mother received him and his family into her house, where he resided until the year 1819. Mrs. Wilson, senior, was a lady whose skill in domestic management was the admiration and wonder of all zealous housekeepers. Under one roof she accommodated three distinct families; and, besides the generosity exercised towards her own, she was hospitable to all, while her charities and goodness to the poor were unceasing. This lady was so well known and so much esteemed in Edinburgh, that when she died, it was, as it were, the

* Wordsworth.

extinction of a "bright particular star;" nor can any one who ever saw her, altogether forget the effect of her presence. She belonged to that old school of Scottish ladies whose refinement and intellect never interfered with duties the most humble. In a large household, where the fashion of the day neither sought nor suggested a retinue of attendants, many little domestic offices were performed by the lady of the house herself. The tea china, for example, was washed, both after breakfast and tea, and carefully put away by her own delicate hands. Markets were made early in the morning. Many a time has the stately figure of Mrs. Wilson, in her elegantly fitting black satin dress, been seen to pass to and from the old market-place, Edinburgh, followed by some favorite "caddie,"* bearing the well-chosen meats and vegetables, that no skill but her own was ever permitted to select. Shrewd sense, wise economy, and well-ordered benevolence marked all her actions. Beautiful and dignified in presence, she at once inspired a feeling of respect. Pious and good, she at the same time knew and understood the world; and false sentiment, or affectation of any sort, was not permitted to live near her; wit and humor she did not lack; but it is doubtful whether poetry was a material of her nature in any shape. Proud as she was of her son John, and great as his devotion was to her, he used always to say that his mother did not understand him. Sometimes, it is no great wonder if his eccentricity might have been a little too much for her order and regularity. It is very doubtful if any lady of the present *régime* could so wisely and peacefully rule the affairs of a household as did this lady,† when, for several years, she had under her roof two married sons, with their wives, children, and servants, along with her own immediate household, a son and two daughters, yet unmarried, making in all a family of fourteen persons. Yet peace and harmony reigned supreme; and there are now not a few of her grandchildren who remember this fine old lady, either as she moved through the active duties of her house, or, seated at the fire-side on a chair, the back of which she never touched, dignified in bearing as a queen, took a short nap, awaking with a kindly smile

* Street porter.

† Mrs. Wilson, senior, was a keen Tory; and it is told of her that on hearing of her son contributing to the *Edinburgh Review*, she said to him significantly, "John, if you turn Whig, this house is no longer big enough for us both." She must have been well pleased with the principles of her daughter-in-law, who, writing after the Reform Bill passed, "thanked God she was born in the reign of the Georges."

at the sound of some young voice demanding a story, in the telling of which, like all good grandams, she excelled.

So, to the pleasant house of his mother, No. 53 Queen street, Wilson changed his abode from dear sycamore-sheltered Elleray.

In 1815 he was called to the bar, along with his friend Patrick Robertson.* John Gibson Lockhart joined them in the year following. For a short time, but only for a short time, Wilson followed the usual routine of a professional promenading in the "*Hall of Lost Steps.*" He did sometimes get cases, but when he found them lying on his table, he said jocularly, when speaking of this afterwards, "I did not know what the devil to do with them!" The Parliament-House life was plainly not the thing which nature meant for him. The restrictions of that arena would not suit his Pegasus, so he freed his wings and took another course.

There are some pleasant fragments of his letters to his wife, written in holiday time, when he would now and then run away for a day or two to saunter, fishing-rod in hand, by the streams of pretty pastoral Peebles, and into Yarrow to visit the Ettrick Shepherd.

He writes from the "Head of the Yarrow," on "Wednesday morning, seven o'clock," in June, 1815:—

"My dearest Jane:—I take time by the forelock merely to inform you that I am still a sentient being. On Sunday, I did not leave Sym's till near twelve o'clock. I called, on my way to Peebles, at Finlay's, at Glencorse, where I sandwiched for an hour, and arrived at Peebles about seven o'clock, a perfect *lameter*, my shoes having peeled my timbers. The walk was rather dreary. At Peebles I had to stop, and remained there all night. On Monday morning, at six o'clock (miraculous!) I uprose from the couch of slumber, and walked along the Tweed to Traquair Knowe (Mr. Laidlaw's). There I fished, and stayed all Monday, the place being very beautiful. Grieve joined the party that night, and several other people. Mr. Laidlaw is married, an insectologist and poet, and farmer and agriculturist. On Tuesday morning I walked to Hogg's, a distance of about eight miles, fishing as I went, and surprised him in his cottage bottling whiskey. He is well, and dressed pastorally. His house is not habitable, but the situation is good, and may become very pretty.

* Among the young men, afterwards distinguished, who passed about the same time, were John Cay, Andrew Rutherfurd, P. F. Tytler, Sir William Hamilton, Thomas Maitland, Alexander Pringle, Archibald Alison, Duncan M'Neill, James Ivory, &c.

There being no beds in his domicile, we last night came here, a farmer's house about a quarter of a mile from him, where I have been treated most kindly and hospitably. The house and entertainment something *à la* Wastdale, but much superior. I have risen at seven o'clock, and am preparing to take a complete day's fishing among the streams near St. Mary's Loch.

"To-morrow night I fish down to Selkirk, to catch the coach to Hawick in the evening; thence on Friday morning to Richmond's, whom I will leave on Sunday evening. So if I can get a seat in the coach on Sunday night at Hawick, you will see me in Edinburgh on Monday morning before breakfast. Mrs. Scott informs me breakfast is ready, so hoping that you will be grateful for this letter, bald as it is, I have the honor to subscribe myself your obedient and dutiful husband, "JOHN WILSON."

On one of these fishing excursions he had proceeded from St. Mary's Loch to Peebles, where he could not at first get admittance to the inn, as it was fully occupied by a party of country gentlemen, met together on some county business; on sending in his name, however, he was immediately asked to join them at dinner. It is needless to say that under his spell the fun grew fast and furious. No one thought of moving. Supper was proposed, and as nothing eatable was to be had in the house, Wilson asked the company if they liked trouts, and forthwith produced the result of his day's amusement from basket, bag, and pocket, in such numbers that the table was soon literally covered. As the Shepherd afterwards said, "Your creel was fu'—your shooting-bag fu'—your jacket-pouches fu'—the pouches o' your verra breeks fu'—half-a-dozen wee anes in your waistcoat, no to forget them in the crown o' your hat, and last o' a', when there was nae place to stow awa' ony mair, a willow-wand drawn through the gills o' some great big anes."

The fresh fragrance of summer, as enjoyed by the running streams and "dowie dens o' Yarrow," combined with the desire to show his English wife something of the beauty of Scotland, suggested about this time an excursion, which was regarded by many as an act of insanity.

About the beginning of July my father and mother set out from Edinburgh on a pedestrian tour through the Western Highlands. That such a feat should be performed by a delicate young Englishwoman was sufficiently astonishing. A little of the singularity, no doubt, arose from the fact, that she was the wife of an eccentric young poet, the strangeness of whose actions would be duly exaggerated. Such a proposal, therefore, could not be made without exciting wonder and talk in the demure circles of Edinburgh society. Mrs. Grant of Laggan thus writes upon the subject to a friend:—

"The oddest thing that I have known for some time is John Wilson's intended tour to the Highlands with his wife. This gentle and elegant Englishwoman is to walk with her mate, who carries her wardrobe and his own,

'Thorough flood and thorough mire,
Over bush, over brier;'

that is, through all the bypaths in the Central Highlands, where they propose to sleep in such cottages as English eyes never saw before. I shall be charmed to see them come back alive; and in the mean time it has cost me not a little pains to explain, in my epistles to my less romantic friends in their track, that they are genuine gentle folks in masquerade. How cruel any authority would be thought, that should assign such penance to the wearers of purple and fine linen, as these have volunteered."

A few facts relative to this romantic walk are not, after a lapse of so many years, lost sight of by those who remember meeting the travellers, and entertaining them kindly. Scotland was dear to Wilson's heart, as was the fair sisterland he was so loath to leave. Who has ever written such words about Highland scenery as he has done? Well he knew all those mist-laden glens in the far west; and the glorious shadows of the great mountains, beneath whose shelter he and his wife would rest after a long day's walk. In this tour they visited the Trosachs, Loch Katrine, and the smaller lochs in that neighborhood, taking such divisions of the Western Highlands as suited their fancy. They did not "chalk out a route," or act as if "they had sworn a solemn oath to follow it." From Loch Lomond westward to Inverary, and thence northward by Loch Awe and Glen Etive, they wandered on—halting when wearied, either for a night, or a day or two, and always well received, strangers though they were; making friends too, in far-off places. Through the wild rampant cliffs and mountains, which lend so awful a grandeur to Glencoe, they proceeded to Ballachulish, billeting themselves upon the hospitable household of Mr. Stewart, where

6

they received such kindness as made the remembrance of that family a bright spot in the wanderings of memory many years after, and meetings with its different members always agreeable. The district of country, however, which seemed to have the greatest charm, and where they lingered longest, was that between Inverary and Dalmally. Loch Awe with its wooded shores, noble bays, beautiful islands, and unsurpassed mountain range, topped by the magnificent crest of Ben Cruachan, whose mighty base, wood-skirted, sends its verdure-clad bounds gently to the margin of the deep waters—was an object too attractive for such lovers of nature soon to part from. Again and again they retraced their steps to this enchanting scene.

In this neighborhood they found a resting-place for a time in Glenorchy, at the schoolmaster's house. Dr. Smith, the present clergyman of Inverary, remembers, when a youth, seeing this devoted pair travelling on foot in these parts; Wilson laden with their travelling gear, and his gentle wife carrying in her hand the lighter portion of it. He says: "I remember well the feelings of wonder and admiration with which I regarded his manliness and her meekness; and whether it be that the thoughts of youth are apt to become indelible impressions, or that what awakened them was a reality in this case, as I am inclined to believe; the thoughts and feelings of youth still remain, so that over and high above all he wrote, I see the man, the earnest, generous man, who though singularly tolerant to others, cared not to measure any odds against his own consciousness of power. It was on this first visit in 1815 that some of those incidents occurred which are not easily forgotten, in a country where the acts of a stranger are narrowly noticed, though kindly interpreted. He and Mrs. Wilson, on their way to Glenorchy, passed a little thatched cottage close by the falls of the Aray. The spot was beautiful; the weather had been wet, and the river rushed along its rocky bed with a fulness that was promising to the angler. It was too attractive to be passed, so they lingered, stopped, and waited for ten days or a fortnight, taking up their quarters at the cottage, and living on the easiest terms with its inmates.

"It is yet told, how on a Sabbath morning the daughter who served came into the room—the only one—where Mr. and Mrs. Wilson slept; and after adjusting her dress at the little mirror hanging by a nail on the unmortared wall, she was unable to hook her gown behind, but went at once to the side of the bed, from which they had not yet risen, saying, 'Do help me to hook my gown.' Mr. Wilson sat up in bed, and served her with the utmost good-nature. In Glenorchy, his time was much occupied by fishing, and distance was not considered an obstacle. He started one morning at an early hour to fish in a loch which at that time abounded in trout, in the Braes of Glenorchy, called Loch Toilà. Its nearest point was thirteen miles distant from his lodgings at the schoolhouse. On reaching it, and unscrewing the butt-end of his fishing-rod to get the top, he found he had it not. Nothing daunted, he walked back, breakfasted, got his fishing-rod, made all complete, and off again to Loch Toilà. He could not resist fishing on the river when a pool looked invitingly, but he went always onwards, reached the loch a second time, fished round it, and found that the long summer day had come to an end. He set off for his home again with his fishing-basket full, and confessing somewhat to weariness. Passing near a farm-house whose inmates he knew (for he had formed acquaintance with all), he went to get some food. They were in bed, for it was eleven o'clock at night, and after rousing them, the hostess hastened to supply him; but he requested her to get him some whiskey and milk. She came with a bottle-full, and a can of milk with a tumbler. Instead of a tumbler, he requested a bowl, and poured the half of the whiskey in, along with half the milk. He drank the mixture at a draught, and while his kind hostess was looking on with amazement, he poured the remainder of the whiskey and milk into the bowl, and drank that also. He then proceeded homeward, performing a journey of not less than seventy miles.*

"On leaving the Glenorchy schoolhouse, they went to Glen Etive. On their way along the banks of Loch Etive, and near the mouth of the river Conglas, they came to a shepherd's house, where they intended to wait for a few days to fish. The shepherd was servant to Mr. Campbell of Achlian. Wilson had a note to him from his master. The morning had been fine, but, as often happens in this climate, it had become very wet towards evening. As the pedestrians reached the cottage drenched, on knocking at the door,

* This adventure is told, with a slight variation, by the Professor himself in his "Anglimania." — *Wilson's Works.*

the shepherd's wife thought not well of them, perhaps startled by the height and breadth of the shoulders of him who stood at the door, for her husband was a little man. She said at once, 'Go on to the farm-house, we cannot take in gangrels here.' The note put all right, and the shepherd with his wife, both dead now, often told the circumstance to enforce hospitality to strangers, as by so doing one might entertain angels unawares."

This kind of reception was at last no novelty to them. A gentleman now residing near Inverness remembers their arriving at Foyers, with a letter of introduction to the late proprietor of that picturesque estate, from their friend Mrs. Grant. Wilson was dressed in sailor fashion, and his wife's attire was such as suited a pedestrian in the mountains. The Highland lassie who received them at the door had not been in the habit of seeing gentlefolks so arrayed, and naturally taking them for "gangrel bodies" from the South, ushered them into the kitchen.

On their returning route they passed through a village where Wilson, on a subsequent expedition, met with adventures to be afterwards recorded. Their appearance is described by the writer of a collection of Highland Sketches,* from whose narrative I borrow the substance of the following account:—

On a fine summer evening, the eyes of a primitive northern village† were attracted by the appearance of two travellers, apparently man and wife, coming into the village, dressed like cairds or gipsies. The man was tall, broad-shouldered, and of stalwart proportions; his fair hair floated redundant over neck and shoulders, and his red beard and whiskers were of portentous size. He bore himself with the assured and careless air of a strong man rejoicing in his strength. On his back was a capacious knapsack, and his slouched hat, garnished with fishing-hooks and tackle, showed he was as much addicted to fishing as to making spoons:—

"A stalwart tinkler wight seemed he,
That weel could mend a pot or pan;
And deftly he could thraw the flee,
Or neatly weave the willow wan'."

The appearance of his companion contrasted strikingly with that

* Mr. William Stewart.

† Mr. Stewart calls it Tomintoul, but that must be a mistake, as at a subsequent date my father speaks of it as a place visited for the first time.

of her mate. She was of slim and fragile form, and more like a lady in her walk and bearing than any wife of a caird that had ever been seen in those parts. The natives were somewhat surprised to see this great caird making for the head inn, the "Gordon Arms," where the singular pair actually took up their quarters for several days. Thence they were in the habit of sallying forth, each armed with a fishing-rod, to the river banks, a circumstance the novelty of which, as regarded the tinker's wife, excited no small curiosity, and many conjectures were hazarded as to the real character of the mysterious couple.

A local hero named the King of the Drovers, moved by admiration of the peculiar proportions of this king of the cairds, felt a great desire to come into closer relations with the stranger. He was soon gratified. A meeting was arranged, in order to try whether the son of the mountain or the son of the plain were the better man in wrestling, leaping, running, and drinking; and in all of these manly exercises the great drover, probably for the first time, found himself more than matched.

After nearly two months' tour, the travellers came down by the low-lying lands of Dunkeld, where Mr. Wilson was somewhat suspiciously regarded, being by some good folks looked upon as a lunatic. Mrs. Izett, a lady of accomplishments and taste, and a great admirer of genius, gives a description of Mr. and Mrs. Wilson's arrival at her house at midnight. She writes to Mr. John Grieve, a friend of my father's, who lived many years in Edinburgh, a man of good judgment, and refined and elegant pursuits:—

"Had you a glimpse of Byron, Southey, etc.? By the way, Southey brings your friend Wilson to my recollection. We had the pleasure of seeing him and his agreeable partner here. Though they were here for several nights, I really could not form an opinion of him. They arrived here late at night. The following day, and *greatest part of the night*, he passed rambling among our glens alone, and the day after, the whole of which he passed within doors, I happened unfortunately to be confined to my room with the headache—at least during the greatest part of it—and thus lost the opportunity you kindly afforded me, of enjoying what I should have considered a great treat. There is something very striking in the countenance of Mr. Wilson, particularly his eye. His head I think quite a model for a minstrel; there is so much of fire, and at the same time so much simplicity. His wanderings, etc., etc., made some people in this quarter—no matter who—think him quite mad, and they will not be persuaded to the contrary. The eccentricities of a poet certainly do bear some resemblance to this at times, and to say truth, Mr. Wilson has his good share of these. I was quite tantalized the day he passed in the house that I was not able to appear, and avail myself of so good an opportunity to become acquainted with him. I saw more of Mrs. Wilson, and was much pleased with her. She made out her *walks* you see, and after this you must allow woman to possess resolution and perseverance. I greatly admired the patience and good-humor with which she bore all the privations and fatigues of her journey. She might make some of your southern *beaux* blush for their effeminacy."

My mother during this tour walked one day twenty-five miles. The travellers had been overtaken by a mist falling suddenly over them when in Rannoch. They missed the beaten track of road, and getting among dreary moors, were long before they discovered footing that could lead them to a habitation. My father made his wife sit down among the moss, and taking off his coat, wrapped her in it, saying he would try and find the road, assuring her, at the same time, that he would not go beyond the reach of her voice. They could not see a foot before them, so dense and heavy was the dreary mist that lay all around. Kissing his wife, and telling her not to fear, he sprang up from where she sat, and bounded off. Not many seconds of time elapsed, ere he called her to come to him—the sound guiding her to where he stood. He was upon the road; his foot had suddenly gained the right path, for light there was none. He told her he had never felt so grateful for any thing in his life, as for that unexpected discovery of the beaten track. He knew well the dangers of those wild wastes when mists fall, and the disasters they not unfrequently cause. A weary walk it was that brought them to "King's House," the only inn at that time for travellers among these Highland fastnesses.

On their return from this wonderful tour, they were quite the lions of Edinburgh. It was fully expected by the anxious community of the fairer sex, that Mrs. Wilson would return weather-beaten and robbed of her beautiful complexion, sunburnt and freckled. But such expectations were agreeably disappointed. One lady who called upon her directly after her return, old Mrs.

Mure of Caldwell, exclaimed, "Weel, I declare, she's come back bonnier than ever!"

My father's own account of their adventures is contained in the following letter to the Ettrick Shepherd, soon after his return, written evidently in the full enjoyment of the highest health and spirits, —to use his own phrase, "strong as an eagle:"—

"EDINBURGH, *September.*

"MY DEAR HOGG:—I am in Edinburgh, and wish to be out of it. Mrs. Wilson and I walked 350 miles in the Highlands, between the 5th of July and the 26th of August, sojourning in divers glens from Sabbath unto Sabbath, fishing, eating, and staring. I purpose appearing in Glasgow on Thursday, where I shall stay till the circuit is over. I then go to Elleray, in the character of a Benedictine monk, till the beginning of November. Now pause and attend. If you will meet me at Moffat, on October 6th, I will walk or mail it with you to Elleray, and treat you there with fowls and Irish whiskey. Immediately on the receipt of this, write a letter to me, at Mr. Smith's bookshop, Hutcheson street, Glasgow, saying positively if you will, or will not do so. If you don't, *I will lick you*, and fish up Douglas Burn before you, next time I come to Ettrick. I saw a letter from you to M—— the other day, by which you seem to be alive and well. You are right in not making verses when you can catch trout. Francis Jeffrey leaves Edinburgh this day for Holland and France. I presume, after destroying the king of the Netherlands, he intends to annex that kingdom to France, and assume the supreme power of the United Countries, under the title of Geoffrey the First. You, he will make Poet Laureate and Fishmonger, and me admiral of the Mosquito Fleet.

"If you have occasion soon to write to Murray, pray introduce something about 'The City of the Plague,' as I shall probably offer him that poem in about a fortnight or sooner. Of course I do not wish you to say that the poem is utterly worthless. I think that a bold eulogy from you (if administered immediately) would be of service to me; but if you do write about it, do not tell him that I have any intention of offering it to him, but you may say, you hear I am going to offer it to a London bookseller.

"We stayed seven days at Mrs. Izett's, at Kinnaird, and were most kindly received. Mrs. Izett is a great ally of yours, and is a fine creature. I killed in the Highlands 170 dozen of trouts. One day nineteen dozen and a half, another seven dozen. I, one morning, killed ten trouts that weighed nine pounds. In Loch Awe, in three days, I killed seventy-six pounds' weight of fish, all with the fly. The Gaels were astonished. I shot two roebucks, and had nearly caught a red-deer by the tail—*I was within half a mile of it at farthest.* The good folks in the Highlands are not dirty. They are clean, decent, hospitable, ugly people. We domiciliated with many, and found no remains of the great plague of fleas, etc., that devastated the country from the time of Ossian to the accession of George the Third. We were at Loch Katrine, Loch Lomond, Inverary, Dalmally, Loch Etive, Glen Etive, Dalness, Appin, Ballachulish, Fort William, Moy, Dalwhinny, Loch Ericht (you dog), Loch Rannoch, Glen Lyon, Taymouth, Blair-Athole, Bruar, Perth, Edinburgh. Is not Mrs. Wilson immortalized?

"I know of 'Cona.'* It is very creditable to our excellent friend, but will not sell any more than the 'Isle of Palms,' or 'The White Doe.'† The 'White Doe' is not in season; venison is not liked in Edinburgh. It wants flavor; a good Ettrick wether is preferable. Wordsworth has more of the poetical character than any living writer, but he is not a man of first-rate intellect; his genius oversets him. Southey's 'Roderic' is not a first-rate work; the remorse of Roderic is that of a Christian devotee, rather than that of a dethroned monarch. His battles are ill fought. There is no processional march of events in the poem, no tendency to one great end, like a river increasing in majesty till it reaches the sea. Neither is there national character, Spanish or Moorish. No sublime imagery; no profound passion. Southey wrote it, and Southey is a man of talent; but it is his worst poem.

"Scott's 'Field of Waterloo' I have seen. What a poem!—such bald and nerveless language, mean imagery, commonplace sentiments, and clumsy versification! It is beneath criticism. Unless the latter part of the battle be very fine indeed, this poem will injure him.

"Wordsworth is dished. Southey is in purgatory; Scott is

* *Cona or the Vale of Clwyd, and other Poems.* Edinburgh. 12mo. The author of this little volume was Mr. James Gray, one of the teachers in the High School, an accomplished man, a friend of my father's. He afterwards took orders in the Church of England, and was appointed to a chaplaincy in India. He died in September, 1830.

† Wordsworth's "White Doe of Rylstone."

dying; and Byron is married. Herbert* is frozen to death in Scandinavia. Moore has lost his manliness. Coleridge is always in a fog. Joanna Baillie is writing a system of cookery. Montgomery is in a madhouse, or ought to be. Campbell is sick of a constipation in the bowels. Hogg is herding sheep in Ettrick forest; and Wilson has taken the plague. O wretched writers! Unfortunate bards! What is Bobby Miller's† back shop to do this winter! Alas! alas! alas! a wild doe is a noble animal; write an address to one, and it shall be inferior to one I have written—for half a barrel of red herrings!‡

"The Highlanders are not a poetical people. They are too national; too proud of their history. They imagine that a *colley-shangy* between the Macgregors and Campbells is a sublime event; and they overlook mountains four thousand feet high. If Ossian did write the poems attributed to him, or any poems like them, he was a dull dog, and deserved never to taste whiskey as long as he lived. A man who lives forever among mist and mountains, knows better than to be always prosing about them. Methinks I feel about objects familiar to infancy and manhood, but when we speak of them, it is only upon great occasions, and in situations of deep passion. Ossian was probably born in a flat country!§

"Scott has written good lines in the 'Lord of the Isles,' but he has not done justice to the Sound of Mull, which is a glorious strait.

"The Northern Highlanders do not admire *Waverley*, so I presume the South Highlanders despise *Guy Mannering*. The Westmoreland peasants think Wordsworth a fool. In Borrowdale, Southey is not known to exist. I met ten men at Hawick who did not think Hogg a poet, and the whole City of Glasgow think me a madman. So much for the voice of the people being the voice of God. I left my snuff-box in your cottage. Take care of it. The Anstruther bards have advertised their anniversary; I forget the day.

* The Honorable William Herbert, Dean of Manchester, died in 1847, in his 70th year. He was author of several volumes or translations from the Icelandic and other northern languages. The poem here referred to is evidently "Helga," which was published in 1815.

† One of the principal Edinburgh booksellers.

‡ An excusable challenge. The "Address to a Wild Deer" is one of his happiest compositions.

§ For a very different and more serious criticism of Ossian's Poems by him, see *Blackwood's Magazine* for November, 1839.

"I wish Lieutenant Gray of the Marines* had been devoured by the lion he once carried on board his ship to the Dey of Algiers, or that he was kept a perpetual prisoner by the Moors in Barbary. Did you hear that Tennant† had been taken before the Session for an offence against good morals? If you did not, neither did I. Indeed it is, on many accounts, exceedingly improbable.

"Yours, truly, JOHN WILSON."

Apparently the *Isle of Palms* had by this time made way with some success, if it did not quite realize the hopes of the author. Previously to the writing of the above letter, he had put himself in communication with Mr. Smith, in reference to the publication of his new volume:—

"EDINBURGH, 53 QUEEN STREET,
September 5, 1815.

"I have as many poems as would make such another volume as the *Isle of Palms*, which I wish to publish this winter. The longest is nearly 4,000 lines. I have as yet spoken of it to no one, friend or bookseller. I have made up my mind not to publish it unless I sell the copyright for a specific sum. I shall not correspond with any other person on the subject till I hear from you, and what your intentions may be concerning it.

"I hope that you are quite well. I have been in the Highlands for two months, with Mrs. Wilson, and am strong as an eagle."

Having received no reply, he wrote a few days later:—

"I felt myself bound by friendship and other ties to acquaint you with my intention before I communicated it to any other person of the trade. As the winter is fast approaching, I wish to have this business settled, ere long, either in one way or another, and will therefore be glad to hear from you as soon as convenient. It is probable that I may appear in Glasgow during the Circuit, to smell the air of the new court, but my motions are uncertain. If I do make it out, I trust the oysters will be in season."

Early in October he writes again, from Glasgow:—

"The volume which I have now ready for the press will contain any number of pages the publisher may think fit, from three to four

* Charles Gray, author of several Scotch ballads, poems, and songs. He died in 1851.

† William Tennant, Professor of Oriental Languages in St. Andrews; Author of "Anster Fair;" died in 1848.

hundred, so as to be sold for twelve shillings, and to be a counterpart of the *Isle of Palms.*

"The first and longest poem is entitled 'The City of the Plague,' is dramatic, and consists of nearly four thousand lines, or between three and four thousand. The scene is laid in London, during the great plague of 1665, and the poem is intended to give a general picture of the situation of a plague-struck city, along with the history of a few individuals who constitute the persons of the drama.

"The second poem, 'The Convict,' is likewise dramatic and in blank verse, and its object is to delineate the passions of a man innocently condemned to death, and the feelings of his dearest relations. It is between two and three thousand lines.

"The third poem is a dramatic fragment, entitled 'The Mariner's Return,' about six hundred lines, and principally consisting of descriptions of sea scenery.

"The remainder of the volume will be made up to the length deemed necessary for poems of a miscellaneous character, in rhyme and blank verse.

"It is not my intention to publish this volume unless I dispose of the copyright; and the sum I have set on it is £200.

"If you feel any inclination to purchase it *of yourself*, one word can do it; if not, one word between friends is sufficient.

"If you determine against purchasing it *of yourself*, then you can inform me whether or not you would be willing, along with Murray, or Miller in Edinburgh, or any other bookseller, to give me that sum for the copyright.

"If you determine against having any thing to do with it, as a principal, on these terms, then, for the present, the subject drops."

Mr. Smith appears to have declined the sole responsibility of the publication, which was ultimately undertaken by Constable, along with whose name those of Smith and of Longman appeared on the title-page. Shortly after this communication my father paid a visit to Elleray, probably for the purpose of inspecting the state of the place, and making arrangements for letting it. On the 31st of October he reports his progress to his wife:—

"ELLERAY, *Friday night, Oct.* 31, 1815.

"DEAREST JANE:—I am not to blame for not having written before this night, owing first to a mistake about the post-night;

and secondly, to the want of sealing-wax or wafer; so, if angry, pray become appeased. On Monday I reached Penrith, the weather being coldish to Hawick; then I took inside to Carlisle, thence outside to Penrith. At Penrith I dined with an old Oxonian, and walked on to Pooley Bridge; there I found Jeany* waiting for me, and proceeded to Patterdale, which I reached about ten o'clock; dark and stormy night. On Tuesday morning I walked to Ambleside, sending Billy (whom I found there) with pony to Elleray. From Ambleside I walked to De Quincey's, with whom I dined; we returned per coach to Ambleside, and drank punch with Dr. Scandler, who is considerably better. The night being indifferent, I stayed all night at Chapman's; on Wednesday I sent for pony and rode to Elleray. I found Mrs. Ritson alive and well. Rode down and called at the parsonage; all glad to see me. Called at the Island; saw Mrs. Curwen and children, well and looking well; W. Curwen in Cumberland; dined therefore at Ullock's; went in the evening to parsonage and drank tea. Thursday, walked about Elleray; dined at Pringle's; met the Baxters and Greaves; pleasant party, Greave falling asleep immediately after dinner. Mr. Pringle is looking tolerably, though I fear he will feel the effects of the accident all his days. Blind of one eye, and confused at times in his head. Mrs. Pringle handsome and kind, and Miss Somerville with her. Friday, have spent all this day along with myself and Mr. Ritson, and Billy at Elleray. The place which had been a wilderness is again trim and neat, and looks as well as possible. The trees are greatly grown, and every thing seems thriving and prosperous. There are eight chickens with whom I am forming a friendship; and I feel as idle as ever.

"I dare say no more about a place so dear to us both; would to God you were here!

"But next time I come, whenever that is, you shall be with me. I have not seen the 'stamp-master.' Saturday and Sunday I intend keeping alone, and at Elleray. Monday I shall probably go to Hollow Oak or Ulverston. The Misses Taylor have gone to Bath. Of the Hardens I know nothing. Mr. Lloyd is worse than ever, and gone to Birmingham; I believe never to return. Kitty Dawes (mother to Dawes) is dead. So is the old miller of Restock, and young Bingham of Kendal, two well-known cockers.

* A favorite pony.

"De Quincey will accompany me to Scotland; but I will write about his rooms in a day or two.

"I have not yet been in the new house. The little detestable bit of avenue looks tolerable. Of Robert and Eliza I know nothing. Kiss everybody you meet for me up-stairs. Write to me, care of Mrs. Ullock, immediately. Thine with eternal affection,

"John Wilson."

Of what happened in the interval between this date and January following there is no record. No doubt he was busy with the proof-sheets of the *City of the Plague*. In January, 1816, he was again at Elleray, and thus relates his adventures to Mrs. Wilson:—

"Bowness, *Sunday*, *January*, 1816.

"Dearest Czarina:—I hope that you received my scroll from Carlisle, which I committed to the custody of Richard, and therefore doubt not that he would fulfil his trust.

"I supped at the Pearsons', and was very kindly received there; Miss Alms being in love with me, which I think I told you before. Going down to their house I fell *upon a slide*, and was most severely bruised, so much so that I had to be carried into a shop, and drink wine which the people very kindly gave me. This was an infernal fall, my rump and head suffering a dire concussion against one of the most fashionable streets. I however made out my visit, though still rather sick and headachy all night. Indeed my journey seemed to consist wholly of disasters. In the morning (no coach going sooner) I pursued my journey to Penrith—day cold and snowy—outside for cheapness. I then got tired of the coach, and, after drinking a glass of wine and water, started on foot for Coleridge's at Pooley Bridge; there I dined, and, at half-past seven in the evening, feeling myself bold and chivalrous, I started again for Patterdale, against the ineffectual remonstrances of the whole family who all prophesied immediate death. The night was not dark, and in two hours I was seated in the kitchen of Mr. Dobson at a good fire. I then proposed crossing Kirkstone, when shrieks arose from every quarter, and I then found a young man had just been brought in *dead*, having been lost on Sunday evening coming from Ambleside, and only found that day. Of course, the melancholy accident made me give up all thoughts of pursuing my journey till daylight, so

I supped and went to bed. Next forenoon at eleven o'clock, a party of men arrived from Ambleside with the Coroner, and I found from them that the road though difficult was passable, so I faced the hill and arrived safe at Chapman's in two hours and ten minutes, having slid along with great rapidity. The thaw was beginning, and had I waited another day, the snow would have been soft and impassable, as it lay in many places ten feet deep, and I walked over two gates. I dined with William Curwen, and walked to De Quincey's, which I reached at half-past one o'clock in the morning; he was at the *Nab*, and when he returned about three o'clock, found me asleep in his bed. I reached Elleray only last night, having spent the whole of Saturday with the lesser man; he walked to Elleray with me, where we drank tea; he then returned to Grasmere; and no sheets being on the bed, I walked to Bowness, and stayed all night. I am still here, and it rains severely. As yet, Elleray is all in the dark. I shall dine there to-morrow alone, but not stay all night, for the lonesomeness is insupportable. I will write a longer letter, and give you news. Nobody, I fear, has died here since I saw you. Billy is well, and his two nephews are at present residing with him at Elleray. His father and mother are expected daily, and a few distant relations.

"Lloyd is in a mad-house; Wordsworth and family from home. Write me on receipt of this (if not before); direct to me at Mrs. Ullock's, Bowness. Eternally thine with all affection,

"J. WILSON."

During the next month he was constantly occupied with the printers, and on the 13th of March he writes to Mr. Smith:—

"I ought long ago to have acknowledged the receipt of your different letters; but I have been busier than any man ever was before.

"My volume went round the trade to-day; with what success I know not. My expectations are but moderate. The volume is too thin and so is the paper, but I believe there is more printing and pages than 10s. 6d. books in general. I put your name into the title page, which I shall ever be happy to do on similar occasions.

"These failures in Glasgow will not be favorable to me as an author."

The reception of the volume was altogether favorable; and it was recognized as indicating a marked increase of power and discipline in the mind of the author. With the exception of that first suggestion of the subject already referred to, I find no allusion to the principal poem nor any trace of it in note-books. Of the other poems, there are but four which correspond in title with any in the "List of Subjects" of 1812. These are "The Children's Dance," "The Convict," "Solitude," and "The Farewell and Return."

In the next number of the *Edinburgh Review*, the volume received a friendly criticism from the hand of Jeffrey, who, in reply to a letter from the author, unfortunately not extant, addressed the following interesting letter to him:—

"MY DEAR SIR:—I am extremely gratified by your letter, and thank you very sincerely, both for the kindness it expresses, and the confidence it seems to place in me. It is impossible, I think, to read your writings without feeling affection for the writer; and under the influence of such a feeling, I doubt whether it is *possible* to deal with them with the same severe impartiality with which works of equal literary merit, but without that attraction, might probably be treated. Nor do I think that this is desirable or would even be fair; for part, and not the least part of the merit of poetry, consists in its moral effects, and the power of exciting kind and generous affections seems entitled to as much admiration as that of presenting pleasing images to the fancy.

"You wish, however, to be treated *as a stranger*, and, I think, I have actually treated you as one, for the partiality which I have already mentioned as irresistibly produced by your writings, certainly has not been lessened by the little personal intercourse we have had. I am not aware that it has been materially increased by that cause, and was inclined to believe that I should have felt the same kindliness towards the author of the work I am reviewing, although I had never seen his face. As to showing you no favor for the future on the score of the past, I am afraid if I do not exactly comply with your request, it will be more owing to my own selfish unwillingness to retract my former opinions and abandon my predictions, than from any excess of good-nature towards their objects. However, your request is very natural and manly, and I shall do what I can to let you have nothing more than justice, and save you from having any other obligations to your critic than for his diligence and integrity.

"As to Wordsworth, I shall only say, that while I cannot at all agree, nor is it necessary, in your estimate of his poetical talents, I love and honor the feelings by which I think your judgment has been misled, and by which I most readily admit that your conduct should be governed. I assure you I am not the least hurt or offended at hearing his poetry extolled, or my remarks upon it arraigned as unjust or erroneous; only I hope you will not set them down as sure proof of moral depravity, and utter want of all good affections. I should be sorry that any good man should think this of me as an individual; as to the opinion that may be formed of my critical qualifications, it is impossible for any one to be more indifferent than myself. I am conscious of being quite sincere in all the opinions I express, but I am the furthest in the world from thinking them infallible, or even having any considerable assurance of their appearing right to persons of good judgment.

"I wish I had more leisure to talk to you of such matters; but I cannot at present afford to indulge myself any further. I think we now understand each other in a way to prevent all risk of future misunderstanding. Believe me always, dear sir, very faithfully yours, "F. JEFFREY.

"92 GEORGE STREET, *Saturday Evening.*"

The pleasant relations thus established between these two men led to a still closer intimacy, which, though unhappily interrupted by subsequent events, was renewed in after years, when the bitterness of old controversies had yielded to the hallowing influences of time.

Whether there was any work done during this year in poetry or prose, I cannot say; but in the way of acquiring materials for future "Recreations of Christopher North" there was undoubtedly a good deal. All the other memorials at least that I have of this year, and a good part of the next, are connected almost entirely with angling, and extensive "raids" into the Highlands. It would almost seem as if there was an unwillingness fairly to cast anchor and remain steadily at work. The stimulus to literary exertion had not yet come with imperative force, and in the interval, before he fairly girded himself up to regular work, he sought strength for it in his love of nature and pedestrian wandering. These excursions, it is but fair to observe, however, appear to have been confined to the proper vacation time of his profession.

Again and again he roams over country he had so often trod before, and in the year following that in which he introduced Mrs. Wilson to the beauties of his native land, he returned to the neighborhood of Loch Awe, extending his tour into Inverness-shire, as we find from the following letters written in the spring and autumn of 1816:—

"ACHLIAN, 29*th April*, 1816.

"DEAR JANE:—I have risen at six o'clock to write to you. Your letter, I find, will not be here till Tuesday morning, I know not why. Curse all country posts!

"To be brief, James Fergusson* and I reached Glasgow on Monday; he went to the play; I did not. On Tuesday, I was tempted to stay in Glasgow, and saw Kean as Zanga in 'The Revenge.' It is heavy work, and he acted poorly, and is in every respect inferior to Kemble. On Wednesday, I went to Greenock by steamboat, of which the machinery went wrong, and blew up part of the deck, on which myself and two fattish gentlemen were sitting. This stopped us, and after a long delay we got into another steamboat, and arrived at Greenock. It was four o'clock. I found that I could only cross the water that night, so I thought it was needless; dined with Bissland, and went to the play, when I again saw Kean. I was too near him; he acted with occasional vigor, and his action is often good, but he rants abominably, and on the whole is no actor at all. On Thursday, I hired a boat and got to Ardentinny—distance eight miles; there fished a few miles, and got six dozen; then walked to Strachur, but on the way cut my foot severely, and awoke on Friday morning dog-lame. With great difficulty I reached, on Friday, the waterfall above Inverary, and was obliged to stop in a small cottage there. On Saturday, I fished up the stream (as when with you), and killed eighteen dozen. When evening came I was eight miles from Achlian, and so lame that I could not walk a step. I procured, therefore, a cart to drag me there, where I arrived at eleven o'clock, and found a warm welcome. Yesterday I rested, and to-day intend going out in the boat for a little fishing. This wound in my heel will render my visit to Megerney impossible, for there is no horse-road, so I will write to-day informing Menzies of my mishap. Is not this a severe trial to one's temper?

* A member of the Scottish bar, who married a sister of my father's friend, William Dunlop.

"The wound is in itself insignificant, but is just on the sole of my heel, and is much festered, about the size of a shilling, so that I cannot walk a single step without the greatest difficulty and pain.

"I shall ride from this, back to Greenock if possible. Immediately on getting this (which I expect will be Thursday forenoon), write that moment—directed to me at Achlian, *by Inverary*. On Wednesday the 8th, write to me at Miss Sym's, Glasgow, where I will be on the 10th, and at Edinburgh, on Saturday the 11th, probably about six o'clock. Your other letters, of course, become useless. I will write again first opportunity.

"Thine with heart and soul till death,

"J. WILSON."

The manner in which he wounded his foot is not a little characteristic. He does not mention the real cause of it to his wife, but curiously enough a story communicated by Dr. Smith, of Inverary, whose reminiscences have been already quoted from, explains this circumstance, the date of the occurrence he relates agreeing with that of the above letter:—

"At a point on the road near to the house which I now occupy, and close by the river-side, as he was on his way to Achlian, a large party of tinkers were pitching their tents. There were men, women, and children—a band—some preparing to go to fish for their supper in the adjoining pool, and some, more full of action, were leaping. They were tall, powerful young men, ready for any frolic, and all the *bonhomie* of Mr. Wilson's nature was stirred in him. He joined the group; talked with them and leaped with them. They were rejoicing in their sport, when he, finding himself hard pressed, stripped off coat and shoes; but the river had had its channel once on the spot; it had left a sharp stone, which was only concealed by the thin coating of earth over it; his heel came down on that stone; it wounded him severely; and, unable to bear a shoe on, he had to go to Achlian. The tinkers would rather that the accident had happened to one of themselves, and they procured a cart in the neighborhood in which he was conveyed to Achlian. The heel was carefully dealt with there by all but himself. Mrs. Smith,* then a little girl, tells me that her mother remonstrated often, but in vain; for he would fish, though scarcely able to limp;

* Then Miss Campbell, daughter of Mr. Campbell, of Achlian.

and one day, as he was fishing from the shore, a large trout, such as Loch Awe is remarkable for, was hooked by him. His line was weak, and afraid to lose it, he cast himself into the loch, yielding to the motions of the strong creature until it became fatigued and manageable. Then he swam ashore with his victim in subjection, and brought it home; but he was without the bandage, and his heel bleeding copiously."

This was no unusual mode of fishing with my father. As the Shepherd remarked: "In he used to gang, out, out, out, and ever sae far out, frae the point o' a promontory, sinking aye further and further doon, first to the waist-band o' his breeks, then up to the middle button o' his waistcoat, then to the verra breist, then to the oxters, then to the neck, and then to the verra chin o' him, sae that you wunnered how he could fling the flee; till last o' a' he would plump richt oot o' sight, till the Highlander on Ben Cruachan thocht him drooned. No he, indeed; sae he takes to the sooming, and strikes awa wi' ae arm, for the tither had haud o' the rod; and could ye believe't, though it's as true as Scripture, fishing a' the time, that no a moment o' the cloudy day micht be lost; ettles* at an island a quarter o' a mile aff, wi' trees, and an auld ruin o' a religious house, wherein beads used to be counted, and wafers eaten, and mass muttered hundreds o' years ago; and getting footing on the yellow sand or the green sward, he but gies himself a shake, and ere the sun looks out o' the clud, has hyucket a four-pounder, whom in four minutes (for it's a multiplying pirn the cretur uses) he lands, gasping through the giant gills, and glittering wi' a thousand spots, streaks, and stars, on the shore."†

With him the angler's silent trade was a ruling passion. He did not exaggerate to the Shepherd in the *Noctes* when he said that he had taken "a hundred and thirty in one day out of Loch Awe," as we see by his letters that even larger numbers were taken by him.

After the lapse of a week he again writes:—

"Dearest Jane:—The Devil is a letter-sorter at the Edinburgh Post-Office, so your Glenorchy letter of Thursday has not been sent to the place of his birth. The Inverary one I got on Saturday, which told me of your welfare, and the brats, which is enough. Where the other is gone is known only to the old gentleman, who will assuredly be hanged one day or other.

* Directs his course. † *Noctes.*

"I promised not to write any more; but thinking you will not be angry with me, I have ventured to scribble a few lines more.

"My heel is in *statu quo* (two Latin words which Robert will explain to you).

"I tried a day's fishing in Loch Awe, and killed a dozen fine ones. Yesterday I rode Achlian's charger to Craig. All here are well, and desire their love to you. Miss Campbell has been poorly, but mends apace. I have received most hospitable welcome. I slept last night in our old room. To-day I limped up to Molloy with my fishing-rod. Mrs. M'Kay there has just been brought to bed of a son, who is doing well. They inquired most kindly for you, and were delighted to see me. What a fishing! In one pool I killed twenty-one trouts, all of them about two pounds each, and have just arrived in time for dinner at Craig, loaded so that I could hardly walk. I have dispatched presents to all around. Miss M'Intyre, with whom we dined, desires her love. Dr. M'Intyre is from home. I shall stay here all night, being tired. On Wednesday, I leave Achlian on horseback, so depend on seeing me on Saturday. That is our marriage-day. In you and in my children lies all my bliss on earth. Every field here speaks of thee. Thine forever,

"J. WILSON."

The next letter is two months later, the Court of Session having sat in the interval. Very probably, however, he was not particular in waiting till the last day of the summer sittings to start once more for his favorite Achlian and Loch Awe. I suspect the idea of eighteen dozen of trout out of the Aray would have influenced him more in these fine days than the mere chance of another brief before "the Lords" dispersed.

"ACHLIAN, *Monday*, 22*d July*, 1816.

"DEAREST JENNET:—Your letter of Thursday I received here on Saturday, and as Sir Richard Strahan said when he fell in with the French fleet, 'We were delighted.'

"The day after I wrote last, namely, Monday, I walked up to the wooden bridge and fished there, killing fifteen dozen. Unluckily the family from home. On Tuesday I dined with Captain Archibald Campbell and his fair daughters at their cottage. We visited on Loch Fyne side, and met a pleasantish, smallish party. On Wednesday I left Inverary at a quarter before four in the morning, with young James M'Nicol, brother to Miss M'Nicol, and fished some moor farms about eight miles off; sport but moderate; fatigue great; slept like a top. On Thursday I dined with Mr. M'Gibbon, the clergyman, who lives in that nice place beyond the wooden bridge. Passed a most social evening, and stayed all night. On Friday I went to another class of moor farms, about eight miles from the wooden bridge, along with young Mr. Bell; had very bad sport indeed; separated from him by chance, and after wandering among the hills for hours, got to the wooden bridge about ten at night. Found Miss Giles Bell and her sister returned; got supper, and in several hours their brother arrived in despair, thinking I was drowned. On Saturday morning returned to Inverary and packed up. Found a gig going to Dalmally which carried me snugly to Achlian, where I found all the worthy inhabitants well. On Sunday, crossed the Loch to Hayfield, and dined with Mr. M'Neill, of that place.* In the evening a most terrific thunder-storm.

"To-day fished in Loch Awe; bad day; killed only one dozen, and returned to dinner; hitherto my sport has been but poorish. I feel unaccountably lazy, and doubt if I shall go to Rannoch at all.

"I am quite well, but more fatigued than you can imagine, so my letter is but shortish.

"Immediately on getting this, write me to Achlian, by Inverary, and send Barton's letter. Let thine be put into the Post-office before seven o'clock in the evening. You will please me by not going on board the 'Ramillies' till I return. But I do not countermand you, nor will I be the least angry if you do go. Bless the small creatures. Everlastingly yours, J. WILSON."

"ACHLIAN, *August* 2, 1816.

"MY DEAREST JANE:—Since I last wrote you I have been where there are no posts or post-offices, and till to-day have had no opportunity of sending you a letter. I suppose you are incensed, and so am I. Your letters have reached me safely, but not Barton's, which I have never seen. Therefore hope you have forgotten to send it to the post; if you have, keep it till I see thee. I have been over the moor of Rannoch, in Glencoe, and other glens near it; at the foot of Loch Ericht, and the country round Loch Treig; I have

* "My poor dear old friend M'Neill, of Hayfield. God rest his soul! It is in heaven. At ninety he was as lifeful as a boy at nineteen." *Noctes.*

seen great scenery, undergone hardships, and am in good health. I returned to Achlian a few days ago, but the post was one day missed, and I sent this by a private hand to Dalmally, and thence to Edinburgh. I have had much good fishing, much bad, and much tolerable—picture of human life. Keep all letters till I see thee. But immediately on getting this write to me, care of Robert Findlay, Esq., Miller Street, Glasgow. I shall be there ere long, day I cannot fix, because conveyances are doubtful, but you will be looking upon me with a pleasant countenance somewhere about the 7th or 8th of this month. Recollect I left you on the 11th, so it is not so long since I went away as you said in your letter.

"I suppose Cadell wished to see me about the *Edinburgh Review*. This is conjecture. What he calls agreeable to me may turn out to be supercilious praise, saying I am not a good boy. Farewell. "J. WILSON."

From Achlian he now worked his way across to Blair Athole, whence he writes to tell how he fares. He is "lame in the knee," and has "not been in bed," but he is just starting, at 6.30 A. M., as if under vow or penance, on a journey of thirty-four miles!

"DEAREST JANE:—It is half-past six morning, and I am just setting off to Braemar, anxious for your letter. I will write you at length first moment I have an opportunity, which will be in two or three days; meanwhile I am well, though lame in my knee.

"Obey all your directions, but, in addition to them, write on Friday (this day week) to me, care of Alexander M'Kenzie, Esq., Millbank, Dingwall. I have not been in bed, and am just setting off thirty-four miles. God bless and preserve thee and ours everlastingly! "J. WILSON.

"BRIDGE OF TILT, BLAIR ATHOLE,
Friday, August, 1816."

So northward he goes with his lame knee, as one burdened with some great exploring quest, which must be fulfilled at all hazards, and through all fatigues. Through the loneliest glens, up the highest mountain-tops, careless of weather, and finding "adventures" in the least likely places, he holds on to the north, and again to the west, till we light on him, after twenty-five miles' walk, sitting down to address his wife from the hospitable abode of his friend Mr. M'Kenzie:—

"MILLBANK, DINGWALL,
Wednesday, 13th August.

"MY DEAREST JANE:—I wrote you last from Abergeldy, and I am afraid you may have been longing for a letter before this reaches you. Such, I hope, is not my vanity, but mutual kind love; may it be our only blessing here and hereafter, and I am satisfied.

"From Abergeldy I started (I think the day after I wrote you) and proceeded to the head of the Don river. My burden was truly insupportable. The same evening I got to Inchrory on the river Aven or Avon, a most lovely place, perhaps the most so in Scotland, where I slept. Next day (Thursday) I got to Tomintoul,* where I slept, a wild and moorland village. Next day was the annual market, and it rained incessantly. My adventures there I will give you afterwards, and they were not to my discredit. On Saturday morning (still most rainy) I proceeded to Grantown, fourteen miles, where I arrived at night, and slept comfortably; the country most wild and desolate. About five miles from this live the Miss Grants, of Lifforchy. Thither on Sunday morning I repaired, and found them all at home and well, with a brother lately arrived from the East Indies. On Monday morning at three o'clock, he and I started to the top of Cairngorm, one of the highest mountains in Scotland, and returned at eight o'clock in the evening; I tired, and he sick even unto death. On Tuesday morning, I left the house and walked on towards Inverness, to a place called Craga, distance twenty-seven miles. It rained incessantly, and I had both toothache and earache. On Wednesday morning I started from Craga, and this same Wednesday reached Millbank, Mr. M'Kenzie's house, from which I now write after a walk of twenty-five miles. So much then for a general sketch, which I will fill up when I am once more with you.

"I find from your letter that our sweet ones are all unwell, and likely to be so. That last letter was dated Friday, August 8th. I am miserable about them. To-morrow, that is, Thursday, August 14th, and that one day, I must rest here, for the fatigue I have lately undergone has been beyond any thing I ever experienced. On Friday, the 15th, I shall start again, and hope to be at Achlian,

* Of this place he says in the *Noctes*:—"Drinking, dancing, swearing, and quarrelling going on all the time in Tomintoul, James, for a fair there is a wild rendezvous, as we both know, summer and winter; and thither flock the wildest spirits of the wildest clans."

Dugald Campbell's, by Inverary, in a week from that time. So *immediately* on receiving this, which I think will be on Saturday, 16th, write to me to that direction. Say you write on the day after you receive mine, whatever that day may be, and I will immediately write you on my arrival there; I will lose no time in getting there, and I think in about a fortnight I shall see you. I trust in God the accounts will be good when I reach Achlian. But to that point I will go as soon as I can. I have undergone great fatigue, and much bad weather, and long for your kind bosom, so help me God! Inverary is nearly 150 miles from this, and no carriages, so I must walk all the way. Once more, I pray to God to take care of our beloved children, and to make them well to us. To take a chance of hearing from you, write one line to Post-Office, Fort-William, the moment you receive this, telling me about the children. But write as above mentioned to Achlian, as I may be at Fort-William before your letter reaches. In short, I will go to Achlian as soon as possible, and from your letter there will judge if I am instantly to return home. No delay will take place. I am most anxious about the children. God bless you! and may the Almighty recover to us all our sweet ones! The chicken-pox is not a bad complaint, so we need not fear; poor Johnny fainting! But they are all dear. So farewell, yours tenderly, JOHN WILSON."

The adventures of which he says "they were not to my discredit," were doubtless made known to Mrs. Wilson, but never came to the ears of the younger generation, being considered either too trivial, or after many years forgotten. They were not forgotten, however, in the North, for in a recent letter from Mr. Alexander M'Kenzie, Dingwall, this very adventure is thus narrated:—

"I am the person specially honored by that visit. Mr. Wilson came to me (then living at Millbank near Dingwall) in such peculiar circumstances as leads me to think he would have made some memoranda about it. He had been fishing in the Dee, and by accident came to a fair at Tomintoul, where he saw a poor man much oppressed and ill-used by another, who was considered the bully of the country, and whose name, I think, he said was Grant. Circumstances led to Mr. Wilson putting off his coat and giving this fellow a thrashing, but on picking up the coat he found it rifled of his pocket-book, containing all his money but a very few shillings! In this state he left for Carrbridge, where he passed the night without more than enough of refreshment. In the morning he left for Inverness, and calling at the Post-Office he found many letters to his address; but not having money to pay the postage, the person in charge declined trusting him! He then crossed Kessock Ferry with only a few pence, and arrived at Dingwall about midday, where I happened to be at the time, and was quite overjoyed at seeing him. He was dressed in white duck trousers covered with mud, and his white hat entirely so with fishing gear!

"As he proceeded to my house, distant about a mile, he shortly detailed his late adventure, and said he was almost famished. My first work was to send to Inverness for his letters, after which we enjoyed one of the most delightful evenings of my life. He kindly rested himself for several days, and I accompanied him through the most romantic and impassable parts of the country to Kintail, where I parted with him at the house of a worthy mutual friend, George Laidlaw.

"In our rambles, which included some curious incidents, and which occupied several days, he fished wherever a loch or stream presented itself. We avoided all *roads* entirely, and lived with the shepherds."

Such stories as these might, to a certain extent, justify that excellent old lady, Mrs. Grant of Laggan, in making the following observations, when, in writing to a friend, she burst forth upon the eccentricities of the young poet:—

"Did I ever tell you of one of the said poets we have in town here—indeed, one of our intimates—the most provoking creature imaginable! He is young, handsome, witty; has great learning, exuberant spirits, a wife and children that he doats on (circumstances one would think consolidating), and no vice that I know of, but, on the contrary, virtuous principles and feelings. Yet his wonderful eccentricity would put anybody but his wife wild. She, I am convinced, was actually made on purpose for her husband, and has that kind of indescribable controlling influence over him that Catherine is said to have had over that wonderful savage the Czar Peter.

"Pray look at the last *Edinburgh Review*, and read the favorable article on John Wilson's 'City of the Plague.' He is the person in question."

In the month of September he again visited Elleray, accompanied by the eldest of his little girls. On his way he wrote to his wife:—

"PENRITH, *Friday, September* 20*th*,
Evening, Nine o'clock, 1816.

"DEAREST JANE:—We got safely to Hawick about ten o'clock; found a comfortable room and fire; supped, and went to bed. Maggy and Mary Topham* drank tea at the fireside in the same room with us, and were in bed by eleven. Maggy stood her journey well; made observations on the moon, and frightened me with the beast several times. We left Hawick in a chaise at ten next morning, and proceeded to Knox's, where we dined. We left that by eight o'clock, and reached Longtown by eleven.

"I supped the ladies and bedded them in half an hour. We left Longtown after breakfast, at ten o'clock; came through Carlisle, and dined at five o'clock. Maggy drank tea at seven, and immediately after retired to bed with Mary Topham, and I believe they are both sound asleep at this moment.

"To-morrow morning at six o'clock we leave this for Patterdale, and I think most probably will remain all night at Bowness. On Sunday will reach Hollow Oak to dinner. Nothing can excel Maggy's behavior—she is perfect; all eyes that looked on her loved her, and Miss Knox, I understand from Mary Topham, cut off a lock of her hair to keep. Merit is sure of being discovered at last.

"She has sat on my knee almost the whole way, and I feel I love her better than ever I did before. She will be an angelic being like her gentle mother. I will write from Hollow Oak on Monday, so you will hear on Tuesday or Wednesday. Write to me on Tuesday, care of Mrs. Ullock, Bowness.

"Give me all family and other news. Love Johnny for my sake, and teach him some prayers and hymns before I return.

"Thy affectionate husband,
"JOHN WILSON."

In another letter a few days later, dated from Elleray, he gives rapid notes of his doings; how he attended a ball which was "most dull, though it gave universal satisfaction;" how next day he "lay in bed all day," and the next "crowed all day like a cock at Elleray, to

* Nursery-maid.

Robertson's* infinite delight;" "the next day De Quincey and William Garnet dined with me here, Billy and Mrs. Balmer officiating." He adds, "Party here very agreeable," which one can well believe. "To-morrow," he goes on, "Garnet, Robertson, and self take coach to Keswick, and thence proceed to Buttermere and Ennerdale. I

* His friend Patrick, afterwards Lord Robertson, one of the most witty and warm-hearted of men. He was born in 1793; called to the Scotch bar in 1815; elected Dean of Faculty in 1842; raised to the bench in 1843; died in 1855. Lockhart wrote many a rhyming epitaph upon him, one of which is quoted elsewhere. On another occasion, he is reported to have written, "Peter Robertson is 'a man'" to use his own favorite quotation, "cast in Nature's amplest mould. He is admitted to be the greatest corporation lawyer at the Scotch bar; and he is a vast poet as well as a great lawyer. Silence, gentlemen, for a song by Peter Robertson:—

"Come listen all good gentlemen of every degree;
Come listen all ye lady-birds, come listen unto me;
Come listen all you laughing ones, come listen all ye grave;
Come listen all and every one, while I do sing a stave.

"One morning, I remember me, as I did lay in bed,
I felt a strange sensation come a throbbing through my head;
And I thought unto myself, thinks I, Where was it I did dine?
With whom? Oh, I recall the name,—'twas Baron Brandywine.

"Let me see: Oh, after turtle we had punch, the spirits' rain,
And, if I'm not mistaken, we had iced hock and champagne,
And sundry little sundries, all which go to make one merry,
An intervening toss, or so, of some superb old sherry.

"Well, then, to be dramatic, we must needs imbibe a dram
(A very sorry sort of pun—the perpetrator Sam);
And then to port and claret with great industry we fell,
Which, sooth to say, appeared to suit our party pretty well.

"Then biscuits all bedevilled we designedly did munch,
To gain a proper relish for that glorious bowl of punch,
But after that I cannot say that I remember much,
Except a hiccup-argument 'bout Belgium and the Dutch.

"Such were my recollections, and such I sing to you,
Good gentlemen and lady-birds—upon my soul it's true;
And if you wish to bear away the moral of my song,
It's this—for all your headaches let the reasons still be *strong*."

I think I detect Mr. Lockhart's hand in the following good wishes:—

"Oh, Petrus, Pedro, Peter, which you will,
Long, long thy radiant destiny fulfil,
Bright be thy wit, and bright the golden ore,
Paid down in fees for thy deep legal lore.
Bright be thy claret, brisk be thy champagne,
Thy whiskey-punch a vast, exhaustless main,
With thee disporting on its joyous shore,
Of that glad spirit quaffing ever more.
Keen be thy stomach, potent thy digestion,
And long thy lectures on 'the general question,'
While young and old swell out the general strain,
We ne'er shall look upon his like again."

will write thee on Saturday, fixing my day of return. I go to Ulverstone to see Maggy, etc. Don't hire a servant without seeing and approving her—mind that. Write me on Saturday as before. Put Elleray on the letter, else a surgeon at Bowness will read it. Love to Ung* and others.

"Eternally yours,

"J. W."

From the excursion with Garnet and Robertson he is hurried back to Elleray on business, and writes in haste:—

"Elleray, *Sept.* 28*th*, 1816.

"My dearest Wife:—I have not half a minute to spare. Immediately on receiving this, send me the inventory of every thing at Elleray. If it is too large to go by post, copy it over in one long sheet, and send it off on Thursday. If it can go by post, write on Tuesday—same day you receive this. On receiving your letter to-morrow, I will write you at length, and tell you when I come home, which will be immediately. It was impossible to leave this hitherto, for reasons I will explain. You will have heard of Maggy since I saw her. I will see her on Wednesday, and tell you all about her. Whatever my anxieties and sorrows are or may be in this life, I have in your affection a happiness paramount to all on earth, and I think that I am happier in the frowns of fortune, with that angelic nature, than perhaps even if we had been living in affluence. God forever bless you, and my sweet family, is the prayer of your loving and affectionate husband,

"J. Wilson."

There are no more letters or memorials of that year. The next brings us into a new field, which calls for a chapter to itself.

* A playful soubriquet for his eldest son.

Patrick Robertson, Esq.—From a sketch by the late Professor Edward Forbes.

CHAPTER VIII.

LITERATURE.—BLACKWOOD'S MAGAZINE.

1817–1820.

With the year 1817 we enter on a new epoch in Wilson's life. Hitherto his literary exertions had been confined almost exclusively to poetry; and the reception of his works, however favorable, had not been such as to satisfy him that that was the department in which he was destined to assert his superiority, or to find full scope for his varied powers. Much as has been said as to the mode in which these were exercised, and the comparative inadequacy of the results, I cannot but think that there is misconception on the subject. I dismiss the question what he or any other man of great powers *ought* to have done: I look simply at what he *did* do, which alone concerns us, now that his work is finished. Whether he might or should have written certain works on certain subjects, for the use or pleasure of his own generation and of posterity, seems to me an idle question. Enough for his vindication, that in a long and laborious literary life he wielded a wholesome and powerful influence in the world of letters; and enough for his fame, that amid the haste and exigencies of incessant periodical composition, he wrote such things as no other man but himself could have written, and which will be read and delighted in as long as the highest kind of criticism and of prose-poetry are valued among men. Periodical literature, it seems to me, was precisely the thing for which he was suited by temperament, versatility, and power; and unless it be broadly asserted, that the service done to letters and civilization through the medium of a great literary organ is unimportant, and unworthy of the efforts of a man of genius, I do not see how it can be maintained that Professor Wilson neglected or threw away his gifts when he devoted them to the establishment and maintenance of the influence of *Blackwood's Magazine.*

Before, however, entering on the less peaceful events which follow, let us have a glimpse of him once more—rod in hand, and knapsack on back—away in the heart of the Highlands towards the close of July, 1817. This time, however, he was burdened with a new load, for he carried besides his wardrobe and fishing-basket, a parcel of books. He had, in fact, come bound to produce an "article" for the *Edinburgh Monthly Magazine*, and that inexorable familiar the printer's devil followed on his heels even into the wilds of Rannoch. There he finished for the August number of that magazine a review of "Lalla Rookh," of which the first part had appeared in June. The following letter is the only memorial of this expedition:—

"MY DEAREST JANE:—On Monday at four o'clock I got to Perth, and during the journey felt much for poor Robert, who must have got dreadfully wet. We dined comfortably there, and walked to Dunkeld in the evening on foot, a very pleasant walk after the rain. On Tuesday, we took the top of the coach to Pitlochry, thirteen miles from Dunkeld, and about six from the bridge, where we got into the coach from Mrs. Izett's. We thence walked by the river Tummel (a scene somewhat like Borrowdale) to an inn at the head of Loch Tummel, where we stayed all night. On Wednesday, we fished up to Kinloch Rannoch, and I killed forty good trouts. I found our worthy friends here in good health and spirits. They have had two children since we saw them, and they inquired very kindly for you. On Thursday, I fished down to Mount Alexander, but the day was cold and unfavorable. Mr. Stewart, of Inverhadden, dined with us at the inn—a rare original. I fear I did not go to bed sober. (*Friday.*)—I have breakfasted with him, and fished; good sport, though, as usual, I lost several large ones. Menzies and his friend left me to-day for Loch Ericht, and I expect to see no more of them. To-morrow I ought to leave this, but that confounded Lalla Rookh is still on my hands; so I shall review it to-morrow, leave it here, and be off to Blair Athole on Sunday. On Monday, I shall be at Captain Harden's, Altnagoich, Braemar, and hope on Wednesday to have good accounts of my sweet girl and the fry. After that my motions are uncertain, but on Sunday evening write to 'Mr. Wilson, Post-Office, Inverness, to lie till called for,' and I hope to be there as soon as the letter. That is the second Sunday after my departure. No mistakes now. Write long and witty letters. The weather has been tolerable, and I am in good health. Give my love to Ung and the others, and God in his mercy keep them all well and happy. Heaven bless you forever, and believe me thy loving and grateful husband.

"KINLOCH RANNOCH *July* 27, 1817."

Here also may come in two pleasant letters from Jeffrey, before we arrive at the point when it became impossible for the editor of the *Edinburgh Review* to exchange confidential and friendly communications with an acknowledged contributor to *Blackwood:*—

"CRAIGCROOK, 10*th October*, 1817.

"MY DEAR WILSON:—Do you think you could be prevailed on to write a review for me now and then? Perhaps this may appear to you a very audacious request, and I am not sure that I should have had the boldness to make it, but I had heard it surmised, and in very intelligent quarters, that you had occasionally condescended to exercise the functions of a critic in works where your exertions must necessarily obtain less celebrity than in our journal. When I apply for assistance to persons in whose talents and judgment I have as much confidence as I have in yours, I leave of course the choice of their subjects very much to themselves, being satisfied that it must always be for my interest to receive all they are most desirous of sending. It is therefore rather with a view to tempt than to assist you, that I venture to suggest to you a general review of our dramatic poetry, a subject which I long meditated for myself, but which I now feel that I shall never have leisure to treat as I should wish to treat it, and upon which indeed I could not now enter, without a pretty laborious resumption of my early and half-forgotten studies. To you, I am quite sure, it is familiar, and while I am by no means certain that our opinions could always coincide, I have no hesitation in saying, that I should very much distrust my own when they were in absolute opposition to yours, and that I am unfeignedly of opinion that in your hands the disquisition will be more edifying and quite as entertaining as ever it could have been in mine. It is the appearance of the weak and dull article in the last *Quarterly*, which has roused me to the resolution of procuring something more worthy of the subject for the *Edinburgh*, and there really is nobody but yourself to whom I can look with any satisfaction for such a paper.

"I do not want, as you will easily conjecture, a learned, ostentatious, and antiquarian dissertation, but an account written with taste and feeling, and garnished, if you please, with such quotations as may be either very curious or very delightful. I intended something of this sort when I began my review of Ford's plays, but I ran off the course almost at starting, and could never get back again.

"Now, pray, do not refuse me rashly. I am not without impatience for your answer, but I would rather not have it for a day or two, if your first impression is that it would be unfavorable. If you are in a complying mood, the sooner I hear it the better.

"Independent of all this, will you allow me again to say, that I am very sincerely desirous of being better acquainted with you, and regret very much that my many avocations and irregular way of life have forced me to see so little of you. Could you venture to dine here without a party any day next week that you choose to name, except Saturday? If you have no engagement, will you come on Monday or Tuesday? Any other day that may be more convenient. If you take my proposal into kind consideration, we may talk a little of the drama; if not, we will fall on something else. Believe me always very faithfully yours, "F. JEFFREY.

"Send your answer to George Street."

The fact that my father agreed to contribute to an organ which soon after became the object of determined hostility in the periodical to which he chiefly devoted his services, will not, I imagine, be now regarded in the same light as it was by the Edinburgh Whigs of 1817. The practice of writing on different subjects in organs of the most hostile opinions is one which is now so universal among men of the highest character in the world of letters, that it needs no vindication here. At the time, too, when my father received this friendly overture from Jeffrey, the Magazine had not assumed that position as a representative of high Tory principles which by and by placed it in direct antagonism to the Review. The subjects on which he agreed to contribute were purely literary, and he was, no doubt, very glad to get the opportunity of expressing his views on poetry in an organ where that subject had not been treated in a style which he could consider satisfactory. It would appear that he had offered to review Coleridge in a friendly manner, which, taken in connection with the fact that a fierce onslaught on that poet appeared in the Number of *Blackwood* at that very time in the press, may furnish matter for unfavorable judgment to any sympathizers in the angry feelings of that period. I have no fear, however, that this circumstance will lead to uncharitable conclusions in the minds of any whose opinion I value. I am content to risk the reader's estimate of my father's generosity and kindliness of nature on the real facts of his life, without keeping any thing in the background that throws light upon them. The following is Jeffrey's reply to his communication, which I regret has not come into my hands :—

"CRAIGCROOK, 17*th October*, 1817.

"MY DEAR WILSON :—I give you up Byron freely, and thankfully accept of your conditional promise about the drama; for Coleridge, I should like first to have a little talk with you. I had intended to review him fairly, and, if possible, favorably, myself, at all events mercifully; but, on looking into the volume, I can discern so little new, and so much less good than I had expected, that I hesitate about noticing him at all. I cannot help fearing, too, that the discrepancy of our opinions as to *that* style of poetry may be too glaring to render it prudent to venture upon it, at least under existing circumstances; and besides, if I must unmask all my weakness to you, I am a little desirous of having the credit, though it should only be an inward one, of doing a handsome or even kind thing to a man who has spoken ill of me, and am unwilling that a favorable review of this author should appear in the *Review* from any other hand than my own. But we shall talk of this after I have considered the capabilities of the work a little further.

"I am very much gratified by the kind things you are pleased to say of me, though the flattering ones with which you have mixed them rather disturb me. When you know me a little better, you will find me a very ordinary fellow, and really not half so vain as to take your testimony in behalf of my qualifications. I have, I suppose, a little more practice and expertness in some things than you can yet have, but I am very much mistaken if you have not more talent of every kind than I have. What I think of your character you may infer from the offer I have made you of my friendship, and which I rather think I never made to any other man.

"I think you have a kind heart and a manly spirit, and feel perfectly assured that you will always act with frankness, gentleness, and firmness. I ask pardon for sending you this certificate, but I do not know how else to express so clearly the grounds of my regard and esteem.

"Believe me always, very faithfully yours,

"F. JEFFREY.

"I hope to see you on your return from Glasgow."

Of the subjects spoken of or contemplated, the only one which he took up was Byron, the review of whom did not make its appearance till August of the following year. That was my father's first and last contribution to the *Edinburgh Review*. Another fragment of a letter from Jeffrey, that must have been written not long after, may also be inserted here for the sake of coherence. It refers to a vindication of Wordsworth by my father, in reply to a letter in the *Edinburgh Magazine* criticising the poet's strictures on the *Edinburgh Review's* estimate of the character of Burns:—

. . . "hear that you had any thing to do with it, and was so far from feeling any animosity to the author that I conceived a very favorable opinion of him. I have not had an opportunity of looking into it since I saw your letter, but I can most confidently assure you that nothing that is there said can break any squares between us, and that you may praise Wordsworth as much as you please, and vilipend my criticisms on him in the most sweeping manner without giving me a moment's uneasiness or offence, provided you do not call me a slanderer, and an idiot, and a puppy, and all the other fine names that that worthy and judicious person has thought fit to lavish on me. I fairly tell you that I think your veneration for that gentleman is a sort of infatuation, but in you it is an amiable one, and I should think meanly of myself indeed if I were to take exception at a man for admiring the poetry or the speculative opinions of an author who, having had some provocation, has been ridiculously unjust to me. One thing I am struck with as a wilful blindness and partiality in the paper in question, and that was your passing over entirely the remarkable fact of the said W—— saying little or nothing of the blasphemies against Burns which occur in the *Quarterly*, and which are far more violent and offensive than mine, and pouring out all the vials of his wrath at the *Edinburgh*, which had given him much less provocation. Is it possible for you in your conscience to believe after this that the tirade against the *Edinburgh* critic was dictated by a pure, generous resentment for the injuries done to Burns, and not by a little vindictive feeling for the severities practised on himself. By the way, I think I am *nearly* right in what I have said of Burns; that is, I think the doctrine and morality to which I object is far oftener inculcated in his writings than any other, and is plainly most familiar to his thoughts, though perhaps it was ungenerous to denounce it so strongly.

"I have not written so long a letter these three years. Pray let me hear that you are writing a review of Lord B—— for me in peace and felicity, and that you have resolved to dirty your fingers no more with the quarrels of magazines and booksellers. God bless you! "Very truly yours, F. JEFFREY."

My father's connection with *Blackwood's Magazine* was such as to make it absolutely necessary, in any record of his life, to give some account of the rise of this periodical, and of the circumstances which led to his becoming so intimately associated with its history. I shall endeavor to do so as briefly as I can. Fortunately, we are now sufficiently removed by time from the controversies of those exciting days, to look at them with perfect calmness, if not impartiality; with something of wonder, it may be, at the fierceness displayed in contests about things which, in our own more peaceful times, are treated with at least the affectation of philosophic indifference; but also, with some admiration of the vigor manifested in supporting what was heartily believed. It is, indeed, impossible for us at this time to realize fully the state of feeling that prevailed in the literature and politics of the years between 1810 and 1830. We can hardly imagine why men, who at heart respected and liked each other, should have found it necessary to hold no communion, but, on the contrary, to wage bitter war because the one was an admirer of the Prince Regent and Lord Castlereagh, the other a supporter of Queen Caroline and Mr. Brougham. We cannot conceive why a poet should be stigmatized as a base and detestable character, merely because he was a Cockney and a Radical; nor can we comprehend how gentlemen, aggrieved by articles in newspapers or magazines, should have thought it necessary to the vindication of their honor, to horsewhip or shoot the printers or editors of the publications in which such articles appeared. Yet in 1817, and the following years, we find such to have been the state of things in the capital of Scotland. Not only was society actually less civilized; but politics, which now happily forms no barrier between men of otherwise congenial minds, then constituted the one great line of demarcation. You were either a Tory and a good man, or Whig and a rascal, and *vice versa*. If you were a Tory, and wanted a place, it was the duty of all good Tories to stand by you; if you were a Whig, your chance was small; but its feebleness was all the more reason why you should be proclaimed a martyr, and all your opponents profligate mercenaries. If I exaggerate, I am open to correction; but such appears to me to have been the prevailing tone among the men who figured most actively in public life about the time to which this chapter relates. In literature, at that time, the *Edinburgh Review* was supreme. Its doctrines were received, among those who believed in them, as oracular; and in the hands of the small retailers of political and literary dogmas who swore by it, these were becoming insufferably tiresome to the Tory part of mankind, who, singularly enough, had no literary oracle of their own north of the Tweed. I suppose the party being strong in power did not feel the want of such influence. The more ardent and active minds on that side, however, were naturally impatient of the dictatorship exercised by Mr. Jeffrey, and wanted only opportunity to establish an opposing force in the interests of their own venerable creed. That opportunity came, and was vigorously used, too vigorously at first, sometimes cruelly and unjustly, but ultimately with results eminently beneficial.

To begin then at the beginning. In the month of December, 1816, Mr. William Blackwood, who had by uncommon tact and energy, established his character in the course of a few years as an enterprising publisher in Edinburgh, was applied to by two literary men to become the publisher of a new monthly magazine, which they had projected.* These gentlemen were James Cleghorn,† who had acquired some literary position as editor of a *Farmers' Magazine*, and Thomas Pringle,‡ a pleasant writer and poet, who afterwards emigrated to South Africa.§ The idea was good, and the time fitting for the "felt want," which is now pleaded about once a week as the ground for establishing some new journal, was then a serious reality; the only periodical in Edinburgh of any mark besides the *Review* being the *Scots Magazine*, published by Constable, once a highly respectable, but at that time a vapid and

* Mr. Gillies in his Memoirs gives the credit of the origin and suggestion to Hogg.—Vol. i., p. 230.

† Mr. Cleghorn was more fortunate in his financial than his literary undertakings, having been the founder of the Scottish Provident Institution, by whom a monument to his memory has been erected in the Edinburgh Warriston Cemetery. He died in May, 1838.

‡ Author of *Narrative of a Residence in South Africa*, *Ephemerides*, &c.; born 1789, died 1834.

§ By a curious coincidence both these gentlemen were lame, and went on crutches, an infirmity to which ludicrous but most improper allusion is made in the Chaldee MS., where they are described as coming in "skipping on staves."

almost "doited" publication. Messrs. Cleghorn and Pringle had secured the co-operation of several clever writers—among others, Mr. R. P. Gillies and James Hogg—and Mr. Blackwood's sagacious eye at once discerned the elements of success in the project. The arrangements were accordingly proceeded with, on the footing that the publisher and the editors were to be joint proprietors, and share the profits, if any. The first number appeared in April, 1817, under the title of *The Edinburgh Monthly Magazine.* The contents were varied and agreeable, but no way remarkable; and a prefatory note to the next number, in which the editors spoke of "Our humble Miscellany," indicates a certain mediocrity of aim which must have been distasteful to the aspiring energy of the publisher, who had very different views of what the Magazine ought to be made. There was no definite arrangement for the payment of contributors. In fact it seems to have been taken for granted that contributions were to be supplied on the most moderate terms, if not altogether gratuitously. I find Mr. Blackwood stating in his subsequent vindication of himself, in reply to the charge of having supplied no money to the editors, that during the six months of their connection, he "had paid them different sums, amounting to £50." He adds, "They will tell you I never refused them any money they applied for. They may perhaps say the money was for contributors; but to this moment I am utterly ignorant of any contributors to whom they either have or were called upon to pay money, excepting some very trifling sums to two individuals."* Perhaps this fact may have something to do with the crisis that soon occurred in the management of the Magazine; at all events, it had not gone beyond two numbers, when editors and publisher found they could not work together. Mr. Pringle was a very amiable man, but his brother editor was a less agreeable person, and with an estimate of his own literary powers considerably higher than that entertained by his sagacious publisher. On the 19th of May the co-editors formally wrote to Mr. Blackwood, letting him know that his interference with their editorial functions could no longer be endured. Mr. Blackwood was probably nothing loath to receive such an intimation, and in the exercise of his rights

* This economical style of work contrasts curiously with the munificence subsequently practised in connection with the Magazine. A few years after this, I find Wilson informing a contributor, "Our pay is ten guineas a sheet," a rate since that time nearly doubled.

as partner and publisher, advertised in the June number of the Magazine that its publication would be discontinued at the end of three months from that date. The editors, thrown adrift by this *coup*, immediately offered their services to Messrs. Constable and Co., as editors of a new series of the *Scots Magazine*, to appear under the title of *The Edinburgh Magazine;* while Mr. Blackwood, after some contention and correspondence, agreed to pay his quondam partners £125 for their share in the copyright of the *Edinburgh Monthly Magazine.** In acquiring the copyright of the Magazine, Mr. Blackwood determined to abandon its old title, and give it a name combining the double advantage that it would not be confounded with any other, and would at the same time help to spread the reputation of the publisher.

Accordingly in October, 1817, appeared for the first time *Blackwood's Edinburgh Magazine* (No. VII. from commencement), and it needed no advertising trumpet to let the world know that a new reign (a reign of terror in its way) had begun. In the previous six numbers there had been nothing allowed to creep in that could possibly offend the most zealous partisan of the Blue and Yellow. On the contrary, the opening article of No. I. was a good-natured eulogium on Mr. Francis Horner; the *Edinburgh Review* was praised for its ability, moderation, and good taste; politics were rather eschewed than otherwise; the literary notices were, with one or two exceptions, elaborately commonplace and complaisant, and, in fact, every thing was exemplarily careful, correct, and colorless. No.VII. spoke a different language, and proclaimed a new and sterner creed. Among a considerable variety of papers, most of them able and interesting, it contained not less than three of a kind well calculated to arouse curiosity and excitement, and to give deep offence to sections more or less extensive of the reading public. The first was a most unwarrantable assault on Coleridge's *Biographia Literaria*, which was adjudged to be a "most execrable" performance, and its

* The sum they had demanded was £300, but according to the publisher's accounts, submitted to the law-agent of the editors, the success of the work had not been such as to justify that estimate. The accounts showed that so far from having made profit, the publisher was nearly £140 out of pocket, and that, "even if the whole impression were sold off, there would not be £70 clear profit." According to this estimate, which seems to have satisfied the agent (no other than the afterwards celebrated George Combe), the half share of the editors at the most would have been worth £35. What the number of copies printed was I have no means of knowing; it was, probably, not large, and the fact that the whole impression was not disposed of, gives some ground for the belief that the publisher had reason to be dissatisfied with the management.

author a miserable compound of "egotism and malignity."* The second was an even more unjustifiable attack on Leigh Hunt, who was spoken of as a "profligate creature," a person "without reverence either for God or man." The third was the famous "Chaldee Manuscript," compared with which the sins of the others were almost pardonable in the eyes of a great portion of the public. The effect of this article upon the small society of Edinburgh can now hardly be realized.†

It was evident, in a word, that a new and very formidable power had come into existence, and that those who wielded it, whoever they were, were not men to stick at trifles. The sensation produced by the first number, was kept up in those that followed. There was hardly a number for many months that did not contain at least one attack upon somebody, and the business was gone about with a systematic determination that showed there was an ample store of the same ammunition in reserve. Most people, however virtuous, have a kind of malicious pleasure in seeing others sacrificed, if the process be artistically gone about, and the *Blackwood* tomahawkers were undeniable adepts in the art. Even those who most condemned them, accordingly showed their appreciation of their performances by reading and talking of them, which was exactly the thing to increase their influence. It must not be imagined, however, that the staple of *Blackwood's* contributions consisted of mere banter and personality. These would have excited but slight and temporary notice, had the bulk of the articles not displayed a rare combination of much higher qualities. Whatever subjects were discussed, were handled with a masterly vigor and freshness, and developed a fulness of knowledge and variety of talent that could not fail to command respect even from the least approving critic. The publisher knew too well what suited the public taste, and had too much innate sense and fairness, to allow more than a reasonable

* It is edifying to find this article criticised thus in "Peter's Letters" two years afterwards:—"This is indeed the only one of all the various sins of the Magazine for which I am at a loss to discover not an apology but a motive. . . . The result is bad, and, in truth, very pitiable."

† It is unnecessary here to give any account of this singular *jeu d'esprit*, the history of which will be found sufficiently detailed in Professor Ferrier's excellent Preface to it, in vol. iv. of Wilson's *Works*. I may add this fact only, that it was composed in 53 Queen street, amid shouts of laughter, that made the ladies in the room above send to inquire, in wonder, what the gentlemen below were about. I am informed that among those who were met together on that memorable occasion was Sir William Hamilton, who also exercised his wit in writing a verse, and was so amused by his own performance that he tumbled off his chair in a fit of laughter.

modicum of abuse in the pages of his Magazine. But he had a difficult task in accommodating the inclinations of his fiery associates to the dictates of prudence and justice; appreciating highly, as he did, their remarkable talents, and unwilling to lose their services, it required great tact and firmness to restrain their sharp pens, and he more than once paid dearly, in solid cash, for their wanton and immoderate expressions.*

The public, whether pleased or angry, inquired with wonder where all this sudden talent had lain hid that now threatened to set the Forth on fire. Suspicions were rife; but Mr. Blackwood could keep a secret, and knew the power of mystery. Who his contributors were, who his editor, were matters on which neither he nor they chose to give more information than was necessary. It might suffice for the public to know, from the allegorical descriptions of the Chaldee MS., that there was a host of mighty creatures in the service of the "man in plain apparel," conspicuous among which were the "beautiful Leopard from the valley of the Palm trees," and "the Scorpion which delighteth to sting the faces of men." As for their leader, he was judiciously represented as a veiled person-

* The early defects of the Magazine are nowhere better analyzed than by the very hands that were chiefly engaged in the work. The authors of "Peter's Letters," after pointing out the faults of the *Edinburgh Review*, go on to say: "These faults—faults thus at last beginning to be seen by a considerable number of the old readers and admirers of the *Edinburgh Review*—seem to have been at the bottom of the aversion which the writers who established *Blackwood's Magazine* had against it; but their quarrel also included a very just disapprobation of the unpatriotic mode of considering the political events of the times adopted all along by the *Review*, and also of its occasional irreligious mockeries, borrowed from the French philosophy, or *soi-disant* philosophy of the last age. Their great object seems to have been to break up the monopoly of influence which had long been possessed by a set of persons guilty of perverting, in so many ways, talents on all hands acknowledged to be great. And had they gone about the execution of their design with as much candor and good feeling as would seem to have attended the conception of it, I have little doubt they would very soon have procured a mighty host of readers to go along with them in all their conclusions. But the persons who are supposed to have taken the lead in directing the new forces, wanted many of those qualities which were most necessary to insure success to their endeavors; and they possessed others which, although in themselves admirably fitted for enabling them to conduct their project successfully, tended, in the manner in which they made use of them, to throw many unnecessary obstacles in their way. In short, they were very young, or very inexperienced men, who, although passionately fond of literature, and even well skilled in many of its finest branches, were by no means accurately acquainted with the structure and practice of literature as it exists at this day in Britain. . . . They approached the lists of literary warfare with the spirit at bottom of true knights; but they had come from the woods and the cloisters, and not from the cities and haunts of active men, and they had armed themselves, in addition to their weapons of the right temper, with many other weapons of offence, which, although sanctioned in former times by the practice of the heroes in whose repositories they had found them rusting, had now become utterly exploded, and were regarded, and justly regarded, as entirely unjustifiable and disgraceful by all who surveyed with modern eyes the arena of their exertions."

Mr. Wilson, *alias* "The Leopard."

age, whose name it was in vain to ask, and whose personality was itself a mystery. On that point the public, which cannot rest satisfied without attributing specific powers to specific persons, refused after a time to acknowledge the mystery, and insisted on recognizing in John Wilson the real impersonation of Blackwood's "veiled editor." The error has been often emphatically corrected: let it once again be repeated, on the best authority, that the only real editor *Blackwood's Magazine* ever had was Blackwood himself. Of this fact I have abundant proofs. Suffice it that contributions from Wilson's own pen have been altered, cut down, and kept back, in compliance with the strong will of the man whose name on the title-page of the Magazine truly indicated with whom lay the sole responsibility of the management.

At what precise date my father came into personal communication with Mr. Blackwood does not appear. Before that, however, he had been an anonymous contributor to the Magazine. In the very first number is a poem entitled, "The Desolate Village, a Reverie," with the initial N., which bears strong marks of his style. Some others, similarly signed, and of similar qualities, occur in subsequent numbers. In the Notices to Correspondents in No. II., it is stated that the "Letter on the proposed new translation of the Psalms" was too late for insertion. That letter, which did not appear, is referred to in the following note, without date or signature, in my father's handwriting:—

"SIR:—I enclose a letter for your Magazine from the same anonymous writer who sent you a communication relative to a new translation of the Psalms. If these communications are inserted, and I feel some confidence that they are fitted for a work like the Edinburgh Magazine, I shall take care to send you some little trifle every month. But I prefer remaining anonymous at present, till I see how my communications are appreciated."

How the monthly trifles were appreciated by Mr. Blackwood's two editors, matters not; that they were appreciated by that gentleman himself soon became apparent. Probably enough, some of the anonymous correspondent's contributions gave rise to those differences of opinion between the publisher and the editors, which ended in their separation. One cannot but suspect that the writer of the paper referred to in the following "Notice to a Correspondent" was either the Leopard or the Scorpion:—"The paper on Craniology by Peter Candid would have appeared in our present number, if it had not contained some improper personal allusions." In the same number (III.), at all events, is a review of "The Craniad," a Poem, which may be given entire.* I have no doubt the cautious editors inserted it with great misgivings as to its containing "improper personal allusions;" very possibly the publisher inserted it without consulting them. It is one of the very few lively things in the *Edinburgh Monthly Magazine.*

In the new Magazine, relieved from the editorial incubus, and the embarrassments of a divided responsibility, the genius of Wilson found free scope. Like a strong athlete who never before had room or occasion to display his powers, he now revelled in their exercise in an arena where the competitors were abundant, and the onlookers eagerly interested. Month after month he poured forth the exuberant current of his ideas on politics, poetry, philosophy, religion, art, books, men, and nature, with a freshness and force that seemed incapable of exhaustion, and regardless of obstacles. It was in fact only a change in the form of his activity. In that new and more exciting field he doubtless dealt many a blow, of which, on calm reflection and in maturer years, he saw reason to repent. But without at all excusing the extravagance of censure and the violence of language which often disfigured these early contributions to the Magazine, I cannot say that I have been able to trace to his hand any instance of unmanly attack, or one shade of real malignity. There did appear in the Magazine wanton and unjustifiable strictures on persons such as Wordsworth and Coleridge, with whom he was on terms of friendship, and for whom, in its own pages and elsewhere, he professed, as he sincerely felt, the highest esteem. But when it is well understood that he was never in any sense the editor, and that in these early days of the Magazine the ruling principle seemed to be that every man fought for his own

* *The Craniad, or Spurzheim Illustrated.* A Poem in Two Parts. 12mo. Blackwood. Edinburgh, 1817. "The Craniad is the worst poem we have now in Scotland. The author has it in his power at once to decide the great craniological controversy. Let him submit his skull to general inspection, and if it exhibit a single intellectual organ, Spurzheim's theory is overthrown." The original of this characteristic bit of criticism occurs in a MS. book, described by Mr. Gillies as an "enormous ledger," which, he says, was taken possession of by my father, and filled with "skeletons" of proposed articles. Of these sketches, however, the much mutilated volume contains none, the existing contents being almost entirely poetry.

Mr. Lockhart, *alias* "The Scorpion."

hand, and was surrounded with a cloud of secrecy even from his fellows, it will appear that he had simply the alternative of ceasing to contribute further to the Magazine, or of continuing to do so under the disadvantage of seeming to approve what he really condemned.* That he adopted the latter course is, I think, no stigma on his character; and in after days, when his influence in the Magazine had become paramount, he made noble amends for its former sins.

The staff of contributors whom Mr. Blackwood had contrived to rally round his standard contained many distinguished men. "The Great Unknown," and the venerable "Man of Feeling," were enlisted on his side, and gave some occasional help. Dr. M'Crie, the biographer of Knox, and Dr. Andrew Thomson, were solemnly and at much length reproved by an orthodox pamphleteer, styling himself *Calvinus*, for their supposed association with the wicked authors of the Chaldee Manuscript. Sir David Brewster contributed scientific articles, as did also Robert Jameson and James Wilson. Among the other contributors, actual or presumed, were De Quincey, Hogg, Gillies, Fraser Tytler, Kirkpatrick Sharpe, Sir William Hamilton, and his brother,† the author of *Cyril Thornton.* But though all these and more figured in the list of Blackwood's supporters, there were but two on whom he placed his main reliance, the most prolific and versatile of all the band, who between them were capable at any time of providing the whole contents of a Number. These were John Wilson and John Gibson Lockhart. Those whose only knowledge of that pair of briefless young advocates was derived from seeing them pacing the Parliament House, or lounging carelessly into Blackwood's saloon to read the newspapers,‡ and pass their jokes on everybody, including themselves,

* Thus it is possible his desire to review Coleridge favorably in the *Edinburgh* may have arisen from a wish to do justice to that great man, the opportunity for which he was denied in the pages of *Blackwood.*

† Thomas Hamilton wrote several works besides *Cyril Thornton;* among others, *Annals of the Peninsular Campaign*, and *Men and Manners in America.* He died in 1842, at the age of fifty-three.

‡ That saloon and its proprietor are thus described by Dr. Peter Morris:—"Then you have an elegant oval saloon lighted from the roof, where various groups of loungers and literary *dilettanti* are engaged in looking at, or criticising among themselves, the publications just arrived by that day's coach from town. In such critical colloquies, the voice of the bookseller may ever and anon be heard mingling the broad and unadulterated notes of its Auld Reekie music; for unless occupied in the recesses of the premises with some other business, it is here that he has his usual station. He is a nimble, active-looking man of middle age, and moves about from one corner to

could have little idea of their power of work, or of the formidable manner in which it was being exercised. That blue-eyed and ruddy-cheeked poet, whose time seemed to hang lightly enough upon his hands, did not quite realize one's idea of the redoubtable critic whose "crutch" was to become so formidable a weapon. Nor did his jaunty-looking companion, whose leisure seemed to be wholly occupied in drawing caricatures,* appear a likely person, when he sauntered home from Princes street, to sit down to a translation from the German, or to dash off at a sitting "copy" enough to fill a sheet of *Blackwood's Magazine*. The striking contrast in the outward aspect of the two men corresponded truly to their difference of character and temperament—a difference, however, which proved no obstacle to their close intimacy. There was a picturesque contrast between them, which might be simply defined by light and shade; but there was a more striking dissimilarity than that which is merely the result of coloring. Mr. Lockhart's pale olive complexion had something of a Spanish character in it, that accorded well with the sombre or rather melancholy expression of his countenance; his thin lips, compressed beneath a smile of habitual sarcasm, promised no genial response to the warmer emotions of the heart. His compact, finely-formed head indicated an acute and refined intellect. Cold, haughty, supercilious in manner, he seldom won love, and not unfrequently caused his friends to distrust it in him, for they sometimes found the warmth of their own feelings thrown back upon them in presence of this cold indifference. Circumstances afterwards conferred on him a brilliant position, and he gave way to the weakness which seeks prestige from the reflected glory found in rank. The gay coteries of London society injured his interest in the old friends who had worked hand in hand with him when in Edinburgh. He was well depicted by his friend through the mouth of the Shepherd, as "the Oxford collegian, wi' a pale face and a black toozy head, but an e'e like an eagle's;

another with great alacrity, and apparently under the influence of high animal spirits. His complexion is very sanguineous, but nothing can be more intelligent, keen, and sagacious than the expression of his whole physiognomy; above all, the gray eyes and eyebrows, as full of locomotion as those of Catalani."—*Peter's Letters*, vol. ii., pp. 187, 188.

* It is said, with what truth I know not, that clever as Mr. Lockhart was with both pen and pencil, he lacked curiously one gift without which no man can be a successful barrister; he could not, like many other able writers, make a speech. His portfolios show that, instead of taking notes during a trial, his pen must have been busily employed in photographing all the parties engaged, judge, counsel, and prisoner. I avail myself of this opportunity to insert here two specimens of his wonderful power, one taken from the Bench, and another from the Pulpit.

A SCOTCH MINISTER.

"When last in Scotland I was advised to look about among the pulpits, to try whether any living specimen could be found resembling the ancient Scottish worthies. I did so, but was not successful."—*Dr. Ulrick Sternstare on the Natural Character of the Scots.—Blackwood*, vol. iv., p. 329.

and a sort o' lauch about the screwed-up mouth o' him that fules ca'ed no canny, for they couldna' thole the meaning o't." I am fortunate enough to be able to give the capital likeness on page 185, drawn by his own hand, in which the satirist who spared no one, has most assuredly not been flattering to himself.

Wilson's appearance in those days is thus described in *Peter's Letters* by Mr. Lockhart:—"In complexion he is the best specimen I have ever seen of the genuine or ideal *Goth.* His hair is of the true Sicambrian yellow; his eyes are of the brightest, and at the same time of the clearest blue, and the blood glows in his cheek with as firm a fervor as it did, according to the description of Jornandes, in those of the 'Bello gaudentes, prælio ridentes Teutones' of Attila." The black-haired Spanish-looking Oxonian, with that uncanny laugh of his, was a very dangerous person to encounter in the field of letters. "I've sometimes thocht, Mr. North," says the Shepherd, "that ye were a wee feared for him yoursel', and used rather, without kennin 't, to draw in your horns." Systematic, cool, and circumspect, when he armed himself for conflict it was with a fell and deadly determination. The other rushed into combat rejoicingly, like the Teutons; but even in his fiercest mood, he was alive to pity, tenderness, and humor. When he impaled a victim, he did it, as Walton recommends, not vindictively, but as if he loved him. Lockhart, on the other hand, though susceptible of deep emotions, and gifted with a most playful wit, had no scruple in wounding to the very quick, and no thrill of compassion ever held back his hand when he had made up his mind to strike. He was certainly no coward, but he liked to fight under cover, and keep himself unseen, while Wilson, even under the shield of anonymity, was rather prone to exhibit his own unmistakable personality.

Such were the two principal contributors to *Blackwood* when it broke upon the startled gaze of Edinburgh Whigdom, like a fiery comet "that with fear of change perplexes monarchs." Not without reason did the adherents of the "Blue and Yellow" wish ill to the formidable new-comer, for, apart from its undeniable offences against good feeling and taste, there was a power and life about the Magazine that betokened ominously for the hitherto unchallenged supremacy of the great Review. In spite of its errors, the substantial merits of the Magazine securely established its popularity, and in the course of a few years it became recognized throughout Britain as the most able and interesting periodical work that had ever been published.

In noticing the early contributors, it would not do to pass over Mr. Robert Sym, whose pseudonym of "Timothy Tickler" became as familiar to its readers as that of Christopher North himself. That "noble and genuine old Tory," as the Shepherd calls him, was Wilson's uncle, and in his hospitable house in George Square, *alias* "Southside," the contributors to the Magazine had many a merry gathering. He was a fine-looking, elderly gentleman, of uncommon height and aristocratic bearing, his white hair contrasting strikingly with the youthful freshness of his complexion. "Tickler," says the Shepherd, "is completely an original, as any one may see who has attended to his remarks; for there is no sophistry there; they are every one his own. Nay, I don't believe that North has, would, or durst put a single sentence into his mouth that had not proceeded out of it. No, no; although I was a scapegoat, no one, and far less a nephew, might do so with Timothy Tickler.* His reading, both ancient and modern, is boundless; his taste and perception acute beyond those of other men; his satire keen and biting; but at the same time his good-humor is altogether inexhaustible, save when ignited by coming in collision with Whig or Radical principles. At a certain period of the night our entertainer knew by the longing looks which I cast to a beloved corner of the dining-room what I was wanting; then with 'Oh, I beg your pardon, Hogg, I was forgetting,' he would take out a small gold key, that hung by a chain of the same precious metal to a particular button-hole, and stalk away, as tall as life, open two splendid fiddle-cases, and produce their contents, first the one and then the other, but always keeping the best to himself. I'll never forget with what elated dignity he stood straight up in the middle of that floor and rosined his bow: there was a twist of the lip and an upward beam of the eye that was truly sublime; then down we sat side by side and began. . . . . . At the end of every tune we took a glass, and still our enthusiastic admiration of the Scottish tunes increased, our energies of execution were redoubled, till ultimately it became, not only a complete and well-contested race, but a trial of strength to deter-

* But all the papers in *Blackwood*, signed "Timothy Tickler," were not written by Mr. Sym, Mr. Hogg notwithstanding.

A SCOTCH JUDGE.

mine which should drown the other. The only feelings short of ecstasy that came across us in these enraptured moments were caused by hearing the laugh and joke going on with our friends, as if no such thrilling strains had been flowing. But if Sym's eye chanced to fall on them, it instantly retreated upwards again in mild indignation."*

The Shepherd himself was not the least remarkable among that set of remarkable men. In spite of qualities that made it impossible perfectly to respect him, his original genius and good-natured simplicity made him a favorite with them all, until his vanity had become quite unendurable. He plumed himself immensely on being the real originator of the Magazine, and of the Chaldee MS. He was a very frequent contributor, but, in addition to his own genuine compositions, he got the credit of numberless performances, both in prose and verse, which he had never beheld till they appeared under his name in the pages of the Magazine. This was a part of that system of mystification practised in the management, which has never been carried so far in any other publication, and undoubtedly contributed very greatly to its success. The illustrious example of Sir Walter Scott had given encouragement to this species of deception, and the editor and writers of *Blackwood* thought themselves quite at liberty, not only to perplex the public by affixing all sorts of fictitious names and addresses to their com-

* The following epitaph on Tickler, from the *Noctes*, is worthy of extraction:—

" Pray for the soul
Of Timothy Tickler;
For the Church and the bowl
A determined stickler.

" Born and bred in the land
Where Fyne herrings they munch,
And a capital hand
At concocting of punch.

" From that great bumper school
To Auld Reekie he came,
And drew in a stool
To his desk in the same.

" But, though W. S.,
And ambitious to thrive,
Even his foes must confess
Cheated no man alive.

" Neither harried poor gentry
Of house or of land,
Nor bolted the country
With cash in his hand.

" Where tall as a steeple,
And thin as a shadow,
He towered o'er the people
In the Links or the Meadow.

(*Chorus.*)—With a pipe in his cheek
And a goblet before him,
Every night of the week
In sæcula sæculorum."

Mr. Sym was born in 1750 and died in 1844.

munications,* but to put forth their *jeux d'esprit* occasionally under cover of the names of real personages who had never dreamed of so distinguishing themselves. This was certainly carrying the system to a most unwarrantable length; but it must be allowed that in the case of the two individuals most played upon in this respect, the liberty was taken by no means amiss. "The Shepherd" was one of these, and he rather enjoyed the fame which was thus thrust upon him in addition to his own proper deserts.† He gives a most amusing account of his sufferings at the hands of Lockhart, whom he describes as "a mischievous Oxford puppy, dancing after the young ladies, and drawing caricatures of every one who came in contact with him." "I dreaded his eye terribly," he says, "and it was not without reason, for he was very fond of playing tricks on me, but always in such a way that it was impossible to lose temper with him. I never parted company with him that my judgment was not entirely jumbled with regard to characters, books, and literary articles of every description."‡ Lockhart continued to keep his mind in the utmost perplexity for years in all things that related to the Magazine. The Shepherd was naturally anxious to know whose the tremendous articles were that made so much sensation monthly, and having found by experience that he could extract no information out of Sym or Wilson, he would repair to Lockhart to ask him, awaiting his reply with fixed eye and a beating heart: "Then, with his cigar in his mouth, his one leg flung carelessly over the other, and without the symptom of a smile on his face, or one twinkle of mischief in his dark gray eye, he would father the articles on his brother, Captain Lockhart, or Peter Robertson, or Sheriff

* In the early numbers of the Magazine one meets a perfect host of these mythical personages, and the impression conveyed to the credulous reader must have been that contributions were flowing in from remarkable persons in all quarters of the empire. There was really so much variety and individuality imparted to these imaginary characters that it was very difficult to perceive that the same writer was assuming the guises of William Wastle, Esq., and Dr. Ulrick Sternstare, and Philip Kempferhausen, and the Baron Lauerwinkel.

† His expressions of opinion on the subject varied according to his mood, but his sober judgment of the matter is on record in his own words:—"My friends in general have been of opinion that he (Wilson) has amused himself and the public too often at my expense; but, except in one instance, which terminated very ill for me, and in which I had no more concern than the man in the moon, I never discovered any evil design on his part, and thought it all excellent sport. At the same time, I must acknowledge that it was using too much freedom with any author to print his name in full to poems, letters, and essays which he himself never saw. I do not say he has done this, but either he or some one else has done it many a time." This was written in 1832. Of Wilson's own kind feeling to Hogg, see letter of 1833.

‡ Hogg's *Memoirs*.

Cay, or James Wilson, or that queer, fat 'body,' Dr. Scott, and sometimes on James and John Ballantyne, and Sam Anderson, and poor Baxter. Then away I flew with the wonderful news to my other associates, and if any remained incredulous, I swore the facts down through them; so that before I left Edinburgh I was accounted the greatest liar that was in it except one."* The simple Shepherd by and by found out that these conspirators had made up their minds to act on O'Doherty's principle, of never denying any thing they had *not* written, or ever acknowledging any thing they *had*. He accordingly thought himself safe in thenceforth signing his name to every thing he published. "But as soon," he says, "as the rascals perceived this, they signed my name as fast as I did. They then continued the incomparable *Noctes Ambrosianæ* for the sole purpose of putting all the sentiments into the Shepherd's mouth which they durst not avowedly say themselves, and these, too, often applying to my best friends."†

A single instance will show to what lengths this system of deception, for it can be called nothing else, was carried. In the articles on Leigh Hunt, already mentioned, he was accused, among other things, of having pestered his friend Hazlitt to review him in the *Edinburgh*. Soon after—I find from Leigh Hunt's "Correspondence," recently published—he wrote to Lord Jeffrey the letter given below.‡ Which of the writers in *Blackwood* perpetrated this very wicked joke I know not, but its point lay in the fact that Sir J. G. Dalyell, with whose name so great a liberty had been taken, was perhaps of all men then in Edinburgh the one who, as a good Whig, regarded *Blackwood's Magazine* with most abhorrence. A cor-

* Hogg's *Memoirs*.

† *Ibid.*

‡ "DEAR SIR:—I trouble you with this, to say, that since my last I have been made acquainted with the atrocious nonsense written about me in *Blackwood's Magazine*, and that nothing can be falser than what is said respecting my having asked and pestered Mr. Hazlitt to write an article upon my poem in the *Edinburgh Review*. I never breathed a syllable to him on the subject, as anybody who knows me would say for me at once, for I am reckoned, if any thing, somewhat over fastidious and fantastic on such matters. I received last night a letter, signed John Erchom (Graham?) Dalyell, advocate, the author of which tells me at last that he is the writer of the article, and that he did not mean to attack my private character! He only attacked the bad principles I evinced in my writings. You may conceive by this that this letter is a strange mixture of affected airs and real paltering. I have written this evening to Edinburgh, according to the signature, to ask whether Mr. Dalyell (if there is such a person) avows himself the author of the letter. But I am taking up your time with these matters. I merely wished, in the first instance, to state what I have mentioned above.

"Believe me, my dear sir, most sincerely yours,

"13 LISSON GROVE, 1817." "LEIGH HUNT.

respondent informs me that he recollects well Sir John coming to him in a state of violent agitation, to show the letter he had just received from Leigh Hunt, enclosing the pretended confession of authorship by himself. "Oh, the villany of these fellows!" exclaimed the persecuted Baronet.* It was in truth a most unscrupulous trick.

But the most elaborate and successful of these mystifications, of all which I suspect the invention must be attributed to Lockhart, was that about Dr. Scott, of Glasgow, or "the Odontist," as he dubbed him. I am not aware, indeed, of any other instance of this kind of joke being carried out so steadily and with such entire success. The doctor was a dentist, who practised both in Edinburgh and Glasgow, but resided chiefly in the latter city,—a fat, bald, queer-looking, and jolly little man, fond of jokes and conviviality, but with no more pretensions to literary or poetic skill than a *street porter*. To his own and his friends' astonishment he was introduced in *Blackwood's Magazine* as one of its most valued contributors, and as the author of a variety of clever verses. There was no mistake about it, "Dr. James Scott, 7 Miller street, Glasgow," was a name and address as well known as that of Mr. Blackwood himself. The ingenious author had contrived to introduce so many of the Doctor's peculiar phrases, and references to his Saltmarket acquaintances, that the Doctor himself gradually began to believe that the verses were really his own, and when called on to sing one of his songs in company, he assumed the airs of authorship with perfect complacency. The "Odontist" became recognized as one of Blackwood's leading characters, and so far was the joke carried, that a volume of his compositions was gravely advertised in a list of new works, prefixed to the Magazine, as "in the press."† Even

* He had been held up to ridicule, under a most horrible disguise, in the "Chaldee MS.," for which, however, he had the satisfaction of receiving damages in an action brought against the publisher.

† Had the volume ever appeared, it would have proved a very unique collection. One of the songs attributed to him became so popular, and is really so admirable in its kind, as to be worth reproducing here as a specimen of these curious lyrics. There is no doubt that Mr. Lockhart was the author.

"CAPTAIN PATON'S LAMENT.

"Touch once more a sober measure, and let punch and tears be shed,
For a prince of good old fellows, that, alack-a-day, is dead!
For a prince of worthy fellows, and a pretty man also,
That has left the Saltmarket in sorrow, grief, and woe.
Oh, we ne'er shall see the like of Captain Paton no mo!

the acute publisher, John Ballantyne, Hogg relates, was so convinced of the Odontist's genius, that he expressed a great desire to be introduced to so remarkable a man, and wished to have the honor of being his publisher. The Doctor's fame went far beyond Edinburgh. Happening to pay a visit to Liverpool, he was immediately

"His waistcoat, coat, and breeches were all cut off the same web,
Of a beautiful snuff-color, or a modest genty drab;
The blue stripe in his stocking round his neat slim leg did go,
And his ruffles of the cambric fine they were whiter than the snow.
Oh, we ne'er shall see the like of Captain Paton no mo!

"His hair was curled in order, at the rising of the sun,
In comely rows and buckles smart that about his ears did run;
And before there was a toupée that some inches up did grow,
And behind there was a long queue that did o'er his shoulders flow.
Oh, we ne'er shall see the like of Captain Paton no mo!

"And whenever we forgathered, he took off his wee three-cockit,
And he proffered you his snuff-box, which he drew from his side-pocket;
And on Burdett or Buonaparte he would make a remark or so,
And then along the plainstones like a provost he would go.
Oh, we ne'er shall see the like of Captain Paton no mo!

"Now and then upon a Sunday he invited me to dine,
On a herring and a mutton-chop, which his maid dressed very fine;
There was also a little Malmsey, and a bottle of Bordeaux,
Which between me and the Captain passed nimbly to and fro.
Oh, I ne'er shall take pot-luck with Captain Paton no mo!

"Or if a bowl was mentioned, the Captain he would ring,
And bid Nelly run to the Westport, and a stoup of water bring;
Then would he mix the genuine stuff, as they made it long ago,
With limes that on his property in Trinidad did grow.
Oh, we ne'er shall taste the like of Captain Paton's punch no mo!

"And then all the time he would discourse so sensible and courteous,
Perhaps talking of last sermon he had heard from Dr. Porteous,
Or some little bit of scandal about Mrs. So and So,
Which he scarce could credit, having heard the *con*, but not the *pro*.
Oh, we ne'er shall hear the like of Captain Paton no mo!

"Or when the candles were brought forth, and the night was fairly setting in,
He would tell some fine old stories about Minden-field or Dettingen;
How he fought with a French major, and dispatched him at a blow,
While his blood ran out like water on the soft grass below.
Oh, we ne'er shall hear the like of Captain Paton no mo!

"But at last the Captain sickened, and grew worse from day to day,
And all missed him in the coffee-room, from which he now stayed away;
On Sabbath, too, the Wee Kirk made a melancholy show,
All for wanting of the presence of our venerable beau.
Oh, we ne'er shall see the like of Captain Paton no mo!

"And in spite of all that Cleghorn and Corkindale could do,
It was plain, from twenty symptoms, that death was in his view;
So the Captain made his testament, and submitted to his foe,
And we laid him by the Ram's-horn kirk; 'tis the way we all must go.
Oh, we ne'er shall see the like of Captain Paton no mo!

welcomed by the literary society of the town as the "glorious Odontist" of *Blackwood's Magazine*, and received a complimentary dinner, which he accepted in entire good faith, replying to the toast of the evening with all the formality that became the occasion.

But the spirit of fun and mischief that prompted these outrageous jokes did not confine itself to practising them on the outer world. The overflowing satire of the inventors was turned by them even upon one another. In a very clever but rather tedious composition of Lockhart's, called the "Mad Banker of Amsterdam," he pokes his fun at his friends all round. There was a society in Edinburgh called the "Dilettanti" club, of which Wilson was President. They came in for a sketch, and he begins with his friend the President:—

"They're pleased to call themselves *The Dilettanti*,
  The President's the first I chanced to show 'em;
He writes more malagrugrously than Dante,
  The City of the Plague 's a shocking poem;
But yet he is a spirit light and jaunty,
  And jocular enough to those who know him;
To tell the truth, I think John Wilson shines
More o'er a bowl of punch than in his lines."

It is said that my father chanced to see the proof-sheet by accident before it went to press, and instantly dashed in immediately after the above stanza, not a little to the chagrin of the author, the following impromptu lines:—

"Then touched I off friend Lockhart (Gibson John),
  So fond of jabbering about Tieck and Schlegel,
Klopstock and Wieland, Kant and Mendelssohn,
  All high Dutch quacks like Spurzheim or Feinagle;
Him the Chaldee yclept the Scorpion;
  The claws but not the pinions of the eagle
Are Jack's; but though I do not mean to flatter,
Undoubtedly he has strong powers of satire."

The troubles in which the publisher and supporters of the Magazine became involved commenced, as has been seen, with its very first number under the new *régime*. The assaults on Coleridge

"Join all in chorus, jolly boys, and let punch and tears be shed,
For this prince of good old fellows that, alack-a-day, is dead!
For this prince of worthy fellows, and a pretty man also,
That has left the Saltmarket in sorrow, grief, and woe!
  For it ne'er shall see the like of Captain Paton no mo!"

For a complete copy of this lyric see *Blackwood*, vol v., p. 735.

Mr. Gibson Lockhart, *alias* Baron Lauerwinkel, *alias* William Wastle, *alias* Dr. Ulrick Sternstare, *alias* Dr. Peter Morris, etc., as sketched by himself.

and Hunt might have been overlooked by the Edinburgh public; but the Chaldee MS., though in reality a joke in comparison, raised a storm of solemn indignation, which it required all the courage and energy of the publisher to bear up against. In a second edition of the Magazine, which was very rapidly called for, the obnoxious article was withdrawn,* doubtless much to the disappointment of purchasers. For in fact the outcry, which at first seemed to threaten the extinction of the Magazine, was the best possible stimulant to its success. It throve on opposition, and waxed more bold and provoking as the enemy showed more sensitive appreciation of its power. But for some time the publisher's position was no enviable one, as may be gathered from the second of two following letters from Mrs. Wilson to her sister in England:—

"EDINBURGH, *December* 18, 1817.

"I hope you got your last number of the Magazine; I have been so busy *working* that I have not had time to look at it. The first thing in it, on the 'Pulpit Eloquence of Scotland,' is written by Mr. Lockhart, a young advocate, a friend of Mr. Wilson's. I believe there is not much of Mr. W.'s in the last number. I think there is something about the Lament of Tasso; that is his. You were right in your conjecture about Mr. Hogg's production; his prose compositions are not in the happiest style; there will be another of his in the next number,—a letter addressed to C. K. Sharpe, Esq. Another article in it, entitled, 'On the late National Calamity,' is Mr. W.'s; and the one on Mr. Alison's pulpit eloquence is written by a son of his. A review of Mandeville is by Mr. Lockhart. There is something besides of Mr. W.'s; but I don't exactly know what it is. I think it is about Old Masters."

"*May* 20, 1818.

"The number that comes out to-day is pronounced a very good one, and I suppose you will soon have it. The articles written by Mr. W. are those 'On Truth,' the 'Fudge Family in Paris,' Childe Harold, canto 4th, and Horace Walpole's Letters. The letter to

* The following note was prefixed to the November number:—"The editor has learned with regret that an article in the first edition of No. VII., which was intended as a *jeu-d'esprit*, has been construed so as to give offence to individuals justly entitled to respect and regard; he has, on that account, withdrawn it in the second edition, and can only add that, if what has happened could have been anticipated, the article in question certainly never would have appeared."

Dr. Chalmers is by Mr. Lockhart. I am not quite sure if Mr. W. will have any thing in the next *Edinburgh Review*, but I hope he will, and I will tell you what it is when I know.

"You asked if Ensign O'Doherty was a fictitious character; he is, and was created by a Mr. Hamilton, a particularly handsome and gentlemanly young man in the army; he is a brother of Sir William Hamilton, a friend of Mr. Wilson's, whom you may have heard me mention. The city of late has been in a state of pleasing commotion owing to a *fracas* which took place last week between Blackwood and a Mr. Douglas from Glasgow, a disgusting, vulgar, conceited writer, whose name was mentioned in one of Nicol Jarvie's letters* in the Magazine, which gave the gentleman such high offence, that after mature deliberation he determined on coming to Edinburgh, and horsewhipping Mr. Blackwood. Accordingly, about a week since he arrived; and one day as the worthy bookseller was entering his shop, Mr. D. followed him, and laid his whip across his shoulder; and before Mr. B. had time to recover from his surprise, Mr. D. walked off without leaving his address. Mr. B. immediately went out and bought a stick; and, accompanied by Mr. Hogg, went in search of Mr. D., whom at last they detected just about to step into a coach on his return to Glasgow. Mr. B. immediately attacked him, and beat him as hard as he could, and then permitted him to take his place in the coach, and proceed home, which he did. I have given you a long story, which I fear you cannot feel the least interest in; but as you take the Magazine, you will not be wholly indifferent to the fate of the publisher, whose conduct on the late occasion is thought perfectly correct; the other man everybody thinks has acted like a fool."

Nothing was left undone to spread the fame and fear of Blackwood. Formidable announcements of forthcoming criticisms were monthly advertised, to keep expectation on the stretch. The very titles of the serial articles indicated uncommon fertility of invention, and a terrible faculty for calling names. There were articles on "The Cockney School of Poetry," on "The Pluckless School of Politics," on "The Gormandizing School of Eloquence." There were letters to literary characters by Timothy Tickler, by Frederick Baron von Lauerwinkel, by Dr. Olinthus Petre, T. C. D., by

* *Blackwood*, January and March, 1818.

Ensign O'Doherty, by Mordecai Mullion, and a host of others too numerous to mention. The variety and mystification thus produced undoubtedly gave great additional zest to the writing; and this apparently multitudinous host of contributors danced about the victims of their satire with a vivacity and gleefulness which the public could not but relish even when it condemned. After all, and giving their full weight to the censures which were justly incurred by many of these compositions, there is much truth in the following remarks, in a vindication of itself prefixed to the Magazine a few years after:—"For a series of years, the Whigs in Scotland had all the jokes to themselves; they laughed and lashed as they liked; and while all this was the case, did anybody ever hear them say that either laughing or lashing were among the seven deadly sins? People said at times, no doubt, that Mr. Jeffrey was a more gentlemanly Whig than Mr. Brougham; that Sydney Smith grinned more good-humoredly than Sir James Mackintosh, and so forth, but all these were satirists, and, strange to say, they all rejoiced in the name." While I cannot agree with the statement following these remarks, that the only real offence of Blackwood's contributors was their being Tories, there is no doubt, I think, that that circumstance greatly aggravated their sins in the eyes of their opponents.*

The faults in question were, however, in themselves sufficiently grave, and may now be referred to, it is hoped, without risk of rekindling the old embers. The worst of them undoubtedly, for which even "Dr. Peter Morris" could afterwards see no apology, was the attack on the venerable Playfair, which appeared in 1818, in the September number of the Magazine, under the guise of a "Letter to the Rev. Professor Laugner, occasioned by his writing in the Königsberg Review: by the Baron von Lauerwinkel."† In

* Insolence and personality have very seldom been altogether wanting in the vigorous youth of journalism, and some of the ablest periodicals that have ever appeared have incurred the most censure in this respect. The *Edinburgh Review* cannot by impartial judges be pronounced to have been immaculate. The *Quarterly* is open to the same remark; and *Fraser's Magazine*, that most philosophic and well-conducted periodical, for some time seemed bent on out-doing the early style of Blackwood, after its older sister had subsided into propriety and self-restraint.

† This mischievous composition professed to be a translation from a German periodical (a literary stratagem, by the way, which probably set the example which Mr. Carlyle, among others, has turned to such frequent and effective purpose), and was thus introduced:—"The Königsberg Review, conducted by the late ingenious M. Mundwerk, was a few years ago very much admired in Germany by numerous readers, who took delight in seeing infidel and unpatriotic opinions maintained by men of acknowledged wit and talent. Strange as the circumstance may appear,

a previous letter under the signature of "Idoloclastes," a strong remonstrance had been addressed to Dr. Chalmers on his support of the *Edinburgh Review*, in which, with great professions of respect and admiration both for Chalmers and Jeffrey, there was mingled a most offensive strain of rebuke on the subject of infidel principles, which were alleged to be characteristic of the Review. In the pretended letter to Professor Laugner, these charges were repeated with still greater violence of language, and combined with the same professions of regret and esteem. The excellent Professor of Natural Philosophy was broadly accused of having turned his back on the faith which he once preached,* and allied himself with a band of unprincipled wits and insidious infidels. The author of both these letters was Mr. Lockhart, and they are striking specimens of that unpleasant power which led his own familiar friends to attribute to him, in their allegorical description, the character of the *Scorpion.* For calm, concentrated sting it would be hard to find six pages to match the Letter of the Baron Lauerwinkel.† The very natural indignation excited by this attack on one of the most amiable and eminent men of whom Edinburgh could then boast, attained its climax in the publication of a pamphlet, called *Hypocrisy unveiled and Calumny detected, in a Review of Blackwood's Magazine.* The author wielded a powerful pen, and fixing on Wilson and Lockhart as the special objects of his criticism, accused them both in very unvarnished terms of conduct disgraceful to men of letters and gentlemen. His own style, indeed, was not the most choice, his elaborate periods being thickly strewed with all the harshest epithets to be found in the dictionary.

it is nevertheless true that this journal numbered among its supporters several clergymen of the Lutheran Church. One of these was the late celebrated preacher, Hammerschlag (Dr. Chalmers was here pointed at), another was Professor Laugner of the University of Königsberg. The indignation of the zealous and worthy Baron von Lauerwinkel was excited," &c.

* Professor Playfair was parish minister of Liff and Bervie from 1773 to 1782. He became assistant to Professor Ferguson in 1785, and in 1805 resigned the chair of Mathematics for that of Natural Philosophy, which he occupied till his death, in 1819.

† Much as these letters were to be condemned, however, it is but fair to observe that the example had been shown on the other side. A voluminous and vehement writer, *Calvinus*, already referred to, had inflicted not less than five pamphlets on the public, addressed to Dr. M'Crie and Dr. Andrew Thomson on their sinful alliance with *Blackwood's Magazine.* In thundering sentences, garnished with plentiful texts of Scripture, he calls upon them to "remember the fate of that priest who associated himself with the infidel compilers of the *Encyclopédie*," and hopes that no priest in this country is willing to let it be supposed that he receives wages from a till that is replenished by the dissemination of blasphemy. Similar remonstrances and insinuations were very frequently levelled against Dr. Brewster; and there can be no doubt that such attacks were calculated to provoke retaliation.

But much of his censure went home to the mark, and he pledged himself, in conclusion, if the subjects of his criticism did not amend their ways, to return to the charge "with less reserve, and more personal effect."* Who the author of this philippic was remained a secret, but there is now no reason to doubt that he was himself a well-known member of the legal body. His allusions to Wilson and Lockhart were too pointed to be passed without notice, and both sought redress in the mode then considered necessary for the vindication of the character of gentlemen. The author of the pamphlet received these communications as might have been expected, he declined to reveal his identity, but printed the correspondence.†

* In furtherance of this purpose he announced as preparing for publication "A Letter to the Dean and Faculty of Advocates on the propriety of expelling the Leopard and the Scorpion from that hitherto respectable body."

† From the *Scotsman*, Saturday, October 24, 1818:

"*To the Author of Hypocrisy Unveiled.*

"SIR:—As it is no part of a manly disposition to use insulting epithets to an unknown enemy, who may perhaps have resolved to remain unknown, I shall not, at present, bestow any upon you. So long as you remain concealed you are a nonentity; and any insults offered by me to a person in that situation might probably not be felt to carry with them any degradation to him, and certainly would not be felt as conferring any triumph upon me. It is probable, however, that you will come forward from your concealment, when you feel that you cannot continue in it without the consciousness of cowardice. I therefore request your name and address, that I may send a friend to you to deliver my opinion of your character, and to settle time and place for a meeting, at which I may exact satisfaction from you for the public insults you have offered to me.

"53 QUEEN STREET, *Friday, Oct.* 23, 1818." "JOHN WILSON.

"*To the Author of Hypocrisy Unveiled.*

"SIR:—I have no wish to apply epithets of insult to you till I know who you are. If you suppose yourself to have any claim to the character of a gentleman, you will take care that I be not long without this knowledge. I remain, sir, your obedient servant,

"23 MAITLAND STREET, *Thursday, Oct.* 22, 1818." "J. G. LOCKHART.

"*To John Wilson, Esq., Advocate.*

"*Friday*, 23*d October*.

"SIR:—The note which I understand to have been forwarded to you by my publisher, will have explained why I did not receive your communication till within these few hours.

"If you *be not* a principal conductor or supporter of *Blackwood's Magazine*, you have no reason for addressing me. If you be not the author or furnisher of materials for an attack on Mr. M'Cormick, which you yourself stated to *be highly unjustifiable*, and of which you denied all knowledge *upon your honor;* if you be not the author of a most abusive attack on your friend, Mr. Wordsworth; if you did not, by an unfounded story, prevail with Mr. Blackwood's former editors to insert that attack; if you be not the secret traducer of Mr. Playfair, Mr. Hazlitt, and Mr. Coleridge; if you be not the wanton and cruel reviler of those gentlemen named in my pamphlet, with whom you had lived in habits of friendship; if you be not one of the principal vomitories of that calumnious and malignant abuse which has, through the medium of *Blackwood's Magazine*, been poured out on all that is elevated, worthy, or estimable; if you be not the writer of one or other of the letters addressed in the name of Z. to Mr. Leigh Hunt, and if you do not take shelter under a quotation from Junius, and submit to be publicly stigmatized by him as a coward and a scoundrel,—then you have nothing to say to me, for I speak only of the writer or writers who have committed these enormities. But if all or any of these things apply

When Mr. Lockhart found that the author would not reveal himself, he appears to have concerned himself no more about the matter, but to have relieved his feelings by caricaturing all the parties concerned in his friend's literary "*Ledger*." "The Leopard" and "The Scorpion," as drawn in the "*Ledger*," will be found on pages 165, 169.

The following admirable letter, addressed at this time to my father, by his friend the Rev. Robert Morehead,* seems, in spite of its length, to be worthy of insertion here. I have no doubt it produced a considerable impression on his mind, though at the time his indignation at the charges of the pamphleteer made him rather impatient of remonstrance:—

to you, in that case you have lost every claim to the character of a gentleman, and have no right whatsoever to demand that satisfaction which is due only to one who has been unjustly accused.

"The cause, besides, in which I have engaged is a public one; it is that of right feeling against all that is vile, treacherous, and malignant. My vocation is not ended; I have pledged myself to the public to watch your proceedings, and, if occasion shall require, to give a more ample exposition of your conduct and character—to inflict a more signal chastisement on your crimes. This pledge *shall be redeemed*.

"Do not think that I shall be deterred, by any threat, from discharging the duty I have thus imposed on myself, or that I shall be so weak as, by a premature avowal of my name, to deprive myself of the means.

"Prove to the satisfaction of the public that the charges which I have made are unfounded, or that they do not apply to you; or, as you yourself ask of Mr. Hunt:—'Confess that you have done wrong,—make a clean breast of it,—beg pardon of your God and of your country for the iniquity of your polluted pen,—and the last to add one pang to the secret throbbings of a contrite spirit,' the first to meet your challenge, if then renewed, shall be, sir, your, etc.,

"THE AUTHOR OF 'HYPOCRISY UNVEILED.'

"*P. S.*—As Mr. Lockhart obviously acts in concert with yourself, I have made the same answer to him which I now make to you."

* This estimable man was for many years an Episcopalian clergyman in Edinburgh. He was presented to the rectory of Easington, Yorkshire, in 1832, and died there in December, 1842.

Mr. Morehead, as may be gathered from the above letter, was a dear friend of my father's, but shortly after this date he became editor of *Constable's Magazine*; and it is to be regretted that, "in that lamentable madness of the time which drove high-minded and honorable men from their propriety," my father, by the unscrupulous liberty of his pen in *Blackwood's Magazine*, gave offence to Mr. Morehead, who, justly displeased, wrote an indignant letter to him, begging that personal allusions should cease as far as he was concerned, and promising that, on his part, he should abstain from any allusion to the Professor in his Magazine. I am happy to be able to say the terms of peace were observed, as their friendship remained unbroken. A notice of Mr. Morehead is made a dozen years later in a *Noctes*, which exhibits my father's real estimate of the author of *Dialogues on Natural and Revealed Religion*.

"*Shepherd.*—I love that man."

"*North.*—So do I, James, and so do all that know him personally—his talents, his genius, and, better than both, his truly Christian character, mild and pure."

"*Shepherd.*—And also bricht."

"*North.*—Yes, bright:

'In wit a man—simplicity a child.'"

—*Noctes*, May, 1830.

"*Sunday Evening.*

"MY DEAR WILSON:—I trust you will forgive me for addressing you on a subject which has been running in my head all week, and has incapacitated me, I believe, from reading or writing, for whenever I attempted either, your image, or the image of some other person or thing connected with *Blackwood's Magazine*, immediately took its station in my brain, and prevented any other idea from obtaining an entrance.

"I have frequently thought of writing to you, yet I have always drawn back, from an aversion to appear to be giving advice or intermeddling in an affair with which I have nothing to do, separate from the interest which every one who knows you must take in you. I hear, however, that you have called on me to-day, and I cannot any longer refrain from saying something to you, though perhaps it may be rather incoherent, on the unpleasant circumstances of the last week. That blame must attach to you and your friend Lockhart for the delinquencies of *Blackwood's Magazine* I am afraid must be admitted; but even if the blame should not go the full length of the accusations which are made against you, I have myself too distinct a conception of the hazards accompanying mysterious and secret composition, and the temptations which it throws in the way of men of imagination and genius (much inferior to either of yours), that I can conceive, in the heat of writing, your trespassing very much upon the limits of propriety or a due regard for the common courtesies and regulations of social life. As it is impossible, too, for another person to enter into all the feelings which may have actuated you on different occasions, I can imagine that you may have done what you are stated to have done, without deserving those imputations which have been thrown upon you. Indeed I cannot, for my own part, think any thing very bad of you. You have always appeared to me a person of high and noble character, and I should be very sorry to view you in any other light. I am not at all, however, surprised that torrents of abuse should be thrown upon you, both in private and public, and I cannot say that the world is unjust in this retaliation.

"The person who has written the anonymous letter to you does not act perhaps in the most chivalrous manner possible, not to let himself be known; but I rather think he is in the right, and as I am one of those people who are disposed to believe all things, I imagine he is really what he gives himself out to be—a person unconnected with the matters in dispute, and determined, from a sense of justice, to defend what he thinks the cause of violated public tranquillity.

"If he had been himself a party, he would have written with more bitterness, and been less disposed to make stupid quotations. All this, however, my dear Wilson, unpleasant as it is at present, may be attended with a very excellent result, if you will allow it to be so. Both you and Lockhart are, I think, designed for much higher things than the game you are playing. I believe that, with the wantonness of youth and conscious power about you, which you do not care much how you exhibit, you are really desirous of doing good; and that you are anxious to root out of the world false sentiments in politics and religion, with a perfect unconcern who may entertain them. This is the best view to take of you; and in this kind of crusade, you are heedless what shock you may give to individuals, whose feelings yet deserve to be consulted, and with whom the public will, in general, take part. I really think nothing less than a Divine commission, such as Joshua received to extirpate the Canaanites, could justify the way in which you are throwing around you poisoned arrows against those whom you surmise to be infidels. When you go beyond a certain mark, you lose your aim. While with all the eloquence that you can muster, you will never persuade the reasonable part of the nation that the *Edinburgh Review* has for its insidious, skulking design to make as many Jacobins and infidels as it can, I suppose the character of that publication is pretty well understood. Nobody takes it up in the notion that they will receive religious instruction from it, or that the writers are very competent to give it; but nobody of sense supposes, whatever slips it may sometimes have made, that its object and secret view is to pull down Christianity; and particularly, no one who knows Mr. Playfair conceives that this is one of his darling contemplations and schemes, whatever may be his opinions upon the subject of Revelation, which nobody has any business to rake out. I believe the only slip he is supposed to have committed in the *Review*, was something on the subject of miracles; and what he says is, I imagine, defensible enough, and reconcilable to a belief in Christianity. Then as to politics, although here, too, there may be various offences, yet I believe the general drift of the politics of the *Edinburgh Review* is felt by the nation to have on the whole a good tendency. If you and your friend persist in writing in *Blackwood's Magazine*, I exhort you strenuously to make that Magazine what you are capable of making it; to take the hint which has been given you; to take warning from the awkward perplexities in which it has involved you, and from which it would be idle to attempt to extricate yourselves entirely, and henceforth to avoid unhandsome personalities. I do not say, spare the *Edinburgh Review;* on the contrary, where you find in it any sentiment that you think militating either against the Constitution or Christianity, by all means expose it; but do not impute motives to the writers which you cannot think exist. Your readers will go more thoroughly along with you if you are temperate, and give that Review the credit which it deserves, and speak of its authors rather as men who do not see the whole truth, than as men who are wittingly blind. If you cannot get the regulation of that Magazine into your own hands, but must have your writings coupled with party politics and personalities, which you yourselves disapprove of, I really think, for your own credit, you should have nothing to do with it; for there is not a piece of abomination in the Magazine which will not be fathered upon one or other of you; and neither Christianity nor Toryism is at present in so low a state that there is any necessity to suffer martyrdom."

The following letter from my father about the same time appears to have been addressed to Mr. Morehead, in reference to a suspicion of Mr. Macvey Napier having been the author of the pamphlet. It betrays the keenness of his feelings on the subject:—

"53 Queen Street,
Half-past Ten, Wednesday, 1817.

"My dear Sir:—Your message to me from Mr. Napier would have been perfectly satisfactory, even had I had any suspicion that he was the author of the pamphlet. But knowing Mr. Napier to be a gentleman and a man of education, I could not have suspected him to be a blackguard and a villain. Had public rumor forced me at any time to ask him if he was the author of that pamphlet, the question would have been accompanied with an ample apology for putting it, for, without that, the question would itself have been an insult. Assure Mr. Napier of this, and that I am sorry he should have been put under the necessity by disagreeable and stupid rumor of disowning that of which I know his nature to be incapable. Had I suspected Mr. Napier, and yet "alluded" to him as the object of my suspicion, I should have acted like an idiot and a coward. In a case like this, suspicion is not to be so intimated. Should I ever suspect any man, I will send with privacy a friend to him; he may be a man of some nerve, and if ever he avows himself he will require them all. My affection and friendship for you never can suffer any abatement. But may I gently say to you, this villanous and lying pamphlet has been read by you with feelings, and has left on your mind an impression, which I did not imagine such a publication could have created in you towards your very attached friend,

"J. WILSON."

Not the least of the ill results of that unhappy letter of the Baron Lauerwinkel was the interruption of the friendly relation between my father and Jeffrey. The latter conveyed his sentiments on the subject in these manly and honorable terms:—

"CRAIGCROOK HOUSE, 13*th October*, 1818.

"MY DEAR SIR:—I take the liberty of enclosing a draft for a very inconsiderable sum, which is the remuneration our publisher enables me to make for your valuable contribution to the last number of the *Edinburgh Review;* and though nobody can know better than I do, that nothing was less in your contemplation in writing that article, it is a consequence to which you must resign yourself, as all our other regular contributors have done before you.

"And now, having acquitted myself of the awkward part of my office with my usual awkwardness, I should proceed to talk to you of further contributions, and . . . to save editorial disquisition on the best style of composition for such a journal, if I had not a still more awkward and far more painful subject to discuss in the first place.

"You are said to be a principal writer in, and a great director and active supporter of Blackwood's *Edinburgh Magazine.* In the last number of that work there is an attack upon my excellent friend Mr. Playfair, in my judgment so unhandsome and uncandid, that I really cannot consent either to ask or accept of favors from any one who is aiding or assisting in such a publication.

"I have not the least idea that you had any concern in the composition of that particular paper, and perhaps I have been misinformed as to the nature and extent of your connection with the work in general. But if it be as I supposed, and if you still profess to take the same interest in that Magazine, I do not see that we can possibly co-operate in any other publication.

"I have no right, certainly, and I am sure I have no intention to rebuke you for any opinions you may entertain, or any views you may have formed of the proper way of expressing them; but if you think the scope and strain of the paper to which I allude in any degree justifiable, I can only say that your notions differ so widely from mine, that it is better that we should have no occasion to discuss them. To me, I confess, it appears that the imputations it contains are as malignant as they are false; and having openly applied these epithets to them, whenever I have had occasion to speak on the subject, I flatter myself that I do not violate the courtesy which I unfeignedly wish to observe towards you, or act unsuitably with the regard which I hope always to entertain for you, if I plainly repeat them here, as the grounds of a statement with which no light considerations could have induced me to trouble you.

"I say, then, that it is *false* that it is one of the principal objects, or any object at all, of the *Edinburgh Review* to discredit religion, or promote the cause of infidelity. I who have conducted the work for nearly fifteen years should know something of its objects, and I declare to you, upon my honor, that nothing with that tendency has ever been inserted without its being followed with sincere regret, both on my part and on that of all who have any permanent connection with the work. That expressions of a light and indecorous nature have sometimes escaped us in the hurry of composition, and that, in exposing the excesses of bigotry and intolerance, a tone of too great levity has been sometimes employed, I am most ready with all humility to acknowledge; but that any thing was ever bespoken or written by the regular supporters of the work, or admitted, except by inadvertence, with a view to discredit the truth of religion, I most positively deny, and that it is no part of its object to do so, I think must be felt by every one of its candid readers.

"In the second place, I say it is false that Mr. P. lent his support to the *Review* in order to give credit and currency to its alleged infidel principles.

"And, finally, it is false that the writings which he has contributed to it have had any tendency to support those principles, or are intended to counteract the lessons which he once taught from the pulpit."

It is much to be regretted that my father's reply to this letter is not extant. What it may have been can only be conjectured. I can have no doubt that he would not attempt to justify the malignant article. But he was not a man to abandon his associates even when he disagreed with them. He had cast in his lot with *Blackwood* and its principles, and was resolved to stand by them at all hazards.

CHAPTER IX.

ANN STREET.—MORAL PHILOSOPHY CHAIR.

1820.

An eventful life seldom falls to the lot of the man of letters. His vicissitudes and excitements are for the most part confined to an arena in which he figures little before the public gaze. In this sense Wilson's life was uneventful; but the constitution of his nature, both physical and mental, made it impossible that it should ever become uninteresting or monotonous. It may be said that he threw himself into the very heart of existence, and found in the lowliest things on earth a hidden virtue that made them cease to be vulgar in his eyes. For fundamentally, though that I know is not the general opinion, he was as much a philosopher as a poet, and had that true instinct, that electric rapidity of glance, that enables a man to penetrate through the forms of things to their real meaning and essence. And when free from the bias of passion or prejudice, his judgment was most accurate. Caprice or change in regard to principles, or persons, or tastes, was no part of his character.

Faults of temper and intolerance sometimes glared forth, finding utterance, it might be, both violent and unreasonable. Thus his highly-strung nervous organization made him keenly alive to all outward impressions, loud laughter, sudden noises, rudeness, affectation, and those offences against minor morals that are generally regarded with indifference or passing disgust, affected him painfully; and if but for a short time exposed to any such annoyances, no self-control prevented him from giving expression to his feelings. But such outbursts, whether manifested in spoken or written words, were as summer storms, that leave the air purer and the sky brighter than before. He was, in fact, too large a man to be unamiable. His natural temper was, in mature life, as it had been in boyhood and youth, sweet and sunny, and, with all his enjoyment of activity and excitement, he never liked any company half so well as that which he found at his own fireside. To that quiet and simple home, in which his happiness was summed up, we now turn for a short time.

Towards the end of the winter of 1819, my father, with his wife and children, now five in number, two boys and three girls,* left his mother's house, 53 Queen street, and set up his household gods in a small and somewhat inconvenient house in Ann street (No. 20). This little street, which forms the culminating point of the suburb of Stockbridge, was at that time quite "out of town," and is still a secluded place, overshadowed by the tall houses of Eton terrace and Clarendon Crescent. In the literary "Ledger," already referred to, which contains all sorts of memoranda in my father's handwriting, there is a page taken up with an estimate of the cost of furniture for dining-room, sitting-room, nursery, servants' room, and kitchen, making up a total of £195, with the triumphant query at the end, in a bold hand, "Could it be less?" Truly, I think not. This little entry throws an interesting light on the circumstances of this devoted pair, who, eight years previously, had started in life so differently under the prosperous roof-tree of Elleray. But the limitation of their resources had, from the beginning, brought with it neither regret nor despondency, and now that they were for the first time fairly facing the cares of life, they took up the burden with hope and cheerfulness. My father felt strong in his own pow-

* Their names, in the order of their ages, were as follows:—John, born April, 1812; Margaret, July, 1813; Mary, August, 1814; Blair, April, 1816; Jane Emily, January, 1817.

ers of work, and his deep affection for his wife and children was a mighty stimulus to exertion. My mother, on the other hand, along with a singular sweetness of disposition, possessed great prudence and force of character; she entered, as her letters indicate, into all that concerned her husband with wife-like zeal, and her sympathy and counsel were appreciated by him above all else that the world could bestow.

In withdrawing from the more fashionable part of Edinburgh, they did not, however, by any means exclude themselves from the pleasures of social intercourse with the world. In Ann street they found a pleasant little community that made residence there far from distasteful; the seclusion of the locality made it then, as it seems still to be, rather a favorite quarter with literary men and artists. The old mansion of St. Bernard's, the property and dwelling-house of Sir Henry Raeburn (the glory of Scotland's portrait-painters) offered them its hospitality and kindly intercourse. No one can forget how, in the circle of his own family, that dignified old gentleman stood, himself a very picture, his fine intellectual countenance lightened by eyes most expressive, whose lambent glow gave to his face that inward look of soul he knew so well to impart to his own unsurpassed portraits. Genius shed its peculiar beauty over his aspect, yet memory loves more than aught else the recollections of the benevolent heart that lent to his manner a grace of kindliness as sincere as it was delightful. The place in Scottish art which he had so long occupied without a fellow was soon to become vacant. But a worthy successor was at that time following his footsteps to fame.

Sir John Watson Gordon lived with his father (then Captain, afterwards Admiral Watson) and a pleasant group of brothers and sisters, in the house adjoining that of Professor Wilson, in whom this rising artist found a warm and kind patron. Not a few of his early pictures were painted under the encouragement and advice of his genial friend. Almost the first subject that brought him into prominent comparison with the best English painters of the day was a portrait of my sister, when seven years of age—a beautifully colored and poetically conceived picture. This gentleman has long since reaped the reward of his industry and talent, and now wears the honor of knighthood, along with the important position of President of the Royal Scottish Academy, continuing still, from time to time, to give evidence to the world, by the admirable vigor and truthful individuality of his portraits, that his eminence is increasing with his years.

Another illustrious name is to be numbered in that coterie of artists. William Allan (who also attained the honor of knighthood and presidentship) was a frequent guest in my father's house. He had not long returned from a residence of some duration in the East. His extended travel and fresh experience of foreign lands, made his society much sought after. He had the advantage of an intimate friendship with Sir Walter Scott, in itself an introduction to intercourse with the best people of the time. Mr. Allan was a man whose intelligence, power of observation, quaint humor, gentle and agreeable manners, made him welcome to all. Many were the pleasant reunions that took place in those days under Professor Wilson's roof, where might be seen together Lockhart, Hogg, Galt, Sir William Hamilton, his brother, Captain Thomas Hamilton, Sir Adam Ferguson, Sir Henry Raeburn, Mr. Allan, and Watson Gordon. In such meetings as these, it may easily be imagined how the hours would pass, the conversation and merriment perhaps continuing till sun-rising.

Wilson had now apparently committed himself to literature as his vocation; and when he removed to Ann Street there seemed no great probability of his being soon called to any more definite sphere of exertion. His professional prospects were not much to be calculated on, for, though fitted in some respects to achieve distinction at the bar, he appears never to have seriously contemplated that as an object of ambition. His aspirations were in a very different direction. Though his pursuits and acquirements had been of a very general and eclectic sort, he had given early proof of his love and capacity for philosophic studies. He had not, it is true, made philosophy his special pursuit, like his illustrious friend Sir William Hamilton, for poetry and literature divided his allegiance. But the science of mind, and more particularly Moral Philosophy, had for him at all times high attraction. Human nature had been in fact his study *par excellence*, and when the prospect opened to him of being able to cultivate that study, not merely as a field of analytical skill, but as a means of practically influencing the minds of others with all the authority of academic position, he eagerly grasped at it as an object worthy of his highest ambition. That prize was not to be won without a desperate struggle, to the history of which a few pages must now be devoted.

In April, 1820, the chair of Moral Philosophy in the University of Edinburgh became vacant by the lamented death of Dr. Thomas Brown. The contest which ensued has had few parallels even in the history of that University, whilst the patronage lay with the Town Council, whose members had to be canvassed personally like the voters in a rotten borough. My father announced himself as a candidate in the course of the month, and so did Sir William Hamilton. Other distinguished men were mentioned as possible competitors, such as Sir James Mackintosh and Mr. Malthus; but it soon became apparent that between these two alone the struggle was to lie. Then came the tug of war. The rivals were intimate personal friends, and between them, happily, no unpleasant word or thought arose during the time that their respective friends were fighting for and against them, like Greek and Trojan. Both had been brilliant Oxonians; but the one was known to have devoted himself to philosophy, with a singleness of aim and a specialty of power, that seemed to his friends, and certainly not without reason, to throw the pretensions of his rival utterly into the shade. Happily for him, too, he had, as became a philosopher, abstained from any interference in public questions, either openly or in secret; and his retired and studious life afforded no possible mark for censure or insinuation even to the most malicious enemy. The other, though reckoned by men well fitted to judge, as a person singularly gifted with philosophic as well as poetic faculty, was better known in the outer world as a daring and brilliant *littérateur*; one of a band of writers who had excited much admiration, but also much righteous censure, and personally as a somewhat eccentric young man of very athletic and jovial tendencies. How these qualities affected his position as a candidate will speedily appear; but all other distinctions were lost sight of in the one great fact of political creed. Sir William was a Whig: Wilson was a Tory. The matter all lay in that. Wilson, too, was not only a Tory, but a Tory of the most unpardonable description; he was one of the leading hands, if not the editor, of that scandalous publication, *Blackwood's Magazine*, a man therefore who needed no further testimonial of being at least an assassin and a reprobate. He, forsooth, a Professor of Moral Philosophy, a successor of Dugald Stewart! The thing was mon-

Sir William Hamilton, at Oxford.—From a sketch by Mr. Lockhart.

strous; an outrage on decency and common sense. Such, without exaggeration, was the view taken by the Whig side in this contest, and strenuously supported publicly in the columns of the *Scotsman*,* and privately in every circle where the name of *Blackwood* was a name of abomination and of fear.

How the proceedings of this election interested my mother may be seen best from her own true womanly feelings expressed without reserve, in a letter to her sister:—

"My mind has been anxiously occupied on Mr. Wilson's account, by an election in which he has, amongst other literary men, started as a candidate. It is for a Professor's Chair in the University here. The Professorship of Moral Philosophy is the situation, which became vacant about six weeks ago, by the death of Dr. Brown. The gift of the Chair is in the power of the Magistrates and Town Council, and I have no doubt there will be a great struggle between the two political parties here. The *Whigs* hitherto have had every thing their own way; and the late Professor was one, as well as the well-known Dugald Stewart, who resigned the situation from bad health, and who has it in his power to resume lecturing if he chooses, and which I fear he will do from party spirit, if he thinks there is any chance of Mr. Wilson's success. Mr. Wilson has been assured of all the support that Government can give him, and Sir Walter Scott has been particularly kind in his exertions for his success. The testimonials which he has received from the Professors at Glasgow, as to his powers for such a situation, are most gratifying and flattering; indeed, his prospects are at present favorable; but I will not allow myself to be sanguine, though I must say that if Mr. Wilson was to

* A single specimen of the rhetoric used may suffice, being the peroration of a long and angry leading article which appeared immediately before the election. The electors were, in conclusion, thus solemnly adjured:—"Again we call upon those members of Council who are fathers of families; who respect the oaths they have taken; who have some regard for religion, morals, and decency, to read the Chaldee MS.; the pilgrimage to the 'Kirk of Shotts;' the attacks on Messrs. Wordsworth, Pringle, Dunbar, Coleridge, and others; to weigh and consider the spirit and character of many other articles in the Magazine, which are either written by Mr. Wilson, or published under his auspices; and if they can possibly excuse him as a private individual, we still put it to them how they can justify it to their conscience, their country, and their God, to select him as the man to fill the chair of Moral Philosophy, and to confide to him the taste, the morals, and the characters of the rising generation."

When the election was over, the public were informed, through the same channel, that the conduct of the electors had "stamped indelible disgrace on the Town Council," and that though it was a prevalent opinion that they were already as low as they could be in the estimation of their fellow-citizens, the proceedings of that day had shown this conclusion to be erroneous, and demonstrated that there is in the lowest depth a lower still.

get such an honorable situation, it would indeed be truly gratifying to me; and I think he is well calculated to fill, with respectability and credit, such a Chair. All the principal men here on the *Government* side are most anxious for his success; and even if he should be disappointed, the handsome manner in which they have come forward, may be as useful to him at some future time as it is satisfactory at the present. The emolument of the situation in itself is nothing, but depends on the number of students who may attend the class. Dr. Brown had about a thousand a year from it. He was brother of the Miss Brown whom you may remember seeing here, and the authoress of *Lays of Affection.*

"If I have any thing to say with regard to Mr. Wilson's affairs, I will let you know soon, but the matter will not be ultimately decided for some time; his *opponents* at present are *few*, and the most formidable is Sir William Hamilton, who is not a Government man, but others may start more appalling. Malthus is one talked of, and Sir James Mackintosh. The latter is an elderly man, who ranks very high in the literary world, and a *Whig.*"

This letter is dated 29th April, 1820. She writes again in July: "I know that you take an interest in all our concerns, or I should not again bore you with the old story of the election, which, when I last wrote to you, I thought was concluded; indeed, the report that Dugald Stewart meant to resume his lectures, came from such good authority that Mr. Wilson set off immediately to Peebles to recover his fatigue. He was no sooner gone than he was sent for back again; for the very next day Dugald Stewart sent in his resignation, and the canvass began instantly in the most determined manner. You can form no idea with what warmth it is still going on, and the Whigs are perfectly mad. The matter is to be decided next Wednesday, and as yet Mr. Wilson has greatly the majority of votes, and I trust will continue to have them, and that his friends will prove stanch. They have been uncommonly active indeed in his behalf, Sir Walter Scott in particular, who says there are greater exertions making by the Whigs now, than they ever made in any political contest in Scotland. The abuse lavished upon Mr. Wilson by them is most intemperate; his greatest crime is that he is a contributor to *Blackwood's Magazine*, that notoriously Tory journal. But I trust all will end well. I shall not write again till the 19th, when our suspense will be at an end."

Hostility on grounds purely political would have been, in the singular state of feeling which then prevailed, more or less excusable. But as the contest deepened, and my father's prospects of success grew stronger, the opposition took a form more malignant. When it was found useless to gainsay his mental qualifications for the office, or to excite odium on the ground of his literary offences, the attack was directed against his moral character; and it was broadly insinuated that this candidate for the Chair of Ethics was himself a man of more than doubtful morality; that he was, in fact, not merely a "reveller" and a "blasphemer," but a bad husband, a bad father, a person not fit to be trusted as a teacher of youth. These cruel charges touched him to the quick. It is difficult now to realize that they could have required refutation; but so far, it appears, did the strength of party bitterness carry men in these angry days. My father found it necessary, therefore, to adduce "testimonials" to his moral character, as well as to his intellectual acquirements. How painfully he felt these malicious attacks may be judged from the following letter to his friend the Rev. John Fleming, of Rayrig, Windermere: its manly spirit and noble tone, under circumstances so trying to the temper, are worthy of remark:—

"53 Queen Street, Edinburgh,
July 2d.

"My dear Sir:—I owe you many thanks for your most kind and friendly letter, which I laid before the electors, along with many others from persons of whose good opinion I have reason to be proud. The day of election is at last fixed, after many strange delays, all contrived by my opponents, who have struggled to obtain time, during which they contrived to calumniate me with a virulence never exceeded and seldom equalled. The election will take place upon Wednesday, the 19th of July, and the contest lies between Sir William Hamilton, Bart., a barrister here, and myself; other four candidates being supposed to have little or no chance of success. I am, unfortunately, opposed by all the Whig influence in Scotland; but, on the other hand, I have the most strenuous support of Government, as far as their influence can be legitimately exercised, and of many of the most distinguished independent men in Scotland. My friends are all sanguine; many of them confident; and I myself entertain strong, and I think well-grounded hopes of success. My enemies have attacked my private character at all

points, and within these few days, have not scrupled to circulate reports that I am a bad husband and a bad father. I confess that this has affected me greatly; as, whatever my faults or errors may have been, it is true as holy writ that I do tenderly love my wife and children, and would willingly lay down my life for their sakes. I need not say that such base insinuations have roused the indignation of my friends; but though calumny is in general ultimately defeated, it often gains its ends for the time being; and in this case it is likely to operate to my disadvantage with some of the electors whose minds are not yet made up. Now you, my dear sir, married me to one of the most sinless and inoffensive of human beings, whom not to love would indeed prove me to be a wretch without a soul, or a heart, or a mind, and to treat whom otherwise than kindly and tenderly would be an outrage against nature. God has blessed me with six innocent children, for whom I pray every night; and all my earthly happiness is in the bosom of my family. But to you I need say no more on such a subject. As an answer to all such calumnies, I fear not that my future life will be satisfactory; but, meanwhile, you will be doing me another friendly office by writing to me another letter, containing your sentiments of me as a man,—such a letter as you would wish to address to a friend who has ever loved and respected you, on understanding that he has been basely, falsely, and cruelly calumniated. The electors are satisfied with my talents, and even my enemies have ceased now to depreciate them; but the attack is now made on my moral character, and they are striving to injure me in the public estimation by charges which, at the same time, cannot, in spite of their falsehood, fail to give me indescribable pain. I am, my dear sir, ever yours affectionately,
JOHN WILSON."

Mr. Fleming's reply is not extant, but the answer to a similar request addressed to Mrs. Grant of Laggan may be given as a curiosity in literature, being, it is to be hoped, the last specimen that will be seen of such a testimonial to any candidate for a professorship. My father wrote to Mrs. Grant as follows:—

"*Sunday Afternoon.*

"MY DEAR MADAM:—During the course of the canvass in which I have for some time past been engaged, I am sorry to know that many calumnies have been industriously circulated against my private character. Among others, it has lately been insinuated that I am a bad husband, a bad father, and, in short, in all respects a bad family man. I believe that I may with perfect confidence assert, that whatever may be my faults or sins, want of affection for my wife and children, my mother, sisters, and brothers, is not of the number. My whole happiness in life is centred in my family, whom God in his infinite goodness has hitherto preserved to me in their beauty, their simplicity, and innocence. I am more at home than perhaps any other married man in Edinburgh; nor is there on earth a human being who feels more profoundly and gratefully the blessedness and sanctity of domestic life. This, my dear madam, must be your conviction; and you would now be conferring upon me a singular favor, by expressing to me in such a letter as I could show to my friends in Council, of whom I have many, your sentiments with respect to me and my character. Your own pure and lofty character will be a warrant of the truth of what you write, and a hundred anonymous slanders will fall before the weight of your favorable opinion. I would not write to you thus, if I were conscious of having done any thing which might forfeit your esteem; but whatever may be thought of my talents or of my poetical genius, neither of which I have ever wished to hear overrated, I have no doubt that I am entitled to the character of a virtuous man in the relations of private life. I am, my dear madam, yours, with true respect,

"John Wilson."

Mrs. Grant thus replied:—

"I have known your family for several years intimately; indeed, through intermediate friends, have known much of you from your very childhood; and in the glow of youth, high spirits, and unclouded prosperity, always understood you to be a person of amiable and generous feelings and upright intentions. Since you married, I have known more of you, and of the excellent person to whom you owe no common portion of connubial felicity; and I always believed her to be the tranquil and happy wife of a fond and faithful husband, domestic in his habits, devoted to his children, and peculiarly beloved by his brothers and sisters, and his respectable and venerated parent. Often have I heard your sisters talk with the warmest affection of you, and praise you, in particular, for your fond and unremitted attention to your wife; and, moreover, remark how quiet and domestic the tenor of your life has been since you left their family, and what particular delight you took in that very fine family of children with which God has blessed you. If you were, indeed, capable of neglecting or undervaluing such a wife and such children, no censure could be too severe for such conduct. But in making an attack of that nature, your enemies have mistaken their point, as your domestic character may be called your strong ground, where you are certainly invulnerable as far as ever I could understand or hear. People's tastes and opinions may differ in regard to talents and acquirements, but as to domestic duties and kind affections, there can be but one opinion among those whose opinion is of any value."

A still higher authority came forward in vindication of his character. The following letter was addressed to the Lord Provost by Sir Walter Scott:—

"EDINBURGH, *8th July*, 1820.

"MY LORD PROVOST:—Some unfavorable reports having been circulated with great industry respecting the character of John Wilson, Esq., at present candidate for the Chair of Moral Philosophy, now vacant in this University, I use the freedom to address your Lordship in a subject interesting to me, alike from personal regard to Mr. Wilson, and from the high importance which, in common with every friend to this city, I must necessarily attach to the present object of his ambition.

"Mr. Wilson has already produced to your Lordship such testimonials of his successful studies, and of his good morals, as have seldom been offered on a like occasion. They comprehend a history of his life, public and private, from his early youth down to this day, and subscribed by men whose honor and good faith cannot be called into question; and who, besides, are too much unconnected with each other to make it possible they would or could unite their false testimonies, for the purpose of palming an unworthy candidate upon the electors to this important office. For my own part, whose evidence in behalf of Mr. Wilson is to be found among certificates granted by many persons more capable of estimating his worth and talents, I can only say that I should have conceived myself guilty of a very great crime, had I been capable of recommending to the Moral Philosophy Chair, a scoffer at religion or a libertine in morals. But Mr. Wilson has still further, and, if possible, more strong evidence in favor of his character, since he may appeal to every line in those works which he has given to the public, and which are at once monuments of his genius, and records of his deep sense of devotion and high tone of morality. He must have, indeed, been a most accomplished hypocrite (and I have not heard that hypocrisy has ever been imputed to Mr. Wilson) who could plead with such force and enthusiasm the cause of virtue and religion, while he was privately turning the one into ridicule, and transgressing the dictates of the other. Permit me to say, my Lord, that with the power of appealing to the labors of his life on the one hand, and to the united testimony of so many friends of respectability on the other, Mr. Wilson seems well entitled to despise the petty scandal which, if not altogether invented, must at least have been strongly exaggerated and distorted, either by those who felt themselves at liberty to violate the confidence of private society by first circulating such stories, or in their subsequent progress from tongue to tongue. Indeed, if the general tenor of a man's life and of his writings cannot be appealed to as sufficient contradiction of this species of anonymous slander, the character of the best and wisest man must stand at the mercy of every talebearer who chooses to work up a serious charge out of what may be incautiously said in the general license of a convivial meeting. I believe, my Lord, there are very few men, and those highly favored both by temperament and circumstances, or else entirely sequestered from the world, who have not at some period of their life been surprised both into words and actions, for which in their cooler and wiser moments they have been both sorry and ashamed. The contagion of bad example, the removal of the ordinary restraints of society, must, while men continue fallible, be admitted as some apology for such acts of folly. But I trust, that in judging and weighing the character of a candidate, otherwise qualified to execute an important trust, the public will never be deprived of his services by imposing upon him the impossible task of showing that he has been, at all times and moments of his life, as wise, cautious, and temperate as he is in his general habits, and his ordinary walk through the world.

"I have only to add, that supposing it possible that malice might have some slight ground for some of the stories which have been circulated, I am positive, from Mr. Wilson's own declaration, and that of those who best know him, that he is altogether incapable either of composing parodies upon Scripture, of being a member of any association for forwarding infidelity or profaneness, or affording countenance otherwise to the various attacks which have been made against Christianity. To my own certain knowledge he has, on the contrary, been in the habit of actively exerting his strong powers, and that very recently, in the energetic defence of those doctrines which he has been misrepresented as selecting for the subject of ridicule.

"I must apologize to your Lordship for intruding on your time such a long letter, which, after all, contains little but what must have occurred to every one of the honorable and worthy members of the elective body. If I am anxious for Mr. Wilson's success on the present occasion, it is because I am desirous to see his high talents and powers of elocution engaged in the important task of teaching that philosophy which is allied to and founded upon religion and virtue.

"I have the honor, etc., "WALTER SCOTT."

The day of success at last arrived; and Mrs. Wilson thus communicates the joyful news to her sister:—

"I am sure you will rejoice to hear that Mr. Wilson was yesterday elected Professor of Moral Philosophy, and that in spite of all the machinations of his enemies, the Whigs. He had twenty-one votes out of thirty,—a majority of twelve, which out of so small a number is pretty considerable. Poor 'Billy Balmer' took such an interest in the thing that he went yesterday morning and stayed near the scene of action till it was all over, and then came puffing down with a face of delight to tell me that 'Master was ahead a good deal.'"

A few days later she writes in a strain of high triumph. Like a good and brave wife she regards her husband's enemies as hers, and under the summary designation of *Whigs* they come in for a proper share of her notice:—

"ANN STREET, *July* 27, 1820.

"MY DEAR MARY:—The want of a decent sheet of paper shall not deter me from immediately thanking you for your and James's kind congratulations on our success in the late canvass, which, thank Heaven, is at last at an end, after a most severe struggle, in which I flatter myself Mr. Wilson has conducted himself with a forbearance and a magnanimity worthy a saint, and which, had he been a Catholic, he would have been canonized for. The pertinacity of his enemies was unprecedented, and I suppose they have not done with him yet; but the Tories have been triumphant, and I care not a straw for the impotent attempts of the scum of the defeated Whigs. I must say I chuckle at the downfall of the Whigs, whose meanness and wickedness I could not give you any idea of were I to write a ream of paper in the cause. In the number of *Blackwood's Magazine* last published they got a rap on the knuckles, just as hints as to what they may expect in future if they persevere in their abuse.* . . . .

"Mr. W. is very well, but as thin as a rat, and no wonder; for the last four months he has had no rest for the sole of his foot. He is now as busy as possible studying. His enemies have given him little time to prepare his lectures—one hundred and twenty in number. The class meets the beginning of November, and he has to lecture an hour every day till April. But for the detestable Whigs the thing might have been settled four months ago, and he would have had ample time for his preparations."

The proceedings at the election need not further be dwelt on. An attempt to rescind the vote at a subsequent meeting of Council was ignominiously defeated. The principal figure in that scene is a certain Deacon Paterson, who appears for once on the stage of history, armed with a "green bag," the contents of which were to annihilate the new Professor's reputation and quash the election. But the Deacon and his bag were very speedily disposed of, and

* Here follow sketches of some of Mr. Wilson's enemies and friends, alluded to in the Magazine, drawn in lively colors, from which we can only find room for that of "The Odontist:"—"The reputed author of the '*Testimonium*' is a good-natured dentist, who lives in Glasgow, whose name is James Scott, and who is the only Scotchman I know, with a very few exceptions, that can understand or relish a joke, and all the *jeux d'esprit* in *Blackwood's Magazine* he enjoys exceedingly, though, poor man, he could not write a line if his salvation depended upon it. . . . 'The Jurist,' who coined the rhymes in praise of *Blackwood*, is one of the great lawyers here, a Mr. Cranstoun."

forthwith disappeared into oblivion, in the midst of a hearty chorus of hisses.

My father lost no time in addressing himself to his important labors, and applied in all quarters, where help was to be relied on, for advice and assistance in collecting materials to guide him in the preparation of his lectures. Three days after the election he writes to his friend, Mr. John Smith, the Glasgow publisher:—

"53 QUEEN STREET, *July* 22.

"MY DEAR SIR:—Many thanks for your very kind letter. The contest was, you know, of a most savage nature, but I never feared for the result. A protest was given in by the defeated party, but that means nothing, and I will be Professor to my dying day.

"It is quite impossible for me to visit you at Dunoon, however delightful it would be. My labors are not yet commenced, but they must be incessant and severe; and I do not intend to leave Edinburgh for one single day till after I have finished the course of Lectures. Nothing but perseverance and industry can bring me even respectably through my toils, and they shall not be wanting.

"What works do you know of on Natural Theology? Ask Wardlaw.

"In short, the next month is to be passed by in reading and thinking alone, and all information you can communicate about books and men will be acceptable."

On the 3d of August he again wrote to Mr. Smith:—

"MY DEAR SIR:—All is now fixed respecting my election, verbally as well as virtually. The Minute of Election is to be read, so says an old and obsolete law, *twice in Council*, and Deacon Paterson, as you probably know, gave notice on the 19th, that he would move to rescind the election. Accordingly, on the first reading of the minute (Wednesday following election), he rose and declared his intention of opening a bagful of charges against me, which, he said, would cause my friends to rescind the election. This he tried to do yesterday, but my friends would not suffer his green bag to be opened. On this, he made a long prepared speech, full of all manner of calumnies against me, during which he was repeatedly called to order even by some of my opponents. At last, a vote of censure upon him was proposed and carried by twenty-one to six. On offering to apologize, this censure was withdrawn, and he did apologize. The vote was then put, 'rescind or adhere,' and carried 'adhere' by twenty-one to six, so that all is settled. The sole object, apparently, in all these proceedings has been to annoy me, my friends and supporters, and to give vent to the wrath of party feeling.

"I am anxious to know if you can get me Mylne's* notes. It is with no view, I need hardly say, of using any thing of his, but merely of seeing his course of discussion.

"I am both able and willing to write my own lectures, every word; but before I begin to do so, I am anxious to have before me a vista of my labors, and this might be aided by a sight of his or any other lectures. But all this is confidential, for my enemies are numerous and ready, and will do all they can to injure me in all things. But they may bark and growl, for it will be to no purpose."

The successor of Dugald Stewart was certain to have all eyes upon him, and the circumstances of the election made him feel all the more imperiously the need of acquitting himself well in a place that had been filled by men so famous; above all merely personal considerations, too, he felt, with almost oppressive anxiety, the sacredness of the trust that had been committed to him as a teacher of that science which embraces all the higher truths and precepts which the light of reason can make known. He accordingly set about his preparations with his usual energy, and for the brief period that intervened before the opening of the session in November, appears to have worked incessantly. His portrait in his study is thus playfully sketched by my mother:—"Mr. Wilson is as busy studying as possible, indeed he has little time before him for his great task; he says it will take him one month at least to make out a catalogue of the books he has to read and consult. I am perfectly appalled when I go into the dining-room and see all the folios, quartos, and duodecimos with which it is literally filled, and the poor culprit himself sitting in the midst, with a beard as long and red as an adult carrot, for he has not shaved for a fortnight."

Of all the friends to whom he applied for counsel in this time of anxiety, there was none on whom he so implicitly relied, or who

* Professor of Moral Philosophy in Glasgow, under whom he had studied in 1801.

was so able to assist him, as Alexander Blair. To him he unbosomed himself in all the confidence of friendship, and in several long and elaborate letters—too long to be given entire—entered minutely into his plans for the course, asking for advice and suggestions with the eagerness and humility of a pupil to his master. He gives a list of the books he has got, and asks his friend to tell him what others he should have; what he thinks of this and that theory; how many lectures there should be on this topic and on that. He sketches his own plan; how he is to commence with some attractive and eloquent introductory lectures "of a popular though philosophical kind," so as to make a good impression at first on his students, and also on the public. Here he purposes to give eight or ten lectures on the moral systems of ancient Greece, which Sir Walter Scott approves of; and which he hopes Blair will also approve of. "The subject is a fine one, and not difficult to write on. These lectures, it might be hoped, would give great pleasure."* Then will commence his own course in good earnest; six or more lectures on the physical nature of man; then twelve more, "though for no cause known," on the intellectual powers. On this he wishes to have Blair's opinion, for at present he sees nothing for it but to tread in the steps of Reid and Stewart; "which to avoid, would be of great importance." "Surely," he says, "we may contrive to write with more spirit and effect than either of them; with less formality, less caution; for Stewart seems terrified to place one foot before another." Then might come some lectures on taste and genius before coming to the moral being. "I believe something is always said of them; and perhaps in six lectures, something eloquent and pleasing might be made out." Let Blair consider the subject. That brings us up to forty lectures. Then comes the moral nature, the affections, and conscience, or "whatever name that faculty may be called." Here seems fine ground for descriptions of the operations of the passions and affections, and all concerned with them. That requires twelve lectures at least; "indeed that is too few, though, perhaps, all that could be afforded." Then comes the Will and all its problems, requiring at least six lectures. "But here I am also in the dark." One more lecture, on man's spiritual nature, gives us

* That anticipation was correct. No part of the course, I am informed, was more valued by his students. His lecture on Socrates, in particular, was considered one of his masterpieces in eloquence and pathos.

fifty-eight in all. The rest of the course will embrace fifty lectures respecting the duties of the human being. "I would fain hope that something different from the common metaphysical lectures will produce itself out of this plan." He will read on, and "attend most religiously to the suggestions" of his friend. Let his friend meantime consider every thing, and remember how short the time is; and that unless he does great things for him, and work with him, the Professor is lost. "I am never out of the house," he adds, "and may not be till winter." He is very unwell, and has just got out of bed; "but the belief that you will certainly be here at the time I fixed, and that you certainly will get me through, has enabled me to rise." So the letter ends that day with a "God bless you!" and the next begins with a recommendation to Blair to read Stewart's argument against the Edinburgh Reviewer's assertion, that the study of Mental Philosophy has produced nothing, and imparted no power. He thinks "that both Jeffrey and Stewart are wrong, probably, however, Stewart most so;" but Blair must examine it, "for it is a subject on which you could at once see the truth." Let him also see what Stewart says on the origin of knowledge, "which seems worth reading;" "indeed," he adds, "these essays, though, I believe, not generally so highly thought of, seem to me to be the best of all Stewart's writings. But I am a miserable judge."* He then goes on with the sketch of the course. "Man's relations to God—Natural Theology, will require say eight lectures. Then his relations to man, and first, the natural relations, say twelve lectures; then the relations of Adoption and Institution, not less than fifteen; this department to embrace discussions about Government, Punishments, and Poor-laws. This gives us thirty-three lectures, leaving seventeen for the discussion of Virtues and Vices, the different Schemes of moral approbation, and other important questions; little enough space." These make up in all one hundred and eight lectures, which he thinks will be about the number required. "I have got notes," he says, "of Stewart's lectures, but they are dull; they are but feeble shadows of his published works, on which he bestowed incredible pains." He inquires about Mylne's lectures.

* This is one of many illustrations of the Professor's genuine humility. The egotism and self-complacency of Christopher North were as ideal as that personage himself. He appears in truth to have been, in metaphysics as in literature, a most acute critic; and some papers by him in *Blackwood*, on Berkeley's Philosophy, were, I believe, referred to by Sir William Hamilton as admirable specimens of metaphysical discussion.

"I believe he followed the French, for he hated Reid. But though an acute man, I cannot think he had any wisdom; he was continually nibbling at the shoe-latchets of the mighty." He again recurs to Stewart's Essays, which Blair is to read and consider, "but only in the conviction that it is necessary for us, which it seems to be. The truth is, that metaphysics must not be discarded entirely, for my enemies will give out that I discard them because I do not understand them. I want, on the contrary, in the midst of my popular views, and in general, to show frequently a metaphysical power, of which, perhaps, Stewart himself does not possess any very extraordinary share. In the first lecture on the Physical Being of Man this must be kept in view."

This letter is dated August 7th, so that it would appear that already, in the course of a fortnight, the Professor-elect had gone pretty deep into his subject, and even got the length of having a complete outline of his proposed course nearly matured. His good friend Blair was not found wanting in this crisis, and appears to have faithfully complied with his wishes, sending a regular series of letters, embodying, in the form of answers and suggestions, the results of his profound and varied study of philosophy, ancient and modern. Of these letters I have no specimen to give; but there is another of my father's sufficiently interesting to be quoted entire. He is at this time apparently (for it is without date) far advanced in his preparations, and has reached that part of his course where the inquiry passed from the region of morals into that of religion.

"My dearest Blair:—I would fain hope that your useful and enabling letters do not interfere too much with your own pursuits, whatever these may be. The morning that brings me a legible sibylline leaf, is generally followed by a more quiet-minded day.

"I wish you to send me two or three letters, if possible, on that division of the passions regarding religion. It is imperfectly done, and altogether the whole subject of Natural Theology and our duties to the Deity is heavy. However, I have remedied that in some measure, and will do so still more this session. What I direct your attention to is the History of Idolatry. Some views of its dreadful, beautiful, reverent, voluptuous character and kind; and some fine things in the mythological system of the Greeks, in as far as feeling, passion, or imagination were concerned. Every thing historical and applied to nations gives a lecture instant effect. Whatever be the true history of all idolatry (Bryant's or others), still the mind operated strongly, and there was not a passive transmission. The impersonalizing of imagination might be expatiated on here, for it was only alluded to in this respect in the Lectures on Imagination. I wish to see stated an opinion as to the power of religion in the ancient world, *i. e.*, in Egypt and Greece, among men in general. Something of the same kind, whatever it was, must have existed and still must exist in Christian countries among the ordinary people, especially in ignorant and bigoted forms of the faith. The image-worship of Catholics is, I presume, susceptible of the holiest emotions of an abstract piety; certainly of the tenderest of a human religion, and in grosser and narrower minds, of almost every thought that formed the faith of an ancient heathen. Many saints, intercessors, priests, etc., I mean no abuse of the Catholic faith, for I regard the doctrines of penitence and absolution and confession as *moral doctrines*, and I wish you would so consider them in an instructive letter. The burden of guilt is fatal, and relief from it may often restore a human soul to virtue. Confession to a friend, to one's own soul, to an elder brother, to a father, to a holy, old, white-haired man (in short, the best view of it), is surely a moral thing, and, as such, ought to be described. Our religious feelings, when justly accordant with the best faith, may be opposite, but true: the simple, austere worship of a Presbyterian, and the richer one of an Episcopalian, and the still more pompous sanctities of Popery. There are deep foundations, and wide ones too, in the soul, on which manifold religions may be all established in truth. We are now speaking not on the question of bestness, but as to fact. Surely the astronomer may worship God in the stars and the manifest temple of heaven, as well as a Scotch elder in a worm-eaten pew, in an ugly kirk of an oblong form, sixty by forty feet; yet the elder is a true man and pure. Sacraments in glorious cathedrals, or upon a little green hillside, which I myself have seen, but cannot describe, as you could do, who have never seen it;* and, above all, funerals; the English service, so affecting and sublime, and the Scotch service, silent, wordless, bare, and desolate—dust to dust in the speechless, formless sorrow of a soul. In that endless emana-

* He had, however, if I am not mistaken, described such a scene with exquisite fidelity, in *Peter's Letters*, vol. iii., p. 75.

tion of feelings, how can reason presume to dictate any one paramount rule to be observed? No. But when by various causes in any nation one tendency runs the one way, then the heart of that nation runs in that channel; all its most holy aspirations join there, and there the sanctity of walls consecrated by the bishops of God, and the sanctity of walls consecrated by no set forms of words, but by the dedication of the place to regular and severe piety,—as in England, the one; in Scotland, the other.* In Scotland, people on week-days walk hatted into churches. Is that, to your mind, an allowable thing? I have seen it done by very religious old men, and not harsh or sullen. To take off their hats would, I think, be reckoned by many a wrong action. This, I conceive, is allowing the inferior motive to prevail over the superior. For they remember the idolatrous practices of the papists whom John Knox overthrew, and rather than resemble them in any degree, they violate the *religio loci*, which is, in the case, this over belief in God. This may seem a trifling concern to you, but it hurts me.

"In the above you will probably see what I want, and perhaps other points may occur to yourself. With respect to metaphysics, do not fear on any subject to write, provided *a conclusion is arrived at.* No letter of yours, *if filled*, can be otherwise than most useful to me. That metaphysical point to which you referred in one of your letters lately, namely, the pure and awful idea of sanctity and reverence to God, which is probably only an extension of a human feeling, is exactly fit for a letter. There is a book called the *Divine Analogy*, by a Bishop Brown, that I do not understand, on this subject. I think you have seen it; and Copleston, I think, touches on it. I intend to put such pieces of the lectures on the Duties to God, as are good, into this part, so that any metaphysical or otherwise important thoughts on our religious emotions or thoughts will be useful. All human emotion towards human beings is fluctuating, and made up of opposite ingredients, even towards our earthly father: towards God, unmingled and one, and this unmingledness and oneness is in truth a new emotion; it exists nowhere else. Men's conduct seldom shows this; but it is in the soul of many, most men. I once saw, in a dream, a most beautiful flower, in a wide bed of flowers, all of which were beautiful. But this one flower was especially before my soul for a while, as I ad-

* This subject is beautifully treated by him in the first number of the "Dies Boreales."

vanced towards the place where they all were growing. Its character became more and more transcendent as I approached, and the one large flower of which it consisted was lifted up considerably above the rest. I then saw that it was Light, a prismatic globe, quite steady, and burning with a purity and sweetness, and almost an affectionate spirit of beauty, as if it were alive. I never thought of touching it, although still I thought it a flower that was growing; and I heard a kind of sound, faint and dim, as the echo of musical glasses, that seemed to proceed from the flower of light, and pervade the whole bank with low, spiritual music. On trying to remember its appearance and essential beauty more distinctly, I am unable even to reconceive to myself what it was, whether altogether different from the other flowers, or of some perfectly glorious representation of them all; not the queen of flowers, but the star of flowers, or flower-star. Now, as I did not, I presume, see this shining, silent, prismatic, vegetable creature, I myself created it, and it was 'the same, but, ah, how different' of the imagination, mingling light with leaf, stones with roses, decaying with undecaying, heaven with earth, and eternity with time. Yet the product, nothing startling, or like a phenomenon that urged to inquiry, What is this? but beheld in perfect acquiescence in its existence as a thing intensely and delightfully beautiful; but in whose perception and emotion, of whose earthly and heavenly beauty, my beholding spirit was satisfied, oh! far more than satisfied, so purer than dew or light of this earth; yet as certainly and permanently existing as myself existed, or the common flowers, themselves most fair, that lay, a usual spring assemblage in a garden where human hands worked, and mortal beings walked, among the umbrage of perishable trees! Perhaps we see and feel thus in heaven, and even the Alexander Blair whom I loved well on earth, may be thus proportionally loved by me in another life. Yours forever,

"J. W."

Among other friends to whom he resorted for advice at this time, was his well-beloved teacher, Professor Jardine. The judicious "Hints" of the old man are given with characteristic method and kindliness, but scarcely call for publication here. So far as the order of the course was concerned, my father preferred to follow his own plan, as sketched in his first letter to Blair. To that plan,

I believe, he adhered ever after, though, in important respects, he completely altered, in subsequent years, the substance of his lectures.

The opening of a new session is always an interesting occasion, and when it is the professor's first appearance the interest is of course intensified. The crowd that assembled to hear my father's introductory lecture proved too numerous for the dimensions of the room, and it was found necessary to adjourn to the more capacious class-room of Dr. Monro, the Professor of Anatomy. Wilson entered, accompanied by Principal Baird, Professors Home, Jameson, and Hope in their gowns, "a thing we believe quite unusual," remarked the *Scotsman*, in whose eyes this trifling mark of respect seemed a kind of insult to the audience, composed as it was, to a large extent, of persons prepared to give the new Professor any thing but a cordial greeting. An eye-witness* thus describes the scene:—"There was a furious bitterness of feeling against him among the classes of which probably most of his pupils would consist, and although I had no prospect of being among them, I went to his first lecture, prepared to join in a cabal, which I understood was formed to put him down. The lecture-room was crowded to the ceiling. Such a collection of hard-browed, scowling Scotsmen, muttering over their knobsticks, I never saw. The Professor entered with a bold step, amid profound silence. Every one expected some deprecatory or propitiatory introduction of himself and his subject, upon which the mass was to decide against him, reason or no reason; but he began in a voice of thunder right into *the matter* of his lecture, kept up unflinchingly and unhesitatingly, without a pause, a flow of rhetoric such as Dugald Stewart or Thomas Brown, his predecessors, never delivered in the same place. Not a word, not a murmur escaped his captivated, I ought to say his conquered audience, and at the end they gave him a right-down unanimous burst of applause. Those who came to scoff remained to praise."

Another spectator of the scene tells me that towards the conclusion of the lecture, the commencement of which had been delayed by the circumstance already mentioned, the Professor was interrupted in the midst of an eloquent peroration by the sudden entrance of Dr. Monro's tall figure—enveloped as usual in his long white

* The author of *The Two Cosmos:* MS. letter.

greatcoat—to announce that his hour had come. Pulling out his watch, the unsympathizing anatomist addressed him: "Sir, it's past one o'clock, and my students are at the door; you must conclude." The orator, thus rudely cut short, had some difficulty in preserving his self-possession, and, after a few sentences more, sat down.

The first lecture and those which followed amply justified the expectations of friends, and completely silenced enemies. Even the unfriendly critic above referred to, while attempting to disparage this first display of his powers, patronizingly assured the new Professor that if he made the exertions he had promised, and demeaned himself as became the successor of Ferguson, Brown, and Stewart, his past errors might be forgotten, and he might obtain that public confidence which was essential to his success as a teacher. No such exhortations were needed to make Wilson feel the gravity of his position, and stimulate him to maintain the glory of the University, on which for the next thirty-one years he reflected so much lustre. When he uttered the confident prediction, "I shall be professor to my dying day," it was in no boastful spirit. He had made up his mind to devote his full strength to the duties of the office, and with all his distrust of his own metaphysical capacity, he had a reasonable confidence in his ability to make the Moral Philosophy class-room, as it had been before him, a place of high and ennobling influence. To himself personally the change of position brought with it a consolidation of character and aims which imparted new dignity to his life and at the same time increased his happiness. In assuming the Professor's gown he did not indeed think it necessary, had that been possible, to divest himself of his proper characteristics, to be less fond of sport, less lively with his pen. His literary activity and influence increased in the years that followed this, for "Christopher North" was as yet but a dimly-figured personage. But from this time "The Professor" is his peculiar, his most prized title; the Chair is the place where he feels his highest work to be. I believe the prejudices and hostility which obstructed his way to it, however triumphantly overcome, threw their shadows forward more than is generally supposed. For, while no one could gainsay the fidelity with which he discharged his duty, and the altogether unrivalled eloquence of his lectures, I believe there were always some people who believed that he was nothing more than a splendid declaimer, and that his course of lectures contained more poetry than philosophy. He was himself aware of this, and refers to it in a letter to De Quincey, in which he naïvely asks his friend to describe him as "thoroughly logical and argumentative," which, he says, "is true; not a rhetorician, as fools aver." The truth is, his poetical and literary fame injured him in this respect as a lecturer; commonplace people thinking it impossible that a man could be both logical and eloquent, an acute metaphysician as well as a brilliant humorist. But among his own students generally there was but one opinion of "The Professor;" to them he was truly *Der Einzige.* Other professors enjoyed their respect and esteem; Wilson took their hearts as well as their imaginations by storm. They may have before this read and argued about philosophy; they were now made to feel it as a power. "The mental faculties" were no mere names; the passions and affections, and the dread mysteries of conscience, ceased to be abstract matters of speculation, and were exhibited before them as living and solemn realities mirrored in their own kindling breasts; and when they found that that formidable personage, of whom they had heard so much, and whose aspect, as he stood before them (he never sat), did not belie his fame, was in private the most accessible, frank, and kindly of men, their admiration was turned into enthusiastic love. There are few who listened to him, whether in the palmy days of his prime, or in the evening of life, when he came to be spoken of as "the old man eloquent," that do not speak of him with glowing cheek and sparkling eye, as they recall the cherished recollections of his moving eloquence, his irresistible humor, his eager interest in their studies and their welfare, his manly freedom of criticism, and his large-hearted generosity. The readiness with which he grasped at any question put to him gave his manner a quickness and animation of expression that at first was somewhat startling. While he had a terrible faculty for *snubbing* any display of conceit or forwardness, diffident talent was set at ease in his presence by the winning sympathy of his look and manner, which at once infused confidence and hope. But I am anticipating what will form the subject of a special chapter, and shall now close this with a brief letter, addressed to his friend Mr. Smith, on Christmas day, 1820:—

"My dear Sir:—If you can send me *instantly*, *i. e.*, by the return of mail or coach, Vince's 'Refutation of Atheism,' you will greatly oblige me. It is not in Edinburgh. Unless, however, you can send it immediately, it will be useless to me.

"I have no time to write. We have ten days of vacation, and I resume my lectures on January 2d. I have delivered thirty lectures, and am now advancing to the moral division of my course. As far as I can learn, my friends highly applaud, and my worst foes are dumb or sulky. The public, I believe, are satisfied. I need not say that my labor is intense. Direct to me at No. 53 Queen street, where I send for my letters every day; and if you have time, tell me how you are, and what doing. Yours very truly,

"John Wilson."

CHAPTER X.

THE PROFESSOR AND HIS CLASS.

It was no temporary enthusiasm that glorified the name of "the Professor" among his students, and still keeps his memory green in hearts that have long ago outlived the romantic ideals of youth. One of the most pleasing results of my labor has been to come upon traces everywhere of the love and admiration with which my father is remembered by those who attended his class. That remembrance is associated in some instances with sentiments of the most unbounded gratitude for help and counsel given in the most critical times of a young man's life. How much service of this sort was rendered during an academical connection of thirty years, may be estimated as something more to be thought of than the proudest literary fame. So, I doubt not, my father felt, though on that subject, or on any claims he had earned for individual gratitude, he was never heard to speak. Of his merits as a teacher of moral philosophy I am not speaking, and cannot pretend to give any critical estimate. I leave that to more competent hands. What I speak of is his relation to his students beyond the formal business of the class; for it is that, I think, that constitutes, as much as the quality of the lectures delivered, the difference between one teacher and another. Here was a poet, an orator, a philosopher, fitted in any one of these characters to excite the interest and respect of youthful hearers. But it was not these qualities alone or chiefly that called forth the affectionate homage of so many hearts; what knit them to the Professor was the heart they found in him, the large and generous soul of a man that could be resorted to and relied on, as well as respected and admired. No man ever had a deeper and kindlier sympathy with the feelings of youth; none could be prompter and sincerer to give advice and assistance when required. Himself endowed with that best gift, a heart that never grew old, he could still, when things were no longer with him "as they had been of yore," enter into the thoughts and aspirations of those starting fresh in life, and give them encouragement, and exchange ideas with them, in no strained or formal fashion. No wonder that such a man was popular, that his name is still dear, and awakens a thrill of filial affection and pride in the hearts of men who once knew him as their preceptor and friend.

I should have liked much, had I been able, to give some account of the Professor's lectures,* and his appearance in his class. But I

* The following is the Syllabus of his course, drawn up by the Professor for the *Edinburgh University Almanac*, as delivered in the session 1833–4, apparently the same in arrangement as originally determined on in his consultations with his friend Blair. In what year he remodelled his course, having previously remodelled his views on the great question of the nature of the Moral Faculty, I have not ascertained. It was at least subsequent to the year 1837, to which Mr. Smith's sketch refers. In later years he began in his first lecture with the subject of the Moral Faculty, the discussion of which extended, Mr. Nicolson informs me, over thirty-seven lectures, occupying the time from the commencement of the session in November to the Christmas recess:

"MORAL PHILOSOPHY.

"*This Class meets at Twelve o'clock.*

"MORAL PHILOSOPHY attempts to ascertain, as far as human reason can do so, the law which must regulate the conduct of Man as a moral being. Inasmuch as it does not derive this law from any authority, but endeavors to deduce it from principles founded in the nature of things, it takes the name of a science. It may be called the Science of Duty.

"The first object, therefore, will be to find those principles on which this law of duty must be grounded. For this purpose we have to consider—1st, The nature of the human being who is the subject of such a law; and 2d, The relations in which he is placed; his nature and his relations concurring to determine the character of his moral obligations.

"When the nature of man has been considered, and also the various relations of which he is capable, we shall have fully before us the ground of all his moral obligations; and it will remain to show what they are, to deduce the law which the principles we shall have obtained will assign. But when we shall have gone over the examination of his nature, the mere statement of his relations will so unavoidably include the idea of the duties that spring from them, that it would be doing a sort of violence to the understanding to separate them; and therefore the consideration of his Duties will be included in the Second Division of the Course.

"But the performance of duty does not necessarily take place upon its being known. There are difficulties and impediments which arise in the weaknesses, the passions, the whole character of him who is to perform it. Hence there arises a separate inquiry into the means to which man is to am saved the risk of attempting to describe what I have not seen, and cannot be expected to be skilled in, by the sketches with which I have been favored from men well able to do justice to the subject, so far as any sketch can be supposed to do justice to an eloquence that required to be heard in order to be appreciated. Of

resort, to enable him to discharge his known obligations. There must be a resolved and deliberate subjection of himself to the known Moral Law; and an inquiry, therefore, into the necessity, nature, and means of Moral Self-government, will furnish the *Third* and last Division of the Course.

"In the *First* Division of the Course, then, we consider the constitution of the Human Being. He has a PHYSICAL NATURE, the most perfect of any that is given to the kinds of living creatures, of which he is one, infinitely removed as he is from all the rest. He has an INTELLIGENCE by which he is connected with higher orders of beings; he has a MORAL NATURE by which he communicates with God; he has a SPIRITUAL ESSENCE by which he is immortal.

"All these natures and powers, wonderful in themselves, are mysteriously combined. The highest created substance Spirit, and Matter the lowest, are joined and even blended together in perfect and beautiful UNION.

"We begin by treating generally of his PHYSICAL CONSTITUTION and POWERS, and showing that much of his happiness—it may be of his virtue—is intimately connected with their healthful condition, as there is a mutual reaction between them and his highest faculties. The APPETITES are explained, and the phenomena of the SENSES; and pains taken to put in a clear light the nature of SIMPLE SENSATION, before proceeding to illustrate the THEORY OF PERCEPTION.

"The impressions received through the senses would be of no use; they could not become materials of Thought, if the mind were not endowed with a power of reproducing them to itself in its internal activity; and this power we consider under the name of CONCEPTION, and very fully the laws by which its action is regulated, the LAWS OF ASSOCIATION.

"We are then led to inquire what is the FACULTY OF THOUGHT itself; and if the different operations of JUDGMENT, ABSTRACTION, and REASONING may all be explained as Acts of this one FACULTY OF INTELLECTION.

"IMAGINATION itself seems to admit of being resolved into the union of this Faculty, with certain Feelings, under the Law of Association; and here an inquiry is instituted into the sources of the SUBLIME AND BEAUTIFUL, an attempt made to define GENIUS and its province, and illustrations are given of the PHILOSOPHY OF TASTE.

"Looking on Man's MORAL NATURE, we seem to see one Principle presiding over and determining the character of all the rest; distinguished by different names, but which no other, perhaps, so well describes as that which expresses it to the common understandings of men—CONSCIENCE. Is it SIMPLE OR COMPOSITE? NATURAL OR ACQUIRED? In endeavoring to answer these questions, we must take a review of all the most celebrated Moral Systems in which it has been attempted to explain its origin, its composition, its growth, and its power.

"From the consideration of this MORAL PRINCIPLE, to which our whole mind is subjected, we pass on to those various POWERS OF PASSION AND AFFECTION which are placed under its jurisdiction, and which, in their endless complexity and infinitely diversified modifications, constitute the strength of the human mind for action, and are the sources of the happiness, the sorrows, and the unfortunate errors of human life. These numerous principles, which have been classed in different manners by Ethical writers, but of which no classification is adequate to represent the variety, are very fully treated of under such great and simple divisions as serve to mark them out for separate discussion; an arrangement and order, which, whether metaphysically just or not, appear to afford facilities for analyzing the processes of nature.

"In treating of Man as a SPIRITUAL BEING, we consider the doctrines of the IMMATERIALITY AND IMMORTALITY OF THE SOUL—doctrines so important and interesting that no argument can be lost that serves to impress them more deeply, and so elevated, that merely to contemplate them, does of itself tend to spiritualize the affection and imagination.

"The *Second* Division of the Course comprehends an inquiry into Man's RELATIONS AND DUTIES. His first RELATION is as a creature to the MAKER AND GOVERNOR OF THE WORLD, and these various reminiscences I shall give three, in the order of the dates to which they respectively relate, viz., 1830, 1837, and 1850, interposing first two characteristic records of earlier relations between the Professor and his students.

therefore it becomes necessary to consider, in the first place, what we are able to know of the Attributes of that Great Being to whom he owes his FIRST DUTY,—a duty which is the foundation of all others.

"The utmost powers of the human mind have always been directed upon this great object. Its Intelligence desires to know the Origin of all things. Its Moral Understanding impels it to seek the Author of all order and law. Its Love and Happiness carry it towards the Giver of all good.

"The chief doctrines which are held concerning the Being and Attributes of Deity, men have conceived might be established by two methods; the first is that which deduces them from the absolute necessity of things, prior to all consideration of the effects in which they are manifested, —the ARGUMENT OR DEMONSTRATION *à priori*. The other method is that to which nature continually constrains us, which may be going on in our minds at every moment, an evidence and conviction collecting upon us throughout life. It deduces the Existence and Attributes of God from their effects in his works, which our Reason can ascribe to no other origin. It reasons from effects to the cause, and is therefore termed the ARGUMENT *à posteriori*.

"The great points established by both these modes of argument are, in the first place, the Existence of God, his Power, and his Wisdom. These may be called the Attributes which our Intelligence compels us to understand, and for which that faculty is sufficient. But there are other perfections which as nearly concern us, and to the contemplation of which we are called by other faculties of our being—His Love, Justice, and Righteousness.

"And here it appears necessary to vindicate the argument of the Evidence of Design from the misrepresentations and sophistries of certain writers by whom it has been impugned, and to expose the unphilosophical and impious spirit of their skepticism.

"When we have considered the grounds on which our natural reason is convinced of these attributes, the *relations* of Man to God are manifest, and his *Duties* rise up in all their awful magnitude to our minds.

"From this part of the Second Division of our Course, which belongs to Natural Theology, we go on to consider the RELATIONS AND DUTIES OF MAN TO HIS FELLOW-CREATURES.

"The division of these relations, with their duties, is determined upon two grounds, being opposed to each other, in one respect, as they are PUBLIC or PRIVATE, and, in another, as they are simply NATURAL, or of HUMAN ADOPTION AND INSTITUTION.

"By the private relations, we understand those by which a man is united to the members of his own family, household, and kindred, as a son, a father, a brother, a kinsman, a master, a servant, a friend. Under each of these relations, the particular circumstances attending it, which constitute the grounds of obligation, are considered, and the duties arising from them explicitly and fully stated, under the head of HOUSEHOLD LAWS.

"By the PUBLIC RELATIONS, we are led to consider him as a Member of a Political Body. There is here a twofold relation—that of RULERS AND SUBJECTS. We shall have to treat of the DUTIES belonging to both; as of Rulers, their first and especial duty to maintain the INDEPENDENCE of the Community among other States, and GOOD GOVERNMENT within their own; as of subjects, the duties of ALLEGIANCE and OBEDIENCE; and here will have to be stated the grounds of obligation on rulers and subjects, namely, MUTUAL BENEFITS; and their duty to their Common Country.

"In the course of these inquiries, questions of vast importance arise as to the ORIGIN AND GROUNDS OF GOVERNMENT; the PRINCIPLES OF LEGISLATION; the PRINCIPAL FORMS which POLITICAL GOVERNMENT has assumed among different nations; and their various adaptation to the essential ends for which they were constituted.

"In this Division of the Course, all those various Theories are strictly examined, which have been offered at different times, of the Nature of Virtue, and the Grounds of Moral Obligation—from Plato and Aristotle, to Stewart and Brown; and especial attention is paid to the Moral Philosophy of Greece.

About a year after he had entered upon his new duties, the Professor was rambling during vacation-time in the south of Scotland, having for a while exchanged the gown for the old "Sporting Jacket." On his return to Edinburgh, he was obliged to pass through Hawick, where, on his arrival, finding it to be fair-day, he readily availed himself of the opportunity to witness the amusements going on. These happened to include a "little mill" between two members of the local "fancy." His interest in pugilism attracted him to the spot, where he soon discovered something very wrong, and a degree of injustice being perpetrated which he could not stand. It was the work of a moment to espouse the weaker side, a proceeding which naturally drew down upon him the hostility of the opposite party. This result was to him, however, of little consequence. There was nothing for it but to beat or be beaten. He was soon "in position;" and, before his unknown adversary well knew what was coming, the skilled fist of the Professor had planted such a "facer" as did not require repetition. Another "round" was not called for; and leaving the discomfited champion to recover at his leisure, the Professor walked coolly away to take his seat in the stage-coach, about to start for Edinburgh. He just reached it in time to secure a place inside, where he found two young men already seated. As a matter of course he entered into conversation with them, and before the journey was half over, they had become the best friends in the world. He asked all sorts of questions about their plans and prospects, and was informed they were going to attend College during the winter session. Among the classes mentioned were Leslie's, Jameson's, Wilson's, and some others. "Oh! Wilson; he is a queer fellow, I am told; rather touched here" (pointing significantly to his head); "odd, decidedly odd." The lads, somewhat cautiously, after the manner of their country, said they had heard strange stories reported of Professor Wilson, but it

"In the *Third* Division of the Course, which runs into the Second, it is attempted to explain some of the chief Means by which Individual and National Virtue and Happiness may be strengthened and guarded: and to point out some of the most fatal causes of the Decline and Fall of Nations.

"At the commencement of each Session several Lectures are delivered, containing a Prospectus of the whole Course, which contains a hundred Lectures.

"Each alternate year the Professor delivers a Course of Fifty Lectures on Political Economy. He follows, in a great measure, the order observed in the *Wealth of Nations;* and, in explaining the doctrines of SMITH, compares them with those of RICARDO."

was not right to believe every thing; and that they would judge for themselves when they saw him. "Quite right, lads; quite right; but I assure you I know something of the fellow myself, and I think he is a queer devil; only this very forenoon at Hawick he got into a row with a great lubberly fellow for some unknown cause of offence, and gave him such a taste of his fist as won't soon be forgotten; the whole place was ringing with the story; I wonder you did not hear of it." "Well," rejoined the lads, "we did hear something of the sort, but it seemed so incredible that a Professor of Moral Philosophy should mix himself up with disreputable quarrels at a fair, we did not believe it." Wilson looked very grave, agreed that it was certainly a most unbecoming position for a Professor; yet he was sorry to say that having heard the whole story from an eye-witness, it was but too true. Dexterously turning the subject, he very soon banished all further discussion about the "Professor," and held the delighted lads enchained in the interest of his conversation until they reached the end of the journey. On getting out of the coach, they politely asked him, as he seemed to know Edinburgh well, if he would direct them to a hotel. "With pleasure, my young friends, we shall all go to a hotel together; no doubt you are hungry and ready for dinner, and you shall dine with me." A coach was called; Wilson ordered the luggage to be placed outside, and gave directions to the driver, who in a short time pulled up at a very nice-looking house, with a small garden in front. The situation was rural, and there was so little of the aspect of a hotel about the place, that on alighting, the lads asked once or twice, if they had come to the right place? "All right, gentlemen; walk in; leave your trunks in the lobby. I have settled with the driver, and now I shall order dinner." No time was lost, and very soon the two youths were conversing freely with their unknown friend, and enjoying themselves extremely in the satisfactory position of having thus accidentally fallen into such good company and good quarters. The deception, however, could not be kept up much longer; and, in the course of the evening, Wilson let them know where they were, telling them that they could now judge for themselves what sort of a fellow "the Professor" was.

Another anecdote of holiday-time relates to a later period, when maturer years had invested the Professor with a more patriarchal dignity and sedateness. True to his love for spring, he had selected that season for an excursion to the pastoral vales of Yarrow and Ettrick, where glittering rivers,

> "Winding through the pomp of cultivated nature,"

attracted more than one poet's admiration; for if Wordsworth sang in verse, Wilson uttered in prose, how "in spirit all streams are one that flow through the forest. Ettrick and Yarrow come rushing into each other's arms, aboon the haughs o' Selkirk, and then flow Tweed-blent to the sea." In the month of May, he sent an invitation to his students resident in the south of Scotland, to meet him at "Tibby Shiels's," where they were to wander a day with him "to enjoy the first gentle embrace of spring in some solitary spot." Where could it have been better selected than at St. Mary's Loch? It was said that the meeting was one of unspeakable delight; the hills were adorned with the freshest green, and the calm, quiet lake reflected the surrounding verdure in its deep waters, and they beheld

> "The swan on still St. Mary's lake,
> Float double swan and shadow."

The Professor spoke of the love of nature, and his words impressed them all, and of the poet of Altrive, "our own shepherd, dear to all the rills that issue, in thousands, from their own recesses among the braes; for when a poet walks through regions his genius has sung, all nature does him homage, from cloud to clod—from the sky to green earth—all living creatures therein included, from eagle to the mole. James knows this, and is happy among the hills." And was that little company then assembled by the "dowie holms," not happy too? Wilson was in his brightest mood; no one was overlooked; joyously and pleasantly passed the day; and before evening laid its westering shadows into gloaming, he called his students around him, and, rising up, "he shook his wild locks among them, blessed them, called them his children," and bade them adieu. Surely a kindly recognition of these young men in manner such as this would bring benefit with it not less lasting, than when, in graver state, he prelected, *ex cathedra*, to his assembled class.

We get an idea of what that class was from the following recollections, which Mr. John Hill Burton has kindly sent to me. He says:—

"I first saw and made the acquaintance of Professor Wilson

when I joined his class in 1830. The occasion was of much more interest to me than the usual first sight of an instructor by a pupil. I do not know if there be any thing of the same kind now, but in that day there was a peculiar devotion to *Blackwood's Magazine* among young readers in the north. All who were ambitious of looking beyond their class exercises, considered this the fountain-head of originality and spirit in literature. The articles of the last number were discussed critically in the debating societies, and knowingly in the supper parties, and the writing of the master-hand was always anxiously traced. To see that master, then, for the first time, was an epoch in one's life.

"The long-looked for first sight of a great man often proves a disappointment to the votary. It was far otherwise in this instance. Much as I had heard of his appearance, it exceeded expectation, and I said to myself that, in the tokens of physical health and strength, intellect, high spirit, and all the elements of masculine beauty, I had not seen his equal. There was a curious contrast to all this in the adjuncts of his presence—the limp Geneva gown, and the square, box-shaped desk, over which he seemed like some great bust set on a square plinth—but I question if any robes or chair of state would have added dignity to his appearance.

"On a very early day in the session—I forget whether it was quite the first—we suddenly came to an acquaintance, on my having occasion to speak with him at the end of the lecture. When he found that I was an Aberdonian, he asked me if I knew Tarland, 'a place celebrated for its markets.' To be sure I did; and Tarland was in those days not a place to be easily forgotten. On the border of the Highlands, it had been a great mart for smuggled whiskey; and though the reduction of the excise duties had spoiled that trade, custom continued it for a while in a modified shape, and the wild ruffianly habits it had nourished were still in their prime, and not likely to disappear until the generation trained to them had passed away. The Professor had seen and experienced the ways of the place. He hinted, with a sort of half-sarcastic solemnity, that he was there in the course of the ethical inquiries to which he had devoted himself; just as the professor of natural history or any other persevering geologist might be found where any unusual geological phenomenon is developed, or the professor of anatomy might conduct his inquiries into some abnormal structure of the human body. His researches might lead him into trials and perils, as those of zealous investigators are often apt to do. In fact, he had to draw upon his early acquired knowledge of the art of self-defence on the occasion, and he believed he did so not unsuccessfully. Here there was a sparkle of the eye, a curl of the lip, and a general look of fire and determination, which reminded one of

'The stern joy which warriors feel
In foemen worthy of their steel.'

"He described the market-day as a sort of continued surge of rioting, drinking, and fighting; and when darkness was coming on, he had to find his way to some distance among unknown roads. A lame man, very unsuited for that wild crowd, had in the mean time scraped a sort of acquaintance with him, and interested him by the scholarship interspersed in his conversation. He was the schoolmaster of a neighboring parish; and as their ways lay together, he was to be the guide, and, in return, to get the assistance of the stalwart stranger. The poor schoolmaster had, however, so extensively moistened his clay, that assistance was not sufficient, and the Professor had to throw him over his shoulder, and carry him. With the remainder of the dominie's physical strength, too, oozed away that capacity for threading the intricacies of the path, which was his contribution to the joint adventure. Assistance had to be got from some of the miscellaneous Highlanders dispersing homewards; and as all were anxious to bear a hand, the small group increased into a sort of procession, and the Professor reached his abode, wherever that might be, at the head of a sort of army of these lawless men.

"A history of this kind was calculated to put a young person at ease, in the presence of the great man and the Professor of Moral Philosophy. We now sailed easily into conversation, and went off into metaphysics. That he should seriously and earnestly talk on such matters with the raw youth was, of course, very gratifying; but there was a sort of misgiving, that he took for granted my knowing more than I did. This was a way of his, however, to which I became accustomed; he was always ready to give people credit for extensive learning. There was no mere hollow courtesy or giving the go-by in his talk on this occasion. He helped me at once to the root of many important things connected with the studies I was pursuing. A point arose, on which he would speak to Sir William Hamilton, who knew all about it; he did afterwards speak to him accordingly, somewhat to my surprise, as I thought he would be unlikely to remember either me or my talk—and I thus made an acquaintance which afterwards strengthened into an admiring friendship for that great man. Then another point came up, on which De Quincey might be consulted, and would give very curious information, if he could be caught. He was then dwelling with the Professor—as much as he could be said to dwell anywhere. Suppose then I should come and dine with them? That would be my best chance of seeing De Quincey. That it was quite right to take advantage of this frank invitation, and, an obscure stranger, to catch at an opportunity of thrusting myself on the hospitalities and the family circle of a distinguished man, may be questioned. But most people will admit that the temptation was great. It was too much for me, and I accepted, with immense satisfaction.

"I went to Gloucester Place accordingly. The poet's residence did not represent the traditional garret, nor his guests the eccentric troop familiar to Smollett and Fielding, although I had gone there to meet one who had the reputation of bringing into the nineteenth century the habits of that age in their most grotesque shape. Him, however, I did not see. The Opium-Eater was supposed to be somewhere about the premises, but he chose neither to appear in the drawing-room nor the dining-room, and years passed before I became acquainted with the most peculiar man of genius, in Britain at least, of the age. Otherwise, there was good company, handsomely housed, and entertained with hospitality thoroughly kind, easy, and hearty, but all in perfect taste and condition.

"It was a sort of epoch to myself, and therefore I remember pretty well who were present. We had Professor Jameson, then at the zenith of his fame as a mineralogist, Lawrence M'Donald, the sculptor, and John Malcolm, then a popular poet and writer of miscellanies, whose fame, though considerable then, has probably been worn out ere this day; he was, as I knew him afterwards, a pleasant, gentle, meditatively-inclined man, though I think he had seen military service, and knew the mess-room of the old war,—a different thing from that of the present day. Youngest, as well as I remember, of these seniors, was a Captain Alexander, whom I take to be the traveller, Sir J. E. Alexander.

"Among my own contemporaries were some representatives of young Edinburgh, of whom a word or two presently, and a Pole, who happened to be the only guest with whom I had any previous acquaintance. His formal designation was Leon Count Lubienski. Seeing a good deal of him afterwards during the five months session, I formed a great idea of his abilities. He had nothing of the imaginative, or of the æsthetic—a term then coming into use from Germany; but for an eye to the practical, and a capacity for mastering all knowledge leading in that direction, it did not happen to me to find his equal among my contemporaries. With all the difficulties of language against him, he carried off from young Edinburgh the first prize in the civil law class. After having astonished us throughout the session, he left us at the end, and I never could discover any thing of a distinct kind about his career, though I have turned up the initials of his name in the many biographical dictionaries of contemporaries which seem to be a specialty of the present day. I heard, many years since, a vague rumor that he had risen in the Russian service. He was just the man, according to the notions of this country, to be useful to such a government, if he would consent to serve it. I feel certain, however, that he was a man who could not have escaped being heard of by the world, had his career in practical life lain elsewhere than in a close despotism.

"Such was the outer circle of guests; within was the Professor's own family. And so hither I found myself transferred, as by a wave of an enchanter's wand, a raw, unknown youth, with claim of no kind in the shape of introduction, with no credentials or testimony to my bare respectability; no name, even of a common friend, to bring our conversation to an anchor with. This success seems far more surprising when looked back upon than it was felt at the time. Young people read in novels of such things, and therefore are not astonished by them; but in after life they become aware of their extreme uncommonness. Nor was it a mere casual act of formal hospitality; I received afterwards many a cordial welcome within those hospitable doors.

"It is possibly its personal bearing that makes me now remember pretty distinctly a good-humored and kindly pleasantry of the Professor's at that first dinner. I have mentioned that there were some representatives of young Edinburgh present. I do not know what precise position towards the rest of the human race the youth of Edinburgh may now claim, but it appeared to me, when I came among them at the time I speak of, that they considered it beyond any kind of question that they were superior to all the rest of the world. To one coming from the common hard drudgery of our classes in the North, where we did our work zealously enough, with plenty of internal rivalry, but thought no more of claiming fame outside the walls than any body of zealous mechanics, it was a great novelty to get among a community, where the High School *dux* of 18—, or the gainer of the gold medal in the —— class, was pointed out to you; nay, further, to meet with lads of your own standing, who were the authors of published poems, had delivered great and telling speeches at the Speculative, or had written capital articles in the *Edinburgh Literary Journal*, or the *University Album*. Whether it were the inheritance of the long hierarchy of literary glory which Edinburgh had enjoyed, or arose from any other cause, this phenomenon was marvellous to a stranger, and rather disagreeably marvellous, because a youth coming into all this brilliant light, out of the Bœotian darkness of Aberdeen, was conscious of being contemplated with compassionate condescension. We had, however, at the University of Edinburgh at that time, a considerable body of Aberdonians, pretty compactly united. At our head was William Spalding, the first among us in learning and accomplishments, as well as in the means of using them. He well justified our expectations by his subsequent career, sadly impeded as it was by bodily ailments, which brought it to an untimely close. I have got into an episode in mentioning him here, but it is not entirely inappropriate, for the Professor was, as I believe he has been in many other instances, the first who, from a high place, took notice of Spalding's capacity.

"Well, emboldened and elated, I suppose, by being brought into social equality with them, it came to pass that, in our after-dinner talk, I threw down the gauntlet to the representatives of young Edinburgh then present, and stood for the equality, at least, if not the superiority of Aberdeen in all the elements of human eminence. In such a contest, a good deal depends on the number of names, in any way known to fame, that the champion remembers; and Aberdeen possessed, especially if one drew on the far past, a very fair stock of celebrities. As I was giving them forth, amidst a good deal of derisive laughter and ironical cheering, the Professor, tickled by the absurdity of the thing, threw himself into the contest, on my side, and tumbled over some of my antagonists in an extremely delectable manner. This was a first revelation to me of a power which I afterwards often observed with astonishment,—a kind of intellectual gladiatorship, which enabled him, in a sort of rollicking, playful manner, to overthrow his adversary with little injury to him, but much humiliation. I can compare it to nothing it so much resembles as a powerful, playful, good-natured mastiff taking his sport with a snarling cur. As I shall have to mention more especially, this was a powerful instrument of discipline in his class. He never had to stand on his dignity. When it was worth his while, he tumbled any transgressor about in a way that made him, though unhurt, thoroughly ashamed of himself, and an example to deter others from doing the like. On the occasion referred to, it was possibly visible to the bystanders, and had I possessed more experience, might have been known to myself, that I also had been gently laid sprawling in the attacks that seemed directed entirely against my adversaries; but I happily saw only their discomfiture, and rejoiced accordingly. All that was done for me was, however, entirely neutralized by a random shaft from the Pole, finding mark he never meant, and piercing more effectually than all the artillery of my opponents. Looking with an air of intense gravity on the whole discussion, he broke in with the inquiry, whether he was right or not in his supposition, that 'Apperdeen was verray illoustrious for the making of stockingks?' After this, there was no use of saying more on either side.

"I wish I had tried to Boswellize, or could now remember the talk of that, as of many other evenings. One little incident I remember distinctly, but I am sure I shall be unable to tell it to any effect. Some priggish remarks having been made by some one on the power of exhaustive analysis, the Professor fell to illustrate it by an attempt, through that process, to send a hired assistant, name unknown, for a fresh bottle of claret. He began calling to him by the ordinary names, John, James, William, Thomas, and so on, but none hit the mark—the man standing by the sideboard, in demure contemplation, as if inwardly solving some metaphysical difficulty. The Professor then passed on in a wild discursive flight through stranger names. At last he seemed to have hit the right one, for the attendant darted forward. It was, in fact, in obedience to a sign by a guest that he was wanted, but it came in immediate response to a thoroughly unconventional designation,—Beelzebub, Mephistophiles, or something of that sort; and the fun was enhanced by the man's solemn unconsciousness that he had been the object of a logical experiment.

"But to come back to the class. It was one that must have been somewhat memorable to the Professor himself, when he looked back upon it in after years. Not only was his son John in it, but it included John Thompson Gordon and William Edmondstoune Aytoun, so that unconsciously the Professor was instructing the future husbands of his daughters. There were others to give it interest and repute—as Archibald Swinton, now Professor of Civil law; the clever Pole I have already referred to; John Walker Ord, who showed poetic powers which promised a considerable harvest; and Thomas Todd Stoddart, who had won laurels, and thoroughly enjoyed them, too, in his published poem of 'The Death Wake.'

"The powers of Wilson, as an instructor and a public speaker, will, of course, be described by others. I may simply say that attendance at his class, at the same time that it was an act of duty, rewarded the student with what duty seldom brings, the enjoyment of an oration alive with brilliant and powerful eloquence.

"Saturday was a great day of enjoyment of a more egotistic kind. Then he spoke on the essays he had received. He gave us a breadth of topics, and allowed us wonderful latitude in the handling of them—but he certainly read them all—and what a mass of trash he must have thus perused! In criticising them, he was charitable and cordial to the utmost stretch of magnanimous charity. I can hardly say what an exciting thrill it imparted to the youth to hear his own composition read out from that high place, and commented on with earnestness, and not without commendation. The recollection of these days sometimes also recalls Boswell's garrulous account of his first symposium with Johnson. 'The Orthodox and High Church sound of THE MITRE; the figure and manner of the celebrated Samuel Johnson; the extraordinary power and precision of his conversation, and the pride arising from finding myself admitted as his companion, produced a variety of sensations, and a pleasing elevation of mind beyond what I had ever before experienced.' But *our* elevation proceeded from entirely intellectual sources, without the aid of the other stimulants which contributed to Boswell's glory. Altogether, that class was a scene of enjoyment which remains in my mind entirely distinct from even the pleasanter portion of other work-day college life.

"The class was a very large one. I have referred to the Professor's peculiar power of preserving discipline, or rather of keeping up good-humor, gentlemanly fellowship, and order, without the necessity of discipline. An instance occurred during the session, when he exercised this power in a matter not peculiar to his own class, not indeed showing itself within the class, but general to the students at large, as a portion of the inhabitants of Edinburgh having a common tie. There was a great snow-ball riot in that session. This is a thing peculiar to Edinburgh, and not easily made intelligible to those who have not witnessed it. As a stranger it surprised me much. In the north we had our old feuds and animosities, often breaking out in serious violence and mischief. But that a set of people—most of them full-grown—should, without any settled feud, utterly change the whole tenor of their conduct, and break into something like insurrection, merely because snow was on the ground, appeared to be a silliness utterly incomprehensible. This snow-ball affair became so formidable-looking that a mounted foreign refugee, with his head full of revolutions, galloped through the streets (I forget if he was in any way armed) calling out 'Barricade—shoot!'

"After it was pretty well over, the Professor made a speech to us on the conclusion of his daily lecture. He did not condemn or even disparage snow-balling; on the contrary, he expressed glowingly his sense of its sometimes irresistible attractions. These he illustrated by what had once occurred to himself and a venerable and illustrious friend; we thought at the time that he meant Dr. Chalmers. In a spring walk among the hills, and in the middle of a semi-metaphysical discussion, they came upon a snow-wreath. By a sort of simultaneous impulse, borne on the recollection of early days, the discussion stopped, and they fell too to a regular hard bicker. After working away till they were covered with snow, panting with fatigue and glowing red with the exertion, they both stopped, and laughed loud in each other's face; just such a laugh as he must have then expressed, did the Professor force upon his class. Then came his contrast between such a scene and a fracas in the dirty streets, where low-bred ruffians took the opportunity to get out some bit of petty revenge or of mere wanton cruelty, or of insolence to those whose character and position entitled them to deference; and so he went on, until there could not be a question that every one in the class who had been concerned in the affair felt ashamed of himself. His practical conclusion was that they should have their bicker, certainly, but—adjourn it from the college quadrangle and the street to the Pentland hills.

"We naturally, among ourselves, talked over any little instances illustrative of the remarkable power of making any one whom he had to rebuke or correct feel foolish. For instance, there used to be a set of dusky personages who then stood at the corner of certain streets, and annoyed the passenger by stepping up right in front of him, like an established acquaintance, and saying, 'Any old clothes?' It was said that the way in which the Professor on such an occasion turned round on the intruder, and said, 'Yes; have you any?' had such an effect, that the word was passed through the tribe, and he never was again addressed by any of its members.

"I remember a very strong negative testimony to this peculiar power, in the circumstance of his entire freedom from the persecutions of two licensed tormentors, who were the terror of all the rest of the professors. They were men of venerable years and weak intellect, who had established a sort of prescriptive right to attend such classes as they might honor with their presence. It was not of course their mere presence, but the use to which it was put by tricky students, that made the standing grief of the professors. One of them was called Sir Peter Nimmo, a dirty, ill-looking lout, who had neither wit himself, nor any quality with a sufficient amount of pleasant grotesqueness in it to create wit in others. I believe he was merely an idly-inclined and stupidish man of low condition, who, having once got into practice as a sort of public laughing-stock, saw that the occupation paid better than honest industry, and had cunning enough to keep it up. He must have had a rather hard time of it, however, in some respects, for it was an established practice to get hold of the cards of important personages—especially if they were as testy as they were important—and to present them to Sir Peter with a request that he would favor the person indicated with his company at dinner. He always went, pretending simplicity, and using a little caution, if he saw symptoms of strong measures. I suppose he sometimes got a meal that way, following an old Scottish saying about taking 'the bite with the buffet.' He always called himself *Sir* Peter. It was said that a man of high title had professed to knight him in a drunken frolic. He wandered about sometimes endeavoring to establish himself as a sponge in country houses. Strangely enough, he thus got the ear of Wordsworth, who showed him attention. He used the Professor's name, and Wordsworth, as I heard, talked of him as a Scotch baronet, eccentric in appearance, but fundamentally one of the most sensible men he ever met with. The Professor remarked that this compliment was no doubt owing to Sir Peter having judiciously preserved silence, and allowed Wordsworth to pour into his ear unceasingly the even tenor of his loquacity.

"The other of this strange pair was a rather more interesting creature. He was called Dr. Syntax. He had of course another name, but of that the public knew nothing. The Tour of Dr. Syntax in search of the picturesque, with its doggerel rhymes and extravagant illustrations, had not then quite lost the great popularity it enjoyed. The representations of the hero were intended to be gross caricatures, but the structure of his namesake was so supernaturally protracted and spidery as closely to approach the proportions of the caricature. His costume, probably by no design of his own, completed the likeness. This being, if seen in the street, was always marching along with extreme rapidity, with his portfolio under his arm, as if full of important business, unless, indeed, he had just got a present of a turban, a yeoman's helmet, or some other preposterous decoration, when he would stand exhibiting himself wherever a crowd happened to pass. He honored the various professors and clergy of Edinburgh with his attendance at their lectures and sermons. He always chose the most conspicuous place he could find. There, with his long, demure, cadaverous face, on which a stray smile would have been at once frozen, he proceeded to business and spread out his portfolio. He sometimes took notes of what was said, at others took the portrait of the speaker; it may be presumed that in church he limited himself to the former function. If it grew dark, he would solemnly draw from his pocket a small taper and strike a light, determined not to be interrupted in his duties, and in the centre of the general gloom a small disk of light would distinguish his countenance, which was as solemn as the grave, yet shed around a degree of restless mirth which spoiled many a lecture, and must have sadly jumbled the devotions of the church-goers. I believe every professor received a full share of this man's attentions except Wilson. His literary ally, the Professor of Civil law, a man endowed with a great fund of humor, which, however, he could not convert like him into defensive armor, suffered dreadfully from Syntax, and when the pale face was visible in the highest desk, we knew that a day was lost, the poor lecturer having enough to do in keeping down internal convulsions of laughter, which seemed as if they would explode and shatter his frame to pieces.

"Both these tormentors, of whom I have, perhaps, said too much, stood in wholesome dread of Wilson. It was, I have no doubt, by effectually treating them according to their folly, that he earned this exemption, in which his brethren must have greatly envied him.

"Before that session came to an end, an event occurred momentous to all of us—the Reform Bill was brought in. We youths had previously indulged in no politics, or if in any, they were of a mild Aristides and Brutus kind, tinged perhaps by De Lolme and the Letters of Junius. Now, however, we were at once separated into two hostile forces. To the liberals, *Blackwood's Magazine*, ceasing to be the guiding-star of literature, had become the watchfire of the enemy. The bitterness of the hostility felt at that time by the young men of the two opposite political creeds cannot easily be understood by those in the same stage of life at the present day. The friendship must have been fast indeed that remained after one friend had become a reformer and the other an anti-reformer. We used to make faces at each other as we passed; and if a few words were exchanged, they were hostile and threatening. I suppose our hostility was a type of a stage of transition between the ferocity of times of civil war and the mild political partisanship of the present day.

"The Professor was known to take his stand against the Bill with great vehemence, but I never knew more than one instance of an approach to an ebullition of it upon any of his friends on our side. There had been many Reform meetings of all kinds, sometimes assembling vast multitudes, when it occurred to attempt a Tory meeting—the word Conservative had not then been invented. A question arose among us whether they should be allowed to have it their own way, and, since they called the meeting public, whether our party should not go and out-vote them. The tactic of public meetings, as simply one-sided demonstrations of the strength of a party, was not then understood, and they were confounded with meetings of representative bodies, where strength is tried by discussing and voting. A friend of the Professor's, older than the youngsters of his class, but a good deal younger than himself, was known strongly to favor an invasion of the meeting from our side. He called on the Professor presently before the meeting; it was a friendly visit, but partially, I presume, for the purpose of sounding the Professor on the exciting question. Just before leaving, he expressed a hope that there would be no disturbance. The Professor, drawing himself up, answered, as well as I can remember having heard, in this wise: 'What any set of blackguards may be prepared to attempt in these days I cannot predict; but I *can* say, that if I see any man who is on terms of acquaintance with *me* go to that meeting to meddle with it, I hope I may be the first—(a pause)—to kick him out into the street.' And the visitor said the Professor looked as if he were so close on the point of rehearsing this performance on the spot, that he involuntarily started a good pace back.

"Though politics entered deeply into our social and literary intercourse at that time, yet the Professor was strong enough in his other elements of distinction to keep himself aloof, and remain untouched in his other relations by the influence of party, without in the least degree putting in question the sincerity of his attachment to his own side. He made in the class just one allusion to politics, and it was emphatic. An ambitious student, in one of his essays, finding his way to the characteristics of democracy, made some allusions to passing events in a tone which he no doubt thought likely to secure the favor of the Professor. We never would have known of this effort had it not been read out in full to us in the class, and followed by a severe rebuke on the introduction of politics to a place where party strife should be unknown."

Another student,* who attended the class seven years later, fortunately preserved his notes, and sends me the following vivid recollections of the winter session of 1837:—

"Of Professor Wilson as a lecturer on Moral Philosophy, it is not easy to convey any adequate idea to strangers,—to those who never saw his grand and noble form excited into bold and passionate action behind that strange, old-fashioned desk, nor heard his

* The Rev. William Smith, of North Leith Church.

manly and eloquent voice sounding forth its stirring utterances with all the strange and fitful cadence of a music quite peculiar to itself. The many-sidedness of the man, and the unconventional character of his prelections, combine to make it exceedingly difficult to give any full analysis of his course, or to define the nature and grounds of his wonderful power as a lecturer. I am certain that if every student who ever attended his class were to place on record his impressions of these, the impressions of each student would be widely different, and yet they would not, taken all together, exhaust the subject, or supply a complete representation either of his matter or his manner. There was so much in the look and tone, in every aspect and in every movement of the man, which touched and swayed the student at the time, but which cannot now be recalled, described, or even realized, that any reminiscence by any one can be interesting only to those whose memories of the same scenes enable them to follow out the train of recollection, or complete the picture which it may suggest.

"I attended his class in session 1837–8. It was the session immediately succeeding the loss of his wife, the thought of which, as it was ever again and again re-awakened in his mind by allusions in his lectures, however remote, to such topics as death, bereavement, widowhood, youthful love, domestic scenes, and, above all, to conjugal happiness, again and again shook his great soul with an agony of uncontrollable grief, the sight of which was sufficient to subdue us all into deep and respectful sympathy with him. On such occasions he would pause for a moment or two in his lecture, fling himself forward on the desk, bury his face in his hands, and while his whole frame heaved with visible emotion, he would weep and sob like a very child.

"The roll of papers on which each lecture was written, which he carried into the class-room firmly grasped in his hand, and suddenly unrolled and spread out on the desk before him, commencing to read the same moment, could not fail to attract the notice of any stranger in his class-room. It was composed in large measure of portions of old letters—the addresses and postage-marks on which could be easily seen as he turned the leaf, yet it was equally evident that the writing was neat, careful, and distinct; and, except in a more than usually dark and murk day, it was read with perfect ease and fluency.

"In the course of lectures which I attended, he began by treating of the desire of knowledge; the feeling of admiration; sympathy; desire of society; emulation; envy; anger; revenge; self; self-esteem; the love of fame or glory, and the love of power.

"The most memorable points in these lectures were: (1.) a highly wrought description of Envy, founded on Spenser's picture of Lucifera riding in the gorgeous chariot of Pride, and preceded by six Passions (the fifth of which is Envy) riding each on an appropriate animal; (2.) a very minute and purely metaphysical analysis of the idea of Self; and, (3.) a highly poetical illustration of the workings of the Love of Power. This last display I can never forget; and sure am I that no one present can ever forget it either. It appeared to have been a lecture whose place in the course and powerful eloquence were previously not unknown to fame. For when I went to the class-room at the usual hour on the last day of November, I found it already overcrowded with an audience, comprising many strangers of note and several professors, all in a high state of expectation. Conspicuous in the centre of the front bench was the new Professor of Logic, Sir William Hamilton, eager with anticipation as the others. At length the door of the retiring-room was thrown open, and with even firmer step and longer stride, and more heroic gait than usual, the Professor, with his flowing gown and streaming locks, advanced to the desk and began the lecture. After a hasty recapitulation of the subjects discussed in previous lectures, he proceeded somewhat thus; I can give but the feeblest sketch of the lecture:—

"'Towards the close of yesterday's lecture we came to the consideration of another active principle, "The Love of Power," and we remarked on the frequent corruption and melancholy degradation of genius through an inordinate love of power. The origin of this love of power is found in the feeling of pleasure which uniformly, and in a proportionably greater or less degree, attends the consciousness of possessing power. Even in lower creation we see this feeling of pleasure shown. The eagle evidently enjoys a deep sensation of pleasure as he cuts his unmarked path through the storm-tossed clouds. The horse also, when in the fulness of his strength he hastens o'er the course, outstripping all his rivals, is a supremely happy as well as an exquisitely beautiful animal. The child too attains a never-failing source of pleasure on his first consciousness of possessing powers, and he is overwhelmed with grief and vexation when he meets with any obstacle which presents an insurmountable obstruction to his free and unfettered exercise of these powers.

"'All the principles which the human being possesses have been given to him for the purpose of enabling him to fight his way through scenes of trouble, and difficulty, and danger, and it has been also wisely decreed that the exercise of these principles or powers, when crowned with success, should afford him pleasure. The woodsman who is engaged in felling pines in the awful depths of the American forest, derives pleasure from the consciousness of power, as he sees giant after giant laid low at his feet by the prowess of his own unaided arm, at the same time that he is usefully employed in clearing out a domain for the support, it may be, of his wife and family. The lonely hunter feels a pleasure in his powers as he brings down the towering bird of Jove by his unerring ball, or as he meets a boar in deadly conflict, and drains the heart's blood of the brute with his spear. The savage fisherman of the far north, as he goes in his frail canoe to pursue the most perilous of all enterprises, feels a pleasure in his powers, as he triumphs by the skill of his rude harpoon over even the mightiest denizens of the deep. The peasant from his conscious feeling of manly power in every muscle of his stalwart frame derives pleasure, and, at the same time, the ability to sustain all the trials and conquer all the difficulties which cross him on his toil-worn path. The life of the scholar is as much a life of difficulty as the life of the traveller who plods on his way through unknown countries, and requires in a high degree the sense of power to cheer and sustain him on his course; for we all know that conquests in the kingdom of intelligence are not to be won by one day's battle. . . .

"'If the mind needs support in its search after virtue, it must much more need it in the ordinary business and pursuits of life.

"'To be weak is miserable, doing or suffering. . . .

"'It has often occurred to us that the most debased and humiliating state in which human nature could be found, is that where men have calmly bowed themselves under the disadvantages in which nature has seen fit originally to place them, without a single stout-hearted effort to relieve themselves from them; as, for instance, in the case of the inhabitants of New Holland, as they were bescribed by those who first visited the island. And what a contrast is visible between their character and that of the North American Indians, vanquishing the feeling of pain in their breasts by the strength of their unconquerable wills; "The Stoics of the wood, the men without a tear."

"'Let us picture to our mind's eye a pampered Sybarite, nursed in all the wantonness of high-fed luxury, dallying on a downy sofa, amid all the gorgeousness of ornamental tapestry, listening to the soft sounds of sweetest music playing in his ears; his eyes satiated with pleasure in contemplating the enchanting pictures that decorate the walls, and the beautiful statues which in pleasing variety fill up the distant vistas of his palace; whose rest would be broken, whose happiness would be spoiled, by the doubling of the highly scented rose-leaf that lies beneath him on his silken couch. Let us by the magic power of imagination transport this man to the gloomy depths of an American forest, where the dazzling glare of a bright fire instantly meets his eye. If he does not forthwith ignominiously expire at the first view, suppose him to survey the characters who compose or fill up the busy scene around it. The barbarous savages of one tribe have taken captive the chief of another engaged in deadly hostilities with them. They have not impaled him alive. That would be to consign him too speedily to unhearing death. But they have tied him fast with bands made of the long and lithe forest grass, which yields not quickly to the fire. They have placed him beside the pile which they kindle with fiendish satisfaction, and feed with cautious hand, well knowing the point or pitch to raise it to, which tortures but not speedily consumes. They have exhausted all their energy in uttering a most diabolical yell, on witnessing their victim first feel the horrid proofs of their resentment, and now, seated on the grass around, they look on in silence. The chief stands firm with unflinching nerve; his long eye-lashes are scorched off, but his proud eye disdains to wink; his dark raven locks have all perished, but there is not a wrinkle seen on his forehead. From the crown of his head to the sole of his foot his skin is one continued blister, but the courage of his soul remains unshaken, and quails not before the tormenting pain. The Sybarite has expired at the mere sight; his craven heart has ceased to beat. The Indian hero stands firm. There is even a smile on his sadly marred cheek, and it is not the smile which is extorted by excruciating pain, and forms the fit accompaniment of a groan, but he smiles with joy as he chants his death-song. He thinks with pride and joy on the heroic deeds he has performed; how he has roamed from sunset to sunrise through the forest depths, and changed the sleep of his foemen into death. He beholds on all sides dancing around him the noble spirits of his heroic ancestors; and nearest to him, and almost, he imagines, within reach of his embrace, he sees the ghost of his father, who first put into his hand and taught him the use of the scalping-knife and tomahawk; who has come from the heavens far beyond the place of mountains and of clouds to quaff the death-song, and to welcome to the land of the great hereafter the spirit of his undegenerate son. The chief is inflamed with a glorious rapture that exalts him beyond the sensation of pain, and conquers agony. "He holds no parley with unmanly fears."

> "The son of Alcnomon has ceased to endure;
> He consented to die, but he scorned to complain."

"'It seems a duty incumbent on us all to think well of ourselves and of our powers. But then comes the question, Where falls the limit to be fixed at which this feeling must cease? We answer, Nature and the real necessities of life discover to a man the actual extent of his powers. Nature, reality, and truth, are the only tests. . . .

"'To show that the innate consciousness of power often sustains a person amidst severely trying difficulties, we may relate a well-authenticated anecdote of Nelson. When a very young man in the rank of midshipman, he was returning from India on sick leave, with his health broken by the climate, and his spirits depressed by the feeling that he was cast off from his profession, and that he could never rise further in it. Sitting one day solitarily, meditating on all this, his thoughts reverted to the great naval heroes who had fought and won his country's battles, and gained for England the empire of the deep; when a bright ray of hope seemed to shine before him, that filled his soul with intense pleasure, and made him exclaim: "I will be a hero; England will not cast me off; England's king will be my patron and my friend." He often after spoke of this ray which did indeed blaze forth, and lighted his path to renown, till the noble watch-word of Trafalgar insured his last and crowning triumph, and the name of Nelson was known as widely as the name of England.'

"This faint sketch taken at the time may serve, with all its imperfections, to give some idea of the substance of this noble lecture, but it cannot convey to any not present the slightest conception of the transcendent power and overwhelming eloquence with which it was delivered, or of its electrifying effects upon the audience. The whole soul of the man seemed infused into his subject, and to be rushing forth with resistless force in the torrent of his rapidly-rolling words. As he spoke, his whole frame quivered with emotion. He evidently saw the scene he described, and such was the sympathetic force of his strong poetic imagination, that he made us, whether we would or not, see it too. Now dead silence held the class captive. In the interval of his words you would have heard a pin fall. Again, at some point, the applause could not be restrained, and was vociferous. Especially when the dying scene in his description of the North American Indian's virtues reached its glorious consummation, the cheers were again and again repeated by every voice, till the roof rang again, and Sir William Hamilton, not less enthusiastic in his applause than the very youngest of the students behind him, actually stood up and clapped his hands with evident delight and approbation.

"I have heard some of the greatest orators of the day,—Lords Derby, Brougham, Lyndhurst; Peel, O'Connell, Sheil, Follett, Chalmers, Caird, Guthrie, M'Neile; I have heard some of these in their very best styles make some of their most celebrated appearances; but for popular eloquence, for resistless force, for the seeming inspiration that swayed the soul, and the glowing sympathy that entranced the hearts of his entire audience, that lecture by Professor Wilson far excelled the loftiest efforts of the best of these I ever listened to; and I have long come to the decided conclusion that if he had chosen the sacred profession, and given his whole heart and soul to his work, he would have raised the fame of pulpit oratory to a pitch far beyond what it ever has reached, and gained a celebrity and success as a preacher second to none in the annals of the Church.

"The course was continued in lectures on, (1.) Jealousy, which was illustrated by a very splendid and elaborate analysis of the character of Othello, in which the erroneousness of the common idea of the Moor as a mere victim of the green-eyed monster was very clearly and convincingly exhibited; (2.) The Love of Pleasure; (3.) Hope; (4.) Fear; (5.) Happiness or Misery in this Life arising from the lower principles of humanity; (6.) Association, discussed at great length and with very great metaphysical acumen, as well as copious illustration; (7.) Imagination, treated in nine most interesting lectures; and, (8.) Conscience; which, with a full and particular consideration of the various moral systems propounded by ancient and modern philosophy, occupied thirty lectures.

"In the next division of the course the Affections were explained and illustrated in a series of sixteen lectures, in which all the wealth of poetry and pathos that were at his command had ample scope and glorious display in picturing scenes of domestic and social life, and in drawing from the whole field of literature examples of family affection and heroic patriotism. Thus we had the picture of a family —with all its interpenetrating relations, of the elder members towards the younger, and of the elder towards each other; the strong hold which any absent member retains over the affections of all at home, and the deep reverence and affectionate love with which they all regard the head of the family—set before us in a manner to rivet attention, by connecting with it a very fine disquisition on Burns's 'Cottar's Saturday Night.' We had the beautiful pictures of filial affection drawn by Sophocles and Shakspere respectively in Antigone and Cordelia, extemporaneously, but most effectively and splendidly described. This *extempore* lecture was immediately followed up by another, delivered also without the aid of any notes, and of a very strange and discursive character, as the heads of it will show:—'Antigone—Electra—Clytemnestra—Agamemnon—Ægisthus—Orestes—Good old Homer who never nods—Ulysses—Achilles—Peleus—The Meeting of Laertes and Achilles—The Lake Poets—Southey and Wordsworth—Apples and Pears—Apple-pie;' but in which the Professor succeeded in demonstrating the vast superiority of the great poets of antiquity, in delineating those simple touches of nature that go to prove the whole world kin. We had then parental affection copiously illustrated in a series of lectures containing highly-wrought pictures of an outcast mother sitting begging by the wayside, of emigrant mothers about to be devoured in a burning ship, and of Virgil's sketches of Evander and Pallas, and Mezentius and Lausus, as contrasted with Wordsworth's sketch of the 'statesman' Michael and his son Luke. One whole lecture was devoted to Shakspere's character of Constance, as exhibiting the workings of maternal affection, and another to Priam's going to ransom the body of Hector from Achilles. The paternal affections and friendship were next dealt with in the same interesting manner, with illustrative references to the writings of Jeremy Taylor, Lord Bacon, Cicero, Shakspere, Dugald Stewart, Thomson, and Coleridge. This part of the course was wound up by three very able lectures on Patriotism, during the delivery of the last of which one of the few memorable 'scenes' during the session occurred in the class. The Professor had begun the lecture by a very earnest and powerful defence of nationality or patriotism against the attacks of those who prefer a spirit of cosmopolitanism. In the course of this, he had occasion to refer to the views of Coleridge and Chenevix on the character of fallen nations, and particularly to the very peculiar relation in which Scotland had long stood to England; and in dealing with this latter point he was proceeding with the remark, that 'the great Demosthenes of Ireland, the ruler of seven millions of the finest peasantry in the world, had presumed to say at a public meeting that the reason Scotland had never been conquered was that Scotland had never been worth conquering.' I do not know how the lecture as written would have dealt with this charge, for the remark led to an interruption of its delivery. Some Irish students, resenting the contemptuous tone in which their great hero was mentioned, and especially taking offence, perhaps justly, at the comical way in which the word '*pizzantry*' was pronounced, raised first a hiss, and then a howl, which provoked counter-cheering from the more numerous Conservatives present, till the class-room became for a few minutes something like Babel or a bear-garden. For a little the Professor looked calmly on; but at last, fairly roused by the unusual uproar, he threw his notes aside, and drowning all noise by the stentorian pitch of voice in which he repeated the sentence that had provoked it all, he on the spur of the moment burst forth in a most eloquent and effective denunciation of all demagogues, and of all Irish demagogues in particular, showing in return for O'Connell's contemptuous remark about Scotland, the exact number of English pikemen and archers that had sufficed for the total subjugation of Ireland; and in castigation of those of his students that had hissed him, launching all the shafts of his raillery, and these were both numerous and sharp, at modern Radicalism, and its cant phrase, 'March of Intellect.' The scene was one not to be forgotten. It was the only occasion any expression of political feeling or bias escaped from him; and yet, though he spoke under great excitement and with merciless severity, he said nothing that made him less respected and admired even by those who differed from him in his political views.*

"The course was concluded by a series of about twenty lectures on Natural Theology, in which that subject was treated in a manner altogether worthy of its vast importance. The great writers, both ancient and modern, were reviewed in a highly philosophical and finely appreciatory spirit. The ability of Hume was fully admitted, and his arguments met as fairly and successfully as they have ever been; but the pretensions of Lord Brougham to authority in the matter were called in question, and some of his views severely criticised. The moral attributes of God; the duties of man to his Maker; religion in the abstract; the immortality and immateriality of the soul; the moral philosophy of the Greeks, and especially the doctrines of Socrates and Plato, were all handled in a way befitting the grandeur and sacredness of these topics, and so as to impress every student with the depth and earnestness of the Professor's religious views and feelings, as well as with the high-toned morality of his whole mind and temperament.

"And now, reviewing generally one's old impressions of the character of the whole course, and qualifying these by the help of subsequent experience and knowledge, there remains a very decided conviction that while the overflowing wealth of poetical reference and illustration, and the somewhat excessive ornamentation of language, were calculated so far to choke and conceal the systematic philosophy of the lectures; to amuse rather than instruct the students; to deprave rather than chasten and purify their style of composition; the high merits and distinguished qualities of the lectures are indisputable, and their tendency to engender free thought, and to encourage large and liberal-minded study of the works of all the

* The obnoxious reference to the "Liberator" appears to have been subsequently omitted from the lecture; but the topic in reference to which it occurred seems to have been one in which the Professor found some difficulty in restraining his contempt for some of the cants of the day about Progress, March of Intellect, &c. Mr. Nicolson gives me the following extract from his notes of the lectures (1848-9), immediately preceding a quotation from M. Chenevix on the benefits of public instruction as the surest basis of stable government:—"These sentiments are not the growth of late years, as some contemptible persons would seem to insinuate."

greatest authors, were of the most decided and purely beneficial nature. It has been the fashion in certain quarters to decry his lectures as loose and declamatory; but only with those whose judgment is based on superficial appearances alone, and who are so destitute of every thing like sympathy, as to be unable to appreciate excellence that squares not in every point with their preconceived idea of it. One indubitable advantage was possessed by all Professor Wilson's students, who had 'eyes to see and ears to hear,' viz., the advantage of beholding closely the workings of a great and generous mind, swayed by the noblest and sincerest impulses; and of listening to the eloquent utterances of a voice which, reprobating every form of meanness and duplicity, was ever raised to its loftiest pitch in recommendation of high-souled honor, truth, virtue, disinterested love, and melting charity. It was something, moreover, not without value or good effect, to be enabled to contemplate, from day to day, throughout a session, the mere outward aspect of one so evidently every inch a man, nay, a king of men, in whom manly vigor and manly beauty of person were in such close keeping with all the great qualities of his soul; the sight at once carried back the youthful student's imagination to the age of ancient heroes and demigods, when higher spirits walked with men on earth, and made an impression on the opening mind of the most genial and ennobling tendency.

"The Professor was not generally supposed to devote much time in private to the business details and work of his class. But all who really worked for him soon discovered the utter erroneousness of this supposition. Every essay given in to him, however juvenile in thought and expression, was read by him with the most patient and judiciously critical care. If any essay afforded proof of painstaking research or of nascent power, its author was at once invited to the Professor's house, to enjoy the benefit of private conversation, and to be encouraged and directed in his studies. I can never forget an evening which I spent alone with him in such circumstances, when, after discussing the subject and views of some essay that had taken his fancy, and favoring me with some invaluable hints on these, he launched out into a long and most interesting discourse on most of the great men of his time; and sent me away at a late hour, not only gratified with his noble frankness of nature and manner, but more than ever convinced of his vast and varied powers in almost every field of knowledge. Though my intercourse with him was limited entirely to student life, I retain for him the deepest reverence and love.

"'I cannot deem thee dead; like the perfumes
Arising from Judea's vanish'd shrines,
Thy voice still floats around me; nor can tombs
A thousand from my memory hide the lines
Of beauty, on thine aspect which abode,
Like streaks of sunshine pictured there by God.'"

The following account of his last year's professional work (the session 1850–1851) is furnished by the medallist of the year:*—

"The first thing that every one remarked on entering his class, was how thoroughly he did his proper work as a Professor of Moral Philosophy. This is not generally known now, and was not even at that time. There was a notion that he was there Christopher North, and nothing else; that you could get scraps of poetry, bits of sentiment, flights of fancy, flashes of genius, and any thing but Moral Philosophy. Nothing was further from the truth in that year 1850. In the very first lecture he cut into the core of the subject, raised the question which has always in this country been held to be the hardest and deepest in the science (the origin of the Moral Faculty), and *hammered* at it through the great part of the session. Even those who were fresh from Sir William Hamilton's class, and had a morbid appetite for swallowing hard and angular masses of logic, found that the work here was quite stiff enough for any of us. It was not till the latter part of the session, in his lectures on the Affections and the Imagination, that he adopted a looser style of treatment, and wandered freely over a more inviting field. But it is not enough to say that he was thoroughly conscientious in presenting to his students the main questions for their consideration; I am bound to add that he was also thoroughly successful. It is well known that his own doctrine (though it was never quite fixed, and he stated publicly to his class at the close of his last session that he had all along been conscious that there was some gap in it) was opposed to the general Scotch system of Moral Philosophy. His

* Mr. Alexander Taylor Innes, who says in reference to that distinction:—"He was specially kind to me, as the youngest who had ever attained that honor, much coveted at that time as coming from *himself;* for when the University offered to give a prize to his class, he declined to discontinue his own, and still year by year awarded 'Professor Wilson's Gold Medal,' giving the other separately or cumulatively."

Eudaimonism was in fact a sublimed Utilitarianism ; so refined and sublimed that it might have appeared quite a fair course to have avoided discussing those metaphysical and psychological questions which lie at the roots of the general controversy. He did not follow this course. On the contrary, he laid bare the whole question: Whether conscience be a product of experience, or an original and intuitive faculty, with a frankness and fairness which are exceedingly rare, and which impressed most those who most differed from him; and at the same time with a perception of the *status quæstionis*, how it bore on all that followed, and how the teaching of each philosopher bore upon it, which makes me regard his lectures as the most comprehensive, and indeed the most *valuable* thing in our language on this particular question, with the single exception of Sir James Mackintosh's Dissertation.

"His appearance in his class-room it is far easier to remember than to forget. He strode into it with the professor's gown hanging loosely on his arms, took a comprehensive look over the mob of young faces, laid down his watch so as to be out of the reach of his sledge-hammer fist, glanced at the notes of his lecture (generally written on the most wonderful scraps of paper), and then, to the bewilderment of those who had never heard him before, looked long and earnestly out of the north window, towards the spire of the old Tron Kirk; until, having at last got his idea, he faced round and uttered it with eye and hand, and voice and soul and spirit, and bore the class along with him. As he spoke, the bright blue eye looked with a strange gaze into vacancy, sometimes sparkling with a coming joke, sometimes darkening before a rush of indignant eloquence; the tremulous upper lip curving with every wave of thought or hint of passion, and the golden-gray hair floating on the old man's mighty shoulders—if indeed that could be called age, which seemed but the immortality of a more majestic youth.* And occasionally, in the finer frenzy of his more imaginative passages—

* Of the "discipline in his class" in 1830, alluded to by Mr. Burton, Mr. Nicholson says, twenty years later:—"I shall never forget the foolish appearance presented one day in the class by an unmannerly fellow, who rose from his seat about ten minutes from the close of the hour, and proceeded to the door. He found some difficulty in opening it, and was returning to his place, when the Professor beckoned him to his desk, and stooping down, asked, in that deep tone of his, kindly, but with a touch of irony in the question, 'Are you unwell, sir?' 'No, sir,' was the answer. 'Then you will have the kindness to wait till the close of the lecture.' The experiment of leaving the class before the termination of the hour was not likely to be again attempted, after such an exhibition."

as when he spoke of Alexander, clay-cold at Babylon, with the world lying conquered around his tomb, or of the Highland hills, that pour the rage of cataracts adown their riven cliffs, or even of the human mind, with its 'primeval granitic truths,' the grand old face flushed with the proud thought, and the eyes grew dim with tears, and the magnificent frame quivered with a universal emotion.

"It was something to have seen Professor Wilson—this all confessed; but it was something also, and more than is generally understood, to have studied under him."

CHAPTER XI.

LITERARY AND DOMESTIC LIFE.

1820–'26.

In July, 1819, the following announcement appeared in the Booklists: "In the press, 'Lays from Fairy Land,' by John Wilson, author of 'The Isle of Palms,'" etc.

> "Doth grief e'er sleep in a Fairy's breast?
> Are Dirges sung in the land of Rest?
> Tell us, when a Fairy dies,
> Hath she funeral obsequies?
> Are all dreams there, of woe and mirth,
> That trouble and delight on earth?"

In the Magazine for January, 1820, one of these lays was published, and it seemed as if the formula, "in the press," really meant something was then preparing for publication, which I believe is all that it generally conveys to the initiated. Beyond that, however, the Lays, if ever in the press, did not show themselves out of it.* From dreams of Fairy Land the author had been roused to the un-

* Unless I except a previous poem, "The Fairies, a Dreamlike Remembrance of a Dream," in the Magazine for April, 1818, with the signature of N., evidently his. The subject was a favorite one with him. In one of his Essays there is a very beautiful and fanciful description of a fairies' burial.

romantic realities of Deacon Paterson and his green bag. The sober certainty of a course of Moral Philosophy lectures took the place of poetic visions, and the "folk of peace" seem thenceforth to have vanished from his view, so far at least as singing about them was concerned. The explanation is cleverly given in the lines of Ensign O'Doherty, in the Magazine for 1821, when the Professor was doubtless still hard at work on the Passions and the Moral Faculty. After "touching off" various other poets, he says:—

"Let Wilson roam to Fairy-land, but that's
An oldish story: I'll lay half-a-crown
The tiny elves are smothered in his gown."

But though the heavy duties of his first session put an end for the time to all other occupations, his literary activity was rather stimulated than otherwise by his elevation to the chair. With trifling exceptions his literary labors were confined exclusively to *Blackwood's Magazine*, and their extent may be guessed from the fact, that for many years his contributions were never fewer on an average than two to each number. I believe that, on more than one occasion, the great bulk of the entire contents of a number was produced by him during the currency of a month. No periodical probably was ever more indebted to the efforts of one individual than "Maga" was to Wilson. His devotion to it was unswerving, and whether his health were good or bad, his spirits cheerful or depressed, his pen never slackened in its service. He became identified with its character, its aims, and its interests; and wearing, as it did, such strong marks of a controlling individuality, it was naturally believed to be under the editorial sway of the hand that first subscribed the formidable initials of "Christopher North." The first conception of that remarkable personage was, however, as purely mythical as the "Shepherd" of the *Noctes*, and "C. N." notes and criticisms were freely supplied by other hands, under the direction of the really responsible editor, Mr. Blackwood. As my father gradually invested his imaginary ancient with more and more of his personal attributes and experiences, the identification became more complete, till at length John Wilson and Christopher North were recognized as names synonymous. Any repudiation of the editorial character essentially associated with the latter was thenceforth regarded as but a part of the system of mystification which had distinguished the Magazine from the beginning. But it was true, nevertheless, that the reins of practical government were throughout in the hands of the strong-minded and sagacious publisher. It lay with him to insert or reject, to alter or keep back; and though of course at all times open to the advice and influence of his chief contributors, his was no merely nominal management, as even they were sometimes made to experience.

The relation between him and my father, considering the character of the two men, was not a little remarkable, and it did equal credit to both. Wilson's allegiance to the Magazine was steady and undivided. He could not have labored for it more faithfully had it been his own property.* This itself would suffice to prove high qualities in the man who owned it. Mere self-interest does not bind men in such perfect mutual consideration and confidence as subsisted between them throughout their lives. It required on both sides true manliness and generosity, combined with tact and forbearance, and every kind feeling that man can show to man. Blackwood's belief in Wilson was unbounded, not simply from admiration of his great powers, but because he knew that he could rely on him to the utmost, both as a contributor and a friend. Wilson's respect and affection for Mr. Blackwood were equally sincere and well founded; and when he followed him to the grave, he felt that no truer friend remained behind. It is pleasant to be able to say that these relations of mutual esteem and confidence were continued uninterrupted after the Magazine came into the hands of Mr. Blackwood's sons, who were able to appreciate the genius and the labor that had done so much to make their own and their father's name famous throughout the world.

In the miscellaneous correspondence that follows, extending over many years, the reader will gather an idea of my father's varied relations, and of the general tenor of his life; but before passing from the subject at present, mention may here be made of the publication in 1822 of a volume of his prose compositions, under the title of "Lights and Shadows of Scottish Life, a selection from the papers of the late Arthur Austin." Some of these had appeared in *Blackwood* under the signature "Eremus," which will also be found affixed to several poems in the very early numbers of the Magazine.

* "Of all the writers in it(the Magazine), I have done *most* for the *least* remuneration, though Mr. B. and I have never once had one word of disagreement on that subject."—MS. letter of Wilson, dated 1833.

These beautiful tales have acquired a popularity of the most enduring kind. They are, indeed, poems in prose, in which, amid fanciful scenes and characters, the struggles of humanity are depicted with pathetic fidelity, and the noblest lessons of virtue and religion are interwoven, in no imaginary harmony, with the homely realities of Scottish peasant life.

The emoluments of his new position, combined with his literary earnings, enabled him, after a few years, to remove from his house in Ann Street to a more commodious residence at no great distance. He was also in a position once more to take up his summer quarters in his beautiful villa at Elleray, the place which he loved above all others on earth; and in the summer of 1823 we find him there, with his wife and children, again under the old roof-tree. After the labors of the College session, and so long a separation from a spot so dear to him, it was not unnatural that he should crave some relaxation from work; and in spite of his publisher's desire to hear from him, the study for a time was deserted for the fields. He was in the habit of sauntering the whole day long among the woods and walks of Elleray. This delightful time, however, had its interruptions. The indefatigable publisher writes letter after letter, reminding him that the Magazine and its readers must be fed. Mr. Blackwood's letters discover the shrewd and practical man of business, temperate in judgment, and reasonable, though a little too much inclined sometimes to the use of strong epithets—a habit too common with literary men of that day, but now fortunately out of fashion. From these letters may be gathered the true relation of Wilson to *Blackwood's Magazine*. On the 15th of May he says :—

"MY DEAR SIR :—For nearly a week I have either been myself, or had one of my sons waiting the arrival of the Carlisle mail, as I never doubted but that you would give me your best help this month. It never was of so much consequence to me, and I still hope that a parcel is on the way.

"That I may be able to wait till the last moment for any thing of yours, I am keeping the Magazine back, and have resolved to let it take its chance of arrival by not sending it off till the 28th, when it will go by the steamboat; this will just allow it time to be delivered on the 31st, and if no accident occur, it will be in time.

"I wrote you on the 3d with Waugh's Review, and a few other

things. I wrote you again with the periodicals on the 6th. Both parcels were directed according to your letter, to be forwarded by Ambleside coach by Mr. —— or Mr. Jackson. I hope you have received them and the former parcel.

"*Quentin Durward* is to be out on Tuesday, when I will send it to you. Reginald* is not quite finished, but will be all at press in a day or two. Mr. Lockhart has done Barry Cornwall† and Tim's‡ Viscount Soligny in good style. My not hearing from you, however, discourages him, and I fear much this number will not be at all what I so confidently expected it would have been.

"I shall be happy to hear that you are all well again.

"I am, my dear sir, yours truly,

"W. Blackwood."

About this time, Mr. Leigh Hunt was advised to threaten legal proceedings against the London publisher of the Magazine, Mr. Cadell, who appears to have been greatly alarmed by this prospect, not having been quite so accustomed to that species of intimation as Mr. Blackwood. He accordingly wrote to Edinburgh, giving a very grave and circumstantial account of the visit he had received from Mr. Hunt's solicitor. Mr. Blackwood and his contributors took the matter much more coolly, as may be seen from the following letter from Mr. Lockhart, whose concluding advice is eminently characteristic. Indeed, all Mr. Lockhart's letters to my father, as will be seen, are marked by the satirical power of the man—piquant, racy, gossiping, clever, and often affectionate and sincere:—

"Edinburgh, *Friday*, *June*, 1823.

"My dear Professor:—Blackwood sends you by this post a copy of the second letter from Cadell, so that you know, ere you read this, as much of the matter as I do.

"I own that it appears to me impossible *we* should at this time of day suffer it to be said that any man who wishes in a gentlemanly way to have our names should not have them. I own that I would rather suffer any thing than have a Cockney crow in that sort.

* *Reginald Dalton.* By Mr. Lockhart.

† *The Flood of Thessaly, The Girl of Provence, and other Poems.* By Barry Cornwall. 8vo.

‡ A *soubriquet* for Mr. Patmore, the reputed author of *Letters on England.* By Victor Count de Soligny. 2 vols. 1823; and *My Friends and Acquaintances.* 3 vols. 1854.

But still there is no occasion for rashness, and I do *not* believe Hunt had that sort of view; at all events, he has not acted as if he had.

"My feeling is that in the next number of the Magazine there should be a note to this effect:—'A certain London publisher has been making some vague and unintelligible inquiries at the shop of our London publisher. If he really wishes to communicate with the author of the article which has offended him, let him not come double-distilled through the medium of booksellers, but write at once to the author of the article in question (he may call him N. B. for the present), under cover to Mr. Blackwood, 17 Princes Street, Edinburgh. He will then have his answer.'

"Whether such a notification as this should or not be sent previously I doubt—but incline to the negative; at all events, the granting of it will save our credit; and as for Hunt, how stands the matter? *First,* Suppose he wishes to bring an action against the author; against you *he* has *no* action, and that he knows; but you would probably give him no opportunity of bringing one; at least, poor as I am, I know I would rather pay any thing than be placarded as the defendant in such an action. *2dly*, Suppose he wishes to challenge the author. He cannot send a message to *you*, having printed the last number of the *Liberal*.* Therefore, either way, the affair *must* come to naught; I mean as to any thing serious.

"Blackwood is going to London next week, and will probably visit you on the way, when you and he can talk over this fully; but ere then, I confess, I should like to have your consent to print such a note as I have mentioned. I cannot endure the notion of these poltroons crowing over us; and being satisfied that no serious consequences *can* result, I do think the thing ought to be done. Read Cadell's letter, and think of it, and write me.

"Above all, for God's sake, be you well and hearty! Who the devil cares for Cockneydom? Write a good article, and take a couple of tumblers. Yours, affly,

"J. G. L.

"*P. S.—Reginald Dalton*† is doing very well. The London subscription was 831, which Ebony thought great for a three-

* The number of the *Liberal*, I presume, containing an article on the Scottish character, in which the Blackwood writers are compared to "a troop of Yahoos, or a tribe of satyrs."

† *Reginald Dalton* and *Adam Blair* were anonymous novels written by Mr. Lockhart.

volume affair. In a new magazine (Knight's) set up by the 'Etonians,' there is an article on *Lights and Shadows*, *Adam Blair*, etc., in which you are larded tolerably, and but tolerably, and the poor Scorpion still more scurvily treated. It is their opening article and their best. The choice exhibits weakness, and conscious weakness. No other news. *Rich and Poor** is a clever book, but very methodistical. I have read about half of it. I will write you a long letter, if you will write me any thing at all."

A fragment of a letter from Mr. Lockhart, written about the same time, contains, like all his effusions, something racy and characteristic. His expressions of interest with regard to Mrs. Wilson's health are more than friendly. The first few lines of this fragment refer to a paper in *Blackwood's Magazine* for July, 1823, "On the Gormandizing School of Eloquence," "No. I. Mr. D. Abercromby." In such scraps as this we find the salt which flavored his letters, and without which he could not have written:—

"Who is Mr. D. Abercromby? You have little sympathy for a brother glutton. What would you think of the Gormandizing School, No. II. 'Professor John Wilson?' I could easily toss off such an article if you are anxious for it, taking one of the *dilettante* dinners, perhaps, and a speech about Michael Angelo by David Bridges,† for the materials. No. III. 'Peter Robertson;' No. IV. 'Wull.' Miss Edgeworth is at Abbotsford, and has been for some time;‡ a little, dark, bearded, sharp, withered, active, laughing, talking, impudent, fearless, outspoken, honest, Whiggish, unchristian, good-tempered, kindly, ultra-Irish body. I like her one day, and damn her to perdition the next. She is a very queer character; particulars some other time. She, Sir Adam,§ and the Great

* *Rich and Poor*, and *Common Events*, a continuation of the former, anonymous novels, which were ascribed to Miss Annie Walker.

† Mr. David Bridges, dubbed by the Blackwood wits, "Director-General of the Fine Arts." For a description of his shop, which was much resorted to by artists, see *Peter's Letters*, vol ii., p. 280.

‡ Miss Edgeworth's visit was in August, 1823. "Never did I see a brighter day at Abbotsford than that on which Miss Edgeworth first arrived there; never can I forget her look and accent when she was received by him at his archway, and exclaimed, 'Every thing about you is exactly what one ought to have had wit enough to dream.'"—*Scott's Life.*

§ Sir Adam Fergusson, the schoolfellow of Scott, died on Christmas day, 1854. Mr. Chambers remarks, in a biographical sketch of the good old knight, published shortly after his death, that "many interesting and pleasant memories hovered around the name of this fine old man, and

Unknown, are 'too much for any company.' Tom Purdie is well, and sends his compts.;* so does Laidlaw.† I have invited Hogg to dine here to-morrow, to meet Miss Edgeworth. She has a great anxiety to see the Bore.

"If you answer this letter, I shall write you a whole budget of news next week; if not, I hope to see you and Mrs. Wilson in good health next 12th of November, till when I shall remain your silent and affectionate brother-glutton, J. G. LOCKHART.

"*N. B.*—Hodge-podge is in glory; also Fish. Potatoes damp and small. Mushrooms begin to look up. Limes abundant. Weather just enough to make cold punch agreeable. Miss Edgeworth says Peter Robertson is a man of *genius*, and if on the stage, would *be a second Liston.* How are the Misses Watson? Give my love to Miss Charlotte when you see her; and do let me know what passed between you and the Stamp-Master,‡ the Opium-Eater, etc., etc. LL. D. Southey is, I suppose, out of your beat."

The remaining portion of this season spent at Elleray contributed (as appears by allusions in the following letters) not a small share of its occupations to the satisfaction and gratitude of Mr. Blackwood:—

in his removal from the world one important link between the Old and the New is severed. It will be almost startling to our readers to hear that there lived so lately one who could say he had sat on the knee of David Hume." He was about a year older than Sir Walter.

* Scott's faithful servant, and affectionately devoted, humble friend, from the time that Tom was brought before Sir Walter in his capacity as Sheriff, on a charge of poaching, and promoted into his service, till his death, which took place in 1829. A full account of his peculiarities will be found in Lockhart's *Life of Scott.*

† William, or, as he was always called, Willie Laidlaw, was the factor and friend of Sir Walter Scott at Abbotsford, and latterly his amanuensis; and in this case "the manly kindness and consideration of one noble nature was paralleled by the affectionate devotion and admiration of another." His family still retains as sacred the pens with which *he* wrote *Ivanhoe* to his master's dictation; and he used to tell that at the most intense parts of the story, when Scott happened to pause, which he very seldom did, running off, as he said, "like lintseed oot o' a pock," Laidlaw eagerly asked, "What next?" "Ay, Willie man, what next! that's the deevil o't!" so possessed with the reality of the tale was the busy penman. It is a curious subject how much and how little an author such as Scott can control his own creatures. If they live and move, they possess him often as much as he them. That "shaping spirit" within him is by turns master and slave. Some one asked the consummate author of *Esmond*, "Why did you let Esmond marry his mother-in-law?" "I! it was'nt I; they did it themselves."

Of his *Lucy's Flitting*, my father said, "'Tis one of the sweetest things in the world: not a few staves of his have I sung in the old days when we used to wash our faces in the Douglas Burn, and you, James, were the herd in the hill. Oh me! those sweet, sweet days o' langsyne, Jamie. Here's Willie Laidlaw's health, gentlemen!"—*Noctes.*

Mr. Laidlaw died in 1845.

‡ Wordsworth.

"EDINBURGH, *September* 6, 1823.

"MY DEAR SIR:—I hope you would receive the coach parcel yesterday or to-day, and I expect I shall have the pleasure of receiving a packet from you by Monday or Tuesday. Being so anxious to make this a very strong number, I have put nothing up yet till I see what you and Mr. Lockhart send me. He is to send me something on Monday, and if I receive Hayley* in time, I intend to begin the number with it. I have time enough yet, as this is only the 6th, but in the beginning of the week I must be getting on. I rely so confidently upon you doing all that you can, that I feel quite at ease, at least as much as ever I can be till I see the last form fairly made up. I have not received the continuation of your brother's article; Mr. Robert promised to write him as he is still in the West. Dr. Mylne told me to-day that he had met him a few days ago at Lord John Campbell's, and that he was pretty well.

"Your friend, Mr. Lowndes from Paisley, was inquiring for you here to-day. I had a letter this morning from Mr. Blair, in which he apologizes for not having fulfilled his engagement, and says, 'It has not been neglect of your claims, to which I have devoted both time and labor, but a complete want of success in every thing I have attempted. I should have written you some apology, but that I had always hopes of completing something before another month, and the only reason I had for sending nothing, seemed almost too absurd to write. I know nothing else I can say till I have something else than excuses to send. I am at this moment engaged on an essay on a question of language, which I shall be glad if I can send for your number now going on, and I have been making remarks on "Hunter's Captivity among the Indians," with the intention of reviewing it, which I shall go on with if I hear nothing from you to the contrary.'

"He gives me no address, but merely dates his letter Dudley. Perhaps you will write him, and tell him not to be over-fastidious, and point out to him something he should do. I have sent Mr. L[ockhart] to-day Alaric's† paper, in which there is a grand puff of 'Maga;' he will forward it to you.

"Maginn writes me in high glee about this number, and says he

* A review of Hayley's *Memoirs*, Art. X., September, 1823.

† Alaric A. Watts, then editor of the *Leeds Intelligencer*.

will send something. I hope I shall have the pleasure of hearing from you very soon, and I am, my dear sir, yours very truly,

"W. BLACKWOOD."

"*Saturday Morning, September* 20, 1823.

"MY DEAR SIR:—Before coming home last night I got all to press, so that I will be able to send you a complete copy of the Number with this, by the mail to-day. You will, I hope, find it a very good one, and though not equal in some respects to No. 79, it is superior in some others. On Wednesday morning I did not expect to have got this length, nor to have had it such a number. By some mistake I did not get back from Mr. L[ockhart] till Wednesday afternoon the slips of O'Doherty on Don Juan and Timothy Tickler. Not hearing from you or him on Tuesday morning, I made up Doubleday's 'Picturesque'* with Crewe's 'Blunt,'† and 'Bartlemy Fair,' by a new correspondent, whom I shall tell you about before I have done; and not knowing how I might be able to make up the Number, I put in Mr. St. Barbe's 'Gallery,'‡ and 'The Poor Man-of-War's Man,' both of which had been in types for three or four months. There being no time to lose, I got these four forms to press; I wish now I had waited another day, and kept 'The Man-of-War's Man,' but still I hope it will pass muster, and I hope you will read it without prejudice. You will naturally be saying, Why did I not, when run in such difficulty, make up and put to press your articles on ———, and the Murderers? Here I am afraid you will blame me, but first hear me. When I first read your terrible scraping of ——— I enjoyed it excessively, but on seeing it in types, I began to feel a little for the poor monster, and above all, when I considered that it might perhaps so irritate the creature as to drive him to some beastly personal attack upon you, I thought it better to pause. I felt quite sure that if published in its present state, he would be in such a state of rage, he would at all events denounce you everywhere as the author. This would be most unpleasant to your feelings, for now that one can look at the article coolly, there are such coarseness and personal things in it as one would not like to hear it said that you were the author of.

* Art. I. in the Number.

† Art. II. a review of Blunt's *Vestiges of Ancient Manners, &c.*

‡ Art. IV. "Time's Whispering Gallery."

There was no time for me to write you with a slip, and I sent it to Mr. ——, begging him to consider it, and write me if he thought he could venture to make any alterations. I did not get his packet till Wednesday, and he then wrote that he could not be art or part in the murder of his own dedicator. In these circumstances, I thought it safest to let the article be for next number, that you might correct it yourself. I hope you will think I have done right, and I would anxiously entreat of you to read the article as if it were written by some other person. Few of the readers of 'Maga' know ——— and weak minds would be startled by some of your strong expressions.* It was chiefly on account of the length of the extracts that I delayed the 'Murderers,' as the extracts from *Don Juan* and *Cobbett* are so very long. The extracts in your article will make eight or nine pages. They are not set up, but I have got them all correctly copied out, and I return you the book. I am not very sure, however, if these horrid details are the kind of reading that the general readers of 'Maga' would like to have. Curious and singular they certainly are; but then the number lies on the drawing-room table, and goes into the hands of females and young people, who might be shocked by such terrible atrocities, but you will judge of this yourself.† Before I received Mr. L.'s MS., I had also made up a very singular story of a suicide, which I received from London, from a person who merely signs himself 'Titus.' O'Doherty's note is by Mr. L. I also wished him to try to make some little alterations in the article, and perhaps add a C. N. note. He had not time, however, to do either the one or the other. Write me what you think of the article, as I fear it will be apt to startle weak minds. However, there is so much talent in it, that I think it will be liked, but not having more I delayed it. 'London Oddities' is by Mr. Croly. 'Timothy, No. IX.' by Dr. Maginn. 'No. X.' by Mr. L. 'Andrew Ardent,' by Stark, and the Answer by Mr. C. Never was any thing better than your 'General Question,' though there are some strong things in it, which you had written in a real savage humor, and which will make certain good folks stare. The 'Director-General' and the 'Prize Dissertation' are capital bits. 'Heaven and Hell' no one could have done but yourself. After getting all these made up, I found I had got ten pages

* These good advices were not lost on the writer.

† The "Murderers" did not appear.

beyond my quantity; and as I could not leave out the small letter this month, I had no room for your articles on 'Tennant' and 'Martin.' I enclose the slips of 'Tennant,' but I have not got 'Martin' set up yet. When you noticed Galt's 'Ringan Gilhaize,' you would recollect, I dare say, Doubleday's 'Tragedy.' I wish much you could give half an hour to it, which would suffice. He has not said much; but in two or three of his letters he has inquired, in his quiet way, if we were not going to have some notice of his Tragedy in 'Maga.' As you probably have not a copy with you, I enclose one, in case you should be tempted to take it up. By the by, the Old Driveller is actually doing an article on 'Ringan Gilhaize.' I have seen him several times lately, and a few days ago, when he stopped half an hour in his carriage at the door, he told me he would give me his remarks on it very soon. I am truly thankful he has not thought of laying his pluckless paws on 'Reginald Dalton.' There really ought to be a splendid article on Reginald. I shall be very anxious till I hear from you, how you like this number.

"W. Blackwood."

"Edinburgh, *October* 18, 1823.

"My dear Sir:—This has been a busy and a happy week with me. Every night almost have I been receiving packets from you, and yesterday's post brought me the Manifesto, which, you will see, closes so gloriously this glorious number.

"It is indeed a number worthy of the ever-memorable month of October. Though I have given twelve pages extra, besides keeping out the lists, I am obliged to keep 'Wrestliana' for next month.

"I have been terribly hurried to get all to press, but I hope you will find your articles pretty correct. I took every pains I could.

"I hope you will write me so soon as you have run through the number, and tell me how you like it. There is so much of your own that your task will be the easier. 'Tennant' is a delightful article, and will make the little man a foot higher. Hogg is beyond all praise, and he will be a most unreasonable porker if he attempt to raise his bristles in any manner of way. I prefixed 'See *Noctes Ambrosianæ*,' and wrote Mr. L. to insert a few words more in the *Noctes* with regard to it. He did not, however, think this necessary. Every one will be in raptures with 'Isaac Walton;' and the *Noctes* is buoyant, brilliant, and capital from beginning to end.

Well might you say that the 'Manifesto'* was very good. I shall weary till I have a letter from you telling me all about the number, and when you think you will be here.

"I enclose you a copy of a letter I had from Mr. Blair a few days ago, with two articles. The one on Language seems very curious, but it is so interlined and corrected, that I must send him a proof of it, and desire him to send me the conclusion, as it would be a pity to divide it. The other article is an account of Raymond Lulli. It is in his sister's handwriting, and is very amusing, but there was not room for it, and it will answer equally well next month.

"I do not know what on the face of the earth to do with the Old Driveller's critique on 'Ringan Gilhaize.' Whenever I hear a carriage stop, I am in perfect horrors, for I do not know what to say to him. I sent the MS. to Mr. L., but he returned it to me, and told me I ought to print it as it is, as it would please both author and critic.

"I send it to you in perfect despair, and I would most anxiously entreat of you to read it, and advise me what I should do. It is as wretched a piece of drivelling as ever I read, and I am sure it would neither gratify Galt nor any one else, while it would most certainly injure the Magazine. If you cannot be plagued with doing any thing to it, you will at all events return it carefully to me by coach as soon as possible.

"I have at last settled with Hook† for *Percy Mallory*. I hope it will do, though it contains not a little Balaam. There are many inquiries about the 'Foresters.' I hope you are going on. It astonishes even me, what you have done for 'Maga' this last week, and if you are fairly begun to the 'Foresters,' Stark will soon be driving on with it.

"I enclose slips of Mr. St. Barbe's article, and an amusing one by Titus. With these and Stark's article, besides several others, I have a great deal already for next number. I am, my dear sir, yours very truly, W. BLACKWOOD."

We come now to the spring of 1824. In the merry month of

* A short article, chiefly addressed to Charles Lamb, on his exaggerated displeasure at a critical observation by Southey.

† *Percy Mallory*, 3 vols., 12mo., published in December, 1823. It was written by Dr. James Hook, Dean of Worcester, brother of Theodore Hook. He was also author of *Pen Owen*, &c. Born 1773, died 1828.

May the usual happy party filling "His Majesty's Royal Mail" set out for the Lakes. Travelling in those days was a matter of more serious consideration than now. The journey to Westmoreland was taken as far as Carlisle per coach; the remaining distance was posted. The arrival at Elleray generally took place between eight and nine o'clock in the evening, long after sunlight had left the skies. A number of trivial associations are remembered in connection with the approach to this beloved place. The opening of the avenue-gate was a sound never to be forgotten. The sudden swing of the carriage at a particular part of the drive, when it came in contact with the low-lying branches of trees (seldom pruned), dripping with a new fallen shower of rain, would send a whole torrent of drops upon the expectant faces that were peeping out to catch a first glimpse of the house, which, lighted up, stood on its elevation like a beacon to guide travellers in the dark.

This new Elleray was as much indebted to natural position as was the old. Trellised all over, there was no more than the space for windows uncovered by honeysuckle and roses. In a very short time it became as great a favorite as the old cottage; which, had it been lost sight of altogether, might have been more regretted. A letter from Mr. Blackwood will show what the Professor had in contemplation for this summer's work.

"EDINBURGH, *6th May*, 1824.

"MY DEAR SIR:—I had so much to do yesterday that I had not time to write you; I hope you got all safe to Elleray, and as the weather is so delightful, I expect to hear in a day or two from you that you have fairly begun to the 'Foresters,'* and are driving on it and every thing else to your heart's content. That you may see what I am doing, I send you what I have made up, and the slips of a long article by Dr. M'Neill,† which I received a few days ago. I am not sure if there will be room for it in this number, but we shall see. It is curious and valuable.

"I wish very much you would write a humorous article upon that thin-skinned person Tommy Moore's 'Captain Rock.' This is the way the book should be treated. We have plenty of the serious *matériel* in Mr. R.'s article, and if you would only take up the

* One of Wilson's tales. It was not published until the following June, 1825.

† The Professor's brother-in-law, now Sir John M'Neill, G. C. B.; at that time in Persia.

Captain in your own glorious way, poor Tommy would be fairly dished. As you probably have not the two last numbers of 'Maga' with you, I enclose them with 'Captain Rock.'

"I have not heard from Dr. Maginn yet, which I am quite annoyed at. He proposed himself that he would send me off regularly every Monday a packet under Croker's cover.

"W. Blackwood."

The next letter is from Lockhart, and is of varied interest:—

"161 Regent Street, *Monday*, 1824.

"Dear Professor:—Many thanks for your welcome epistle, which, on returning from Bristol yesterday, I found here with 'Maga,' and a note of Blackwood's. By the way, you will be glad to hear I found poor Christie doing well, both in health and business. I spent three very pleasant days with him. I have seen a host of lions, among others, Hook, Canning, Rogers, Croly, Maginn, Captain Morris* (not the Dr.), Botherby, Lady Davy, Lady C. Lamb—* * * * (I copy these stars from a page in *Adam Blair*), Miss Baillie, old Gifford, Matthews, Irving, Allan Cunningham, Wilkie, Colburn, and Coleridge. The last well worth all the rest, and 500 more such into the bargain. Ebony should merely keep him in his house for a summer, with Johnny Dow† in a cupboard, and he would drive the windmills before him. I am to dine at Mr.

* Charles Morris, once the idol of clubmen in London, was born in 1745, and died on July 11, 1838, ninety-three years of age! Mr. Lockhart's parenthetical reference to the Doctor is, of course, to his own *nom de plume* as Dr. Peter Morris, of Pensharpe Hall, Aberyswith. The following allusion to the "Captain" is taken from M. Esquiros' *English at Home*:—

"Among the last names connected with the Beef-steak Club figures that of Captain Morris. He was born in 1745, but survived most of the merry guests whom he amused by his gayety, his rich imagination, and his poetical follies. He was the sun of the table, and composed some of the most popular English ballads. The Nestor of song, he himself compared his muse to the flying-fish. At the present day his Bacchic strains require the clinking of glass, and the joyous echoes of the Club, of which Captain Morris was poet-laureate. Type of the true Londoner, he preferred town to country, and the shady side of Pall Mall to the most brilliant sunshine illuminating nature. Toward the end of his life, however, he let himself be gained over by the charms of the rural life he had ridiculed, and retired to a villa at Brockham given him by the Duke of Norfolk. Before starting, he bade farewell to the Club in verse. He reappeared there as a visitor in 1835, and the members presented him with a large silver bowl bearing an appropriate inscription. Although at that time eighty-nine years of age, he had lost none of his gayety of heart. He died a short time after, and with him expired the glory of the Club of which he had been one of the last ornaments. Only the name has survived of this celebrated gathering where so much wit was expended, but it was of the sort which evaporates with the steam of dishes and bowls of punch."

† An Edinburgh short-hand writer.

Gillman's one of these days. Irving,* you may depend upon it, is a pure humbug. He has about three good attitudes, and the lower notes of his voice are superb, with a fine manly tremulation that sets women mad, as the roar of a noble bull does a field of kine; but beyond this he is nothing, really nothing. He has no sort of real earnestness, feeble, pumped up, boisterous, overlaid stuff is his staple; he is no more a Chalmers than ——† is a Jeffrey. I shall do an article that will finish him by and by. * * * Neither Maginn nor any one else has spoken to me about the concerns and prospects of our friend. My belief is, that he has come over by Croker's advice to assist Theodore in *Bull*,‡ and to do all sorts of by jobs. I also believe that Croker thinks he himself will have a place in the cabinet in case of the Duke of York's being King, and of course M. looks forward to being snugly set somewhere in that event. It is obvious that Hook, Maginn, and all this set hate Canning; and indeed a powerful party of high *ton* (Duke of York at head thereof) *is* forming itself against his over-conciliation system. I am not able to judge well, but I still believe that Canning is the man no Tory Ministry can do without; moreover, that the Marquis of Hertford (the great man with Croker's party, and the destined *Premier* of Frederick I.) has not a character to satisfy the country gentlemen of England. I met Canning at dinner one day at Mr. Charles Ellis's; the Secretary asked very kindly after you, and mentioned that 'he had had the pleasure of making acquaintance with Mr. Blackwood, a very intelligent man indeed.' I am to dine with him on Saturday, when I shall see more of him. He was obviously in a state of exhausted spirits (and strength indeed) when I met him. Rogers told me *he knew* that Jeffrey was mortally annoyed with Hazlitt's article on the periodicals being in the *Edinburgh Review*, and that it was put there by Thomas Thomson and John A. Murray,§ who were co-editors, while 'the king of men'

* Edward Irving, the celebrated preacher, was at this time sailing onwards on the full tide of popularity. Mrs. Oliphant, in her recent biography, writes thus regarding his famous sermon preached during this year to the London Missionary Society: "There can be little doubt that it was foolishness to most of his hearers, and that after the fascination of his eloquence was over, nine-tenths of them would recollect, with utter wonder, or even with possible contempt, that wildest visionary conception."

† A well-known Whig lawyer.

‡ The *John Bull* newspaper, edited by Theodore Hook.

§ Afterwards Lord Murray.

was in Switzerland.* Wordsworth is in town at present, but confined with his eyes. I thought it might appear obtrusive if I called, and have stayed away. John Murray seems the old man; the *Quarterly* alone sustains him. Maginn says he makes £4,000 per annum of it, after all expenses, and as they really sell 14,000, I can easily credit it. Colburn is making a great fortune by his Library and altogether. I meet no one who ever mentions his magazine but to laugh at it. The No. of Ebony is fair, but not first-rate. Your talk of Murders is exquisite, but otherwise the *Noctes* too local by far. Maginn on Ritter Bann not so good as might be. The article on Matthews (I don't know whose) is just, and excellent criticism. This wedding of James's came on me rather suddenly. Perhaps you will be delayed in Auld Reekie for the sake of witnessing that day's celebration. My own motions are still unfixed, but I suspect I shall linger here too long to think of a land journey or the lakes. More likely to make a run in September, and see you in your glory. De Quincey is not here, but expected. Yours,

"J. G. L.

"I don't hear any thing of *Matthew Wald* here, but I would fain hope it may be doing in spite of that. Ask Blackwood to let me hear any thing. Can I do any thing for him here? I am picking up materials for the Baron Lauerwinkel's or some other body's letters to his kinsfolk, 3 vols. post 8vo. Pray write a first-rate but *brief* puff of *Matthew* for next number *Blackwood*, or if not, say so, that I may do it myself, or make the Doctor.† I shall write B—— one of these days if any thing occurs, and at any rate he shall have a letter to C. N. speedily, from Timothy, on the *Quarterly* or *Westminster* Reviews. A *Noctes* from me positively."

Passing over the various other topics touched on in this letter, how strangely do these words about "Frederick I." now sound upon the ear! How little did the sagacious foresight of politicians calculate that every day an invisible hand was preparing the crown for a little child of five years of age, and that in the short space of eighteen years, no fewer than five heirs of the royal line should

* From Mr. Innes's *Memoir of Thomas Thomson*, I see that the editorship of the *Edinburgh Review* was left in his hands more than once. "This foremost of Record scholars, the learned legal antiquarian, and constitutional lawyer," died in 1852, aged eighty-four.

† *The History of Matthew Wald*, a novel by Mr. Lockhart. It was reviewed in the May number of *Blackwood*.

pass away, leaving a clear and uninterrupted passage for the Princess Victoria to the throne of these realms!

The next letter is equally characteristic:—

"ABBOTSFORD, *Sunday*, 2d *January*, 1825.

"MY DEAR WILSON:—I left London on Wednesday evening, and arrived here in safety within forty-six hours of the 'Bull and Mouth.'

"Our friend the Bailie* might probably show you a letter of Dr. Stoddart† about getting some *literary* articles for the *New Times*. I saw Old Slop, and introduced Maginn to him. What the Doctor and he might afterwards agree about I can't say, but I do hope there may be a permanent connection between them, as among newspeople there is no doubt Stoddart is by far the most respectable man, and there is every reason to fear M.'s propensities tending more frequently to the inferior orders of the *Plume*.

"For myself, I accepted Dr. Stoddart's offer of his newspaper, to be repaid by a few occasional paragraphs throughout the year; and upon his earnest entreaty for some introduction to you, I ventured to say that I thought you would have no objection to receive the *New Times* on the same terms.

"Whether he has at once acted on this hint I know not, but thought it best to write you *in case*.

"After all, it is a pleasant thing to have a daily paper at one's breakfast-table all the year through.

"It can cost us little trouble to repay him by a dozen half-columns—half of these may be puffs of ourselves, by the way—and Southey and others have agreed to do the same thing on the same terms. So if the *New Times* comes, and you don't wish it upon these terms, pray let me know this, that I may advise Slop.

"London is deserted by the gentlefolks in the Christmas holidays, so that I have little news. I placed my brother, quite to my satisfaction and his, at Blackheath. As for the matter personal to myself, of which I spoke to you, I can only say that I left it in Croker's

* Mr. Blackwood.

† Sir John Stoddart (at this time editor of *The New Times*, a morning paper, which was started about 1817, and continued until 1828) was born in 1773, and died in 1856. Besides his political writings, he was the author of *Remarks on Local Scenery and Manners in Scotland in* 1799 *and* 1800. 2 vols. 1801; *An Essay on the Philosophy of Language;* and some translations. In the political caricatures and satires of that day, he was continually introduced as "Dr. Slop."

hands; he promising to exert himself to the utmost whenever the high and mighty with whom the decision rests should come back to London. I think, upon the whole, that there is nothing to be gained or denied except Lord Melville's personal voice; and it will certainly be very odd if, every thing else being got over, he in this personal and direct manner shows himself not indifferent, but positively adverse. I entertain, therefore, considerable hope, and if I fail shall not be disappointed certainly, but d—d angry.

"I shall be in Edinburgh, I think, on Thursday evening, when I hope to find you and yours as well in health, and better in other respects, than when I left you. May this year be happier than the last! Yours always, J. G. LOCKHART."

A letter from Mr. De Quincey, after a long silence, again brings him before us, as graceful and interesting as ever, though also, alas! as heavily beset with his inevitable load of troubles. His letter is simply dated "London;" for obvious reasons, that great world was a safer seclusion than even the Vale of Grasmere :—

"LONDON, *Thursday. February* 24, 1825.

"MY DEAR WILSON :—I write to you on the following occasion:— Some time ago, perhaps nearly two years ago, Mr. Hill, a lawyer, published a book on Education,* detailing a plan on which his brothers had established a school at Hazelwood, in Warwickshire. This book I reviewed in the *London Magazine*, and in consequence received a letter of thanks from the author, who, on my coming to London about midsummer last year, called on me. I have since become intimate with him, and excepting that he is a sad Jacobin (as I am obliged to tell him once or twice a month), I have no one fault to find with him, for he is a very clever, amiable, good creature as ever existed; and in particular directions his abilities strike me as really very great indeed. Well, his book has just been reviewed in the last *Edinburgh Review* (of which some copies have been in town about a week). This service has been done him, I suppose, *through* some of his political friends (for he is connected with Brougham, Lord Lansdowne, old Bentham, etc.), but I understand *by* Mr. Jeffrey. Now Hill, in common with multitudes in this

* The work referred to here is, "Plans for the Government and Liberal Instruction of Boys in large numbers, drawn from Experience." 8vo. London. 1823.

Babylon—who will not put their trust in Blackwood as in God (which, you know, he ought to do)—yet privately adores him as the devil; and indeed publicly, too, is a great *proneur* of Blackwood. For, in spite of his Jacobinism, he is liberal and inevitably just to real wit. His fear is, that Blackwood may come as Nemesis, and compel him to regorge any puffing and cramming which Tiff has put into his pocket, and is earnest to have a letter addressed in an influential quarter to prevent this. I alleged to him that I am not quite sure but it is an affront to a Professor, to presume that he has any connection as contributor or any thing else, to any work which he does not publicly avow as his organ for communicating with the world of letters. He answers that it would be so in him—but that an old friend may write *sub rosâ*. I rejoin that I know not but you may have cut Blackwood—even as a subscriber—a whole lustrum ago. He rebuts—by urging a just compliment paid to you as a supposed contributor, in the *News of Literature and Fashion*, but a moon or two ago. Seriously, I have told him that I know not what was the extent of your connection with Blackwood at *any* time; and that I conceive the labors of your Chair in the University must now leave you little leisure for any but occasional contributions, and therefore for no regular cognizance of the work as director, etc. However, as all that he wishes—is simply an interference to save him from any very severe article, and not an article in his favor, I have ventured to ask of you if you hear of any such thing, to use such influence as must naturally belong to you in your general character (whether maintaining any connection with Blackwood or not), to get it softened. On the whole, I suppose no such article is likely to appear. But to oblige Hill I make the application. He has no *direct* interest in the prosperity of Hazelwood: he is himself a barrister in considerable practice, and of some standing, I believe: but he takes a strong paternal interest in it, all his brothers (who are accomplished young men, I believe) being engaged in it. They have already had one shock to stand: a certain Mr. Place, a Jacobin friend of the school till just now, having taken pet with it—and removed his sons. Now this Place, who was formerly a tailor—leather-breeches maker—and habit-maker—having made a fortune and finished his studies—is become an immense authority as a political and reforming head with Bentham, etc., as also with the *Westminster Review*, in which quarter he is supposed to have the weight of nine times nine men; whence, by the way, in the 'circles' of the booksellers, the Review has got the name of the *Breeches Review*.

"Thus much concerning the occasion of my letter. As to myself —though I have written not as one who labors under much depression of mind—the fact is, I *do* so. At this time calamity presses upon me with a heavy hand:—I am quite free of opium:* but it has left the liver, which is the Achilles' heel of almost every human fabric, subject to affections which are tremendous for the weight of wretchedness attached to them. To fence with these with the one hand, and with the other to maintain the war with the wretched business of hack author, with all its horrible degradations—is more than I am able to bear. At this moment I have not a place to hide my head in. Something I meditate—I know not what—'Itaque e conspectu omnium abiit.' With a good publisher and leisure to premeditate what I write, I might yet liberate myself: after which, having paid everybody, I would slink into some dark corner—educate my children—and show my face in the world no more.

"If you should ever have occasion to write to me, it will be best to address your letter either 'to the care of Mrs. De Quincey, Rydal Nab, Westmoreland' (Fox Ghyll is sold, and will be given up in a few days), or 'to the care of M. D. Hill, Esq., 11 King's Bench Walk, Temple:'—but for the present, I think rather to the latter: for else suspicions will arise that I am in Westmoreland, which, if I were not, might be serviceable to me; but if, as I am in hopes of accomplishing sooner or later, I should be—might defeat my purpose.

"I beg my kind regards to Mrs. Wilson and my young friends, whom I remember with so much interest as I last saw them at Elleray,—and am, my dear Wilson, very affectionately yours,

"THOMAS DE QUINCEY."

In the following letter from my father to his friend, Mr. Findlay, of Easter Hill, he refers to the death of his venerable mother, which took place in December, 1824. The accident to my mother, to which allusion is made, occurred in the previous summer; he was driving with her and the children one day in the neighborhood of Ambleside, when the axletree gave way, and the carriage was over-

* To the very last he asserted this, but the habit, although modified, was never abandoned.

turned while ascending a steep hill. No very bad consequences to any of the party ensued at the time. Mrs. Wilson, however, felt the shock to her nervous system, which affected her health so as to cause her husband much anxiety.

"29 ANN STREET, *March* 2, 1825.

"MY DEAREST ROBERT:—Much did I regret not being at home when you called upon us lately. Both Mrs. Wilson and myself felt sincerely for your wife and yourself on your late affliction. I had heard from Miss Sym that there were few hopes, but also that the poor soul was comfortable and happy, and now no doubt she is in heaven.

"I am sure that you too would feel for all of us when you heard of my mother's death; she was, you know, one of the best of women, and although old, seventy-two, yet in all things so young that we never feared to lose her till within a few days of her departure; she led a happy and a useful life, and now must be enjoying her reward. I have suffered great anxiety about Mrs. Wilson; that accident* was a bad one, and during summer she was most alarmingly ill. She is still very weak, and her constitution has got a shake, but I trust in God it is not such as may not be got over, and that the summer will restore her to her former health. She

* The following letter from Principal Baird alludes to the same accident:—

"UNIVERSITY CHAMBERS, *July 23d*, 1824.

"MY DEAR SIR:—In the first place, to begin methodically, I beg to congratulate you on the hair-breadth escape which the newspapers told us you so happily made when your horse was restive and your gig on the brink of a precipice; and, in the second place, I beg to remind you that the best expression of your gratitude for the deliverance, will be to—to compose some paraphrases and translations for the use of the Church. I shall be glad to learn, and to see proof that you are thus employed.

"I have got several excellent pieces from Mrs. Hemans and Mrs. Grant, of Laggan, lately, in addition to those which I had formerly from Miss Joanna Baillie, &c.

"I am at present busy in the transmission of papers through the Church in respect to the General Assembly's plan for increasing the means of education, of religious instruction chiefly, in the Highlands and Islands. In three contiguous parishes there is a population of about 20,000, and above 18,000 of these poor people have never been taught to read. In another district about 47,000 out of 50,000 have not been taught. Ought these things so to be?

"I am particularly interested in the state of Iona. Ill supplied with a single school, it has no place of worship. The minister is bound to preach to them only four times in the year. He preaches on a hill-side, and from that neighboring coast of the mainland; he has an audience on that hill-side of never less than 1,000 persons. This is the state of Iona, from which came at a remote day to our mainland the light of literature and religion. I wish you would write a petition by Iona for consideration and help. St. Kilda's privations have been supplied by public sympathy and bounty. Let us not neglect Iona, amid the 'ruins of which whose plaids would not grow warmer?'

"I am, with great regard, yours most faithfully,

"GEORGE BAIRD."

looks well, but is not so, and many a wretched and sleepless hour do I pass on her account.

"It is so long since the meeting of the good old Professor's* friends, that I need now say no more than that all the arrangements met with my most complete approbation, that I read the account with peculiar pleasure, and especially your speech and Dr. Macgill's. Whatever was in your hands could not be otherwise than proper and right. I have been much worried with my own affairs, ——— having entangled me in much mischief, even after he had ruined me, but I am perfectly reconciled to such things, and while my wife and family are well and happy, so will I be. Could I see Jane perfectly restored, I should dismiss all other anxieties from my mind entirely.

"I should like much indeed to see you at Easter Hill for a day or two; my plans are yet all unfixed. Perhaps I may take a walk as far early in May.

"I am building a house in Gloucester Place, a small street leading from the Circus into Lord Moray's grounds. This I am doing because I am poor, and money yielding no interest. If Jane is better next winter, I intend to carry my plan into effect of taking into my house two or three young gentlemen. Mention this in any quarter. Remember me kindly to your excellent wife. Your family is now most anti-Malthusian. Believe me ever, my dearest Robert, your most affectionate friend, JOHN WILSON."

The house in Gloucester Place was completed and ready for habitation in 1826, and thenceforth was his home during the remainder of his life. The plan of receiving young gentlemen into his house was never put into execution.

About this time a proposal was made that a separate Chair of Political Economy should be instituted in the University of Edinburgh, and that the appointment should be conferred upon Mr. J. R. M'Culloch, then editor of the *Scotsman* newspaper. Wilson's professorship combined the two subjects of Moral Philosophy *and* Political Economy, but up to this period he had not lectured on the latter topic: he therefore resented the movement as an interference with his vested rights, and by appealing to Government succeeded in crushing the project. After this controversy (which

* Professor Jardine.

included a sharp pamphlet, in which the Professor, under the *nom de plume* of Mordecai Mullion, dealt somewhat freely with Mr. M'Culloch), he lectured on political economy. Two years later, we find that he was an advocate of free trade, as may be seen from his letter to Dr. Moir in the next chapter. Could his new studies—consequent upon complying with his friend Patrick Robertson's advice to prepare a course of lectures on political economy—have led to this result? It is more than probable that De Quincey may also have influenced his opinions on this head.

The following letters, from Mr. Patrick Robertson, Mr. Huskisson, Mr. Canning, and Mr. Peel, will show the interest taken by Wilson's personal and political friends as to the proposed Chair:—

"EDINBURGH, *Tuesday*, 14*th June*, 1825.

"MY DEAR WILSON:—I have your last. Lockhart and Hope concur with me in thinking that the idea of a petition is out of the question. It would not do to enter the field in this way, unless victory were perilled on the success; and what will be the lethargy of our leading Tories and the activity of the Whigs? I should fear the result of a contest in this form. You seem to me to have made every possible exertion; and there is only one thing more I must urge upon you, a positive pledge to lecture on this subject *next winter*. You are quite adequate to the task, and this without leaving Elleray. Books can easily be sent; and if you don't know about corn and raw produce, and bullion and foreign supplies, so as to be ready to write in December, you are not the man who went through the more formidable task of your first course. A pledge of this kind would be useful, and when redeemed (if the storm were now over), would be a complete bar against future invasions of your rights. Think of this, or rather determine to do this without thinking of it, and it is done.

"I don't see why you should leave your charming cottage to come down here at present, nor how you can be of any further service than you have been. It is strange there is no answer from the Big Wigs. Lord Melville writes nobody, and I fancy William Dundas has his hands full enough of his city canvass since that insane ass, ——, started. I am in hopes you will hear soon. Both Hope and Robert Dundas are anxious to do all in their power, and expect this plot will be defeated; but I see no way of preventing it ultimately, except your actual lectures on the subject. None of us will come up this year, that you may have time to study, so study you must; and don't you understand the old principle upon which the whole of this nonsensical science hangs? I assure you, without jest, we all deeply feel the insult thus offered to you and the party, and I cannot believe it will ever be carried through. My hope is in Peel more than all the rest. Oh, for one dash of poor Londonderry! Ever yours faithfully, PAT. ROBERTSON."

"BOARD OF TRADE, 15*th June*, 1825.

"SIR:—I have had the honor to receive your letter of the 8th instant, stating the grounds on which you conceive that the erection of a new professorship in the University of Edinburgh, for the purpose of lecturing on Political Economy, would be an unfair interference with the rights, and consequent duties, which belong to the Chair of Moral Philosophy.

"Without feeling it necessary to go into the question how far the mode of lecturing on political economy which has hitherto prevailed in the University of Edinburgh is the most desirable, and exactly that in which I should concur, if the whole distribution of instruction in that University were to be recast, I have no difficulty in stating that every attention ought to be paid, in looking at the present application, to the circumstances and consideration which you have stated.

"The state of this case, as far as I know, is this:—An application has been made by memorial, from certain individuals, to the Government, for the sanction of the Crown to establish a professorship of Political Economy in the University, the subscribers offering to provide a permanent fund for founding the new Chair, in like manner as has been done by a private gentleman (Mr. Drummond) in the University of Oxford.

"This memorial has been referred by Lord Liverpool to the University of Edinburgh for their opinion, and no final decision will be taken by the Government until that opinion shall be received. Should the Senatus Academicus not recommend a compliance with the prayer of the Memorial, I have every reason to believe that it will not receive the sanction of Government, and I have conveyed that impression to the person who had put the memorial into my hands.

"I must therefore refer you, as one of that Senatus Academicus, to your colleagues, who will, I have no doubt, give that opinion which shall appear to them most conducive to the furtherance of the important duties of the University, without prejudice to the individual right of any member of that learned body. I have the honor to be, sir, your most obedient servant,

"W. HUSKISSON."

FROM MR. CANNING.

"FOREIGN OFFICE, *June* 21, 1825.

"DEAR SIR:—The alarm under which your letter of the 8th was written, has, I think, subsided long ago, in consequence of the answers which your representations received from other quarters. I only write lest you should think that I had neglected your letter, or felt no interest in your concerns. I am, dear sir, your obedient and faithful servant, GEO. CANNING.

"MR. PROFESSOR WILSON."

FROM SIR ROBERT PEEL.

[*Private.*] "WHITEHALL, *June* 21, 1825.

"SIR:—The project of establishing a new and separate Professorship of Political Economy in the University of Edinburgh did not receive any encouragement from me. I understand that it is altogether abandoned; and I have only, therefore, to assure you, that before I would have given my assent to it under any circumstances, I should have considered it my duty to ascertain that the institution of a new Chair was absolutely necessary for the purposes for which it professed to be instituted, and that the just privileges of other professors were not affected by it. I have the honor to be, sir, your obedient servant, ROBERT PEEL.

"PROFESSOR WILSON, ETC., ETC., *Edinburgh.*"

He did not "leave his charming cottage," but very soon found more interesting work than political economy to occupy his thoughts. Mr. Blackwood soon after writes of his "going on with another volume," and also says, "I rejoice, too, that you are preparing your Outlines."* Of the "other volume" nothing more was heard. Some small portion of its intended contents was probably con-

* In December, 1825, I find advertised as "speedily to be published, in one vol., 8vo., *Prospectus of a Course of Moral Inquiry*, by John Wilson, Professor of Moral Philosophy in the University of Edinburgh;" this book, however, never appeared.

tributed to a work presently to be spoken of; but from the letters in reference to that subject, it may be conjectured that some tales were written by him, which, if they ever appeared in print, are not hitherto identified with his name. Besides the three tales which had already been published, *Lights and Shadows*, *Margaret Lyndsay*, and *The Foresters*, and two volumes of poems, no separate works of his appeared until the *Recreations of Christopher North*, in 1843. That he did not carry out his intention of preparing his Outlines is cause of regret.

The next letter from Mr. Lockhart contains some reference to a literary project, of which the first idea appears to have originated with him. The name of *Janus* will doubtless be entirely new to the readers of this generation, and there are not many now living who are aware of the fact that the volume published under that name, in November, 1825, was chiefly the composition of Wilson and Lockhart. The fact that the publication was intrusted to any other hands than those of Mr. Blackwood I can only attribute to the fact—apparent, from some allusions in Mr. Lockhart's letters—that he had by this time become rather impatient of Mr. Blackwood's independent style of treating his contributions. But for him the book would never have appeared, and as certainly my father would never have contributed. The plan was suggested apparently by the popularity of a class of books that began to appear in London in the preceding year, under the title of Annuals, such as the *Forget Me Not*, the *Amulet*, and *Friendship's Offering*. They were adorned with engravings, and contained contributions from the pens of distinguished writers. The projectors of *Janus* thought it most prudent to make the success of their Annual depend on its literary merits alone, but it turned out that they were mistaken. Lockhart and Wilson undertook the editorship, and contributed the great bulk of the articles.* The following is a letter from Mr. Lockhart bearing on this subject. He was on the eve of starting for Ireland with Sir Walter Scott:—

"EDINBURGH, *July 8th*—(Starting).

"MY DEAR WILSON:—I am exceedingly sorry to find myself

* Several letters on the subject have been sent me, through the kindness of John Boyd, Esq., of the firm of Oliver & Boyd, the publishers of *Janus*, which show the interest and zeal with which the work was carried through.

leaving Edinburgh without having seen again or heard from you. I have no time to write at length, so take business in form.

"1*st*. I have seen Dr. Graham and David Ritchie to-day. They both are in spirits about the affair of the P. E.* chair. Peel has written to the Principal *most favorably* for you, and they both think the matter is settled. However, it is still possible a Senatus Academicus may be called, in which case you will of course come down.

2*d*. I have seen Boyd. He is in high glee, and has got many subscriptions already for *Janus*. I have settled that I shall, on reaching Chiefswood by the 12th of August, be in condition to keep *Janus* at work regularly, and therefore you must let me have, then and there, a quantity of your best MS. If you think of any engravings, the sooner you communicate with Boyd as to that matter the better, as he will send to London for designs, and grudge no expense; but this is a thing which does require timely notice.

"I confess I regard all that as a very secondary concern. In the mean time I have plenty of things ready for *Janus;* and the moment I have from you a fine poem or essay, or any thing to begin with (for I absolutely demand that you should *lead*), I am ready to see the work go to press.

"I therefore expect, when I reach home, to find there lying for me a copious packet from Elleray.

"3*d*. Constable is about to publish a *Popular Encyclopædia*, in 4 vols. 8vo, and he has been able to get Scott, Jeffrey, Mackenzie to contribute. The articles are on *an average* one page and a half each, but each contributor, having undertaken a number of articles, is at liberty to divide the space among *them* as he pleases. I have undertaken a few heraldic and biographical things, and he is very anxious that you should do the same.

"For example, *Locke*, *Hobbes*, *Dr. Reid:* Would you take in hand to give him two or three pages each (double columns), condensing the most wanted *popular* information as to these men? If so, he would gladly jump, and I should certainly be much gratified, because I perceive in him the most sincere desire to have connection literary with your honor.

"Pray address to me, care of Captain Scott, 15th Hussars, Dublin, if you wish to write to me immediately; if not, my motions are so uncertain that you had much better write to Constable himself, or

* Political Economy.

to me when I return. As to the articles, nine of them are wanted *this year*.

"I beg my best respects to Mrs. Wilson, and to all the bairns, greeting. Yours affectionately, J. G. LOCKHART."

About that time there was no small excitement at Elleray in the anticipation of a visit from Sir Walter Scott. Mr. Canning was also in the neighborhood, and there was a desire to do honor to both by some grand demonstration. On the 17th August, Lockhart writes to Wilson, "On board the steamboat 'Harlequin,' half-way from Dublin to Holyhead:"—

"MY DEAR WILSON:—Here we are, alive and hearty. Sir Walter Scott, Anne Scott, and myself; and I write you at the desire of the worthy Baronet to say, that there has been some sort of negotiation about meeting Mr. Canning at your friend Bolton's. He fears Mr. Canning will be gone ere now, but is resolved still to take Windermere *en route*. We shall, therefore, sleep at Lancaster on Friday night, and breakfast at Kendal, Saturday morning. Sir W. leaves it to you to dispose of him for the rest of that day. You can, if Mr. Canning is at Storrs, let Col. Bolton know the movements of Sir W., and so forth; or you can sport us a dinner yourself; or you can, if there is any inconvenience, order one and beds for us at Admiral Ullock's. We mean to remain over the Sunday to visit you, at any rate; so do about the Saturday as you like. I believe Sir W. expects to call both on Wordsworth and Southey in going northwards; but I suppose if Canning is with you, they are with you also. Canning in his letter to Scott calls you 'Lord High Admiral of the Lakes.'

"I am delighted to find that there is this likelihood of seeing you, and trust Mrs. Wilson is thoroughly restored. I have heard from nobody in Scotland but my wife, who gives no news but strictly domestic. Perhaps this will not reach you in time to let us find a line at Kendal informing us of your arrangements. Yours always,

"J. G. LOCKHART."

Sir Walter, with his daughter, Miss Scott, and Mr. Lockhart, visited Elleray, as was promised, and remained there for three days. Of this meeting Mr. Lockhart writes:—"On the banks of Windermere we were received with the warmth of old friendship by Mr. Wilson and one whose grace and gentle goodness could have found no lovelier or fitter home than Elleray, except where she now is."*

All honor was done to the illustrious guest, and my father arranged that he should be entertained by a beautiful aquatic spectacle. It was a scene worthy a royal progress, and resembled some of those rare pageants prepared for the reception of regal brides beneath the dazzling sunshine of southern skies. "There were brilliant cavalcades through the woods in the mornings, and delicious boatings on the lake by moonlight, and the last day 'The Admiral of the Lake' presided over one of the most splendid regattas that ever enlivened Windermere. Perhaps there were not fewer than fifty barges following in the Professor's radiant procession when it paused at the Point of Storrs, to admit into the place of honor the vessel that carried kind and happy Mr. Bolton and his guest. The three Bards of the Lakes led the cheers that hailed Scott and Canning; and the music and sunshine, flags, streamers, and gay dresses, the merry hum of voices, and the rapid splashing of innumerable oars, made up a dazzling mixture of sensations, as the flotilla wound its way among richly-foliaged islands, and along bays and promontories peopled with enthusiastic spectators."†

My father invited various friends from Scotland at this gay and notable time, to join in the general welcome given to Scott; among others, he asked his old and esteemed friend the Professor of Natural History, Mr. Jameson,‡ who was reluctantly detained by his duties as editor of *The Edinburgh Philosophical Journal:* his letter is of sufficient interest to be given here:—

"My dear Sir:—I have delayed from day to day answering your kind letter, in expectation of being able to make such arrangements as would allow me the pleasure of visiting you, but in vain; and now I find, from unforeseen circumstances, that I must forego the happiness of a ramble with you this season. My sister, or rather sisters, who were to accompany me, and who beg their best wishes and kindest thanks to you for your polite invitation, wish all printers, and printers' devils, at the bottom of the Red Sea. They have been in a state of semi-insurrection against me for some

* *Life of Scott.* † *Ibid.*

‡ Professor Jameson died in 1853, *ætat* eighty.

time, owing to the putting off of the expedition, but are now resigned to their fate.

"Edinburgh is at present very dull, and very stupid, and we are only kept alive by the visits of interesting strangers.

"The adventures of the regatta have reached this, and my sisters expect to hear from Miss Wilson, who, they presume, acted a distinguished part in the naval conflict, an animated account of all that befell the admirals. Some German philosophers say that a man—that I presume does not exclude a professor—may be in many places at the same time. I was rather inclined to doubt the accuracy of this notion, but now it seems to be confirmed in yourself, for, on the *same day*, you were buried at Edinburgh, and alive and merry at Elleray.*

"All here join in best wishes to your family and Mrs. Wilson, and believe me to remain yours faithfully and sincerely,

"ROB. JAMESON.

"My dear sir, I hope you will not forget your promise of a paper for *The Edinburgh Philosophical Journal.* The effects of the scenery of a country on its population would form a very interesting topic, and one which affords an ample field for interesting observation."

Soon after returning to Scotland, Lockhart writes, not in the best of spirits. What the opening allusion is to, I do not know:—

"CHIEFSWOOD, *Wednesday*, 1825.

"MY DEAR WILSON:—I have received your letter, and shall not say more in regard to one part of its contents than that I am heartily sensible to your kindness, and shall in all time coming re-

* This refers to a practical joke of Mr. Lockhart's, but not known at the time to have originated with him; a joke which might have ended in painful results had it come untimeously to the ears of any one nearly connected with its object. It was no less than a formal announcement of Professor Wilson's sudden death in the leading columns of *The Weekly Journal*, along with a panegyric upon his character, written in the usual style adopted when noting the death of celebrated persons. I have not been able to find the paper, but I believe it was only inserted in a very few copies. On a later occasion Mr. Lockhart amused himself in a similar manner, by appending to a paper on Lord Robertson's poems in *The Quarterly Review*, the following distich:

"Here lies the peerless paper lord, Lord Peter,
Who broke the laws of God, and man, and metre."

These lines were, however, only in one copy, which was sent to the senator; but the joke lay in Lord Robertson's imagining that it was in the whole edition.

spect most religiously the feelings which I cannot but honor in you as to that matter. I hope I may be as brief in my *words* about Mrs. Wilson. I trust the cool weather, and quiet of a few weeks, will have all the good effects you look forward to, and that I shall have the pleasure of seeing you all well and gladsome, in spite of all that hath been in the month of November. As for *you*, I do think it is likely we may meet earlier. All I know of Canning's motions is, that Sir W. Scott expects him at Abbotsford very early in October; the day not fixed that I know of. I cannot help thinking that you would be much out of your duty, both to others and to yourself, if you did *not* come down; for there *is* to be at least one public dinner in C.'s offer—I mean from the Pitt Club—and I think he can't refuse. You must come down and show that we have one speaker among us—for *certes* we have but one—unless the President himself should come forth on the occasion, which I take to be rather out of the dice. I know Sir W. also will be particularly gratified in seeing you come out on such a field-day. I wish you would just put yourself into the mail and come to *me* here when C. leaves Storrs, and then you would see him at Abbotsford, and at Edinburgh also, without trouble of any kind. The little trip would shake your spirits up, and do you service every way. I assure you it would do me a vast deal of good too. I have been far from well either in health or spirits for some time back, and indeed exist merely by dint of forcing myself to do something. I have spent five or six hours on Shakspere regularly, and have found that sort of work of great use to me, it being one that can be grappled with without that full flow of vigor necessary for any thing like *writing;* and I wish you had some similar job by you to take up when the spirit is not exactly in its highest status. I heard grand accounts of you the other day from the young Duke of Buccleuch and his governor, Blakeney—a very superior man, by the way. It would make *me* happy indeed to see you here, and I may say the same of not a few round about me.

"I shall not fail to write you again, if I hear any thing worth telling as to C.; but I think it more likely you should than I, and I hope you will write *me* if that be the case.

"One word as to Ebony.* It is clear he must go down now. Maginn, you have heard, I suppose, is universally considered as the

* The *soubriquet* by which Mr. Blackwood was known by his contributors.

sole man of the *John Bull Magazine;* a most infamous concern, and in general displaying a marvellous lack of every thing but the supremest impudence. I foresee sore rubs between Ebony and him. ——— is exceedingly insolent when he has nobody near him, as is the case at present—cuts and maims—keeps back, etc., etc.; in short, is utterly disgusting.

"You will have perceived that I have done very little this summer. How could I? I am totally sick of all that sort of concern, and would most gladly say, 'farewell forever.'

"Yours affectionately always, J. G. LOCKHART."

It appears that Mr. Canning did not visit Abbotsford, and the anticipated opportunity of showing that there was "one speaker" in Scotland did not therefore occur.

The brilliant and versatile, but somewhat dangerous pen of Maginn,* was at this time in full employment for the Magazine. In

* William Maginn, *alias* Ensign O'Doherty, *alias* Luctus, *alias* Dr. Olinthus Petre, Trinity College, Dublin, &c., &c., was born at Cork in 1794, and died in London in 1842. This versatile writer and singular man of genius began to contribute to *Blackwood* in November, 1819. Dr. Moir says that his first article was a translation into Latin of the ballad of "Chevy Chase," which was followed by numerous articles containing both wit and sarcasm, which Mr. Blackwood had to pay for in the case of Leslie *v.* Hebrew. Although he continued to write for *Blackwood*, the publisher was not acquainted with his real name, and the account of their first interview is amusingly told by Dr. Moir:*—

"I remember having afterwards been informed by Mr. Blackwood that the Doctor arrived in Edinburgh on Sunday evening, and found his way out to Newington, where he then resided. It so happened that the whole family had gone to the country a few days before, and in fact the premises, except the front gate, were locked up. This the Doctor managed, after vainly ringing and knocking, to open, and made a circuit of the building, peeping first into one window and then another, where every thing looked snug and comfortable, though tenantless. He took occasion afterwards to remark, that no such temptations were allowed to prowlers in Ireland.

"On the forenoon of Monday he presented himself in Princes street, at that time Mr. Blackwood's place of business, and formally asked for an interview with that gentleman. The Doctor was previously well aware that his quizzes on Dowden, Jennings, and Cody of Cork (perfectly harmless as they were), had produced a ferment in that quarter, which now exploded in sending fierce and fiery letters to the proprietor of the Magazine, demanding the name of the writer, as he had received sundry notes from Mr. Blackwood, telling him the circumstances; and on Mr. Blackwood appearing, the stranger apprised him of his wish to have a private conversation with him, and this in the strongest Irish accent he could assume.

"On being closeted together, Mr. Blackwood thought to himself—as Mr. Blackwood afterwards informed me—'Here, at last, is one of the wild Irishmen, and come for no good purpose, doubtless.'

"'You are Mr. Blackwood, I presume,' said the stranger.

"'I am,' answered that gentleman.

"'I have rather an unpleasant business, then, with you,' he added, 'regarding some things which appeared in your Magazine. They are so and so, would you be so kind as to give me the name of the author?'

* *Dublin University Magazine*, January, 1844, which contains the fullest account of Maginn's life and writings I have seen.

the *Noctes* in particular, where the character of the composition allowed most freedom of expression, he took his full swing, and laid about him in true Donnybrook style. Whether the "sore rubs" anticipated by Lockhart occurred, I have no means of knowing; probably they did. That he sometimes caused considerable annoyance to the judicious editor will appear from the following brief note to Wilson about this very time. The reference in the conclusion is to Mr. Blackwood's candidature for the office of Lord Provost, in which he was unsuccessful.

"EDINBURGH, *August* 22, 1825.

"MY DEAR SIR:—I received your packet in time, and I hope you will find the whole correctly printed, though I was obliged to put to press in a great hurry. I only got Maginn's Song on Saturday night, after I had put the sheets to press.

"On Thursday I received from him some more of the *Noctes*, but I did not like them, as he attacked Moore again with great bitterness for his squibs upon the King, and charged the Marquis of Hastings as a hoary courtier, who had provoked Moore *with his libels upon the King*. I have written him that it really will not do to run a-muck in this kind of way. I hope you will, on the whole,

"'That requires consideration,' said Mr. Blackwood; 'and I must first be satisfied that—'

"'Your correspondent resides in Cork, doesn't he? You need not make any mystery about that.'

"'I decline at present,' said Mr. B., 'giving any information on that head, before I know more of this business—of your purpose—and who you are.'

"'You are very shy, sir,' said the stranger; 'I thought you corresponded with Mr. Scott, of Cork,' mentioning the assumed name under which the Doctor had hitherto communicated with the Magazine.

"'I beg to decline giving any information on that subject,' was the response of Mr. Blackwood.

"'If you don't know him, then,' sputtered out the stranger, 'perhaps, perhaps you *could* know your own handwriting,' at the same moment producing a packet of letters from his side-pocket. 'You need not deny your correspondence with that gentleman; I am that gentleman.'

"Such was the whimsical introduction of Dr. Maginn to Mr. Blackwood; and after a cordial shake of the hand and a hearty laugh, the pair were in a few minutes up to the elbows in friendship."

From this time, 1820, till 1828, he continued his contributions more or less frequently. In 1824, about the time Mr. Lockhart writes of him, he was appointed foreign correspondent of *The Representative;* but as this newspaper was not long-lived, he was again thrown upon his resources, and he earned a scanty livelihood by writing for the periodicals. He assisted, as Mr. Lockhart says, Theodore Hook, in the *John Bull*, and obtained so much reputation as a political writer, that on the establishment of the *Standard*, he was appointed joint editor of the latter. He was ultimately connected with the foundation of *Fraser's Magazine*, in 1830, and along with Father Mahony, Mr. Hugh Fraser, and others, gave that periodical his heartiest support. He was then in the zenith of his fame, and his society courted; but in 1834 he was again corresponding with Mr. Blackwood, dating his contributions from a garret in Wych street, Strand, and from this time till his death his condition was one of wretchedness.

like this number, and that you will be in good spirits to do something very soon for next one. I fully expected to have had the pleasure of a letter from you either yesterday or to-day.

"A letter from you, however short, is always a treat. The canvass for the Provostship is as hot as ever, but the result does not now appear so certain as when I last wrote you; still, I do not despair, and I trust we shall be successful.

"I am, my dear sir, yours truly, W. BLACKWOOD."

Mr. Lockhart's temporary disgust at magazine writing did not affect his productive activity. Very soon after writing the foregoing letter, he was hard at work writing articles for *Janus*, which began to be printed early in September, and was published about the close of November, 1825. The various letters which passed between the editors and the publisher on the subject are entirely occupied with the details of "MS.", "slips," "proofs," and "forms." They contain, however, the materials for ascertaining the contributions of the two principal writers, a list of which will be found in the Appendix. The following letter from my father to Delta is given, as being the first communication between them which I have found, and as illustrating his mode of discharging the delicate duty of telling a friend that his MS. is not "suitable." It is also his first letter dated from Gloucester Place:—

"GLOUCESTER PLACE, No. 8, *Friday*.

"MY DEAR SIR:—On my arrival here, a few days ago, I found in the hands of Messrs. Oliver and Boyd, an extract from a tale intended for *Janus*. As I take an interest in that volume, I trouble you with a few lines, as I know your handwriting.

"I had intended writing to you to request a contribution to *Janus*, but delayed it from time to time, uncertain of the progress that double-faced gentleman was making towards publicity.

"Copy for 350 pages is already in the printer's hands, and I have about 120 pages of my own MS., and of a friend, to send in a few days, which, owing to peculiar circumstances, must make part of the volume, so that 470 pages may be supposed to be contributed. A number of small pieces too are floating about, which it is not easy to know how to dispose of.

"I am, however, anxious that something of yours should be in this volume, and if it be possible, there shall be, if you wish it.

"The funeral scene is certainly good, natural, and true, and as part of a tale, I have no doubt it will be effective. Standing by itself it does not strike me as one of your best things (many of which are most beautiful and most lively), and I should wish to have in *Janus* one that *I* at least like better.

"I had in my possession, some time ago, a MS. volume of yours containing several prose tales, one of which,* about a minister, a bachelor, I think, or widower, loving or being made to love his housekeeper, or somebody else, I thought admirable. Another tale, too, there was, of a lively character that I liked much, but I forget its name.† I generally forget, or at least retain an indistinct remembrance of what gives me most pleasure. Had I that volume I would select a tale from it for *Janus*. The worst of *Janus* is, that a page holds so little in comparison with a magazine page, that even a short story takes up necessarily great room.

"Should the volume prove an annual, I hope you will contribute.

"This is not a confidential communication. Mr. Lockhart and I have no objections to be spoken of as friends and contributors to *Janus*, but, on the contrary, wish to be. But let all contributors keep their own counsel. I am, my dear sir, yours with much regard,

JOHN WILSON."

On her way to Edinburgh from Elleray, my mother was taken alarmingly ill, and was for some time in a very precarious state. This, combined with the labors of the opening University session, left little leisure for literary work; MS. for *Janus* was therefore in great demand, and proof-sheets had to be revised after the class hour in the Professor's "retiring-room." Some contributions had also been expected from Mr. De Quincey, which, however, did not make their appearance. The work at last came out in the form of a very finely-printed small octavo volume of 542 pages, which was sold at the price of 12s. There were no embellishments beyond a vignette representation of the two-faced god, and no names were given on the title-page or in the table of contents. The preface announces that the volume is intended to be the first of a series, to be published annually early in November. It never went, however, beyond its first number, not having received encouragement enough

* This appeared in the volume under the title, "Saturday Night in the Manse."

† Probably "Daniel Cathie, tobacconist."

to warrant the risk of a second trial. As the publisher dealt liberally with the authors, we may infer that the book did not pay so well as it might have done with poorer matter and a lower price. There was, in fact, *too much* good writing in this now little-known volume: such a crop could not be "annual," and so it came up but once. Its name suggests the character of the subjects contained in its pages, which vary in range between the seriousness of philosophy and the facetiousness of genuine humor; as free from dulness in the one kind as from flippancy in the other. Among the shorter and lighter papers, there is one from the French, but not a translation, that gives the history of a dog, "Moustache," whose characteristic individuality is as skilfully portrayed as if it had come from the hand of a literary "Landseer."* From the list of contents it will be seen that nearly the whole was produced by the editors. Of the few contributions by other hands, are Miss Edgeworth's witty "Thoughts on Bores," and one or two pleasant sketches by Delta.

Mr. Lockhart left Chiefswood for London in December, 1825, to assume the editorship of the *Quarterly Review.* The following letter appears to have been written the day after he had taken possession of the editorial chair:—

"25 PALL MALL, 23*d December*, 1825.

"MY DEAR WILSON:—It was only yesterday that we got ourselves at length established under a roof of our own, otherwise you should have heard from me, and, as it is, I must entreat that whatever you do as to the rest of my letter, you will write *immediately*, to say how Mrs. Wilson is. I have often thought with pain of the state in which we left her, and, through her, you, and I shall not think pleasantly of any thing connected with you, until I hear better tidings.

"Murray, from what he said to me, would answer Boyd's letter in the affirmative. I did not choose to press him, but said what I could with decency.†

"As I feared and hinted, you are rather in a scrape about the

* Of such is Dr. John Brown, who, in *Our Dogs*, has unravelled the instinctive beauties and touching sagacity of the canine race, with a delicacy of perception and cunning workmanship of thought truly admirable. "Rab" and "Moustache," in their devotion of purpose, would perfectly have appreciated each other; but, alas! the faithful companion of "Ailie," and the brave "Moustache," must remain for ever the heroes of their own tales. These are not dogs to be met with every day; they come, like epic poems, after a lapse of ages, and like them are immortal.

† Probably refers to Murray becoming the London publisher of *Janus*.

Uranus poem, the proprietor of it being some old Don, who for these seven years had dunned Murray constantly, the bookseller in the mean time writing, he says, to Blackwood, equally in vain.

"One thing remains; that the whole *MS.* be *forthwith* transmitted to Murray; in that case the old gent. may probably never know of the printing of any part. I fear the volume is heavy on the whole; but I know the deepness of my own prejudice against metaphysical essays, and would fain hope it is not largely partaken.

"Maginn is off for Paris, where I hope he will behave himself. He has an opportunity of retrieving much, if he will use it. I think there can be nothing in his removal to injure his writings in *Blackwood*, but *au contraire*, and certainly nothing to diminish their quantity.

"Mr. ——— has yesterday transferred to me the treasures of the Review; and I must say, my dear Wilson, that his whole stock is not worth five shillings. Thank God, other and better hands are at work for my first number, or I should be in a pretty hobble. My belief is that he has been living on the stock bequeathed by Gifford, and the contributions of a set of d—d idiots of Oriel. But mind now, Wilson, I am sure to have a most hard struggle to get up a very good first Number, and, if I do not, it will be the Devil. I entreat you to cast about for a serious and important subject; give your mind full scope, and me the benefit of a week's Christmas leisure.

"Murray's newspaper concerns seem to go on flourishingly. The title, I am rather of belief, will be 'The Representative,'* but he has not yet fixed.

"I shall write you in due time, and at length, as to that business.

"As for me personally, every thing goes on smoothly. I have the kindest letters from Southey, and indeed from *all* the real sup-

* Murray's newspaper concerns did not go on "flourishingly," as may be gathered from the following note:—"With Mr. Benjamin Disraeli for editor, and witty Dr. Maginn for Paris Correspondent, John Murray's new daily paper, *The Representative* (price 7d.), began its inauspicious career on the 25th January, 1826. It is needless to rake up the history of a dead and buried disaster. After a short and unhappy career of six months, *The Representative* expired of debility on the subsequent 29th of July. The Thames was not on fire, and Printing House Square stood calmly where it had stood. When, in after years, sanguine and speculative projectors enlarged to John Murray on the excellent opening for a new daily paper, he of Albemarle street would shake his head, and with rather a melancholy expression of countenance, pointing to a thin folio on his shelves, would say, 'Twenty thousand pounds are buried there.'"—"Histories of Publishing Houses," *Critic*, January 21, 1860.

porters of the Review. Give my love to Cay, and do now *write, write, write* to yours affectly., J. G. Lockhart."

During the following year my father contributed no less than twenty-seven articles, or portions of articles, to the Magazine, including the following, afterwards republished, in the collected works by Professor Ferrier:—"Cottages," "Streams," "Meg Dods," "Gymnastics." The only month in which nothing of his appeared was May; the month of April, which closed the session, being his busiest at the College, except November. During the autumn of this year, business of some importance obliged him to go into Westmoreland. He was accompanied by his daughter Margaret and his son Blair, and during his absence wrote regularly to his wife, giving pleasant local gossip and descriptions of the improvements at Elleray. The dinner at Kendal, of which he speaks, was one of political interest connected with the Lowther family, at which he, as a matter of course, was desirous to be present. Mrs. Wilson's brother-in-law, Mr. James Penny Machell of Penny Bridge, was High Sheriff that year at the Lancaster Assizes, which accounts for the allusions to the trials, besides that some of them excited unusual interest.

"Kendal, 22*d August*, 1826,
Tuesday Morning, Half-past Three.

"My dearest Jane:—I wrote you a few lines from Carlisle, stating our successful progress thus far, and we arrived here same night at half-past eleven. Not a bed in the house, nor any supper to be got, the cook having gone to bed. I however got Maggie and Blair a very nice bed in a private house, and saw them into it. I slept, or tried to do so, on a sofa, but quite in vain. In a quarter of an hour we set off for Elleray in a chaise, which we shall reach to breakfast about half-past ten. We are all a good deal disgusted with our reception last night in this bad and stupid inn.

"It is a very fine day, and Elleray will be beautiful; I should think of you every hour I am there, but to-morrow you know I am to be in Kendal again, and shall write to you before the *dinner*. I have seen nobody in the town whatever, and, of course, heard nothing about the intended meeting. The Mackeands were hanged yesterday (Monday), and I have just been assured that the *brother* Wakefield, who was to have been tried on Saturday, has forfeited his bail, and is off, fearing from the judge's manner that he would be imprisoned—if he stood trial—five years.* So there will be no trial at all at Lancaster. I hope, therefore, yet to be at Hollow Oak.

"Think of my bad luck in losing seven sovereigns from there being a hole in my lecturing pantaloons. All the silver fell out of the one pocket, which Blair picked up, but the sovereigns had dropped forever through the other.

"I will write as often as possible, and tell you all that I hear about the various places and people. Kindest love to Johnny and Mary, who will have their turn some day, and also to the lovely girl and George Watson.

"The chaise is at the gate, and is an open carriage.

"I am, my dearest Jane, ever your affectionate husband,

"JOHN WILSON."

"KENDAL, *August* 23, 1826,
Wednesday Night, Twelve o'clock.

"MY BELOVED JANE:—The dinner is over, and all went well. Your letter I have just received, of which more anon. Why did you not write on Monday night? but thank God it is come now. We are all well, and my next, which will be a post between, shall be a long, descriptive, full and particular account of every one thing in the country. It is your own fault that this is not a long letter, for my misery all day has been dreadful. Mr. Fleming was with me all day, and was the kindest of friends; and George Watson will, I am sure, write for you.

"I shall see the Machells, who have returned home, and well, I understand. Once more, God bless and protect you! and get your spectacles ready for next letter, which I shall have time to write at length. Hitherto I have not had an hour.

"To-morrow, at Elleray, I shall write an admirable epistle.

"Your affectionate husband,

"JOHN WILSON.

"Love to Johnny, Mary, Umbs, and George Watson."

* The two Mackeands were brothers, who had committed an atrocious murder on the inhabitants of a wayside inn, in Lancashire. The "brother Wakefield" was no less a person than Edward Gibbon Wakefield, whose shameful deception wove a strange romance around the life of Helen Turner, and furnished to the annals of law one of the most peculiar cases that has ever been recorded.

"ELLERAY, *August 24th*, 1826,
Thursday Forenoon.

"MY DEAREST JANE:—I shall give you a sort of *précis* of our movements. On Tuesday morning, at nine o'clock, we left Kendal in an open carriage, and reached Elleray before eleven. The day was goodish, indeed excellent at that time, and the place looked beautiful as of old. A handsome new rail runs along from the junction of the new avenue, all along to front of the new house, and has a parkish appearance—painted of a slate color. The house we found standing furnished and in all respects just as we left it, so that, I suppose, the family have just walked out. The plants in the entrance reach near the roof, one and all of them, but have few flowers, and must be pruned, I fear, being enormously lank in proportion to their thickness, but all in good health. The little myrtles are about a yard high, and in high feather. The trees and shrubs have not grown very much—it seems a bad year for them; but the roses and smaller flowers have flourished, and those sent from Edinburgh were much admired. The walks in the garden are all gravelled neatly; the bower is as green as the sea, and really looks well. The hedge lately planted round the upper part is most thriving, and strawberry-beds luxuriant; in short, the garden looks pretty. The crops in the fields are bad, as all in the country are.

"In an hour or two after our arrival it began to rain and blow and bluster like Brougham, so I left the house. Dinner was served in good style at six; fowls, fish, and mutton. In the evening William Garnet came up, and was, as you may suppose, in a state of bliss. The boy is well, and I am to be his godfather by proxy. On Wednesday morning, I never doubted but there would be a letter from you, as I made you promise to write every night at six; but I never make myself understood. It gave me great pain to find there was none; but this I alluded to before, so say no more now, but will give you a *viva voce* scold for it. Fleming went with me in the chaise to Kendal, and at half-past three we sat down to dinner: Lord Lowther and Portarlington (pronounced Polington), Colonel Lowther, Henry Lowther, Howard of Levens, Colonel Wilson, Noel of Underlay, Bolton, the little Captain, and fifty-six others. It went off with *éclat*, and I speechified a little, but not too much, and gave satisfaction. Barber came over on purpose, and is evidently in the clouds about what I said of his cottage, although he made no allusion to it. The ball in the evening was apparently a pleasant one, but thin, as it was only fixed *that morning* that there was to be one. At twelve o'clock the mail came in, and I went down myself to the Post-Office, and got the postmaster to open the bag, and, lo and behold, your letter of Tuesday, which took a load of needless anxiety off my soul. God bless you! I returned to the inn, and Barber took me immediately in his chaise to Elleray, which we reached about two, and had a little supper; he then went on, and I to bed.

"I am now preparing, after sound sleep, to call at the Wood and Calgarth. We shall dine at the Wood. The children were to have dined there yesterday, but the rain prevented them. Mrs. Barlow came up in the evening, they tell me, with Miss North. Gale was found guilty of two assaults at Lancaster, but the anti-Catholic doctor allowed him to get off without fine. How absurd altogether the quarrel originating in Catholic Emancipation. I shall probably go to Penny Bridge on Saturday, but will write again to-morrow, so send to the Post-Office on Saturday evening, and on Sunday too, for letters are not delivered till Monday. But be sure you, or Mary, or Johnny, or George Watson, write every night, till farther orders. The little pony, Tickler, and Nanny, the cow, are all well, so is Star; Colonsay is sold for four pounds. The last year's calf is as large as any cow, and there is another calf and two pigs. I shall give you any news I hear in my next. I will write to Johnny soon. Your affectionate and loving husband, JOHN WILSON."

The "Colonsay" mentioned here as sold "for four pounds," had been at one time a pony of remarkable strength and sagacity. A few summers previously, my father became acquainted with a Mr. Douglas, who, with his family, was then residing near Ambleside. This gentleman possessed a handsome and prepossessing appearance; beyond that he had not much to recommend him, being nothing but a sporting character, and was after a time discovered not to be *sans peur* and *sans tache*. However, he visited in all directions, frequently coming to Elleray. One day he appeared, mounted on a very fine animal, which he said was thorough-bred, and an unrivalled trotter. This statement gave rise to some discussion on the subject of trotting, *à propos* of which, Wilson brought forward the merits of a certain gray cob in his possession, half jestingly proposing a match between it and the above-mentioned "thoroughbred."

Mr. Douglas was delighted to meet with an adventure so entirely to his taste, so then and there the day and hour was fixed for the match to come off—a fortnight from that time.

It is a long-ago story, but I well remember the excitement it created in the *ménage* at Elleray, and the unusual care bestowed upon the cob,—how his feet were kept in cold cloths, and how he was fed, and gently exercised daily. In short, the mystery about all the ongoings at the stable was most interesting, and we began to regard with something akin to awe the hitherto not more than commonly cared for animal.

At last the day anxiously looked for arrived. Full of glee and excitement we ran—sisters and brothers—down the sloping fields, to take a seat upon the top of a wall that separated us from the road, and where we could see the *starting-point*. "Colonsay" was led in triumph to meet his fashionable rival, whose "get-up" was certainly excellent. Both rider and horse wore an air of the turf, while my father, in common riding dress, mounted his somewhat ordinary-looking steed, just as a gentleman would do going to take his morning ride. At last, after many manœuvres of a knowing sort, Mr. Douglas declared himself ready to start, and off they set, in pace very fairly matched,—at least so it seemed to us from the Elleray gate.

To Lowood, as far as I remember, was the distance for this trial. Umpires were stationed at their respective points on the road, and Billy Balmer kept a steady eye from his station upon "Colonsay," whose propensity for dashing in at open gates was feared might ruin his chance of winning. Meantime, the juvenile band on the wall, along with Mrs. Wilson, were keeping eager watch for the messenger who was to bring intelligence of the conquering hero; and how great was their delight when in due time they heard that "Colonsay" had won the day; Mr. Douglas's much boasted of trotter having broken into a canter.

This trotting match with the handsome adventurer, was the origin of "Christopher on Colonsay" in the pages of *Blackwood*, which did not appear, however, till ten years afterwards.

CHAPTER XII.

LITERARY AND DOMESTIC LIFE.

1827–'29.

One who knew my father well, said, "That in the multiform nature of the man, his mastery over the hearts of ingeneous youth was one of his finest characteristics. An essay or poem is submitted to him by some worthy young man, he does not like it, and says so in general terms. The youth is not satisfied, and, in the tone of one rather injured, begs to know specific faults. The generous aristarch, never dealing haughtily with young worth, instantly sits down, and begins by conveying, in the most fearless terms of praise, his sense of that worth; but, this done, woe be to the luckless piece of prose or numerous verse! Down goes the scalpel with the most minute savagery of dissection, and the whole tissues and ramifications of fault are laid naked and bare. The young man is astonished, but his nature is of the right sort; he never forgets the lesson, and, with bands of filial affection stronger than hooks of steel, he is knit for life to the man who has dealt with him thus. Many a young heart will recognize the peculiar style of the great nature I speak of. This service was once done to Delta; he was the young man to profit by it, and the friendship was all the firmer."* Mr. Aird probably alludes to the following letter, written by Professor Wilson in January, 1827, to his friend Dr. Moir:—

"My dear Sir:—Allow me to write you a kind letter, suggested by the non-insertion of your Christmas verses in the last number of 'Maga'—a letter occasioned rather than caused by that circumstance—for I have often wished to tell you my mind about yourself and your poetry.

"I think you—and I have no doubt about the soundness of my opinion—one of the most delightful poets of this age. You have not, it is true, written any one great work, and, perhaps, like myself, never will; but you have written very many exquisitely beautiful poems which, as time rolls on, will be finding their way into

* Thomas Aird's *Memoir of D. M. Moir.*

the mindful hearts of thousands, and becoming embodied with the *corpus* of true English poetry. The character and the fame of many of our finest writers are of this kind. For myself, I should desire no other—in some manner I hope they are mine; yours they certainly are, and will be more and more as the days and years proceed.

"Hitherto, I have not said as much as this of you publicly, and for several good reasons. *First.* It is best and kindest to confer praise after it is unquestionably due. *Secondly.* You, like myself, are too much connected with the Magazine to be praised in it, except when the occasion *either* demands it or entirely justifies it. *Thirdly.* Genevieve is not my favorite poem, because the subject is essentially *non-tragic to my imagination*, finely as it is written. *Fourthly.* I shall, and that, too, right early, speak of you as you ought to be spoken of, because the time has come when that can be done rightfully and gracefully. *Fifthly.* I will do so when I feel the proper time has come; and, *lastly*, As often as I feel inclined, which may be not unfrequent. I love to see genius getting its due; and, although your volume has not sold extensively, you are notwithstanding a popular and an admired writer.

"Having said this much conscientiously, and from the heart, I now beg leave to revert to a matter of little importance, surely, in itself, but of some importance to me and my feelings, since, unluckily, it has rather hurt yours, and that too, not unnaturally or unreasonably, for I, too, have been a *rejected contributor.* In one respect you have altogether misconceived Mr. Blackwood's letter, or he has altogether misconceived the very few words I said about the article. I made no comparison whatever between it and any other article of the kind in 'Maga,' either written by you or by any one else. But I said that the Beppo or Whistlecraft measure had become so common, that its sound was to me intolerable, unless it was executed in a transcendent style, like many of Mr. Lockhart's stanzas in the Mad Banker of Amsterdam, which, in my opinion, are equal to any thing in Byron himself. Your composition, I frankly and freely say now, will not, in my opinion, bear comparison, for strength and variety, with that alluded to. I said further, that there had been poems, and good ones too, without end, and also in magazines, in that measure; that it had, for a year or so, been allowed to cease, and that I wished not to see its revival, except in some most potent form indeed. That is all I said to Mr. Blackwood. I will now say, further, in defence or explanation of the advice I gave him, that the composition is not, in my opinion, peculiarly and characteristically *Christopherish*, and therefore, with all its merit, would not have greatly delighted the readers of 'Maga' at the beginning of a new year. *Secondly.* The topics are not such as Christopher, on looking back for two or three years, could have selected, and many important ones are not alluded to at all. That to me is a fatal objection. *Thirdly.* There are occasional allusions that are rather out of time and place, and seem to have been—as I believe they were—written, not lately, but a good while ago. So that I do not now, as I did not then, think it a composition that would have graced and dignified a new year's number, preceding all other articles, as a sort of manifesto from the pen of C. N., and this, partly from its not being very like him in style, but chiefly from its being very unlike him in topics.

"Having said so much, I will venture to say a little more, well knowing that my criticism will not offend, even although it may not convince.* Of the first four stanzas, the first is to me beautiful, the second moderately good, the third, absolutely bad, and the fourth, not very happy, Irving and Rowland Hill being better out of North's mind altogether on a Christmas occasion. The nineteenth stanza is, I think, very bad indeed, no meaning being intended, and the expression being cumbrous and far from ingenious. Twentieth stanza I see no merit in at all, nor do I understand it, I hope, for I trust there is more meaning in it than meets my ear. Jeffrey's age was a bad joke at the first, worse when repeated in a Christmas Carol for 1827–28. The whole stanza displeases me much. Twenty-four is pretty well, but by no means equal to what would have been the view-holloa of old C. N. on first tally-hoing a Whig. The last line of it does not tell, or point to any one person; if so, not distinctly. Twenty-fifth contains a repetition of what has been many thousand times repeated in 'Maga,' *usque ad nauseam*, by that eternal Londoner from Yorkshire, and wants the free freshness with which C. N. would have breathed out himself on such a topic, if at all. Perhaps I dislike twenty-eighth stanza, because I am by no means sure of its political economy, and never can join in the cry

* Then follows a minute criticism of the poem, stanza by stanza, too detailed to be given entire. A few touches may suffice, indicating that in politics the extreme opinions of Christopher North, as expressed in *Blackwood*, were not always those of John Wilson.

in the Magazine against free trade. Twenty-ninth stanza is neither good nor bad perhaps, but it leans towards the latter. Thirty-third is written, I fear, in the same vein with much of our enemies' abuse against us. Thirty-fourth opens inefficiently with Eldon. He is a fine old fellow, but in some things a bigot, and getting very old; yet I love and respect him, as you do. Still this, and stanzas thirty-fifth, thirty-sixth, and thirty-seventh are not glorious, and free, and exulting, but the contrary, and the list of our friends is too scanty. Thirty-sixth is unworthy of Sir Walter, and Δ, and C. N., and J. W. Pardon me for saying so. In stanza fortieth I did not expect any thing more about Time, and be damned to him! All the stanzas that follow to forty-sixth, inclusive, are excellent, and in themselves worthy of Δ. But what if there be no snow and no skating at Christmas? No appearance of it at present. Besides, in such an address, they are too numerous. Forty-seventh, forty-eighth, and forty-ninth are feeble in the extreme; and the recipe for hot-pint, although correct, especially so.

"Finally, the composition, as a whole, is of a very mediocre character, in the opinion of your kind friend and most sincere admirer, Professor Wilson.

"I have never, in the whole course of my life, given an opinion in writing more than three lines long, of any composition of any man, whom I did not know to be a man of genius and talents. I have given you this long, scrawling, imperfectly expressed opinion of your verses, because I had already let you know that it was unfavorable, and therefore there is no impertinence in giving some of the reasons of my belief.

"That you should agree with me wholly is not to be expected; but that you will agree with me partly, I have no doubt, by and by. I say so from experience, for I have often and often seen, all at once, compositions of my own to be good for little or nothing, which I had at the time of writing them thought well of, and even admired.

"One thing I *know* you are wrong in, and that is in your preferring this composition to all you ever wrote for 'Maga.' You have written for 'Maga' many of the most delightful verses that are in the English language, and as for 'Mansie Waugh,'* it is inimitable,

* *The Life of Mansie Waugh, Tailor in Dalkeith.* 12mo. Edinburgh, 1828. A work full of humor, and abounding in faithful sketches of Scottish life and manners.

and better than Galt's very best. That it should have stopped—if the fault of Mr. Blackwood—is to me inexplicable and very displeasing, and I have more than once said so to him, for nothing better ever was in 'Maga' since she was born. Mr. Blackwood certainly thought the rejected composition a good one, and it was owing to me that it was rejected. I take that on my own head. But that 'Mansie Waugh' should be stopped, is to me disgusting, because it was stopped in my teeth, and in yours who have the glory of it.

"Let me conclude with the assurance of my esteem for you, my dear sir, no less as a man than an author. I am happy to know that you are universally esteemed where you would wish to be, in your profession, and in your private character, and that your poetical faculty has done you no harm, but on the contrary great good.

"I wish you would dine with us on Saturday *at six o'clock.* I expect De Quincey, and one or two other friends, and there is a *bed* for *you*, otherwise I would not ask you at so late an hour.

"I am yours affectionately, JOHN WILSON."

With the above exception, the memorials of this year are confined to the pages of *Blackwood*, to which he contributed in one month (June), when a double number was published, six of the principal articles. How little he thought of knocking off a *Noctes* when in the humor, may be judged from a note to Mr. Ballantyne, the printer, in which he says:—"I think of trying to-day and to-morrow to write a 'Noctes.' Would you have any objection to be introduced as a member? Would your brother? Of course I need not say, that, with a little fun, I shall represent you both in the kindest feeling. Pray let me know.

"Yours very truly, JOHN WILSON.

"*Subject*:—A party are to assemble in the *New Shop* to dinner."

The following note to the same gentleman may come in as a minor illustration of the "calamities of authors:"—

"Last night *about eleven* o'clock, I got two proofs to correct, which took me nearly *three hours.* I ordered the boy, therefore, to go away, and come early in the morning. It is exactly half-past eight, and I have had the luxury of three hours' work after supper for no end whatever, instead of indulging in it before breakfast.

Yet to get on is, I understand, of great importance. Here, then, are hours on hours lost, not by me assuredly; then by whom?

"Why the devil does not the devil hasten himself of an August morning? What right can any devil, red-hot from Tartarus, have to disturb me, who never injured him, for three long hours including midnight, *all for no purpose but to make me miserable?*

"I am, my dear sir, very wroth; therefore, see henceforth, that delays of this kind do not occur, for though I am willing to work when necessary, I am not willing to sacrifice sleep, and sometimes suffer, which is worse, from want of arrangement or idleness in the infernal regions. Yours sincerely,

"JOHN WILSON.

"*Thursday morning.*—With two corrected proofs lying before me for several hours needlessly at a time when they are most wanted in the Shades."

In the month of July of this year, my mother writes to her sister:—

"We are all quite well, and looking forward to a few weeks' stay on the banks of the Tweed with great pleasure. I forget whether I mentioned when I last wrote to you that Mr. Wilson had taken lodgings at Innerleithen (about six miles from Peebles). We go on the 2d of August, the day after the boys' vacation commences.

"Mr. and Mrs. Lockhart and their two children are come here this summer, I am sorry to say the latter in search of health. Mr. L. is looking well, and not a bit changed in any respect.

"Ebony has presented me with the *Life of Napoleon*, 9 vols.; everybody is now devouring it, but what is thought of it I have not heard; it will last me some years to get through it if I live; at least, if I read at my customary pace."

The three autumnal months were spent at Innerleithen, the Professor visiting Edinburgh from time to time, to attend to his literary affairs, finding on his return relaxation in his favorite amusement of fishing, or rambling over the hills to St. Mary's Loch, and not unfrequently spending a day at Altrive with the Ettrick Shepherd. He had intended, in the following year, to let Elleray; but not having found a suitable tenant, he spent the autumn there himself with his family.

From a letter to his friend, the Rev. Mr. Fleming of Rayrig, written in the spring of 1828, it will be seen how fondly he clung to the place, after having made up his mind as a matter of duty to sacrifice the pleasure of spending his summers there. Referring in this letter to the Magazine, he says:—

"Of *Blackwood's Magazine* I am not the editor, although, I believe, I very generally get both the credit and discredit of being Christopher North. I am one of the chief writers, perhaps the chief, and have all along been so, but never received one shilling from the proprietor, except for my own compositions. Being generally on the spot, I am always willing to give him my advice, and to supply such articles as may be most wanted when I have leisure to do so. But I hold myself answerable to the public only for my own articles, although I have never chosen to say, nor shall I ever, that I am not editor, as that might appear to be shying responsibility, or disclaiming my real share in the work. To you, however, I make the avowal, which is to the letter correct, of Christopher North's ideal character. I am in a great measure the parent nevertheless, nor am I ashamed of the old gentleman, who is, though rather perverse, a thriving bairn.

"I shall be at Elleray, with my daughters Margaret and Mary, about the 18th or 20th of April, and hope to stay a month. I intend to let Elleray, if I can get a suitable tenant, for *three years.* My children are all just growing up, and I cannot remove them from Edinburgh, nor can I leave them, even if the expense of having two houses were such as I could prudently encounter. I have therefore brought my mind to make the sacrifice of my summers, nowhere else so happy as on the banks of beautiful and beloved Windermere. My visit is chiefly to make arrangements for letting Elleray during the period now mentioned.

"I feel great delicacy in asking any questions of a friend relative to concerns of his friends. But I hope you will not think me guilty of indelicacy in writing to know on what terms Bellfield was let to Mr. Thomson. I am wholly at a loss to know what to ask for Elleray, and Bellfield would be a rule to go by in fixing the rent. I am anxious you will do me the justice to think that I am one of the last men in the world to seek to know any thing of the kind, except in the case like the present, where it would be of advantage to my interests and that of my family; or if there be any objection to your informing me of the point, perhaps you would have the goodness to give me your opinion of what might be the annual rent of the house, garden, and outhouses of Elleray. Whoever takes it must keep the place in order, and therefore must keep on my gardener on his present wages. The land I could either keep myself, or let it along with the house, the whole or in part.

"Mr. —— would act for me, I know, but ——, like other idle people, is too free of his tongue about my intentions, of which he knows nothing, and has been busy telling all people that I am never again to return to Elleray, and that Elleray is to be sold. This rather displeases me. Mr. —— would oblige me in any thing, but is not very skilled in character, and might, I fear, be imposed upon if he met with people wishing to impose. The idea of making Mr. Fleming useful to me has something in it abhorrent to my nature. Do, however, my dear sir, forgive my natural anxiety on this point, for if I should let Elleray to a family that would injure it, it would make me truly unhappy. I love it as I love life itself; and, in case I leave Elleray unlet, in your hands I would feel that it was as safe as in my own. I am, however, I repeat it, duly sensible of the delicacy of making such a request to such a friend; and one word will be sufficient. My intention is to keep the cottage in my own hands, with the privilege to inhabit it *myself* if I choose for a month or two, which will be the utmost in my power; although that privilege I will give up if necessary.

"Mrs. Wilson is much better in her general health than she has been since her first unhappy illness; but is still far from being well, and my anxieties are still great. I am, however, relieved from the most dreadful of all fears, and I trust in God that the fits will not again return. Her constitution would seem to have outlived them, but they have been of a most heart-breaking kind, and I look on all life as under the darkness of a shadow. John, my eldest boy, is five feet ten inches tall, and goes to College next winter. My daughters you will, I hope, see soon, and yours must come up to Elleray and stay a day or two with them, while they will be but too happy to be again at sweet Rayrig. I hear of a house having been built below Elleray by Mr. Gardiner. I hope it is not an eyesore. If it be, my eyes, I am sorry to state, will not be often offended by it for some years to come. A curious enough book on transplanting trees has been published here lately, which I will bring you a copy of. Sir Henry Stewart, the author, has made a place well wooded and thriving out of a desert, and has removed hundreds of trees of all kinds, from twenty to fifty years old, with underwood, all of which have for years been in a most flourishing condition.

"I think you will get this letter on Sunday morning. I shall think of you all in church. Your affectionate friend,

"John Wilson."

As soon as his college duties were over, he set out for Elleray. He writes from Bowness to my mother, May 16, 1828:—

"My dear Turkess:—I have this morning received your long and kind letter; and though I wrote to you yesterday, I do so again. First, then, I enclose a twelve-pound note, which, I hope, will settle the accounts, though you don't mention the amount of the rendering one. I will thank you to write to Robert as follows:—'Dear Robert, be so good as send to me the ten-pound receipt to sign, if convenient, and I will return it by post. Jane is to tell you to do so, to save you a postage. If you can give her the money *first* it will be convenient; if not, she will wait till I return the paper. Yours, J. W.' Your taste in furniture is excellent, being the same as my own; so choose a paper of a bluish sort, and don't doubt that I will like the room the better for its being entirely your taste, carpet and all. Johnny may go to the fishing whenever you think it safe; but remember wet feet are dangerous to him at present. If he goes, tell him to go and come by the coach, and give him stockings to put on dry. To fish there with dry feet is not possible; and he is not strong yet. Send him to school, with a note saying it was but an eruption, for I cannot think it was the small-pox. If it was, he is cured now. I hope they are good boys. God bless them both, Umbs, and their good mother!

"Yesterday, we rode to Ambleside—Mary on Blair's pony, which is in high health and very quiet, and spirited too, Maggie on the nondescript. We called on the Lutwidges, whom we saw. They are all well—she looking very beautiful, and in the family-way of course. On the Edmunds, too. We called on the Norths, and were most kindly received. I left the girls there, and proceeded to Grasmere, along the new road by the lake-side, which is beautiful. Found Hartley Coleridge, a little tipsy, I fear, but not very much; went with him to Sammy Barber's. Sammy was delighted to see me. He has unroofed his house, and is raising it several feet. He has built a bed-room for himself, thirty feet long, by twenty wide, with two fireplaces, and one enormous window commanding a view of the whole lake. It is the most beautiful room I ever saw. All the rest of the house is equally good, and still the external look improved.

"Wordsworth is in London. I called for the nymphs at eight o'clock, and we reached Elleray about ten o'clock—all well. Both nymphs are recovered, though Mary has still a little sore-throat left. To-day, we have walked to Bowness, and made some calls. We visited the Island, and Miss Curwen comes to Elleray next Wednesday to stay all night. She is a sweet girl, modest, sensible, amiable, and English. They are a worthy family. The girls are just now gone on to Rayrig with Miss Taylor, and I shall join them there. I wait behind to write to the Turkess. The country now is in perfect beauty; and I think of one who has been a kind, and affectionate, and good wife to me at all hours. If I do not, may the beauty of nature pass away from my eyes! To-morrow we dine at Calgarth. On Tuesday next, Sammy Barber and H. Coleridge dine with us. Neither Wellock nor M'Neil has appeared, and I shall wait for them no more. Captain Hope and his lady and a piccaninny have just driven up to the door of the inn; he is a son of the Lord President's, and brother of the Solicitor-General, and a friend of mine. They are just off again. Write as soon as you can or choose, and tell Johnny or Blair to write too—a conjoint letter. Once more, love to you all. Your affectionate husband,

"JOHN WILSON."

The following letters show how well he knew to adapt his communications to the taste of his correspondents:—

TO HIS SON BLAIR.

"ELLERAY, *Friday Afternoon, May* 23, 1828.

"MY DEAREST BLAIR:—Your very entertaining and witty letter came in due course at the breakfast hour, and made us all laugh till we were like to burst our sides; and Mary had very nearly broken a tea-cup. It was, however, rather impertinent. Your pony is in capital health and spirits, and Mary rides him very gently and not too fast. Maggy rides a chestnut cow, which George declares is a horse, and it certainly is rather like one sometimes. There are two cats, both very tame—a black, and a white one with a red tail. I fear the latter kills small birds. The young thrushes have flown, and so have a nest of linnets in the front of the house. The thrush is building again in another place. We had a gooseberry-tart yesterday, which you would have liked very much. On Saturday, we dined at Calgarth, and found all the people there exceedingly well and happy. On Sunday we went to church, and dined at home. On Monday we also dined at home; and on Tuesday, Hartley Coleridge came to dine with us, without Mrs. Barlow, who was ill. On Wednesday we all dined at home; and yesterday Fletcher Fleming and Mr. Harrison from Ambleside dined with us. To-day we are all going to drink tea with Miss Taylor at Bowness, and to go to a children's ball in the evening. Hartley Coleridge is still with us, and sends his love to your mamma and all yourselves. To-morrow we are going down to Penny Bridge, and will return on Monday or Tuesday. On Wednesday, which is Ambleside Fair, I am going there. On Thursday, there is to be wrestling there. On Friday, Mr. Garnet gives us a dinner; and after that we shall be thinking of coming home again pretty soon. I am happy to hear you and Johnny are good boys. Tell Johnny I am very angry with him for not writing. Tell mamma that I like the paper; and got her last letter this morning. God bless her, and you, and Johnny, and Umbs, and keep you all well and happy till we return. Love, too, to Miss Penny, that is, Aunt Mary; and kind compliments to Mrs. Alison. I will write to mamma from Penny Bridge. I am, my dear little boy, your most loving and affectionate father,

"THE OLD MAN."

TO HIS SON JOHN.

"ELLERAY, *Monday Afternoon, June* 2, 1828.

"MY DEAR JOHNNY:—I received your letter this morning, from which I find you are well, and in good spirits. I am satisfied with your place in the Academy, which I hope you will keep till the end, or rather steal up a little. I presume Mr. Gunn intends going on the stage. We left Penny Bridge on Tuesday, and dined at the Island with a large party. On Wednesday, I went to Ambleside fair, and settled a few bills. Richard Sowden dined with me at

Elleray on that day, and kept furnishing me with his talk till one o'clock in the morning—the girls being at the Miss Bartons'. On Thursday, I went again to Ambleside, with William and George Fleming, to see the wrestling. It was very good. A man from Cumberland, with a white hat and brown shirt, threatened to fling everybody, and 'foight' them afterwards. The 'foighting' I put a stop to. He stood till the last, but was thrown by a schoolmaster of the name of Robinson, cousin to the imp who used to be at Elleray, who won the belt with a handsome inscription—'From Professor Wilson.' We had then a number of single matches, the best of three throws; and Collinson of Bowness threw Robinson easily, he himself having been previously thrown by the Cumbrian for the belt. One Drunky, who had also been thrown for the belt, then threw Collinson, and a tailor called Holmes threw Cumberland. A little fellow about the size of Blair, or less, threw a man about six feet high, and fell upon him with all his weight. Holmes, the tailor, threw Rowland Long. The wrestling, on the whole, 'gave the family great delight.' On Friday, we all sailed with Captain Stamp in the 'Emma,' and ran aground at the water-head, but got off in about an hour without damage. The 'Emma' is an excellent, safe, roomy boat, and draws more water than the 'Endeavor.' On the same Friday, we dined with William Garnet, and at tea met some young ladies, the Miss Winyards, and Lady Pasley. We rode home in the dark and the wet. On Saturday we gave a party in the evening to the Flemings, Bellasses, and Miss A. Taylor from Ambleside. We had the band, and danced, and the party was pleasant. On Sunday we stayed at home, the day being blowy; and Miss A. Taylor is still with us. To-day some gentlemen dined at Elleray; so you see we are very gay. To-morrow we are all going a pic-nicking on the Lake. God bless you, my dear Johnny! Mind all your dear mother says, and be kind in all things, and attentive to her till we return. Love to Blair and Umbs. Your affectionate father, JOHN WILSON.

"The cross lines are for your mamma."

"MY DEAREST JANE:—I intend riding into Kendal on Wednesday, to meet our Edinburgh friends, as it will be satisfactory to hear how you all are. I shall be kept here a few days longer than I intended, because of the want of the needful, which I want to sponge out of Ebony. I shall also send to Robert for the £10, in case you have not got it. I will write to you on Thursday, fixing the day for our return, The girls are both well, and everybody is kind to them. They are just gone to call at Calgarth, with Alicia Taylor on horseback, with John Alexander with them on foot. Owen Loyd, and Joseph Harding, and some others, are to dine with us to-day. Summer is come, and really the most beautiful time of the year is past. Write to me on *Sunday evening*, for we shall not leave this till Tuesday, at the earliest. If you write the day you get this, too, or bid Blair do so, so much the better, for that day is always a happy one on which I hear from you. You are a most unaccountable niggard. Direct Mr. Hood's letter to me here, and send it to me by post. Tell Johnny to call and inquire for Captain Watson, or do so yourself, my dear Jane, first good day. I am glad to hear such good accounts of him. Keep sending me the *Observer* and *Evening Post.* My expectations of my room are very high. I intend to get John Watson to give me a head of you, to hang up over the chimney-piece. What think you of that? The little man does not sleep well here by himself. I do not fear that I shall find you well and happy. Yours till death.

"John Wilson."

The allusions to Hartley Coleridge awaken mingled feelings of pain and pleasure in remembrance of his frequent visits to Elleray, where he was ever a welcome guest. The gentle, humble-hearted, highly gifted man, "Dear Hartley," as my father called him, dreamed through a life of error, loving the good and hating the evil, yet unable to resist it. His companionship was always delightful to the Professor, and many hours of converse they held; his best and happiest moments were those spent at Elleray. My father had a great power over him, and exerted it with kind but firm determination. On one occasion he was kept imprisoned for some weeks under his surveillance, in order that he might finish some literary work he had promised to have ready by a certain time. He completed his task, and when the day of release came, it was not intended that he should leave Elleray. But Hartley's evil demon was at hand; without one word of adieu to the friends in whose presence he stood, off he ran at full speed down the avenue, lost to sight amid the trees, seen again in the open highway still running, until the sound of his far-off footsteps gradually died away in the distance, and he himself was hidden, not in the groves of the valley, but in some obscure den, where, drinking among low companions, his mind was soon brought to a level with theirs. Then these clouds would after a time pass away, and he again returned to the society of those who could appreciate him, and who never ceased to love him.

Every one loved Hartley Coleridge; there was something in his appearance that evoked kindliness. Extremely boyish in aspect, his juvenile air was aided not a little by his general mode of dress—a dark blue cloth round jacket, white trousers, black silk handkerchief tied loosely round his throat; sometimes a straw hat covered his head, but more frequently it was bare, showing his black, thick, short, curling hair. His eyes were large, dark, and expressive, and a countenance almost sad in expression, was relieved by the beautiful smile which lighted it up from time to time. The tone of his voice was musically soft. He excelled in reading, and very often read aloud to my mother. The contrast between him and the Professor, as they walked up and down the drawing rooms at Elleray, was very striking. Both were earnest in manner and peculiar in expression. My father's rapid sweeping steps would soon have distanced poor Hartley, if he had not kept up to him by a sort of short trot; then, standing still for a moment, excited by some question of philosophical interest—perhaps the madness of Hamlet, or whether or not he was a perfect gentleman—they would pour forth such torrents of eloquence that those present would have wished them to speak forever. After a pause, off again through the rooms, backwards and forwards, for an hour at a time would they walk; the Professor's athletic form, stately and free in action, and his clear blue eyes and flowing hair, contrasting singularly with Hartley's diminutive stature and dark complexion, as he followed like some familiar spirit, one moment looking vengeance, the next humble, obeisant. Is it not true that the sins of the fathers are visited upon the children? Certain it is that the light of genius he inherited was dimmed from its original source. He found no repose upon earth, but wandered like a breeze, until he was laid down in the quiet churchyard of Grasmere, close beside the resting-place of William Wordsworth.*

* Hartley Coleridge, son of Samuel Taylor Coleridge, born 1796, died 1851.

My father's contributions to the Magazine this year were very extensive, and several of them of enduring interest. They include "Christopher in his Sporting Jacket," "Old North and Young North," "Christmas Dreams," "Health and Longevity," "Salmonia," and "Sacred Poetry." My mother, writing to her sister in September, asks her:—"Have you read Blackwood's last number? I mean any of it. 'Christopher in his Sporting Jacket' is thought very good; and Mr. W. expressed a sort of wish our nephew John might like it. The Dean of Chester thinks it about one of the best things the author has produced."

Another of her letters about this time contains some pleasant home gossip. A baby niece is of course a principal topic:—"Mr. Wilson feels a great interest in her, poor little thing, and is never annoyed by any of her infantine screams or noises, which is more than I can say of him towards his own when of that age. This is a comfort to me, because I shall have true delight in having the little darling here as often as she is allowed to come; and you may well suppose that I am always anxious, when the pen is, as it *must* be, in Mr. Wilson's hand often, that he has nothing to disturb him." The mother's heart is shown in the following lines:—"Johnny is preparing for the University. As Mr. Wilson only expects and *exacts* common diligence from him, I do not fear he will do well." After mentioning the classes, she says:—"The three last-mentioned accomplishments (drawing, fencing, and dancing) are only recreations, but there is no harm in them; and I believe a greater blessing cannot befall a young man than to have every hour harmlessly if not usefully employed. You cannot think how much pleased I was with a letter Mr. W. received from Miss Watson the other day, speaking of the boys. I dare say it was flattering, but she has a way of saying things that appears as if they were not flattering. I would copy it now for you, but that I think you must be tired of the old mother's egotism. I have not mentioned the girls, but they are well. M. has two pupils, Jane and M. De Quincey, to whom she gives daily lessons in reading, writing, geography, grammar, and spelling; this occupies good part of the forenoon, and practising, mending old stockings, millinery, and such like, fill up some of the remaining hours of the day."

The four following letters from Allan Cunningham tell their own story:—

"27 LOWER BELGRAVE PLACE,
11*th September*, 1828.

"MY DEAR FRIEND:—I have cut and cleared away right and left, and opened a space for your very beautiful poem, and now it will appear at full length, as it rightly deserves. Will you have the goodness to say your will to the proof as quickly as possible, and let me have it again, for the printer pushes me sorely.

"You have indeed done me a great and lasting kindness; you have aided me, I trust effectually, in establishing my Annual Book,* and enabled me to create a little income for my family. My life has been one continued struggle to maintain my independence and support wife and children, and I have, when the labor of the day closed, endeavored to use the little talent which my country allows me to possess as easily and as profitably as I can. The pen thus adds a little to the profit of the chisel, and I keep head above water, and on occasion take the middle of the causeway with an independent step.

"There is another matter about which I know not how to speak; and now I think on't, I had better speak out bluntly at once. My means are but moderate; and having engaged to produce the literature of the volume for a certain sum, the variety of the articles has caused no small expenditure. I cannot, therefore, say that I can pay you for Edderline's Dream; but I beg you will allow me to lay twenty pounds aside by way of token or remembrance, to be paid in any way you may desire, into some friend's hand here, or remitted by post to Edinburgh. I am ashamed to offer so small a sum for a work which I admire so much; but what Burns said to the Muse, I may with equal propriety say to you:—

"'Ye ken—ye ken
That strong necessity supreme is
'Mang sons of men.'

"Now, may I venture to look to you for eight or ten pages for my next volume on the same kind of terms? I shall, with half-a-dozen assurances of the aid of the leading men of genius, be able to negotiate more effectually with the proprietor; for, when he sees that Sir Walter Scott, Professor Wilson, Mr. Southey, Mr. Lockhart, and one or two more, are resolved to support me, he will comprehend that the speculation will be profitable, and close with me

* *The Anniversary.*

accordingly. Do, I beg and entreat of you, agree to this, and say so when you write.

"Forgive all this forwardness and earnestness, and believe me to be your faithful servant and admirer,

"Allan Cunningham."

"27 Lower Belgrave Place,
November 7, 1828.

"My dear Friend:—My little Annual—thanks to your exquisite Edderline, and your kind and seasonable words—has been very successful. It is not yet published, and cannot appear these eight days, yet we have sold 6,000 copies. The booksellers all look kindly upon it; the proprietor is very much pleased with his success; and it is generally looked upon here as a work fairly rooted in public favor. The *first* large paper proof-copy ready shall be on its way to Gloucester Place before it is an hour finished. It is indeed outwardly a most splendid book.

"I must now speak of the future. The *Keepsake* people last season bought up some of my friends, and imagined, because they had succeeded with one or two eminent ones, that my book was crushed, and would not be any thing like a rival. They were too wily for me; and though I shall never be able to meet them in their own way, still I must endeavor to gather all the friends round me that I can. I have been with our mutual friend Lockhart this morning, and we have made the following arrangement, which he permits me to mention to you, in the hope you will aid me on the same conditions. He has promised me a poem, and a piece of prose to the extent of from twenty to thirty pages, for £50, and engaged to write for no other annual. Now if you would help me on the same terms, and to the same extent, I shall consider myself fortunate. It is true you kindly promised to aid me with whatever I liked for next year, and desired me not to talk of money. My dear friend, we make money of you, and why not make some return? I beg you will, therefore, letting bygones be bygones in money matters, join with Mr. Lockhart in this. I could give you many reasons for doing it, all of which would influence you. It is enough to say, that my rivals will come next year into the field, in all the strength of talent, and rank, and fashion, and strive to bear me down. The author of 'Edderline,' and many other things equally delightful, can prevent this, and to him I look for help.

"I shall try Wordsworth in the same way. I am sure of Southey and of Ed. Irving. I shall limit my list of contributors, and make a better book generally than I have done. I am to have a painting from Wilkie, and one from Newton, and they will be more carefully engraved too.

"I am glad that your poem has met with such applause here. I have now seen all the other Annuals, and I assure you that in the best of them there is nothing that approaches in beauty to 'Edderline.' This seems to be the general opinion, and proud I am of it. I remain, my dear friend, yours ever faithfully,

"Allan Cunningham."

"27 Belgrave Place Lower,
November 19, 1828.

"My dear Friend:—I send for your acceptance a large-paper copy of my Annual, with proofs of the plates, and I send it by the mail that you may have it on your table a few days before publication. You will be glad to hear that the book has been favorably received, and the general impression seems to be, that while the *Keepsake* is a little below expectation, the *Anniversary* is a little above it. I am told by one in whose judgment I can fully confide, that *our* poetry is superior, and 'Edderline's Dream' the noblest poem in *any* of the annuals. This makes me happy; it puts us at the head of these publications.

"I took the liberty of writing a letter to you lately, and ventured to make you an offer, which I wish, in justice to my admiration of your talents, had been worthier of your merits. I hope and entreat you will think favorably of my request, and give me your aid, as powerfully as you can. If you but knew the opposition which I have to encounter, and could hear the high words of those who, with their exclusive poets, and their bands of bards, seek to bear me down, your own proud spirit and chivalrous feelings would send you [quickly] to my aid, and secure me from being put to shame by the highest of the island. One great poet, not a Scotch one, kindly advised me last season, to think no more of literary competition with the *Keepsake*, inasmuch as *he* dipt *his* pen exclusively for that publication. I know his poetic contributions, and fear them not when I think on 'Edderline.'

"I hope you will not think me vain, or a dreamer of unattainable things, when I express my hope of being able, through the aid of my friends, to maintain the reputation of my book against the fame of others, though they be aided by some who might have aided me. Should you decline—which I hope in God you will not—the offer which I lately made, I shall still depend upon your assistance, which you had the goodness to promise. Another such poem as 'Edderline' would make my fortune, and if I could obtain it by May or June it would be in excellent time.

"If you would wish a copy or two of the book to give away, I shall be happy to place them at your disposal. I remain, my dear friend, your faithful servant,

"ALLAN CUNNINGHAM."

"27 LOWER BELGRAVE PLACE,
12th December, 1828.

"MY DEAR FRIEND:—I enclose you some lines for your friend's paper, and am truly glad of any opportunity of obliging you. I like Mr. Bell's *Journal** much. He understands, I see, what poetry is; a thing not common among critics. If there is any thing else you wish me to do, say so. I have not the heart to refuse you any thing.

"I was much pleased with your kind assurances respecting my next year's volume. Mr. Lockhart said he would write to you, and I hope you will unite with him and Irving in contributing for me alone. As I have been disappointed in Wordsworth, I hope you will allow me to add £25 of his £50 to the £50 I already promised. The other I intend for Mr. Lockhart. This, after all, looks like picking your pocket, for such is the rage for Annuals at present, that a poet so eminent as you are may command terms. I ought, perhaps, to be satisfied with the kind assurances you have given, and not be over greedy.

"One word about Wordsworth. In his last letter to me, he said that Alaric Watts had a prior claim, 'Only,' quoth he, 'Watts says I go about depreciating other Annuals out of regard for the *Keepsake*. This is untrue. I only said, as the *Keepsake* paid poets best, it would be the best work.' This is not depreciating! He advised me, before he knew who were to be my contributors, not to think of rivalry in literature with the *Keepsake*. Enough of a little man and a great poet. His poetic sympathies are warm, but his heart, for any manly purpose, as cold as a December snail. I had to-day

* *The Edinburgh Literary Gazette.*

a very pleasant, witty contribution, from Theodore Hook. I remain, my dear friend, yours faithfully,

"ALLAN CUNNINGHAM.

"*P. S.*—I have got Mr. Bell's letter and Journals, and shall thank him for his good opinion by sending *him* a trifle some time soon for the paper. If you think my name will do the least good to the good cause, pray insert it at either end of the poem you like. A. C."

The *Anniversary*, of which the editor wrote so anxiously, was not the only literary work this year that had requested the Professors's powerful aid. "Edderline's Dream," unfortunately, a fragment, some cantos having been lost in MS., was followed in the month of December by two beautiful little poems, one called "The Vale of Peace," the other "The Hare-Bells," written for *The Edinburgh Literary Gazette*, then edited by Mr. Henry Glassford Bell, whose abilities as a student in the Moral Philosophy class had attracted Professor Wilson's notice. He frequently visited at his house in Gloucester Place, and very soon evinced qualities more worthy of regard than a cultivated mind and a refined poetical taste. This acquaintanceship ripened into a friendship warm and sincere. Support in affairs of literature was not long a binding link; letters were forsaken for law, and, after a few years' practice in Edinburgh, Mr. Bell removed to Glasgow, having obtained a Sheriffship in that important city, where he has long enjoyed the respect due to an admirable judge, and an accomplished man of letters.

It has already been mentioned that my father had prepared sketches for the composition of various poems; why he did not follow further his original impulses in this direction has been matter of surprise. So strong a genius as his can hardly be supposed to have quite missed its proper direction. Yet from the date of the publication of the "City of the Plague," up to 1829, there is no indication of his having seriously bent his mind to poetical composition. In the autumn of that year, at Elleray, he was again visited by the muse, and my mother thus mentions the fact to her sister:—

"Mr. W. has been in rather a poetical vein of late, and I rather think there will be a pretty long poem of his in the next number of *Blackwood*, entitled, 'An Evening in Furness Abbey,' or something of that kind. It will be too long for *you* to read, but perhaps Ann will do so, and tell you what it is about." From the publication of this beautiful poem, the tender domestic allusions in which would alone make it of peculiar interest and value in the eyes of the present writer,* down to 1837, when he composed his last poem, "Unimore," he did not again exercise his poetic faculty in the form of verse. Late in life, he thought much of a subject which he wished to shape into verse, "The Covenanters," but he said that he found in it insuperable difficulties.† "The Manse" was another subject he used to speak of, adding jocularly, "he was obliged to leave that, owing to the *Disruption*."‡

How far we have got beyond the days when criticism of the Ettrick Shepherd required remonstrance to subdue it, may be gathered from the next letter, received during this holiday time at Elleray:—

"MOUNT BENGER, *August* 11, 1829.

"MY DEAR AND HONORED JOHN:—I never thought you had been so unconscionable as to desire a sportsman on the 11th or even the 13th of August to leave Ettrick Forest for the bare scraggy hills of Westmoreland!—Ettrick Forest, where the black cocks and white cocks, brown cocks and gray cocks, ducks, plovers, and peaseweeps and whilly-whaups are as thick as the flocks that cover her mountains, and come to the hills of Westmoreland that can nourish nothing better than a castril or stonechat! To leave the great yellow-fin of Yarrow, or the still larger gray-locher for the degenerate fry of Troutbeck, Esthwaite, or even Wastwater! No, no, the request will not do; it is an unreasonable one, and therefore not unlike yourself; for besides, what would become of Old North and Blackwood, and all our friends for game, were I to come to Elleray just now? I know of no home of man where I could be so happy within doors, with so many lovely and joyous faces around me; but this is not the season for in-door enjoyments; they must be reaped on the

* Contrasting his present experience with his early poetic dreams, he says:

"Those days are gone,
And it has pleased high Heaven to crown my life
With such a load of happiness, that at times
My very soul is faint with bearing up the blessed burden." . . .

† He corresponded with Mr. Aird a good deal on this subject. His letters are too lengthy for insertion, but it is refreshing to find in them an occasional hearty outburst of indignation at the persecuting government of Charles and James. "Ought there not to be some savage splendid Covenanters introduced somewhere or other? Pray, consider with yourself how far they ever carried retaliation or retribution. I believe not far. Besides, under such accursed tyranny, bold risings up of men's fiercest and fellest passions were not wrong."

‡ The split in the Church of Scotland in 1843.

wastes among the blooming heath, by the silver spring, or swathed in the delicious breeze of the wilderness. Elleray, with all its sweets, could never have been my choice for a habitation, and perhaps you are the only Scottish gentleman who ever made such a choice, and still persists in maintaining it, in spite of every disadvantage. Happy days to you, and a safe return! Yours most respectfully,

"JAMES HOGG."

The following letter, written about the same time, from my father to his friend Mr. Fleming, is unfortunately torn at the conclusion, but what remains of it is sufficiently interesting to be given:—

"MY DEAR FLEMING:—I much fear that it will not be possible for me to join your party on Tuesday, which I should regret under any circumstances, and more especially under the present, when you are kind enough to wish my presence more than usual. I have tried to arrange my proceedings, in twenty different ways, with the view of returning on Tuesday, but see not how I can effect my object. Mr. Benjamin Penny and his wife come to us to-morrow, and leave us on Friday. I cannot therefore go to Keswick till Saturday, and from Keswick I have to go to Buttermere and Cromack, and, if possible, Ennerdale and Wastwater. The artist who accompanies me, or rather whom I accompany, is unfortunately the most helpless of human beings, and incapable of finding his way alone among mountains for one single hour. I am, therefore, under the absolute necessity of guiding him every mile of the way, and were I to leave him he might as well be lying in his bed. His stay here is limited by his engagements in Edinburgh, and we shall have to return to Elleray on Thursday, without having an opportunity of going again into Cumberland. Were I therefore to leave him on Tuesday, great part of my object in bringing him here would be defeated, and, indeed, even as it is, I have little hope of his achieving my purpose. He can neither walk nor ride, nor remember the name of the lake, village, vale, or house, and yet he is an excellent artist, though a most incapable man. I returned from a three days' tour with him on Saturday night, and would have immediately written to you, but expected to have called on you on Sunday evening, to tell you how matters stood. Mrs. Wilson, John, and one of the girls, or indeed any part of the family you choose, will be with you on Tuesday; and if Tuesday be a bad day, so that Mr. Gibb cannot draw, and the distance be such as I can accomplish, I will exert some of my activity, a little impaired now, though not to any melancholy extent, and appear at Rayrig at five o'clock.

"It would have been pleasant had the three friends met, in a quiet way, at Rayrig; and I do not doubt that, in spite of all, we might have been even happy. But our meeting was prevented. Watson, I am sure, regretted it; and as for myself, I trust you will believe in the warmth and sincerity of my affection.

"With regard to the conversation of Calgarth about the Edinburgh murderers,* I had quite forgotten it, till the allusion to it in your kind letter recalled it to my memory. I do not believe that there is any difference of opinion in our minds respecting those hideous transactions, that might not be reconciled in three minutes' uninterrupted conversation. But I never yet recollect a single conversation in a mixed company, on any subject on which some difference of opinion between two parties had been expressed or intimated, where it was not rendered impossible to reconcile it by the interposition of a third or fourth party taking up some point connected with, perhaps, but not essentially belonging to the point at issue. The argument, if there has been one, is thus broken in upon, new topics introduced, and, without tedious explanations, it is scarcely possible to get back to the real question. Something of this kind occurred, I remember, at Calgarth. Watson and Lord De Tabley joined in with certain remarks—right enough, perhaps, in their way—but such as involved and entangled the thread of our discourse. And thus you and I appeared, I am disposed to think, to have adopted different views of the matter; whereas, had we been left to ourselves, we should either have agreed, or at least had an opportunity of letting each other clearly understand what the point was on which we disagreed, and the grounds of that disagreement. In early life I fear that my studies were not such as habituated my mind to the very strictest and closest reasonings; nor perhaps is it the natural bent . . . ."

The artist, Mr. Gibb, whose incapacity in travelling is thus hu-

* Burke and Hare, who were tried in Edinburgh, in 1829, for a series of murders perpetrated for the purpose of supplying the medical school with anatomical subjects.—See *Noctes Ambrosianæ*. 190.

morously described, was taken to Westmoreland by Professor Wilson, in order to make drawings for an intended work descriptive of lake scenery; a design, however, that came to an end, owing to an untimely disaster that overtook the numerous illustrations that had been made.

A letter from so celebrated a man as Thomas Carlyle naturally awakens interest, to know how he and Professor Wilson regarded each other. The terms of affection expressed in this epistle would lead to a supposition that there had been an intimate intercourse between them. But either want of opportunity or other circumstances prevented the continuance of personal friendship. It seems that these two gifted men never met, at least not more than once again after their first introduction, which took place in the house of Mr. John Gordon, at one time a favorite pupil, and ever after a dearly-loved friend of my father.

"CRAIGENPUTTOCK, DUMFRIES,
19*th December*, 1829.

"MY DEAR SIR:—Your kind promise of a Christmas visit has not been forgotten here; and though we are not without misgivings as to its fulfilment, some hope also still lingers; at all events, if we must go unserved, it shall not be for want of wishing and audible asking. Come, then, if you would do us a high *favor*, that warm hearts may welcome in the cold New-Year, and the voice of poetry and philosophy, *numeris lege solutis*, may for once be heard in these deserts, where, since Noah's deluge, little but the whirring of heath-cocks and the lowing of oxen has broken the stillness. You shall have a warm fire, and a warm welcome; and we will talk in all dialects, concerning all things, climb to hill-tops, and see certain of the kingdoms of this world, and at night gather round a clear hearth, and forget that winter and the devil are so busy in our planet. There are seasons when one seems as if emancipated from the 'prison called life,' as if its bolts were broken, and the Russian ice-palace were changed into an open sunny *Tempe*, and man might love his brother without fraud or fear! A few such hours are scattered over our existence, otherwise it were too hard, and would make us too hard.

"But now descending to prose arrangements, or capabilities of arrangement, let me remind you how easy it is to be conveyed hither. There is a mail-coach nightly to Dumfries, and two stagecoaches every alternate day to Thornhill; from each of which places we are but fifteen miles distant, with a fair road, and plenty of vehicles from both. Could we have warning, we would send you down two horses; of wheel carriages (except carts and barrows) we are still unhappily destitute. Nay, in any case, the distance, for a stout Scottish man, is but a morning walk, and this is the loveliest December weather I can recollect of seeing. But we are at the Dumfries post-office every Wednesday and Saturday, and should rejoice to have the quadrupeds waiting for you either there or at Thornhill, on any specified day. To Gordon, I purpose writing on Wednesday; but any way I know he will follow you, as Hesperus does the sun.

"I have not seen one *Blackwood*, or even an Edinburgh newspaper since I returned hither; so what you are doing in that unparalleled city is altogether a mystery to me. Scarcely have tidings of the *Scotsman-Mercury* duel reached me, and how the worthies failed to shoot each other, and the one has lost his editorship, and the other still continues to edit.* Sir William Hamilton's paper on Cousin's Metaphysics I read last night; but, like Hogg's Fife warlock, 'my head whirled roun', and ane thing I couldna mind.' *O curas hominum!* I have some thoughts of beginning to *prophesy* next year, if I prosper; that seems the best style, could one strike into it rightly.

"Now, tell me if you will come, or if you absolutely refuse. At all events, remember me as long as you can in good-will and affection, as I will ever remember you. My wife sends you her kindest regards, and still hopes against hope that she shall wear her Goethe brooch this Christmas, a thing only done when there is a man of genius in the company.

"I must break off, for there is an Oxonian gigman coming to visit me in an hour, and I have many things to do. I heard him say the other night that in literary Scotland there was not one such other man as ——— !—a thing in which, if ——— would do himself any justice, I cordially agree. Believe me always, my dear sir, yours with affectionate esteem, THOMAS CARLYLE."

* One of the pleasant little incidents of those agreeable times, when it was considered necessary that the editors of the *Scotsman* and the *Caledonian Mercury* should exchange shots to vindicate a fine-art criticism. The principals were Mr. Charles Maclaren and Dr. James Browne. The "hostile meeting" took place at seven o'clock in the morning, on the 12th of November, 1829.

About this time I find another letter from Mr. Lockhart, referring to the contest for the University of Oxford in 1829, when Sir Robert Peel was unseated:—

"London, 24 Sussex Place, Regent's Park,
Sunday.

"My dear Wilson:—I am exceedingly anxious to hear from you, firstly about Landor, what you have done, or what I really may expect to count on, and *when?* You will see Blanco White's review ere this reaches you. I think it won't do, being full of coxcombry, and barren of information, and in all the lighter parts *mauvais genre.* It's, however, supported by all the Coplestons, Malthuses, etc.; and to satisfy ——, I must make an exertion, in which, as you love me, give me your effectual aid—for you can. I know you will.

"I take it for granted you have been applied to both for Peel and Inglis. What do you say on that score? I am as well pleased I don't happen to have a vote. To have one, would cost me near £100; more than I care for Peel, Inglis, and the Catholic Question, *tria juncta in uno.* The Duke now counts on forty majority in the Lords, but his cronies hint he begins to be sorry the opposition out of doors is so *weak*, as he had calculated on forcing, through the No Popery row, the Catholics to swallow a bill seasoned originally for the *gusto* of the Defender of the Faith.

"How are you all at home? Ever yours,

"J. G. Lockhart.

"*P. S.*—If you go to Oxon, come hither *imprimis*, and I will go with you."

The next letter is addressed to Mr. De Quincey, dated June, 1829, and alludes to the "sketch of the Professor," of which I have made partial use in a previous chapter:—

"*Sunday Evening, June,* 1829.

"My dear De Quincey:—I had intended calling at the Nab to-morrow, to know whether or not you had left Edinburgh; but from the *Literary Gazette*, received this morning, I perceive you are still in the Modern Athens. I wish, when you have determined on coming hitherwards, that you would let me have intimation thereof, as an excursion or two among the mountains, ere summer fades, would be pleasant, if practicable.

"Your sketch of the Professor has given us pleasure at Elleray. It has occurred to me that you may possibly allude, in the part which is to follow, to the circumstance of my having lost a great part of my original patrimony, as an antithesis to the word 'rich.' Were you to do so, I know it would be with your natural delicacy, and in a way flattering to my character. But the man to whom I owed that favor *died* about a fortnight ago, ———, and any allusion to it might seem to have been prompted by myself, and would excite angry and painful feelings. On that account I trouble you with this perhaps needless hint, that it would be better to pass it over *sub silentio*. Otherwise, I should have liked some allusion to it, as the loss, grievous to many minds, never hurt essentially the peace of mine, nor embittered my happiness.

"If you think the *Isle of Palms* and the *City of the Plague* original poems (in design), and unborrowed and unsuggested, I hope you will say so. The Plague has been often touched on and alluded to, but never, that I know of, was made the subject of a poem, old Withers (the City Remembrancer) excepted, and some drivelling of Taylor the Water-Poet. Defoe's fictitious prose narrative I had never read, except an extract or two in Britton's *Beauties of England*. If you think me a good private character, do say so; and if in my house there be one who sheds a quiet light, perhaps a beautiful niche may be given to that clear luminary. Base brutes have libelled my personal character. Coming from you, the truth told, without reference to their malignity, will make me and others more happy than any kind expression you may use regarding my genius or talents. In the *Lights and Shadows*, *Margaret Lyndsay*, *The Foresters*, and many articles in *Blackwood* (such as Selby's 'Ornithology'*), I have wished to speak of humble life, and the elementary feelings of the human soul in isolation, under the light of a veil of poetry. Have I done so? Pathos, a sense of the beautiful, and humor, I think I possess. Do I? In the *City of the Plague* there ought to be something of the sublime. Is there? That you think too well of me, is most probably the case. So do not fear to speak whatever you think less flattering, for the opinion of such a man, being formed in kindness and affection, will gratify me far beyond the most boundless panegyric from anybody else. I feel that I am totally free from all jealousy, spite, envy, and un-

* November, 1826.

charitableness. I am not so passionate in temper as you think. In comparison with yourself, I am the Prince of Peacefulness, for you are a nature of dreadful passions subdued by reason. I wish you would praise me as a lecturer on Moral Philosophy. That would do me good; and say that I am thoroughly logical and argumentative—for it is true; not a rhetorician, as fools aver. I think, with practice and opportunities, I would have been an orator. Am I a good critic? We are all well. I have been very ill with rheumatism. God bless you, my dear friend, and believe me ever yours affectionately, J. W."

The friendship subsisting between Mr. De Quincey and my father has already been mentioned. From 1809, when he was his companion in pedestrian rambles and the sharer of his purse, till the hour of his death, that friendship remained unbroken, though sometimes, in his strange career, months or years would elapse without my father either seeing or hearing of him. If this singular man's life were written truthfully, no one would believe it, so strange the tale would seem. It may well be cause of regret that, by his own fatal indulgence, he had warped the original beauty of his nature. For fine sentiment and much tender kindliness of disposition gleamed through the dark mists which had gathered around him, and imperfectly permitted him to feel the virtue he so eloquently described. For the most part his habit of sympathy was such that it elevated the dark passions of life, investing them with an awful grandeur, destructive to the moral sense. These beautiful writings of his captivate the mind, and would fain invite the reader to believe that the man they represent is De Quincey himself. But not even in the "Autobiography" is his *personnel* to be found. He indeed knew how to analyze the human heart, through all its deep windings, but in return he offered no key of access to his own. In manner no man was more courteous and naturally dignified; the strange vicissitudes of his life had given him a presence of mind which never deserted him, even in positions the most trying. It was this quality that gave him, in combination with his remarkable powers of persuasion, command over all minds; the ignorant were silenced by awe, and the refined fascinated as by the spell of a serpent. The same faults in common men would have excited contempt; the same irregularities of life in ordinary mortals would have destroyed interest and affection; but with him patience was willing to be torn to tatters, and respect driven to the last verge. Still Thomas De Quincey held the place his intellectual greatness had at first taken possession of. Wilson loved him to the last, and better than any man he understood him. In the expansiveness of his own heart, he made allowances for faults which experience taught him were the growth of circumstance. It may seem strange that men so opposite in character were allied to each other by the bonds of friendship; but I think that all experience shows that sympathy, not similarity, draws men to one another in that sacred relation.

I remember his coming to Gloucester Place one stormy night. He remained hour after hour, in vain expectation that the waters would assuage and the hurly-burly cease. There was nothing for it but that our visitor should remain all night. The Professor ordered a room to be prepared for him, and they found each other such good company that this accidental detention was prolonged, without further difficulty, for the greater part of *a year*. During this visit some of his eccentricities did not escape observation. For example, he rarely appeared at the family meals, preferring to dine in his own room at his own hour, not unfrequently turning night into day. His tastes were very simple, though a little troublesome, at least to the servant who prepared his repast. Coffee, boiled rice and milk, and a piece of mutton from the loin, were the materials that invariably formed his diet. The cook, who had an audience with him daily, received her instructions in silent awe, quite overpowered by his manner; for, had he been addressing a duchess, he could scarcely have spoken with more deference. He would couch his request in such terms as these:—"Owing to dyspepsia afflicting my system, and the possibility of any additional disarrangement of the stomach taking place, consequences incalculably distressing would arise, so much so indeed as to increase nervous irritation, and prevent me from attending to matters of overwhelming importance, if you do not remember to cut the mutton in a diagonal rather than in a longitudinal form." The cook—a Scotchwoman—had great reverence for Mr. De Quincey as a man of genius; but, after one of these interviews, her patience was pretty well exhausted, and she would say, "Weel, I never heard the like o' that in a' my days; the bodie has an awfu' sicht o' words. If it had been my ain maister that was wanting his dinner, he would ha' ordered a hale table-fu' wi' little mair than a waff o' his haun, and here's a' this claver aboot a bit mutton nae bigger than a prin. Mr. De Quinshey would mak' a gran' preacher, though I'm thinking a hantle o' the folk wouldna ken what he was driving at." Betty's observations were made with considerable self-satisfaction, as she considered her insight of Mr. De Quincey's character by no means slight, and many was the quaint remark she made, sometimes hitting upon a truth that entitled her to that shrewd sort of discrimination by no means uncommon in the humble ranks of Scottish life. But these little meals were not the only indulgences that, when not properly attended to, brought trouble to Mr. De Quincey. Regularity in doses of opium was even of greater consequence. An ounce of laudanum per diem prostrated animal life in the early part of the day. It was no unfrequent sight to find him in his room lying upon the rug in front of the fire, his head resting upon a book, with his arms crossed over his breast, plunged in profound slumber. For several hours he would lie in this state, until the effects of the torpor had passed away. The time when he was most brilliant was generally towards the early morning hours; and then, more than once, in order to show him off, my father arranged his supper parties so that, sitting till three or four in the morning, he brought Mr. De Quincey to that point at which in charm and power of conversation he was so truly wonderful.*

CHAPTER XIII.

LITERARY AND DOMESTIC LIFE.—A CRUISE WITH THE EXPERIMENTAL SQUADRON.

1830–'37.

In 1830, we get some glimpses of home life in Gloucester Place, from my mother's letters to Miss Penny. She says, in reply to an invitation for her sons to Penny Bridge:—"The boys are transported with the idea of so much enjoyment, and I hope they will

* Mr. De Quincey died at Edinburgh, December 8, 1859.

not be disappointed indeed. I do not think Mr. Professor can refuse them, but I have not yet had time to talk the matter over with him; for at the time the letter came he was particularly busy, and the day before yesterday, he and Johnny left us for a week to visit an old friend, Mr. Findlay, in the neighborhood of Glasgow, from whose house they mean to go and perambulate all the old haunts in and about Paisley, where Mr. W. spent his boyhood, and particularly to see the old minister Dr. M'Latchie, whom I dare say you have heard him mention often; he lived in his house for several years before he went to Glasgow College." My father really must have been "particularly busy" at this time, and his powers of working seem to me little short of miraculous; he had two articles in *Blackwood* in January; four in February; three in March; one each in April and May; four in June; three in July; *seven* in August (or 116 pages); one in September; two in October; and one in November and December: being thirty articles in the year, or 1,200 columns. To give an idea of his versatility, I shall mention the titles of his articles in the Magazine for one month, viz., August:—"The Great Moray Floods;" "The Lay of the Desert;" "The Wild Garland, and Sacred Melodies;" "Wild Fowl Shooting;" "Colman's Random Records;" "Clark on Climate;" "Noctes, No. 51." My mother, while all this literary work was going on, was too good a housewife to be able to spare time for more than the most notable works of the day. She, however, says jocularly to her correspondent: "I think I must give you a little literature, as I shine in that line prodigiously; I have read, with intense interest, as everybody must do, Moore's *Life of Lord Byron.* Mr. W. had a copy sent to him, fortunately; for strange as it may appear, it is not to be had in the booksellers' shops here, and I suppose will not be till the small edition comes out."

In September and October, the Professor writes, from Penny Bridge and Elleray, the following letters to his wife:—

"Penny Bridge, *Tuesday, September*, 1830.

"My dearest Jane:—We came here yesterday; and my intention was to take Maggy back to Elleray with me to-day, and thence in a few days to Edinburgh. But I find that that arrangement would not suit, and therefore have altered it. Our plans now are as follows:—We return in a body to Elleray (that is, I and Maggy, and James Ferrier) this forenoon. There is a ball at Mrs. Edmund's (the Gale!) to-night, where we shall be. On Thursday, there is a grand public ball at Ambleside, where we shall be; and I shall keep Maggy at Elleray till Monday, when she and the boys will go in a body to Penny Bridge, and I return *alone* to Edinburgh.

"From your letters I see you are well; and I cannot deny Maggy the pleasure of the two balls; so remain on her account, which I hope will please you, and that you will be happy till and after my return. The session will begin soon, and I shall have enough to do before it comes on. Dearest Jane, be good and cheerful; and I hope all good will attend us all during the winter. Such weather never was seen as here! Thursday last was fixed for a regatta at Lowood. It was a dreadful day, and nothing occurred but a dinner-party of twenty-four, where I presided. On Friday, a sort of small regatta took place. A repast at three o'clock was attended by about seventy-five ladies and gentlemen, and the ball in the evening was, I believe, liked by the young people. The 'worstling' took place during two hours of rain and storm. The ring was a tarn. Robinson, the schoolmaster, threw Brunskil, and Irvine threw Robinson; but the last fall was made up between them, and gave no satisfaction. The good people here are all well and *kind.* Maggy has stood her various excursions well, and is fat. I think her also grown tall. She is a quarter of an inch taller than Mrs. Barlow. Colonel B—— lost his wife lately by elopement, but is in high spirits, and all his conversation is about the fair sex. He is a pleasant man, I think, and I took a ride with him to Grasmere t'other day. The old fool waltzes very well, and is in love with Maggy. He dined with us at Elleray on Sunday. I have not seen the Watsons for a long time, but shall call on them to-morrow. The weather and the uncertainty of my motions have stood in the way of many things. I have constant toothache and rheumatism, but am tolerably well notwithstanding. Give my love to Molly and Umbs. Tell them both to be ready on my arrival, to help me in arranging my books and papers in the garrets and elsewhere. My dearest Jane, God bless you always. Your affectionate husband,

"J. Wilson."

A few days later he writes:—

"Elleray, *Monday Afternoon*,
October, 1830.

"My dearest Jane:—The ball at Ambleside went off with great *éclat*, Maggy being the chief belle. The Major is gone, and proved empty in the long-run. We all dined at Calgarth on Saturday—a pleasant party. On Sunday, a Captain Alexander (who was in Persia) called on us, and we took him to the Hardens' to dinner. We were all there. To-day, Maggy and Johnny made calls on horseback, and we in the 'Gazelle.' We took farewell of the Watsons. Mr. Garnet dines with us at Elleray, and the boys at Lowood with the Cantabs. To-morrow they go to Penny Bridge, and J. Ferrier to Oxford, and I to Kendal. So expect me by the mail on Wednesday, to dinner, at five, if I get a place at Carlisle. I found the Penny Bridge people were anxious, so I let the bairns go to them till after the Hunt ball; and no doubt they will be happy. Have all my newspapers from the 'Opossum' on Tuesday before I arrive. Tell Molly to get them in a heap. Have a fire in the front drawing-room and dining-room, and be a good girl on my arrival. Have a shirt, etc., aired for me, for I am a rheumatician; a fowl boiled. I got your kind letter yesterday. Love to Moll and Umbs. God bless you! I am, your affectionate husband,

"Johnny Wilson."

"Elleray, *Monday*, 1830.

"My dearest Jane:—I had a letter this morning from Maggy, dated Saturday, Bangor Ferry, *all well;* and I suppose that she would write to you some day. She told me not of her plans, but I understand from Belfield, that the party are expected there on Thursday. I think I shall stay till she arrives. We dined at Penny Bridge on Thursday, having called at Hollow Oak, and found all the family at both places well.

"Miss Penny is looking very well. We returned that night to Elleray. On Friday, for the first time—no, for the second—we took a sail in the 'Gazelle,' the Thomsons' boat, for an hour or two, and then dined in a body at Lowood. On Saturday we rode (all five) to Grasmere, walked up Easdale—fell in with a man and his wife, or love-lady—Englishers apparently, named Brodie, who were anxious to see Langdale. We told them to join us, and all seven rode to the head of it, across by Blea-Tarn, and down little Langdale to Ambleside.

"It was a delightful day as to weather, and we enjoyed ourselves considerably.

"At Ambleside, where we arrived about half-past six, we dined in great strength. The Carr surgeon, the Costelloe ditto, John Harden, Fletcher Fleming, another person, I think, and ourselves five. I got home about twelve, all steady. Sunday, that is yesterday, was one of the most complete things of the kind I remember to have seen; and I presume the floods in Morayshire were in high health and spirits. We lay on sofas all day. To-day, Monday, is stormy and showery, and I never left the dining-room great chair. Tell Mary to write to me the night she gets this, and that, I think, will be to-morrow, and I shall get it on *Thursday*. Write you on *Thursday night*, and I shall get it on Saturday, on which day I shall probably leave Elleray, but I will fix the day as soon as Maggy comes. I shall, on my arrival, have plenty to do to get ready for November 4th; so shall not most probably go to Chiefswood at all. Hartley Coleridge came here on Saturday, and is looking well and steady. He sends his kindest regards to you, Mary, and Umbs. Do you wish me to bring Maggy with me? Yours, most affectionately,

J. WILSON.

"I got your kind letter duly this morning."

"DEAREST MOLL:—Write me a long letter, and on Wednesday night, if you have not time on Tuesday. Give my love to your Mamma and Umbs. Your affectionate father,

J. W."

Next year he paid another visit to Westmoreland, from which he writes to his wife:—

"PENNY BRIDGE, *Sunday*, 26*th Sept.*, 1831.

"MY DEAR JANE:—I delayed visiting this place with Mary till I could leave Elleray, without interruption, for a couple of days. T. Hamilton stayed with us a fortnight, and, as he came a week later, and stayed a week longer than he intended, so has my return to Edinburgh been inevitably prevented. Mary and I came here on Thursday, since which hour it has never ceased raining one minute, nor has one of the family been out of doors. They are all well, including Mrs. and Miss Hervey, who have been staying about a month. It now threatens to be fair, and I purpose setting off by and by on foot to Elleray, a walk of fifteen miles, which perhaps may do me good; but if I feel tired at Newby Bridge, I will take a boat or chaise. Mary I leave at Penny Bridge for another week. The boys will join her here next Thursday, and remain till the Monday following, when they will all return to Windermere. On that Monday, Mary will go to Rayrig for two days or three, and either on Thursday or Friday arrive together in Edinburgh. I and Gibb will most probably be in Edinburgh on *Thursday first*, unless I find any business to detain me at Elleray for another day, on my return there to-night. If so, you will hear from me on *Wednesday*. As Mary wrote a long letter on Tuesday last, full, I presume, of news, I have nothing to communicate in that line. Birkbeck has been at Elleray for two or three days, and Johnny says he expects Stoddart, who perhaps may be there on my return to-night. We all went to the Kendal ball, which the young people seemed to enjoy. Twenty-six went from Bowness, forming the majority of the rank and beauty. I hope you have been all quite well since I saw you, as all letters seem to indicate, and that I shall find you all well on my return. A severe winter lies before me, for I must lecture on Political Economy this session, as well as Moral Philosophy; and that Magazine will also weigh heavy on me. I certainly cannot work as I once could, and feel easily wearied and worn down with long sitting; but what must be must, and toil I must, whatever be the consequence. The month before the Session opens will be of unspeakable importance to me, to relieve if possible my miserable appearance in College beginning of last Session. I wish to do my duty in that place at least, and change and exposure there are hard to bear, and of infinite loss to my interests. I feel great uneasiness and pain very often from the complaint I spoke of; but how else can I do what is necessary for me to do? Whatever be the consequence, and however severe the toil, I must labor this winter like a galley-slave; and since it is for us all, *in that at least*, I shall be doing what is at once right and difficult, and in itself deserving of commendation. If I fall through it, it shall only be with my life, or illness beyond my strength to bear up against. I hope Maggy's playing the guitar and singing frequently, and that Umbs is a good boy. Kindest love to them. I should like to have a few kind lines from you, written *on Monday*, the evening you receive this, and sent to post-office then. I may, or rather *must* miss them, but if any thing prevents it I shall conclude you are undoubtedly all well. You need not send any newspapers after recei t of this, but please to keep them together. Do not say any thing about my motions to the Blackwoods, as I wish to be at home a day or two *incog.* I shall get my room done up when I arrive, which will save me trouble perhaps afterwards in looking out for papers. Mary is getting fat, and looks well, and the boys are all right. I am, my dearest Jane, yours ever affectionately, JOHN WILSON."

Two days later he writes :—

"MY DEAR JANE :—I expect to be at home on Friday per mail, or 'Peveril,' to dinner. I purpose riding over to Penrith with Garnet on the ponies on Wednesday, and thence on, which saves me Kendal, a place abhorred. The family leave Elleray that day for Penny Bridge. I was so knocked up with my walk therefrom as to be stiff and lame yet. My walking day is over. The shrubs in the entrance are all well, but too tall, and want to be cut over. The myrtle is in excellent health and beauty, though it seems less.* Charlie† is in high glee and condition. The avenue is beautiful, and the gate pretty, the low walls being covered with ivy, and other odoriferous plants and parasites. The ponies and cows are all well-to-do, five of the former and two of the latter. Of the five former, one is an 'unter, and two are staigs. I called to-day at the Wood, and found all the Watsons well. I have frequently done so. I have not been in Ambleside since Hamilton left us; and we have seen nobody for a long time, it being supposed that I am gone, whereas I am just going. I wish no dinner on Friday, but a *foal,* as F. calls it. Mary is to write to you on Friday next, so you will hear of the boys a day later than by the Professor. Weir must have been a bore. I like Otter; Starky is in treaty for Brathay for nineteen years. He is seventy-two. Rover is pretty bobbish. Star is at Oldfield in high spirits, and neighs as often as we pass the farm. Love to Maggy and Umbs. I expect to find you all well, and if possible alone and in good humor on Friday, for I shall be very tired. Stoddart brought letters. I opened Mag's and yours, but not the other two, which being about eating had no charms. Yours affectionately, J. WILSON."

That the Magazine did weigh heavily upon him I do not wonder,

* The myrtle was my mother's favorite plant.
† A spaniel belonging to my mother.

as he had already written twenty articles during 1831, five of which were in the August number.

During this year, too, he commenced those noble critical essays on "Homer and his Translators,"* which scholars have remarked "contain the most vivid and genial criticisms in our own or any other language."† I believe deep thought and careful philosophical inquiry, combined with stirring vivacity, are nowhere more attractively displayed than in these essays of my father. But not to the learned alone do they give delight, for my humble admiration makes me turn to them again and again.

The following letter from Mr. Sotheby, relating to these papers, may come in here :—

"13 Lower Grosvenor Place, *October* 8, 1831.

"My dear Sir :—One month, two months, three months' grievous disappointment, intolerable disappointment, Homer and his tail, Chapman, Pope, and Sotheby in dim eclipse. What becomes of the promise solemnly given to the public, that the vases of good and evil, impartially poured forth by your balancing hand, were ere Christmas to determine our fate? I long doubted whether I should trouble you with a letter, but the decided opinion of our friend Lockhart decided me. And now hear, I pray, in confidence, why I am peculiarly anxious for the completion of your admirable remarks.

"I propose, ere long, to publish the Odyssey, and shall gratify myself by sending you, as a specimen of it, the eleventh book. It will contain, *inter alia*, a sop for the critics, deeply soaked in the blood of a fair heifer and a sable ram, and among swarms of spirits, the images of the heroes of the Iliad, completing the tale of Troy divine. After the publication of the Odyssey, it is my intent, by the utmost diligence and labor, to correct the Iliad, and to endeavor to render it less unworthy of the praise you have been pleased to confer on it. Of your praise I am justly proud ; yet for my future object, I am above measure desirous of the benefit of your censures. The remarks (however flattering) with which I have been honored by others, are less valuable to me than your censures ; of this, the proof will be evident in the subsequent edition.

* The first appeared in April, followed by Numbers 2 and 3, in May and July. In August, a critique on the Agamemnon of Æschylus interrupted the essays, but they were resumed again in December, continued at intervals from 1832 to 1834, making in all seven papers.

† Gladstone's *Studies on Homer and the Homeric Age.*

"You must not, you cannot leave your work incomplete. How resist the night expedition of Diomede and Ulysses?—Hector bursting the rampart—Juno and the Cestus—Hector rushing on, like the stalled horse snapping the cord—The death of Sarpedon—The consternation of the Trojans at the mere appearance of the armed Achilles—The Vulcanian armor—Achilles mourning over Patroclus—The conclusion of the twentieth book—The lamentations of Priam, and Hecuba, and, above all, of Andromache—Priam at the feet of Achilles—Andromache's lamentation, and Helen's (oh, that lovely Helen!) over the corse of Hector—can these and innumerable other passages be resisted by the poet of the 'City of the Plague?' No, no, no.

"In sooth, I must say, I had hope that at Christmas I might have collected, and printed for private distribution, or, far rather, published, for public delight and benefit, with your express permission, the several critiques in one body, and then presented to the world a work of criticism unparalleled.

"I dine this day at Lockhart's, with my old and dear friend, Sir Walter. His health has improved since his arrival. Perhaps your cheeks may burn. I beg the favor of hearing from you. I remain, my dear sir, most sincerely yours, WM. SOTHEBY."*

Miss Watson, the writer of the following letter, was a lady whose name can scarcely be permitted to pass without some notice. She was eldest daughter of the Bishop of Llandaff, and a woman of high mental attainments. When my father resided as a young man in Westmoreland, she was then in the flower of her age, and in constant communion with the bright spirits who at that time made the Lake country so celebrated. Mr. De Quincey, in writing of Charles Lloyd, and mentioning Miss Watson as his friend, says she "was an accomplished student in that very department of literature which he most cultivated, namely, all that class of works which deal in the analysis of human passions. That they corresponded in French, that the letters on both sides were full of spirit and originality." Miss Watson's life, with all the advantages which arise from a highly endowed nature, was but a sad one, for her temperament was habitually melancholy, and her health delicate. She has long since found repose. The speech which she alludes to in her letter, was

* William Sotheby, born November 9, 1757; died December 30, 1833.

one made by Professor Wilson at a public meeting which had been projected by a number of individuals, to give vent to their sentiments upon the effect of the reform measures in the contemplation of Government:

"*December* 3, 1831.

"MY DEAR PROFESSOR:—I suppose it is to yourself I owe the Edinburgh papers containing your own eloquent and elegant speech. Many thanks; I admire it much. If you were not born a prince you deserve to be one. Mr. Bolton was here when I was reading it, and he said, 'I do assure you, Miss Watson, that Mr. Canning never made a finer speech, and I shall drink the Professor's health in a bumper to-day.' I really am not capable of understanding what Englishmen mean by all this nonsense. We are like the Bourbons, of whom it may be said, 'that they had learnt nothing by the French Revolution.' Is it possible that the system of equality (at which a child of five years old might laugh) can still delude the minds of men now? I have no news worth sending; all is quiet. The cholera frightens no one. We laugh at it as a good joke. God help our merry hearts! there is something ludicrous in it, I suppose, which I can't find out. Blackwood sent me *Robert of Paris*, etc., which I am very much pleased to have. I have not begun it yet; indeed, I am not well, nor would have sent you so dull a letter, but that I could not delay saying how much I was gratified by the papers. Ever believe me yours affectionately, D. WATSON.

"Kind remembrances to Mrs. Wilson and Margaret. It is bitter, bitter cold in this pretty house. As for you and the Shepherd (to whom I would send my thanks for the most gratifying letter I ever received, but that it is rather too late in the day), I advise you both to shut yourselves up in Ambrose's for a month to come, and keep clear of all the nonsense that will be going on in the shape of Reform; and every night put down your conversation, and let me see it in *Blackwood*. You shall be two philosophers enchanted like Durandarte, and not to be disenchanted till all is over. Truly I do think you eat too many oysters! How much I do like those 'Noctes.' Write one, and let it be a good one. Wordsworth says 'that the booksellers are all aghast! and that another *dark* age is coming on.' I think he is not far wrong. He is a wonderful creature when he will deign to be what nature made him, not artificial society. He read one of his poems to me. The subject was some

14*

gold-fish, but the latter stanzas were magnificent! Oh, what a pity it is to see so noble a creature condescending to be the ass of La Fontaine's Fable! Adieu! I have written beyond my power of hand. I would rather far listen to you than write to you. I cannot now make up a letter, but my heart is still the same. It was the only talent I ever possessed in this world. It *must* be hid under a bushel. How is Mrs. Hamilton? I am ashamed to send such a scrawl, but indeed I am very poorly, as the old nurses say."

The following passages from the Professor's oration, which, on referring to the papers, I see was *the* speech of the day, are worth reproducing. He said, among other good things, that "Often have I heard it said, and have my eyes loathed to see it written, that we of the great Conservative party are enemies of education, and have no love for what are called the lower orders—orders who, when their duties are nobly performed, are, in my humble estimation, as high as that in which any human being can stand. I repel the calumny. I myself belong to no high family. I had no patronage beyond what my own honorable character gave me. I have slept in the cottages of hundreds of the poor. I have sat by the cotter's ingle on the Saturday night, and seen the gray-haired patriarch with pleasure unfold the sacred page—the solace of his humble but honorable life. I have even faintly tried to shadow forth the lights and shades of their character; and it is said I belong to that class who hate and despise the people. . . . Must I allow my understanding to be stormed by such arguments as that the chief business of poor men is to attend to politics, or their best happiness to be found in elections? I know far better that he has duties imposed on him by nature, and, if his heart is right and his head clear, while he is not indifferent to such subjects, there are a hundred other duties he must perform far more important; he may be reading ONE BOOK, which tells him in what happiness consists, but to which I have seen but few allusions made by the reformers in modern times. In reading those weather-stained pages, on which, perhaps, the sun of heaven had looked bright while they had been unfolded of old on the hill-side by his forefathers of the Covenant; when, environed with peril and death, he is taught at once religion towards his Maker, and not to forget the love and duty he owes to mankind; to prefer deeper interests, because everlasting, to those little turbulences which now agitate the surface of society, but which, I hope, will soon subside into a calm, and leave the country peaceful as before."*

I fear, however, his political opponents, in that time of madness, did not look upon his words with the same loving eyes as his amiable correspondent, as I see in a letter of my father's at this time a reference to a rhyming criticism of the Conservative proceedings any thing but flattering, from which I give two lines as a specimen:—

"The Professor got up and spoke of sobriety,
Religion, the Bible, and moral propriety."

"I need not point out to your disgust," parenthetically observes the Professor to a friend, "the insinuations conveyed in that wretched doggerel, nor express my own that they could have been published by a man who has frequently had the honor of sitting at my table, and of witnessing my character in the domestic circle."

In this excited period I find ladies writing strongly on political matters. For example, even the gentle spirit of my mother is roused. She says to my aunt:—"I hope you are as much disgusted and grieved as we all are with the passing of this accursed Reform Bill. I never look into a newspaper now; but we shall see what they will make of it by and by."

Among my father's contributions to the Magazine this year, there appeared in the May number an article which attracted considerable attention. It was a review of Mr. Tennyson's Poems,† the first edition of which had appeared two years previously. The critique was severe, yet kindly and discriminating. The writer remarking good-humoredly at its close, "In correcting it for the press, we see that its whole merit, which is great, consists in the extracts, which are 'beautiful exceedingly.' Perhaps in the first part of our article we may have exaggerated Mr. Tennyson's not unfrequent silliness, for we are apt to be carried away by the whim of the moment, and, in our humorous moods, many things wear a queer look to our aged eyes which fill young pupils with tears; but we feel assured that in the second part we have not exaggerated his strength, and that we have done no more than justice to his fine faculties." It says much for the critic's discriminating power that he truly foretold of the future Laureate, that the day would come when, beneath sun and

* *Edinburgh Advertiser*, Nov. 29, 1831.

† *Poems, chiefly Lyrical.* By Alfred Tennyson. London: E. Wilson. 1830.

shower, his genius would grow up and expand into a stately tree, embowering a solemn shade within its wide circumference, and that millions would confirm his judgment "that Alfred Tennyson is a poet." The young poet, although evidently nettled,* received the criticism in good part, and profited by it. On reading the paper once more, I observe that, with scarcely a single exception, the verses condemned by the critic were omitted or altered in after editions.†

In June, 1832, my mother writes:—"Mr. Wilson has long and earnestly wished to have a cruise with the experimental squadron, which I believe will sail by the end of this month; but unfortunately he was late in applying to Sir P. Malcolm."

In July he left home for the purpose of joining the squadron, and the result of his naval experience will be found in the following communications sent from time to time to Mrs. Wilson:

"UNION HOTEL, CHARING CROSS,
Wednesday, July 11, 1832.

"MY DEAREST JANE:—I have received your favor of last Saturday, and rejoice to find that you are all well, and in as good spirits as can be expected during my absence. Had I known what bustle and botheration I should be exposed to, I hardly think I should have left Edinburgh. Every day gives a different account of the movement of the squadron. The 'Vernon,' who is at Woolwich, was to have dropt down to-day to Sheerness, but it is put off till Friday, and even that is uncertain. She has then to get all her guns and powder on board, and her sails set, and other things, which will take some days, I guess; and this morning it is said the squad-

* In the edition of his poems, published in 1833, the following somewhat puerile lines appeared, which I quote as a literary curiosity:—

"TO CHRISTOPHER NORTH.

"You did late review my lays,
Crusty Christopher;
You did mingle blame with praise,
Rusty Christopher:
When I learned from whom it came,
I forgave you all the blame,
Musty Christopher;
I could *not* forgive the praise,
Fusty Christopher."

† "The National Song;" "English War Song;" "We are Free;" "Love, Pride, and Forgetfulness;" Sonnet, "Shall the hag Evil," &c.; "The 'How' and the 'Why;'" "The Kraken," &c., &c., are all consigned to oblivion, or to our acquisitive brethren on the other side of the Atlantic, who may have preserved these youthful effusions in the American editions.

ron are to meet at Plymouth. All this keeps me in a quandary, and I have not been able to see Sir F. Collier, the captain of the 'Vernon,' but possibly shall to-morrow. Since I wrote I have been again at Woolwich, and seen the officers of the 'Vernon.' They were at first rather alarmed at the idea of a professor, and wondered what the deuce he wanted on board. I understand that they are now in better humor; but the truth is, that *pride* is the leading article in the character of all sailors on their own ship; and I am told these dons are determined to take nobody else but myself. Captain Hope (not the President's son) and Andrew Hay were with me at Woolwich, and there we picked up Captain Gray* of the Marines (you will remember his singing), who dined with us at Greenwich. I see Blair every day, and pass my time chiefly with *offishers*, the United Service Club being close at hand. The literary people here seem cockneys. I called yesterday on Miss Landon, who is really a pleasant girl, and seemed much flattered by the old fellow's visit. To-day Blair and I, along with Edward Moxon, (bookseller), take coach for Enfield (at three o'clock), to visit Charles Lamb. We return at night, if there are coaches. On Thursday, I intend going to the Thomsons' down the river, and shall call again on my way on the 'Vernon,' to see what is doing. Meanwhile, you will get this letter on *Friday, and be sure it is answered that evening, and sent to the General Post-Office.* I shall thus hear from you on Monday, and shall then (if not off) have to tell you all our future intentions. Meanwhile it is reported that *the cholera is on board the 'Vernon.'* If so, I shall not go, but proceed to the Tyne. But say nothing of this to anybody. Yesterday I visited Kensington Gardens with Captain Hope, but saw nobody like Maggy, Mary, Umbs, and yourself. I met there Lord Haddington, and am to dine with him, if I can, before sailing; but I hope we shall be at rendezvous by Monday night. Tell Maggy to give me all news, and if you have heard again from Johnny. I will send you in my next my direction when we set sail; and I am not without hopes the squadron may land me in Scotland. Some say there will be *fighting*, and that the 'Vernon' will lead the van, being, though a frigate, as powerful as a line-of-battle ship. I will write to Ebony about money for the house after I hear from Maggy, and hope you will go on pretty well till I return. Tell Maggy to be civil to Bob,

* Charles Gray, see p. 132.

and he will be my banker for small sums. I will also send a receipt, which you will get on the *6th of August, for £30 odd;* but I will explain how in my next.

"Take good care of all yourselves, and be good boys and girls. Love to Mag, Moll, and Umbs. As for *Blair, he* cuts me so up that I fear to send him even my compliments. I am glad to hear of Moll's voice being high. Keep Mag to the *guitar* and new songs. Yours ever affectionately, JOHN WILSON."

The next is to his daughter Mary:—

"UNION HOTEL, CHARING CROSS,
July 16, 1832.

"MY DEAR MARY:—I have received your kind epistle, and am rather pleased to find you all well. I write these few lines in a great hurry, to tell you to *wrap up in a parcel, two silver soup-spoons, two tea-spoons, and two silver forks,* and direct them to me at Union Hotel, Charing Cross, per mail, without delay. *See them booked at the Office.* Young ladies take such things to school, and young gentlemen, it seems, to sea. See that the direction is distinct. Write to me by the same post, or if any thing prevent, by the one following; but direct my letter, care of Captain Tatnal, No. 5 Park Terrace, Greenwich. I have just time to say God bless you all, but in a few days will write a long letter telling you of our intended motions, as we hope to be off by the 26th. Don't believe any thing about the 'Vernon' in any newspaper. Be good girls and boys till my return, and do not all forget your old Dad. Love to mamma, and tell me if you have heard farther from Johnny. Thy affectionate father, J. WILSON."

TO MRS. WILSON.

"NO. 2 PARK TERRACE, GREENWICH,
Friday.

"MA BONNE CITOYENNE:—I am now fairly established here in lodgings, that is, in a room looking into Greenwich Park, with liberty to take my meals in a parlor belonging to the family. The master thereof is a Frenchman, and a Professor of Languages, and the house swarms with frogs, that is, children. I pay fourteen shillings a week for lodging, which is a salutary change from the hotel. I dine with Tatnal or Williams, or at a shilling ordinary, and hope to be able to pay my bill to Monsieur Gallois when I take my departure. I walk to Woolwich daily (three miles), and board the 'Vernon,' who now assumes a seaward *seeming*. Her gun-carriages are on board, but not the guns themselves, which are to be taken in at Sheerness. I have seen Sir F. Collier, who behaves civilly, but he cannot comprehend what I want on board the 'Vernon,' neither can I. Her destination is still unknown, but she is to have marines and artillerymen on board, which smells of fighting. But with whom are we to fight? My own opinion is, that we are going to cruise off Ireland, and to land troops at Cork. Williams thinks we are going to Madeira, to look after an American frigate, and Tatnal talks of the Greek Islands. Meanwhile, Sir P. Malcolm, I hear, is enraged at being kept tossing about in the 'Donegal,' without knowing why or wherefore; and nobody knows where the 'Orestes' has gone. The 'Tyne' sails to-morrow for Plymouth. The 'Vernon,' it is thought, cannot be off before the 27th, so that there will be time to write me again before I go to sea. You will get this on Monday morning, and I hope some of you will answer it that night. Direct it to me at Captain Tatnal's, No. 5 Park Terrace, Greenwich, in case I should be off. If our destination be merely Ireland, there is every probability of our touching at some Scotch port. I have been several times at Sir Henry Blackwood's, in Regent Park; pleasant family, and fashionable. I forgot if I mentioned that I went to the Opera, singing and dancing, and *tout-ensemble* beautiful. A Miss Doyle (a Paddy about thirty-five), at Sir H. B.'s, plays the harp ten times better than Taylor. She is held to be the finest harpist we have. Miss Blackwood is very pretty, and clever. I go up to town to-day to dine with Mrs. Burke, and to-morrow a party of us eat white bait at the 'Crown and Sceptre' here. Besides the 'Vernon,' there are lying at Woolwich two new gun-brigs, also built by Symonds, called the 'Snake' and the 'Serpent.' They go with us to compete with the 'Orestes.' The squadron, therefore, at first, will consist of the 'Donegal,' 84, the 'Vernon,' 50, the 'Castor,' 44, the 'Tyne,' 28, the 'Orestes,' 'Serpent,' and 'Snake,' 18; and we expect to be joined by the 'Britannia' and 'Caledonia,' 120; but that is uncertain. The hatred felt for the 'Vernon' is wide and deep, and all the old fogies predict she will capsize in a squall. This is all owing to her incomparable beauty. You have just to imagine the 'Endeavor' magnified, and you see her hull, only she is sharper. She is very wide in proportion to her length, and also deep; so the devil himself will not be able to upset or sink her. She has the masts and spars of a 74, and yet they seem light as lady-fern. I am sorry, however, to say, that there have been twelve cases of cholera on board, and three deaths. The disease, however, is now over, and I have no doubt arose from the dreadful heat of the weather acting on the new paint. She is now dry as a whistle, and the crew is the finest ever seen. I hope you will get up a long letter among you in reply to this, and I shall be expecting it anxiously, as the last I can receive for some time. I will write again before one o'clock, sending you my direction, and also a receipt, which will enable you to get some money, I think, on the 6th of August. Be sure to tell me of Johnny, and when he returns I hope he will write me an account of his route and his exploits. Blair, too, might write me a letter, I think. Kindest love to them all. Keep Maggie at her music, and tell me how Molly is getting on with Miss Paton. Perhaps Umbs has a voice! Tell her to try. Compliments to Rover.* God bless you all, and believe me, dearest Jane, yours ever most affectionately,

"JOHN WILSON."

"SHEERNESS, *August* 4, 1832.

"MY DEAREST JANE:—I have delayed writing to you from day to day, in hourly expectation of being able to tell you something decisive of our mysterious motions, but am still in ignorance. In a few days you may expect another and very long epistle; but I write now just to say that we are weighing anchor from Sheerness for the Nore, and that to-morrow we set sail down the Channel, either for Cork or Madeira, or somewhere else, for nobody knows where. I never knew what *noise* was, till I got on board the 'Vernon.' But all goes on well; the particulars in my next. I enclose you a five-pound note just to pay the postage. I cannot get on shore, else I would send a stamp for some money due to me on the 6th. But I will send it first port we touch on. Meanwhile Maggy must, when necessary, get a small supply from Bob.

"You will not think this short letter unkind, for we are ordered off in half an hour. You may depend on my next being rather amusing.

* One of the dogs.

"I shall be most anxious to hear from you, and of you all, immediately. You are all at leisure, and must get up a long joint letter, telling me of every thing. Get a long sheet from Ebony, and cross it all over. Enclose it (directed to me in H. M. S. 'Vernon') to Mr. Barrow, Admiralty, and he will transmit it duly. Do not lose time. God bless you all, one and all, and believe me, my dearest Jane, ever yours affectionately, JOHN WILSON."

"——, 1832.

"MY DEAREST JANE:—I wrote to you a few days ago from Sheerness, and now seize another hour to inform of our motions since I wrote from London. I found my lodgings at Greenwich very comfortable, but experienced almost as many interruptions there as in town. I dined with Charles Burney one day, and found the family the kindest of the kind, and pleasant. I forget if I told you that the Literary Union gave me a dinner, with T. Campbell in the chair. At last, after many a weary delay, the 'Vernon' left Woolwich on *Sunday*, 29*th July*, in tow of two steamboats, which took her to the Nore. On Monday, 30th, she was taken into dock at Sheerness, and then, after some repairs in her copper, anchored within cable-length of the 'Ocean,' of 100 guns. Some of us amused ourselves with walking about the place; but it is somewhat dullish, though the docks, etc., are splendid. On *Tuesday*, 31*st*, we took our guns on board, fifty 32-pounders, the method of doing which was interesting to me, who had never seen it before; and then lunched with the officers of the 'Ocean,' and inspected that magnificent ship 'The Flag Ship'—Admiral Sir J. Beresford. I dined with the Admiral in his house on shore, and met a pleasant party of males and females. We had music and dancing, and the family proved agreeable and amiable. At midnight we reached the 'Vernon,' all tolerably steady, that is to say, Mr. Massey, the first lieutenant, the captain, and myself.

"On *Wednesday*, 1*st* of August, I breakfasted with the officers of the 'Ocean,' and Lieutenant Carey (brother of Lord Falkland) took me in his cutter to Chatham, during which sail we saw about a hundred ships of war, of the line and frigates, all moored like models along both shores. The chaplain (Falls) and I then inspected Chatham and Rochester, and walked to Maidstone, where were the assizes; so we proceeded to a village wayside inn, where we slept comfortably. This walk gave us a view of the Vale of Alesford and the richest parts of Kent.

"On *Thursday*, 2*d*, we returned to the 'Vernon,' through a woody and hedgy country, and the hottest of days, and in the afternoon saw the powder taken aboard. The officers of the 96th gave me a dinner at the barracks, and a jovial night we had of it. On rowing back to the ship, one of our lieutenants fell overboard, but we picked him up without loss of time, and had him resuscitated. On *Friday*, 3*d*, I called on the Admiral, and chatted with his three daughters, about the corresponding ages of your three—pretty, and well brought up, elegant, and without *hauteur*. They have no mother, but an aunt lives with the Admiral, who is a kind-hearted soul as ever lived. I also called on Captain Chambers, captain of the 'Ocean,' who lives on shore, and chatted with his daughters, three in number, and agreeable—eldest pretty and rather literary—good people all. I also called on Mr. Warden, surgeon, who used to live in Ann Street. I found him and his wife and family snugly situated in a good house, and civil to a degree. I dined on board the 'Ocean:' officers of that ship delightful fellows, and overwhelmed me with kindness.

"*Saturday, the* 4*th.*—The 'Snake' gun-brig from Woolwich appeared in the offing going down the river, and the 'Ocean' saluted her with twelve guns. At midday the 'Vernon' manned her yards, a beautiful sight, while we received the Admiral. I lunched on board the 'Ocean,' and dined in the 'Vernon,' having inspected all the docks and the model-room, and seen Sheerness completely. In the evening we were towed out to the Nore. *On Sunday, the* 5*th*, we weighed anchor by daylight, and the 'Vernon' for the first time expanded her wings in flight. She was accompanied by the Duke of Portland's celebrated yacht the 'Clown,' whom she beat going before the wind, but we had no other kind of trial till we cast anchor off the Sark in the 'Swin' off Norwich. *Monday, the* 6*th.*—Weighed anchor at daylight with a fine breeze, and went into the Downs. Off Ramsgate, were joined by the 'Snake' and 'Pantaloon' gun-brigs, the latter the best sailer of her size ever known. It came on to blow fresh, and for several hours we tried it on upon a wind, having been joined by a number of cutters. The 'Vernon' rather beat the rest, but in my opinion not very far, the 'Pantaloon' sticking to her like wax. But our sails are not yet stretched, and the opinion on board is, that she will, in another week or so, beat all opponents. The day was fine, and the sight beautiful, as we cruised along the white cliffs of Dover, and then well over towards the French coast. At sunset we returned before the wind to the Downs, and the squadron ('Vernon,' 'Snake,' 'Pantaloon,' and 'Clown') cast anchor off Deal, surrounded by a great number of vessels.

" *Tuesday, the 7th.*—The squadron left their anchorage before Deal about twelve o'clock, with a strong breeze; the 'Clown' and 'Pantaloon' being to windward of the 'Vernon,' and the 'Snake' rather to leeward. This position was retained for nearly two hours, when the 'Snake' dropped considerably astern, and the 'Vernon' weathered the 'Pantaloon,' the 'Clown' still keeping to windward and crossing our bows. At this juncture it blew hard, and I went down with Collier and Symonds to dinner in their cabin. The 'Vernon' was now left in charge of the first lieutenant, and in tacking missed stays. The 'Snake' and 'Pantaloon' immediately went to windward, and we were last of all. It still blew very fresh, and in about two hours we again headed the squadron, all but the 'Clown,' who continued first all along. Towards sunset the wind came off the land, where the 'Snake' and 'Pantaloon' were, and brought them to windward of us about two miles, and so ended the day's trial, with alternate success. The 'Snake' and 'Pantaloon' then came down by signal under the 'Vernon's' stern, and we continued all night in company under easy sail, the wind having slackened, and the moon being clear and bright.

" *Wednesday, 8th.*—At seven o'clock found ourselves off Beachy Head, with the 'Clown' a long way to leeward, the 'Snake' to windward, and the 'Pantaloon' in our wake. The wind had shifted during the night, and we had the advantage of it. But towards morning it had fallen, and we made but two knots an hour. The calm continued during the day, and we made but little way. Early in the afternoon a miserable accident occurred. The crew were up aloft lowering the main top-gallant yard. It is a spar about seventy feet long, and about sixty feet above the deck. As it was coming down, a man slid along it to release a rope from a block, when, by some mistake, the men above cut the rope he was holding by, and in sight of us all he descended with great velocity, clinging to the spar till he came to the end of it, and then with outstretched arms fell about forty feet upon the deck, within three yards of where I was standing. The crash was dreadful, and he was instantly carried below, affairs going on just as if he had been a spider. It was found that his right arm was shattered to pieces, and his whole frame shook fatally. He continued composed and sensible for three hours, when he began to moan wofully, and in half an hour expired. He was a Scotsman of the name of Murray, one of the best men in the ship, and brother, it is said, of a clergyman. No doubt many felt for him, but the noise, laughter, swearing, and singing, went on during all the time he was dying.

"*Thursday*, 9*th*.—The ship has been making considerable way during the night, and at eight o'clock we are off the Isle of Wight; 'Snake' and 'Pantaloon' about two miles behind, all three going before the wind. The dead man is lying on the gun-deck, separated from where I now sit by a thin partition. The body is wrapped in flags, and the walls at his head and back are hung with cutlasses and the muskets of the marines. His weatherbeaten face is calm and smiling, and 'after life's fitful fever he sleeps well.' The night before, he was one of the most active in a jig danced to the fifes. The wind is freshening, and we expect to be off Plymouth (120 miles) by midnight. We have sprung one of our yards, and the fore-mast seems shaken, so we shall put into Plymouth to refit, and probably remain there *three* days. It is not unlikely that the Admiral (Malcolm) may join us there. If not, we shall sail for Cork (distant 300 miles), and then, perhaps, the experimental squadron will begin its career. We have no more fear of fighting, neither do we know where we may be going, but my own opinion is that we shall cruise in the Channel. I do not see that I can be at home sooner than a month at the soonest, as all that I came to see remains yet to be seen. I am not without hopes of getting a letter from you before we leave Plymouth. I meet with all kindness from everybody, and am pleased with the on-goings of a sea-life, though the bustle and disturbance is greater than I had imagined, and the noise incessant and beyond all description. But my appetite is good, and I am never heard to utter a complaint. All day wind light, but towards evening it freshened, and at seven we committed the body of the poor sailor to the deep. The funeral ceremony was most impressive. Before nightfall the 'Snake' came up with a fresh breeze, and we had another contest, in which the 'Vernon' was fairly beaten. In smooth water and moderate winds the 'Snake' is at present her master, much to my surprise; when it blows hard we are superior. *Friday*, 10*th*.—This morning at four we entered Plymouth. The country around is very beautiful, and young Captain Blackwood and I are proposing to go on shore. How long we remain here seems uncertain. I hope it may not be above a day or two.

"Captain Blackwood and self have been perambulating Plymouth, and intend to dine at the hotel thereof.

"I have written a tolerably long letter. God bless you all, and true it is that I think of you every hour, and hope you now and then think of me too. Kindest love to all the progeny, John, Mag, Moll, Blair, and Umbs, and believe me yours most affectionately,

"J. WILSON.

"Write to me again on receipt of this, and enclose as before to Mr. Barrow of the Admiralty. The enclosed signature of my name, Johnny will give to Robert Blackwood, who will get my half-year's salary from the City Chamberlain, which you will get from the said Bob. Send £10 to Elleray, and account to me for the rest of the enormous sum.* I enclosed £5 in my last from Sheerness. Once more love to yourself and to children, and farewell. I will write from Cork. Yours, J. W."

"PLYMOUTH, *August* 23*d*.

"MY DEAREST JANE:—I have, as you know, received your first long united epistle, and answered it in a hurried letter, telling you to write to me direct to Plymouth. Before that I wrote a long journal letter enclosing my signature for a receipt, which no doubt you have received. To wait for the post of that era (the day after my long letter, August 10), I went up the Tamar with Captain Blackwood, and after an excursion of three days returned to Plymouth. On Tuesday the 14th I dined on board the 'Malta,' Captain Clavell, with a large party, and that evening went aboard the 'Campeadora' schooner, a pleasure-yacht belonging to Mr. Williamson, from Liverpool (nephew to old Shaw thereof, who, I understand, was a rich and well-bred personage), and sailed with him to Portsmouth, distant from Plymouth 150 miles. I passed two days at Portsmouth viewing all the great works there; and returned to Plymouth on Saturday, the 17th, by a steamer; a most stormy

* The Professor's "salary" was £72 4s. 4d. per annum.

passage. Saturday and Sunday I dined on board the 'Vernon;' and on the Sunday I wrote to you the hurried letter above alluded to. On Monday, the 19th, I dined with Mr. Roberts, the master ship-builder of the docks, and met some naval and military officers. Tuesday the 20th was an a'-day's rain, and I kept all day in a lodging-room with Captain Williams, R. N., and his brother, the purser of the 'Vernon.' Wednesday the 21st was a fine day, but I went nowhere, except on board a few ships; and it being electioneering time here, I heard some speeches from Sir Edward Codrington and others. I dined with a party of *offishers* at the hotel. To-day (Thursday the 22d) I saw Sir F. Collier, who informed me that the squadron of Sir P. Malcolm, consisting of seven sail, were in the offing, and that the 'Vernon' is to join them to-morrow at 12 A. M. We are consequently all in a bustle; and my next letter will be from the first port we put into. This is the night of the said Thursday; I am on shore writing this. I hope that a letter from you will reach us to-morrow before we sail, though I *fear* not, because Mr. Barrow is at Portsmouth, and that may have delayed your letter. The letter which you were to write *direct* according to former instructions, to Plymouth, will be sent after us ere long. On receiving this please to write to me, *directed to me under cover to Mr. Barrow, Admiralty*, and it will be forwarded with the Admiral's letters. *The cruise* begins *to-morrow*, and two months have been spent, as you will see, in another way. I shall take two or three weeks of the cruise, as it would be stupid to return without seeing the experimental squadron. I shall write to you by the first steamer or tender that takes letters from the squadron. I do not think we are going very far. Several balls and concerts were about to be given to us, but our orders have come at last rather unexpectedly, and all the ladies are in tears. I forgot to say that on Monday, the 13th, I dined, not on board the 'Vernon,' but in the Admiral's house, with a splendid party. The 'Vernon' has been much attacked in the newspapers, but my account of her in my long letter is the correct one. I think in strong breezes she will beat the squadron. In light winds she may prove but an 'Endeavor.' I shall say no more of my hopes and fears about your letter to-morrow; but this I will say, and truly, that I think of you all three or seven times a day, or haply twenty-one. I suppose the lads have gone to Elleray, according to my permission in my last, and with the means of doing so afforded by the stamp-receipt. I will write to you again before long; I hope it will not be very long before I return. Tell the girls to be sensible and good *gals*. Love to them and the lads, if these latter be with you; and do not doubt, my dearest Jane, that I am, and ever will be, your affectionate JOHN WILSON."

"CAMPEADORA SCHOONER, PLYMOUTH,
August 31, 1832.

"MY DEAREST JANE:—After some anxiety from not hearing from you, your letter of the 23d, direct to Plymouth, reached me the day before yesterday, and informed me that all are well. I cannot conjecture what has become of your other letters, but I have received only one long one written conjunctly, and your own of the 23d. Any or all intermediate must still be with Mr. Barrow. I presume that Sym has told you within these few days that he has heard from me, and I now sit down to inform you further of my proceedings. The squadron are now collected, and we have been sailing with strong breezes. The first day there was no right trial; the second, from Torbay to near Plymouth and back again, was also inconclusive. The chief struggle was between the 'Snake,' 'Castor,' and 'Vernon.' When going under full sail, in the same tack, close-hauled to the wind, the 'Vernon' was considerably ahead, the 'Castor' next, and the 'Snake' trying to shoot across the 'Castor's' bow, but without success. The 'Castor' carried away her jib-boom, and signal was thereupon made by the Admiral for us to *put about*. The 'Castor' stood in, and we crossed her to windward only fifty yards. As she was more than fifty yards behind when we started, her people claimed the victory, but it was obviously no go. The day grew very boisterous, and we got safe at sunset into Torbay. On Sunday (the day following), I visited the Admiral, as told in my letter to Sym. On Monday we lay at rest. I am sorry to say, that on entering Torbay, on Saturday night, a man fell overboard, and was drowned. On Wednesday morning, at four o'clock, the squadron got under weigh and left Torbay. I had gone on board the 'Campeadora' the night before, and slept there on condition that a look-out should be kept on the movements of the 'Vernon.' Judge of my feelings (mixed) when awakened at seven, and told all the ships had been gone for several hours. At eight we weighed anchor and followed the fleet. The tide favored us, and so did a strong breeze from the land, and in a few hours we discovered the squadron some leagues ahead, but to leeward, and they were all racing, and, as we neared, I had a beautiful view of all their motions. The 'Snake' was two miles ahead of all the others; the 'Vernon' and 'Prince' were next, and close together. The 'Trinculo' followed, then the 'Nimrod;' next came the 'Castor,' and, finally, the 'Donegal;' the 'Dryad' had been sent to Portsmouth, and the 'Tyne' to Plymouth the day before. It now came on to blow very hard, and the waves ran hillocks high; frequent squalls darkened the sky, and shut out the ships, which ever and anon reappeared like phantoms. They seemed to retain their positions. Meanwhile we kept to windward, and ahead of them all, but with a pitching, and a tossing, and a rolling no mortal stomach could withstand. Still, though occasionally sick, I enjoyed the storm. My hat flew overboard, and we were all as wet as if in the sea. There was no danger, and the vessel was admirably managed, but she was liker a fish than a bird. Between four and five in the afternoon the 'Campeadora' dropt anchor behind the breakwater in Plymouth Sound. In rather more than half-an-hour the 'Snake' did the same; in another half-hour in came the 'Prince;' in quarter of an hour more the 'Vernon;' and shortly after the 'Trinculo' and the 'Nimrod;' the 'Castor' and 'Donegal' were obliged to lie off during the night. The race was fifty miles, beating to windward, and in blowy weather. The 'Vernon' was, at the end, seven miles ahead of the 'Castor,' her chief competitor, they being the only two frigates, and built by rivals, Symonds and Jeffrys. As soon as I got myself dried, and my hunger appeased, I joined the 'Vernon,' and joined the officers in the gun-room, crowing over the 'Castor.' They had sold all my effects by auction, and had considered me a deserter. The night was passed somewhat boisterously, *but the name of the Campeadora never once mentioned!!!!* She had beaten them all *like sacks*, and I therefore behaved as if I had come from Torbay in a balloon. Next day (Thursday) we remained all anchored behind the breakwater. Your welcome letter I received on board the 'Vernon,' the evening of the race. I asked one of the officers what he thought of the 'Campeadora,' who had left Torbay three hours after the squadron, and anchored in the Sound of Plymouth half-an-hour before the 'Snake.' His answer was, '*That he had not seen her!* that we had not sailed with the squadron at all; and had been brought in by the tide and the land breeze'!!! The tide and land breeze had helped to bring us up with the squadron; but for five hours we beat them all, as I said, *like sacks* into our anchorage. The whole officers joined with my antagonist in argument, and it has been settled among them that the 'Campeadora' did not sail with the squadron, and that she beat nobody! Such, even at sea, is the littleness of men's souls; it is worse even than on Windermere at a regatta. This is Friday (the 31st), and I slept last night in the 'Campeadora.' I shall keep this letter open till I hear something of our intended motions, which I hope to do on boarding the 'Admiral.' The 'Vernon' is said to be *wet*, because when it blows hard, and she sails upon a wind, the spray spins over her main top-gallant mast. This it seems is reckoned a great merit. As to the noise on board—for it consists of everlasting groaning, howling, yelling, cursing, and swearing, which is the language in which all orders are given and executed—never less than 200 men are *prancing* on her decks, and occasionally 500; windlasses are ever at work, and iron cables are letting out and taking in, which rumble like thunder. Gun-carriages (two ton and a half heavy) are perpetually rolled about to alter her *trim*, and ever and anon cannon fired close to your ears (32-pounders) which might waken the dead. Drums, too, are rolling frequently, and there are at all times the noise of heavy bodies falling, of winds whistling, and waves beating up to any degree. But all these noises are nothing compared to *holy-stoning!* This is the name given to scrubbing decks. A hundred men all fall at once upon their knees, and begin scrubbing the decks with large rough stones called holy-stones; this continues every morning from four o'clock to five, and is a noise that beggars all description. I sleep in the cock-pit, a place below both decks, in a swinging cot, which is very comfortable. But as soon as the decks are done, down come a dozen Jacks, and *holy-stone* the floor of the cock-pit, without taking any notice of me, who am swinging over their heads. That being over, all the midshipmen whose chests are in the cock-pit, come in to wash, and shave, and dress. You had better not imagine the scene that then ensues. As soon as the majority of them are gone I get up, and, at half-past seven, Captain Coryton of the Marines gives me his cabin to wash and dress in. I do so every morning, and the luxury of washing too became known to me for the first time; for you get covered with dust, and sand, and paint by day and night, to say nothing of tar and twine; in short, every thing but feathers. The eating is excellent, and the drinking not bad, though sometimes rather too much of it.

"I have, since writing the above, seen Sir F. Collier, who informs me we start to-morrow forenoon (September 1st) for the coast of Ireland. I shall go; and if the squadron does not return soon to Portsmouth, I shall sail from Cork to some northern port, and so home. I will write to you by the first opportunity, and I believe one will occur in a week. Love to the girls. I am happy to hear that Molly is getting on with her singing, and she may depend on my being pleased with her *chanson.* Meg is, no doubt, now a Sontag; perhaps Umbs may also prove a songstress. The boys by this time have, I suppose, been a while at Elleray. *Narcotic* is a good word for the Opium-Eater, but I read it hare-skin. I have just heard that another letter is lying for me on shore. I hope it is from some of you; but I cannot get it, I fear, till the morning, and I am this hour again on board the 'Vernon,' and it is blowing so hard that no boats are going on shore.

"I therefore conclude with warmest and sincerest affection for thyself and all our children. Give my kindest remembrances to my sister Jane, who, I devoutly trust, will continue to improve in health, and, ere long, be well. You are now but a family of four females, so be all good boys, and believe that I will be happy to be with you again, when I hope you will be happy to see again the old man. Once more, with love to you and the three Graces, I am, my dearest Jane, ever yours most affectionately,

"John Wilson.

"'Vernon,' off Plymouth, *August 31st.*"

"Land's End, *Tuesday Evening,*
September 4th.

"About eight o'clock morning we were off the Scilly Isles, and observed a steamer. It contained the Admiralty and other grandees. Sir C. Paget, Sir F. Maitland, and Admiral Dundas, came on board at nine, and at ten signal was made for all ships to close upon the 'Vernon.' The wind was light but steady, and the day beautiful. We sailed till five o'clock (seven hours) in charming style, but it would take a volume to narrate all our evolutions. For the greater part of the time the 'Waterwitch' kept first, and then the 'Vernon,' the 'Snake' having outmanœuvred herself by passing too close to windward. The 'Castor' sailed well, but kept dropping to leeward. At half-past four the 'Vernon' weathered the 'Waterwitch' and 'Snake,' and led the squadron. This was done by fair sailing, on which the Admiral made signal to shorten sail, which was done; and the grandees left us and went on board the steamer, which set off for Portsmouth. Sir Pulteney then came on board the 'Vernon,' and acknowledged we had beaten the squadron. The 'Castor' was four miles to leeward, the 'Stag' six, and the 'Donegal' eight: the 'Nimrod' as far; but the 'Waterwitch' and 'Snake' were only a quarter of a mile under our lee. The triumph of the 'Vernon' is declared complete, but, in my opinion, the 'Waterwitch' and 'Snake' may beat her another day; the 'Castor' cannot, in any wind. The Admiral has just left us, and, if weather permit, Sir F. Collier and the Professor will dine to-morrow on board the 'Donegal.' We are now making sail back to the 'Lizard,' where, in the morning, a boat will come from shore for our letters. We will then put about for the coast of Ireland, as Sir Pulteney himself has told me; and therefore, my dearest Jane, either yourself or the lasses, that is, the gals, must write to me, if possible, the evening you receive this—*His Majesty's Ship 'Vernon,' Cork*—without any reference to Barrow, and I shall get it probably before we leave that harbor. That will be the last time I shall hear from you before I return; and from Cork I will write to Sym, who will probably send you my letter or part of it. Pray keep my letters for sake of the dates, for I have not been able to keep a journal. A good many things have occurred on board within these few days, but I have no room to narrate them. Warmest love to the progeny, who, I hope, do not forget him who tenderly loveth them. I expect to find them all grown on my return, and Catalani jealous of Sontag. I send them all kisses and prayers for their happiness, and for that of one of the best of wives to her affectionate husband,

"JOHN WILSON."

"OFF THE LIZARD, *September* 5, 1832.

"MY DEAREST JANE:—I wrote a tolerably long letter the day before we left Plymouth, which was on Tuesday, the 4th. I had then received three letters from you, including one that had been sent to Cork. I therefore knew that you were all well on the 23d

August, and trust I believe you are so *now*. The squadron left port with a light leading wind, consisting of 'Donegal,' 'Vernon,' 'Castor,' 'Stag' (a 46 frigate), 'Nimrod,' 'Snake,' and 'Waterwitch.' The 'Dryad' is paid off, being a bad sailer, and the 'Tyne' sails for South America in a few days, and belongs no more to our flag. The 'Trinculo' has gone to Cork, and the 'Prince' is at Plymouth. In beating out, 'Vernon' missed stays, and drifted, stern foremost, aboard the 'Castor,' with no inconsiderable crash, staving her boat in the slings, and making much cordage spin. We got off, however, without damage of any consequence, and towards night were off the Eddystone lighthouse. There was very little difference in the rate of going between 'Vernon' and 'Castor.' The 'Castor' rather beat us the first two hours, but at sunset (when sail is always taken in) we were to windward about 200 yards; the 'Snake,' as usual, a mile at least ahead, and to windward of us all. All night we kept under easy sail in 'our Admiral's lee,' and on Monday morning at six o'clock, signal was made for us to spread all our canvas, and try it before the wind. We soon got into a cluster, the breeze being so light as to be almost a calm, and so we carried on in a pretty but tedious style for the greater part of the day, our prows being in the direction of Falmouth. The Lords of the Admiralty are there at present, and I suppose we shall touch in this evening. They were at Plymouth, and I was introduced to one of them, Admiral Dundas, who was very civil; so was Sir C. Page; and Sir F. Maitland, the latter of whom invited me to see him at Portsmouth on our return, he being Admiral on that station. Sir J. Graham I did not see, as we were at dinner when he came on board the 'Vernon.' Sir Pulteney has been extremely kind, and is a good old man. I had not heard of poor Minna's death, and asked how she was, when he gave me the intelligence. She was a good woman, in my opinion. She died of dropsy, and had suffered much, but bore it like a Christian. We have just caught sight of an enormous lizard, so large that it is called 'The Lizard,' and we are all to lie under its shadow till morning, so good-night."

"CORK, *Friday*, 14*th Sept.*, 1832.

"MY DEAREST JANE:—I wrote to you on the 5*th*, *off the Lizard*, and since then have enjoyed *a week's capital cruising* in all kinds of winds, except a positive storm. Your last letter received was the 29*th* *of August;* and I am in hopes of getting your answer to mine of the 5th to-night. If I do not, I shall leave orders at the post-office to send it on to London, where I hope to be in a week from this day. But in case any accident should happen, I wish *one of you* to write to me, the *same day you get this, directed to me at 'Union Hotel, Charing Cross, London, to lie till called for,'* telling me that you are all well. I shall be at Portsmouth (necessarily) a day or two before I go to London, but shall not stay in the metropolis more than *one day.* I rather think I shall come down to Edinburgh by land, for a steamboat after the 'Vernon' will be rather dull, and at this season rolls most infernally. In that case I shall go by York; for I do not wish to trouble Elleray at present, for sufficient reasons. As I shall travel *outside*, I shall probably stay a day at York: but I will write you a day before I leave London, communicating particulars, and you will see me before long.

"On Tuesday, the 11th, we entered the Cove of Cork at sunset; the squadron at four o'clock. On Wednesday, the 12th, I set off on foot for the city of Cork, distant thirteen miles, a most beautiful walk. At nine o'clock, I took a seat in the mail-coach, and was off for Killarney. In the coach were a Captain and Mrs. Baillie, young people who had been in India, and near relatives of the Major and Mrs. Barlow. We became friends.

"At Killarney found that Mrs. Cashel* *was not there!* ought to have known that before. Stormy night, so kept snug in a good inn. Thursday, 13th, left Killarney in a jingle at five o'clock in the morning, and arrived at Marino Lodge, on the Kenmare, distance twenty miles, before nine o'clock. Found the family all well, except Mrs. Cashel, who has an asthmatic cough, *which mention to nobody.* I will amuse you *when we meet* with my account of my visit to that quarter. Nothing could exceed their kindness, and she admires you beyond all. On Friday, the 14th, left Marino Lodge in a taxed cart at five o'clock, and went nearly twenty miles through mountains to a place on the Cork road, where the mail overtook us. Got in—and afterwards out—after being *twice upset*, and three times half upset. More of that anon; no bones broken. I have just dined in the coffee-room with three very agreeable Irishmen, whose names I do not know, but who asked me to drink wine as *the Professor.* I am just about to set off for the

* His sister.

'Vernon' in a jingle; and I hear that we sail to-morrow (Saturday, the 15th), at five o'clock A. M. Indeed, Sir F. Collier told me so before I left the ship. I thought it would or might seem unkind not to see Grace when I was in Ireland, and therefore I travelled 160 miles for that purpose, being with them just twenty hours. You must not be incensed with the shortness of this letter, for you must perceive that I have been in a dreadful racket. I intend writing another letter to Sym on our way up to Portsmouth; but do not say any thing about it. If your letter has come thus far, it will be lying for me to-night on board the 'Vernon.' Tenderest love to the Graces, and also to the lads at Elleray. I hope you will be kind to the old man on his return—all of you. Yours ever, most affectionately, JOHN WILSON."

"UNION HOTEL, CHARING CROSS,
Tuesday Afternoon, September 25th, 1832.

"MY DEAREST JANE:—The 'Vernon' anchored at Spithead this day week, and the day following I wrote to Sym, who would tell you of my welfare. I got your Cork letter on the Thursday, and on Friday I bade farewell to the 'Varmint' (as she is called), and dined on shore with the Williamses, who have a house at Portsmouth. That night I took coach to London, where I arrived about six o'clock, and went to bed for some hours. I found your letter lying for me soon after breakfast, and was rejoiced to find you were all well. On Saturday, Dr. Maginn dined with me; and on Sunday I called on Mrs. S. C. Hall and husband, Miss Landon, and Thomas Campbell, with the last, not least, of whom I passed the evening. There is a Captain Coryton (of the Marines) on board the 'Vernon,' whose wife and family live at Woolwich. I promised to call on them to tell them about him, and his mode of life, and did so on Monday, having walked thither and back (about twenty miles). He is to be absent for three years in South America. I returned to London by seven, and dined with a German Baron, whose name I can neither spell nor pronounce, a Polish Patriot, (not Shirma), and a French royalist. On Tuesday, that is, this day, after some business connected with my cruise, I called on Mrs. Jamieson, author of *King Charles's Beauties*. She is very clever, middle-aged, red-haired, and agreeable, though I suspect you would call her a conceited minx. She is to send some Italian airs to the guitar for Maggie, to the hotel this evening. I am going to dine to-day at the Literary Union, with Campbell and some others. To-morrow I shall be busy all day, calling on naval officers, and at the Admiralty, nor could I have sooner done so. And on Thursday, I shall leave London for York in one of the morning coaches. This will enable me to stop some hours there to rest, and I shall be in Edinburgh on Saturday afternoon; I do not know at what hour, but I believe *two or three after the mail,* unless I take my place *in the mail from York.* The gals can ask Bob at what hour any coach arrives in Edinburgh from York, besides the mail. I should think he will know. But should any thing detain me, it will only be my not getting a place at York. The gals may take a look at the mail, perhaps on Saturday. I need say no more than that I shall be truly happy to find you all well and happy, as you deserve to be. God bless you all! Yours ever affectionately,

"JOHN WILSON."

CHAPTER XIV.

LITERARY AND DOMESTIC LIFE.

1832–'37.

THE following letter will be read with interest:

"LONDON, *November* 30, 1832.

"SIR:—You have often, and 'on the *Rialto*' too, twitted me with an addition to Sonnets, and 'such small deer' of poetry, sometimes in a spirit of good-humor, at others in that tone of raillery which is so awful to young gentlemen given to rhyming *love* and *dove*. Yet, notwithstanding the terrors of your frown, I think there is so much of the milk of human kindness blending up with that rough nature of yours, as would prevent you from willingly hurting the weak and the defenceless; on the contrary, if Master Feeble acknowledged his failing in a becoming manner, I can believe that you would put the timid gentleman on his legs, pat his head, cocker his alarmed features into a complacent smile, and, giving him something nice, washing it down with a jorum of whiskey-toddy, send him home to his lodgings and landlady with your compliments, so that I, you will perceive, have no bad opinion of your lionship.

"You can do me a great good; and when I assure you, which I do seriously and in all sincerity, that I seek not your favor in the spirit of vanity, that I may plume myself with it hereafter; and when I tell you that I have ventured on this publication not to exalt myself, but, if possible, to benefit some poor relations, weighed down by the pressure of our bad times, I am sure that I may rely on your appreciating my motive, whatever you may think of the means I have taken to work it out.

"One thing more I would say; these poems, such as they are, are the productions of a self-educated man, who, in his tenth year of childhood, with little more than a knowledge of his *Reading Made Easy*, was driven out into the world to seek his bread, and pick up such acquirements as he could meet with; these are not many, for he was not lucky enough to meet with many. This is a fact which I do not care that the public should know, for what has that monster so well off for heads to do with it; nor, perhaps, have you; I have mentioned it merely because I could not conceal it at this moment, when the disadvantages it has surrounded me with return upon me like old grievances for a time forgotten, but come back again to 'sight and seeing,' as palpable as ever, and as provoking.

"Enough of myself. There are many errors in the book staring me out of countenance. While it was in the press I was dangerously ill, and, therefore, paid but little and distracted attention to it. Think, then, as mercifully of me and mine as you can; and though, when you are frolicsome, you love to spatter us poor cockneys, sometimes justly enough, at others not so, believe that I can candidly appreciate the power and the beauty of some parts of *Blackwood's Magazine*, and that I am, all differences notwithstanding, your humble servant, —— ——."*

In my mother's letters during 1833 and 1834, the strong political feelings of the time are occasionally exhibited. In one she says:

* The signature of this letter has been torn off, but the letter itself is indorsed "from Charles Lamb to Professor Wilson." I am, however, afraid that it is not the production of "Elia," and as I am not familiar with the handwriting, I cannot say who is the writer, or whether the appeal was responded to.

"We are all terribly disgusted and annoyed at the result of the late elections. I never look into a newspaper now; and my only comfort is in reading the political papers in *Blackwood*, and remembering that I have lived in the times of the Georges." Again she writes: "What do you think of Church and State affairs? We are in a pretty way; oh, for the good old times! Thank Heaven, while Mr. Wilson can hold a pen, it will be wielded in defence of the right cause." His pen, indeed, was not allowed to lie idle at this time, as the reader will find by referring to his contributions. During 1833–'34 he wrote no fewer than fifty-four articles for *Blackwood*, or upwards of 2,400 closely printed columns on politics and general literature. Among these were reviews of Ebenezer Elliot* and Audubon, the ornithologist, which called forth interesting and characteristic replies.

FROM EBENEZER ELLIOT.

"SHEFFIELD, 8*th May*, 1834.

"MR. PROFESSOR:—I do not write merely to thank you for your almost fatherly criticism on my poetry, but to say, that when I sent that unhappy letter, addressed, I suppose, to the Editor of *Blackwood's Magazine*, I knew not that the Professor was the editor. I had been told that the famous rural articles were yours, and the 'Noctes.' This was all I knew of that terrible incarnation of the Scotch Thistle, Christopher North. I had judged from his portrait on the cover of the Magazine. I understand it is a true portrait of Mr. Blackwood, whose name even now involuntarily brings before my imagination a personage ready to flay poor Radicals alive. When at length I understood you was the editor, I still thought you was only the successor of C. North, the dreadful. The letter must have been the result of despair. The *Monthly Review* had stricken me on the heart with a hand of ice, but I had failed to attract the attention of the critics generally; and perhaps I then thought that even an unfavorable notice in *Blackwood* would be better than none. But when I was told, a few days ago, that I was reviewed in 'Maga,' I expected I was done for, never to hold up my head again. Having no copy of the letter I know not what vileness it may contain, besides the sad vulgarity† unfortunately

* Ebenezer Elliot, the Corn-Law Rhymer, was born in 1781; he died in 1849.

† "Mr. Elliot was pleased, a good while ago, in a letter, the reverse of flattering, addressed to

quoted, and for which I blush through my marrow; but on the word of a poet, whose fiction is truth, when I wrote it I was no more aware, than if you had never been born, that I was writing to Professor Wilson. I should hate myself if I could deliberately have sent a disrespectful letter to the author of those inimitable rural pictures, which, before God, I believe have lengthened my days on earth.

"After your almost saintly forbearance, I must not bother you about the Corn-Laws; but I will just observe that in our Island of Jersey, where (perjury [*sic*] excepted) the trade in corn is free, land lets much higher than in England. But is it not a shame that wheat should be sent from Holland to Jersey, after incurring heavy charges, and the Dutchman's profit, and then be sent to England as the produce of Jersey? Poor John Bull paying for all out of his workhouse wages, or the sixteen-pence which he receives for fourteen hours' factory labor in the climate of Jamaica.

"What is to follow such legislation? I am, with heartfelt respect and thankfulness, EBENEZER ELLIOT."

I cannot resist giving a passage from an article which afforded the author of the *Corn-Law Rhymes* so much genuine pleasure:—

"Ebenezer Elliot does—not only now and then, but often—ruralize; with the intense passionateness of a fine spirit escaping from smoke and slavery into the fresh air of freedom—with the tenderness of a gentle spirit communing with nature in Sabbath-rest. Greedily he gulps the dewy breath of morn, like a man who has been long suffering from thirst drinking at a wayside well. He feasts upon the flowers—with his eyes, with his lips; he walks along the grass as if it were cooling to his feet. The slow typhus fever perpetual with townsmen is changed into a quick gladsome glow, like the life of life. A strong animal pleasure possesses the limbs and frame of the strong man released from labor, yet finding no leisure to loiter in the lanes—and away with him to the woods and rocks and heaven-kissing hills. But that is not all his pleasure—though it might suffice, one would think, for a slave. Through all his senses it penetrates into his soul—and his soul gets wings and soars.

us, and written with his own hard hoof of a hand, to call us a 'big blue-bottle,' but we bear no resemblance to that insect," &c.—From "Poetry of E. Elliot," in *Blackwood's Magazine*, May, 1834.

Yes; it has the wings of a dove, and flees away—and is at rest! Where are the heaven-kissing hills in Hallamshire? Here, and there, and everywhere—for the sky stoops down to kiss them—and the presence of a poet scares not away, but consecrates their embraces

'Under the opening eyelids of the morn.'

Of such kind is the love of nature that breaks out in all the compositions of this town-bred poet. Nature to him is a mistress whom he cannot visit when he will, and whom he woos, not stealthily, but by snatches—snatches torn from time, and shortened by joy that 'thinks down hours to moments.' Even in her sweet companionship he seems scarcely ever altogether forgetful of the place from which he made his escape to rush into her arms, and clasp her to his breast. He knows that his bliss must be brief, and that an iron voice, like a knell, is ringing him back to dust and ashes. So he smothers her with kisses—and tearing himself away—again with bare arms he is beating at the anvil, and feels that man is born to trouble as the sparks fly upwards. For Ebenezer Elliot, gentle reader, is a worker in iron; that is—to use his own words—'*a dealer in steel, working hard every day; literally* laboring *with my head and hands, and alas, with my heart too! If you think the steel-trade, in these profitless days, is not a heavy, hard-working trade*, come and break *a ton*.'

"We have worked at manual labor for our amusement, but, it was so ordered, never for bread; for reefing and reeving can hardly be called manual labor—it comes to be as facile to the fingers as the brandishing of this present pen. We have ploughed, sowed, reaped, mowed, pitchforked, threshed; and put heart and knee to the gavelock hoisting rocks. But not for a day's darg, and not for bread. Now here lies the effectual and vital distinction between the condition of our poet and his critic—between the condition of Ebenezer Elliot and that of all our other poets, except Robert Burns."*

The next letter is from Mr. Audubon;†—

"My dear Friend;—The first hour of this new year was ushered to me surrounded by my dear flock, all comfortably seated around

* *Blackwood's Magazine*, May, 1834.
† J. J. Audubon, author of *The Birds of America*, &c., died in 1831.

a small table, in a middle-sized room, where I sincerely wished you had been also, to witness the flowing gladness of our senses, as from one of us 'Audubon's Ornithological Biography' was read from your ever valuable Journal. I wished this because I felt assured that your noble heart would have received our most grateful thanks with pleasure, the instant our simple ideas had conveyed to you the grant of happiness we experienced at your hands. You were not with us, alas! but to make amends the best way we could, all of a common accord drank to the health, prosperity, and long life, of our generous, talented, and ever kind friend, Professor John Wilson, and all those amiable beings who cling around his heart! May those our sincerest wishes reach you soon, and may they be sealed by Him who granted us existence, and the joys heaped upon the 'American woodsman' and his family, in your hospitable land, and may we deserve all the benefits we have received in your ever dear country, although it may prove impossible to us to do more than to be ever grateful to her worthy sons.

"Accept our respectful united regards, and offer them to your family, whilst I remain, with highest esteem, your truly thankful friend and most obedient servant, JOHN J. AUDUBON."

The next letter is from the Rev. James White:*—

"LOXLEY, STRATFORD-ON-AVON,
4th November, 1834.

"MY DEAR SIR:—The last was an admirable 'Noctes,' and in my opinion, makes up for the one for July. After describing the party at Carnegie's, who did you mean by the ass that, after braying loud enough to deafen Christopher, went braying all over the

* The Rev. J. White, of Bonchurch, Isle of Wight, author of *Sir Frizzle Pumpkin*, *Nights at Mess*, *&c.*, and other stories, died March 28, 1862, aged fifty-eight. "Mr. White, says the *Edinburgh Courant*, who was a native of this country, where his family still possess considerable property, was born in the year 1804. After studying with success at Glasgow and Oxford, he took orders in the Church of England, and was presented by Lord Brougham to a living in Suffolk, which he afterwards gave up for another in Warwickshire. On ultimately succeeding to a considerable patrimony, he retired from the Church and removed with his family to the Isle of Wight, where Mrs. White had inherited from her father, Colonel Hill, of St. Boniface, a portion of his estate, Bonchurch, so celebrated for its beauty and mild climate. His retirement enabled him to devote a considerable share of his time to literary pursuits, which he prosecuted with much success. The pages of *Blackwood* were enlivened by many of his contributions of a light kind, too popular and well known to require to be enumerated; and his later works, including the *Eighteen Christian Centuries* and the *History of France*, showed that his industry and accuracy, as well as his good sense and sound judgment, were not inferior to his other and more popular talents."—*Gentleman's Magazine*.

Borders? You unconscionable monster, did you mean me? Vicar of the consolidated livings of Loxley and Bray! I console myself with thinking it is something to be mentioned in the 'Noctes,' though in no higher character than an ass.

"Have you ever thought of making Hogg a metempsychosist? what a famous description he would give of his feelings when he was a whale (the one that swallowed Jonah), or a tiger, or an antediluvian *aligautor* near the Falls of Niagara, his disgust after being shot as an eagle, to find himself a herd at the head of Ettrick!*

"Do you think of coming to England next year? Remember, whenever you do, you have promised me a benefit. Has Blair come up to college yet? If he has, I wish you would for once write me a letter with his address; for, as I am only a day's drive from Oxford, I should be most happy to show him this part of the country in the short vacation. My wife desires to be very kindly remembered to you and Mrs. Wilson, not forgetting the young ladies. And I remain, ever yours very truly,

"JAMES WHITE."

Attention to the ordinary course of duties, and the numerous occupations which engrossed his daily life, never stood in the way of my father's endeavors to be useful to his fellow-men. An example of this may be seen in his correspondence with a mutual friend, in order to pacify and to restore Mr. Hogg to his former position with Mr. Blackwood. This labor, for such it was, ended ultimately to the satisfaction of all parties, and the correspondence which led to that result is truly honorable to the writers.

"MY DEAR SHEPHERD:—From the first blush of the business, I greatly disliked your quarrel with the Blackwoods, and often wished to be instrumental in putting an end to it, but I saw no opening, and did not choose to be needlessly obtrusive. Hearing that you would rather it was made up, and not doubting that Mr. Blackwood would meet you for that purpose in an amicable spirit, I volunteer my services—if you and he choose to accept of them—as mediator.

"I propose this—that all mere differences on this, and that, and

* This hint appears to have been acted upon, as those who are interested may read the Shepherd's transmigrations fully detailed in the "Noctes" of February, 1835.

every subject, and all asperities of sentiment or language on either side, be at once forgotten, and never once alluded to—so that there shall be asked no explanation nor apology, but each of you continue to think yourself in the right, without taking the trouble to say so.

"But you have accused Mr. Blackwood in your correspondence with him, as I understand, of shabbiness, meanness, selfish motives, and almost dishonesty. In your Memoir there is an allusion to some transaction about a bill, which directly charges Mr. Blackwood with want of integrity. In that light it was received by a knave and fool in *Fraser's Magazine*, and on it was founded a public charge of downright dishonesty against a perfectly honorable and honest man. Now, my good sir, insinuations or accusations of this kind are quite 'another guess matter' from mere ebullitions of temper, and it is impossible that Mr. Blackwood can ever make up any quarrel with any man *who doubts his integrity*. It is your bounden duty, therefore, to make amends to him on this subject. But even here I would not counsel *any apology*. I would say that it is your duty as an honest man to say fully, and freely, and unequivocally that you know Mr. Blackwood to be one, and in all his dealings with you he has behaved as one. This avowal is no more than he is entitled to from you; and, of course, it should be taken in lieu of an apology. As to writing henceforth in 'Maga,' I am sure it will give me the greatest pleasure to see the Shepherd adorning that work with his friends again; and, in that case, it would be graceful and becoming in you to address Mr. Blackwood in terms of esteem, such as would remove from all minds any idea that you ever wished to accuse him of want of principle. I should think that would be agreeable to yourself, and that it would be agreeable to all who feel the kindest interest in your character and reputation. In this way you would both appear in your true colors, and to the best advantage.

"As for the *Noctes Ambrosianæ*, that is a subject in which I am chiefly concerned; and there shall never be another with you in it, *if indeed that be disagreeable to you!!!* But all the idiots in existence shall never persuade me that in those dialogues you are not respected and honored, and that they have not spread the fame of your genius and your virtues all over Europe, America, Asia, and Africa. If there be another man who has done more for your fame than *I* have done, let me know in what region of the moon he has taken up his abode. But let the 'Noctes' drop, or let us *talk* upon that subject, if you choose, that we may find out which of us is insane, perhaps *both*.

"Show this letter to the Grays—our friends—and let them say whether or not it be reasonable, and if any good is likely to result from my services. I have written of my own accord, and without any authority from Mr. Blackwood, but entirely from believing that his kindness towards you would dispose him to make the matter up at once, on the one condition which, as an honest man, I would advise him to consider essential, and without which, indeed, he could not listen to any proposal. I am, my dear sir, your affectionate friend, JOHN WILSON."

"MY DEAR MR. HOGG:—Your letter in answer to mine is written as mine was, in a friendly spirit; but on considering its various contents, I feel that I can be of no use at present in effecting a reconciliation between you and Mr. Blackwood. I was induced to offer my services by my own sincere regard for you, and by the wishes of Mrs. Izett and Mr. Grieve; but it rarely happens that an unaccredited mediator between offended friends in a somewhat complicated quarrel can effect any good. Should you, at any future time, wish me to give an opinion in this matter, or advice of any sort, you will find me ready to do so with the utmost sincerity. I will merely mention to Mr. Grieve, who was desirous of having you and Mr. Blackwood and myself to dinner, that I wrote you, and had an answer from you; but I shall leave you to tell him or not, as you please, what passed between us. That I may not fall into any unintentional mis-statement, I will likewise tell Mr. Blackwood the same, and no more, that I may not do more harm than good by having taken any step in the affair. If you never have made any accusation of the kind I mentioned against Mr. Blackwood, then am I ignorant of the merits of the case altogether, and my interference is only an additional instance of the danger of volunteering counsel, with erroneous impressions of the relative situation of the parties. I proposed a plan of reconciliation, which seemed to me to make no unpleasant demand on either party, and which was extremely simple; but it would seem that I took for granted certain accusations or insinuations against Mr. Blackwood's character as a man of business, which you never made. I am, therefore, in the dark, and require to be instructed, instead of being privileged to counsel. With every kind sentiment, I am, my dear sir, yours most sincerely, JOHN WILSON."

In a long letter to Mr. Grieve, my father is at great pains to clear up the matter, and effect the much-desired reconciliation on terms honorable to both parties. He says:—

"If Mr. Hogg puts his return as a writer to 'Maga,' on the ground that 'Maga' suffers greatly from his absence from her pages, and that Mr. B. must be very desirous of his re-assistance, that will at once be a stumbling-block in the way of settlement; for Mr. B., whether rightly or wrongly, will not make the admission. No doubt Mr. H.'s articles were often excellent, and no doubt the 'Noctes' were very popular, but the Magazine, however much many readers must have missed Mr. Hogg and the 'Noctes,' has been gradually increasing in sale, and therefore Mr. B. will never give in to that view of the subject.

"Mr. Hogg, in his letter to me, and in a long conversation I had with him in my own house yesterday after dinner, sticks to his proposal of having £100 settled on him, on condition of writing, and of becoming again the hero of the 'Noctes,' as before. I see many, many difficulties in the way of such an arrangement, and I *know* that Mr. Blackwood will never agree to it in that shape; for it might eventually prove degrading and disgraceful to both parties, appearing to the public to be a bribe given and taken dishonorably.

"But nothing can be more reasonable than for Mr. Hogg to make £100 or more by 'Maga,' and by the *Agricultural Journal.* If he writes again for both, Mr. B. is bound to pay him handsomely and generously, as an old friend and man of genius; and no doubt he will do so, so that if Mr. Hogg exert himself to a degree *you and I* think reasonable, there can be no doubt that he will get £100 or more from Mr. Blackwood, without any positive bargain of the kind above mentioned, which might injure Mr. Hogg's reputation, and appear to the public in a degrading light.

"To insure this, *none of Mr. Hogg's articles should ever again be returned.* If now and then any of them are inadmissible *they should still be paid for*, and Mr. Blackwood, I have no doubt, would at once agree to that, so that at the end of the year Mr. Hogg would have received his £100 or more, without any objectionable condition, and on reasonable exertions.

"And now a few words about myself. The Shepherd, in his letter to me (which you have seen, I believe), seems to say that *I* ought to settle the £100 a year on him, and that he is willing to receive it from me, if I think it will be for my own benefit. I have said nothing about this *to him*, but to *you* I merely say that I never did and never will interfere in any way with the pecuniary concerns of the Magazine, that being the affair of Mr. Blackwood; *secondly*, that of all the writers in it, *I* have done *most* for the *least* remuneration, though Mr. B. and I have never once had one word of disagreement on that subject; and *thirdly*, that it is a matter of the most perfect indifference to me, whether or not I ever again write another 'Noctes,' for all that I write on any subject seems to be popular far above its deserts; and considering the great number of 'Noctes' I have written, I feel very much indisposed ever to resume them.* My own personal gain or loss, therefore, must be put out of sight entirely in this question; as I can neither gain nor lose by any arrangement between Mr. B. and Mr. Hogg, though the Shepherd thinks otherwise.

"This, likewise, must and will be considered by Mr. Blackwood, whether the 'Noctes' *can* be resumed, for if the public supposed that *I* were influenced by a regard to my own interests in resuming them, I most certainly never would; and were I to resume them, and Mr. Hogg again to prove wilful, and order them to be discontinued, I should feel myself placed in a condition unworthy of me. I wrote the 'Noctes' to benefit and do honor to Mr. Hogg, much more than to benefit myself; and but for them, he with all his extraordinary powers would not have been universally known as he now is; for poetical fame, you well know, is fleeting and precarious. After more than a dozen years' acquiescence and delight in the 'Noctes,' the Shepherd, because he quarrelled with Mr. Blackwood *on other grounds*, puts an end to them, which by the by he had no *right* to do. It is for me to consider whether I *can* resume them; but if I do, it must be clearly understood that I am not influenced by self-interest, but merely by a desire to bring back things as they

* My father never wrote another "Noctes" after the Shepherd's death, which took place in 1835.

were before, and to contribute my part to an amicable arrangement.

"But I will say *to you* what must not be said to anybody else, that if it be necessary, owing to Mr. Hogg not writing a sufficient number of articles fit for insertion, to make up some considerable sum towards £100 per annum being given to him, I will certainly contribute half of it along with Mr. Blackwood.

"There are various other points to be attended to. The Magazine *now* is the least *personal* periodical existing, and it will continue so. Now Mr. Hogg may wish to insert articles about London and so on, that may be *extremely personal*. Mr. Blackwood could not take such articles. He *has himself* reason to be offended with Mr. Hogg's writings about himself, and could not consistently in like manner offend others. Suppose that the Shepherd sent such MS. for the first year as could not be inserted at all, is Mr. Blackwood to be paying him £100 for nothing? The *kind*, therefore, of his contributions must be considered by 'James,' though he may still be allowed considerable latitude.

"With respect to past quarrels, they should at once be forgotten by both parties, and not a word said about them, except *if* Mr. Hogg has published any thing reflecting on Mr. Blackwood's *integrity*. *I think he has*. *That*, therefore, must be done away with by the Shepherd in the Magazine itself, but not in the way of *apology*, but in a manly manner, such as would do honor to himself, and at once put down all the calumnies of others, to which Mr. Blackwood has been unjustly exposed, especially in *Fraser's Magazine*. All abuse of Mr. Blackwood in that work, *as founded on his behavior to Mr. Hogg*, must, by Mr. Hogg, be put a stop to; for if he continues to write in *Fraser*, and to allow those people to put into his mouth whatever they choose (and they hold him up to ridicule every month after a very different fashion from the NOCTES!!), their abuse of Mr. Blackwood will seem to be sanctioned by Mr. Hogg, and neutralize whatever he may say in 'Maga.' This is plain.

"Consider what I have said attentively, and I will call on you *on Tuesday at two o'clock*, and will explain a few other matters perhaps tedious to write upon. After that, the sooner you see Mr. B. the better, and I think an arrangement may be made, in itself reasonable and beneficial to all parties, on the above basis. Yours ever affectionately,

JOHN WILSON."

The result of these friendly negotiations may be gathered from the "Noctes" of May 1834, in which there is a lively and most amusing description of the Shepherd's return to the bosom of his friends in the tent at the Fairy's Cleugh.*

I make use of my mother's words to tell of the plans for the summer of 1834:—"Our own plans for the summer are, to spend four months of it at least, that is, from the 20th June till the 20th October, in Ettrick Forest. The house we have taken, which is furnished, belongs to Lord Napier, who is at present in China, and he wished to get it let for the summer; but, from the retirement of the situation, hardly expected to meet with a tenant for that time. It is called Thirlstane Castle; the country around is all interesting, being pastoral, with no lack of wood and water, and a great lack of neighbors; we all like retirement, young and old, and look forward, with great satisfaction, to spending a quiet summer."

We accordingly took up our quarters at Thirlstane, and enjoyed Ettrick Forest vastly; the boys had their fishing and shooting; the very dogs were happy. "The dowgs," as James Hogg called them, shared in all our amusements; it was here that Rover had his adventure with the witch transformed into a hare. "She was sitting in her ain kail-yaird, the preceese house I dinna choose to mention, when Giraffe, in louping ower the dyke, louped ower her, and she gied a spang intil the road, turning round her fud within a yard o' Clavers,†—and then sic a brassle; a' three thegither up the brae, and then back again in a hairy whirlwind; twa miles in less than ae minute. She made for the mouth of the syver,‡ but Rover, wha had happened to be examining it in his inquisitive way, and kent naething o' the course, was coming out just as she was gaun in, an' atween the twa there ensued, unseen in the syver, a desperate battle. Well dune witch; well dune warlock; and at ae time I feared, frae his yelping and yowling, that Rover was getting the worst o't,

* The whole dialogue, which will be found in the *Noctes*, May, 1834, is too long for quotation, but a few lines of the apology may be given:—

"I'll never breathe a whisper even to my ain heart, at the laneliest hour o' midnight, except it be when I am saying my prayers, o' ony misunderstanding that ever happened between us twa, either about 'Mawga' or ony ither topic, as lang's I leeve, an' am no deserted o' my senses, but am left in full possession of the gift of reason; and I now dicht aff the tablets o' my memory ilka letter o' ony ugly record that the Enemy, taking the advantage o' the corruption o' our fallen nature, contrived to scarify there wi' the pint o' an airn pen, red-het frae yon wicked place. I now dicht them a' aff, just as I dicht aff frae this table the wine-drops wi' ma sleeve; and I forgive ye frae the very bottom o' ma sowle," &c., &c.

† The Shepherd's colleys.

‡ A covered drain.

and might lose his life. Auld poosies* cuff sair wi' their fore-paws, and theirs is a wicked bite. But the outlandish wolfiness in Rover brak forth in extremity, and he cam rushing out o' the syver wi' her in his mouth, shaking her savagely, as if she had been but a ratton, and I had to choke him off. Forbye thrappling her, he had bit intil the jugular; and she had lost sae meikle bluid, that you hae eaten her the noo roasted, instead o' her made intil soup."

Rover was a colley from the beautiful pastures of Westmoreland; he had succeeded Brontë† in the Professor's affections. He had all the sagacity of his species; he was generally admired, but strictly speaking he was not beautiful, as the Shepherd remarked that he had "a cross o' some outlandish blood" in his veins; he, however, walked with a stately, defiant air, and was very "leesh;" his coat was black and glossy, it gleamed in the light; a white ring surrounded his neck, and melted away into the depths of his muscular chest; he was very loving and affectionate, and as we children told him every thing that was going on, these communications quickly opened his mind, and Rover increased so much the more in intelligence. We never doubted in his humanity, and treated him accordingly; animation of spirit and activity of body combined to give him a more than usual share of enjoyment. Rover's companion in dog-life was Fang the terrier. Poor Fang was one of the victims in Hawthornden garden; but at Thirlstane he, like Rover, and like us all, old and young, enjoyed himself vastly. Poor Rover fell sick in the spring of the following year, and struggled for many days with dumb madness. I remember that shortly before the poor creature died, longing for the sympathy of his master's kind voice, he crawled up stairs to a room next the drawing-room; my father stood beside him, trying to soothe and comfort the poor animal. A very few minutes before death closed his fast-glazing eye, the Professor said: "Rover, my poor fellow, give me your paw." The dying animal made an effort to reach his master's hand; and so thus parted my father with his favorite, as one man taking farewell of another. My father loved "both man, and bird, and beast;" he could turn at any moment from the hardest work, with playful tenderness, to some household pet, or any object colored by home affection.‡

* Hares.

† A favorite dog of my father's, of whom more anon.

‡ It is worth observing how close in description two students of dog-life have approached each

Wife, children, pets, idealized as they sometimes are, play through many of his most beautiful and imaginative essays. Memory revives in his soul matters trivial enough; but to those familiar with his ways, these little touches, embalming the fancy or taste of some cherished friend, are deeply interesting. For example, my mother's favorite plant was the myrtle: we find it peeping out here and there in his writings, thus—

North.—"These are mere myrtles."

Shepherd.—"Mere myrtles! Dinna say that again o' them—mere; an ungratefu' word, of a flowery plant, a' fu' o' bonny white starries; and is that their scent that I smell?"

North.—"The balm is from many breaths, my dear James. Nothing that grows is without fragrance."

In a letter written by my mother this autumn she says:—"We like our residence exceedingly, notwithstanding its great retirement and moist climate: the latter we were prepared for before we came, and have certainly not been disappointed, for we have had rather more of rain than fair weather. The house is situated in a narrow valley in Ettrick, with high hills on every side, which attract the clouds. We, however, contrive to amuse ourselves very well, with books and work, music and drawing; and when fair and fine, the boys and girls have their ponies, and the old people a safe low open carriage, yclept a drosky, in which they take the air. The walks are quite to my taste, and without number in the wood which surrounds the

other. Every one remembers the celebrated contest in *Rab and his Friends;* here is my father's description of a dog-fight from the *Noctes.* No one was more amused at the resemblance than the genial author of *Rab*, when the writer pointed out that he had been anticipated by the "Shepherd:"—

"Doun another close, and a battle o' dowgs! A bull-dowg and a mastiff! The great big brown mastiff mouthin' the bull-dowg by the verra haunches, as if to crunch his back, and the wee white bull-dowg never seeming to fash his thoomb, but sticking by the regular set teeth o' his under-hung jaw to the throat o' the mastiff, close to the jugular, and has to be drawn off the grip by twa strong baker-boys pu'in' at the tail o' the tane, and twa strong butcher-boys pu'in' at the tail o' the tither; for the mastiff's maister begins to fear that the viper at his throat will kill him outright, and offers to pay a' bets, and confess his dowg has lost the battle. But the crowd wish to see the fecht out—and harl the dowgs that are noo worrying ither without any growling—baith silent, except a sort o' snorting through the nostrils, and a kind o' guller in their gullets,—I say the crowd harl them out o' the midden, ontil the stanes again—and, 'Weel dune, Cæsar!' 'Better dune, Vesper!' 'A mutchkin to a gill on Whitey!' 'The muckle ane canna fecht!' 'See how the wee bick is worrying him noo, by a new spat on the thrapple!' 'He wud rin awa', gin she wud let him loose!' 'She's just like her mother, that belanged to the caravan o' wild beasts!' 'O, man, Davie, but I wud like to get a breed out o' her by the watch-dowg at Bellmaiden Bleachfield, that killed, ye ken, the Kilmarnock carrier's Help in twenty minutes at Kingswell!'"—*Noctes.*

house, and there is one delightful walk, the avenue, which is the approach, and which, from one lodge to the other, is rather more than a mile of nice dry gravel, and quite level, or nearly so, which suits me vastly well; there is a beautiful flower-garden close to the house and a very pretty brawling stream, which reminds one of Stockgill at Ambleside; there is a very good waterfall likewise in the grounds, about a mile from the house, which I have not yet seen, the path being very steep, and, owing to the rains, very wet; it is called the Black Spout. The boys have abundance of amusement in fishing and shooting, there being plenty of game—hares and rabbits. John has the Duke of Buccleuch's permission to shoot, and therefore we expect to have plenty of grouse. . . . . Our neighbors, who are few and far between, consist of respectable farmers, who have showed us great attention, indeed, Mr. Wilson was known to all the neighborhood long ago, in his pedestrian perambulations. The church is about a mile and a half from us, a neat little building, with a comfortable manse attached. Mr. Smith, the minister, is a very favorable specimen of a Scotch clergyman, with a modest, hospitable wife, and two children.

"Mr. Wilson was obliged to go to Edinburgh last Saturday, but I hope he will be here again on Wednesday. He is staying at the Bank. Poor Mr. Blackwood is very ill; indeed, I fear dangerously so. It is a surgical case, and though his general health has not as yet suffered, should that give way there is no chance for him. He would be an irreparable loss to his family, and a serious one to Edinburgh, being an excellent citizen, a magistrate, and highly respected even by his enemies."

My father's spirits were at this time very much disturbed at the prospect of soon losing his kind and long-tried friend, the gradual increase of whose illness he writes of with much feeling to his wife:—

"Gloucester Place, *Thursday Night.*

"My dear Jane:—I found Mr. Blackwood apparently near his dissolution, but entirely sensible, and well aware of his state, which indeed he had been for a long time, though, till lately, he had never said so, not wishing to disturb his family. He was very cheerful, and we spoke cheerfully of various matters; this was on Monday, on my arrival from Peebles in a chaise, the coach being full. Tuesday was a day of rain, and being very ill, I lay all the day in bed. I did not, therefore, see any of the Blackwoods, nor anybody else, but heard that he was keeping much the same. On Wednesday I saw Alexander and Robert, and found there was no change. This morning (Thursday) I called, and found him looking on the whole better than before, stronger in his speech and general appearance. I had much conversation with him, and found him quite prepared to die, pleased with the kindness of all around him, and grateful for all mercies. It is impossible, I think, that he can live many days, and yet the medical men all declared on Sunday that he could not hold out many hours. A good conscience is the best comforter on such a bed as his, and were his bed mine to-morrow, bless God I have a conscience that would support me as it supports him, and which will support me till then, while I strive to do my duty to my family, with weakened powers both of mind and body, but under circumstances which more than ever demand exertion. I have been too ill to write one word since I came, and have seen nobody, nor shall I till I return to Thirlstane. Not one word of the Magazine is written. Last night I made an effort and walked to the Bank through a tremendous storm.

"I was in bed to-day till after bank hours, and could not disturb the Blackwoods, of whom I have not heard since the morning. I have consulted Liston. Sedentary employments are bad for that complaint, but sedentary I must be, and will work till I can work no longer. It is necessary that I should do, and better men have done so, and will do so while the world lasts. Thank God, I injure nobody in thought, word, or deed. I am willing to die for my family, who, one and all, yourself included, deserve all that is good at my hands. I believe that poor Mr. Blackwood's exertions have caused his illness, and after his death my work must be incessant, till the night comes in which no man can work. I have been interrupted all summer, but winter must see another sight, and I will do my utmost. I will write again by Ebenezer Hogg, and shall not, indeed cannot, leave this before Mr. Blackwood's death. He cannot survive many days, but I do not think the boys and Mr. Hay need come in. I will speak of that again in my letter. I am yours affectionately, JOHN WILSON."

"BANK, *Thursday Night.*

"MY DEAR JANE:—I arrived at the Bank at half-past twelve on

Monday with a violent toothache; dined there alone; saw the Blackwoods, and went to bed at nine. On Tuesday called on Mr. Blackwood, and found him tolerably well. Lost all that day in being unable to settle to any thing; finding the bank-house most uncomfortable in all respects—no pillows to the beds, no sofas, no tables on which it was possible to write, from their being so low and the chairs so high. I did nothing. On Wednesday did a little, but not much; and dined, perhaps injudiciously, with Liston,* to meet Schetky;† stayed till one o'clock; and to-day had an open and confused head; wrote in the back shop, but not very much. I sent for Nancy to the Bank, and found from her that she was picking currants in Gloucester Place, and told her that I would be there to-morrow (Friday) at nine o'clock, and write in my room, which, she says, is open, and sleep at the Bank. I dine at Mr. Blackwood's. Mr. Hay called on me at the shop to-day, and is well, having been ill with cholera or colic. The Magazine is in a sad state, and entirely behind, and as yet I have done little to forward it. I am not quite *incog.*, I fear, but have avoided seeing any of my old friends of the Parliament House. I will write by Sunday's mail, so you will hear from me on *Tuesday*, telling you when to send the gig to Innerleithen. I think it will be on Wednesday night, therefore keep it disengaged for that day; but I will mention particulars in my next. My face is swelled, but not so bad as before nearly. The Whigs are all *in* again, or rather were never out, except Lord Grey, who remains out. Poor Blackwood looks as well as ever, and there seem to be hopes, but the disease is very, very bad, and I do not know what to say. Love to all. Yours ever affectionately,

"JOHN WILSON."

"*Saturday Evening.*

"MY DEAR MAGGIE:—Mr. Blackwood is in the same state, wear-

* Robert Liston, the celebrated surgeon; died in 1847.

† John Schetky, an artist, a friend of my father's.—"I have no conceit of those 'who are all things to all men.' Why, I have seen John Schetky himself in the sulks with sumphs, though he is more tolerant of ninnies and noodles than almost any other man of genius I have ever known; but clap him down among a choice crew of kindred spirits, and how his wild wit even yet, as in its prime, wantons! playing at will its *virgin* fancies, till Care herself comes from her cell, and sitting by the side of Joy, loses her name, and forgets her nature, and joins in glee or catch, beneath the power of that magician, the merriest in the hall."—*Noctes*, No. lxvi., 1834.

"A gentleman who served with our army in the Spanish campaigns, and has painted several wild scenes of the Pyrenees in a most original manner. He is, I imagine, the very finest painter of sky since Salvator Rosa."—*Letters on the Living Artists of Scotland.*

ing away gradually, but living longer than any of the medical people thought possible. Last Sunday, it was thought he could not live many hours.

"I enclose £10 for present use, and shall write to your mamma on Monday, so that you will hear from me on Wednesday.

"This goes by Ebenezer Hogg, and two other letters; and Nancy, I understand, is sending clothes to Bonjeddard, from which I gather you are going to the ball, which is right. Love to all. Use the gig as you choose, for I shall not want it for some time. Thine affectionately, JOHN WILSON."

"GLOUCESTER PLACE, *Monday Evening.*

"MY DEAR JANE:—I shall be in Innerleithen on Thursday per coach, so let the gig be there the night before. I have been writing here since Friday, with but indifferent success, and am at this hour worn out. Nancy has done what I asked her to do, and I have let the bell ring 10,000 times without minding it.

"Billy called, with Captain Craigie, on Sunday, and, after viewing them from the bedroom window, I let them in. I have seen nobody else, not even Sym, but intend to call to-morrow night. I have slept here, and in utter desolation, as at Blackwood's it was too mournful to go there.

"What is to become of next Magazine I do not know. If I come here again, I will bring Maggie with me. Five hours of writing give me a headache, and worse, and I become useless. I do not think Blackwood will recover, but Liston speaks still as if he had hopes. Nobody writes for the Magazine, and the lads are in very low spirits, but show much that is amiable. I believe Hogg and his wife and I will be in the coach on Thursday morning to Innerleithen; so Bob told me. The printers are waiting for MS., and I have none but a few pages to give them; but on Wednesday night all must be at press. I hope to find you all well and happy. Yours ever affectionately, JOHN WILSON."

Mr. Blackwood died on the 16th of September, 1834. "Four months of suffering, in part intense, exhausted by slow degrees all his physical energies, but left his temper calm and unruffled, and his intellect entire and vigorous even to the last. He had thus what no good man will consider as a slight privilege, that of contemplating the approach of death with the clearness and full strength of his mind and faculties, and of instructing those around him, by solemn precept and memorable example, by what means alone humanity, conscious of its own frailty, can sustain that prospect with humble serenity."* This event made no change in my father's relations with the Magazine, but two years later a trial came that deadened his interest, and the willingness of his hand to work.

"What is to become of next Magazine?" was the question on Monday evening, while the printers were waiting for MS., and he had but a few pages to give them. How he worked that night and next two days may be seen by examining the number of the Magazine for October, of which he wrote with his own hand 56 out of the 142 pages required. His articles were: "A Glance at the Noctes of Athenæus;" and a "Review of Coleridge's Poetical Works."

For the remainder of this year, and for the two subsequent years, he gave the most unequivocal proofs of his regard for his friend's memory, and his interest in his family, by continuing his labors with unflagging industry. In glancing over his contributions for 1835, I perceive that in January he had three; in February five; in March two; in May two; in July five; in August four; in September three; and in October and November one in each month, making a total of twenty-six articles during the twelve months. Of all these criticisms I have only space to allude to the very brilliant series of papers on Spenser, regarding which Mr. Hallam remarks, that "It has been justly observed by a living writer of the most ardent and enthusiastic genius, whose eloquence is as the rush of mighty waters, and has left it for others almost as invidious to praise in terms of less rapture, as to censure what he has borne along in the stream of unhesitating eulogy, that 'no poet has ever had a more exquisite sense of the beautiful than Spenser.' "†

In 1836 and 1837, he continued to contribute an article at least once a month until his own great loss paralyzed him.

The following letters were written in the autumn of 1835 from the banks of the Clyde:—

"THE BATHS, HELENSBURGH,
1835, *Tuesday*, 12 *o'clock.*

"MY DEAR JANE:—I dined with Miss Sym on Sunday, and was kindly received by her and Mr. Andrew.

* *Blackwood*, October, 1837. † *Literature of Europe*, vol. ii., p. 136.

"Dinner was over (half-past four), but the Howtowdy and pigeon-pie brought back, and having cast the coat to it, much to the old lady's amusement, I made a feast. I left Glasgow at half-past six on Thursday morning, and reached Helensburgh about nine. I forgot to say that Blair was at the Mearns, so I did not see him. Monday (that is yesterday) was a broiling day without wind; not a breath till about twelve, when some yachts started for a cup; the heat was intense, though there was a canopy over the *Orion*, in which the party was gathered. We had every thing good in the upper and lower jaw-most line; and the champagne—a wine I like—flew like winking. This continued till six o'clock, and I had a mortal headache. Race won by the 'Clarence' (her seventh cup this summer), the 'Amethyst' (Smith's yacht) being beaten. At seven we sat down forty-five to dinner in the Baths, so the hotel is called, and we had a pleasant party enough, as far as the heat would suffer."

"LARGS, *Sunday, August* 2, 1835.

"MY DEAR MAGG!—I duly received the governess's letter, and write now to say that two gentlemen are to dine with us in Gloucester Place on Wednesday first, viz., Wednesday, August 5th, at six o'clock. Get us a good dinner. It was my intention to write a long letter about *us*, but how can I? We have all been at church, and the room is filled with people, and the post goes in an hour. Blair and Frank Wilson and Willy Sym came down per steamer last night, and return to Glasgow to-morrow morning, but Blair has no intention, as far as I know, of returning to Edinburgh. I have just seen him, and no more. The Regatta is over, and Umbs was at the ball here; 200 people present. To-day is a storm. To-morrow I hope to get to Glasgow, and be home to dinner on Tuesday per mail—sooner not possible—so do try all of you to be contented till then without me. All are well. Your affectionate father,
JOHN WILSON,
"Who sends love to the lave, chickens and dogs included."

In August, 1836, the Professor, with his wife and two eldest daughters, visited Paisley, where a public dinner was given to him, to which he was accompanied by his friend Thomas Campbell. The meeting was numerously attended, and went off with *éclat*.

The following note to Mr. Findlay accompanied a report of the speeches on this occasion:—

"6 Gloucester Place, *September* 1.

"My dear Friend:—The pen is idle; not cold the heart! I forget not ever the friends of my heart. This report is a very imperfect one, but I thought you might not dislike to see it. I *will* write very soon, and at length. We are all well, and unite in kindest regards and remembrances. Ever yours most affectionately,

"John Wilson."

As an illustration of his humorous post-prandial speeches, I give an extract from the report:—"Mr. Campbell had been pleased to give them an animated character of his physical power; all he would say was that nature had blessed him with a sound mind in a sound body, and he had felt her kindness in this, that it had enabled him in his travels and wanderings to move with independence and freedom from all the restraints that weakness of body might imply. He remembered seeing it mentioned in the public prints some years ago that he resembled the wild man of the wood, but little did he dream that at last he was to grow into a resemblance of their immortal Wallace." After some further observations, in which the learned Professor spoke warmly and eloquently of the genius of Mr. Campbell, he referred to the remarks of that gentleman about the circles of reputation that surrounded him, and his reception at the dinner of the Campbell Club. Perhaps, he observed, it was not so great an achievement for Mr. Campbell to come 400 miles to receive the honors awaiting him, as it was for him (Mr. W.) to go forty miles to see those honors bestowed upon him; while the little discharge of applause with which his appearance was welcomed, was to be regarded only as a humble tribute due to Mr. Campbell's superior artillery. He gave Mr. Campbell willingly the possession of all the outer circles. He gave him London—undisputed possession of London—also of Edinburgh; he did not ask for Glasgow; but here in Paisley (tremendous cheering which drowned the rest of the sentence), they would agree with the justice of the sentiment, when he said that had he been born in the poorest village in the land, he would not have cause to be ashamed of his birthplace; nor, he trusted, would his birthplace have cause to be ashamed of him (cheers). But when he considered where he was born—the town of Paisley—where he had that morning walked along the front of his father's house—itself no insignificant mansion—a town of the very best size—not like the great unwieldy Glasgow, or Edinburgh, where (while fears were entertained of the failure of the crops in the country) a crop was going on in the streets of the city (cheers and laughter), but turned he to his native town, "Ah, seest'u! seest'u!"* (tremendous cheering and laughter). Politics were very properly excluded from that meeting, etc., etc.

After the festivities at Paisley were over, they took a short excursion to Loch Lomond, Glen Falloch, Killin, Loch Earn, Crieff, Comrie, Perth, and homewards; nor was it then imagined that one of that happy party was so soon to be removed from the honored and loved place she held in her family.

On New Year's day, 1837, my mother wrote her last letter to her dearly loved sister; and the correspondence, which had continued without interruption for twenty-five years, was now to cease:—

"My dear Mary:—With the exception of Mr. Wilson, we are nearly as well as usual. I cannot get Mr. W. to take proper care of himself; he would put you out of all patience, as he really does me, and neither scolding nor persuasion avail, and I am obliged to submit, and so must he; he consents to stay in the house, which is one comfort, and therefore I trust his cough will soon disappear.

"Frank says the preparations in Glasgow for the reception of Sir R. Peel will be splendid. Mr. Wilson and John will be both there. I believe there will be at least 2,000 at the dinner, and the demand for tickets is unprecedented. I will take care to send you a newspaper, with the best account of the meeting that can be had. There is some anticipation, I hear, that the Radicals will try to make some disturbance, but there is no fear but their attempts will be soon put a stop to.

"I am just now reading a delightful book; if you have not already seen it, pray try and get it; it is Prior's '*Life of Goldsmith*.' Do you remember how you used to like Goldsmith? and I never read a line of this book without thinking of you, and wishing we were reading it together. You will love him better than ever after reading these Memoirs.

"A thousand thanks for your welcome letter, and for all the good

* This is a Paisley expression peculiar to the people, and means "Seest thou, seest thou?"

and kind wishes therein contained. In return, pray accept all our united and most cordial wishes, which are offered in all sincerity and affection to yourself and all our well-beloved friends at Penny Bridge, that you may enjoy many, many happy returns of this blessed season. Your affectionate sister, J. WILSON."

My mother's illness was not at first of a nature to alarm the family; but my father was always nervous about her, when any thing more than usual disturbed her health; she had been for some years delicate, and took less exercise than was perhaps for her good. We thought that the little tour, made in the autumn of 1836, had been very beneficial, and hoped that this would in future tempt her to move more frequently from home. About the middle of March, little more than two months after sending an affectionate greeting at the beginning of a new year to the beloved friends at Penny Bridge, she was taken ill with a feverish cold, which, after a few days, turned to a malady beyond the aid of human skill. Water on the chest was the ultimate cause of her death, which sad event took place on the 29th of March, and was communicated to her sister Mary in the following touching letter by a relative, who could well understand the irreparable loss that had befallen husband and children by the passing away of this gentle spirit:—

"My letter, written last night, will have prepared you to hear that our worst fears have been confirmed; our dearest Jane expired last night at half-past twelve o'clock. Immediately after writing to you, I went, along with my husband, to Glo'ster Place, trusting that she might once more know me. She had been sleeping heavily for two or three hours, but when I went into her room, she was breathing softer though shorter, and a kind of hope seized upon me. The physician had ordered a cordial to be given her every hour; for this purpose it was necessary to rouse her from her sleep, and it was at this time a trial was to be made whether she would know me; how anxiously I hoped to exchange one kind look with her, to kiss her again, but it was not God's will it should be so. Her husband was just going to raise her head, that he might enable her to taste the draught, when she breathed three sighs, with short intervals, and all was over before we who were around her bed could believe it possible that her spirit had fled. We were stunned with the unexpected stroke, for none of us had anticipated any change last night. The Professor was seized with a sort of half delirium, and you can scarcely picture a more distressing scene than him lying on the floor, his son John weeping over him, and the poor girls in equal distress. His first words were those of prayer; after that he spoke incessantly the whole night, and seemed to recapitulate the events of many years in a few hours. They were all calmer this morning. Maggy tells me that she scarcely ever spoke except when addressed; that she did not think herself in danger, and had even yesterday morning spoken of getting better. But she did not know any of them, at all times, for the last day or two, and I believe *none* of them *yesterday*. The funeral, I believe, will take place on Saturday. God bless you both;—with kindest love to all."

So passed away from this earth the spirit of his idolized wife, leaving the world thenceforth for him dark and dreary. This bereavement overwhelmed him with grief, almost depriving him of reason, nor, when the excess of sorrow passed away, did mourning ever entirely leave his heart. When he resumed his duties next session, he met his class with a depressed and solemn spirit, unable at first to give utterance to words, for he saw that he had with him the sympathy and tender respect of his students. After a short pause, his voice tremulous with emotion, he said, "Gentlemen, pardon me, but since we last met, I have been in the valley of the shadow of death."

CHAPTER XV.

LITERARY AND DOMESTIC LIFE.

1837–'44.

"Pictures and visions which fancy had drawn and happy love had inspired, came now in fierce torrent of recollection over the prostrate and afflicted soul. Though sorrow had no part in them before, it possesses them now. Thus, one idea, and the pain which is now inseparable from it, reign over all changes of thought—though these thoughts in themselves have been fixed in their connection with one another, and image linked to image long before; they rise up by those connections, but they are determined to arise and depart by that one fixed conception which holds its unshaken seat in the sorrow of the soul."* It is quite evident from these words, written a year after that great domestic affliction had befallen him, that my father had not shut out from his heart the image of his wife. How he thought and felt at the moment when the shadow of death darkened his life, may be gathered from the following touching lines copied from the public journals of the day:—

"Last week a paragraph appeared describing the painful situation to which Professor Wilson had been reduced from deep mental affliction. The following extract from a letter to a friend, written by himself, is the best evidence of the error into which our contemporary had fallen:—

"'It pleased God on the 29th of March to visit me with the severest calamity that can befall one of his creatures, in the death of my wife, with whom I had lived in love for twenty-six years, and from that event till about a fortnight ago, I lived with my family, two sons and three daughters, dutiful and affectionate, in a secluded house near Roslin. I am now in Edinburgh, and early in November hope to resume my daily duties in the University. I have many blessings for which I am humbly thankful to the Almighty, and though I have not borne my affliction so well, or better than I have done, yet I have borne it with submission and resignation, and feel that though this world is darkened, I may be able yet to exert such faculties, humble as they are, as God has given me, if not to the benefit, not to the detriment of my fellow-mortals.'"

That letter leads one irresistibly back to one written in May, 1811, when he stood on the threshold of a new life full of anticipated happiness. Where was that solemn, calm spirit, now that she—the best and gentlest of wives—was gone? Did he say, "Comfort's in heaven, and we on earth?" True it was, he suffered as such a soul must suffer at such a loss, and it was for a long time a terrible storm of trouble. But he gave evidence in due time that he was not forever to be overcome with sadness.

It is necessary, in order to relate some of the events of this summer, that we should follow him to the secluded house near Roslin, where he went immediately after my mother's death, doubtless

* "Our Two Vases," *Blackwood*, April, 1838.

hoping to find, as he had done of old, some comfort in communion with outward nature. It was Spring, too, his very love for which carried with it a vague presage of evil.

> "Yea! mournful thoughts like these even now arise,
> While Spring, like Nature's smiling infancy,
> Sports round me, and all images of peace
> Seem native to this earth, nor other home
> Desire or know; yet doth a mystic chain
> Link in our hearts foreboding fears of death,
> With every loveliest thing that seems to us
> Most deeply fraught with life."

Thus did he meet the fair season so loved of old, sighing—

> "O the heavy change, now thou art gone;
> Now thou art gone, and never must return!"

I may observe here, without any unfilial disrespect, that his deep sorrow was not without its good influence on the sufferer. Those who had known him were well aware of the sincerity of his religious belief, and of his solemn and silent adoration of the Saviour; but it was observed from this time that his faith exercised a more constant sway over his actions. The tone of his writings is higher, and they contain almost unceasing aspirations after the spiritual. The same humility, which in a singular degree now made him so modest and unobtrusive with the public, ordered all his ways in private life. The humble opinion he had of himself could have arisen from no other source than from reverence to God, whose servant he felt himself to be, and debtor beyond all for the possession of those gifts which, in the diffidence of his soul, he hoped he had used, "if not for the benefit, not for the detriment of his fellow-mortals." As a specimen of his thoughts, and as introductory to the life of peace and charity which he led in his seclusion at Roslin, I refer my readers to a noble passage on Intellect;* it forms a touching contrast to the simplicity and tenderness of disposition which caused him to turn aside from these lofty communings to the common humanities of nature. He was well known in the houses of the poor. No humble friend was ever cast aside if honest and upright. During the summer, an old servant of my mother's, who had formerly lived many years in her service, had fallen into bad health, and was ordered change of air. She was at once invited to

* "Our Pocket Companions," *Blackwood's Magazine*, vol. xliv., 1838.

Roslin, and Jessie willingly availed herself of my father's kindness, and came to his house; but the change was of little service; consumption had taken firm hold, and soon the poor invalid was confined to bed never more to rise. That she was considerately attended and soothed during those long watches—the sad accompaniment of this lingering disease—was only what was to have been expected, but it was no unfrequent sight to see my father, as early dawn streaked the sky, sitting by the bedside of the dying woman, arranging with gentle but awkward hand the pillow beneath her head, or cheering her with encouraging words, and reading, when she desired it, those portions of the Bible most suitable to her need. When she died, her master laid her head in the grave in Lasswade churchyard.

This whole season was burdened with one feeling which tinged all he wrote, and never quite left him.* In October, he returned to Edinburgh and resumed his college duties, how, we have already seen in Mr. Smith's reminiscences. About this time circumstances occurred that in a measure removed the gloom which had settled upon his mind. Two of his daughters were married,† and the pleasant interchange of social civilities, which generally takes place on these occasions, led him into a wider circle of friends than formerly.

* "There is another incident of that period which brings out the profound emotion in a way too characteristically singular to be repeated, were it not known beyond the private circle:—how two pet dogs, special favorites of Mrs. Wilson's, having got astray within the preserve-grounds of an estate near which their owner was then staying in the country, were shot by the son of the proprietor, while engaged in field-sports with other gentlemen, and were afterwards ascertained, to their extreme regret, to belong to Professor Wilson, to whom they sent an immediate explanation, hastening to follow it up afterwards by apologies in person. His indignation, however, it is said, was uncontrollable, and we can conceive that leonine aspect in its prime—dilating, flaming, flushed with the sudden distraction of a grief that became rage, seeing nothing before it but the embodiment, as it were, of the great destroyer. The occasion, it was gravely argued by a mediator, was one for the display of magnanimity. 'MAGNANIMITY!' was the emphatic reply,—'Why, sir, I showed the utmost magnanimity this morning when one of the murderers was in this very room, and I did not pitch him out of the window!' As murder he accordingly persisted in regarding it, with a sullen obstinate desire for justice, which required no small degree of management on the part of friends, and of propitiation from the culprits, to prevent his making it a public matter. Untrained to calamity, like Lear, when all at once—

"'The king is mad! how stiff is our vile sense
That we stand up, and have ingenious feeling
Of our huge sorrows! Better we were distract:
So should our thoughts be severed from our griefs;
And woes, by wrong imaginations, lose
The knowledge of themselves.'"

—From Mr. Cupple's graceful "*Memorial and Estimate of Professor Wilson, by a Student.*" 4to. Edinburgh.

† The eldest, Margaret Anne, to her cousin, Mr. J. F. Ferrier, now Professor of Moral Philosophy, St. Andrews; the second, Mary, to Mr. J. T. Gordon, now Sheriff of Midlothian.

By the marriage of his second daughter, who, along with her husband, found a home for eleven years in her father's house, a change was wrought in the feelings of some of the chief men of the Whig party towards him. It has already been shown to what an extent the bitterness of party spirit had separated good men and true from each other, not only in public matters but in private life. That spirit was now dying out, and the alienation which had for some years existed, more through force of habit than inclination, was soon to cease, as far as my father was concerned. Mr. Gordon was a Whig, and connected with Whig families; he introduced to his father-in-law's house new visitors and new elements of thought; old prejudices disappeared, and "Christopher North" was frequently seen in the midst of what once was to his own party the camp of the enemy. Many a pleasant day they spent in each other's houses; and no observer, however dull, could fail to be struck even by the aspect of the four men who thus again met together, Jeffrey, Cockburn, Rutherfurd, and Wilson. I think I may venture, without partiality, to say that my father was the most remarkable of the four. There was a certain similarity of bearing and manner in the three great lawyers which was not shared by him: he was evidently not one of the family. I shall never forget his manly voice, pleasantly contrasting with Jeffrey's sharp silvery tones, as they mingled sparkling wit with their more serious discourse, which was enlivened by the quaint humor and Doric notes of Cockburn, that type of the old Scottish gentleman, whose dignified yet homely manner and solemn beauty gave his aspect a peculiar grace—Rutherfurd also, to whose large mind, consummate ability, rich and ripe endowments, I most willingly pay a most sincere and affectionate tribute of true regard and respect.* It will not do for me to dwell on these things, however pleasant to myself would be a digression into this fairy-land of reminiscence.†

* The mutual appreciation and familiar friendship of Wilson and Rutherfurd was as instant as are question and answer to-day by telegraph; and I cannot now recall, without emotion, the fond and constant attachment which the great and busy lawyer felt and manifested to "Christopher North." I have before me at this moment letter after letter, written during a course of years to my husband from his uncle in London, in the din of the heaviest seasons of official duty, not one of which ever concludes without some special message to or inquiry about the "Professor."

† Nobody, however, will grudge me a few words in honor of that amiable and admirable man, the late Lord Murray, who may be said to have lived in the open air of universal and cheerful hospitality. His heart and his hearth were alike open, with an equal warmth of welcome, to all, old and young, big or little. None understood or relished better than he did the joyous benevolence of my father's disposition. I wish I could linger a little over the agreeable *réunions* in

My father, since the days when he wrote in the *Edinburgh*, had achieved a position in letters not only different from Jeffrey's, but higher and more enduring. As a critic, he had worked in a deeper mine than the Edinburgh Reviewer, dealing less with mere forms, and more with the true spirit of art.

His great work, indeed, was that which to me seems the highest destiny of man, to teach; and his lessons have spread far and near. In the limitations of his genius lay its excellence; it made him patriotic; and if, for example, his name is not linked with individual creations of character such as bind the name of Goethe with Faust or Werther or Wilhelm Meister, yet his immediate influence extends over a wider sphere of life. These creations of the great German, though quite accordant with nature, speak but to a high order of cultivation. They are works containing a spirit and action of life, the sympathies of which can never enter the hut of the peasant or the homes of the poor. On the other hand, Wilson is thoroughly patriotic; there is not a class in the whole of Scotland incapable of enjoying his writings; and I believe his influence in the habits and modes of thought on every subject, grave or gay, is felt throughout the country. Be it politics, literature, or sport, there is not one of these themes that has not taken color from him—a sure test of genius. In the "Noctes" alone is seen his creative power in individual character; yet its most original conception is not a type, but a being of time and place. The Shepherd is not to be found everywhere in Scotland, either sitting at feasts, or tending his flocks on the hill-side. We are not familiar with him as we are with the characters of Charles Dickens. We have to imagine the one; we see and know the others. Christopher himself is typical of what has been; he presides at these meetings, when philosophy mounts high, with the dignity of a minister of blue-eyed Athene. The spirit of the Greek school is upon him, and we can fancy, that, before assembling his companions together, he invoked the gods for eloquence and wisdom. There he was great; but in his tales, his *Recreations*, and his poetry, the true nature of the man, as he lived at home, is to be found. In the simple ways of his daily life, I see him as he sometimes used to be, in his own room, surrounded by his family—the

Jeffrey's house in his latter years, which, under the mellowed lustre of a simple domestic fireside, rivalled the sprightliest fascinations of a Hôtel Rambouillet. No friend went to them, or was there greeted, with more cordial sympathy than Professor Wilson.

prestige of greatness laid aside, and the very strength of his hand softened, that he might gently caress the infant on his knee, and play with the little ones at his feet. And many a game was played with fun and frolic; stories were told, *barley-sugar* was eaten, and feasts of various kinds given. "A party in grandpapa's room" was ever hailed with delight. There was to be seen a tempting display of figs, raisins, cakes, and other good things, all laid out on a table set and covered by himself; while he, acting on the occasion as waiter, was ordered about in the most unceremonious fashion. After a while, when childhood was passing away from the frolics of the nursery, and venturing to explore the mysteries of life, he would speak to his little friends as companions, and passing from gay to grave, led their young spirits on, and bound their hearts to his.

In speaking of his kindness to *human pets*, I may mention a very delightful instance of his love to the inferior animals. I remember a hapless sparrow being found lying on the door-steps scarcely fledged, and quite unable to do for itself. It was brought into the house, and from that moment became a *protégé* of my father's. It found a lodging in his room, and ere long was perfectly domesticated, leading a life of uninterrupted peace and prosperity for nearly eleven years. It seemed quite of opinion that it was the most important occupant of the apartment, and would peck and chirp where it liked, not unfrequently nestling in the folds of its patron's waistcoat, attracted by the warmth it found there. Then with bolder stroke of familiarity, it would hop upon his shoulder, and picking off some straggling hair from the long locks hanging about his neck, would jump away to its cage, and depositing the treasure with an air of triumph, return to fresh conquest, quite certain of welcome. The creature seemed positively influenced by constant association with its master. It grew in *stature*, and began to assume a noble and defiant look. It was alleged, in fact, that he was gradually becoming an *eagle*.

Of his dogs, their name was Legion. I remember Brontë, Rover, Fang, Paris, Charlie, Fido, Tip, and Grog, besides outsiders without number.

Brontë comes first on the list. He came, I think, into the family in the year 1826, a soft, shapeless mass of puppyhood, and grew up a beautiful Newfoundland dog. "Purple-black was he all over, except the star on his breast, as the raven's wing. Strength and sagacity emboldened his bounding beauty, and a fierceness lay deep down within the quiet lustre o' his een that tauld you, even when he laid his head upon your knees, and smiled up to your face like a verra intellectual and moral creature—as he was—that had he been angered, he could have torn in pieces a lion."* He was brave and gentle in disposition, and we all loved him, but he was my father's peculiar property, of which he was, by the way, quite aware; he evinced for him a constancy that gained in return the confidence and affection of his master. Every day for several years did Brontë walk by his side to and from the College, where he was soon as well known as the Professor himself. This fine dog came to an untimely end. There was good reason to believe that he had been poisoned by some members of Dr. Knox's class, in revenge for the remarks made by my father on the Burke and Hare murders.† I remember the morning we missed Brontë from the breakfast-room, a half-formed presentiment told us that something was wrong; we called, but no bounding step answered the summons. I went to look for him in the schoolroom, and there he lay lifeless. I could not believe it, and touched him gently with my foot; he did not move. I bent down and laid my hand on his head, but it was cold; poor Brontë was dead! "No bark like his now belongs to the world of sound;" and so passed Brontë "to the land of hereafter." It was some time ere he found a successor; but there was no living without dogs, and the next was Rover, of whom I have already spoken.

The house in Gloucester Place was a rendezvous for all kinds of dogs. My father's kindliness of nature made him open his house for his four-footed friends, who were too numerous to describe. There was Professor Jameson's Neptune, a Newfoundland dog, Mrs. Rutherfurd's Juba, a pet spaniel, and Wasp, a Dandy Dinmont, belonging to Lord Rutherfurd, who were constant visitors; but the most notorious *sorner* of the whole party was Tory, brother to Fang, both sons of Mr. Blackwood's famous dog, Tickler. Tory paid his visits with the cool assurance of a man of the world, the agreeableness of whose society was not to be questioned for a moment; he remained as long as he wished, was civil and good-humored to every one, but, as a matter of course, selected the master of the house as his chief companion, walked with him, and patron-

* *Noctes Ambrosianæ.* † Ibid.

ized him. I think he looked upon himself as the binding link between the bitter Tory of the old *régime*, and the moderate Conservative of the new. There was evidently a feeling of partisanship in his mind as he took up his position at the door of Mr. Blackwood's shop, either to throw the Professor off or take him up, as the case might be. I never knew so eccentric a dog as Tory; he had many friends, but his ways were queer and wandering. There was no place of public amusement he did not attend; his principles were decidedly those of a dog about town; and though serious, grave, and composed in deportment, he preferred stir and excitement to rest and decorum. Tory was never known to go to church, but at the door of the theatre, or at the Assembly Rooms, he has been seen to linger for hours. He was a long-backed yellow terrier, with his front feet slightly turned out, and an expression of countenance full of mildness and wisdom. Tory continued his visits to Gloucester Place, and his friendship for the Professor, for several years, but he did not neglect other friends, for he exhibited his partiality for many individuals in the street, accompanying them in their walk, and perhaps going home with them. This erratic and independent mode of existence brought him much into notice. There must be many in Edinburgh who remember his knowing look and strange habits.

One other such companion must be mentioned, the last my father ever had; he belonged to his son Blair, and was originally the property of a cab-driver in Edinburgh. Grog was his name, and it argues the unpoetical position he held in early life. He was the meekest and gentlest, and almost the smallest doggie I ever saw. His color was a rich chestnut brown; his coat, smooth and short, might be compared to the wing of a pheasant; and as he lay nestling in the sofa, he looked much more like a bird than a dog. I think he never followed my father in the street, their intimacy being confined entirely to domestic life; he was too *petit* to venture near Christopher as he strode along the street, but many a little snooze he took within the folds of his ample coat, or in the pocket of his jacket, or sometimes on the table among his papers. I cannot pretend to say of what breed Grog had come; he had little, comical, turned-out feet; he was a cosy, coaxing, mysterious, half-mouse, half-bird-like dog; a fancy article, and might have been bought very fitly from a bazaar of lady's work, made up for the occasion, and sold at a high price on account of his rarity. He died easily, being found one morning on his master's pillow lifeless; his little heart had ceased to beat during the night. The Professor was very sad when he died, and vowed he never would have any more dogs—and he kept his vow.

In connection with this subject, there remains something to be said of his continued devotion to the birds mentioned in an earlier part of this Memoir. I think it was the love of the beautiful in all created things that made my father admire the glossy plumage, delicate snake-like head, and noble air of game birds—the aristocracy of their species. For many months he pampered and fed no fewer than *sixty-two* of these precious bipeds in the back-green of his house. The noise made by this fearful regiment of birds beggars all description, yet, be it said, for the honor of human patience and courtesy, not a single complaint ever came from friend or neighbor; for months it went on, and still this

"Bufera infernal"

was listened to in silence.*

Fearing lest any of his pets should expand their wings and take flight, their master sought to prevent this by clipping a wing of each. He chanced to fix upon a day for this operation when his son-in-law, Mr. Gordon, was occupied in his room with his clerk, the apartment adjoining which was the place of rendezvous. Chanticleer, at no time "most musical, most melancholy" of birds, on this occasion made noise enough to "create a soul under the ribs of death." Such an uproar! sounds of fluttering of feathers, accompanied by low chucklings, half hysterical cackling, suppressed crowing, and every sign of agitation and rage that lungs not human could send forth. During the whole of this proceeding, extraordinary as it may have appeared to the uninitiated ear, not an observation escaped the lips of the clerk, who for more than an hour was subjected to "this lively din."

If, however, the silence of neighbors did honor to their virtue, there were distresses and perplexities which domestic tongues

* His medical attendant naïvely relates that one day when the Professor took him into his "aviary," and pointed out the varied beauties of his birds, the Doctor asked, "Do they never fight?" "Fight!" replied the Professor, "you little know the noble nature of the animal; he will not fight unless he is incited; but," added he, with a humorous twinkle of the eye, "put a hen among them, and I won't answer for the peace being long observed ——and so it hath been since the beginning of the world," added the old man eloquent.

found no difficulty in expressing. Two of the birds fell sick, and change of air was considered necessary for their restoration to health. A happy thought suggested to the Professor, that an hospital might be found for the invalids in a room of the attic story, where boxes and various unused articles of the *ménage* were kept, in short, the lumber-room, not unfrequently, however, a repository for very valuable articles—so far belying its name. In this apartment, for more than a week, walked in undisturbed quiet the two invalids, tended, fed, and visited many times during each day by their watchful patron. Health by those means was restored, and nothing now remained but to remove the pets to their old abode in the back-green, where they crowed and strutted more insolently than ever. A few days after the lumber-room had been evacuated by its feathered tenants, the Professor's daughters ascended to the said apartment, happy in the possession there—secure in a well-papered trunk—of certain beautiful ball-dresses to be worn that very night in all the freshness of unsullied crape and ribbons. What sight met their eyes on opening the door of the room! Horrible to say, the elegant dresses were lying on the floor in a corner, soiled, torn, and crumpled, in fact useless. The box in which they had been so carefully laid, had been, on account of its size, at once secured by the Professor as an eligible coop for his birds. The dresses were of no value in his eyes; probably he did not know what they were; so tossing them ruthlessly out, he left them to their fate. It was quite evident, from the appearance they presented, that along with the empty trunk—according to the caprice of the fowls—they had been used as a *nest*. To imagine the feelings of the young ladies at the sight of their fair vanities, "all tattered and torn," is to call up a subject which, even at this distant date, causes a natural pang. It was a trial certainly not borne with much patience, and no doubt, in the hour of disappointment, called forth expressions of bitter and undisguised hatred towards all animated nature in the shape of *feathers*. The *aviary* was after a time shut up, and all its inhabitants were sent off in various directions. The following note to Dr. Moir will show how they were disposed of:—

"6 GLOUCESTER PLACE, *Monday*.

"MY DEAR SIR:—I have a game-cock of great value which I wish to walk (as it is technically termed) for a few months. Can you take him in? This will depend entirely on your setting any value on the bird you now may have, and who, I presume, is Dunghill. If you do, on no account displace him from his own throne. If you do not, I will bring mine down on Thursday, and see him safely deposited in your back court. In that case, his present majesty must either be put to death or expatriated, as if put together they will fall by mutual wounds. Yours affectionately,

"J. Wilson."

Apparently the only article from his pen during 1840 in *Blackwood* was a review of "A Legend of Florence," by Leigh Hunt. If he had not long ere that made the *amende honorable* for the unjust bitterness of the past, he certainly in this review used "the gracious tact, the Christian art," to heal all wounds, illustrating finely his own memorable words, "The *animosities* are mortal, but the *humanities* live forever."

Preparatory to beginning an essay upon Burns, which he had engaged to write for the Messrs. Blackie, he was desirous to seek the best domestic traces of him that could be found, and naturally turned to Dumfriesshire for such information. Two interesting letters to Mr. Thomas Aird, will, better than words of mine, show how earnestly he set about his work, although I cannot, at the same time, avoid drawing attention to certain expressions of anxious interest concerning the better part of the man. For example, his desire to hear "if Burns was a church-goer, regular or irregular, and to what church." All his inquiries show a tender sympathy, a Christian desire to place that erring spirit justly before men, for well did he know how in this world faults are judged. There is a touching simplicity, too, in the personal allusions in these words, "*Her* eyes never having looked on the Nith."

"*May* 3, 1840.

"My dear Mr. Aird:—I have been ill with rose in my head for more than a fortnight, and it is still among the roots of my hair, but in about a week or so, I think I shall be able to move in the open air without danger. I have a leaning towards Dumfriesshire, it being unhaunted by the past, or less haunted than almost any other place, *her* eyes never having looked on the Nith. Perhaps thereabouts I might move, and there find an hour of peace. Is Thornhill a pleasant village? and is there an inn between it and Dumfries? Is there an inn in the pass of Dalvine? Is Penpont habitable quietly for a few days, or any of the pretty village-inns in that district? Pray let me hear from you at your leisure *how the land lies.* Perhaps I may afterwards step down to your town for a day, but I wish, if I make out a week's visit to Nithsdale or neighborhood, to do so unknown but to yourself. Affectionately yours, JOHN WILSON."

Four months later we find him writing again to the same friend:—

"EDINBURGH, *Sept.* 24, 1840.

"MY DEAR MR. AIRD:—I have at last set to work—if that be not too strong an assertion—on my paper about Burns, so long promised to the Messrs. Blackie of Glasgow, for *The Land of Burns.* They have in hand about fifty printed quarto pages, but some of it has not been returned to me to correct for press. They expect, I believe, thirty or fifty more.

"Can you find out from good authority in Dumfries (Jessie Lewars, they say, is yet alive, and is Mrs. Thomson) if Burns was a church-goer at Dumfries, regular or irregular, and to what church? 2. If he was on habits of intimacy with any clergyman or clergymen in the town—as, for example, Dr. Burnside? In 1803, I stayed two days with the Burnsides—all dear friends of mine *then*, and long afterwards, though *now* the survivors are to me like the dead. I then called with Mary Burnside,* now Mrs. Taylor, in Liverpool, on Mrs. Burns. Robert I remember at Glasgow College, but hardly knew him, and I dare say he does not remember me. 3. Did any clergyman visit him on his dying bed; and is it supposed that when dying the Bible was read by him more than formerly or not? 4. Had Burns frequent, rare, or regular family worship at Dumfries? At Ellisland I think he often had. If these questions can be answered affirmatively, in whole or in part, I shall say something about it; if not, I shall be silent, or nearly so. In either case I hope I shall say nothing wrong.

"I have not left Edinburgh since I saw you, but for a day or so, and I won't leave it till this contribution to *The Life of Burns* is finished. Then I intend going for a week to Kelso, and from the 20th October to ditto April, if spared, be in this room, misnamed a

* Mary Burnside was the friend and confidante of the "Orphan Maid," whose image was so hard to tear from his young heart.

study—it is a sort of library. I am alone with one daughter, my good Jane; her mother's name, and much of her nature—but not . . . Yours affectionately, JOHN WILSON."

During this summer he went into Dumfries and Galloway, accompanied by his two sons. I have an interesting account of a visit he paid to the Rev. George Murray of Balmaclellan, Glenkens, with a day's fishing in Lochinvar, but it is too long for insertion.

In speaking of his room, which he calls "a sort of library," something may be said of that careless habit which overtook him in his later years, and gave to his whole appearance an air of reckless freedom. His room was a strange mixture of what may be called order and untidiness, for there was not a scrap of paper, or a book, that his hand could not light upon in a moment, while to the casual eye, in search of discovery, it would appear chaos, without a chance of being cleared away.

To any one whose delight lay in beauty of furniture, or quaint and delicate ornament, well-appointed arrangements, and all that indescribable fascination caught from *nick-nacks* and articles of *vertu*, that apartment must have appeared a mere lumber-room. The book-shelves were of unpainted wood, knocked up in the rudest fashion, and their volumes, though not wanting in number or excellence, wore but shabby habiliments, many of them being tattered and without backs. The chief pieces of furniture in this room were two cases: one containing specimens of foreign birds, a gift from an admirer of his genius across the Atlantic, which was used incongruously enough sometimes as a wardrobe; the other was a book-case, but not entirely devoted to books; its glass doors permitted a motley assortment of articles to be seen. The spirit, the tastes and habits of the possessor were all to be found there, side by side like a little community of domesticities.

For example, resting upon the *Wealth of Nations* lay shining coils of gut, set off by pretty pink twinings. Peeping out from *Boxiana*, in juxtaposition with the *Faëry Queen*, were no end of delicately dressed *flies;* and pocket-books well filled with gear for the "gentle craft" found company with Shakspere and Ben Jonson; while fishing-rods, in pieces, stretched their elegant length along the shelves, embracing a whole set of poets. Nor was the gravest philosophy without its contrast, and Jeremy Taylor, too, found innocent repose in the neighborhood of a tin box of barley-sugar, excellent as when bought "at my old man's." Here and there, in the interstices between books, were stuffed what appeared to be dingy, crumpled bits of paper—these were bank-notes, his *class fees*—not unfrequently, for want of a purse, thrust to the bottom of an old worsted stocking, when not honored by a place in the book-case. I am certain he very rarely counted over the fees taken from his students. He never looked at or touched money in the usual way; he very often forgot where he put it; saving when these stocking banks were his humor; no one, for its own sake, or for his own purposes, ever regarded riches with such perfect indifference. He was like the old patriarch whose simple desires were comprehended in these words:—"If God will be with me, and keep me in the way I am to go, and give me bread to eat, and raiment to put on"—other thought of wealth he had not. And so there he sat, in the majesty of unaffected dignity, surrounded by a homeliness that still left him a type of the finest gentleman; courteous to all, easy and unembarrassed in address, wearing his *néglige* with as much grace as a courtier his lace and plumes, nor leaving other impression than that which goodness makes on minds ready to acknowledge superiority; seeing there "the elements so mixed in him, that nature might stand up and say to all the world, This was a man."

"Writing for Blackwood" were words that bore no pleasant significance to my ears in the days of childhood. Well do I remember, when living long ago in Ann Street, going to school with my sister Margaret, that, on our return from it, the first question eagerly put by us to the servant as she opened the door was, "Is papa busy to-day; is he writing for Blackwood?" If the inquiry was answered in the affirmative, then off went our shoes, and we crept up stairs like mice. I believe, generally speaking, there never was so quiet a nursery as ours. Thus "writing for Blackwood" found little favor in our eyes, and the grim old visage of Geordie Buchanan met with very rough treatment from our hands. If, as sometimes happened, a number of the Magazine found its way to the nursery, it never failed to be tossed from floor to ceiling, and back again, until tattered to our hearts' content. In due time we came to appreciate better the value of these labors, when we learned what love and duty there was in them; and a good lesson of endurance and power the old man taught by the very manner of his work. How he set about it, *à propos* of his study, may claim a few words of description.

His habit of composition, or rather I should say the execution of it, was not always ordered best for his comfort. The amazing rapidity with which he wrote, caused him too often to delay his work to the very last moment, so that he almost always wrote under compulsion, and every second of time was of consequence. Under such a mode of labor there was no hour left for relaxation. When regularly in for an article for Blackwood, his whole strength was put forth, and it may be said he struck into life what he had to do at a blow. He at these times began to write immediately after breakfast, that meal being dispatched with a swiftness commensurate with the necessity of the case before him. He then shut himself into his study, with an express command that no one was to disturb him, and he never stirred from his writing-table until perhaps the greater part of a "Noctes" was written, or some paper of equal brilliancy and interest completed. The idea of breaking his labor by taking a constitutional walk never entered his thoughts for a moment. Whatever he had to write, even though a day or two were to keep him close at work, he never interrupted his pen, saving to take his night's rest, and a late dinner served to him in his study. The hour for that meal was on these occasions nine o'clock; his dinner then consisted invariably of a boiled fowl, potatoes, and a glass of water—he allowed himself no wine. After dinner he resumed his pen till midnight, when he retired to bed, not unfrequently to be disturbed by an early printer's boy; although sometimes, these familiars did not come often enough or early enough for their master's work,* as may be seen from the following note to Mr. Ballantyne:—

* That these familiars were not always so dilatory, the following humorous description will testify:—"O these printers' devils! Like urchins on an ice-slide *keeping the pie warm*, from cock-crow till owl-hoot do they continue in unintermitting succession to pour from the far-off office down upon Moray Place or Buchanan Lodge, one imp almost on the very shoulders of another, without a minute devil-free, crying, 'Copy! copy!' in every variety of intonation possible in gruff or shrill; and should I chance to drop asleep over an article, worn down by protracted sufferings to mere skin and bone, as you see, till the wick of my candle—one to the pound—hangs drooping down by the side of the melting mutton, the two sunk stories are swarming with them all a-hum! Many, doubtless, die during the year, but from such immense numbers they are never missed any more than the midges you massacre on a sultry summer eve. Then the face and figure of one devil are so like another's—the people who have time to pay particular attention to their personal appearance, which I have not, say they are as different as sheep. That tipsy Thammuz is to me all one with Bowzy Beelzebub," &c.—*Noctes*.

"The boy was told to call this morning at seven, and said he would, but he has not come till . . . . I rose at five this morning on purpose to have the sheets ready. I wish you could order the devils to be more punctual, as they never by any accident appear in this house at a proper time. The devil who broke his word is he who brought *the first packet last night.* The devil who brought the second, is in this blameless. I do not wish the first devil to get more than his due: but you must snub him for my sake. For a man who goes to bed at two, does not relish leaving it at five, except in case of life or death. Would you believe it, I am a *little* angry just now?

J. W."

I do not exaggerate his power of speed, when I say he wrote more in a few hours than most able writers do in a few days; examples of it I have often seen in the very manuscript before him, which, disposed on the table, was soon transferred to the more roomy space of the floor at his feet, where it lay "thick as autumnal leaves in Vallombrosa," only to be piled up again quickly as before. When I look back to the days when he sat in that confused, dusty study, working sometimes like a slave, it seems to me as if Hood's "Song of the Shirt," with a difference of burden, would apply in its touching words to him; for it was

"Write, write, write,
While the cock is crowing aloof;
And write, write, write,
Till the stars shine through the roof;"

And so was his literature made, that delightful periodical literature which, "say of it what you will, gives light to the heads and heat to the hearts of millions of our race. The greatest and best men of the age have not disdained to belong to the Brotherhood; and thus the hovel holds what must not be missing in the hall—the furniture of the cot is the same as that of the palace; and duke and ditcher read their lessons from the same page."

He never, even in very cold weather, had a fire in his room; nor did it at night, as most apartments do, get heat from gas, which he particularly disliked, remaining faithful to the primitive candle—a large vulgar tallow, set in a suitable candlestick composed of ordinary tin, and made after the fashion of what is called a kitchen candlestick. What his fancy for this was I cannot say, but he never did, and would not, make use of any other.

From 1840 to 1845 there were only two papers contributed by him to Blackwood, viz., the review of Leigh Hunt's *Legend of Florence*, already spoken of, and a laudatory criticism of Macaulay's *Lays of Ancient Rome.* The latter appeared in December, 1842. This cessation from labor arose in the first instance from a paralytic affection of his right hand, which attacked him in May, 1840, and disabled him for nearly a year. It was the first warning he received that his great strength and wonderful constitution lay under the same law as that which commands the weakest. Writing thenceforward became irksome, and the characters traced by his pen are almost undecipherable. This attack gradually wore away, but it was during its continuance, and for years after, that he imposed upon himself rules of total abstinence from wine and every kind of stimulant. Toast and water was the only beverage of which he partook.

I have nothing more to relate of this time, nor are there any other traces of literary occupation beyond that belonging directly to his College duties. The remaining portion of this year must be permitted to pass in silence; and not again till the summer of 1841, is there a trace of any thing but what belongs to a retired and quiet life.

In June, 1841, he presided at a large public dinner given in honor of Mr. Charles Dickens,* and immediately afterwards started for the Highlands. The following letter to Mr. Findlay recalls recollections of that delightful tour. I was then with him at Rothesay, as his communication shows, on occasion of a melancholy nature, which, however, at that period did not result as was anticipated, and left the summer months free from any other sorrow than that of anxiety. Mrs. Gordon rallied for a time, and was well enough to bear removal to Edinburgh in the autumn, but the sad condition in which she was brought friends around her, of whom my father was one; and on one of these visits to Rothesay, he made from thence a short detour by Inverary and Loch Awe, taking me with him, along with his eldest son John.

"ROTHESAY, *Thursday Night,*
July 1, 1841.

"MY DEAR ROBERT:—Gordon and I left Edinburgh suddenly by

* Reported in *Scotsman*, June 26, 1841

the night mail on Monday, and arrived here on Tuesday forenoon. Dr. Hay and my daughter Mary followed in the afternoon, in consequence of the illness of Mrs. Gordon, senior, who, I fear, is dying. To-day, Mary and Gordon had nearly met a fatal accident, having been upset in a car, over a considerable depth among rocks on the shore-road, along with their friend Mr. Irvine, and his son. All were for a while insensible except Mary, and all have been a good deal hurt. Mary was brought home in Mrs. T. Douglas's carriage, and is going on well. In a day or two she will be quite well; and Gordon is little the worse. It was near being a fatal accident, and had a frightful look. I was not of the party. Mrs. Gordon's condition and Mary's accident will keep me here a day or two, so my plans are changed for the present, and I shall not be at Easter Hill till next week. Be under no anxiety about Mary, for she has recovered considerably, and will soon again be on her feet. My hand is not so well to-day, and I fear you will hardly be able to read this scrawl. Yours affectionately, JOHN WILSON."

At no time did my father ever appear so free from care as when communing with nature. With him it was indeed communion. He did not, as many do when living in the presence of fine scenery, show any impatience to leave one scene in order to seek another; no restless desire to be on the top of a mountain, or away into some distant valley; but he would linger in and about the place his heart had fixed to visit. All he desired was there before him; it was almost a lesson to look at his countenance at such moments. There was an expression, as it were, of melancholy, awe, and gratitude, a fervent inward emotion pictured outwardly. His fine blue eye seemed as if, in and beyond nature, it saw some vision that beatified the sight of earth, and sent his spirit to the gates of heaven.

I remember walking a whole day with him, rambling about the neighborhood of Cladich; scarcely a word was uttered. Now and then he would point out a spot, which sudden sun-gleams made for a moment what he called a "sight of divine beauty;" and then again, perhaps when some more extended and lengthened duration of light overspread the whole landscape, making it a scene of matchless loveliness, gently touching my arm, he signified, by a motion of his hand, that I too must take in and admire what he did not express by words; silence at such moments was the key to more intense enioyment. We sat down to rest on an eminence at the head of Loch Awe, when the midday sun glittered over every island and promontory, streaking the green fields with lines of gold. Not a sound escaped his lips; but when, after a while, the softening shades of afternoon lent a less intense color to the scene, he spoke a few words, saying: "Long, long ago, I saw such a sight of beauty here, that if I were to tell it no one would believe it; indeed, I am not sure whether I can describe what I saw; it was truly divine! I have written something very poor and feeble in attempt to describe that incomparable sight, which I cannot now read; but to my dying day I shall not forget the vision."

Did this vision suggest "Lays of Fairyland?"—taking too, in after years, another form than verse. It appeared in one of the most beautiful morsels of prose composition he ever wrote, which so impressed Lord Jeffrey's mind, he never was tired of reading it.

It is a description of a fairy's funeral, and rather than refer the reader to the volume and page where it is to be found, I give the extract, as in fitting association with Loch Awe and the unforgotten vision or poet's dream near the brow of Ben Cruachan:—

"There it was, on a little river island, that once, whether sleeping or waking we know not, we saw celebrated a fairy's funeral. First we heard small pipes playing, as if no bigger than hollow rushes that whisper to the night winds; and more piteous than aught that trills from earthly instrument was the scarce audible dirge! It seemed to float over the stream, every foam-bell emitting a plaintive note, till the fairy anthem came floating over our couch, and then alighting without footsteps among the heather. The pattering of little feet was then heard, as if living creatures were arranging themselves in order, and then there was nothing but a more ordered hymn. The harmony was like the melting of musical dewdrops, and sang, without words, of sorrow and death. We opened our eyes, or rather sight came to them when closed, and dream was vision. Hundreds of creatures, no taller than the crest of the lapwing, and all hanging down their veiled heads, stood in a circle on a green plat among the rocks; and in the midst was a bier, framed as it seemed of flowers unknown to the Highland hills; and on the bier a fairy lying with uncovered face, pale as a lily, and motionless as the snow. The dirge grew fainter and fainter, and then died quite away; when two of the creatures came from the circle, and took their station, one at the head, the other at the foot of the bier. They sang alternate measures, not louder than the twittering of the awakened woodlark before it goes up the dewy air, but dolorous and full of the desolation of death. The flower-bier stirred; for the spot on which it lay sank slowly down, and in a few moments the greensward was smooth as ever, the very dews glittering above the buried fairy. A cloud passed over the moon; and, with a choral lament, the funeral troop sailed duskily away, heard afar off, so still was the midnight solitude of the glen. Then the disenthralled Orchy began to rejoice as before, through all her streams and falls; and at the sudden leaping of the waters and outbursting of the moon, we awoke."

I know not what the custom of authors is with regard to their own works, but this is true, that Professor Wilson never read what he wrote after it was published. He never spoke of himself but with the greatest humility. If egotism he possessed, it belonged entirely to the playful spirit of his writings, as seen in the lighter touches of the "Noctes." It was this humility that gave so great a charm to his graver conversation; and in listening to him, you felt perfectly convinced that truth was the guiding principle of all he said. There was no desire to produce an impression by startling theories, or by careless off-hand *bits* of brilliancy—the glow without heat. Simple, earnest, eloquent, and vigorous, his opinion carried the weight with it which belongs to all in whom implicit confidence rests. I never knew any one the *truth* of whose nature, at a glance, was so evident; not a shadow of dissemblance ever crossed that manly heart. His sympathies are best understood in examples of the love which gentle and simple bore to him.

Fortunately, one of the few letters I ever received from him has been preserved. It brings the reader to 1842, when it will show him in one of his happiest moods. He has shaken the dust of the pavement from his feet, and pitched his tent for the time being on the pastoral slopes of a retired valley, the beautiful boundary of the river Esk, renowned in story for the adventures of "Young Lochinvar." There, in the spring of the year, he rambled, full of interest and occupation, not angling, or loitering through day-dreams by holm or shaw, but looking on with approving eye, suggesting and aiding, as circumstances required, in the appointment of a new house for his son John, who had just entered upon the pleasant, though anxious, toil of a farmer's life.

As the summer advanced I was to join him there. Meanwhile he writes a description of the *locale*, so beautifully minute in character that it may stand as a daguerreotype of the scene. I offer the letter as one of the best specimens of his domestic correspondence:—

"BILLHOLM, LANGHOLM,
Friday Forenoon, May 27, 1842.

"MY DEAR MARY:—We left Linhope on Wednesday, dined at the farmer's ordinary in Langholm, and came to Billholm in the evening. Yesterday we were all occupied all day taking stock on the hills—sixty score; twelve gentlemen dined, thirty-four shepherds and herdsmen, ten horses, and twenty-five dogs. The scene surpassed description, but it is over. This morning the party (with Billholm and Menzion at their head) went off for a similar purpose to Craighope, distant some ten miles; and Billholm, I believe, will return with Mr. Scott (the outgoing tenant) in the evening. Meanwhile I am left alone, and shall send this and some other letters to Langholm by a lad, as *there is no post.* That is inconvenient—very.

"In a day or two we shall be more quiet, but you can have no idea of the bustle and importance of all at this juncture, nor has John an hour to spare for any purpose out of his own individual concerns.

"This place is, beyond doubt, in all respects sweet and serene, being the uppermost farm in the valley of the Esk before it becomes bare. It is not so rich or wooded as a few miles farther down, but is not treeless; the holms or haughs are cultivated and cheerful; the Esk about the size of the Tweed at the Crook, and the hills not so high as the highest about Innerleithen, but elegantly shaped, and in the best style of pastoral.

"The house 'shines well where it stands,' on a bank sloping down to the river, which is not above twenty yards from the door, so Goliah* has nothing to do but walk in and float down to Langholm. But after Port Bannatyne he is safe against water. It fronts the river; many pleasant holms in the middle distance, and the aforesaid hills about a mile off, surrounding the horizon. Sufficient

* One of his grandchildren.

trees up and down the banks; but the view in front open, not exposed. The house was originally of this common kind: door in the middle, window on each side, three windows above, and windowless roof. A stone portico, since erected, takes away the formality, and breaks the blast. Freestone, neat with a window, good place for a clock, or even a 'beetle.' Entering through a glass door into the passage, to the left is the drawing-room, about sixteen feet square, I think, though I have not measured it yet; one window looking to the front, another up the river into a close scene pretty with trees; a most pleasant parlor.

"To the right is *the* parlor, 15 feet by 12, small no doubt, but lodgeable and comfortable. Up-stairs (which face you on your entrance) are four bedrooms, all comfortable; the two to the front excellent and fit for anybody; one of them with a small dressing-room with a window. I forgot to say, that behind the drawing-room is a pretty little room for a boudoir, study, or bedroom. All these rooms are papered, not, perhaps, as we would have papered them, but all neat and tidy, and not to be needlessly found fault with. So done only two years ago; so is the passage and staircase. An addition had been made to the house at the end to the right hand; and on the ground floor is the dining-room, into which you enter through the aforesaid parlor. It is, I believe, 18 feet by 16. One window looks to the front, and one into a grove of trees. It is oil-painted, of the color of dark brick-dust, with a gilt moulding; rather ugly at first sight, but I am trying to like it, and, for the present, it will do. Doors, etc., of all the rooms, good imitation of oak.

"Above the dining-room, and behind it overhead, are two largish rooms, very low in the roof, communicating with one of the best bedrooms aforesaid, and used formerly as nurseries.

"So there are, in fact, seven bedrooms.

"There is a good kitchen (fatally to me, not to John) near the dining-room, and back kitchen, also servants' hall, as it is called, or rather *butler's* pantry—a very comfortable and useful place—and fitted up with presses, which John bought. There is a woman-servant's room, with two beds; ditto, ditto, man-servant's. A storeroom—good size—and a large dark closet, fit to hold the six tin canisters, though they were sixty, and other things besides. Behind are a few out-houses in rather a shaky condition. The farm-offices are about 100 or 150 yards from the house. The garden is an oblong, containing, I should think, about 1½ acres. One end joins the house; one side is walled, and the farther end; the other side, hedged prettily, and with many lilacs, runs along the banks of the river, and 'tis a very pretty garden indeed. Fruit-trees rather too old, and gooseberry-bushes too; but the latter show a pretty good crop, and I counted 120 bushes. There are also currants and *rasps*, and a promising strawberry bed. Every thing in it will be late this season, as it was dressed since John came here, only three weeks ago, but every thing is growing. The furniture has not yet made its appearance, but I believe is at Langholm, and I shall hear about it by return of my messenger.

"I will write again first opportunity, and expect to be at home by the middle of the week. Observe the directions in my last letter. Love to Blair and Umbs, Gordon and Goliah, Lexy and Adele, Taglioni, Mary Anne, and the rest.

"Your affectionate father, JOHN WILSON."

Almost the whole of this summer was spent at Billholm. The winter, coming again with its usual routine of work, calls him to town somewhere about October. In December his fine "Roman hand" strikes fire once more through the languid ribs of "Maga," and he greets with good heart and will the *Lays of Ancient Rome*. No *arrière pensée* of political differences obtrudes its ill-concealed remembrance through his words. What is it to him whether it be Whig or Tory who writes, when genius, with star-like light, "flames in the forehead of the morning sky?" "What! poetry from Macaulay? Ay, and why not? The House hushes itself to hear him, even when 'Stanley is the cry.' If he be not the first of critics (spare our blushes), who is? Name the young poet who could have written *The Armada*, and kindled, as if by electricity, beacons on all the brows of England till night grew day! The young poets, we said, all want fire. Macaulay is not one of the set, for he is full of fire."

And so does he proceed, with honest words of praise, to the end, giving what is due to all. More of his treatment of this noble enemy in another place.

As I have already remarked, there was nothing written for *Blackwood* during the years 1842–'44. What was he about?

What right has such a question to be put? Is literature worked as if on a tread-mill, under the hand of a task-master; or is the public voice never to cease from the weary cry of "give, give?"

The contents of the following letter to Dr. Moir will show that he was not absolutely idle:—

"*4th Oct.*, 1842.

"MY DEAR SIR:—I have lost several days in looking over till I am sick, all *Blackwood*, for a description of Christopher's house in Moray Place. It is somewhere pictured as the House of Indolence, and with some elaboration, as I once heard Horatio Macculloch, the painter, talk of it with rapture. I wish you would cast over in your mind where the description may be, as I would fain put it into a chapter in vol. iii. of 'Recreations' now printing. Sometimes a reader remembers what a writer forgets. It is not in a 'Noctes.' I read it with my own eyes not long ago; but I am ashamed of myself to think how many hours (days) I have wasted in wearily trying to recover it. Perhaps it may recur to you without much effort of recollection. Yours affectionately,

"JOHN WILSON."

CHAPTER XVI.

LITERARY AND DOMESTIC LIFE.

1844–'48.

WE now come to February, 1844, where an old correspondent reappears, whose letters, if not written in the sunny spirit of *bonhomie*, have a peculiar excellence of their own. Never did graver's tool give more unmistakable sharpness to his lines, than the pen of John Gibson Lockhart gave to his words. The three following letters are as characteristic of his satirical power as any of those off-hand caricatures that shred his best friends to pieces, leaving the most poetical of them as bereft of that beautifying property, as if they had been born utterly without it. I have seen various portraits of my father from that pencil, each bearing the grotesque image of the artist's fancy, yet all undeniably like. So was it his humor, nearly to the end, to look upon men and things with the chilling eye of the satirist.

"25*th March*, 1844.

"MY DEAR WILSON:—I have spelt out your letter with labor,* but great ultimate contentment.

"Alexander Blackwood had given me, by yesterday's post, my first information touching that enormous absurdity of —— *in re* Kemp deceased, and I answered him, expressing my deep thankfulness for the result of your interference; but I had not quite understood with how much difficulty you contended, and how nearly you were alone in the fight against eternal desecration. If Kemp had been put there, —— must in due time have polluted the same site *à fœculentiore.* Of the *other* suggestion nipt in the bud, never shall I breathe a whisper to any human being. For some time I have fancied Scotland must be all mad; I never see a Scotch paper without being strengthened in that conviction, but this is the *ne plus ultra!*

"I have not read any novel lately, far less written one. I do not even guess to what new book you allude in your last page. You address me by the name of some *hero*, I suppose, but that is undecipherable by my optics. No bamming here. Do name the book. Is this your sly way of announcing to me some new escapade of the long-haired and longish-headed?

"By the by, Swinton has depicted both hair and head with very admirable skill. I had no notion that there was such stuff in the lad. He will, I am confident, soon be on a par here with Frank Grant, who is clearing £5,000 or £6,000 per annum. I like the C. N. a thousandfold better than Lauder's, and hope to have an engraving of it, same size, very speedily.

"I showed the 'Poemata'† some weeks ago to John Blackwood, and bade him send you a copy. Perhaps to me you owe your knowledge, therefore, of the novel epithet. Horace, however, has 'teterrima belli causa' and I rather suspect *teterrima* carries a delicate *double entendre* in that classical *loc. vald. cit.*

"You have not read the title-page correctly. First, the book is

* This difficulty arose from the circumstance of his correspondent suffering, as has been told, from the weakness in his hand.

† *Poemata Lyrica. Versa Latina Rimante Scripta.* By H. D. Ryder. Simpkin, Marshall, and Co.

published by Simpkin, Marshall, *et Co.* 2d. The author is not Moore, *Dean* (to whom it is dedicated, as a compliment to his 'zeal for the Apostolical succession'), *but* H. Ryder, Canon of Lichfield, son of the late Bishop of Lichfield, and nephew of Lord Harrowby. I fancy the man is simply mad; if not, Lonsdale must handsel his jurisdiction by overwhelming a scandal not inferior to the other Fitz-Eveque H. Marsh's *in re* Miord. That case, by the by, goes to confirm another of my old doctrines, viz., that the Trial by Jury is the grossest of all British humbugs. I forget if it is Swift or Scorpio who sang—

"'Powers Episcopal we know
Must from some apostle flow;
But I'll never be so rude as
Ask how many draw from Judas.'

"Here is another fine spring day. Why don't you come up with Lord Peter for a week or two; or without him? The Government is in a tarnation fix. I suspect Ashley has got very wild, poor fellow —a better lives not; and that we shall have by and by Jack Cade in right earnest. Gleig is chaplain-general of the forces; keeping Chelsea and his living in Kent too. * * * * * Ever yours affectionately, J. G. L.

"Alone and dreary; both my young away from me; I shall soon be left entirely alone in this weary world.

"You read in the papers about Louis Philippe giving Brougham a piece of Gobelins Tapestry, but they did not mention the subject. It is a very fine *picture* indeed—of a worrying-match between two dogs!

"Now I went, a few nights ago, to a large dinner at Brougham's house, and on entering the inner room, there was he with a cane, holding aside the curtains, and explaining the beauties of this masterpiece to—*Plain John!!*

"Literal truth; but absurder than any fiction. The company seemed in agonies of diversion at the unconsciousness of the pair of barons.

"*That week* both *H. B.** and *Punch* had been caricaturing them as the Terriers of the *Times* disgracing a drawing-room!

"All true, as I shall answer, etc."

* Mr. John Doyle, the father of Richard Doyle, author of *Brown, Jones, and Robinson,* "is generally believed to be the author of the celebrated H. B. political sketches, which were a few

There are one or two allusions in this letter which may require a word of explanation.

The first paragraph refers to a proposition made by some parties in Edinburgh, that the remains of Mr. Kemp, the architect of the Scott monument, should have interment beneath it, he having come to an untimely end not long after the completion of his design. Professor Wilson had some trouble in preventing this absurd project being carried out. In the second, there are some playful remarks about a novel; *à propos* of which I may say, that novel-reading was a mental dissipation my father seldom indulged in, regarding that sort of literature, in general, as enervating to the mind and destructive to the formation of good taste. Now and then he was prevailed on to open one, when recommended as very good. *Whitefriars* had just been published; he was delighted with it, and sat down, on the impulse of the moment, to congratulate the author (who could be no other than John G. Lockhart) on his success; and in this belief he addresses him by the title of his hero.*

This letter is almost immediately followed by another:—

"*March* 28, 1844.

"MY DEAR WILSON:—It is not easy to judge of the merit of an architectural design until one (I mean an ignoramus) has seen it in actual stone. I thought the drawing of Scott's monument very good, and I suppose, from what is now executed, you can form a fair opinion. All my remaining anxiety is that the statue should be in *bronze*. Marble will last very few years before you see the work of decay on the surface. Is it too late to make a vigorous effort for this, in my mind, primary object? I have no fear about *money*. I met . . . yesterday at dinner at . . . , and gave her your love. She is a fine creature. I see nothing like her, and were I either young or rich, I should be in danger. She told me Brewster, Chalmers, and all the Frow Kirk are going to start a new Review. How many Reviews are we to have? Is not it odd that the old ones keep afloat at all? but I doubt if they have lost almost any thing as yet. The *Q. R. prints* nearly 10,000, I know, if not quite. Nor have I

years ago so remarkably popular, and which, while exhibiting with abundant keenness the prominent features and peculiarities of the persons caricatured, were always gentlemanly in feeling, and free from any appearance of malice."—Knight's *English Cyclopædia.*

* *Whitefriars* has been ascribed to Miss E. Robinson.

heard that Ebony is declining, in spite of these Hoods and Ainsworths, etc., etc.

" . . . showed me a lot of Edinburgh daguerreotypes—the Candlishes, etc.; that of Sir D. Brewster is by far the best specimen of the art I had ever seen. It is so good, that I should take it very kind if you would sit to the man whom Brewster patronizes *for me.** I should like also to have Sheriff Cay. This art is about to revolutionize book-illustration entirely.

"There is very great uneasiness here about this ten hours' affair. I really expect to see the Government displaced sooner or later by this coalition of Johnny Russell with Ashley, Oastler, and the *Times*. Your old friend, Sir James Graham, is terribly unpopular with both sides of the House. Yet I think his demeanor in private society infinitely more agreeable than Peel's, who, somehow, is not run upon in the same style by any party. Inglis takes kindly to the name of Jack Cade. We shall have him H. B.'d, of course. Ashley speaks well, he has a fine presence, good voice, and his zeal gives him real eloquence now and then; but he has slender talents, and his head has been quite turned by the popularity he has acquired. I seriously fear he will go mad. He lives and moves in an atmosphere of fanaticism, talks quite gravely about the Jews recovering Jerusalem, the Millennium at hand, etc., etc.

"Brougham goes to Paris this week to (*inter alia*) take counsel with Guizot and Dupin about a great humbug (I believe), his new Society for the Amendment of the Law; and, learning that Lyndhurst, Denman, etc., approved, I agreed to be a member on Brougham's request, and went to a meeting yesterday, where he was in the chair. What a restless, perturbed spirit! * * * * *

"Nothing could surprise me now-a-days. The Government have allowed B. to be their saviour so often in the H. of Lords, that they may by and by find it impossible to refuse him even the Seals. I am, you see, idle, and in gossiping vein this morning, having just got rid of a d—d thick Quarterly, I fear, a dull one. Ever affectionately yours, J. G. LOCKHART."

In the next letter, which is the last of this correspondence that has been preserved, it will be seen how pain and inward yearning

* My father did so, and the frontispiece to the present *Memoir* is engraved from Mr. Hill's calotype, by the artist's kind permission.

for things gone from before his eyes had softened a stern nature, bringing it through trials which left him a sadder and a wiser man :—

"FAIR LAWN, TUNBRIDGE,
Easter Wednesday, 1844.

"MY DEAR WILSON :—I had your kind letter here yesterday, and the *resolutions* as to the Scott and Kemp affairs, which seem to me drawn up in the best possible taste, not a word to give offence, and much very delicately calculated to conciliate. I came to this place a week ago, utterly done up in body and mind; but perfect repose and idleness, with cold lamb and home-brewed beer, and no wine nor excitement of any sort, have already done wonders, and in fact convinced me that I might have health again, if I could manage to cut London, and Quarterly Reviews. As for any very lively interest in this life, that is out of the question with me as with you, and from the same fatal date, though I struggled against it for a while, instead of at once estimating the case completely as I think you did. Let us both be thankful that we have children not unworthy of their mothers. I reproach myself when the sun is shining on their young and happy faces, as well as on the violets and hyacinths and bursting leaves, that I should be unable to awaken more than a dim ghost-like semi-sympathy with them, or in any thing present or to come, but so it is. No good, however, can come of these croakings. Like you, I have no plans now—never. Walter must fag hard all this summer in Essex with a Puseyite tutor, if he is to go to Balliol in October with any advantage, and therefore I think it most likely I shall not stir far from London. * * * *

" * * * * I used to have a real friendship for the water of Clyde and some half-dozen of its tributary Calders and Lethans, familiar from infancy; and, most of all, for certain burns with deep rocky beds and cold invisible cascades. As it is, I could be well contented to abide for the rest of this life in such a spot as this same Fairlawn —well named. It is a large ancient house built round a monastic court, with a good park, most noble beeches, and limes and oaks, looking over the rich vale of the Medway, with a tract of rough heath, and holt, and sand-hill, lying behind it, six or seven miles in length, and about two in breadth. This was the original seat of the Vanes; and old Sir Harry lies buried here with many of his ancestors. It is now possessed by Miss Yates, cousin-german to Sir R.

Peel, an excellent, sensible, most kind old lady; stone blind from five years of age, and otherwise afflicted, but always cheerful; too high a Tory to admire the premier, and, *inter alia*, of old Sir Robert's opinion as to the Children question. I am going to-day for a few days to another house in this neighborhood, and shall be in London again by this day week.

"Sir W. Allan writes he has a picture of Sir W. and Anne Scott for the Exhibition. I hope rather than expect to be pleased therewith.

"So Abinger *exit.* He wedded a spry widow who had been anxious for his third son on last August; and on landing at Calais for the honey trip, put herself down 'age 55;' but the Fates were not to be gammoned, nor Lady Venus neither, and the coffin-plate will tell truly: Ann. Ætat. 76. I suppose Pollock will take the place, yet it is not impossible that *H. B.* may fancy it, and if he does, it might not be easy for Peel to give him a rebuff. Ever affectionately yours, J. G. L."

Lockhart's very sorrows are a contrast to those of his friend. There is something of a listless bitterness in the words, "I should be unable to awaken more than a dim ghost-like semi-sympathy with them, or in any thing present or to come." He is stricken, as it were, and will not look up. But my father, with that healthful heart of his, that joyous nature that smiles even in the midst of tears, had scarcely yet laid aside the strong enthusiasm which belonged so remarkably to his youth. His energies are, as may be seen from the following letter to his son John, still directed to the "Kemp affair." The subject is pleasantly mingled with domestic interests concerning Billholm:—

"6 Gloucester Place, *Saturday*, 6*th*, 1844.

"My dear John:—On looking over the portfolio of prints, I thought Harvey's Covenanters, Baptism, and Allan's Burns worth framing, and have got them framed in same style with Allan's Scott in the dining-room. These three make a trio, with Harvey in the middle, which will hang, I think, well on the drawing-room wall opposite the front window.

"The Polish Exiles will hang, I think, well to the right of the door, as you enter the drawing-room, if in the middle, so as at any time to allow of two appropriate pendants. The demure Damsel may range with Victoria. But follow your own taste, which is as good, or better than mine.

"The five will make the room look gay, and they leave this by the wagon on the 8th instant, directed to be left at Langholm till called for.

"I close my session on Friday, the 12th, or perhaps a day or two sooner. The weather here is fine, and I trust you will have a good lambing season in spite of the severities since you left us. I see prices are somewhat better, and trust this year may be considerably more favorable than the last two. My own motions are not fixed for the future; but I shall not leave this before the latter end of May for any other quarter. Four hundred persons were assembled to inter Kemp in the Scott Monument. I heard of it at eleven o'clock; saw M'Neill, and after much angry discussion with a deputation, stopped the funeral, and turned it into the West Kirkyard. They had got leave from . . . and some other fools, and had kept the public ignorant of the proceedings. Very general approbation of our interference is not unmixed with savage or sulky exasperation among the ten-pounders who stood up for their order. It would have been a vulgar outrage. Next day's *Witness* was insolent, but since, there has been a calm sough. The general committee have since passed resolutions approving our conduct. We passed them ourselves, and I moved them in a strong speech, to which there was no reply.

"A Professor of Music was to be chosen on Saturday, the 3d March. We were all met; but neither party could tell how it might go, as there were two doubtful votes. The Bennettites boldly moved, on false and foolish pretence of giving time to a new candidate named Pearson, to postpone the election till the 1st of June; and this motion was carried *by one*. They hope something may occur before then, to give Bennett a better chance; and they expect to have the vote of the Chemical Professor, who is to be elected in a few weeks, which may turn the scales. . . . We are all well, and Mary will visit you soon. I leave Blair, who is well, to speak for his own motions. He has been talking of going to Billholm for some days past. With love from all here and in Carlton Street—I am, your affectionate father, J. WILSON."

Soon after this home-loving spirit has assisted in making the pretty pastoral farm "look gay," we find him in the full energy of his ardent nature, awakening the sympathies of all around him on a subject that moved the whole Scottish nation as with one heart, and ultimately brought a stream of sympathetic souls together to the banks of Doon, till it seemed as if all Scotland had poured its life there to do honor to the memory of Burns.

The Burns Festival was an occasion fitted to call forth the zeal of Wilson's nature, and he worked heart and soul in the cause, with vigor little less than that which impelled him, in "his bright and shining youth," *to walk seventy miles* to be present at a Burns meeting, which he "electrified with a new and peculiar fervor of eloquence, such as had never been heard before."* We have three letters relative to this great gathering; one is addressed to his son-in-law, Mr. Gordon, before it took place, with a view to arranging the toasts:—

"My dear Sheriff:—The toasts now stand well, and we shall not try to improve the arrangement. What you say about the poor dear Shepherd is, I fear, true, though his fame will endure. Neither will his memory have to come in till after Scott and Campbell; and we all know, that even on a generally popular theme, it is very difficult to secure attention and interest far on in the 'Course of Time.' Perhaps the memory of the Shepherd cannot be given at all, for if some prosing driveller, without name or influence, were to give it, it would not do at all. If so, I shall speak of him during what I say of Burns. Will that do? I desire to have your opinion of this; for if you think it would not do, I shall look about for a proper person to give his memory after Alison has spoken. William Aytoun? What should follow? 'The Peasantry,' etc. That toast I recommended to Mr. Ballantine, and we leave it in his hands, or any one he may select to do it for him. If the Justice-General or Lord Advocate were to give 'Lord Eglinton' in a few sentences, it

* Of the Professor's walking feats I have not been able to gather many authentic anecdotes. Mr. Aird mentioned the fact quoted here in his speech at the Burns Festival, and my brother writes me on the subject:—"I have often heard him mention the following. He once walked forty miles in eight hours, but when or where he did it I cannot recollect. On another occasion he walked from Liverpool to Elleray, within the four and twenty hours. I do not know what the distance is, but think it must be somewhere about eighty miles. You are correct about his walking from Kelso to Edinburgh—forty miles, to attend a public dinner. It was in 1822, when the King was there. Once, when disappointed in getting a place in the mail from Penrith to Kendal, he gave his coat to the driver, set off on foot, reached Kendal some time before the coach, and then trudged on to Elleray."

would do well. But such toast is not necessary; for the names might be merely mentioned, and the thanks carried by acclamation. So with all others. These toasts might be set down and assigned, and given as circumstances may permit.

"I shall write to Ballantine to that effect, subject to any alterations; and there is no need to print the toasts, etc., tunes, etc., till all is fixed, a few days before the 6th; vice-chairman, stewards, etc., as no man of course would, on such an occasion, speak of himself, the place assigned him, whatever that may be, speaking for itself.

"Finally, we propose 'The Provost and Magistrates of Ayr and other Burghs,' and 'The Ladies,' of course, with shouts of love and delight. And so finis."

The next letter is from Sergeant Talfourd,* whom he had invited to join the meeting at Ayr:—

"OXFORD, *July* 14, 1844.

"MY DEAR SIR:—Your very kind letter respecting the festival on the banks of the Doon has reached me at this city, where I am on the circuit; and if it were possible for me to meet the wish it so cordially expresses, I should at once recall the answer I felt compelled to give to the invitation of the committee, and look forward with delight to sharing in the enjoyments of the time. When, however, I tell you the sad truth, that on the 6th August we (*i.e.*, the Circuit) shall be at Shrewsbury, and on the 7th shall turn southward to Hereford, so that it will be impossible for me to be in Scotland on the 6th by the utmost exertion, and all the aid of steamboats and railways, without entirely absenting myself from both the Shrewsbury and the Hereford Assizes, and causing serious inconvenience to many, besides the loss to myself, I am sure you will sympathize with the conviction I have reluctantly adopted, that *I cannot* be with you at your most interesting meeting. Our long circuit, which is this year somewhat later than usual, in consequence of the Irish Writ of Error, will not close before the 22d or 23d August, when I hope to take my family to the country you know so well in the neighborhood of Windermere, where Mr. Wordsworth has taken a cottage for us for the holidays. If your festival had, happily for me, occurred while I was there at liberty, I should have embraced, with pleasure I cannot express, the opportunity of

* Sir Thomas Noon Talfourd died in the discharge of his professional duties at the Assizes, 1854.

meeting you under circumstances so original as the celebration of one of the truest poets who ever lived, and of beholding his genius by the light of yours, and then I might perhaps have hoped to induce our great living poet to accompany me. But I am tantalizing myself by fancying impossibilities, and can only hope that Wordsworth may grace your festival, and that all happiness may attend it, and you and yours.

"Believe me to remain, my dear sir, most truly and respectfully yours, T. N. TALFOURD."

The last from the Professor to Aird is characteristic of that gentle courtesy which the chivalry of his nature ever showed to woman. Such traits of kindliness may seem almost too trifling to draw attention to, but they are unfortunately not so common in the routine of intercourse with our fellow-creatures as could be wished:—

"EDINBURGH, *Saturday Evening, August* 17*th*, 1844.

"MY DEAR MR. AIRD:—I looked about for you in all directions, but could not see you on the field or in the Pavilion. I wished most to have had you on the platform, as the procession passed by before the Adelphi. It was very affecting.

"I told the Committee a week or two before the Festival, to invite Mrs. Thomson (Jessie Lewars), and no doubt they did so. But I could get no information about her being there from anybody, so did not allude to her in what I said, lest she might not be present.

"I spoke to a lady in the Aulds' cottage, thinking she was Mrs. Begg, but she told me she was not; giving me her name, which I did not catch. Perhaps she was Mrs. Thomson? I wish you would inquire, and, if so, tell her that I did not hear the name; for, if it was she, I must have seemed wanting in kindness of manner. I saw it stated in a newspaper that she was seated in the Pavilion with Mrs. Begg. I wished I had known that—if it was so; but nobody on the morning of the Festival seemed to know any thing, and Mr. Auld in his cottage naturally enough was so *carried*, that he moved about in all directions with ears inaccessible to human speech.

"A confounded bagpipe and a horrid drum drove a quarter of an hour's words out of my mind, or rather necessitated a close, leaving out a good deal to balance what I did say.

"I intend publishing my address in Blackwood's next number, properly corrected, along with all the others; and, if you can find a place for it in the *Herald*, I wish you would, for I wish the people in the country to see it, if they choose, in right form. Speakers are at the mercy of the *first* reporter, and at the mercy of circumstances.

"I am not without hopes of seeing you at Dumfries this month—or early next. 'Twas a glorious gathering. Yours affectionately,

"John Wilson."

My father was always glad to escape from Edinburgh during the summer, but latterly he required other inducement than the "rod" to take him from home; a solitary "cast" was losing its charm, and he now liked to find companions to saunter with him by loch and stream. This summer his old friend, Dr. Blair, had been visiting him, and was easily prevailed on to take a ramble to the Dochart before returning south. The following letter to his daughter Jane (Umbs or "Crumbs"), tells of his own sport and of the *Wizard's* walks:—

"Luib, *Sunday, June* 1, 1845.

"Dear Crumbs:—We arrived at Luib (pronounced Libe) on the Dochart, foot of Benmore, on Tuesday afternoon at three o'clock, *via* Loch Lomond and Glenfalloch. We soon found ourselves ensconced in a snug parlor looking into a pretty garden, and in every way comfortable. Our bedroom is double-bedded—small; but such beds I have not slept in for one hundred years. Since our arrival till this hour there has not been above twenty drops of rain, and the river (the Dochart) has not been known so low by the oldest inhabitant, who is the landlord—aged eighty-five—deaf and lame—but hearty and *peart*. Wednesday, Thursday, Friday, and Saturday, after breakfast, *I* walked *three* miles up the river, which flows past the inn, and fished down, killing each day with midges about three dozen good trout, like herrings, of course, and about ten dozen of fry—a few of about a pound; none larger. The natives are astonished at my skill, as in such weather fish were never caught before. The Wizard* disappears in the morning, and returns to dinner about six. On Thursday he left Luib about nine, and returned at half-past seven, having been over a range of mountains

* Dr. Alexander Blair.

and back again, certainly two thousand feet high. But on Friday he was much fatigued and kept to the valley, and even yesterday he had not recovered from his fatigue. With respect to myself, I am always knocked up at night, and fresh in the morning. I made right down the middle of the river among huge rocks and stones, avoiding all the pools twenty feet deep, of which there are hundreds, many places utterly dried up, others not a foot deep. In flood or rains it must be a most tremendous river. On Monday I think of going to Loch Narget (Maragan?), about eight miles over the hills, but only if windy and cloudy.

"On the whole, this is the pleasantest inn I ever was at, and the station in all respects delightful. The Wizard takes a *gill of whiskey* daily. I have given up all hopes of rain, and intend staying here a few days longer. We shall be at Cladich on Thursday."

"PORT SONACHAN, *June* 9.

"MY DEAR UMBS:—We left Luib on Thursday, the 5th instant, and reached Cladich at half-past seven. No Williams, nor room for ourselves, so we proceeded three miles to Port Sonachan, where we have been ever since. Friday was a day of storm, and no fishing. Having allowed my boat to drift a few miles to leeward, it took two boatmen three hours to bring me back to port, during which time it rained incessantly, and was bitter cold. I suffered much, and was in fits on Saturday. The fishing was bad, and I only killed nine; but one was a noble fellow, upwards of two pounds. On Monday kept the house all day. To-day fished eight miles down the lake to Castle Ardchonnel, a very fine old ruin on an island, which I had never seen before; landed and dined in the castle with Archy and Sandy, time from three to four o'clock; wound up and returned before the wind, homeward-bound; beheld the Wizard on a point of the loch, and took him in; reached Port Sonachan before seven, and dined sumptuously. Angling had been admirable; sixty-one trout crammed into the basket, which could not have held another. Of these, thirty were from one-half to three-quarters and one pound each; the rest not small; they covered two large tea-trays. It reminded me of the angling thirty and thirty-five years ago. The natives, especially Archy, were astonished.

"I understood the Wizard wrote to Blair yesterday; he enjoys himself much, and walks about from morning to night."

We shall now follow him through a small portion of the year 1845, when he appears to have resumed his work with steady purpose, as may be seen by looking at the Magazine for seven consecutive months. North's Specimens of the "British Critics" make a noble contribution to that periodical. Those papers, along with too many of equal power and greater interest, have found jealous protection within the *ceinture* of its pages, and seem destined to a fate which ought only to belong to the meagre works of mediocrity. The eighth number of "British Critics" was written at Elleray, whither he had gone for a few weeks, tempted by a beautiful summer, and the natural longing of his heart to roam about a place full of so many images, pleasant and sad, of the past. The following note to Mr. Gordon refers to this article:

"ELLERAY, *Wednesday.*

"MY DEAR GORDON:—I am confidently looking for best accounts of dear Mary every day.

"Pray, attend! I have sent a long article to Blackwood—'No. VIII. on Critics,'—about MacFlecnoe, but chiefly the 'Dunciad.' It will be very long—far longer than I had anticipated, or he may wish. It cannot be sent here for correction, and I wish much you would *edit it.*

"Blackwood will give it to you when set up—and I hope corrected in some measure by the printer—along with the MS.; and perhaps *on Tuesday* you may be able to go over it all, and prevent abuses beyond patience. I will trust to you. I also give you power to *leave some out*, if absolutely necessary. Don't let it be *less than thirty-two pages*—if the MS. requires more. In short, I wish the article in this number, and all in if possible. If not, I leave omission to your discretion; but read it all over carefully first, that you may not leave out something referring to something remaining in. 'We ship on the 24th.' Yours ever, in haste for post,

"J. W."

In the same year (1847), when the Philosophical Institution was established in Edinburgh, he was elected its first President, and delivered the opening address. To this honorable office he was re-elected by the members every year as long as he lived.

We have now come to a longer blank, relieved by no letter, by no work. From the autumn of 1845 till that of 1848 there is nothing but silence. Alas! this was but the beginning of the end. Ten years ago, while yet strong in body, though suffering and sad of heart, the melancholy of his mind gave a similar tone to his words, and he wrote of himself as if his days were being consumed swifter than a weaver's shuttle:—"Day after day we feel more and more sadly that we are of the dust, and that we are obeying its doom. This life is felt to be slowly—too swiftly wheeling away with us down a dim acclivity—man knoweth not into what abyss. And as the shows of this world keep receding to our backward gaze, on which gathers now the gloom, and now the glimmer, of this world, hardly would they seem to be, did not memories arise that are realities, and some so holy in their sadness that they grow into hopes, and give assurance of the skies."

With thoughts such as these ever springing from the pure region of his soul, did he go on meeting the common day with hope brightened into cheerfulness, until existence was beautified once more by the conviction that duties were still before him—though one was gone whose approving smile had given impetus to all he did.

The first break to this silence comes in a short letter, written to his old friend Mr. Findlay, inviting him to be present at the marriage of his son John, which took place in July, 1848. This relation was one conducive to his happiness—a fresh tie to keep him hale and strong of heart—making the summer visits to Billholm all the more agreeable by a welcome from its new occupant, whose gentle companionship often cheered his rambles by the river side, or made pleasant a rest beneath the shade of its trees:—

"*Friday, June* 9, 1848.

"My dear Robert:—My son John is to be married on the 22d of this month, at the house of his father-in-law, Mr. G. Bell, 43 Melville Street. We are sorry not to have beds to offer our friends, and a journey to and from Edinburgh may not be convenient to you at this time; but if you, your good lady, and one of your dear daughters, can assist at the ceremony (twelve o'clock) I need not say how welcome will be your presence, and that we shall hope to see you after it at Glo'ster Place.

"Ever affectionately yours, J. Wilson."

It may be seen from a letter to his son Blair, that he had lost no time in paying a visit to the newly-married pair; for he writes from their home on the 28th September, 1848, having taken a peep of the pastoral hills on his way from Elleray, where he had been in the earlier part of the season. His letter speaks of domestic matters only; but it is easy to see a change in his spirit, and that he clings more and more to the circle of young lives around him. Loneliness, as time crept on, was a feeling that easily affected him, so much so, that sometimes on his return from the College, if he found no one in the house, he would turn from the door, and retrace his steps through the streets, until he met with his daughter, or some of his little grandchildren; then all was right, and a walk with them restored him to his wonted spirits. How sadly comes the confession from his lips of the dreariness which fell upon him at Elleray, a place at one time enjoyable as paradise, but where now he could not rest, as these touching words tell: "I have resolved not to return to Elleray, as I should not be able to be there if you had left it. I slept at Bowness the fifth night after my return to Elleray from Hollow Oak; the silence and loneliness of myself at night not being to be borne, though during the day I was tranquil enough." He makes allusion to his hand, "it is very poorly," and so indeed it was, for he had been unable to use it, saving with difficulty, for nearly three years. This weakness annoyed him very much, not more than was natural, if it appeared to him to be the commencement of a greater evil—that fatal breaking up, which saps the strength, and brings age before its time.

His accustomed work goes on, but by fits and starts, according to his bodily vigor. This autumn only one paper was written for *Blackwood*, upon Byron's "Address to the Ocean," one of those beautiful critiques which go so deeply into the true principles of poetry. Its severity may startle at first, but can hardly fail to be acknowledged as just.

His whole heart and soul were in poetry, and he threw out from the intensity of that feeling a hundred little side-lights, that sparkled and danced on and about the commonest things in nature, till, like a long-continued sunbeam, they lengthened and deepened into a broad light, the happiest, the most joyous in the world, radiant with fun, careering, playing the strangest pranks, showing at last, in shape unmistakable, that enviable property which cannot by any skill in the world be planted in a nature that has it not from its cradle. I do not agree with those who hold that humor is the best part of human nature, and that the whole meaning of a man's character may be traced to his humor. But it is an element coming and going, with other qualities, with all that composes the inner spirit; often, it is true, in abeyance, but never crushed; always asserting its rights, not unfrequently with an incongruity which, in its unexpected intrusion, does not rob it of charm, but rather adds to its power.

Wilson's humor has been described as being sometimes too broad; perhaps, in the "Noctes," he occasionally makes use of an *impasto* laid on a little too roughly. But who ever enjoyed his conversation at home or abroad, among the woods and wilds of nature, or on the busy streets of Edinburgh, that was not as often overpowered by his humor as by his wit, by his wisdom as by his eloquence? His manner in mixing the talk with the walk was peculiar. He took several steps alongside of you, conducting you on to the essential point, then, when he had reached that, he stopped, "right-about faced," stood in front of you, looking full at you, and delivered the conclusion, then released you from the stop you were forced to make, walked on a few paces, and turned in the same manner again.

Latterly, a walk to the College was rather too much for him, and he generally took a cab from George Street. This in time became his habit, and gave rise occasionally to the most riotous behavior among the cab-drivers, who used to be on the look-out for his approach, all desirous of driving him. The moment that well-known figure was seen, an uproar began. His appearance and dress were too peculiar not to be recognized a good way off, for no one wore a hat with so broad a brim, covered with such a deep crape, his long hair flowing carelessly about his neck, and his black coat buttoned across his chest, now somewhat portly. Still, despite increasing infirmity, his step was free, and he looked leonine in strength and bearing. So did he when he sat for his photograph to Mr. D. O. Hill, an engraving from which is prefixed to this work. In this product of that wonderful art, then in its infancy, comes out the character of the man; the block, as it were, from nature, not softened down or refined away by that delicacy which so often makes portrait-painting insensate, but great in its original strength; with a something, perhaps more of the man, and a little less of the poet in his look, than painting would have given, yet unmistakable to the very character of the hands, broad and beautiful in form. The hair, not so fine, is rather lost in the hazy shadows of the photograph, but all else is good and true. Why, some one may ask, are those "*weepers*"* on his sleeves?† This was a mark of respect he paid to the memory of his wife, and which he continued to wear as long as he lived, renewing these simple outward memorials with tender regularity. The solicitude he showed about his weepers was very touching. Many a time I have sewed them on while he stood by till the work was finished, never satisfied unless he saw it done himself.

A street scene was described to me by a lady who saw it take place:—

One summer afternoon, as she was about to sit down to dinner, her servant requested her to look out of the window, to see a man cruelly beating his horse. The sight not being a very gratifying one, she declined, and proceeded to take her seat at table. It was quite evident that the servant had discovered something more than the ill-usage of the horse to divert his attention, for he kept his eyes fixed on the window; again suggesting to his mistress that she ought to look out. Her interest was at length excited, and she rose to see what was going on. In front of her house (Moray Place) stood a cart of coals, which the poor victim of the carter was unable to drag along. He had been beating the beast most unmercifully, when at that moment Professor Wilson, walking past, had seen the outrage and immediately interfered. The lady said, that from the expression of his face, and vehemence of his manner, the man was evidently "getting it," though she was unable to hear what was said. The carter, exasperated at this interference, took up his whip in a threatening way, as if with intent to strike the Professor. In an instant that well-nerved hand twisted it from the coarse fist of the man, as if it had been a straw, and walking quietly up to the cart he unfastened its *trams*, and hurled the whole weight of coals into the street. The rapidity with which this was done left the driver of the cart speechless. Meanwhile, poor Rosinante, freed from his burden, crept slowly away, and the Professor, still clutching the whip in one hand, and leading the horse in the other, pro-

* "Weepers" are "stripes of muslin or cambric stitched on the extremities of the sleeves of a black coat or gown, as a badge of mourning."—*Jamieson.*

† They do not appear in the engraving, as the page is too small to contain the whole photograph.

ceeded through Moray Place to deposit the wretched animal in better keeping than that of its driver. This little episode is delightfully characteristic of his impulsive nature, and the benevolence of his heart. No weak appeal, through the gossiping columns of newspapers, to humane societies for the suppression of cruelty to animals; but action on the spot, with instantaneous aid to the oppressed. Such summary measures, however, are not always taken. Moral courage is required to face bystanders; and not many would care to be seen with a carter's huge whip, leading a miserable raw-boned old horse through the fashionable streets of Edinburgh. But he despised nothing that was just, even to the meanest of created things; and had a supreme contempt for the observance of conventional formalities, when they interfered with good and honest feelings of the heart.

It may seem somewhat strange, as I advance towards the later years of my father's life, that I can relate nothing of foreign travel; or even of recurring visits to London. Only twice after his marriage did he go to the metropolis, and then, not for any lengthened period, nor with the purpose of keeping himself in the world, or gathering gossip from that great whirlpool of tongues. He never, as far as I can remember, at any time thought of or cared to associate his name with circumstances likely to bring him into contact with that huge centre of the world—the first entrance to which he so beautifully describes in his "Recreations," written in 1828; too long to give here, and yet almost too fine to be omitted. But those who do not know it, will do well to learn how a nature such as his was affected, by what scarcely now awakens more than a certain curiosity, that ere long takes the shape of *blasé* indifference. I doubt very much if any spirit, even beyond the common mould, ever had such emotions awakened within it as those Wilson felt when, "all alone and on foot," he reached that mighty city, where every sight he saw called up some thought of wonder from the treasures of his ardent mind.

Here is a portion of his powerful description; to convey the idea how, without fear yet trembling, he left the world of his dreams, the "emerald caves," the "pearl-leaved forests," and "asphodel meadows," and opened his eyes upon that which was no longer a shadow. "Now were we in the eddies—the vortices—the whirlpools of the great roaring sea of life! and away we were carried, not afraid, yet somewhat trembling in the awe of our new delight, into the heart of the habitations of all the world's most imperial, most servile, most tyrannous, and most slavish passions! All that was most elevating and most degrading, most startling and most subduing too; most trying by temptation of pleasure, and by repulsion of pain; into the heart of all joy and all grief; all calm and all storm; all dangerous trouble and more dangerous rest; all rapture and all agony—crime, guilt, misery, madness, despair." This fragment is part of one of those prose poems which he has so often composed, and which many of his imaginative essays may be called. What visions foreign shores would have brought to his mind, can from such morsels as this be imagined. But the plans of his youth, sketched out no doubt during a period of mental disquietude, and broken up forever, were not likely to be again suggested to one who had found in domestic life so much happiness. Thus, all thoughts of travel were dissipated from his mind when excitement ceased to be necessary for the preservation of his peace. So time passed away, and no new place rose up to tempt him from home. I believe, however, if his health had continued unbroken, or even been partially restored, he would have crossed the Atlantic.

There is no literary man of our land more highly prized or better appreciated in America than Professor Wilson. In that country his name is respected, and his writings are well known. It is doubtful if in England he has so large a circle of admirers. I have often heard him speak of Americans in terms of admiration. He knew many, and received all who came to see him with much interest and kindness; loving to talk with them on the literary interests of their country; giving his opinion freely on the merits and demerits of its writers, for they were well known to him. Of one of them he always spoke with profound respect, as a man whose spiritual life and great accomplishments, pure philosophical inquiries and critical taste, had given him a lofty position among his countrymen—Dr. Channing, the piety of whose character made his life upon earth one of singular beauty. Of his peculiar religious tenets I never heard my father speak. Nobility of nature, and aspirations directed to high aims in exercising influence for good over his fellow-creatures, were virtues of a kind, taken in combination with intellectual power, sufficient to win favor from him.

The autobiographical nature of my father's writings permits me, to a certain extent, to make use of such passages as I know are not only the expression of his sentiments, but likewise a reflex of his conduct in life. Then he had a simple habit of seeking pleasure in communion with his own people above all others, finding their society sufficient for the interest and enjoyment of life. Thus it is that I have no record to give of his mixing in circles composed of those above him in station; no *bons mots* from noble wits; no flashes of repartee from dames of high degree; at home and abroad he walked a simple, unaffected, *unfashionable* man. With gracious respect to rank, he held aloof from the society of the great; admiring, from the distance at which he stood, the great and illustrious names that adorned his land; doing homage in the silence of his heart to all that makes aristocracy admirable and worthy of good report, yet preferring to remain true to his own order.

It was this loyalty that gave him power over the hearts of men, and, I believe, this influence it was which, beyond the respect that knowledge wins, enabled him to render such valuable assistance to art in Scotland. Though he was not (beyond opportunities found in youth) cultivated as many are in the deeper parts of art, such as can only be fathomed by long study and unwearied research, he nevertheless possessed an intuitive feeling for it; he loved it, and brought an intimate knowledge of nature in all her humors, to bear upon what was set before him. The poet's eye unravelled the painter's meaning, and if minute detail escaped the expression of his admiration, as not being significant of the moving spirit of the painter's soul, it was because this careful transcription merged its beauty into greater and more touching effect; even as in contemplating nature, our first feeling is not to sit down to trace the delicate pencillings of flowers, or count the leaves of the dark-belted woods, or yet pick out the violet from its mossy bed. In the perfect landscape we know how much lies "hidden from the eye," and so with the perfect tableau. Our first impression is taken from the general effect, and if one of delight, fails to be recognized until our transport has subsided; then from delight to wonder are the senses changed, and the handiwork of nature in art is acknowledged by one acclamation of praise. It was this love of nature, this devotion to the beautiful, the *truth*, as I have before observed, that made my father welcome to that body of men who form so interesting a portion of the community—our painters. Their social gatherings, their public meetings, even the "annual Exhibition," was confessed to be benefited by his presence. That hearty sympathy, the genial smile, and the ready joke, are all remembered as something not soon to be seen again. The artist's studio was a resort well known to him, and many an hour did he spend within its pleasant enclosures.

On one occasion when sitting to Mr. Thomas Duncan for his portrait,* entering his studio, he said, "I am sorry, my dear sir, that my sitting must to-day be a short one; I have an engagement at two o'clock, I have not a moment after that hour to spare." Mr. Duncan, of course, expressed his regret; and at once arranged his easel, placed his subject in the desired position, and began his work. Never had an hour passed away so rapidly. The Professor was in excellent spirits, and the painter, delighted with his sitter, was loath to say that two o'clock had struck. "Has it?" said the Professor, "I must be off;" and forthwith began to re-arrange his toilette, looking at himself in the large pier-glass, stepping backwards and forwards, making remarks upon his appearance, tying his neckcloth, brushing back his hair, then turning to Mr. Duncan with some jocular observation on the subject of dress. Sitting down for a moment led on to something about art; then perhaps a story. Rising up, his waistcoat, still in his hand, was at last put on; a walk for a moment or two about the room; another story, ending in laughter; beginning again some discourse upon graver matters, till he fell into a train of thought that by degrees warmed him into one of those indescribable rushes of eloquence, that poured out the whole force of his mind; turning the studio into a lecture-room, and the artist to one of the most delighted of his students.

"Bless me, my dear sir," he said, rising suddenly; "give me my coat, I fear it is long past two o'clock, I had almost forgotten my engagement."

Mr. Duncan, smiling, handed him his coat, saying, "I fear, sir, your engagement must be at an end for to-day; it is now five o'clock."

Many a story, I believe, of this sort could be told of him.

There is nothing in the world so difficult to call up and retain as a passing gleam of fun or humor. We require the accessories of the moment, the peculiar little touch, the almost invisible light, that, gleaming athwart the mind, kindled it into that exuberance out of

* Christopher in his Sporting Jacket. Mr. Thomas Duncan, an accomplished artist, died in 844. His portrait, painted by himself, hangs in the National Gallery, Edinburgh.

which comes the story, the jest, the speaking evidence of the man. Better is it to be silent forever than destroy the meaning of such words. Wilson's conversational powers, his wit, his humor, cannot, save in general terms, be described. I humbly confess my own unfitness for such an undertaking; and I have not been able to meet with any one who by faithful repetition can give me aid in this way. I doubt very much if there is one alive who could. Mr. Lockhart was the only person, who, had he survived to do honor to his friend, might, from the clearness of his perceptive qualities, the pungency of his wit, and the elegance of his language, have done him justice.

Two friends have sent me their reminiscences of social meetings with him about this time. One of them says:—

"During his last five or six years, in common, I believe, with the rest of the world, I saw him in society very rarely. It was said that he came to be fond of solitude, and much to dislike being intruded on. I remember Lord Cockburn giving a picturesque account of an invasion of his privacy. It was something, so far as I can recall the particulars, in this way. There was a party which it was supposed he should have joined, but he did not. They forced their way to his den, and, he being seated in the middle of the room, walked round and round him in solemn, silent, and weird-like procession, he equally silent and regardless of their presence, only showing, by a slight curl of the corner of his mouth, that he was internally enjoying the humor of the thing.

"The last time I met him in society was an occasion not to be easily forgotten. It was one of those stated evening receptions (Tuesdays and Fridays) which brightened the evening of Jeffrey's life. Nothing whatever now exists in Edinburgh that can convey to a younger generation any impression of the charms of that circle. If there happened to be any stranger in Edinburgh much worth seeing, you were sure to meet him there. The occasion I refer to was dealt with exactly as the reception of a distinguished stranger, though he was a stranger living among ourselves. There came a rumor up-stairs that Professor Wilson had arrived, and a buzz and expectation, scarcely less keen among those who had never met him, than among others who wondered what change the years since they had last met him in festivity had wrought. I could see none. He was on abstinence regimen, and eschewed the mulled claret consecrated to those meetings, but he was genial, brilliant, and even jovial. If he had become a hermit, it was evident that solitude had not visited him."

My other correspondent met the Professor at a dinner-party at Lord Robertson's, the last party of the kind, I think, he ever was induced to be present at. "The party was especially joyous and genial. After the ladies had left the room, the host, in a short mock-heroic speech,* moved that I should 'take the chair of the meeting,' which was duly seconded by the Honorable Lauderdale Maule, of the 79th Highlanders. Upon modestly declining to accept of the honor, I was informed that, if I persisted in my refusal, I should be removed from the room by a policeman for contempt of court! I then at once moved up to the head of the table and seated myself, having on my right hand the gallant and accomplished officer above mentioned, and on my left the grand-looking old Professor, with his eye of fire, and his noble countenance full of geniality and kindness. Lord Robertson, as was his wont several years before his death, sat on the left-hand side, two or three seats from the top. Of that goodly company, those three I have just mentioned have passed away. One incident I remember of that dinner-party. Robertson, with affectionate earnestness, but from which he could

* Of Lord Robertson's mock-heroic speeches, Mr. Lockhart gives a vivid description in his account of the Burns dinner of 1818:—"The last of these presidents (Mr. Patrick Robertson), a young counsellor, of very rising reputation and most pleasant manner, made his approach to the chair amidst such a thunder of acclamation, as seems to be issuing from the cheeks of the Bacchantes, when Silenus gets astride on his ass, in the famous picture of Rubens. Once in the chair, there was no fear of his quitting it while any remained to pay homage due to his authority. He made speeches, one chief merit of which consisted (unlike Epic Poems) in their having neither beginning, middle, nor end. He sang songs in which music was not. He proposed toasts in which meaning was not. But over every thing that he said there was flung such a radiance of sheer mother-wit, that there was no difficulty in seeing the want of *meaning* was no involuntary want. By the perpetual dazzle of his wit, by the cordial flow of his good humor, but, above all, by the cheering influence of his broad, happy face, seen through its halo of punch steam (for even the chair had by this time got enough of the juice of the grape), he contrived to diffuse over us all, for a long time, one genial atmosphere of unmingled mirth." The remarks I have already made, as to the difficulty of adequately recording the expressions of original humor, where the felicity consists in the expression and accessories as much as in the mere words, apply equally to the wit or humor of Robertson. I venture, however, to give one example that occurs to me, out of perhaps hundreds that might be remembered, of his peculiar and invincible power of closing all controversy by the broadest form of *reductio ad absurdum*. At a dinner party, a learned and pedantic Oxonian was becoming very tiresome with his Greek erudition, which he insisted on pouring forth on a variety of topics more or less recondite. At length, at a certain stage of the discussion of some historical point, Robertson turned round, and fixing his large eyes on the Don, said, with a solemnly judicial air, "I rather think, sir, Dionysius of Halicarnassus is against you there." "I beg your pardon," said the Don, quickly, "Dionysius did not flourish for ninety years after that period." "Oh," rejoined Patrick, with an expression of face that must be imagined, "I made a mistake. I meant *Thaddeus of Warsaw*." After that the discussion went no farther in the Greek channel.

not altogether exclude his peculiar humorous style of illustration, proposed the health of his friend, Professor Wilson. The Professor replied with feeling, but, at the same time, gave Robertson a rejoinder in Patrick's own style. 'I have known him,' said the Professor, 'since his early manhood; I remember his beautiful hair—intensely red! Knew him! I produced him; I educed him; and I occasionally snuffed him' (here the Professor stretched out his arm in the direction of Robertson's head, making the motion with his hand as if it held snuffers). 'It is said, I believe, my friend is a wit; this I deny; he never was, is not, and never can be a wit; I admit his humor, humor peculiarly his own—unctuous and unmistakable.' In the course of the evening, the Professor sang his favorite song of the 'Sailor's Life at Sea,' and with what power, with what sailor-like *abandon*, and in the concluding stanzas, when he describes the 'Sailor's death at Sea,' with what simple pathos! it is indescribable, but the effect was visible on every one who heard him. Later on, he volunteered 'Auld Lang Syne,' and often as I have heard the song, and by many good singers, I never heard before, nor ever will again, such a rendering of it. Burns himself would have been glad and proud to have joined in the chorus! I met Wilson one or two days after in Hanover Street. He accosted me. I remarked that never till that night at Robertson's had I ever really met '*The Professor*.' He said it was a pleasant evening, and that 'Peter' was very good. 'But, sir,' said he, 'a very curious circumstance happened to myself; I awoke next morning singing, ay, and a very accurate version too of the words and music of that quaint ballad of yours, "The Goulden Vanitee;" curious thing, sir, wasn't it?' and with a sly look of humor, he turned and walked away."*

* This quaint ballad, the author of which is unknown, is worth giving in a note, but without the magic of the singer's voice it reads but tamely.

THE GOULDEN VANITEE.

There was a gallant ship,
And a gallant ship was she,
Eek iddle dee, and the Lowlands low;
And she was called "The Goulden Vanitee,"
As she sailed to the Lowlands low.

She had not sailed a league,
A league but only three,
Eek, etc.,
When she came up with a French Gallee
As she sailed, etc.

Out spoke the little cabin-boy,
Out spoke he,
Eek, etc.;
"What will you give me if I sink that French Gallee,"
As ye sail, etc.

Out spoke the captain,
Out spoke he,
Eek, etc.;
"We'll gi'e ye an estate in the North Countree,"
As we sail, etc.

"Then row me up *ticht*
In a black bull's skin,
Eek, etc.,
And throw me o'er deck-buird, sink I or swim,"
As ye sail, etc.

So they've row'd him up *ticht*
In a black bull's skin:
Eek, etc.,
And have thrown him o'er deck-buird, sink he or soom,
As they sail, etc.

About and about,
And about went he,
Eek, etc.,
Until he came up with the French Gallee
As they sailed, etc.

Oh! some were playing cards,
And some were playing dice:
Eek, etc.,

CHAPTER XVII.

CLOSING YEARS.

1849–'54.

In the year 1849, the first of a series of beautiful papers from my father's pen appeared in *Blackwood*, entitled "Dies Boreales." They are ten in number, and to me are more attractive than any of his other writings, as they are not only the result of the last efforts of his matured strength, put forth ere the night came, but contain the very essence of his experience. Some, no doubt, will be ready to compare them with the "Noctes," and complain that they contain less variety of character and stirring incident. To compensate for that want, however, they have certain deeper qualities. The discussions they contain on some of the highest questions of morals, and the criticisms on some of the masterpieces of ancient and modern poetry, appear to me to be of the very highest value. In the first of these papers some noble thoughts will be found upon the rituals of the Church, from which I should like to extract his definition of what composes the Scottish service :—

"The Scottish service comprehends prayer, praise, doctrine; all three necessary verbal arts amongst Christians met, but each in utmost simplicity. The praise, which unites the voices of the congregation, must be written. The prayer, which is the turning towards God of the soul of the shepherd upon behalf of the flock,

When he took out an instrument, bored thirty holes at twice!
As they sailed, etc.

Then some they ran with cloaks,
And some they ran with caps,
Eek, etc.,
To try if they could stap the saut-water draps,
As they sailed, etc.

About and about,
And about went he,
Eek, etc.,
Until he cam back to the Goulden Vanitee,
As they sailed, etc.

" Now throw me o'er a rope,
And pu' me up on buird;
Eek, etc.,
And prove unto me as guid as your word:"
As ye sail, etc.

" We'll no' throw you o'er a rope,
Nor pu' you up on buird,
Eek, etc.,
Nor prove unto you as guid as our word,"
As we sail, etc.

Out spoke the little cabin-boy,
Out spoke he,
Eek, etc.,
" Then hang me I'll sink ye as I sunk the French Gallee,"
As you sail, etc.

But they've thrown him o'er a rope,
And have pu'd him up on buird,
Eek, etc.,
And have proved unto him far better than their word:
As they sailed, etc.

I am indebted for the words and the music to my friend Mr. P. S. Fraser.

and upon his own, must be unwritten, unpremeditated, else it is not prayer. Can the heart ever want fitting words? The teaching must be to the utmost forethought, at some time or at another, as to the matter. The teacher must have secured his intelligence of the matter ere he opens his mouth. But the form, which is of expedience only, he must very loosely have considered. That is the theory. It presumes that capable men, full of zeal, and sincerity, and love—fervent servants and careful shepherds—have been chosen under higher guidance. It supposes the holy fire of the new-born Reformation—of the newly regenerated Church, to continue undamped, inextinguishable.

"The fact answers to the theory more or less. The original thought—simplicity of worship—is to the utmost expressed when the chased Covenanters are met on the greensward between the hillside and the brawling brook, under the colored or uncolored sky. Understand that, when their descendants meet within walls beneath roofs, they *would* worship after the manner of their hunted ancestors."

My inclination would lead me to say something more of the "Dies," but I must leave them, trusting that fresh readers of my father's works will seek them out, and read him in the same spirit as he himself did those great minds that preceded him.

One more domestic change took place to make him for a time feel somewhat lonely. His youngest daughter, Jane Emily, left him for a home of her own. On the 11th of April, 1849, she was married to Mr. William Edmondstoune Aytoun, Professor of Belles Lettres in the University of Edinburgh. But his second son, Blair, was yet left to cheer him in his now circumscribed household; discharging with devotion duties of affection, until broken health obliged him unwillingly to leave Edinburgh, and seek change of scene. The remaining portion of this year, like many others, was spent at his own fireside; the coming and going of his family forming the only variety of the day, not unfrequently concluded by some amusement for his grandchildren. A favorite walk with them was to the Zoological Gardens. Wonderful diversions were met with there, and much entertaining talk there was about the wild beasts; not always, however, confined to the amusement of the little children who walked with him; for he generally managed to find auditors who, if not directly addressed, were willing to linger near and listen.

There is something expressive in the words, "Little Ways." Every one has seen, in intimate intercourse with his fellow-creatures, habits and peculiarities that are in themselves trifling enough, but so belonging to the person that they can be looked upon only as his "ways," and are never for an instant disputed, rather encouraged. My father had a number of these "ways," all of so playful a kind, so much proceeding from the affection of his nature, that I can scarcely think of him without them, coming, as they do, out of the heart of his domesticities, when moving about his house, preparing for the forenoon lecture, or sitting simply at home after the labor of the day. I would not as a matter of taste introduce an ordinary toilette to the attention of the reader, but with the Professor this business was so *like himself*, so original, that some account of it will rather amuse than offend. By fits and starts the process of shaving was carried on; walking out of his dressing-room into the study; lathering his chin one moment with soap, then standing the next to take a look at some fragment of a lecture, which would absorb his attention, until the fact of being without coat, and having his face half-covered with soap, was entirely forgotten, the reverie only disturbed by a ring at the bell, when he would withdraw to proceed with the "toilette's tedious task," which, before completion, would be interrupted by various caprices, such as walking out of one room into another; then his waistcoat was put on; after that, perhaps, he had a hunt among old letters and papers for the lecture, now lost, which a minute before he held in his hand. Off again to his dressing-room, bringing his coat along with him, and, diving into its pockets, he would find the lost lecture, in the form of the tattered fragment of a letter, which, to keep together, he was obliged to ask his daughter to sew for him with needle and thread, an operation requiring considerable skill, the age of the paper having reduced the once shining Bath post to a species of crumbling wool, not willing to be transfixed or held in order by such an arrangement as that of needlework. At last, he would get under weigh; but the tying of his shoes and the winding-up of his watch were the finishing touches to this disjointed toilette. These little operations he never, as far as I remember, did for himself; they were offices I often had the pleasure of performing. The watch was a great joke. In the first place, he seldom wore his own, which never by any chance was right, or treated according to the natural properties of a watch.* Many wonderful escapes this ornament (if so it may be called) had from fire, water, and sudden death. All that was required of it at his hands was that it should go, and point at some given hour. His own account of its treatment is so exactly the sort of system pursued, that this little imaginative bit of writing will describe its course correctly:—"We wound up our chronometer irregularly, by fits and starts, thrice a day, perhaps, or once a week, till it fell into an intermittent fever, grew delirious, and gave up the ghost." His snuff-box, too, was a source of agony to him; it was always lost, at least the one he wished to use. He had a curious sort of way of mislaying things; even that broad-brimmed hat of his sometimes went amissing; his gloves, his pocket-handkerchief, every thing, just the moment he wished to be off to his class, seemed to become invisible. No doubt all these minor evils of life were vividly before him when he makes his imaginary editor give occasional vent to his feelings in the "Noctes."†

These are some of the "ways." Gas, as I have said, he could not endure, having once blown it out, and nearly suffocated a whole family. It was the first duty of the servant to place the tin candlestick and snuffers on his table in the morning. That and his inkstand were two articles of *vertu* not to be removed from his sight. The inkstand, a little earthenware image of Arion on his dolphin, I preserve with care and pride.‡

* A sufferer sends me the following anecdote:—"While delivering one of the Inaugural Addresses to the Philosophical Institution, of which he was president, in the full career of that impassioned eloquence for which he was so distinguished, he somewhat suddenly made a pause in his address. Looking round on the platform of faces beside him, he put the emphatic question, 'Can any of you gentlemen lend me a watch?' Being very near him I handed him mine, but a moment had hardly passed ere I repented doing so. Grasping the chronometer in his hand, the Professor at once recommenced his oration, and, in 'suiting the action to the word,' I expected it would soon be smashed to pieces; but I was agreeably disappointed, as, after swaying it to and fro for some time, he at last laid it gently down on the cushion before him."

† "Who the devil has stolen my gloves? cries the same celebrated literary character, as, stamping, he blows his nails, and bangs the front door after him, sulkily shaking his naked mawlies on the steps with Sir John Frost.

"Hang it! had we three hundred and sixty-five snuff-boxes, not one of them would be suffered to lie still on this table; but the whole gang shall be dismissed, men and women alike, they are all thieves. You have not seen my slippers, you say, sirrah?—Well, then, we shall use our interest to get you admitted into the Blind Asylum.

"Hold your confounded tongue, sir, and instantly fetch us our hat. What else have you got to do in this life, you lazy hound, but attend to our hat? And have you no fears, you infidel?"

‡ It was bought by my mother, in a small shop in Stockbridge, in 1820. That shop was then kept by a young man, who has since risen to great eminence in the world, having gained by his acquirements, and extensive antiquarian knowledge, a name of European fame. In his private life he is beloved and respected by all who know him, and among my own friends there is no one I esteem more highly than Mr. Robert Chambers.

He was in his latter years passionately fond of children: his grandchildren were his playmates. A favorite pastime with them was fishing in imaginary rivers and lochs, in boats and out of them; the scenery rising around the anglers with magical rapidity, for one glorious reality was there to create the whole, fishing-rods, reels and basket, line and flies—the entire gear. What shouts and screams of delight as "the fun grew fast and furious," and fish were caught by dozens, Goliah getting his phantom trout unhooked by his grandfather, who would caution him not to let his line be entangled in the trees; and so they would go on. The confidence which children place in their elders is one of the most convincing proofs of the love bestowed on them. At that period of life no idea of age crosses the mind. The child of six imagines himself surrounded by companions of his own age in all he sees. The grandfather is an abstract of love, good humor, and kindness; his venerable aspect and dignified bearing are lost sight of in the overflowing benevolence of his heart. Noah's ark, trumpets, drums, pencils, puzzles, dolls, and all the delightful games of infant life are supposed to possess equal interest in his eyes. I have often seen this unwearied playmate sitting in the very heart of all these paraphernalia, taking his part according to orders given, and actually going at the request of some of these urchins up-stairs to the nursery to fetch down a forgotten toy, or on all-fours on the ground helping them to look for some lost fragment. With all this familiarity there was a certain feeling of awe, and care was taken not to offend. Sometimes the little group, becoming too noisy, would be suddenly dispersed: Christopher, being in no humor to don his "sporting-jacket," closed for a brief season the study-door, intimating that serious work had begun.

A nervous or fidgety mother would have been somewhat startled at his mode of treating babies; but I was so accustomed to all his doings that I never for a moment interfered with them. His granddaughter went through many perils. He had great pleasure in amusing himself with her long before she could either walk or speak. One day I met him coming down-stairs with what appeared to be a bundle in his hands, but it was my baby which he clutched by the back of the clothes, her feet kicking through her long robe, and her little arms striking about evidently in enjoyment of the reckless position in which she was held. He said this way of carrying a child was a discovery he had made, that it was quite safe, and very good for it. It was all very well so long as he remembered what he was about; but more than once this large good-natured baby was left all alone to its own devices. Sometimes he would lay her down on the rug in his room and forget she was there; when, coming into the drawing-room without his plaything, and being interrogated as to where she was, he would remember he had left her lying on the floor; and bringing her back with a joke, still maintaining he was the best nurse in the world, "but I will take her up-stairs to Sally," and so, according to his new discovery, she was carried back unscathed to the nursery. He did not always treat the young lady with this disrespect, for she was very often in his arms when he was preparing his thoughts for the lecture-hour. A pretty tableau it was to see them in that littered room, among books and papers—the only bright things in it—and the SPARROW, too, looking on while he hopped about the table, not quite certain whether he should not affect a little envy at the sight of the new inmate, whose chubby hands were clutching and tearing away at the long hair, which of right belonged to the audacious bird. So he thought, as he chirped in concert with the baby's screams of delight, and dared at last to alight upon the shoulder of the unconscious Professor, absorbed in the volume he held in his hand.

Such were the little scenes that recall "the grandfather" to me; and I hope I have not wearied my readers by this detail about babies and children, but that I may have added, by common facts, a tenderer association to his name, claiming from those who only knew his intellect respect for the loving sympathies that made home so sweet.

I have now come to the year 1850, when my father was living alone in his house in Gloucester Place, leaving it occasionally to visit his son John at Billholm, as two letters bearing the date of that year show. They are both addressed to his second son, Blair, and are written in his usual kind and home-loving spirit. One of them announces the death of his faithful old servant, Billy Balmer:—

"LIXMOUNT, 14*th August*, 1850.

"MY DEAR BLAIR:—Poor Billy died here yesterday night about nine o'clock, so quietly, that we scarcely knew when he was gone.

On Friday, he is to be interred in the adjacent cemetery. His wife had come from Bowness.

"I think of going to Billholm *on Saturday* for ten days. Perhaps you will write to me there *on getting this*, and tell me how you are going on. Your letter to Jane was most acceptable to all of us.

"I will write to you from Billholm on receiving a letter from you. All well. Jane Aytoun and Golly left for Billholm yesterday. Kind regards to all friends at Kirkebost, and believe me ever, your most affectionate father, J. W."

Of Billy a few more words may be said. The last time my father visited Westmoreland was in the year 1848. Whether his old boatman fancied, from being no longer young, that he would soon be separated from his master forever I cannot say, but soon after he took a longing to visit Scotland. The railway from Kendal to Edinburgh had been open some short time, but Billy was a stern Conservative, and could not suffer the idea of modern reform in any shape; he considered railways generally not only destructive to the country at large, but to individual life in particular—a species of infernal machine for the purpose of promoting sudden death.* With these feelings, perfectly orthodox in the breast of such a primitive son of creation, it is natural to suppose that he would shun the locomotive. So one fine day he bade farewell to "pretty Bowness," and trudged manfully on foot all the way into Eskdale Muir, arriving, weary and worn out, after a couple of days' walking, at the hospitable door of Billholm. There he was received, and he tarried for some months; but kind though the young master was, he longed for the old. After a time he left the "house that shines well where it stands," and made his way to Edinburgh. True devotion like that met with the reward due to it, and Billy was re-established in his master's service, dressed after the fashion of his early days, in sailor guise, with pleasant work to do, and a glass of ale daily to cheer his old soul.

I never knew of any love to mortal so true as that of Billy for my father. It was like that of David for Jonathan, "passing the

* Billy's horror at railways appears to have been shared by others who ought to have known better. Witness Wordsworth's lines on the projected Kendal and Windermere Railway, commencing—

"Is there no nook of English ground secure from rash assault?"

love of women." Cheerful reminiscences he had of past labor by the lake-side; then came kindness and care to soothe the weakness and troubles of advancing age; and, last of all, the touch of a tender hand by the dying bed. Poor old man; he had come to pay me a visit at Lixmount, where I was then residing, when he took his last illness; he lay some weeks, fading gradually away. Before his last hour came, I sent to let my father know I thought it was at hand; my message brought him immediately. He walked the distance—about two miles from Gloucester Place; and walking at that time was beginning to fatigue him, so he arrived heated and tired, but went at once, without taking rest, to his old comrade's room, where he found him conscious, though too weak to speak. Billy's eye lighted up the moment it rested on the beloved face before him, and he made an effort to raise his hand—the weather-beaten hand that had so often pulled an oar on Windermere; it was lying unnerved and white, barely able to return the pressure so tenderly given. The other held in its helpless grasp a black silk handkerchief which he seemed desirous of protecting. As the day wore on life wore away. The scene was simple and sad. Pale and emaciated, the old man rested beneath the white drapery of his bed, noiseless almost as a shadow; while my father sat beside him, still fresh in face and powerful in frame, exhibiting in his changing countenance the emotions of solemn thought and a touched heart. Soon the change came; a stronger breathing for a moment, a few faint sighs, and then that unmistakable stillness nowhere to be heard but in the chamber of death. The old boatman had passed to other shores. The handkerchief he grasped in his hand was one given to him by his master; he had desired his wife to lay it beside him. It was a something tangible when memory was leaving him, that revived in his heart recollections of the past. Billy Balmer was interred in the Warriston Cemetery. My father walked at the head of his coffin, and laid him in his grave.

The next letter is written in September:—

"My dear Blair:—Golly and Jane having both written to you from Billholm, I need say little of my visit to it. You know, too, of the sudden appearance of the dear Doctor.* We left them all well on the Wednesday preceding the Queen's arrival. But we

* Dr. Blair.

did not go to see her *entrée* on Thursday, and so missed what I hear was a sight worth seeing. On Friday I attended, with about twelve other professors, the stone-laying,* which was pretty. The Prince spoke well, and to the purpose. On Saturday we dined with Mrs. R. Chambers, and met De Quincey and his daughters and a few others. In the evening dropt in about 150 literary persons of all ages and sexes; and I never saw the Doctor in such force. His tongue never lay, and he would have sat till midnight; but Sabbath broke up the party. Next day Mary came for us in her carriage, but no Doctor was to be found, so we went to Lixmount without him, and at half-past seven he appeared in a brougham, having lost himself in some quarries. On Tuesday, he dined with Mrs. Pitman, and to-day accompanies her to the Horticultural; so I do not expect to see him again till Friday. He is stronger than I ever knew him, and in great spirits; and I am as kind to him as possible. I expect he will stay yet for ten days, when he returns to Abberly to accompany Mrs. Busk to London. I am not without hopes that he will pay us a visit early in spring. He sends his love to you.

"Gordon is the greatest man in Edinburgh—next to him the Provost and Mr. Moxey.† The place seems quiet again as before, but the excitement was great. Dear Jane had a bad attack two days before we left Billholm, but was up the day we left, and I trust quite hardy again. I am much the better of the dear Doctor's visit, and am in good spirits. You are not forgotten in Skye by any of us; and we all rejoice to think what a stock of health you are laying in for the winter. I am glad the guardsman and lady are pleasant. When the Doctor goes I shall be able to know my own motions. I must go then for a few days to St. Andrews. After that I will write to you. Meanwhile God bless you, ever prays your affectionate father, J. W.

"Give my very kindest regards to the Doctor and good lady."

The "dear Doctor," whose name has so frequently been mentioned in these pages, claims a few more words here. The schoolboy of olden days, beloved by all for his gentleness and goodness, singing out, as Miss Sym describes him, "Ohon a ree! ohon a ree!" whom she finds "groping in the press, howking out a book, part

* The foundation-stone of the new National Gallery on the Mound.

† Superintendent of Police.

of which was read with his peculiar burr." These simple words give us the impression that there was a something about him different from other boys. As a man, I never saw any one like him; and truly he continued his love for "howking out books." How much he read, and to what purpose, may be clearly seen from the correspondence between himself and his friend, to whom, in exterior and manner, he formed a strange contrast. The gentleness of his movements was remarkable. There was almost a timidity of character expressed in his bearing at first sight; but the wonderful intelligence of his countenance, the fine formation of his head, dispelled that impression, and the real meaning was read in perceiving that modesty, not fear, conquered his spirit, taking from him that confidence which the consciousness of power almost always gives. It was similarity of studies and sentiments that made them so much one; for of athletic sports in any shape, Dr. Blair knew nothing practically, nor cared. The course and habit of his life were like the smooth, deep water; serene, undisturbed to outward eye, and the very repose that was about him had a charm for the restless, active energy of his friend, who turned to this gentle and meek nature for mental rest. I have often seen them sitting together in the quiet retirement of the study, perfectly absorbed in each other's presence, like schoolboys in the abandonment of their love for each other, occupying one seat between them, my father, with his arm lovingly embracing "the dear Doctor's" shoulders, playfully pulling the somewhat silvered locks to draw his attention to something in the tome spread out on their knees, from which they were both reading. Such discussions as they had together hour upon hour! Shakspere, Milton—always the loftiest themes—never weary in doing honor to the great souls from whom they had learnt so much. Their voices were different too: Dr. Blair's soft and sweet as that of a woman; my father's sonorous, sad, with a nervous tremor: each revealing the peculiar character of the man. Much of the Professor's deep thought and love of philosophy grew out of this friendship. The two men were mutually invaluable to each other. The self-confidence of the stronger man did not tyrannize over the more gentle, whose modesty never sunk into submission, nor quailed in presence of a bolder power. Their knowledge was equal; the difference lay in their natural powers. The one bright, versatile, and resolute, has left his works behind him; while the other, never satisfied, always doing and undoing, has unfortunately given but little to the world; and it is to be feared the grave will close over this remarkable man, leaving no other trace of his rare mind and delightful nature than that which friendship hallows in its breast. The last visit Dr. Blair paid to his friend, their time was exclusively devoted to the study of Milton, and the result of these hours finds noble record in the "Dies Boreales." The subject is approached with a reverence such as ever marks a spirit willing to bow before a great power. The inner purpose of the poet's soul claims the critic's every thought, and he advances with well-ordered steps from the beautiful portals, opened by invocation to the muse, into the heart of the splendid structure, leading his reader with unrivalled skill into lofty chambers of thought and imagery.

It is now time to speak of those days in which the sand was running quickly down in the glass. A change which the eye of affection is not always the first to mark, could not, however, be concealed from his family. In the winter of 1850, symptoms of breaking up of health obliged the Professor, for the first time, to absent himself from College duties. I have received an account of one particular illness, the exact statement of which did not, at the time it took place, come from his lips. Indeed, as his health decidedly weakened, so did he in proportion try to rise above it. The same interest in his work which kindled his energies in early years, glowed with unabated ardor in old age. I give it as it was sent to me:*—

"One day Professor Wilson was late in appearing; perhaps ten or twelve minutes after the class hour—an unusual thing with him, for he was punctual. We had seen him go into his private room. We got uneasy, and at last it was proposed that I should go in, and see what it was that detained him. To my latest hour I will remember the sight I saw on entering. Having knocked and received no answer, I gently opened the door, and there I found the Professor lying at full length on the floor, with his gown on. Instinctively I rubbed his head and raised it up, kneeling with the noble head resting on my breast. I could not, of course, move. But in a few minutes in came other students, wondering in turn what was keeping *me*, and we together raised the Professor up into his chair. I caught the words 'God bless you!' Gradually he got better, and

* By the Rev. A. B. Grosart, Kinross.

we forced him to sit still, and never dream of lecturing that day or for a time. He was very reluctant to consent. I remember too that we spoke of calling a cab, but he said 'No,' it would shake him too much. In about half-an-hour he walked home. We announced to the class what had taken place, and very sore our hearts were. I think the Professor remained away three weeks, and on his return expressed glowingly and touchingly his gratitude to 'his dear young friends.'"

This was his last year of public labor. The whole session had been one of toil to him, and the exertions he made to compass his work could not be concealed.

His last Medallist says:*—

"The end did not come till his work for that session was done. On Friday he distributed prizes, and heard the students read their essays; taking particular interest in those of one gentleman who, with great ability, attacked his whole system, and of another who fancied that he had discovered a *via media* between the two great factions. Then he dismissed us, and the cheers and plaudits of his class rang in his ear for the last time. On Monday I called to get his autograph on one of my books; but the blow had already to some extent fallen, for he was unable even to write his name. Twice after this I saw him, at his own request, and always on the subject of his lectures; for he was bent on what he called a 'reconstruction' of his theory for the ensuing session; while it was but too plain to those around him that he was not likely to see the College again. The old lion sat in his arm-chair, yellow-maned and toothless, prelecting with the old volubility and eloquence, and with occasionally the former flash of the bright blue eye, soon drooping into dullness again. I still remember his tremulous 'God bless you!' as the door closed for the last time. How different from that fresh and vigorous old age in which he had moved among us so royally the year before!"

The relaxation of summer holidays brought no satisfactory improvement in his health. The truth lay heavy on his spirit—that the usefulness of his life was drawing to its close. Day by day some strength went out of him, and he must bid farewell to "his children," as he was wont to call his students. The freshness of his glory was no longer in him; "the bow was not renewed in his hand." Long and mournful meditation took possession of him; days of silence re-

* Mr. Taylor Innes.

vealed the depth of his suffering; and it was only by fits and starts that any thing like composure visited his heart. Still did he speak of returning to his labors at the commencement of the session; and, in order to regain strength, he proposed to make an excursion into the Highlands, provided that a family party went with him. There was no difficulty in arranging this; and in June, accompanied by his two eldest daughters, his sons John and Blair, his son-in-law Professor Ferrier, his brother James, and his niece Henrietta Wilson, he set out for Luib; at which rendezvous he was joined by Mr. Glassford Bell and his eldest daughter. Luib, as we have seen from his letter in 1845, is a pretty wayside hostelry in the central Highlands of Perthshire, about seven miles beyond Killin. There we encamped for a fortnight, encountering such caprices of weather as generally pass over the mountain districts of Scotland. The more adventurous of the party treated the weather with contempt, taking long walks. Of these were Mr. James Wilson and his niece, who wandered over large stretches of ground: but few of the others could compare notes of adventure with them. Had my father been able to endure fatigue, we too would have had something to boast of; but he was unable to do more than loiter by the river-side close in the neighborhood of the inn—never without his rod. Alas, how changed the manner of his sport from that of his prime! We must make use of his own illustration as he speaks of the past and present; for North's exploits in angling are varied enough to be brought forward at any point of his life. He says to the Shepherd:—

"In me the passion of the sport is dead—or say rather dull; yet have I gentle enjoyment still in the 'Angler's silent Trade.'" So seemed it then on the banks of the Dochart.

"But Heavens, my dear James! How in youth, and prime of manhood too, I used to gallop to the glens, like a deer, over a hundred heathery hills, to devour the dark rolling river, or the blue breezy loch! How leaped my heart to hear the thunder of the nearing waterfall! and lo, yonder flows, at last, the long dim shallow rippling hazel-banked line of music among the broomy braes, all astir with back-fins on its surface; and now the *feed is on*, teeming with swift-shooting, bright-bounding, and silver-shining scaly life, most beauteous to behold, at every soft alighting of the deceptive line, captivating and irresistible even among a shower of natural leaf-born flies, a swarm in the air from the mountain woods."

A picture of the past visiting the present, as time glides on, making more perceptible the cruel changes which come to mortal strength. How now do his feet touch the heather? Not as of old, with a bound, but with slow and unsteady step, supported on the one hand by his stick, while the other carries his rod. The breeze gently moves his locks, no longer glittering with the light of life, but dimmed by its decay. Yet are his shoulders broad and unbent. The lion-like presence is somewhat softened down, but not gone. He surely will not venture into the deeps of the water, for only one hand is free for "a cast," and those large stones, now slippery with moss, are dangerous stumbling-blocks in the way. Besides, he promised his daughters he would not wade, but on the contrary, walk quietly with them by the river's edge, there gliding "at its own sweet will." Silvery bands of pebbled shore, leading to loamy-colored pools, dark as the glow of a southern eye, how could he resist the temptation of near approach? In he goes, up to the ankles, then to the knees, tottering every other step, but never falling. Trout after trout he catches, small ones certainly, but plenty of them. Into his pocket with them, all this time manœuvring in the most skilful manner both stick and rod; until weary, he is obliged to rest on the bank, sitting with his feet in the water, laughing at his daughters' horror, and obstinately continuing the sport in spite of all remonstrance. At last he gives in, and retires. Wonderful to say, he did not seem to suffer from these imprudent liberties. Occasionally he was contented to remain away from the water, enjoying the less exciting interest of watching others. His son John delighted him by the great achievement of capturing two fine salmon, their united weight being about forty-five pounds. It was a pleasant holiday-time. There was no lack of merriment, and though my father was not in his best spirits, he rallied now and then from the gloom that oppressed him at the outset of the excursion.

On his return to Edinburgh, he was prevailed on by his brother Robert to pay him a visit at Woodburn. While there, the painful question of his retirement from public life was agreed on, and caused him much mental distress. He sent in his resignation, after thirty years' service. The remaining portion of this autumn was spent at Billholm. His retirement from active life was a step that interested all parties, and Government was not backward in rewarding the faithful services of one who, though not of their party, merited grateful consideration. The following letters will explain my words. One is addressed to Sheriff Gordon; the other to James Moncreiff, Esq., Lord Advocate:—

"GWYDYR HOUSE, WHITEHALL,
August 30, 1851.

"MY DEAR GORDON:—The enclosed will show you with what great cordiality my suggestion has been received by Lord John, and this post conveys directly to Professor Wilson an intimation from Lord John Russell, conceived in terms which, I think, cannot fail to be most gratifying to him, that the Queen has granted him a pension of £300 a year. I have sent Lord John's letter direct, as I think it will in that way best bear its real character of being a spontaneous tribute by the Government and the country.

"And now let me say that nothing that has happened to me since I held office has given me so much real pleasure as being permitted to convey to so old and steadfast a friend as yourself, intelligence which I am sure must greatly gratify you. I trust, under Providence, it may be fruitful to your illustrious relative of a long and honored old age, and of comfort and happiness to all your circle. Believe me ever, yours very sincerely, J. MONCREIFF."

"HOLYROOD PALACE, 28*th August*, 1851.

"MY DEAR LORD ADVOCATE:—I have complied at once with your wishes, and immediately obtained the Queen's approbation. I send the enclosed letter to you, that there may be no unfair surprise in communicating the Queen's intentions to Professor Wilson. Be so good as to take care that this letter is given him in such a manner as may be most agreeable to his feelings. Yours truly,

"J. RUSSELL."

As soon as Mr. Gordon received the intelligence that it had pleased her Majesty to bestow her bounty on Professor Wilson, he and I set off immediately to Billholm as messengers of the pleasant news. We arrived there late at night, and found every one in bed. The reason for our sudden appearance was not long in being made known, and in a short time the whole household was astir. The Professor rose from his bed, supper was set out before us, and a very joyful repast we had; every one expressing their grateful pleasure at this unexpected recognition of his public services. We were scarcely inclined to retire to our rooms, and remained talking till early morning. My father was much touched by the delicate tact of Lord John Russell's communication to the Lord Advocate, couched in terms indicative of a tender nobility of soul.

I know not if the acknowledgment of her Majesty's bounty is a fragment, or the whole of a letter addressed to Earl Russell, but it came into my hands lately, and as being written by my father, I imagine it was a copy of the letter sent, or at least part of it. Whatever the case may be, it will at least be interesting, and I therefore give it:—

"Billholm, Langholm.

"My Lord:—That her Majesty has been graciously pleased to bestow on me, in the evening of my life, so unexpected a mark of her bounty, fills my heart with the profoundest gratitude, which will dwell there while that heart continues to beat. I beg your Lordship to lay this its poor expression with reverence at her Majesty's feet.

"For your kindly sentiments towards my professional and literary character, I would return such acknowledgment as is due from one who knows how to estimate the high qualities of the house of Russell."

We remained a week or two at Billholm, my father returning with us to Edinburgh. As winter approached, many a thought crossed his heart of his lost labor, and cheerfulness was hard to keep up. He seemed disinclined for any sort of amusement, and remained within doors almost entirely; unable to find pleasure even in the pastimes of his grandchildren, at one time so great an amusement to him. Something of a settled melancholy rested on his spirit, and for days he would scarcely utter a word, or allow a smile to lighten up his face. He was as a man whose "whole head is sick and the whole heart faint." That such a change for a time should take place, was by no means unnatural. He was not yet stricken in years, the glow within the great mind was still strong, but the pulses of life were weak. So ardent and impulsive a nature could not be expected to lay aside its harness without a pang. Religion alone supported him in the solitude of that altered existence. These dark clouds were possibly as much due to his enfeebled health as to the belief that the usefulness of his life was over. His brother Robert, who had ever loved him with the tenderest affection, and who sought by every means to soothe his spirit and restore his health, proposed that he should again make his house a home. He did so, taking up his abode at Woodburn,* where, from the closing year of 1851 until the autumn of 1852, he resided. If unwearied care and devoted affection could have stayed the increasing malady, which with certain, though often invisible, steps was wearing him away, he had never died. While under that kind roof, there were many days of calm happiness, mingled with others sad enough. The restlessness attending nervous disease is almost as distressing as pain; of which I believe he had but little during the whole course of his decline. He rallied so far when at Woodburn as to be able to write his last papers for *Blackwood's Magazine*—numbers IX. and X. of "Dies Boreales." There was nothing in that house to disturb study when he was inclined for it. He had a suite of rooms to himself; no noise, no interruptions molested the quiet of his days. Pleasant and cheerful faces surrounded him at a moment's notice. His nieces rallied about him as loving daughters, often watching through the weary hours of sleepless nights by his bedside. Nothing was wanting, yet did the heart "know its own bitterness," in those moments when the cruelty of his disorder laid hold of his spirits, and plunged him, as he expressed it, into a state of "hopeless misery." "Nothing," he said to me, "can give you an idea of how utterly wretched I am; my mind is going, I feel it." Then coming directly to the burden of his soul, he would say, "Yes, I know my friends thought me unfit to hold up my head in the class as I ought to do;" then continuing, with an expression of profound solemnity, "I have signed my death-warrant; it is time I should retire." This was so evidently a morbid state of feeling induced by disease, that, distressing as it was to those who witnessed it, one could not but feel satisfied that ere long it would pass away, and a more placid frame of mind ensue. When these brighter hours came—which they did —nothing could be more delightful than his aspect, more playfully charming than his spirit. He scarcely looked like an invalid, or one who would be tormented by the fluctuations of moody humors. Altogether there was a something about him different from his days of defiant strength. Massive as his frame still remained, its power was visibly gone, and a gentle air of submission had taken

* Mr. R. S. Wilson's residence, near Dalkeith.

the place of that stately bearing. His step, that once seemed to ignore the ground beneath his feet, was feeble and unsteady. He no longer had the manner of one who challenged the inroads of time. In these moments he presented a serene and beautiful picture of calm and genial old age. He had not lost his interest in outward things nor yet in those of literature. He writes the subjoined playful note to his son Blair, or rather causes it to be written. The contents of it are evidence of how he intends to occupy his time:—

"WOODBURN, DALKEITH, *4th December*, 1851.

"MY DEAR BLAIR:—Anne's* fair hand holds the pen. The supply of books was most acceptable. The volume of Pascal was right; but I see there are two others by the same translator, viz., vol. 1st, 'Provincial Letters;' vol. 2d, 'Miscellaneous Letters.' Have you a translation of Cicero's 'De Finibus?' Is there a volume on Philosophy by Price or Dring? also by one Dymond, a Quaker? also by one Oswald, a Scotchman? Sir William Drummond's 'Academical Questions?' That vol. of Lord Jeffrey's collected works containing a Review of Sir William Drummond? That vol. of Lord Jeffrey's works containing a Review of Bishop Warburton? Send the above to my brother Robert. Come out, if convenient, on Saturday. Yours affectionately, JOHN WILSON.

"(Signed by order of the Presbytery.)

"*P. S.*—You may give my regards to Mary, and perhaps to Gordon,—Golly,† Adel, Pa, Charles Dickens, and the young lady.

"JOHN WILSON."

He also kept himself *au courant* with public affairs by reading the journals of the day. His political ardor was not so much abated as to prevent him from expressing his sentiments with his usual animation; and he found an opportunity of giving one last memorable proof of his independence and magnanimity of spirit in favor of an illustrious political adversary. In 1852 the representation of the city of Edinburgh became vacant by the dissolution of Parliament. There were three candidates, and one of them was Thomas Babington Macaulay. During the summer the Professor was more than usually feeble, seldom taking exercise out of doors, but preferring

* His niece, the eldest daughter of Mr. R. S. Wilson.

† His five grandchildren.

to remain in his own room. Possibly the languor of disease made exertion painful to him, for it was difficult to prevail on him, in the latter portion of his life, to drive or even to sit in the open air. Much to the surprise of the household, he one morning this summer expressed a desire to go into Edinburgh. Unfortunately, Mr. Wilson's carriage was not at hand, some of his family having gone into town to make calls. This *contretemps* it was supposed would have diverted his intention to another day. Not so. He sent to Dalkeith for a conveyance, and on its arrival set off with his servant upon his mission, giving no hint as to its nature, but evidently bent upon something of the most engrossing interest and anxiety to himself. On arriving in Edinburgh he drove to Mr. Blackwood's, in George Street, to rest before proceeding farther. Every one rejoiced to see him; and as he drove along many a respectful and glad recognition he received, people wondering if he had come to live and move among them once more. But what had brought him through the dusty roads and hot midday sun? He looked wearied and feeble as he got into his carriage to drive away from George Street, apparently without any particular object in view. So might it have been said, for he had not mentioned to any one what had brought him so far—far for an invalid, one who had almost risen from a sick-bed. His mysterious mission to Edinburgh was to give his vote for Thomas Babington Macaulay. When he entered the Committee-room in St. Vincent Street, supported by his servant, a loud and long cheer was given, expressive both of pleasure at seeing him, and of admiration at the disinterested motive which had brought him there. Mr. Macaulay's recognition of this generous action supplies an interesting sequel to the incident:—

"ROYAL HOTEL, CLIFTON,
July 16, 1852.

"MY DEAR MR. GORDON:—I am truly grateful for your kindness in letting me know how generous a part Professor Wilson acted towards me. From my school-days, when I delighted in the *Isle of Palms* and the *City of the Plague*, I have admired his genius. Politics at a later period made us, in some sense, enemies. But I have long entertained none but kind feelings towards him, and his conduct on Tuesday is not the first proof which he has given that he feels kindly towards me. I hope that you will let him know how much pleasure and how much pride I felt when I learned he had given me so conspicuous a mark of his esteem.

"With many thanks for your congratulations, believe me, yours most truly, T. B. MACAULAY."*

This autumn my father's hand ceased forever from work. Writing had now become a painful exertion, and nothing shows it more than his manuscript. The few notes he wrote at this time to his son Blair, and now lying before me, are almost undecipherable, the characters evidently written by a weak and trembling hand. There is nothing of moment in any of them; but as they refer to the work which occupied him at that time, I subjoin them with feelings of painful interest, as the last words his hand ever transcribed.†

Few as the words of these notes are, we can perceive that his work is one of much interest to him, and that he is bestowing the usual care on its preparation.

There is only one passage which I shall make use of from these last articles, the *Dies Boreales*. Not because it is so beautiful in itself, but by reason of the tender character of the subject. That deep and lasting love which the grave did not destroy—the lost image of his wife—was an ever present theme for the exercise of his soul's submission. Tempered though his sorrow was, he carried it in the recesses of his heart perpetually, and his last thoughts have been embalmed in this fine passage. The forlorn and widowed heart speaks in every word:

"When the hand of Death has rent in one moment from fond

* Besides the laudatory critique of the *Lays of Ancient Rome* in *Blackwood*, for December, 1842, my father, unless I am misinformed, had once more at least acted a generous part to a political opponent, by reviewing "Croker's Criticisms" on Macaulay's *England*, in two letters addressed to the editor of the *Scotsman*, April 18th and 28th, 1849, signed *Aliquis*.

"*July 22d.*

† "MY DEAR BLAIR:—I took from Gloucester Place three volumes of Milton, of which one is the second volume of 'Paradise Lost,' 4th edition, Thomas Newton. It contains the first six books, and the note and letter. The first volume must contain the first six. Can you get it for me, and send it out without delay per train? Yours affectionately, J. WILSON.

"I want to have Addison's Essay on 'Paradise Lost.'"

"WOODBURN.

"MY DEAR BLAIR:—Your active kindness has done all that could be done about Milton. Look in my room for 'Payne,' Knight's 'Principle of Taste,' and for Kames's 'Elements.'

"Yours affectionately, J. WILSON."

"WOODBURN, *Thursday Afternoon.*

"MY DEAR BLAIR:—Call at Blackwood's on your way to College (on Saturday), and ask John or the Captain if they have a parcel *for me at Woodburn* from the printer's in the evening; if so, you may stay and bring it by railway, the latest one going.

"Yours affectionately, J. WILSON."

affection the happiness of years, and seems to have left to it no other lot upon Earth than to bleed and mourn, then, in that desolation of the spirit, are discovered what are the secret powers which it bears within itself, out of which it can derive consolation and peace. The Mind, torn by such a stroke from all those inferior human sympathies which, weak and powerless when compared to its own sorrow, can afford it no relief, turns itself to that Sympathy which is without bounds. Ask of the forlorn and widowed heart what is the calm which it finds in those hours of secret thought, which are withdrawn from all eyes? Ask what is that hidden process of Nature by which Grief has led it on to devotion? That attraction of the Soul in its uttermost earthly distress to a source of consolation remote from Earth, is not to be ascribed to a Disposition to substitute one emotion for another, as if it hoped to find relief in dispelling and blotting out the vain passion with which it labored before; but, in the very constitution of the Soul, the capacities of human and divine affection are linked together, and it is the very depth of its passion that leads it over from the one to the other. Nor is its consolation forgetfulness. But that affection which was wounded becomes even more deep and tender in the midst of the calm which it attains."*

All earthly things now wore for him a solemn aspect. His mind was evidently inclined to meditate upon those truths by which religion exalts moral perceptions, and to bring all his force to test how he could elevate the soul's aspirations before he retired from the field in which he had so long labored. He humbly looked in the coming days of darkness for the light that rises to the upright, and hopefully awaited the summons that should call him to rest from his labors, and enter into the joy of his Lord.

He remained at Woodburn until the end of the autumn of 1852. Before he left it he had received visits from various old friends. Among the last was his old partner in literature and all the wild audacities of its then unlicensed liberty, John Gibson Lockhart. Much changed he was; more so even than his friend. It was a kind and pleasant meeting. I had prepared Mr. Lockhart to find my father greatly altered, as we drove out together. He afterwards told me he saw no change mentally, but considered him as bright and great as ever. Yet time had done much to destroy the

* *Dies Boreales*, August, 1852.

fine frame of the one; the heart-energies and interests of the other; nor could it be but a melancholy retrospect which crossed their thoughts in looking back to the days of gigantic strength in "life's morning march when the spirit was young." There was the same contrast between them as of yore, attributable to the different condition of their mental health. The indestructible buoyancy of my father's spirit gave to his mind an almost perennial freshness, and he was not less susceptible to emotions of joy and sorrow than in the passionate days of old. But now all within was tempered by the chastening hand of time, and the outward expression showed it. There was no more exuberant happiness, but a peaceful calm; no violent grief, but a deep solemnity. Mr. Lockhart, on the other hand, seemed to live with a broken heart, while all about him had a faded and dejected air. He spoke despondingly of himself. Health, happiness, and energy, he said, were gone; he was sick of London, its whirl and its excitements.

"I would fain return to Edinburgh," he said, "to be cheered by some of your young happy faces, but you would have to nurse me, and be kind to me, for I am a weary old man, fit for nothing but to shut myself up and be sulky." He certainly looked very much out of health and spirits at that time; indeed, he was like a man weighed down by inward sorrow. The momentary vivacity which lightened his countenance was almost more painful to witness than the melancholy natural to it. Now and then, some of the old sarcastic manner came across him, and as he sat at the writing-table, with the once tempting pen and ink before him, one could fancy him again dashing off one of those grotesque sketches in which he had delighted to commemorate friends and foes. But the stimulus was gone. A few hours were spent together by these old friends, during which there was much talk of bygone days. They parted as they met, with kindness and affection, expressing hopes that renewed health might enable them to meet again. My father stood at the door while Lockhart got into his carriage, and watched him out of sight. He never saw him again.*

As long as my father's mind remained unclouded, he continued to take an interest in the welfare of his friends, participating with unaffected sincerity in their pleasures, and rejoicing in their affection. The following little note to Mr. Robert Findlay, says more than

* Mr. Lockhart died at Abbotsford, November 25, 1854, about seven months after the Professor.

many words, and is significant of that *love* which was so large an element of his nature:*—

"MY DEAREST ROBERT:—I rejoice in my soul to learn that your son Charles has married a wife to his own entire satisfaction, and I trust to his father's, mother's, sisters', and brother's, and all friends. Kindest love to Mrs. Findlay and the rest. God bless you, and her, and them. Much love in few words. Your friend of friends,

"J. W."

And so with these kind words he took farewell of the friend, the "brother," of his youth. What thoughts of the past would revisit his memory in writing that little missive, we can imagine, taking him back to the sunlit hills which enclosed the home of his prime, from whence his "friend of friends" heard of a wedding morning, bright as the good deserve, and radiant with happiness; more serene, because it had come to close sorrow long and stoutly borne.

A yearning for home still lingered amidst the fading joys of memory; and the old man, standing on the threshold of another life, sighed to set his house in order. He must return to Edinburgh; so, bidding adieu to the kind brother who had so gently met all the caprices of his illness, and to whom the happier condition of a docile spirit had endeared him more than ever, he left the devoted circle of that household towards the close of the year 1852, and once again established himself in Gloucester Place.

For the first few months after his return, he appeared to rally, and gained strength; so much so as to inspire his family with hopes that better days were yet in store; but, like the sudden reanimation of a dying light, the glow proved tremulous and uncertain. Anxiety and watching still continued; the gloom and depression of his mind coming and going from time to time, leaving with the struggle of each beating wave, a melancholy evidence that a wreck lay there. How was such a trial borne? As all others had been. Grief deep as death was overcome in the end by patience. That great and lustrous mind felt day by day how its might was sinking;

* Since I wrote the above this dear friend has also been laid in his grave. Mr. Robert Findlay died on the 27th of June, 1862, having reached the advanced age of seventy-eight. As one of my father's earliest and dearest friends, I would have respected his memory; but personal knowledge of his high worth, and all those amiable qualities which endeared him to his family and friends, claims expression of sorrow.

while no outward complaint came to tell of the agony within; but efforts more trying and perplexing than can be told were made to test the amount of power yet remaining. He would read, or rather cause to be read aloud, books upon the same subject, as differently treated by their various authors, chapter by chapter. Philosophical works were tried first, but confusion was the result of this process of inquiry, as to his mental strength. The attempt was too much. With a sigh of despondency the volumes were laid aside, ordered to be taken away, and were not again brought out. A short period of repose, that might in ordinary cases have been beneficial, seemed only to fret and disturb him. There was no allaying that long-fostered passion for communion with the immortals. Thus, for a period almost covering the year, were such afflicting struggles continued. Nothing was ever seen more touching than the gradual undoing of that lofty mind; the gradual wasting of that powerful strength. One looked on, and felt as David did of old when the Lord's anointed fell. "How are the mighty fallen!" were words that sent a sound as a solemn dirge to our hearts. Yet was there no rebellion in this desire to hold fast the gifts that were his from heaven: who would part willingly with such powers?*

Such usefulness was about to pass away: he had parted from "his children." In the silence of his more composed hours, God be praised, the "storm was tempered," and a quiet sunshine shed its peaceful radiance over his spirit, nor have I reason to believe that other than happy thoughts visited him, mingled with the brightest and most joyous of the past—of those days when "our parish" was little less than Paradise in his eyes.

Certain it was the "Mearns" came among these waking dreams, and then he gathered around him, when the spring mornings brought gay jets of sunshine into the little room where he lay, the relics of

* I remember having once heard an instance of his having effected a happy cure in a case of severe mental trouble. The subject was a student whom he had recognized as showing great promise in his earlier career, but whose subsequent exertions had not answered his expectations. Inquiring of the youth the cause of this falling off, he learned that his mind had been overpowered, as many are on entrance into thinking life, by doubts and difficulties leading to darkness and disbelief, verging in despair. Fitful glimpses of light had crossed his dreary path, but still he found no comfort or rest. The Professor listened to the tale of grief with tender sympathy. His steady faith and long experience, his knowledge of how doubts and fears assail the hearts even of the high and pure, enabled him to enter into the very depths of that woe-stricken soul. With words of wisdom he consoled the wandering spirit, while he led him by the power of persuasion, the force of truth, and the tenderness of love, to the clear upper light, there leaving him to the blessing of the Father. The clouds broke away, and the day-spring from on high revisited that darkened spirit.

a youthful passion, one that with him never grew old. It was an affecting sight to see him busy, nay, quite absorbed, with the fishing-tackle scattered about his bed, propped up with pillows—his noble head, yet glorious with its flowing locks, carefully combed by attentive hands, and falling on each side of his unfaded face. How neatly he picked out each elegantly dressed fly from its little bunch, drawing it out with trembling hand along the white coverlet, and then, replacing it in his pocket-book, he would tell ever and anon of the streams he used to fish in of old, and of the deeds he had performed in his childhood and youth.* These precious relics of a by-gone sport were wont to be brought out in the early spring, long before sickness confined him to his room. It had been a habit of many years, but then the "sporting jacket" was donned soon after, and angling was no more a mere delightful day-dream, but a reality, "that took him knee-deep, or waistband-high, through river-feeding torrents, to the glorious music of his running and ringing reel." This outward life was at an end. With something of a prophetic spirit did he write in former days, when he affected the age he had not attained—how love for all sports would live in his heart forever: "Our spirit burns within us, but our limbs are palsied, and our feet must brush the heather no more. Lo! how beautifully these fast travelling pointers do their work on that black mountain's breast! intersecting it into parallelograms, and squares, and circles, and now all a stoop on a sudden, as if frozen to death! Higher up among the rocks, and cliffs, and stones, we see a stripling whose ambition it is to strike the sky with his forehead, and wet his hair in the misty cloud, pursuing the ptarmigan now in their variegated summer dress, seen even among the unmelted snows. Never shall Eld deaden our sympathies with the pastimes of our fellow-men any more than with their highest raptures, their profoundest griefs." Nor did he belie the words.

We were naturally desirous of keeping from his knowledge any thing that would surprise him into agitation. This could not, however, always be done, for family distress, as a matter of course, he must participate in. The day which brought us intelligence of Mrs. Rutherfurd's death was one of startling sorrow to him. His own

* A year or two earlier he writes to his youngest daughter:—"I took stock, and find I have forty-four dozen loch flies and fifty-six of stream flies. Of the latter six dozen are well adapted for our river; but 'Lord Salton' is nearly done, and must be renewed. Into the Yarrow I shall never again throw a fly."

widowed life had been one of long and faithful mourning; and the bereavement which his friend, Lord Rutherfurd, was called upon to endure, filled his mind with the most poignant pain, and it was with difficulty he could banish the subject from his thoughts. Other men's sorrows, in the unselfishness of his nature, he made his own. More unbounded sympathy I never knew. Therein lay the feminine delicacy of his nature, the power of winning all, soothing the sad, encouraging the weak, scorning not the humble. With heart and hand alike open, he knew and acted up to the meaning of one simple rule—Do unto others as ye would that they should do unto you. So, through another spring into summer, and once again to the mellowed autumn and winter snows, he lingered on contented, almost cheerful, but also sometimes very sad. At such times he never spoke. Can we doubt that these visitations of solemnity had a meaning? The veil which it had pleased God to draw over the greater power of his mind had not left it without a lesser light. He still knew and loved his friends, and found pleasure in their occasional visits. The presence of his children and his grandchildren continued to cheer and interest him almost to the end. That silence, so incomprehensible to common minds, looking too often for consolation in the recited words of Scripture, which they convey to curious ears as expressing the last interest and hope of dying hours, was no other than the composing of his spirit with the unseen God.

There is little more to tell. The last time my father was seen of familiar faces was on the 13th of October, 1853. I drove with him to Mr. Alexander Hill's shop in Princes Street, in order to see a painting of Herrings' then being exhibited there. He did not take so lively an interest in the picture as I had anticipated, but soon grew wearied, and evidently unable to rouse himself from a certain air of indifference which, when disappointed, he generally wore. Yet he was not always untouched by the efforts which love made to cheer and please him; and his moistened eye told more than a thousand words how he felt and followed the little entertainments got up for this end. Young children were at all times attractive to him, and though now unable to do more than stroke their heads or touch their little hands, still he loved to look upon them; smiling a gentle adieu when their prattle became too much for him. One day I thought to amuse him in one of his gloomy moments by introducing his youngest grandchild, some four years of age, dressed as "Little Red Riding-hood." This picturesque small figure, in a scarlet cloak, with a shock of long curls hanging about his merry face, made his *entrée* into grandpapa's room, holding up in his chubby hands a basket neatly adorned with leaves, out of which peeped sticks of barley-sugar and other bon-bons. Trotting to the bedside where the old man lay, he offered his dainty repast with a sort of shy fear that the wolf was actually there, and was greatly relieved by the kind caresses and good welcome he received, observing that grandpapa's hands were so white, and that he never once *growled.*

The tender and anxious question which he asked concerning Robert Burns, "Did he read his Bible?" may, perhaps, by some be asked about himself. On a little table, near his bedside, his Bible lay during his whole illness, and was read morning and evening regularly. His servant also read it frequently to him. In the strong days of his prime, he wrote, not without experience, these words in reference to sacred poetry:—

"He who is so familiar with his Bible, that each chapter, open it where he will, teems with household words, may draw thence the theme of many a pleasant and pathetic song. For is not all human nature and all human life shadowed forth in those pages? But the heart, to sing well from the Bible, must be imbued with religious feelings, as a flower is alternately with dew and sunshine. The study of *The Book* must have begun in the simplicity of childhood, when it was felt to be indeed divine, and carried on through all those silent intervals in which the soul of manhood is restored, during the din of life, to the purity and peace of its early being. The Bible to such must be a port, even as the sky—with its sun, moon, and stars—its boundless blue—with all its cloud mysteries—its peace deeper than the grave, because of realms beyond the grave—its tumult louder than that of life, because heard altogether in all the elements. He who begins the study of the Bible late in life must, indeed, devote himself to it night and day, and with a humble and a contrite heart, as well as an awakened and soaring spirit, ere he can hope to feel what he understands, or to understand what he feels; thoughts and feelings breathing in upon him, as if from a region hanging, in its mystery, between heaven and earth."

On Christmas day, 1853, he assembled around him his entire family, sons and daughters, with their children, to spend the day in his house. It was almost merry. His servant decorated the rooms with evergreens, and one little garland, with touching love, he ordered to be laid on his wife's picture, which hung over the chimney-piece in his bedroom. He was unable to dine down-stairs, but we visited him after dinner, and rejoiced in the cheerfulness that lighted up his countenance. It seemed a harbinger of coming peace, and we felt no strangeness in wishing him a happy Christmas, nor thought, as we gazed upon that beautiful face, that the snows of another such season would fall upon his grave. My brother John, with his wife and some of his infant family, spent this New Year with him. This was a great happiness; and for some time the old fervor and animation of his spirit seemed to return. They remained with him to the end. There were two subjects he had been wont to dwell on with affecting tenderness—the memory of his wife, and his beautiful home on Windermere. Had they faded from his vision now, or were they only more sacred as sights now connected with the glories of another world, purified in his thoughts from all earthly contact, renewed in spirit and in beauty, just as his sight was about to close, and his heart to cease from participation in things here below? I cannot say, but the name of "Jane" and of "Elleray" never more escaped his lips.

Another spring is announced amid sunshine, and the cheerful twittering of birds. Even in towns the beautiful influence of this season is felt, for the very air has caught up the fresh loamy perfume from the far-off fields, and a feeling of exhilaration is participated in by all creatures. The languid invalid is not indifferent to this emotion, and, with reanimated nature, new life invigorates every sentient being. And so did we hope that this advent of spring would cheer, and for a time console the heart of him whose eyes, yet able to bear the light of day, were often turned from the bed where he lay to the window, as if he wandered again in the faintness of memory to the freedom of outward nature. But these impulses were gone, and the activity which once bore him gladly along to the merry music of streams "to linger by the silent shores of lochs," rested now forever. On the 1st of April I received a message that my father had become worse. I hurried immediately to Gloucester Place. On entering the room a sad sight caught my eye. He had risen to breakfast much in his usual state of health, but, while taking it, a stroke of paralysis seized him. When I arrived, his bed was being prepared for him, and he still lay in his large chair. A mortal change was visible over his whole frame. The shock affected one entire side, from his face downwards, and at that moment he appeared quite unconscious. We laid him gently in bed, composing that still powerful-looking body as comfortably as possible, and in a few moments the medical attendants arrived. There was no hope given us; his hour had come. All that were near and dear to him were in the house. Not a sound was heard but the heavy and oppressed breathing of the dying man. No change took place the whole of that day. His brother Robert never left his bedside, but sat there holding the big hand, now able only to return the pressure given it; the last grateful sign of still conscious love.

We all watched through the night while some hours of natural sleep fell upon him. Next day the same sad scene; no change; morning's dawn brought no comfort. It was now Sunday; time hurried on, and we still hoped he knew us as we laid our hands upon his, but he was unable to speak. The only sign we had that consciousness had not left him was, that he continued to summon his servant, according to his old habit, by knocking upon the small table at his bedside. Several times during the day he made that signal, and on its being answered, I could not say that it meant more than that he desired his servant should now and then be in the room. She had served him long, faithfully, and with a true woman's kindness. It was the only way in which he could thank her. At five o'clock his breathing became more difficult. Evening sent its deepening shadows across his couch—darker ones were soon to follow. Still that sad and heavy breathing, as if life were unwilling to quit the strong heart. Towards midnight he passed his hand frequently across his eyes and head, as if to remove something obstructing his vision. A bitter expression for one instant crossed his face—the veil was being drawn down. A moment more, and as the clock chimed the hour of twelve, that heaving heart was still.

The following lines came into my hands after my father's death. They were written in youth; but the fact that his prayer was grant ed, makes these beautiful words, as it were, the parting farewell which his lips were not permitted to utter to those he loved:—

"When nature feels the solemn hour is come
That parts the spirit from her mortal clay,
May that hour find me in my weeping home,
'Mid the blest stillness of a Sabbath-day!
May none I deeply love be then away;
For through my heart the husht though sobbing breath
Of natural grief a holy calm will send;
With sighs from earth will heavenly voices blend,
Till, as on seraph fair, I smile on death,
Who comes in peace, like an expected friend.
Dipt in celestial hues the wings of love
Will o'er my soul a gracious shade extend;
While, as if air were sun, gleams from above
The day with God, the Sabbath without end!"

APPENDIX.

I.

PUBLIC FUNERAL AND PROPOSED STATUE.

I AM indebted for the following account to a friend:—

"On the 7th of April, 1854, the mortal remains of Professor Wilson were laid in the Dean Cemetery. Seldom has such a procession wended through the streets of Edinburgh as passed, in the soft sunshine of that April afternoon, from Gloucester Place up Doune Terrace, Moray Place, and Randolph Crescent, on to that lovely sequestered ground, where now repose a goodly company of men whose names will not soon die—Jeffrey, Cockburn, Rutherfurd, Thomas Thomson, Edward Forbes, David Scott, John Wilson, and his well-loved brother James. Students were there from many a distant place, who had come to pay the last tribute to 'the Professor,' whom they loved, and, for old Scotland's sake, were so proud of. Tears were shed by manly eyes; and none were there who did not feel that the earth closed, that day, over such a man as the world will not soon see again.

"That Edinburgh, rich in monuments for a northern city, should unhesitatingly determine to add to these a statue of John Wilson, was most fitting and natural. The resolution was not only at once formed, but speedily acted upon. Shortly after his death a public meeting was held, the Lord Provost (M'Laren) presiding, at which it was formally resolved that such a statue should be erected 'on a suitable and conspicuous site.' A committee was appointed with that view, consisting of the Right Hon. the Lord Justice-General (M'Neill), Lord Neaves, Sir John Watson Gordon, P. R. S. A., R. A., Mr. John Blackwood, Mr. Robert Chambers, Mr. P. S. Fraser, and Dr. John Burt. Much time was necessarily occupied in the receipt of subscriptions, and other arrangements; but early in 1857, the committee found themselves in a position to commission Mr. John Steell, R. S. A., Her Majesty's Sculptor for Scotland, to execute a bronze statue, ten feet in height, with a suitable pedestal, to be placed at the north-west corner of East Princes Street Gardens. The statue is now approaching completion; and will be erected on the appointed site a few months hence. As the work has not yet, however, left the artist's studio—has not, indeed, received the final touches from his hands—it would be presumptuous to speak of it further than to say that it promises to prove worthy alike of the sculptor, of his noble subject, and of the very 'suitable and conspicuous site' it is destined to occupy. In a representation of a man whose notable person is so fresh in the recollection of many hundreds of his fellow-citizens, exact portraiture was indispensable; and it was well that the sculptor, in presenting to us that memorable figure in his habit as he lived, was able also, even by faithful adherence to that habit, to attain much of the heroic element. The careless ease of Professor Wilson's ordinary dress is adopted, with scarcely a touch of artistic license, in the statue; a plaid, which he was in the frequent habit of wearing, supplies the needed folds of drapery, and the trunk of a palm-tree gives a rest to the figure, while it indicates, commemoratively, his principal poetical work. The lion-like head and face, full of mental and muscular power, thrown slightly upward and backward, express fervid and impulsive genius evolving itself in free and fruitful thought—the glow of poetical inspiration animating every feature. The figure, tall, massive, athletic; the hands—the right grasping a pen, at the same time clutching the plaid that hangs across the chest, the left resting negligently in the leaves of a half-open manuscript; the limbs, loosely planted, yet firm and vigorous;—all correspond with the grandly elevated expression of the countenance. To his contemporaries the statue will vividly recall Professor Wilson, at once in his everyday aspect, and as he was wont to appear in his class-room or on the platform, in the very fervor of his often fiery oratory; while to succeeding times it will preserve a vivid and worthy representation of one who, apart from all his other claims to such commemoration, was universally recognized as one of the most striking, poetic, and noble-looking men of his illustrious time."

II.

CORRESPONDENCE RELATING TO JANUS.*

MR. LOCKHART TO MR. BOYD.

"CHIEFSWOOD, *4th September*.

"DEAR SIR:—I am much surprised at the Professor's silence. However, time must not be lost needlessly, so I send you to be put up in slips, 1st, 'Thoughts on Bores,' which paper is by Miss Edgeworth, who, I *believe*, will allow that to be said when you publish your volume.

"2d, Hints on the Universities; 3d, Rabbinical Apologue; 4th, Maxims from Goethe; 5th, Ordeal by Fire; 6th, Five Sonnets from the German.

"I have chosen these as they would illustrate the different methods of printing to be employed in the book. You will consult only your own convenience as to your choice of that, or those to be put in slips at present.

"Yours truly,
"J. G. L."

WILSON TO THE SAME.

"*Wednesday, Two o'clock.*

"DEAR SIR:—I send the revised sheets corrected for press. I have seen Mr. Lockhart, and find you have an Arabian tale of his in hand, which put in any-

* "Janus, or the Edinburgh Literary Almanac." Oliver & Boyd, 1826. Foolscap, 8vo.

where you choose, either after or before the order I gave you in my last note. The 'Bohemian Gardener' is not finished, I understand, so it can go in afterwards. Do not set into form the Sceptical Estimate of the Fine Arts. Mr. Lockhart leaves town to-morrow, and I believe he intends to *alter* a little the poem on Lord Byron. Brown on Beauty may be put into forms; a few corrections will be made on it. Make a new paragraph near the beginning, 'When we speak of the emotion,' &c.

"Yours truly,
"J. WILSON."

WILSON TO MR. BOYD.

"ELLERAY, KENDAL,
Thursday, 6*th October*, 1825.

"DEAR SIR:—Along with this you will receive three papers, two of them complete, and one not so. The incomplete one is 'Poetry and Prose,' of which I will send the conclusion in a few days along with a quantity of matter.

"Whatever arrangement Mr. Lockhart may have made about the upmaking of the articles, you will follow it. If he has made no arrangement final and decisive, then I think his own 'Hints' would open the volume as well or better than any thing else, being excellent in itself, and on a subject of great interest; then might follow the other articles sent by him indifferently, or in any order. After these may come my two papers entitled 'Rise and Decline of Nations,' and on the 'Prime Objects of Government,' which set up into forms, and send to me without delay per mail, letting me know, *by letter*, the day they leave Edinburgh.

"They shall be returned instantly, corrected for press. Send also the incomplete Essay on Poetry and Prose along with them. I shall leave Elleray on the 27th, and be in Edinburgh on the 29th; but you had better send me the articles without delay, as you will be receiving copy from me before I come down, and instantly after. I shall send four short tales in the manner of 'Lights and Shadows,' which you will make up as they arrive, either after my other articles or on any other plan, for the order signifies nothing. Owing to the length of several of the articles, the volume should be 530 pages, that shorter and lighter articles may have room. The volume will conclude with a poem of mine in four parts, of a romantic character, of which I will send you the first part along with my next packet.

"I have written to Mr. Lockhart by this day's post, informing him of the contents of this letter.

"Yours very truly,
"JOHN WILSON."

THE SAME TO THE SAME.

"ELLERAY, 16*th October*, 1825.

"DEAR SIR:—Yesterday I sent per coach three articles for *Janus*, and I have got so many more finished, or in hand, that I wish to see Mr. Lockhart before I send them to you.

"I am not without hopes of seeing him here in a few days; but, at all events, shall know what articles he has done in addition to those he sent you. From the list of articles he sent me a few days ago, which he is doing, or to do, and from those I have in hand, the volume cannot easily be less than 550 pages, which, since there are to be no embellishments, may probably be got up so as to sell at the price you would like to fix. I shall be in Edinburgh on the 29th, and the printing may then go on as rapidly as you choose, as I shall have more copy than can be used for this volume.

"You will oblige me greatly by sending me a bill for £150, which I could discount at Kendal, at Messrs. Wakefield. This would be a great convenience for me, just at present, on the eve of my leaving the neighborhood. This request is rather before date, but I will send my receipt for the money, and in final settlement consider the former.

"As I leave this on Thursday, the 27th, I hope to hear from you a few days before in answer to this.

"I am, my dear sir, yours very truly,

"JOHN WILSON."

MR. LOCKHART TO MR. BOYD.

"CHIEFSWOOD, *Saturday Evening.*

"MY DEAR SIR:—I was just about to lose all patience, or to take it for granted the Professor was defunct, when I received this evening a letter from him, in which he announces his having sent to you *three* articles, and his intention to send more in a few days. He also says he has told you to begin the volume with my 'Hints on Universities.' Since he thinks so, so be it. After the 'Hints,' please set up in the following order:—

"Article 2. Ordeal by Fire; 3. Specimens of the Rabbin Apologue; 4. Sonnets from the German; 5. Thoughts on Bores; 6. Maxims, after which (as mentioned on the slip) the little article 'Leaves,' now sent; 7. Then set up *one* of the Professor's articles, a longish one, whichever of the three you like; 8. Then the Friesland Proverbs, now sent; 9. Moustache, now sent; 10. The Player and his Poodle, now sent; 11. The Return, from Goethe, now sent; 12. Jews of Worms, now sent; 13. Another of Mr. Wilson's articles, now sent; 14. To Death, from the German, now sent; 15. Glasgow Revisited, now sent; 16. Maclean of Aros, now sent; 17. Serenade, from Goethe, now sent; 18. Another of the Professor's articles, now sent; 19. Song of the Gipsy King, now sent; 20. Inscription at Hoch-heim, now sent; 21. Epitaph of De Ranzau, now sent; 22. Epigrams, now sent; 23. Essence of the Opera, now sent; 24. Ballad from the Norman French.

"In regard to all these you need not bother yourself with slips, but set up in sheets. That sent as specimen is most beautiful, and I never saw proofs that needed so little correction. I am called from home for some days, but if I be not back very soon I shall let you know where to address (when I am concerned with the correcting of them). In the mean time, don't send any to this place until you hear from me. I have corrected the proofs formerly sent, so that you may at once go on as merrily as you choose.

"Of course you will send the Professor proofs of every thing.

"Yours truly,

"J. G. LOCKHART.

"From Mr. Wilson, 17th October, 1825:—

"Antipathies; Dante and Milton; on the character Buonapartic."

WILSON TO THE SAME.

"ELLERAY, *Saturday*, *October* 22, 1825.

"DEAR SIR:—Many thanks for your kind letter, and enclosure of £150 on account of *Janus.*

"In sheet 6, I agree with the compositor that the white lines should be taken out. Fill up the space with the 'Player and Poodle,' and 'The Return.' After the article on the Rise and Fall of Nations, 'German Sonnets,' and a pretty poem in print, now sent; then on the 'Prime Objects of Government;' then Milton and Dante, Buonaparte, and Antipathies, and any other short articles. These last three I have not yet received, but put them into forms, for very few corrections will be made on them. Then prose and poetry, which I now return corrected, and without any addition, as the intended conclusion forms another article, which I now send incomplete, entitled 'Sceptical Estimate of the Fine Arts,' which put into slips. 'Brown on Beauty,' now sent, you will put up into forms after the other mentioned. That will bring the forms to about 240 pages, I suspect. I will send more MS. without much delay. The order I have sent of the short articles is of no consequence, if you have set up in forms in any other order; but keep it if you have not. The next 60 pages will be pathetic and picturesque tales. After that, 50 pages of lively articles, all written by me. Mr. Lockhart will then contribute a hundred pages of excellent articles, and the remainder also I expect will be good. The volume should not be less than 550 pages, which I hope you can afford at twelve shillings. I delayed writing for two posts, in hopes of getting the three articles, but they have not come to hand. I will be in Edinburgh on the 29th, in my house in Gloucester place, so send nothing here after receipt of this.

"I am, dear sir, yours truly,

"JOHN WILSON."

WILSON TO MR. BOYD.

"GLOUCESTER PLACE, 2*d November*, 1825.

"DEAR SIR:—I got home this evening, after a melancholy delay of some days at Hawick, owing to the sudden and alarming illness of Mrs. Wilson. Thank God, she is wonderfully recovered, and restored to a state free from all danger.

"I shall correct all revises to-morrow, and send them to you before dinner.

"I send you some more MS., namely, 'Pins,' 'Antiquity,' 'Love Poetry,' 'Preface to any New Work of Imagination.' These may go into forms forthwith after 'Beauty.' 'Medals,' and the two poems in the same hand, from some quarter unknown to me, you had better put up after the articles before mentioned, and in forms at once. They are good articles, and such a correspondent deserves encouragement. The other articles are not good, but I know the quarter from which one of them comes, and will write to the author, who is a man of genius. By the time the MS. now sent is in types, I shall send you more; and I have reason to think what will add greatly to the value of *Janus.* Remember not to scrimp it, and I presume it will be in time if shipped by the end of the month. I shall see Mr. Lockhart to-morrow at one o'clock.

"*Wednesday Morning.*—I wrote this last night.

"Yours truly, J. WILSON."

To the Same.

"15*th November*, 1826.

"Dear Sir:—I have hardly had a moment to myself since I saw you, but hope in two days or so to have a little leisure. I have corrected or looked at the two poems. You will correct Δ's sheets by his MS. No word yet from the Opium-Eater.

"I hope to send some MS. in a couple of days, as not much time now remains.

"Yours truly,

"John Wilson."

To the Same.

"Dear Sir:—Set up as much of the enclosed as will finish the half-sheet in question. Send the half-sheet itself to-morrow to the class-room, at one o'clock, for correction, and along with it all the enclosed MS., for I want it to go on with.

"Yours truly,

"J. Wilson.

"*Thursday*, 17*th November*, 1825.—*P. S.*—I will send back the other things to-morrow, for I cannot lay my hands on them just now."

To the Same.

"21*st November*, 1825.

"Dear Sir:—I send the conclusion of the tale (Miles Atherton). After it, set up 'Haco's Grave,' the 'Home Star,' 'To the Spirit of Health,' 'Genius.' After these a paper now sent about Cambridge. The paper on 'Crusades' I wish put into slips. The other may go into forms at once.

"Yours truly,

"J. Wilson."

To the Same.

"6 Gloucester Place,
26*th November*, 1825.

"My dear Sir:—I have been hindered by many causes, among the worst my wife's indisposition, from doing what I intended. I am in daily expectation of hearing from Mr. Lockhart of the Opium-Eater. I can have now no hope. I shall do four *Lights and Shadows*, and Mr. Lockhart will be sending in something good to conclude. Send down to-morrow night, and you will get whatever is ready.

"Yours truly,

"John Wilson."

To the Same.

"28*th November*, 1825.

"Dear Sir:—Enclosed is the corrected sheet, also three articles. The first, entitled 'Action and Thought,' will follow what is already in hand.

"Neither of the other two articles, 'Country Life' and 'Something Scottish,' is finished, but set them up, and the conclusion will be sent to you in the afternoon.

"Yours truly,

"J. W."

To the Same.

"28th November, 1825.

"Dear Sir:—I send corrected slips. After it set up the article on the 'Study of History,' on which I took much pains for another work that will not be gone on with. After it the other article now sent.

"Then will come four stories, making about twenty-six pages; and Mr. Lockhart, I hope, will send what will conclude the *tottle* (with 550) of the whole. I have been cruelly interrupted in all my work by Mrs. Wilson's indisposition. But she is pretty well to-day. Yours truly, J. W."

CONTENTS.

Hints concerning the Universities.
Church Service for the Ordeal by Fire.
Specimens of the Rabbinical Apologue.
Sonnets from the German of Glück.
Thoughts on Bores.
Maxims—from Goethe.
Leaves.
On the Rise and Decline of Nations.
Old Freezeland Proverbs.
Moustache.
The Player and his Poodle.
The Return—from Goethe.
The Jews of Worms in the year 1348.
Marco Bozzaris.
On the Prime Objects of Government.
Dante and Milton.
Napoleon.
Antipathies.
To Death—from the German of Glück.
Glasgow Revisited.
Lament for Maclean of Aros.
Serenade—from Goethe.
Poetry and Prose.
Song of the Gypsy King.
Inscription on a Tombstone in the Churchyard at Hoch-heim.
The Epitaph of De Ranzau.
Epigrams, &c.
The Essence of Opera.
Song from the Norman-French.
The History of Alischar and Smaragdine.
The Western Campaign.
Brown on Beauty.
Antiquity.
Pins.
Love Poetry.
A Preface that may serve for all Modern Works of Imagination.
Medals, or Obverses and Reverses.
The Beasts *versus* Man.
Stanzas on Freedom.
Saturday Night in the Manse.
Daniel Cathie, Tobacconist.
On the Death of Lord Byron.
The Bohemian Gardener.
Miles Atherton.
Haco's Grave.
The Home Star.
To the Spirit of Health.
Genius.
New Buildings at Cambridge.
The Crusades—Chivalry—Fiction.
Observations on the Study of History.
Influence of Luxury on Religion.
Action and Thought.
Country Life.
Something Scottish.
Effect of Growing Prosperity.
The Transport.
Pastorall; extracted from Uranus and Psyche, a MS. religious poem.

III.

LIST OF PROFESSOR WILSON'S CONTRIBUTIONS TO BLACKWOOD'S MAGAZINE FROM 1826.*

		PAGES.
1826.		
January.	Nine pages of Preface,	9
	Christmas Gifts,	10
February.	Birds,	8
	Moore's Sheridan, 5 pages—Galt, 5, besides omissions—Croly, 8,	5
	Noctes,	17
March.	Cottages,	25
	Saint and Demon,	1
	Remains of Wolfe,	12
	Byron Papers,	9
	Naval Sketch-Book,	21
April.	Streams,	29
	Noctes,	21
June.	Meg Dods' Cookery,	10
	Wilson's Ornithology,	10
	Noctes,	20
July.	Hints for the Holidays,	12
	Noctes, 15—Moir or Hogg, 3,	15
Aug. P. 1.	Gymnastics,	23
	Wilson's Ornithology,	11
2.	Hints for the Holidays, 2,	26
	Letter to Mrs. M. on the Sexes,	1½
	The Four Shops,	3½
Sept.	Hints for the Holidays, 3,	28½
October.	Noctes, 16½—Hogg, 1¾—Mr. C. Croker, 1¾,	16½
November.	Glance over Selby's Ornithology,	24
	Noctes,	23
December.	Christmas Presents, entd. Mr. Wilson,	11
1827.		
January.	Noctes,	16
March.	Noctes,	17
April.	Do.	17
May.	May Day,	19
June.	Persian Women,	12
	Aird's Characteristics,	18
	The Navy, No. 1,	8
June. P. 2.	Cruickshank on Time,	16
	Pollok's Course of Time, 2—Aird, 10,	2
	Richardson's Sonnets,	2
	Dr. Phillpott's Letters,	25
	The Reigning Vice,	13
	Noctes,	21
July.	Real State of Ireland,	14
	Cyril Thornton,	20
	Noctes,	30

* I had hoped at one time to be able to give a complete list of my father's contributions from the commencement of the *Magazine*, but the materials for fixing the authorship with certainty, in every instance, do not exist.

		PAGES.
1827.		
Sept.	Moore's Epicurean,	29
October.	The Traveller's Oracle,	20½
	Schmelzle's Journey,	22
	Montgomery's Poems,	20¾
November.	Preface and Review of Chronicles,	52
	Heber's Hymns,	17
1828.		
January.	Christmas Dreams,	6
	Christmas Presents,	7
	Health and Longevity,	15
	Noctes,	25
February.	Postscript,	1
March.	Leigh Hunt's Byron,	47
April.	Sir H. Stuart's Book,	24
	Anatomy of Drunkenness,	18⅛
May. 2.	Life of Burns,	46
	Noctes, No. 36, L. 13, with pieces from Hogg, C. Croker,	10
June.	Old North and Young North,	19
	The Man of Ton,	21
	Wilson's Illustrations,	18
July.	Dr. Phillpotts,	28
	Monkeyana,	10
	Huskisson's Complete Letter-Writer,	15
August.	Bremhill Parsonage,	22
	Salmonia,	25
Sept.	Christopher in his Sporting Jacket,	40
October.	Noctes, 20½—17—White, 3—Hogg, 1,	20
November.	Interscript and Postscript,	2
	Noctes, 21—Mr. Coleridge, 12—Mr. Johnston, 4,	21
December.	Noctes,	32
P..1.	Sir R. Inglis's Speeches,	21
	Sacred Poetry,	22
1829.		
January.	Edinburgh Sessional School,	29
March.	Noctes,	30
April.	Do.	24
May.	Do.	15
	Note,	½
Sept. P. 2.	Loves of the Poets,	16
	Furness Abbey,	21
	Noctes,	
December.	Noctes,	34
	The Annuals,	29
1830.		
January.	Education of the People,	16
	The Age—a Poem,	11
Feb. 1.	The Fall of Nineveh,	36
	The Young Lady's Book,	12
2.	Banwell Hill,	27
	Moore's Byron,	32
March.	Do. do.	34
	Annals of Peninsular War,	31
	Notice,	2
April.	Noctes,	36
May.	Do.	31

			PAGES.
1830.			
June.		The Christian Year,	16
		On the Punishment of Death,	14
		The Mariner's Return,	11
		Noctes,	32
July.		Bear-Hunting,	23
		Sadler on Balance of Food,	27
		Notice to Correspondents,	9
August.		The Great Moray Floods,	38
		The Lay of the Desert,	8
		Wild Garland, etc.,	5
	2.	Wild Fowl Shooting,	11
		Colman's Random Records,	2½
		Clarke on Climate,	9
		Noctes, 43—L. 9—Hogg, 2,	43
September.		Day at Windermere,	12
October.		The Moors,	33
		Expiation,	16
November.		Noctes,	25
December.		Winter Rhapsody,	32
1831.			
January.		Noctes,	35
		L'Envoy,	2
February.		Noctes,	22
	2.	Winter Rhapsody,	40
		Mr. Sadler and Edinburgh Reviewer,	37
March.		Noctes,	37
April.		Sotheby's Homer,	20
		Noctes,	33
May.		Reformers and Anti-Reformers,	16
		Sotheby's Homer,	37½
June.		Edinburgh Election,	34
		Lord Advocate on Reform,	31
July.		Sotheby's Homer,	33
		Audubon's Ornithological Biography,	16
Aug.	1.	Audubon and Wilson,	34
		Unimore,	53
	2.	Friendly Advice to the Lords,	19
		Greek Drama, No. 1,	41
Sept.		An Hour's Talk about Poetry,	16
		American and Whig on the Bill,	23
October.		Tod's Rajast'han,	16
November.		Noctes,	43
December.		Sotheby's Homer,	43
		Curliana,	21
1832.			
January.		Protestant Affairs in Ireland,	14
		Reply to Lord Brougham,	28
February.		Sotheby's Homer,	36
		Noctes,	33
	P. 2.	L'Envoy,	1½
March.		Balance of Parties,	23
April.		American Poetry,	19
		Miss F. Kemble's Tragedy,	20
		Noctes,	28
May.		Tennyson's Poems,	21

		PAGES.
1832.		
June.	Christopher at the Lakes,	24
	Living Poets and Poetesses,	8
	Maid of Elvar,	22
July.	Griffin's Remains,	30
	Christopher at the Lakes,	18
August.	Do. do.	16
	Upper Canada,	25
November.	Noctes,	29
1833.		
January.	Characteristics of Women,	19
Feburary.	Do.	27
March.	Do.	28
April.	The Factory System,	32
	Characteristics of Women,	22
P. 2.	Motherwell's Poems,	14
	Devonshire and Cornwall,	16
May.	On Poor Laws and Ireland,	33
	Twaddle on Tweedside,	17
June.	Greek Anthology with Hay,	24
	Loch Awe,	16
July.	Sir Henry Blackwood,	24
	Greek Anthology with Hay,	26
August.	Do. do.	27
September.	Northern Lighthouses,	15
	Greek Anthology,	56
October 1.	Morning Monologues,	40
	False Mediums,	
	America, No. 2,	21
2.	English Cathedral Establishments,	38
November.	The Hindu Drama,	24
	Spenser, No. 1,	33
December.	Retribution,	8
	Greek Anthology,	38
1834.		
January.	Sotheby's Odyssey,	26
	Hindu Drama,	29
February.	Odyssey,	30
	Aria,	4
March.	Whig Prosecutions of the Press,	18
	Refutations of Stewart,	28
	Conspiracy against Mr. Sheil,	10
April.	Baron Smith,	11½
May. 1.	Loudon on Education of Gardeners,	19
	Admission of Dissenters,	15
2.	Stephen Oliver on Angling,	16½
	Moral of Flowers,	13
	Poetry of Ebenezer Elliott,	21
	Combinations,	16
	Noctes—Hogg and Mag. 12,	31
June.	Aurora—A Vision,	10
	Christopher on Colonsay,	17
July.	Do. do.	14
	Noctes—Hogg, a small part,	29
August.	Do.	32
	Campbell's Siddons,	24

		PAGES.
1834.		
September.	Campbell's Siddons,	17
	Edmund Spenser,	23
October.	Glance at the Noctes of Athenæus,	27
	Coleridge's Poetical Works,	29
November.	Noctes,	29
	Spenser,	24
December.	Do.	33
	Orphan's Song,	1
	Noctes, &c.,	28
1835.		
January.	Edmund Spencer, Part V.,	23
	Audubon's Ornithological Biography,	18
	Noctes, etc.,	17
Feb. 1.	Bishop of Exeter and Lord John Russell,	8
	Roscoe's Poems,	8
	Noctes, etc.,	31
2.	Ancient Scottish Poetry, No. 1, Dunbar,	32
	Dana's Buccaneer,	12
March.	Shall we have a Conservative Government?	30
	Edmund Spenser, Part VI.,	17
May.	Wordsworth's New Volume,	24
	Female Characters in our Modern Poetry, No. 1,	28
July.	Life of Edmund Kean,	12½
	Tomkins on the Aristocracy of England,	14½
	Anniversary of Waterloo,	7
	Stoddart's Angling,	9
August.	Anglimania,	22
	Female Characters in our Modern Poetry, No. 2,	14
	Clare's Poems,	16
	Willis's Poems,	12
	The Doctor, First Dose,	20
September.	The Modern Dunciad,	12
	De Berenger's Helps and Hints,	8
	Justin Martyr and other Poems,	12
October.	The Doctor, Second Dose,	26
November.	Sacred Poetry of Seventeenth Century,	
1836.		
January.	Baillie's Dramas,	16
February.	Do.	16
March.	Swan's Views of the Lakes of Scotland,	15
May.	Alford's Poems,	17
June.	The Metaphysician, No. 1,	8
	Definitions of Wealth,	9
	The Siller Gun,	15
July.	The Metaphysician, No. 2,	9
August.	Do. " 3,	21
September.	Do. " 4,	19
October.	Do. " 5,	13
November.	Do. " 6,	17
December.	Do. " 7,	10
	Epigrams of Theocritus,	9
	The Mountain Decameron,	20
1837.		
January.	Do.	27
February.	The Metaphysician, No. 8,	7

		PAGES.
1837.		
March.	The Birth-Day,	24
April.	Our Two Vases,	20
October.	Do.	24
November.	Poetry by Our New Contributor, 10—Sterling, 16½	10
1838.		
February.	Loss of Our Golden Key,	33
April.	The Latin Anthology,	44
May.	Our Two Vases,	28
June.	Our Two Panniers,	32
July.	Extracts,	20½
August.	Christopher in His Cave,	17
September.	Christopher among the Mountains,	32
October.	A Glance over Thomas Warton,	20
November.	Our Pocket Companion,	29
December.	Tupper's Geraldine,	18
1839.		
February.	New Edition of Ben Jonson,	25
April.	Christopher in his Alcove,	33
May.	Our Descriptive Poetry,	13
July.	The Antediluvians, or the World Destroyed,	25
August.	Our Pocket Companions,	23
November.	Have you read Ossian?	22
1840.		
March.	Leigh Hunt's Legend of Florence,	16
1842.		
December.	Lays of Ancient Rome,	22½
1845.		
February.	North's Specimens of the British Critics,	26
March.	Do. do.	32
April.	Do. do.	26
	Extracts from the Drawer of our What-not.	
May.	North's Specimens of British Critics,	30
June.	Do. do.	23
July.	Do. do.	15
August.	Do. do.	28
September.	Do. do.	23
1848.		
October.	Byron's Address to the Ocean,	16
1849.		
June.	Dies Boreales,	26
July.	Do.	32
August.	Do.	28
September,	Do.	28
November.	Do.	35
1850.		
April.	Dies Boreales, No. 6,	32
May.	Do.	18
October.	Do.	20
1852.		
August.	Christopher under Canvas,	30
	Dies Boreales—The Last,	24

INDEX.

ACCIDENT to Mrs. Wilson, 276, 277.
— to Mrs. Gordon, senior, 401.
Achlian, visits to. *See* Campbell.
Aird, Thomas, 299, 319, 415.
— letters to, on Burns, 394–396.
— on the Festival, 417, 418.
Alison, Sir A., 111, 121, 415.
Allan, Mr., of the *Caledonian Mercury*, 98.
Allan, Sir William, 201, 413.
Ambleside, fair at, 309, 310. *See* Elleray.
America and the Americans, 426.
Anderson, Samuel, 181.
Anecdotes of College life, 49–55.
Anglers' Tent, the, 84.
Angling, early fondness for, 3, 4, 7, 12. *See* Fishing Excursions.
— his last "cast," 446.
Animals, love of—
— the peaseweep in the moor, 9.
— cock-fighting, 45.
— spiders and their habits, 92.
— game-cocks, 92, 116.
— ponies and cows, calves and pigs, 297.
— chickens and dogs, 379.
— the dog Rover and the witch, 371, 372.
— two pet dogs shot, 386.
— list of dogs, 389.
— his four-footed friends, 390.
— Brontë, Tory, and Grog, 389–392.
— his "aviary" in the back-green, 392–394.
— interference in behalf of an ill-used horse, 424, 425.
Anniversary, The, an annual of Allan Cunningham's, 314–318.
"Apperdeen stockingks," 237.
Aristocracy, the, Wilson admired from a distance, 427.
Art, love of, 427, 428, 458.
Astley, the Messrs., 84.
Audubon, John James, the ornithologist, 361, 363, 364.
"Auld lang syne," as sung by Wilson, 431.
Authors, calamities of, 303, 304, 398, 399.
"Aviary," the, 392.
— treatment of its invalids, 393.
Awe, Loch, 139–142, 154, 400–402.
Aytoun, Professor W. E., 238.
— marriage of, to Jane Emily Wilson, 434.

BABIES, the Professor's "way" of carrying, 437, 438.
Bachelor degree, examination for, at Oxford, 72–74.
Baillie, Joanna, 112.
Baird, Principal, 222.
— letter from, 277.
Ballantynes, the, 103, 108, 110, 112, 115, 181, 183, 303.
Balmer, Billy, a boatman on Windermere, 88–90, 134, 136, 149, 212.
— some account of, 438–440.
Bar, Scottish, called to the, 117, 121.
Barber, Samuel, 297, 308, *et seq.*
Barley-sugar, fondness for, 23, 389.
Barlow, Mrs., 309, 330.
Barton, Mr., 143.
Baxter, Mr., 134.
Bell, Henry Glassford, 317, 318, 421.
Bell, Mr., 143.
Ben Cruachan, 124.
Bentham, Jeremy, 274, 275.
Beresford, Admiral Sir J., 345.
Berkeley's philosophy, papers on, in *Blackwood*, 217.
Bible, remarks on the, 459.
Billholm, the residence of his son John, description of, 404–406.
— a summer at, 407.
— letter to, 413, 414.
— visits to, 438, 447.
Blackwood, Captain, 349.
Blackwood, Sir Henry, 343.
Blackwood, John, 463.
Blackwood, William, 115, 164, 167.
— his saloon described by Lockhart, 171.
— letters from, 259, 260, 264–270, 289–290.
— his illness and death, 374–378.
Blackwood's Magazine versus *Edinburgh Review*, 156, 164, 175.
— account of the rise of the Magazine, 160 162.
— its early defects, 164.
— contributors to, 171.
— fictitious names used in, 176, 180.
— troubles occasioned by its assaults, 184–198.
— Wilson's allegiance to, 258.
— his contributions to, 294, 313, 329, 334, 335, 361, 378, 394, 400, 406, 420, 422.
— his last papers, 449.
— For titles of contributions *see* APPENDIX III., 470–475.
Blair, Dr. Alexander, 25, 98.
— letters to Findlay on Wilson's attachment to Margaret of Dychmont, 65–73. *See* Love episode.
— visit to Elleray, 84. 85.
— letter from, 117.

Blair, Dr. A.; correspondence with, when preparing Moral Philosophy Lectures, 216–221.
—— mentioned, 341, 365, 440, 441.
—— accompanies Wilson to the Highlands, 418, 419.
—— reminiscences of his friendship with Wilson, 441–443.
Blantyre Priory, 21.
Boating, love of, 88–90.
Bothwell Banks, 37, 56.
Boxing—Wilson "a varra bad un to lick," 23, 45, 95.
Boyd, John, 282.
Boyhood, 1–14.
"Breeches Review," the, 276.
Brewster, Sir David, 171, 411.
"British Critics," North's Specimens of the, 420.
Bridges, David, 262.
Brontë, the dog, 389.
Brougham, Lord, 94, 252, 409, 411.
Brown, Dr. John, 292, 372, 373.
Brown, Peter, Bishop of Cork, 220.
Brown, Dr. Thomas, 202, 206, 222, 223.
Browne, Dr. James, editor of the *Caledonian Mercury*, 323.
Bryant, Jacob, 219.
Bull, midnight chase of a, 90–92.
Bull (John) Magazine, 271, 287, 288.
Burke and Hare, the Edinburgh murderers, 321, 390.
Burney, Charles Parr, Archdeacon of Colchester, 49, 74, 345.
Burns Festival, 415–418.
Burns, Robert, 158.
—— essay on, 394, 395.
Burnside, Mary, the friend of the "Orphan Maid," 395.
Burt, Dr. John, 463.
Burton, John Hill, his reminiscences of the Professor and his class, 231–243.
Byron, Lord, 131, 158.
—— paper on his "Address to the Ocean," 422.

Cab-drivers on the look-out for Wilson, 423.
Cadell, T., 144, 260, *et seq.*
Caird, the great, and his wife, 127.
Calder Bank, 21, 34.
Calderwood, 34.
Calvinus, attack by, on Drs. M'Crie and Andrew Thomson, 171, 190.
Campbell, Captain Archibald, 142.
Campbell, Dugald, of Achlian, 125.
—— visit to, 139–144, 146.
Campbell, Thomas, 345, 358, 379.
Canning, George, 271.
—— letter from, 281,
—— visit to Elleray, 284, 285.
—— mentioned, 287, 288.
Carlisle, sports at, 94.
Carlyle, Thomas, letter from, 322, 323.
Carter, a speechless, looking after the Professor with his horse, 424, 425.
Cashel, Mrs. (Grace Wilson), 2, 357.
Cay, Sheriff, 121, 181, 411.
"Chaldee Manuscript," 163, 171, 187.
Chambers, Robert, 436, 463.
Channing, Dr., 426.
Cheese, Rev. Benjamin, 73.
Children, the Professor's love of, 437, 438, 458, 460.
Christmas vacations, 19, 20; his last Christmas day, 460.
"Christopher North," 257.
—— letter on, 305.
—— portrait of, in his Sporting Jacket, 428.
Church service, Scottish, 433, 434.
"City of the Plague," publication of, 133, 137. *See also* 117.
Cladich, 401.
Cleghorn, James, 160–162.
Cockburn, Lord, 387, 429, 463.
Cock-fighting, 45, 46.
Cocks, establishment of, at Elleray, 46, 92, 93.
Codrington, Sir Edward, 350.
Colburn, Henry, 272.
Coleridge, Hartley, 307, *et seq.*, 311, 312, 332.
Coleridge, Samuel Taylor, 81, 134, 135.
—— his *Biographia Literaria*, 162.
—— review of his poetical works, 378.
College life at Glasgow, 14–26.
—— at Oxford, 37–77. *See* Oxford.
Collier, Sir F., 341, *et seq.*
"Colonsay, Christopher on," origin of, 297, 298.
Combe, George, 162.
Commonplace-books, begun at Oxford, plan of, 40–43, 67.
—— extracts from, in prose and verse, 85–88.
Composition, habits of, 398–400.
Constable, Archibald, 115, 133, 162, 283.
Coop, the, in the attic, 393.
Copleston, Rev. Edward, 220.
"Copy, copy!" 398.
Cranstoun, Mr., 112, 213.
Critic, Wilson as a, 299, 359, 360.
Croker, John Wilson, 271, 273.
Cruikstone, 37.
Cunningham, Allan, 270.
—— letters from, 313–318.
Cupple, Mr., extract from his "Memorial" of Wilson, 386.
Curwen, William, 134, 136.

Dalyell, Sir J. G., 181, 182.
Dasent, Dr., 48.
Death of a sister, 14.
—— of Wilson's father, 14, 15.
—— of his mother, 277.
—— of his wife, 382, 383.
—— of Professor Wilson, 461.
"Delta," *see* Moir, Dr
De Quincey, Thomas, remarks of, on Wilson's pugilistic and leaping attainments, 46–48.
—— on his friends at Oxford, 49.
—— description of Elleray, 78, 79.
—— first meeting with Wilson, 82–84.
—— story of the bull-chase, 90–92.
—— remarks on Wilson as a naturalist, 92.
—— letters to, 101, 113, 324–326.
—— mentioned, 134, 135, 149, 171, 224, 234, 279, 291, 336, 441, 468.
—— letter from, 274–276.
—— friendship with Wilson, 326–328.
De Tabley, Lord, 321.
Diary in 1801, 17. *See* Memorandum-book.
Dickens, Charles, 45, 388.
—— public dinner to, 400.
"Dies Boreales," composition of the, 432, 433.
—— the last contributions to *Blackwood*, 449, 452, 453.
"Dilettanti Club," 184.
"Dim acclivity," the, 421.
Disraeli, Benjamin, 293.
Dixon, Rev. Richard, 73.

Dobson, Mr., 135.
Dogs, the, at Thirlstane Castle, 371–373.
—— anecdote of two shot at Roslin, 386.
—— list of Wilson's dogs, 389.
Douglas, Mr., of Glasgow, his *fracas* with Mr. Blackwood, 188.
Dow, John, 270.
Doyle, John, 409, 410.
Doyle, Richard, 409.
Drawing, early attempts at, 4. *See* Art.
Dress, peculiarities of, 423.
Drovers, King of the, Wilson's match with, in a Highland village, 127.
Drummond, Mr. Home, 49.
Dumfries, visit to, 396.
Duncan, Thomas, Wilson in his studio, 428.
Dundas, Admiral, 354.
Dundas, Robert, 279.
Dundas, William, 279.
Du Perron, Cardinal, as a leaper, 47.
Dunlop, William, 24, 26, 72, 139.
Dunlops, the, of Garnkirk, 2.
Dychmont, 22.
—— the ladies of, 33–37.

Early companions, 25, 26.
"Edderline's Dream," 316–318.
Edgeworth, Miss, 262, 292.
Edinburgh, removal of the family to, 118–121.
—— Ann street and its associations, 198–201.
—— removal to Gloucester Place, 278.
Edinburgh Monthly Magazine, 154, 160–162.
Edinburgh Review, strictures of, on education at Oxford, 55.
—— "Isle of Palms" reviewed in, 115.
—— Wilson's contributions to, 120, 158. *See* Jeffrey.
—— review of the "City of the Plague," 137.
—— the *Review* versus *Blackwood*, 156, 164.
Elleray, purchase of, 68, 69.
—— description of, by De Quincey, 78, 79.
—— society in the district, 81, 96.
—— excursions around, 84, 87, 88, 149, 150.
—— boating on Windermere, 88–90.
—— regattas, 97, 285.
—— plans of composition at, 116.
—— departure from, 117–119.
—— visits to, 133–136, 148–150, 259, 269.
—— the new house at, 269.
—— visit of Sir Walter Scott, 284, 285.
—— letters to Mrs. Wilson and family from, 294–297, 307–311, 331, 332; to Sheriff Gordon, 420, 421.
—— intention to let, 305.
—— visits in 1845 and 1848, 420, 422.
—— resolution not to return, 422.
Elliot, Ebenezer, the Corn-Law Rhymer, 361–363.
Ellison, Nathaniel, 49.
Eloquence, the Gormandizing School of, 262.
Equestrian adventure, 90.

Fairy, funeral of a, described, 402, 403.
Fairy-land, Lays from, 256.
Fang, the dog, 372, 389.
Father, death of Wilson's, 14, 15.
Ferguson, Dr. Adam, 223.
Fergusson, Sir Adam, 201, 262, 263.
Fergusson, James, 112, 139.
Ferrier, Professor, 163, 294, 330.
—— marriage of, to Miss Wilson, 386.
Findlay, Robert, 24, 25.
—— correspondence with, on the Orphan Maid, 60–77. (*See* Love episode.)
—— letter to, on his marriage with Miss Penny, 105.
—— letter to, on the death of Mrs. Findlay, senior, and of Mrs. Wilson, senior, 277, 278.
—— mentioned, 329.
—— note to, 380.
—— letter to, from Rothesay, 400.
—— invited to the marriage of John Wilson, jun., 421.
—— letter to, congratulating him on his son's marriage, 455.
—— his death, 455.
Finlay, John, a young poet, 68, 71, 101, 104.
Finlay, Mr., of Glencorse, 121.
Fish, the first, 3.
Fishing excursions—to the Tweed and Yarrow, 121.
—— to the Highlands, 126.
—— to Loch Awe, 138–142.
—— to the wilds of Rannoch, 154.
—— to the Dochart, 418, 419, 445.
—— his last excursion, 445, 446.
Fleming, Rev. John, of Rayrig, 81.
—— letters to, 207, 208, 304–307, 320, 321.
Forbes, Professor Edward, 151.
"Foresters, The," 268, 269, 282.
Fortune, unencumbered, 39.
—— circumstances connected with the loss of it, 118.
Fraser, P. S., 433, 463.
Fraser's Magazine, 189, 289, 366, 370.
Free Trade, views on, 279, 301, 302.
Friend, The, a serial of Coleridge's referred to, 85.

Gaisford, Dr. Thomas, 50.
Gale House and its inmates, 96, *et seq.*
Galt, John, 201, 267, 268.
"Gangrel bodies" from the South, 126.
Garnet, William, 149, 296, 309, 310, 331.
Gas *versus* Candle, 399, 400, 436.
"Gemm eggs, a pouchfu' o'," 94.
Gibb, Mr., an Edinburgh artist, 320–322, 333.
Gill, Mr., 112.
Gillies, R. P., 160, 161, 168, 171.
Gipsies, the Howitts' story of his joining a gang of, 48.
Gladstone, W. E., 335.
Glasgow University, enters, 15.
—— college life, 14–26.
—— recollections of, 38, 39.
Glassford, Mr., 112.
Gleniffer, 1.
Gloucester Place, removal to new house in, 278.
"Gold Medal, Professor Wilson's," 254.
Gordon, Sir John Watson, 200, 463.
Gordon, Mrs., senior, accident to, 401.
Gordon, John Thomson, 238.
—— marriage of, 386.
—— letters to, 415, 416, 420.
—— letter to, from the Lord Advocate, intimating the grant of a pension to Wilson of £300 per annum, 447.
Gordon, John, 322.
"Goulden Vanitee, The;" music and words of this quaint ballad, 431–433.
Graham, Dr., 283.
Graham, Sir James, 356, 411.

Grahame, Rev. James, author of "The Sabbath," publication of "Lines" to his memory, 110-112.
Grandfather, Wilson as a, 437, 438, 458, 459, 460.
Grant, Mrs., of Laggan, 123, 126, 147, 208-210.
Grants of Lifforchy, 145.
Gray, James, author of "Cona," 130.
Gray, Lieutenant Charles, 132, 341.
Greave, Mr., 134.
Grenville, Lord, 99.
Grey, Sir Charles E., 49, 74.
Grieve, John, 121, 127.
— letter to, on Hogg's dispute with Blackwood, 368-370.
Grog, the dog, 391.
Grosart, Rev. A. B., of Kinross, his account of an illness of the Professor, 443, 444.

Haddington, Lord, 341.
Hall, Mrs. S. C., 358.
Hallam, Henry, 378.
Hallside, Professor Jardine's residence, society and diversions at, 21, 22, 34.
Hamilton, Archibald, 26.
Hamilton, Captain Thomas, 171, 188, 201.
Hamilton, Sir William, 121, 163, 171, 201.
— contest with, for the Chair of Moral Philosophy, 202, *et seq.*
— at Wilson's lectures, 245, 249.
Harden, Allan, of Brathay, 85.
— letter to, 99, 100.
Harden, Captain, of Altnagoich, 154.
Hawick fair, adventure at, 229, 230.
Hay, Andrew, 341.
Hazlitt, William, 181.
H. B. political sketches, 409.
Health giving way, 443, *et seq.*
— residence at Woodburn, 449-455.
— return to Edinburgh, 455.
— paralytic stroke, 461.
Heber, Reginald, 49.
Helensburgh, regatta at, 379.
Herbert, William, Dean of Manchester, 131.
Highlands, tour in the, 71.
— pedestrian tour, accompanied by Mrs. Wilson, 122-129.
— tour of 1816, 139-147.
— of 1817, 153, 154.
— short excursion in 1836, after the Paisley festivities, 381.
— and again in 1841, 400, 401.
— his last excursion to, in search of health, 445.
Hill, D. O., his calotype of Wilson, 411, 423.
Hogg, James, the Ettrick Shepherd, visit to, 121.
— letters to, 129-132, 365-368.
— writes for the *Edinburgh Magazine*, 161, and for *Blackwood*, 171, 179, 181.
— letter from, 319, 320.
— his quarrel with the Blackwoods, 365-371.
Home, Wilson at, 328, 329, 388, 389.
Home, Professor James, 222.
"Homer and his Translators," Essays on, 335.
Hook, Dr. James, 268.
Hook, Theodore, 271, 318.
Hope, Captain, 308.
Hope, Captain (Experimental Squadron), 341.
Hope, Professor T. C., 222.
Horner, Francis, 162.
Horner, Leonard, 2[illegible].
Howitt, William and Mary, 48.
Hume, David, 263.
Humility, his, in speaking of himself, 408.
Humor, Wilson's, 422, 423, 428, 429.
Humphries, Mr., 84.
Hunt, Leigh, attack on, in *Blackwood*, 163, 181, 182, 260, 261.
— review of his *Legend of Florence*, 400.
Huskisson, W., letter from, on the proposal for a separate Chair of Political Economy, 280, 281.
"Hypocrisy Unveiled," the pamphlet so called, and its author, 190-192.

Inkstand, the Professor's, 436.
Innerleithen, residence at, 304.
Innes, Alex. Taylor (his last Medallist), reminiscences of the Professor and his class, 254-256, 444.
Ireland, rambles in, 68, 69.
— visits to his sisters in, 115, 357.
Irving, Rev. Edward, his preaching described, 271.
"Isle of Palms," original draught of, 43.
— correspondence on its publication, 101-104, 107-116.
Ivory, James (Lord), 121.
Izett, Mrs., 127, 129, 154, 367.

Janus, publication of, 282-284, 290-292.
— correspondence relating to, 464-469.
— contents of, 46[illegible].
Jameson, Professor Robert, 171, 222.
— letter from, 28[illegible], 286.
Jamieson, Mrs., author of "King Charles's Beauties," 358.
Jardine, Professor George, residence in the family of, 15, *et seq.*
— first published poems dedicated to, 113,
— his "Hints" for Moral Philosophy Lectures, 221.
— mentioned, 278
Jeffrey, Lord, 112.
— his review of the *Isle of Palms*, 115.
— visit to the Continent, 129.
— letter on Wilson's poems, 137, 138.
— letter from, on Contributions to the *Edinburgh Review*, 155.
— letter vindicating the *Review* from the charge of infidelity, 196-198.
— *réunions* at his house, 387, 388.
— his evening receptions, 429.
Jenner, Dr., of Oxford, 52.
Jones, Sir William, 42.

Kean, Charles, 139.
Keepsake, The, an annual, 316-318.
Kemp affair and Scott Monument, 408, *et seq.*
Kinnaird, Mr., 44.
Knox, Mr., 148.

Ladies and Politics, 336-339, 361.
Laidlaw, George, of Kintail, 147.
Laidlaw, Mr., of Traquair Knowe, 121.
Laidlaw, William, Scott's amanuensis, 263.
Lake escapades, 88, *et seq.*
"Lalla Rookh," review of, 154.
Lamb, Charles, 44, 238, 341, 360.

"Lament, Captain Paton's,"—verses by Lockhart, attributed to the Odontist, 182–184.
Landon, Miss, 358.
Leaping, attainments in, 47, 48.
Lectures on Moral Philosophy, preparation of, 215–225.
"Leopard, the," 164, 168.
Lewis, Mr., 44.
"Lights and Shadows," publication of, 258, 259, 282.
Liston, Robert, the celebrated surgeon, consultation with, 375, 376.
Literature and politics, 159.
Litt's *Wrestliana*, 94.
Lloyd, Charles, of Low Brathay, 81, 97, 111, 136, 336.
Lloyd, William H., 25.
Lockhart, Captain, 180.
Lockhart, J. G., 121, 149, 171–175.
—— letters from, 260–263, 270–272, 273, 274, 282–284, 286–288, 292–294, 324, 408–413.
—— becomes editor of the *Quarterly Review*, 292.
—— his last interview with Wilson, 453, 454.
—— his death, 454.
London, visits to, 55, 425.
Love episode in early life: Margaret of Dychmont, 32–37.
—— poems dedicated to, 35–37.
—— letters addressed to, 43, 44, 57–60.
—— letters on, to Findlay, 60–65, 68–71, 74–77.
—— correspondence between Blair and Findlay, 65–68, 72, 73.
Lowndes, Mr., 264.
Lowther, Lord, 94, 294, 296.
Lubienski, Leon Count, a Polish student, 235, 237.
Luib, visits to, 418, 419, 445.
Lyndsay, Mr., brother-in-law of Professor Jardine, 21. *See* Palmes.

Macaulay, T. B.; his *Lays* criticized, 400, 406.
—— candidate for the representation of Edinburgh, 450.
—— Wilson's mysterious mission to Edinburgh to vote for, 451.
—— letter to Sheriff Gordon, expressing his kindly feelings towards the Professor, 451, 452.
Macculloch, Horatio, 407.
Machell, James P., 96, 294.
Mackenzie, Henry, the "Man of Feeling," anecdote of, 45, 46.
—— referred to, 171.
Mackintosh, Sir James, 206, 255.
Maclaren, Charles, editor of the *Scotsman*, 323.
Macleod, Rev. Dr. Norman, sen., 24.
M'Culloch, J. R., editor of the *Scotsman*, 278.
M'Crie, Rev. Dr., 171, 190.
M'Donald, Lawrence, 234.
M'Gibbon, Rev. Mr., 143.
M'Intyre, Dr., 142.
M'Kenzie, Alex., of Dingwall, 144–147.
M'Laren, Duncan, 463.
M'Latchie, Rev. Dr. George, of Mearns, Wilson's second instructor, 5–8, 112, 329.
M'Neill, Mr., of Hayfield, 143.
M'Neill, Duncan, Lord Justice-General, 121, 463.
M'Neill, Sir John, 2, 269, 414.
M'Nicol, James, 143.

Magdalen College, *see* Oxford.
Maginn, Dr. William, 270, 288, 289, 293, 358.
Maitland, Sir F., 354, 356.
Maitland, Thomas, 121.
Malcolm, John, 234.
Malcolm, Sir P., 340.
Malthus, Rev. T. R., 206.
"Mansie Waugh," 302.
Margaret of Dychmont, *see* Love episode.
Marriage, 105, 106.
—— of his daughters Margaret and Mary, 386.
—— of his son John, 421.
—— of his daughter Jane Emily, 434.
"Mathetes," a letter on Education by Blair and Wilson, 85.
Maule, Hon. Lauderdale, 430.
Maxwell, Sir John, of Pollok; his reminiscences of Wilson at Mearns, 6, 7.
Mearns manse, education at, 5.
—— physical features of the parish, 5, 6.
—— reminiscences of, 7, 8, 456, 457.
—— account of his feelings on bidding it farewell, 12–14.
Melville, Lord, 274, 279.
Memorandum-book, an early, 17, 33.
—— extracts, 20–25.
Menzies, Mr., 154.
"Mill, a little," 229.
Miller, Robert, bookseller in Edinburgh, 131, 133.
Millheugh, 34.
Moir, Dr. (Delta), 279, 288.
—— letters to, 290, 291, 299–303, 393, 394, 407.
Moncrieff, James (Lord Advocate), his letter to Sheriff Gordon intimating the grant of a pension to Wilson of £300 per annum, 447.
—— letter from Lord John Russell to, on the pension, 447.
Monro, Dr. Alex., Professor of Anatomy, 222.
Montrose, Marquis of, 2.
Monument to Professor Wilson, 463, 464.
Moore, Thomas, 44, 269, 270, 289.
Moors, "Wee Kit" lost on the, 8–10.
Moral Faculty, origin of the, 254.
Moral Philosophy Chair in Edinburgh University: becomes a candidate for, 202.
—— his competitors, 202, 206.
—— Whig opposition, 202, 206.
—— his moral character attacked, 207.
—— preparation of lectures, 214–225.
—— the opening lecture, 222, 223.
—— syllabus of his course, 226–229.
—— reminiscences by old students of the Professor and his class, 231–256.
—— his last year of public labor, 443, *et seq.*
—— resignation of his chair, 446.
—— correspondence relating to the Queen's pension, 447, 448.
Morehead, Rev. Robert, 111, 112, 192.
—— letter from, on the attack on Playfair, 193–195.
—— letter to, on the same, 195.
Morris, Captain Charles, 270.
Mourning, wearing of, 424.
Moxon, Edward, 341.
"Muckle-mou'd Meg" of the Mearns manse, 10 11.
Muir, Leezy, in search of Wee Kit, 9.
Mure, Mrs., of Caldwell, 129.
Murray, Rev. George, of Balmaclellan, 396.
Murray, John A. (Lord), 271, 387.
Murray, John, publisher, 272, 292, 293.
Music, love of, 22, 431.

Mylne, Dr., 264.
Mylne, Professor James, 215.
Mystification connected with *Blackwood's Magazine*, 163–167, 180–182, 188, 189.

Napier, Andrew, 24.
Napier, Macvey, 196.
Naturalist, qualifications as a, 92, 93.
Nature, communion with, 401.
Naval experience, 340–359.
Neaves, Lord, 463.
Newby, James, 93.
Newdigate prize at Oxford, 73, 74.
Newton, Mr., 316.
Nicolson, Alexander, reminiscences of the Professor and his class, 252, 255.
"Nimmo, Sir Peter," an eccentric visitor of the College classes, 240.
—— his interview with Wordsworth, 241.
Nursery, pulpit oratory in the, 3, 4.

O'Connell, Daniel, reference to, in a Lecture, and its effects on the class, 251, 252.
"Odontist, The," 182–184, 213.
O'Doherty, Ensign, 188.
Old Clothes—"Have you any?" 240.
Old Slop and the *New Times*, 273.
Orator, Wilson's power as an, 249.
Ord, John W., 238.
"Orphan-maid," the, of Dychmont, 33–35. *See* Love episode.
"Outlines of a Course of Moral Inquiry," projected, 281.
Oxford: entered at Magdalen College, 37.
—— recollections of, in after life, 37, 38.
—— studies and manner of life at, 39–77.
—— expenditure at, 39.
—— sketches of companions, 43, 44.
—— amusements at, 45, *et seq.*
—— friends and acquaintance at, 49.
—— reminiscences of a fellow-student, 50–55.
—— long solitary rambles, 62–64.
—— examination for Degree of Bachelor, 72–74.

Paget, Sir C., 354, 356.
Paisley, town of, 1, 2.
—— public dinner, 379–381.
Palmes, Mrs. (Margaret Lyndsay), 21.
Paralysis, seized with a shock of, 461.
Paralytic affection of the right hand, 400, 422.
Park, Mungo, Wilson's project of accompanying him to Africa, 59, 60.
Parliament-House life, 125.
Paterson, Deacon, and his "green bag," in Edinburgh Town-Council, 213–215.
Paton's (Captain) Lament, 182–184.
Pearson, Mr., 135.
Peddie, James, Wilson's first English teacher, 4, 5.
Pedestrianism, feats of, 24, 55, 62–64, 101, 122, *et seq.*, 415,
Peebles, an adventure at, 122.
Peel, Sir Robert, letter from, 281.
—— reception of, in Glasgow, 381.
Penny, James, 104.
Penny, Miss Jane, first meetings with, 96, *et seq.* *See* Wilson, Mrs., junior.
Penny, Miss, letters of Mrs. Wilson to, 187, 188, 205 206, 212 :304, 313, 318, 328, 329, 381.
Penny Bridge, Wilson's visits to, and letters from, 329, 330, 332–334 *See* Elleray.
Periodical literature, Wilson's connection with, 158, *et seq.*, 399.
Peter's Letters. quoted, 16, 17, 164, 171, 172, 175.
Philosophical Institution of Edinburgh, presidency of, 420.
Physical characteristics, 39, 44–48.
"Pizzantry," the Irish, 251.
Plans of composition: List of Subjects for meditation, 116, 117.
Playfair, Professor John, attacked in *Blackwood*, 189, 190.
—— the excitement caused by it, 190–195.
Poetry, early love of, 22, 26–32.
—— MS. volume of, dedicated to "Margaret," 35–37.
—— verses from commonplace-book, 85–87.
—— correspondence as to his first publication, 101–104, 107–116.
—— proposed poems, 116, 318.
—— a second volume contemplated, 132.
—— publication of, 132, 133, 136.
—— subsequent poems, 318, 319.
—— principles of, 422.
Poets, criticism on the, 130, 131.
Political Economy, proposal for a separate Chair of, 278–281, 333.
Politics and Literature, 159, 160.
—— among students, 242, 243.
Poor, kindness to the, 385, 386.
Portraits of Wilson; by Raeburn, 17.
—— Hill's calotype, 411.
Portrait of Christopher in his Sporting Jacket, 428.
Power, the love of, illustrated, 245–249.
Pringle, Alexander, 121.
Pringle, Mrs., 134.
Pringle, Thomas, 161, 162.
Printers' devils, 304, 398, 399.
Proctor, mode of shutting up a, 49.
Pseudonyms of Lockhart, 180, 185.
Pugilistic skill, 46, 47, 229.
Purdie, Tom, 263.

Quarterly Review, Lockhart becomes editor of, 292, *et seq.*

Raeburn, Sir Henry, his portrait of Wilson, 17, 57.
—— mansion at St. Bernard's, 200.
Regattas at Windermere, 97, 285.
—— at Helensburgh, 379.
"Representative" newspaper, 293.
Richmond, Mr., 122.
Ritchie, David, 283.
Ritson, William, 95, 93, 134.
Robertson, Patrick (Lord), 121, 149, 151, 180, 409.
—— letter from, 279, 280.
—— Lockhart's joke on, 286,
—— his mock-heroic speeches at social gatherings, 430.
Roger, Rab, in search of little Kit, 9.
Roslin, life at, after his wife's death, 384–386.
Routh, Dr. M. J., President of Magdalen College, 16, 49, 73.
Rover, the dog, and the witch, 371, 372, 389.
Russell, Lord John, 411.
—— letter to the Lord Advocate on Wilson's pension, 447.

Russell, Lord John; Wilson's letter to, 448.
Russell, Rev. William, 73.
Rutherfurd, Andrew (Lord), 121, 387, 463.
—— death of Mrs. Rutherfurd, 457, 458.

"SAILOR'S Life at Sea," a favorite song of the Professor's, 431.
Saturday in the class, 238, 239.
Scandler, Dr., 134.
Schetky, John, 376.
"Scorpion, the," 164, 168.
Scott, Dr. James, of Glasgow, "the Odontist," 181, 182–184, 213.
Scott, Sir Walter, 112, 130, 171, 179.
—— letter to the Lord Provost of Edinburgh, recommending Wilson for the Chair of Moral Philosophy, 210–212.
—— his visit to Elleray, 284, 285.
Scots' Magazine, 160.
Sharpe, C. Kirkpatrick, 171, 187.
"Shaving" and its interruptions, 435.
Shepherd, G., Wilson's examiner at Oxford, 73.
"Shiells, Tibby," visit of the Professor and his students to, 231.
Sibthorpe, Mr., 49.
Smith, Dr. Colin, of Inverary; his reminiscences of Wilson, 124–126, 140, 141.
Smith, John, publisher in Glasgow, 71.
—— letters to, on the publication of his poems, 101–104, 107–116.
—— offered a second volume, 132, 133, 136.
—— letters on the Moral Philosophy Chair, 214, 215, 224, 225.
Smith, Rev. William; his reminiscences of the Professor and his class, 243–254.
Snow-ball riot, 239, 240.
Social hours at *Maudlin*, 50, 51.
Social meetings, reminiscences of, 429–431.
Sonnet on the hour of death, 462.
Sotheby, William, 72.
—— letter from, 335, 336.
Southey, Robert, 81, 130, 314, 316.
Southwell, R. H., reminiscences of Wilson at Oxford, 50–55.
Spain, expedition to, meditated, 98, 100.
Sparrow, a domesticated, 389, 438.
Speculative Society, 117.
Speed in composition, 399.
Spenser, series of papers on, 378.
Spiders and their habits, 92.
Sporting-Jacket, the Professor in his, 229.
—— portrait of, 428.
Sports, early development of his passion for, 3, 4, 11, 12, 24, 45.
—— pugilistic skill, 46, 47.
—— attainments as a leaper, 47, 48, 95. *See* Pedestrianism.
—— skill in wrestling, 45, 94, 95, 127, 310, 330.
—— yachting, 379.
Squadron, Experimental, cruise with the; letters to Mrs. Wilson during, 340–359.
Stanley Shaw, 1.
Statue, proposed, of Wilson, 463, 464.
St. Mary's Loch, the Professor and his "children" at, 231.
Steell, John, R. S. A., 463.
Stewart, Dugald, 205, *et seq*.
Stewart, Mr., of Inverhadden, 154.
Stewart, Mr., of Ballachulish, 123.
Stewart, William, author of Highland Sketches, 126.
Stewart, Sir Henry, 307.
Stoddart, Sir John, 273.
Stoddart, T. T., 238.
Street scene, a, 424, 425.
Strolling players, 48.
Student, character as a, *see* College life.
Students, intercourse with, 231, 234–238.
—— care in examining their essays, 253.
Study, the Professor's, 396, 397.
Swinton, Professor Archibald, 238.
Syms, the, 2.
—— grandfather and grandmother of Wilson, 20, 21.
Sym, Catharine, 21, 140.
Sym, Robert ("Timothy Tickler"), 2, 20, 176, 179.
Synge, Edward, 50.
"Syntax, Dr.," an Edinburgh character, 241, 242

TALFOURD, Sir Thomas Noon, letter from, on his absence from the Burns Festival, 416, 417.
Tarland, market-days at, 232.
Taylor, Misses, 134.
"Teegar, oure John's," 4.
Tennant, Professor William, of St. Andrews, 132.
Tennyson, Alfred, review of his Poems, 339, 340.
Thirlstane Castle, a summer at, 371–374.
Thomson, Rev. Dr. Andrew, 171, 196.
Thomson, Thomas, 271, 272, 463.
Thorp, Rev. Charles, 73.
"Timothy Tickler," *see* Sym, Robert.
Tinkers, adventure with, 140.
Tipperary shillelaghs, 49.
Toilette, peculiarities of Wilson's, 435.
Tomintoul, 126, 145.
—— adventure at the fair, 146, 147.
Torrance, 34, 71, 77.
Tory, anecdotes of the dog, 390, 391.
"Trials of Margaret Lyndsay," 282.
Tytler, Fraser, 121, 171.

ULLOCK, Mrs., 134, 135.

W., MISS, of Dychmont, 33, 34.
Wakefield, Edward Gibbon, 294, 295.
Wales, excursion in, 67.
Warden, Mr., 346.
Wardlaw, Rev. Dr., 214.
Watch, the Professor and his, 435, 436.
Watson, Bishop, 81, 114.
Watson, George, 295, 297.
Watson, Richard, 90, 93, 321.
Watson, Miss D., letter from, 336, 337.
Watts, Alaric A., 264, 317.
Waugh, Edwin, 95.
Whigs, their opposition to Wilson when candidate for the Chair of Moral Philosophy, 202, 206.
White, Rev. James, of Bonchurch, 364, 365.
Wilkie, Sir David, 316.
Wilson, Andrew, 2, 115.
Wilson, Blair, 434.
—— letters to, 308, 309, 438–441, 450, 452.
Wilson, James, 171.
Wilson, Robert Sym, of Woodburn, 446.
Wilson, Mrs., senior, family of, 2.
—— removes with the family to Edinburgh, 19.
—— her domestic management, 119–121.
—— her death, 276, 277.

Wilson, Mrs., junior, 105, 106, 112.
—— her pedestrian tour in the Highlands, 122–129.
—— accident to, 276, 277.
—— letters to her sister, Miss Penny, 187, 188, 205, 206, 212, 328, 329, 381, 382.
—— her death, 382, 383.
Wilson Family, 2.
Wilson's Hall, Paisley, 1.
Windermere Lake, 69, 78.
—— boating on, 88.
—— regattas at, 97, 285.
Woodburn, visit to his brother at, 446.
—— takes up his abode there, 446–455.
Wordsworth, William, letter to, 26–32.
Wordsworth, William; first meeting with, 81.
—— his "White Doe," 130.
—— Jeffrey's estimate of his poetry, 188.
—— mentioned, 312, 317.
"Writing for Blackwood," its significance in the family, 397.

YARROW, excursion to the, 121.
York, Duke of, 271.
Young, Professor, of Glasgow, 15, 16.
—— Wilson's reminiscences of, 16.
—— first published poems dedicated to, 113.
Youth, remarks on the importance of this period of life, 8.

THE END.

www.ingramcontent.com/pod-product-compliance
Lightning Source LLC
LaVergne TN
LVHW020915110826
845150LV00004B/678

* 9 7 8 1 4 2 5 5 5 5 6 1 0 *